IAN PETHERS

1

Foreword by Edward Woodward OBE.

It is quite astounding how much our country has to offer the visitor these days. Whether you are after some time away from it all, a chance to delve into Britain's history, or the opportunity to walk amongst some of the many areas of outstanding natural beauty, rural or urban, we really do have it all, whether we get the chance to appreciate it or not!

I have stayed in most parts of Britain at one time or another. There is nothing more frustrating than the inevitable conversation shortly after you have returned from an area which makes you aware of what you have missed. You know the sort of thing; an assumption that you cannot possibly have visited such a town without seeing the superb orchards, ancient remains or perhaps modern shopping village. By then it is too late, and you silently vow to be much better prepared before future visits. I have made that promise many times, but seldom kept it!

I like the series of guides of which you are now holding a volume simply because they represent an attempt to give any visitor a comprehensive reference work for what can be found in a given area, but without sticking to dry facts alone. After all, what do you remember most about a particular visit, be it for work or holiday? Every town, city and village has its own atmosphere, its own stories from past and present, and its own unique setting in our equally varied countryside. The most famous attraction may be the most remembered, but any two people will describe it differently, focusing on their own preferred details. When I hear mention of a particular town or city it is often a hotel room that comes to mind, or a certain street, theatre, or restaurant.

The authors of the Four Seasons Guides have put some real flavour into what they have written; a mixture of personal comment, recollection and opinion with the solid base ingredients necessary to any guide book; relevant and up to date information about attractions, places to visit and to stay in. So many places are covered, but each has retained some of its individuality even in the midst of such a multitude.

These are books into which you can dip now and then for a little entertainment or information. You may then find yourself reading for longer than you at first intended, as one anecdote, piece of folklore or description leads you onto another. Any book which can make you smile at one moment, and at the next form a determination in your mind to visit somewhere new, must be a welcome addition to the bookshelf, or travelling bag.

Edward Woodward OBE.

Dear Reader

I hope you enjoy reading and using this guide as much as I have enjoyed compiling its contents.

To help make future editions even better, I would appreciate it if you would suggest suitable venues and places to visit for possible inclusion.

I look forward to hearing from you.

Yours sincerely
Nicola Miles - *Editor.*
Bon Appetit and a fond Bon Voyage.

Dear Contributors

I would like to thank all those involved in the production of this guide, especially Valerie for her support, Paul Bugge and Leigh Walsh for the technical advice, Ian Pethers and Sharon Bradley for the illustrations, Kevin Gotts and Harry Derby for the many miles they travelled, many times to the detriment of their social lives, and Sue Hanson & staff at Kingsley Media Ltd for their hard work and enthusiasm.

Editor.

ISBN 0-9526555-4-3
The Discerning Visitor *(A Four Seasons Guide)*
Published by Kingsley Media Ltd - Plymouth, Devon

British Library Catalogue-In-Publication Data
Catalogue Data is available from the British Library

Origination and typesetting by TYPEstyle - Ivybridge, Devon
Printed and bound in the United Kingdom by
The Devonshire Press Limited, Torquay, Devon

Concept by M Willcocks PhD • Editor - Nicola Miles

TOURIST INFORMATION CENTRES

SUFFOLK
ALDEBURGH - 01728 453637
BECCLES - 01502 713196
BURY ST EDMUNDS - 01284 764667
FELIXSTOWE - 01394 276770
HADLEIGH - 01473 823284
IPSWICH - 01473 258070
LAVENHAM - 01787 248207
LOWESTOFT - 01502 523000
NEWMARKET - 01638 667200
SOUTHWOLD - 01502 724729
STOWMARKET - 01449 676800
SUDBURY - 01787 881320
WOODBRIDGE - 01394 382240

ESSEX:
BRAINTREE - 01376 550066
COLCHESTER - 01206 282920
HALSTEAD - 01787 476480
SAFFRON WALDEN - 01799 510444

CAMBRIDGESHIRE & S. LINCOLNSHIRE:
BOSTON - 01205 356656
CAMBRIDGE - 01223 322640
ELY - 01353 662062
HUNTINGDON - 01480 388588
PETERBOROUGH - 01733 452336
ST NEOTS - 01480 388788
SPALDING - 01775 725468
WISBECH - 01945 583263

NORFOLK:
ATTLEBOROUGH - 01953 452404
AYLSHAM - 01263 733903 *
CROMER - 01263 512497
DEREHAM - 01362 698992 *
DISS - 01379 650523
DOWNHAM MARKET - 01366 387440
FAKENHAM - 01328 851981 *
GREAT YARMOUTH - 01493 846345
HOLT - 01263 713100 *
HOVETON - 01603 782281 *
HUNSTANTON - 01458 532610
KING'S LYNN - 01533 763044
LODDON - 01508 520690 *
MUNDESLEY - 01263 721070 *
NORTH WALSHAM - 01692 407509 *
NORWICH - 01603 66607
RANWORTH - 01603 270453 *
SHERINGHAM - 01263 824329 *
SWAFFHAM - 01760 722255 *
THETFORD - 01842 752599
WALSINGHAM - 01328 820510 *
WATTON - 01953 882058 *
WELLS NEXT THE SEA - 01328 710885 *
WYMONDHAM - 01953 604721 *

Indicates summer opening only, where 'summer' stretches generally from the end of March to September, although some offices may still be open until October or early November. Other offices are open throughout the year.

ABOUT THIS GUIDE

This guide is designed to be user- friendly, each featured hotel etc., has either a full or half dedicated page, together with an illustration and Quick Reference panel, including the tariff. Each county is separated into chapters, making it easy to find an area, or particular activity of interest to the user. The chapters commence with an index of the selected venues pertinent to the area covered in the specific chapter, this is followed with a summary of the area, including potted history, folklore and anecdotes etc., places to visit, attractions and activities, all with telephone numbers, where available.

To locate a particular destination, turn to page 8.
To locate a particular region, City, town or village, turn to page 588.
To find locations or a map reference turn to page 598.
To locate activities not covered in the chapters, turn to page 595.
To locate a Tourist Information centre, turn to page 6.
To locate a particular Hotel, Inn etc., turn to pages 9-12.
To purchase other editions in this series, turn to page 593.
To write to the Editor, turn to page 594.
To make notes etc., turn to page 602.

Whilst every precaution has been taken in selecting venues for this guide, the publishers can not accept responsibility if you are not satisfied. To ensure standards are maintained, you comments (good or otherwise) would be immensely appreciated, and passed on to the venues concerned. Should you visit venues that have particularly impressed you, which are not included in this guide, but you feel should be, please write to us, and accept our sincere thanks.

Please turn to page for readers comments 594.

To book accommodation, please contact the venue directly, or for your convenience :- E-mail Kingsley Media Ltd, **(kingsley@hotels.u-net.com)**, your enquiry will be passed to the venue of your choice.

WHEN BOOKING PLEASE MENTION THIS GUIDE. THANK YOU.

Please remember when booking accommodation, a booking made by any means is legally binding, and may render you liable for the full cost of the period you have booked. It is a wise precaution to insure against unforeseen circumstances, and please contact the venue as soon possible if you can not arrive on the day you have booked. Kinsley Media Ltd., does charge a fee to accept bookings, accept deposits, or accept any responsibility with regard to availability etc., or any other facet of a booking.

Index to Chapters and Destinations in this Guide

INDEX TO SELECTED VENUES

9

INDEX TO SELECTED VENUES

INDEX TO SELECTED VENUES

Author's Acknowledgements

To Gill, who became indispensable as a travelling companion, her research, ideas, encouragement, and extraordinary perception was inspirational to the nth degree. My thanks also to Nikki and Sue for their help and technical knowledge and to the research staff at Kingsley Media, for their support and patience. My special thanks to Ian & Sharon the artists, for producing illustrations that brought my text to life, and to John who taught me how to convert from the quill to a word processor. Finally, to the people in all the Tourist Information Centres from Colchester to Cromer, who enthusiastically responded to my insatiable quest for facts and figures.

Thank you.

INTRODUCTION

This edition in the Discerning Visitor *series* takes the reader to East Anglia. As a broad introduction to the region, it answers the most important questions asked by discerning visitors before setting out on their travels. Where shall we stay? Where shall we eat? When shall we go, so as not to miss the main local events? What are the special attractions of the towns and villages that surround the Fens, the Broads, the Brecks? What makes the coasts of Norfolk and Suffolk so different from those elsewhere in Britain? Why are the rivers and the Broads so well known amongst anglers and small boat sailors throughout Europe? And how have the many events in the region's rich history left their mark on the town and landscape?

I have taken four centres as bases for the tours which I describe, to split the region into more manageable areas, from the driver's point of view. One part will be based on the village of Dersingham, near King's Lynn, which is as convenient for the Fens as it is for the North Norfolk coast round to Cromer, the Brecklands, and Thetford. Then there will be Gorleston, where we will hear travellers' tales of the Norfolk Broads, explore the coast and, finally, devote time to absorbing the ancient and modern attractions of Norwich and its surroundings.

Further north we will have to face a difficult decision - and it is a hard one - between Ely and Cambridge as our Fenland base. Cambridge's claim is obvious whenever we think of England's culture, learning and traditions. Yet that claim could be a point in Ely's favour: It is not well known and its character, history and atmosphere don't enjoy the high reputation they deserve. We will see - as the roads unwind we may decide to restore the balance a bit On the other hand, it could be a touch perverse to come this far and not spend a night in a city where so many famous heads have rested from the exhausting mix of intense study and socialising . Then again, to wax independent, and find a bed in the shadow of the 'Lantern of the Fens', the Cathedral recognised as one of the finest feats of engineering of the Middle Ages, has its own appeal. Yes, it is a hard choice. If in doubt - don't, as they say, so, let's procrastinate - once we take to the road.

Ancient Bury St Edmunds will be our third base, an obvious Choice and , at some stage, we will turn our backs on the North Sea and drive a short way inland to Colchester, the last base on our list. This Essex town is our gateway to yet another expanse of very different countryside, running down from the picturesque villages in the north west to the ebullient high spots of the coastal region, which will ensure our travels end with a touch of drama, and last visit to
John Constable country.

East Anglia presents more extensive vistas of farmland than anywhere else in Britain. The shades of green, umber, ochre and gold patchwork their way from horizon to horizon with the gentle perfection of a classical oil painting. The land lies like a ruffled rug: more flat at the coast and in the central Fens, then rolled up elsewhere into soft, shaded ridges. Broad heath lands and parochial valleys adjoin the hills, all mastered by stout church towers, visible for miles.

Away from the main centres, the travelling by road is easy and the driver can find miles of peaceful lanes and by ways to take him to his destination - without a hint of road rage!

Although, in some areas of East Anglia, the concentration on cereal crops has had a damaging visual effect, this is fertile country and, elsewhere, flowers, fruit and vegetables are seen on every hand - on roadside stalls or awaiting harvest from the broad fields and orchards. Nevertheless, it is a land of surprises and so, before one can be mesmerised by the flatness, the winding ways of Norfolk and Suffolk suddenly twist free of arable acres to reach points of vantage that draw the eye to wide pasture lands, focused on villages whose unbroken history slips back and back to the early days of human settlement.

Despite the welcome undulations, however, one must admit that the general impression is of an endless plain with woods and spinneys, however dense, as the exception - and as prominent as the church towers, if it only because of their rarity. So, this becomes 'Sky Country' - and 'sky' becomes an experience of greater significance, perhaps, than anywhere else in England. The dizzying vastness of the domed blue of summer is suspended between the spectacular, swift variations from hour to hour of spring and autumn, when the sun from one quarter is almost blinding while the rainbows and overbearing darkness of a dying storm in another are fit for the end of the world. Again, at days' beginnings and ends, there are dawns and sunsets that would be hard to equal from Cape Wrath to the Lizard.

BURNHAM DEEPDALE CHURCH

Nature is not the whole story, though. There are towns and cities where our entire architectural history seems alive, respected and put to good use, even if it is a bit hard to find, sometimes. Nearby, are villages whose churches, pubs and half-timbered cottages keep a record in flint, brick, wood, thatch and tile of the lives of families whose ancestors first settled in the area before the birth of Christ.

This is the land of Boadicea, queen of the Icenii, the British tribe that stubbornly resisted the Roman invaders from within their virtually impregnable natural defences. To the north and east, as ever, was the sea; to the west, the undrained swamps - whilst no invader it in his right mind would ever have attempted to hack his way northwards through the dense forests of Essex.

The Romans left plenty of evidence of their occupation throughout the region, as did the waves of other invaders from Scandinavia and Germany, who followed them. The last to come were the Normans, and they, too, met a stout reluctance to be absorbed on the part of the East Anglian Saxons. Their leader, Hereward the Wake, by his heroic exploits, earned a permanent place in the nation's folklore and history books.

Much later, in the 17th century, other arrivals from Europe - the more peaceful immigrants from Holland - wrought a further major change on the region. Having reclaimed much flooded land in their native country, the newcomers set about draining the Fens - a task which had been considered impossible by the local population, up to then. Once established, these ties with the 'low countries' were strengthened as trade blossomed via the ports of Harwich, Felixstowe, Great Yarmouth and King's Lynn. This rich and varied culture sired many famous sons and daughters. Among them, Nelson, Wolsey, Oliver Cromwell, Elizabeth Fry and Thomas Clarke, a leading figure in the fight for the abolition of slavery, are all remembered with pride.

In the arts, the tranquillity of the rural life, the intellectual fireworks of Cambridge and, above all of them, the awe-inspiring sky with its unforgettable and unique quality of light, have inspired painters from Constable and Gainsborough to the Norwich School of Cotman and Crome. Similarly, writers from Pepys and Cowper to Rider Haggard and Rupert Brooke have all been drawn to this part of England. Finally, one must not forget the centuries-old musical tradition that reached its pinnacle, perhaps, in the work of Benjamin Britten, whose name will always be linked with Aldeburgh.

The region may have a reputation as the driest in Britain - but you'd never guess it from the number and variety of its wildlife population. [Perhaps they're unimpressed by statistics]. For the student of natural history, East Anglia acts like an irresistible magnet. Nature reserves abound. The Fens, Broads and coastal marshes offer the best bird-watching opportunities in Britain - a fact recognised throughout the world - while even the tiniest creek is home to a host of creatures whose daily round delights the enthusiast.

With this background to guide us, then, it is time to move from the general to the specific, to start, in short, to plan our exploration of these unique and fascinating Eastern Counties. We could start anywhere from Colchester to Cambridge, from Yarmouth to The Wash. We have only to pick our base. As that's the case, I propose casting my vote in favour of the King's Lynn area, because of an interest in this part of Norfolk that dates from my childhood and is based on nothing more substantial than family legends of a wealthy Hugenot ancestor who fled from France, settled to the west of Norwich, made his fortune - and has defied every attempt made by my relatives to establish a claim on his estates, as he was wise enough to leave behind little more trace of his passing than hints on a tombstone and a few entries in parish records. Ah......., but you should hear the stories!

So please follow me on what promises to be an eventful and unforgettable experience.

Bon Voyage.

Selected venues in this chapter

"And Noah he ofen said to his wife when he sat down to dine,
I don't care where the water goes........
if it does't mix with the wine"
G.K. Chesterton

CHAPTER 1
Exploring the North of the Region
North Norfolk "Nature to be Enjoyed"

I have chosen **DERSINGHAM** as my first base for exploring the north of the region for its ease of access. King's Lynn, to the south, is a more intensive introduction to the history and character of old Norfolk towns. It seems likely, though, after a day's exploration, tramping through nature reserves, and absorbing the atmosphere of country houses, that it would be wise to avoid congested major roads in the rush hour. Dersingham is an attractive little village off the A149 midway between Lynn, as it is known locally, and Hunstanton, to the north. Perhaps its main claim to fame is its proximity to Sandringham, which must be the most famous country home in England. Of course we don't just need good access for our daily pilgrimages: the 'town down the road' is also handy for shopping expeditions, eating out and visits to the theatre. Once we have secured our base, we can begin our first sortie. We will travel south a short way, past the Royal residence, turn onto the A148 and enter King's Lynn along Benefer Way.

NORFOLK COTTAGES

All English history from the Domesday Book onwards can be conjured up from the many pointers found within the boundaries of **KINGS LYNN** [Information - 01553 763044]. At the time of Domesday, it was known as Lynn Episcopi - Bishop's Lynn - to confirm its role in the manor of the Bishop of Norwich.

The town was famous for its harbour in the middle ages - by the 14th century it was the third most important port in England. It became Lynn Regis - King's Lynn - in a charter from Henry VIII, after the Dissolution of the Monasteries in 1537. The town continued to prosper, mainly as a centre for grain exports, throughout the 17th, 18th and 19th centuries, as we can see from the fine buildings set off by its 'labyrinth of tiny streets'.

Today King's Lynn is an expanding port and a centre of growth for the area, in terms both of tourism and carefully blended industrial development. For example, the modern glass-making factory, the latest feature in a 300 year-old tradition, has already become a tourist attraction where visitors can see the entire process involved in the creation of Caithness Crystal.

Amongst the many imposing buildings, three are outstanding. The 15th century GUILDHALL OF ST GEORGE, the largest ancient structure of its kind in the country, nowadays houses the town's ARTS CENTRE on which the annual festival is focused, amidst a year-round programme of music, comedy and cinema. Lynn's medieval prosperity was expressed in its spectacular chequered flint work and so, when the Town Hall was built five hundred years later, a style was chosen to match its predecessor. Further reflections of the town's historical importance are the 1683 CUSTOM HOUSE and England's only surviving Hanseatic warehouse.

Of course, Norfolk is also famous for its churches - and Lynn is no exception. The parish church of St. Margaret, dating from the 12th century, reveals many stages of the town's evolution in the styles of its later additions. Not least of these is the Georgian 'Gothic' nave of 1740, built to replace the original, which was destroyed when a storm felled the spire right across it!

One cannot move on from King's Lynn without mentioning its markets. The Tuesday market, dating again from the 12th century, is held in a spacious square near the town's other main church, whose patron saint is Nicholas. This square is also the site of the old CORN EXCHANGE [Information - 01553 766202], which has been refurbished as a magnificent concert hall. The even older Saturday market takes place at the southern end of the High Street, close to St. Margaret's. In fact, Lynn has one of the widest ranges of shopping facilities in the area, as the markets are supplemented by a pedestrian precinct and many stores and smaller shops which blend in with the splendid Vancouver Centre.

So, having chosen a base, and explored its better known neighbour, it is time to head north, back up the A149 to Hunstanton, regarded by some as King's Lynn's seaside resort. Leaving the town by our chosen road, with the marshy fringes of the Wash to our left, within a matter of minutes we reach our first stop: **CASTLE RISING**.

Set among defensive earthworks that may have been built by the Romans, the castle's impressive Norman keep stands as a monument to its builder, the 12th century William de Albini. He became Earl of Sussex, following his marriage to the widow of

Henry I. Edward III later obliged his machiavellian mother, Isabella, 'The She-Wolf of France', to make it her 'home' after he had dealt with her lover and accomplice, Roger Mortimer, the murderer of her husband, Edward II. It is said, locally, that on many a night Isabel's ghost may be seen prowling around the ramparts.

The castle changed hands under the Tudors. It was granted to the Duke of Norfolk by Henry VIII in 1544 and stayed in the Howard family for four hundred years, until the Ministry of Public Building and Works took it over in 1958.

CASTLE RISING

Entry is by the ruined gate house, from which one gains access to the hall - keep, of which only the lower two carved and decorated stages remain. A great stone staircase takes the visitor to the upper level, to an intriguing series of rooms, galleries and minor staircases which are well worth exploring. The view from the ramparts, alone, is probably enough justification for the climb. Now just a hamlet, Castle Rising once rivaled King's Lynn as a port. Sadly, the Babingley River, which was its lifeline to the sea, silted up and became non-navigable to boats which, by then, had become much larger than those of its heyday.

After visiting the castle, we return to the A149 and head north to a right turn leading to **SANDRINGHAM** [Enquiries - 01553 772675], the royal home which is so familiar as a setting for the informal family pictures that have become an integral part of the English tradition. The house and grounds of the Queen's Norfolk residence are open to the public during the summer, if no member of the Royal Family is staying there. The 7,000 acre estate covers seven parishes, although there is no actual village of Sandringham. The best point of entry, from the Castle Rising - Dersingham road, takes one through luxuriant woodland to the house itself, set in superb grounds. It is a mid-Victorian re-creation of a Jacobean design, financed by the then Prince of Wales - later, Edward VII - using Duchy of Cornwall funds that accumulated whilst he was a minor.

As long as the family is away, visitors are welcome in the house, gardens, park and museums of motor cars and dolls. Although the main attraction, perhaps, is the insight gained into the off-duty life of the Queen, her husband and children from the very personal nature of all to be seen in the public rooms, the keen gardener will find the grounds just as rewarding. The sixty glorious acres are beautifully landscaped, with walks amongst rhododendrons, azaleas, camellias, magnolias, fuchsias and hydrangeas set out around the lakes, along the stream and through the woods.

Whilst in the area, there is a further attraction worthy of consideration. Across the main road from the house, is SANDRINGHAM WARREN, a spread of woodland, heath and clumps of rhododendrons offering nature trails, less serious walks and many spots for picnics. At the far side of the Warren is the Edwardian station where the royal family used to arrive, before transferring to carriages for the final stage of the journey to their country home. The line was closed in 1969, and the station, which was bought by a private owner, is now a railway museum. After our tour of the royal home, the route continues in the direction of Hunstanton. As our Sandringham detour took us from the A149 onto the B1439 we must remain on that minor road through Dersingham for a mile or two, which, in passing, provides an extra bonus. Near the junction of the A and B roads, lies **SNETTISHAM**, with its 18th century water mill, art gallery, river walks and, at the distance of a mile or two, the RSPB bird sanctuary, where four hides surround a disused shingle pit. Among the many species to be seen here are common terns in summer and wildfowl and waders during the winter.

Travelling north again, we reach **HEACHAM**, a large seaside village with good walks along its sea wall in both directions. Here is the centre of Norfolk's lavender industry, one of the area's major attractions. In mid-summer, the sight of the fields around the village and at Chosely Farm, five and a half miles to the east, is breathtaking. All the shades of mauve and purple shimmer in the sunlight, until the crop is harvested in early August. It is then taken either to Caley Mill on the main King's Lynn - Hunstanton road for packing and dispatch, or distilling, or to another small distillery at **FRING**, four miles to the south east.

CALEY MILL [Enquiries - 01485 570384], the headquarters of Norfolk Lavender, was built from local carrstone as a corn mill early in the 18th century. Today, in its setting of rose, lavender and herb gardens, it has a unique reputation for the quality of its products and its specialist services to gardeners. Also in the grounds is the National Collection of Lavenders, where fifty species or varieties are nurtured in individual beds - although, if there's a danger of frost the more fragile ones are shifted indoors. Guided tours can be arranged, and these also take in the Herb Garden and the Fragrant Meadow Garden. Having taken in the sights and scents of these displays, visitors will almost certainly want to call in at the Fragrant Plant Centre to choose some samples for their own gardens from the range on sale - or to pop into the Gift Shop where the Mill's hand-made soaps, perfumes and other products are available.

Heacham's place in history is further strengthened by its connections with the Red Indian Princess, Pocahontas, whose life was celebrated in the 1997 King's Lynn pageant. Pocahontas married John Rolf at Heacham Hall in 1614. She died three years later, at the age of only 22, but left a son, Tom, who went back to his mother's homeland, and has since been claimed as an ancestor by many famous families throughout the United States. The hall itself was destroyed by fire during World War II.

As we turn into **HUNSTANTON** [Information - 01485 532610], we are approaching an area of serious beaches. The town itself is the largest of the resorts along this section of coast. Incidentally, it is also the only East Anglian seaside town which actually faces west! This spectacular expanse of sand stretches for miles, past Old Hunstanton Village and Holme-next-the-Sea to Brancaster, all of which will be visited in due course.

Although these natural features have attracted the familiar developments of fun fairs and caravan parks, they have been absorbed into the rest of the waterfront so as to leave a significant reminder of the gentler air of the town's Victorian past. This quality, however, should not be taken as backward-looking: in keeping with the latest concerns for the quality of the environment, Hunstanton has won Seaside Awards for its cleanliness and amenities for the past six years. It is a friendly, tidy and welcoming place - if a bit brash - offering a great deal to those who enjoy the more active aspects of the seaside, as well as much to those who prefer to relax when on holiday.

A short walk northwards along the golden sands brings us to Hunstanton's famous striped cliffs. Formed about a hundred million years ago, these present a 'sandwich effect', with carrstone - a sandstone cemented by iron oxide or rust - set between two layers of chalk, one of which has been stained red by the presence of the iron. Below this 60ft elevation the rock has collapsed into huge boulders at the top of the beach as well as many rockpools, which are exposed when the clear, shallow water drops at low tide. These features, though they may seem only a backdrop to the bustle of the holidaymakers' activities, come into their own as evening approaches, presenting another facet of the area's appeal. Because of its orientation, the resort basks in sunshine long after the bustle along the promenade has quietened down. Seemingly endless, lazy summer evenings develop an intensely romantic atmosphere, until the entire sea and landscape combine to afford a perfect setting for incomparably spectacular sunsets.

Local landowner Henry Styleman Lestrange was the driving force behind the town's early development from 1846. With the arrival of the railway in 1862, and the burgeoning fashion for seaside holidays, Hunstanton experienced a boom. Many of its most attractive architectural features date from this period and the following decade or two. As hereditary Lord High Admirals of the Wash, the Lestrange family had a significant influence on the area. In theory these dignitaries can claim ownership of anything on the beach or in the sea 'as far as a man could ride his horse into it at low tide and then throw his spear!' Notices on the sands suggest this right even extends to all the oysters and mussels taken along the foreshore! Finally, further up the coast, at the adjacent OLD HUNSTANTON, the family's name is further commemorated by an antiques, arts and crafts centre.

The cliff-top remains of ST EDMOND'S CHAPEL, where Edmond, king of the East Angles, is said to have landed in AD850, are a pointer to the more distant history which the town shares with much of Norfolk, whose origins stretch back into mists beyond remembrance. OLD HUNSTANTON HALL, a moated mansion, dates to more recent, Tudor, times.

Nonetheless, today's Hunstanton is about the beach and sea, from the remains of the old pier, which now houses an amusement centre, to facilities for water sports and the SEA LIFE CENTRE, which presents a spectacular insight into the underwater world of the Norfolk coast. Unwinding after the day's activities will tend to focus on the food, drink and conviviality of the town's pubs and renowned family 'chippies'. There are also restaurants catering for a wide range of more sophisticated palates. Finally, to complete the evening, the PRINCESS THEATRE [Information - 01485 532252] offers a variety of 'spectaculars' around the year, featuring artists from Joe Loss to Julie Felix.

After exploring Hunstanton, it's time to prepare for a major change of emphasis. Much of West Norfolk, particularly the coastline, is designated an Area of Outstanding Natural Beauty. So, having left the interactive human and natural elements of a true seaside town, we enter the world of sand dunes, reed beds and clear horizons which lead us to infinitely peaceful beaches.

Old Hunstanton, Brancaster and Holkham form an area of stunning coastal scenery and spaciousness that cries out to be explored. Walkers, in particular, will love discovering the wonders of the miles of shoreline. At Holme-next-the-Sea, the ancient PEDDARS WAY joins the NORFOLK COAST PATH which runs from Hunstanton to Cromer. Even a casual stroll reveals a wealth of wild flowers. Rabbits, foxes and other animals are often seen here, as are larks, plovers, kestrels, magnificent pheasants and, in autumn, the many migrants for whom this is a main point of departure. Historically, Peddars Way is worthy of note, as its ancient track way seems to have been a major line of communication as far back as pre-Roman times, linking Holme with Knettishall, near Thetford, fifty miles away in Suffolk. Of course, as well as being the best way to become acquainted with the wildlife of the coastal region, these walks also offer sweeping views of the historic, exhilarating waterfront. So, having been led by the Peddars Way or the Coast Path to **HOLME-NEXT-THE-SEA**, what do we find? A pretty village, perhaps not as 'next' as its name suggests, owing to changes in local topography over the centuries. In fact, the beach can only be reached by crossing the HUNSTANTON CHAMPIONSHIP GOLF COURSE where one is warned to keep an eye open for the little white projectiles!

It is worth digressing for a moment at this stage, to draw attention to the general architectural characteristics of this part of North Norfolk. Even when travelling in the midst of winter, one is astounded by the unique quality of the light which makes the stunning views across flat or gently undulating landscapes so spectacular. It is within these landscapes, however, that the true jewels are located. A mixture of flintwork and brick, capped with terra-cotta pantiles, is found in villages whose small cottages front the road that either passes through them as a kind of rural highway , or else winds beguilingly from the church to the pub, then onto the store and the gateway to the manor.

Time and again one encounters reminders of the 'Dutch connection', in the shape of stepped gable- ends, tall, narrow windows and extended, ornamented chimney stacks. These are romantic and, by and large, unspoilt places from which it is hard to tear oneself away. Cley, Blakeney, Stiffkey - home of the renowned Stiffkey Blue cockles - and Thornham are classic examples of this style that, more than once, leave one wondering if one has not taken a wrong turning and ended up somewhere near Amsterdam.

To return to Holme: while the village has its own appeal, one must admit that the joint attractions of the HOLME DUNES NATURE RESERVE and the HOLME BIRD OBSERVATORY are all but irresistible. Somewhere near five hundred acres of sand-dune and salt marsh are entered by a bumpy one mile track that leads first to the Nature Reserve and then to the Observatory, for which joint permits are available from either warden. The richness of plant, animal and bird life under the administration of the Norfolk Naturalists' Trust and the Norfolk Ornithologists' Association is worthy of the famous Guinness book: 279 species of birds, including ospreys, hoopoes, the rare collared flycatcher, the red-rumped swallow and numerous species of warbler have been recorded, as have 363 species of moth and plants ranging from sea buckthorn and sea lavender to bee and pyramid orchids .

It's possible, after so much fresh air, that we need a touch of man built environment, to achieve a balance, if nothing else! At such a moment, one or more of the villages known as the Seven Burnhams verges on the magnetic in its attractions: a pub, a beer or coffee and some food garnished with revelations of more recent, human, history, perhaps. This might be a wish beyond contradiction, but we still need to be a little patient. En route to the Burnhams we ought to pause at Titchwell and Brancaster - each of which merits its special inclusion in our tour - rather than hurtle by along the A149 in search of refreshment.

TITCHWELL MARSH RESERVE marks the RSPB's response to a tidal surge in January 1953, which inundated land first reclaimed for agriculture by the building of sea walls in the 1780's. The Reserve car park lies down a track a quarter of a mile west of the village and there one will also find a useful information centre. Guidelines are important if one is to make the best of one's time amidst the shingle beach, reed beds, marsh land and salt and fresh water lagoons. In summer, the area is home to ringed plovers, bearded reedlings and little terns. In winter, Brent geese, avocets and shore larks are among the many interesting inhabitants. One should note, however, that while the reserve is open daily, the information centre is only open in summer.

Our last pause before the break is at **BRANCASTER** - which really needs a day's visit just to be able to cope with its geography. It is all a matter of the scale of one's aspirations: to see everything involves, at the outset, the one mile drive from the centre of the neat red-roofed village with its 14th century church, through a thicket of reeds and across the salt marsh to the beach car park behind the dunes. From here, one gains access to wide sands backed by a massive sea wall. As swimming from the beach is extremely dangerous, because of the swift incoming tides which soon cut off and then cover the sands, we may prefer to return to the village at this point rather than dally longer than is necessary to absorb the main features of this section of coast. Yet, on a sunny day, this is as good a spot as any for just being, for floating in the imagination somewhere between sea, sand and sky.

BRANCASTER STAITHE, one and a half miles east of the village, presents a small, all but land-locked harbour, home to a remnant of its once significant shellfish-gathering industry, whose origins are said to go back to Roman times, as does so much in the area. It flourished when access was much better. From the hard foreshore, small boats now take visitors to the National Nature Reserve on SCOLT HEAD ISLAND, at the entrance to BRANCASTER HARBOUR. The reserve is owned jointly by the National Trust and the Norfolk Naturalist's Trust, and is managed by the Nature Conservancy. Established in 1923, its reputation is based largely on its nesting colonies of common and sandwich terns, breeding on a four acre ternery near the landing stage, which also marks the start of the three-quarter mile nature trail. Before setting out it should be noted that, as at BRANCASTER BEACH, the low tides are to be treated with extreme caution - indeed, it is dangerous even to walk across to the island at such times - especially if one lacks local knowledge. Finally, it should also be noted that there are two further restrictions: dogs are not allowed onto the island, and the ternery is strictly out of bounds during May, June and July, when the birds are breeding.

We may well be heading to the Seven Burnhams for a breather after all these spectacles of nature, but we shouldn't forget the villages' claims to fame in their own right. Of the seven, that is, Burnhams Norton, Othery, Sutton, Thorpe, Ulph, Westgate and Deepdale, three seem particularly interesting. Whichever one is chosen, though, no doubt the pleasure of resting one's limbs will be just as great.**BURNHAM DEEPDALE** is a trim little village with an eye-catching parish church. Built soon after the Conquest, it is of flint with an unusual, circular tower. Inside is one of North Norfolk's chief treasures: a seasonal font, carved from a single, solid block of stone. On it are depicted twelve figures carrying out tasks appropriate to each month of the year.

BURNHAM THORPE, two miles inland, is renowned as the birthplace of Horatio Nelson. Although the old rectory where the event took place, in 1758, was pulled down in 1802, the village's All Saints Church, which stands a short distance from its gathered cottages, still has the font where he was christened, as well as a crucifix carved of wood from the 'Victory' and a bust of Nelson in its chancel.

BURNHAM OVERY STAITHE, in contrast, is impressive as a pleasant little sailing village, where boats are launched either side of high water from its wide slope of hard sand. Appropriately, it attracts attention each year with its regatta. Richard Woodget, one-time master of the 'Cutty Sark', lived here from 1899 to 1926 and there is a plaque to indicate his house. As one absorbs the village's atmosphere and delights in the views across the coast, one can see that a clipper captain would have a job to find a better location for his own mooring place. Tracks from the village lead out onto the marshes and one, called 'Cockle Path', has been restored as far as Scolt Head. Boat trips to Scolt Head Island are available, weather permitting.

The next call on our tour brings us to a scene of total delight. Soon after leaving the Burnhams, we arrive at **HOLKHAM** and turn right, off the A149 into the grounds of HOLKHAM HALL [Enquiries - 01328 710227]. The manor was originally bought in 1610 by Edward Coke, a famous jurist, who later became Lord Chief Justice. The present Palladian mansion was built by the first Earl of Leicester over a period of thirty years, from 1734. The family's direct line failed and the estate passed to Thomas Cook [1752 - 1842] who seized this opportunity to practice his skills as an agricultural reformer. The estate wasteland was transformed into scientifically cultivated areas. Whilst crop changes included a shift in emphasis from rye to wheat, developments in breeding led to the evolution of improved livestock breeds. His family then reclaimed more of the OVERY MARSHES, which were first drained in 1639, as their part of the process. Unfortunately, thanks to their efforts, Wells and Cley were left high, dry, and somewhat speechless, with their original 'Next the Sea' labels rather wide of the mark. Coke of Holkham's achievements are commemorated by a 100ft high monument crowned with a wheatsheaf and surrounded at its base corners by a Devon ox, a Southdown sheep, a plough and a seed drill.

HOLKHAM HALL

The Hall, which is open from May to September plus the four bank holidays, houses a superb art collection, including works by Rubens, Van Dyck, Claude, Poussin and Gainsborough, as well as pieces from the Greek and Roman eras, all displayed in sumptuous settings amongst examples of William Kent's furniture. As an introduction to this experience of 2,000 years of fine art, access to the building is via a stunning alabaster entrance hall. Elsewhere on the estate, attractions include an exhibition featuring the history of farming which, amongst other things, shows how Coke's new four-course crop rotation system worked. There is also a Bygones Museum, which houses more than 4,000 domestic and agricultural artefacts, presenting a panorama of seven generations of living history. Other features embrace an art gallery of new work, a pottery and the inspired gardens, as well as a garden centre. In fine weather, one can enjoy the lakeside walks or take to the water for a short cruise. A deer park completes the outstanding spectrum of attractions.

Across the road from the gate to the hall, the half-mile long Lady Anne's Drive leads to HOLKHAM GAP and the HOLKHAM NATURE RESERVE. The entire twelve miles of coast, from Overy Staithe to Blakeney, apart from the Channel entrance to Wells Next The Sea, forms the largest coastal nature reserve in England and Wales: its 10,000 acres of dunes, glorious beaches and salt marshes must be all but unequalled anywhere. The Wells Channel winds down to pine-fringed HOLKHAM BAY, with good, safe swimming from its half-moon sweep of firm sand. It is hardly an exaggeration to suggest that one could spend one's entire time in North Norfolk in the Holkham area and consider it to have been a thoroughly worthwhile experience.

WELLS-NEXT-THE-SEA [Information - 01328 710885] - which is strictly speaking 'inland' not 'next', because of the effects of reclamation over the years -

though hardly larger than an average village, must be considered in three parts. The quayside, the old street behind the quay and the beach area have individual characters that are quite distinct from those of their neighbours.

The quay is a jumble of cafes, ships' chandlers and amusement arcades overlooked by the harbour master's office. Here one also finds stalls selling mussels, dressed crab, cockles and samphire. Words like 'bright', 'brash' and 'breezy', come readily to mind when taking in the overall effect. It's rather surprising, therefore, to discover that the old streets and Georgian houses surrounding 'Buttlands' - a green probably named from 16th century long bow practice - have a quite different dignity and style about them. Just as different is the High Street which winds up from the large parish church of St. Nicholas.

One mile away from the village, the beach area is sandy and inviting - provided one remembers not to swim near the lifeboat house. There is also a large boating lagoon known as 'Abraham's Bosom'. If you propose to spend some time on the beach be warned about the sand bank known as Bob Hall's Sand. It might look inviting for a pleasant stroll on a sunny day; if it does, don't hang about if you want to stay dry. Make it a swift stroll or you'll be cut off by the incoming tide! One further attraction draws numbers of enthusiasts to the village, the seaward terminus of the WELLS AND WALSINGHAM LIGHT RAILWAY [Talking timetable - 01328 856506], whose eight-mile return journey along old Great Eastern track makes it one of the longest ten and a half inch gauge railways in Britain.

Having left the bustle on the quayside at Wells and returned to the main road, a few minutes' drive brings us to a village whose renown is out of proportion to its comparatively small size: **STIFFKEY**. While there is some debate as to whether the village's name should be pronounced as its spelling would suggest rather than as the traditional 'Stewkey', there is no such conflict regarding the fame of its cockles, known far and wide as 'Stewkey Blues'. The colour of the cockles derives from material in the tidal areas where they are gathered at low water. It only affects the shells and is, apparently, completely harmless. The flavour, according to connoisseurs , is worth travelling miles to experience. Stiffkey is not to be missed for reasons other than the purely gastronomic. It is a totally unspoilt place of brick and flint, straddling a road which undulates from the first houses to the last. On the seaward side, in July, a further interesting phenomenon occurs. The marshes, owned by the National Trust, are covered with purple sea lavender; which is completely [and surprisingly] scentless!

Having come this far along the North Norfolk coast from King's Lynn, it seems a good idea to stop for a moment and just look around. It cannot escape even the most casual and hurried observer that, despite the charm of the villages and the magnificence of the country houses, this is wild country on which man's grip is tenuous. Ever since people first settled here they have been engaged in a constant war with the sea whose tides and changes of mood they have learned, at best, to respect, and, very often, to dread. Daniel Defoe, after a visit to North Norfolk, claimed that his most persistent memories were of the flavour of the lobsters; and of the terror of the sailors! Off Cromer, the site of one of the busiest lifeboat stations in the British Isles, lies a stretch of shoals and sand banks known as 'The Devil's Throat' - and local comments suggest that this appellation borders on the charitable.

Nor is this state of affairs stable enough for a long-term plan to allow man to come to terms with it. The tides change. Mud, sand, clay and shingle - all are driven by the sea into long desolate strips which emerge from the water only to be sucked back from time to time and dashed away into oblivion. Examples of this process are Scolt Head and Blakeney Point, whose constantly changing outlines make any map of them virtually meaningless.

Such is human perversity that, as we have seen, this has been one of the most consistently populated areas in Britain, as well as one of the most prosperous. The unbroken line of habitation and the changes of fortune have left well-defined traces in the landscape and architecture, which have a unique attraction and charm, regardless of the horrors of the tideline. Were one delivered blindfold to some parts of England, and then allowed to see, one might have some difficulty in deciding where one had ended up; not so in North Norfolk.

At first glance the location is obvious. For example, nowhere else would one find such widespread use of flint as in the West of this county. From a distance, some towns and villages look like shuffled up piles of pebbles. Pebbles, that on closer inspection reveal strong and peculiar design elements: chequer - boards of alternate flint and stone here, more random designs with squared off, brick door and window frames there. Each had a specific significance for the hands and minds of the builders of the houses and churches all those years ago, today these are not even remembered. Truly fascinating - yet one cannot forget the lobsters [or the seafarers].

Throughout our travels we have seen many wild birds and have become familiar with the wild flowers of heath, wood and marsh land. As we approach the little village of **MORSTON**, there is an opportunity to encounter other creatures frequently associated with this stretch of the coast. A lane from the village runs down to a tidal creek and to the 540 acres of MORSTON MARSH, bought together with MORSTON QUAY by the National Trust in 1973. The real attraction, however, lies offshore. We can take a boat from the foreshore out to BLAKENEY POINT, and stand a good chance of seeing seals basking on the exposed sandbanks. The colony was badly hit by a virus during the summer of 1988. To deal with the outbreak, the National Trust, the Sea Mammal Research Unit in Cambridge, the RSPCA and Greenpeace joined forces to establish a Seal Assessment Centre at Docking. This work, and the crisis itself, attracted a great deal of media coverage and aroused much public interest in seals. By 1990, the virus seemed to have worked its way through the seal population, but careful observation has been kept up nevertheless.

If the weather has been kind, and the voyage has been fruitful, the benign air that this will have created will be enhanced at our next destination: the village of **BLAKENEY**. For at least eight hundred years the name of this village has been synonymous with sailing. Currently, its reputation stands as a centre for yachting and cruising, but, in the Middle Ages, it was known throughout East Anglia as a port second only to King's Lynn in significance. While fishing has been a continuing activity, in those days the village's major role was trading in wool and grain with Europe. Today's recreational sailors are the descendants of those men who fought their way back and forth across the North Sea to bring wealth and security to the region.

The history of Blakeney goes back more than a thousand years before its days of maritime prosperity. There are many traces to be found of occupation long before the Romans arrived. With the collapse of the Latin empire, the Vikings took an interest in the region, as did the Angles, after whom it came to be named. The village is mentioned in the Domesday Book of 1086 and scholars suggest the name derives from 'Blak Snitt', meaning 'Black Isle'. An element of controversy has crept in even here, as others suggest that particular name might have referred to 'Snitterley'; which could have been another place altogether, subsequently washed out to sea.

In the 13th century, all the coast villages - Weybourne, Salthouse, Cley, Wiveton and Blakeney - were combined into a single port. This had considerable prestige, and the entry from the sea was BLAKENEY HAVEN, opposite Cley. At this time, in 1292, the area attracted the Carmelite Friars, who established a very important foundation on the ground running from the present church to the quay. By the time of the dissolution in 1538 this had grown to an estate of sixty five acres. It is possible that the chancel of the present church is part of the original building which, in medieval times, had a light on top of its tower to guide shipping. More recently, its churchyard was chosen as the last resting place of Sir Henry 'Tim' Birkin, who made his name racing Bentleys during the golden age of the track at Brooklands in the 1920's and 30's.

In 1222, Henry III granted a market charter to Blakeney. This aspect of the village's significance is marked by the establishment of the Guildhall in the mid- 14th century. It can be seen today near the quay. Although wrecking and smuggling occasionally offered additions to the local income, by Tudor times it was primarily for fish that the village was best known, with a reputation for quality that extended throughout England. Henry VIII gave a charter to Blakeney to sell fish to Binham Priory and Walsingham Abbey. Indeed, so important was the fishing trade considered to be, that, from the time of Richard II, the fishermen of Blakeney, Cley, Cromer and the adjacent ports were exempt from being impressed into the Navy. Moreover, there is a traditional tale which says that when Blakeney was asked to provide ships to fight the Armada, the mayor of Lynn said they were too busy fishing off Iceland to be involved in such matters.

Three local men became great admirals in the British Navy. Sir Christopher Myngs was baptised at Salthouse in 1625, and saw much action before he was killed at the battle of North Foreland in 1666. Sir John Narborough, baptised at Cockthorpe in 1640, again saw much active service before his death in 1688. His second wife married the most famous of the three: Sir Cloudesley Shovell. He was knighted for his gallantry at the battle of Bantry Bay [1689] and died in 1707 in a shipwreck off the Isles of Scilly. The press gang exemption had gone during the eighteenth-century and local men, by Nelson's day, played as important a part in the defeat of the French navy as men from any other area of the country.

Blakeney has its fair share of old tales and legends concerning, for example, the deeds of highwaymen and the appearance of strange apparitions with mystical powers. One that sticks in my mind is the legend of Black Shuck, said to appear as a huge black dog. The name- deriving, apparently, from the Anglo-Saxon word 'socca', meaning 'demon' - has attached itself to the story of a dog found drowned with his master on the shoreline after a great storm in 1709. His spirit is said to haunt the coast, howling over his loss and foretelling disaster.

Trade at Blakeney declined from the 17th century onwards. The process started when the Calthorpe family began to carry out land enclosures which destroyed the viability of Salthouse, Wiveton and then Cley. Up to the end of the 19th century, large coal ships delivered their cargoes to Blakeney, but eventually the silting up of the access channel meant that even this source of trade came to a close. The building of the flood banks, together with the silting process, has led to the evolution of a new era for the village: today it has become popular as a spick and span holiday resort with much to offer the dinghy-sailing fraternity. The main street of Blakeney has adopted the brick and flint style, with a steep drop down to the harbour. The parish church of Saint Nicholas is vast and impressive, having an unusual second, much smaller tower built at the east end. This tower was probably used as a beacon.

One need not be actively involved with boats to enjoy the pleasant atmosphere of this part of the coast. There is much to be said for just sitting on the quay and watching the dinghies tacking their way along the twisting inlet of the River Glaven, and then taking a boat to Blakeney Point to watch the wild fowl. As with Marston, there is also a chance to watch the seals on the offshore banks, having made the four mile boat trip north west from the mouth of the Haven.

All in all Blakeney is a place which, once visited, is not easily forgotten. It has, in abundance, that combination of interesting features and Norfolk charm which remains fresh however many times one returns.

Having left Blakeney, and still heading broadly east along the A149, we come to **CLEY-NEXT-THE-SEA** - remembering to pronounce it 'Cly', if we don't want to be marked down instantly as 'trippers'. We can see at a glance that there's not very much that is 'next' about this village either, if we're talking about proximity to the tideline. Again, because of the 17th century land reclamation , the former nautical focus of the place is but a fond memory. Instead, there is a pleasant assembly of flint houses on a dog-leg bend in the road, where traffic and pedestrians compete uneasily, and the remains of a quay on which sits a rather splendid 18th century windmill. From here, a smaller road leads across the saltings for about a mile to a long shallow, shingle beach which shelves markedly and can make for dangerous swimming. Known as CLEY EYE, this stony barrier to the sea's inroads is enough of an attraction to justify its own car park, from which one may set out on the five mile walk to Blakeney Point.

BIRDWATCHING ON THE SALTINGS

As might be expected along this coast, much of the marsh has become a bird sanctuary, offering a haven to bitterns and bearded tits among others. The CLEY AND SALTHOUSE MARSHES constitute a 650 acre Norfolk Naturalist' Trust nature reserve between the A149 and the sea. The abiding memory, however, is probably that of the startling changes that have occurred as a result of actions that seemed, at the time, no doubt, to make economic sense amidst a plethora of good intentions - and yet had unforeseen side effects . Does that have a familiar ring, one wonders. Thus the once bustling port is reduced to a cluster of houses and the sea is out of sight. Very pretty, certainly, in an eco-friendly sort of way - but food for thought, for all that.

On from Cley, we come to two or three more villages separating us from the town of Sheringham. Amongst these is **SALTHOUSE**, with its village pond accommodating swans and cygnets, where one must be on one's guard to avoid frightening the ducks that seem to take crossing and re-crossing the road as a natural part of their fun. Nearby is **KELLING**, another pleasant village worth a pause, not least for the sake of some interesting shops whose contents will delight collectors.

Our drive leads next to a village with dramatically different claims to fame - **WEYBOURNE**. Because of its steep beach, which allows ships of a reasonable size to come in quite close, Weybourne was once considered important enough to be garrisoned, particularly against the Spanish in 1588. Now it draws attention on two main counts: the NORTH NORFOLK RAILWAY [Enquiries - 01263 822045] and the MUCKLEBURGH COLLECTION [Enquiries - 10263 588210]. Once a part of the Midlands and Great Northern Railway, the preserved line, operated by a group of enthusiasts since 1960, offers a three mile trip on steam or diesel trains from Holt to Sheringham stations. The journey takes approximately 16 minutes, end to end, and Weybourne lies roughly mid-way. There is a station car park in the village, as there is at each of the termini.

Close by, at Weybourne Military Camp, the Muckleburgh Collection must be a major draw to anyone who has an interest in military history. Amidst Britain's largest privately owned working military collection, may be found examples of many kinds of military hardware operating on land or in the air, as well as a display of model ships. This offers interesting comparisons between, say, early and modern tanks, or second World War and contemporary artillery tactics.

NORTH NORFOLK RAILWAY

We now experience another one of those unexpected Norfolk changes. Having spent some time amidst the wild terrain of bird sanctuaries, nature reserves and little picturesque villages, we are about to be brought back to a taste or two of the lifestyle of more urban coastal resorts. The first of these is **SHERINGHAM** [Information - 01263 824329].

As so often in this part of the world, we find that the coming of the railway, towards the end of the 19th century, transformed what, for centuries, had been a comparatively quiet fishing village. This transformation is visible as a spreading out of squares of holiday makers' houses from the lower town, which still consists, to a great extent, of the traditional cottages of the fisher folk who used to be the sole inhabitants. The newer, upper part of the town focuses on the High Street, which has a neat clock tower at one end and the seafront at the other. **UPPER SHERINGHAM** was once an agricultural area but is now almost entirely residential. Obviously, the visitors staying in these houses and hotels are attracted by the beach, which has extensive, clean sand at low tide. At high tide, however, there is little more than a ridge of shingle, a feature for which provision has been made in the range of other attractions available elsewhere in the town.

Away from the seaside, these other aspects are well worth considering. SHERINGHAM HALL is set in a delightful park designed by Humphrey Repton, and famed for its splendid rhododendrons. Just under a mile to the east of the town are the ruins of the 13th century BEESTON PRIORY, where carpets of wild flowers can be found on the surrounding common, from spring to autumn. The pretty corner offers fine views of heath, woods and sea. Finally, there are woodland walks on the ridge above the town, leading from the remains of a Roman camp. Between Sheringham and Holt runs the North Norfolk Railway, to which we have already referred in describing the attractions of Weybourne, its mid point.

Having left the town, still on the ubiquitous A149, our next goal is **CROMER** [Information - 01263 512497], with a somewhat different approach to the serious business of holiday making. Between the two towns, the discerning visitor may wish to make haste and avert the eye from the prospect of EAST and WEST RUNTON, which may once have had their share of appeal. Heavily wooded country runs down to safe beaches, through one of the few gaps along the coast here, but this has been somewhat camouflaged by the spread of caravans and mobile homes. In any case, Sheringham has given us a taste for a touch more urban living, so we must head on eastwards; but not before dropping in at the NORFOLK SHIRE HORSE CENTRE [Enquiries - 01263 837339]. Whatever the weather, this is one of those places that's full of fascination for the car-mad generation, with enough points of interest to take up half the day.

The story of the 'Gem of the Norfolk Coast' - Cromer - parallels that of our last port of call. Perhaps the new fashion for seaside holidays intervened in its lifestyle somewhat earlier, in that the 18th century saw the first appearance of smart houses for summer visitors around the old port cottages, but yet again it was the arrival of the railway that lit the fuse of development. The streets of the old town form a maze twisting around the 14th century Church of St Peter and St Paul, whose 160ft high perpendicular tower is the highest in Norfolk and a familiar indicator of Cromer's early importance. Unlike similar locations along the coast, however, the effect of the sea over the ages at Cromer was not to silt up the access and thereby gradually destroy the possibility for sailors and fishermen to maintain their way of life - but quite the reverse. As originally established, Cromer was some way inland, but the intervening town of SHIPDEN was gradually washed away by the sea in the Middle Ages.

Cromer is now best known for two things: the crabs and the bravery of its lifeboatmen, amongst whose endeavours the saving of 450 lives in World War Two stands pre-eminent. In considering the dangers of this coast, it seems ironic that the very sands that attract the holidaymakers also form the banks offshore which are such a peril to sailors. For example, not only has the stretch known as 'The Devil's Throat' made the Cromer lifeboat one of the busiest in Britain, it was also the scene of numerous rescues led by the country's most decorated lifeboatman, Henry Blogg, a Cromer man who was coxswain of the boat from 1909 to 1947. There is a bronze bust in the town's NORTH LODGE PARK, looking out to sea, as a witness to his heroic efforts which led to his being awarded the George Cross as well as many lifeboat medals. The old lifeboat house is now a museum at the foot of The Gangway, there is a grooved stone path built to enable horses to pull heavy cargo from the beach.

CROMER

So, what of the town's contemporary attractions? There is safe swimming from a good, sandy beach with numerous shallow pools. As befits a bustling family holiday resort, there are places of interest for people of all ages, including a small zoo and a museum. This last is focused on the late Victorian fishermen's way of life , their cottages and the provision for their descendants to trace family trees with the help of a computerised photo library. In addition, there is a range of entertainment offered during a summer season at the PAVILION THEATRE [Enquiries - 01263 512495]. Finally, the town's accommodation offers a range of facilities ranging from all you would expect at a large hotel to the more straightforward approach of modest boarding houses.

One should also note that Cromer is not just a resort in which to while away the hours of sunshine in an aimless, if apparently busy, kind of way. There are well organised provisions for a range of physical activities, including walking, riding, boating and golf at the ROYAL CROMER GOLF CLUB. It's a pleasant place, is Cromer, where the traditional concept of 'seaside' is still very much alive and well - and never more than at CARNIVAL time. This landmark in the Norfolk year holds a special appeal and suggests planning an August visit carefully, so as not to miss it.

As we leave Cromer, it's time to turn away from the sea and head inland along the A148. Shortly, we arrive at HOLT [Information - 01263 713100], which is one of the most attractive small towns in the whole of Norfolk, with its main street, enlivened by a variety of intriguing, small shops, creating as one authority has put it, 'a little Soho in the heart of rural Norfolk'. The architecture is mostly Georgian, as a large part of the area was destroyed in a fire in 1708.

Historically, Holt was a market town, and the home of Gresham's School, founded in 1555 by Sir Thomas Gresham, who was born here in 1519 and went on to be Lord Mayor of London, having established the Royal Exchange. The school was originally housed in an 1850s Tudor style building but was moved half a mile along the Cromer Road in 1900. This road runs through avenues of beech and pine trees, broken by stretches of heather and bracken, to Sheringham. Another road worth exploring would take us four miles north-west amidst rolling fields and woodlands, above the saltings, to Cley, although just as appealing an alternative might be the Blakeney road, which crosses the River Glaven, running through the gardens of the eighteenth-century LETHERINGSETT HALL. Further attractions could include the moated ruin of the 15th century BACONSTHORPE CASTLE and KELLING PARK [Enquiries - 01263 712235] home of the EAST ANGLIAN FALCONRY CENTRE, the largest sanctuary of its kind in the country. There are over two hundred birds in residence, many of which can be handled. The sanctuary also cares for injured owls and other birds of prey. While one is in the area, it would be as well to make the slightly longer detour, along country lanes through **GRESHAM** village, to the 1750 acre FELBRIGG ESTATE [Enquiries - 01263 837444] of woods, parks and gardens, not forgetting the chance for a tour of the Hall itself. This unspoilt 17th century house is the setting for a superb collection of 18th century furniture and paintings, while its grounds offer an opportunity for delightful strolls through the walled garden, the woodland and around the lake. It is open throughout the spring and summer, from March to November, although, even then, it is closed on Thursdays and Fridays.

As we head down from Holt, on the final stretch of our circuit which leads, eventually, back to King's Lynn, our interest takes a different focus from the one we enjoyed while following the line of the coast. In this area, attention is drawn primarily to human efforts to relate to an environment where farming has replaced fishing as the major occupation. Furthermore, the buildings and other aspects of human habitation are at least as significant in this context, as were the natural attractions of the marshes, dunes, and seashore. As we'll see, there is a great deal of history set out along this part of our journey, too.

Time for another detour, in reality rather than the imagination. On our way to Thursford, mid-way between Holt and Fakenham, it's worth striking off to the right, along the B1156, to LANGHAM GLASS, said to be one of Norfolk's finest working craft factories. The three main aspects of the centre are equally appealing, though very different in their focal points. Within the collection of restored 18th century barn workshops one can admire a variety of crafts not exclusively connected with glass. Then, in the main Glass House, one can watch craftsmen producing the now famous Langham Glass. Finally, there are several shops where visitors can buy gifts they have seen being made, bargain gifts, mainly made in Norfolk and unavailable elsewhere and antiques and collectibles ranging from Victorian china to Lalique. Naturally, as with most such attractions in the area, the day can be rounded off with a meal in the restaurant.

The next call has rather more to do with spectacle than any more earnest human endeavour. **THURSFORD**, is the home of THE THURSFORD COLLECTION [Enquiries - 01328 878477] which pays a quite remarkable tribute to one element in the glitz and glamour of show business. The collection, which has won a number of tourism awards, houses a unique range of mechanical organs and other fairground memorabilia. There is a Christmas spectacular each year and a range of special events including the Wurlitzer show, where the attractions of this particular instrument are dramatically highlighted. For railway enthusiasts, the collection also houses examples of 2ft gauge locomotives and rolling stock.

Although the collection itself is somewhat dazzling, in the light of our travels so far our amazement is mainly generated by the county's capacity to surprise yet again with the variety and range of its features. Such thoughts become particularly compelling, now, as we move on from the halls of mechanical music, in their rural setting, to the deeply abiding sensations generated by a stretch of country where mankind's eternal involvement with mysticism and the spiritual quest for enlightenment become pre-eminent. As we shall see, this quest has generated more than one strange aspect of its own. In short, we are about to arrive at the **WALSINGHAMS**, in an attempt to share their experience of visions and the subsequent evolution of faith.

To begin our change of mood, with the sound of the mighty Wurlitzer possibly still ringing in our ears, we must leave Thursford behind us, along with the A148, and set out once again into the country. The transition will be less sudden if we begin it with a short visit to **GREAT WALSINGHAM**, the terminus of the preserved railway line that links it with Wells. Perhaps it is tempting, if unfair, to suggest at this stage that having stated that fact, you have said all there is to say about the village, despite its other attractions. In a sense, its main misfortune is to exist in the shadow of its now inappropriately prefixed neighbour which, considering its size, has attracted more attention than one might expect. There is a GALLERY and a TEXTILE CENTRE here though, and it's worth pausing if one is looking for examples of a wide range of excellent traditional crafts.

To arrive at **LITTLE WALSINGHAM** is to encounter, in and around the old tiled, brick and timber cottages of the village, what amounts to a montage of the history of the established church in England. Of most widespread significance is the shrine of Our Lady of Walsingham, established in 1061 by the then lady of the manor, Lady Richeld. She had a vision in which she was commanded by the Virgin Mary to establish a 'Santa Casa', that is, a replica of the Nazarene House of Annunciation. From this moment, the village's church history mirrored, in its small way, that of the bulk of the country.

For example, the shrine was later added to by the Augustinians and the Franciscans. Some time after, it had acquired such a reputation that Henry VIII felt obliged to make a pilgrimage while on a visit to East Barsham. Notwithstanding this, after he quarrelled with Rome and embarked on the Dissolution of the Monasteries, his minions destroyed the shrine before which he had once stood in reverence. Separated in this way from its Roman origins, the spiritual life of the village pursued a similar course to that of most Anglican parishes.

Catholicism may have been down, however, but it was most definitely not out - which became most evident in the latter part of the 19th century when a kind of revival began, in a form which came to be known as Anglo Catholicism. As a result of the resurgence, a new Italianate shrine was built between 1931-37 and that has continued Little Walsingham's role to this day. Currently, the role has been extended into the practice amongst the faithful of making a similar pilgrimage to the Slipper Chapel at Houghton St Giles. This is the NATIONAL SHRINE OF OUR LADY and is visited by Roman Catholics to affirm their beliefs within the confines of its small structure, which dates from the 14th century. Today, pilgrims making their way to Houghton stop at Walsingham to remove their shoes before completing the last few miles barefoot.

There is some element of mysticism in the atmosphere of both locations, which one can almost reach out and touch. It's as though the repeated expression of faith by a large enough number of people over the centuries has created a new element, added to by each of them, which now affects all who go there. Having shared as much as we can in the corporate experience of the pilgrims all that is left to do is to complete the brief circle away from the main road and resume the line of progress towards **FAKENHAM** [Information - 01328 851981], our last major stopping place before returning to Dersingham.

FAKENHAM MARKET

One must acknowledge at the outset that Fakenham's claims to fame make strange bedfellows. Historically, it was a market town, lying some three miles to the north east of RAYNHAM HALL, which is still the ancestral home of the Townshend family. The 2nd Viscount, who resided there in the early 18th century, was something of a politician - but he is most vividly remembered as an agricultural innovator with a specific interest, which led to his acquiring the nickname 'Turnip'. His most important contribution to farming improvements - and this certainly puts him on a par with Coke of Holkham - grew from his enthusiasm for turnip growing. Eventually, from his experiments with this crop, he developed what came to be an all but universal crop rotation system.

Another of Fakenham's neighbours which is much in keeping with the town's Georgian buildings and part 15th century church, is BARSHAM MANOR, a sumptuous Tudor red-brick mansion. Yet, given such obvious attributes, based with equal firmness on the nurture of the land and on the trade arising from its produce, fate seems somewhat perverse in decreeing that the town be equally well known for a unique historical collection of gas appliances. The FAKENHAM MUSEUM OF GAS AND LOCAL

HISTORY (Enquiries - 01328 863150), housed within the boundaries of the defunct - but now restored - gas works, is unique. Nowhere else in the country can one see so clearly how our urban gas was produced for many years. By means of demonstrations of plant, cookers, heaters and other items of equipment, some of which are more than a hundred years old yet still in perfect working order, the entire process is shown clearly and with a fetching eye for detail. While this is yet another experience not to be missed, there are other features of Fakenham that might, at the very least, dictate the day chosen for our visit. Thursday is market day, an important weekly event renowned throughout the area.

Browsing amongst the stalls is one very effective way to see how the town functions and, while we are there, we might do well to attend an auction and visit the antique shops for which the town is regarded as a centre for the county. Then, appropriately enough, if we need some respite from the bustle, we can pop across to the A1067 for a brief spin down to PENSTHORPE WATERFOWL PARK and NATURE RESERVE [Enquiries - 01328 851465]. Beloved of Richard Branson, Pensthorpe offers the magic of the water's edge all the year round. There are more than 120 species of waterfowl from around the world to be seen - it is, in fact, Europe's finest collection of endangered and exotic water birds. There are all the usual facilities, from an exhibition gallery to a restaurant and gift shop. Don't forget to check the date of your visit against the Park's calendar - in 1997, it hosted many remarkable displays and exhibitions, from wildlife paintings and photographs to patchwork and garden sculptures - and subsequent years are likely to be just as busy.

Back down the A148 again, in the direction of King's Lynn, we'll pause only at **HOUGHTON ST GILES** before taking the B1440 , on the right, to Dersingham, where we hope that at least a cup of tea - if not something rather stronger - will be waiting. Having this vision of bliss in the front of the mind, and having, perhaps, had something of a surfeit of very mixed experiences, we may choose to keep the number of further visits to the bare minimum. As it happens, that choice fits in well with what is left to be seen - and Houghton will definitely be our last call before serious refreshment and rest.

Even this last experience of the day should not be overlooked. We have already discussed the SLIPPER CHAPEL as one of the twin focal points of pilgrimage in the area. As interesting in its own way is HOUGHTON HALL, another example of the majestic Norfolk country house, this time dating from the early 18th century. While the claim of its gardens and architecture are undeniable, it offers in addition to such familiar attractions a quite extraordinary collection of model soldiers and a fine range of stables, currently housing a number of superb heavy horses. Once again, the experience of such a visit - coming after Fakenham's gasworks and Walsingham's shrine - says a great deal about the variety of points of interest which await discovery around every Norfolk corner. Finally we return, via Sandringham, to the point where we began.

THE BLAKENEY HOTEL
The Quay
Blakeney
Norfolk
NR25 7NE
Tel: 01263 740797 Fax: 01263 740795

AA *** RAC ***

Blakeney, once a port of importance in medieval times, has largely retained its period charm but now is only accessible to small craft and is a popular centre for yachting and bird-watching. The Blakeney Hotel with its Quayside location has magnificent views across the estuary and salt marshes to Blakeney Point which is an area of outstanding natural beauty owned by the National Trust and part of the Heritage Coastline. The Point can be reached either by ferry boat from the Quay or on foot from the neighbouring village of Cley. There are numerous historic places to visit in North Norfolk including the Halls at Holkham, Blickling, Felbrigg and Houghton, the Sandringham Estate and many interesting Norfolk villages and churches. Norwich and Kings Lynn are both within an hour's drive and the market towns of Holt, Sheringham, Aylsham and Cromer are full of interest. Many sports and other activities are available locally including bird-watching, bowling, cycling, fishing, golf, horse riding, sailing, wind surfing and tennis.

The Blakeney is a delightful, relaxed, traditional hotel run immaculately and offering high standards of hospitality and service whilst giving value for money. Many guests have been coming here for years and they represent all age groups It is just that sort of hotel that makes you feel you want to come back as quickly as possible. Sensibly the tariff varies by season, by weekend or midweek, by length of stay and the category of room, which offers guests a wide choice. The staff are friendly and efficient, with receptionists who make you genuinely welcome, porters who offer a twenty four hour service and nothing is too much trouble for any of them. The Hotel's sixty bedrooms all have private bathrooms, central heating and double glazing, colour television, direct dial telephones, tea and coffee making facilities, bathrobes and a baby listening service. Many of the bedrooms have delightful views over the estuary and the salt marshes to Blakeney Point and the sea. There are south facing rooms looking onto the gardens, rooms with four poster beds, and some with antique furniture. There is a ground floor room suitable for wheelchair access and others with patio doors on to a separate garden. A few rooms are in an adjacent annexe, some with enclosed patios, ideal for dogs. Comfortable lounges, one non-smoking and both with glorious views, are much used for afternoon tea. The Bar and Restaurant occupy the entire front of the hotel and both have splendid views. The restaurant serves delicious food both from an a la carte menu and from the table d'hôte menu. Breakfast is scrumptious, light lunches are served daily except for Sunday when lunch is a traditional affair. The wine list complements the food perfectly. With a heated indoor swimming pool and jacuzzi, saunas and a mini gym, a billiard room, games room and private gardens in which to relax, The Blakeney offers everything anyone could possibly want.

USEFUL INFORMATION

OPEN; All year

RESTAURANT; Excellent food both

CHILDREN; Welcome A la carte & table d'hôte

CREDIT CARDS; All major cards

VEGETARIAN; Choices available

LICENSED; Yes. Fine wine list

WHEELCHAIR ACCESS; Yes. Ramp

ACCOMMODATION; 60 ensuite rooms

GARDEN; Yes. Swimming pool etc.

RATES: from £61 pp D.B&B minimum 2 nights

Midweek & weekend breaks 4 & 7 day holidays Senior Citizen Breaks .

BAYLEAF
10 Saint Peters Road
Sheringham
Norfolk
NR26 8QY

Tel: 01263 823779

One Crown Commended

Bayleaf is well situated in Sheringham for those who stay in this friendly home from home atmosphere. It is close to the shops and the sea front, backing on to the park and putting green, one mile from the much visited Sheringham Park, near the Little Theatre and Splash Leisure Complex as well as being adjacent to the popular 'Steam Railway'. Sheringham has a coveted Blue Flag Beach and currently the cleanest sea in the country.

Paul and Maureen Pigott are the owners of Bayleaf Guest House and the run it immaculately, doing everything needed themselves. Their standards are very high and this is reflected throughout the house. Both keen gardeners, guests have the great pleasure when dining of looking out over the patio and well stocked flower beds full of interesting shrubs and flowers which provide a blaze of colour. Inside the house the furniture is mainly Victorian in keeping with the age of the building. The large Bar Lounge and Dining Area are comfortable, relaxed places and have an unusual collection of books, Anything from Enid Blyton and Rupert Bear to Golf! The food is excellent. Maureen is an experienced and talented chef and delights in producing interesting meals. Breakfast each day is a feast and self-service from the bar. There are no limitations; you simply have as much as you want. The house is licensed and there is always a selection of fine wines and vintage ports.

Seven ensuite, charmingly furnished bedrooms are availale. Two of these are on the ground floor with wheelchair access. Each bedroom has television and a hostess tray. Children over ten years are very welcome and so are pets at a charge of £1.50 a day.

USEFUL INFORMATION

OPEN: All year

CHILDREN: Over 10 years

VEGETARIAN: On request

WHEELCHAIR ACCESS: Yes

GARDEN: Yes PETS: Yes £1.50 daily

ACCOMMODATION: 7 ensuite rooms

RATES: From £19pp B&B

DINING ROOM: Good food, well presented

CREDIT CARDS: None taken

LICENSED: Yes

SMOKING: Bar & Bedroom

CAMBRIDGE HOUSE
Sea Front
East Cliff
Cromer
Norfolk
NR27 9HD

Tel:01263 512085
Internet:http//:www.broadland.com.cambridge house

Two Crowns Commended. Tourist Award 'Welcome Host'

A mother and daughter team, Olive and Liz Wass, run this attractive Victorian residence, pleasantly situated on the sea front overlooking the pier and east beach with steps to the promenade opposite the front door. Built in 1887, the house which is strictly non-smoking has retained the charm and atmosphere of that period but now has the additional facilities that the modern day traveller requires.

Winner of a tourism award for excellence Cambridge House has a delightful, homely, relaxed atmosphere and is an ideal place in which to stay for a holiday or short break at anytime of the year except between Christmas and New Year. Cromer is a fascinating place in its own right with many associations with the sea, its lifeboats and crews have become famous throughout the world. You can visit the lifeboat museum on the gangway or discover the modern lifeboat station on the end of the pier. The Pavilion Theatre is home to the popular Seaside Special End of the Pier Show. Cromer fishermen still haul their boats up onto the beach to land their catch of crabs and sell them to the local shops and hotels for holiday makers to enjoy. There are endless pursuits and entertainments on offer. Regular train and bus services run to and from Cromer so you do not have to use your car to discover North Norfolk's coast or the beauty of the Norfolk Broads. Much of North Norfolk is designated as an area of outstanding natural beauty, unspoilt villages and seaside towns, steam railways, historic houses, craft centres and lots more besides.

Cambridge House has five comfortably furnished bedrooms, three of which are ensuite, all have televisions and they all have a generously supplied hostess tray. An excellent full English breakfast is served every morning and at night a three course dinner is served with predominantly traditional British fare. There is a table licence. It really is a lovely house in which to stay and the sea views are stunning.

USEFUL INFORMATION

OPEN: All year except Christmas & New Year
CHILDREN: Welcome
VEGETARIAN: By arrangement
WHEELCHAIR ACCESS: No
ACCOMMODATION:5 rooms 3 ensuite

RATES: From £20.pp B&B

DINING ROOM: Good, traditional fare
CREDIT CARDS: None taken
LICENSED: Table Licence
GARDEN: No, but Beach at front door
A STRICTLY NON-SMOKING
HOUSE

THE COBBLERS GUEST HOUSE
Standard Road
Wells-next-the-Sea
Norfolk
NR23 1JU

Tel/Fax: 01328 710155
E Mail: ina@cobblers.co.uk

Crab Award North Norfolk Hotel
& Guest House Association

Within a few minutes walk of the quay you will find Cobblers Guest House in Standard Road. It is one of those friendly, immediately welcoming establishments that one always hopes to find. Owned by Ina and Mike, the house was built in 1924 in a peaceful situation close to the centre of Wells and has private off street parking at the front of the house - something to be cherished in Wells which does not have the best of parking facilities. Both Ina and Mike are interesting people who have done much with their lives and have found a special quality of life in caring well for their many guests who like the easy informality that is apparent from the moment of arrival. Mike is a keen ornithologist and photographer with several awards for his natural history work. He could not have found a better spot to be than Wells-next-the-Sea which lies at the centre of the North Norfolk Coast, midway between the Bird Reserves of Cley and Titchwell. It is a knowledge he will happily share with you.

There are eight prettily appointed bedrooms in total; two family rooms, three double rooms, one twin-bedded and two single rooms. The two family/double rooms and one single are ensuite. Every room has its own wash basin and there are two bathrooms and three loos. Colour television and tea and coffee facilities as well as many other touches complete the picture . There are two Guest lounges, a conservatory and a delightful garden - all available at any time to guests. In the morning you will come down to the light, spacious dining room ready to enjoy a very good, freshly cooked breakfast with several choices and at night home-cooked evening meals are available with an eclectic menu of Continental, English and Vegetarian dishes. Dietary requirements will always be taken into consideration when menus are being planned.

It is unthinkable that anyone could ever find the sea boring but if you want to explore further away from Wells then you are spoilt for choice. There are some charming villages, fascinating museums including the Thursford Collection at Fakenham, the Muckelburgh Collection at Weybourne and Holkham Hall Bygones Museum at Holkham as well as the fine Norfolk Rural Crafts at Langham Glass, Near Holt. The North Norfolk Railway always pleases visitors and then there is Sandringham House and Country Park, Felbrigg Hall Garden & Park, Pensthorpe Waterfowl Park and Blickling Hall Gardens Park. It is a wonderful area for walking, there is fishing, sailing and many other activities as well.

USEFUL INFORMATION

OPEN: All year
CHILDREN: over 4 years
CREDIT CARDS: None at present
LICENSED: Restaurant/Residential
ACCOMMODATION: 8 rooms 3 ensuite
RATES: B&B from £15. children 1/2 price
Short breaks: 3 nights for 2 Mon-Thurs. Nov-Feb.

DINING ROOM: Good home-cooked fare
VEGETARIAN: Yes & dietary needs
WHEELCHAIR ACCESS: No
GARDEN: Yes & Conservatory
PETS: No
Smoking only in the Conservatory

CROWMERE HOUSE
4 Vicarage Road
Cromer
Norfolk
NR27 9DQ

Tel: 01263 513056

Listed and Commended

Built in 1876 Crowmere House is the home of Sallyanne Marriott and her husband. Sallyanne is one of life's naturally outgoing and friendly people who runs Crowmere House as a relaxed informal guest house. She will tell you that she is the chief cook and bottle washer of the household; this may be so but she is much more. She cares for her guests and is intent on making their stay a happy, memorable time. The house is just five minutes from the mixed sand and flintstone beach and its scenic cliff top walk. Cromer, of course, is famous for its Victorian Pier, its Theatre and more recently for its flagship RNLI Station. The Victorian Town Centre is a gem dominated by the magnificent flint church which boasts the highest tower in Norfolk. There is so much to see and do in this area including a plethora of National Trust Properties. A great place for a holiday made even better by staying at Crowmere House.

The house is attractively decorated throughout with a feeling of light and spaciousness about it. There are four ensuite rooms, three doubles and one twin-bedded. Two family suites, the first with a double bedroom, a single bedroom and private bathroom. The second has a double bedroom, a triple bedroom and a private bathroom. All the rooms have television and a hospitality tray. Breakfast is served in a bright dining room and Sallyanne uses fresh local produce whenever possible. It is a delicious meal and certainly more than sufficient to set one up for the day. Special dietary needs are also catered for with prior notice. Evening meals are not available but Cromer has many good eateries and is famous for its seafood especially crabs. Crowmere House is open all the year round and as it is centrally heated, it is a warm, cosy place to be in winter when many think this part of Norfolk is at its best.

USEFUL INFORMATION

OPEN: All year
CHILDREN: Welcome
CREDIT CARDS: None taken
LICENSED: No
PETS: No

DINING ROOM: Great breakfast
VEGETARIAN: Catered for
WHEELCHAIR ACCESS:
GARDEN: No.
ACCOMMODATION: 4 ensuite
2 Fmk with private bathroom

RATES: B&B Low season £14 pp High Season £19pp
Children from £5 depending on age

FISHES RESTAURANT
Market Place
Burnham Market
Kings Lynn
Norfolk
PE31 8HE

Tel: 01328 738588

Good Food Guide. Egon Ronay

If you enjoy seafood of any kind there is probably not a better restaurant specialising in the fruits of the sea than the aptly named Fishes Restaurant, at Burnham Market owned and run for almost a quarter of a century by Gillian Cape. It is the perfect place in which to enjoy a meal. The 18th century building stands on the village green, very much part of the busy village of Burnham Market. Inside it is the sophisticated simplicity which strikes one. The floor is cork, there are big windows creating a sense of space, the solid tables are attractively set and throughout there is a sense of well-being, civilised and not one jot of pomposity. In summer it is always busy but in winter you can enjoy sitting in front of a log fire perhaps reading one of the many good books lying around whilst you wait for your meal. Gillian Cape has built a tremendous reputation which is why you will always find a regular clientele among diners. She, and her friendly, well-trained staff know exactly how to treat people and ensure that their needs are met.

The ever changing menu includes fresh fish and therefore changes regularly to accommodate the catch. You may well start at lunch-time with crab soup or smoked fish pate and move on to oysters and mussels baked in garlic or delicious salmon fish cakes with crab sauce. The sweets are delectable with some irresistible home-made ice creams and sorbets or perhaps a light Chocolate Mousse with Amaretti biscuits. Lunch is a set price but each dish can be ordered individually. At Dinner the choice is even larger with Potted brown shrimps (from Holkham Bay), King scallop and prawn au gratin, Brancaster mussels, Dover sole, Sea bass, Monkfish and much more. The wine list is well chosen to complement the food and at sensible prices.

Burnham Market is just two miles from unspoilt sand dunes, creeks and marshes in an area of 'outstanding natural beauty. The children enjoy building sand castles in summer whilst their elders sunbathe or sail. It is great walking country and in winter provides excitement for bird-watchers. Holkham Hall and its estate is four miles away and there are other historic houses, round tower churches, flint faced cottages, pretty villages, quaint hostelries and much more to enchant the visitor before or after a meal at Fishes.

USEFUL INFORMATION

OPEN: 12-2pm & 6.30-9.30pm (9pm Winter) RESTAURANT: Specialises in Seafood
Closed 3 weeks in January CHILDREN: Well behaved welcome
CREDIT CARDS: All major cards VEGETARIAN: By arrangement
WHEELCHAIR ACCESS: Yes LICENSED: Yes
PETS: No

HARVEST FIELDS
61A Manor Road
Dersingham
Norfolk
PE31 6LH

Tel: 01485 541123

Harvest Fields is much more than a house offering Bed and Breakfast. Built in the 1600s it had a small shop attached to it and then was considerably extended over the next two hundred years. For the last five years it has been the home of David and Jill Tatham and their friend and partner Sue Megahy. They are still restoring the house to its former glory and at the same time have opened up their home to visitors. Bed and Breakfast here is a cheerful, happy experience where the hospitality and warmth of the welcome is totally genuine. The shop, in use in the 1600s, is now a Christian Book shop combining its role with a Craft Shop and a Coffee Shop. The latter, housed in part of the Barn serves delicious food, especially home-made cakes, and is known widely for its speciality - apple cake! In addition to this there is a comprehensive needle craft area and both picture and embroidery framing are done on the premises. Demonstrations are available for needlework and rubber stamping. In fact if you are interested the gang of three will be only too delighted to induct you into their multi-talented arts.

In spite of their busy lives, Harvest Fields is run immaculately. There are three, comfortably furnished guest rooms each with a wash basin and hot and cold water. There is a family room with a double bed, cot and a folding bed is available. The other rooms are a twin room and a single room. All of them have television and a hostess tray. Breakfast is a great meal with everything freshly cooked to your order. No evening meals are served but there are good local places in which to eat.

The area could not be better for visitors with the desire to explore. It is within easy reach of the North Norfolk coastal resorts and coastal walks. Great for bird-watching and within easy reach of reserves. Sandringham House and Gardens are within ten minutes walk and are open during the summer but there are extensive woodland walks all year. The old, historic town of King's Lynn with its fine old buildings and old working port is only ten miles distant.

USEFUL INFORMATION

OPEN: All year
CHILDREN: Welcome No evening meals
CREDIT CARDS: None taken
LICENSED: No
ACCOMMODATION: 1fml 1 tw 1sgl
Not ensuite PETS: By arrangement
RATES: £14.50pp B&B

DINING ROOM: Great breakfast

COFFEE SHOP: Home-made cakes
WHEELCHAIR ACCESS: No
GARDEN: Yes

HIDEAWAY
Red Lion Yard
Wells-Next-The Sea
Norfolk
NR231 AX

Tel: 01328 710524

2 Crowns Commended
East Anglian Tourist Board

Wells-Next-The-Sea is a delightful seaside town with a host of interesting places to visit including Fellbrigg, Blickling Hall, Houghton Hall, Sandringham, the fascinating Thursford Collection, Langham Glass, and the Bird Sanctuarys at Titchwell, Pensthorpe, Cley and Blackney and many others. The old town of Walsingham is five miles away and if Admiral Lord Nelson has always been your hero, 'Nelson Country' is a few miles from Wells.

With so much to see and do Hideaway makes an ideal place to stay. It is a bed and breakfast establishment but also offers very good evening meals. Owned and run by Madeleine Higgs, it is a friendly welcoming house where the informality masks the efficient way in which this genial lady organises the establishment. You will find that many guests find it a home from home. Madeleine is also the cook and her love of good food is quite obvious in the range and standard of what she provides. Her menu changes every day and takes into account the excellent local produce including fish from the boats on the shore. The wine list allows you to choose from a selection which covers wines from around the world. The guest accommodation is in an annexe which was originally a stable area with its own entrance for which each guest has a key. There is an Honesty Bar and a sitting area where there are facilities for making drinks, concocting food for a picnic, and a refrigerator to keep it all fresh. A Sauna and Spa complete the facilities for guests. Three pretty and well furnished ensuite guest rooms have television and a hostess tray. This is somewhere that one can stay at any time of the year in comfort and enjoy the spectacular beauty of this part of Norfolk. Short Mid-week Breaks and special weekends are available out of season.

USEFUL INFORMATION

OPEN: Jan5th-Dec 20th
CHILDREN: Over 12 years
CREDIT CARDS: None taken
LICENSED: Residential
ACCOMMODATION: 1dbl 2tw en suite   Ground floor room
RATES: From £36 per room

DINING ROOM: Delicious home-cooked fare. Evening meal optional
VEGETARIAN: Yes
WHEELCHAIR ACCESS; No.

THE JOLLY FARMERS
1 Burnham Road
North Creake
Fakenham
Norfolk
NR21 9JW

Tel: 01328 738185

Member of CAMRA

The Jolly Farmers lives up to its name! It is a friendly, happy inn in a pleasant village in the rural part of North Norfolk but within easy reach of the sea either at Wells-next-the Sea or Burnham Overy Staithe. There are many Nature Reserves in the area and the open countryside is ideal for bird-watching or walking. Mr and Mrs Savage, the landlords of the pub are experienced ornithologists and happy to pass on their knowledge. Mrs Savage is a skilful wildlife illustrator and designer who exhibits her work with other local artists. 'Jolly Jo's' gallery and craft shop will be opening within the court yard of the Inn from Easter 1998 featuring work by the landlady Jo, also other local artists.

The inn is a friendly place to be both for locals and visitors. The well-stocked bar is known for the excellence of its Real Ale and is recognised by CAMRA. Food, either in the Restaurant or the Bar is good, home-cooked, wholesome English fare with Daily Specials marked up on a board daily. The menu has many traditional favourites as well as some innovative ones which are very popular. Great packed lunches are available every day for those going walking or fishing - the Savages just need a little advance warning. Vegetarians can be catered for as well. The Jolly Farmers is family run with help from the Savages seventeen year old daughter who is in the process of working her apprentice scheme within the business. Their son is at University before joining the Royal Marines but can also be seen to lend a hand at busy times. It makes for a great atmosphere and it is no wonder that it is beloved by locals. In the summer the garden is a favourite place in which to enjoy a drink or eat. Quiet and restful but with enough going on around you to prevent boredom!

USEFUL INFORMATION

OPEN: 11.30-2.30pm 6-11pm 10.30Sun   RESTAURANT: Good home-cooked
CHILDREN: Welcome English fare
CREDIT CARDS: None taken   BAR FOOD: Good value. Daily
LICENSED: Full On   VEGETARIAN: By arrangement
GARDEN: Yes   PETS: Yes

KNIGHTS HILL HOTEL
South Wootton
King's Lynn
Norfolk
PE30 3HQ

Tel: 01553 675566
Fax: 01553 675568

RAC***AA. EATB
4 Crowns Commended

Set atop one of the highest points in West Norfolk, enjoying magnificent views of The Wash and overlooking Castle Rising is Knights Hill Hotel. It stands within eleven acres of parkland and gardens and is one of those blissful places to stay which is a happy combination of rural relaxation, efficient service and facilities that will satisfy the most travel weary guest. As far back as 1588 Knights Hill, formerly Rising Lodge, has featured prominently in the history of the local area as the residence and meeting place of persons of note. The house, reputed to be on the site of the Kings Hunting Lodge in Rising Chase, has grown with the increasing success of the farm. The original farm cottage dating from the 17th century, now adjoins the main house with its classic dimensions and Georgian facade. There are fifty seven ensuite bedrooms, fully equipped and charming furnished, decorated in a country style. Kinghts Hill combines, with skill, the role of country pub, restaurant, hotel and health and leisure club. The food is delicious, the wines well chosen. It is a great place for holidaymakers and business visitors to West Norfolk. Whether you travel here by car, or train to King's Lynn or use the private landing pad, the warmest welcome awaits you.

USEFUL INFORMATION

OPEN: All year 11am-11pm
CHILDREN: Welcome
CREDIT CARDS: All major cards
LICENSED: Full On
ACCOMMODATION: 57 ensuite rooms
RATES: Sgl from £80-105 Dbl. from £85-£120
Special weekend breaks& tennis

RESTAURANT: International menu
BAR FOOD: Grill type menu, roasts
and daily specials
VEGETARIAN: Always a choice
WHEELCHAIR ACCESS: Yes
GARDEN: Yes. Swimming
PETS: In some rooms

LAKESIDE
Waterworks Road
Old Hunstanton
Norfolk
PE36 6JE

Tel: 01485 533763

3 Crowns Commended

Lakeside is a really unusual property. Converted from the Old Hunstanton Waterworks it is now a stylish and essentially comfortable hotel in which Liz and Keith Clayson-Hoffbauer, the owners, welcome guests. A spring rises in the grounds and feeds a small lake which attracts birds from the local Nature Reserves, Titchwell, Holme and Snettisham. Lakeside is a few yards away from Hunstanton Golf Club and a few miles from the Royal West Norfolk at Brancaster. The Norfolk Coastal Path which meets Peddars Way in the next village, is almost on the hotel's doorstep. Energetic walkers will enjoy the walk to Morston Quay where boat trips will take you to the Seal Beaches. The National Trust properties, Felbrigg, Blickling and Oxburgh Halls are within easy reach. Sandringham, the home of Her Majesty the Queen, is a few minutes drive away and within twenty minutes drive you can be in King's Lynn, a medieval port in the Hanseatic League, with its beautiful old streets.

Liz and Keith have recently acquired Lakeside and they plan to improve the decor considerably over the next few years in order to give each room its own individual character. The Lounge was the first room to be tackled and with its attractive leather chesterfields and upholstered sofas, it shows what excellent taste they both have. Liz is a multi linguist and also is a pianist and sings alto in a choir. Keith paints and works in stained glass. They have travelled extensively particularly in Europe, North Africa and South East Asia. It is on this that they base their ideas of hospitality. If people are well fed they are content is a philosophy which might be applied here. There is a super breakfast and dinner is a set menu using fresh vegetables in season and much use of Elizabeth David's recipes. Vegetarian options are always available. The small wine list has been carefully chosen to complement the menu. There are eight guest bedrooms, the four doubles and two twin rooms are all ensuite whilst the two single rooms share a bathroom. Television and a Hostess tray is in every room and it is hoped that a video library and hiring facilities will be established shortly. The beautiful guest lounge has patio doors over looking the lake as does the conservatory type Dining Room. Plans for the future include a quiet Reading Room overlooking the garden. A truly delightful place in which to stay with a great atmosphere.

USEFUL INFORMATION

OPEN: All year
CHILDREN: 8 years upwards fare
VEGETARIAN: Yes. Menu changed daily
WHEELCHAIR ACCESS: No
GARDEN: Yes
ACCOMMODATION: 4dbl 2tw ensuite - 2sgl with shared bathroom
RATES: From £19 pppn B&B Special breaks available

DINING ROOM: Excellent home-cooked

CREDIT CARDS: Not yet established
LICENSED: Hotel/Restaurant
PETS: No

LOWER FARM
Harpley
King's Lynn
Norfolk
PE31 6TU

Tel: 01485 520 240

Something that strikes you immediately as you drive up to Lower Farm, is the total sense of peace and tranquillity that surrounds the house. It is set in two-three acres of garden and lovely woodland and inside it is warm and welcoming. Amanda and Robert Case are your hosts. The Case family has been farming in Norfolk for a very long time and this comes over in the welcoming atmosphere of the house. It is an ideal place for anyone on holiday or on business. There is so much to do including visiting Sandringham which is only five miles away. It is also half a mile from Houghton Hall, the home of the Marquess of Cholmondly. The coast is twenty minutes distant. Then there is Peddars Way for walking enthusiasts and riding. Lower Farm has stabling for horses and dogs are welcome but not in the house. There is plenty of space for parking horse boxes and cars.

All the rooms at Lower Farm and large and airy. There are three guest rooms, each furnished attractively with the emphasis on comfort. One double has bath, shower, basin and loo. Another double has shower, basin and loo and the twin-bedded room has a private bathroom. All the rooms have television, hairdryers, radios, refrigerators and a generously supplied hostess tray. Sleep comes easily in such quiet surroundings and when you wake to the sounds of the farm and countryside in the morning you will be ready to come down to a true Farmhouse Breakfast or a simpler Continental meal, served in the large Dining Room. Everything is freshly cooked to your order and local or farm produce is used including free range eggs. There are no evening meals but Robert and Amanda will happily recommend you to one of the many eateries within easy distance.

USEFUL INFORMATION

OPEN: All year except Christmas week
CHILDREN: Over 12 years
CREDIT CARDS: None taken
LICENSED: No
ACCOMMODATION: 2dbl 1tw
RATES: Dbl. £25pp Tw £18pp £5 sgl supplement
Special out of season Breaks - details on request

DINING ROOM: Great Farmhouse Breakfast. No evening meal
VEGETARIAN: Upon request
WHEELCHAIR ACCESS: No
GARDEN: Yes 2-3 acres
PETS: Outside only

MIRABELLE RESTAURANT
7 Station Road
West Runton
NR Cromer
Norfolk

Tel: 01263 837396

This small privately owned restaurant has grown from humble beginnings, until twenty four years later it is known, and respected, in a very wide area. Quite rightly so, for the chef proprietor is a man who believes that quality is paramount but it must be accompanied by value for money. His delectable food has made many people come to the restaurant on a continuing basis and over the years his clientele have learnt that if they wish for something extra special in the way of a celebration, perhaps for a Golden Wedding, the chef will surpass even his own very high standards.

The set menu is not vast but it is well chosen with six or seven starters, which will always include a particularly good home-made soup and usually Scampi Viennoise. From the main courses, there is an unbeatable Fillet of Beef Wellington which is for two and must be ordered in advance, well worth taking the trouble to do so. Less exotic but equally delicious is the Emince of Chicken Andrea. Lobster Thermidor is always a popular choice and local fish, available in the summer months, is very much a speciality of the house including a Dover Sole Meuniere.

Vegetarians are not forgotten. The two dishes most frequently on the menu are Nutburgers with Provencale Sauce or Vegetable Vol au Vent with Basil Sauce. In addition during the winter months, you will find local game features on the menu. If you have room for dessert you will undoubtedly be tempted by Brandy Cream Pancakes, Crepes Suzettes or Sabajon au Marsala- all dishes for two people. It is good to see that there are two savouries on the menu as well as Welsh Rarebit or Mushrooms on Toast. The extensive wine list of fine wines comes from all over the world including California, Austria, Australia and New Zealand.

USEFUL INFORMATION

OPEN; Lunch 12.30-2pm
Dinner 7-9.30pm
CHILDREN; Yes
CREDIT CARDS; Visa/Master/
AMEX/Diners
LICENSED; Fine wines, bottled beers

RESTAURANT; English & Continental
High quality
BAR FOOD; Not applicable
VEGETARIAN; Always 3 dishes
DISABLED ACCESS; Yes
GARDEN; No

NICHOLSONS SHOP AND CAFE
33 High Street
Holt
Norfolk
NR25 6BN

Tel: 01263 711230
Fax: 01263 711721

Email nicholson@netcom.co.uk
Internet :
netcom.co.uk/business/nicholson

Individuality is the essence of Nicholson's. In the mass-market mega-world of the nineties, visiting the shop at 33 High Street, Holt must be one of life's more refreshing experiences. Witnessing the public's response is reassuring too: shoppers are returning there in steadily increasing numbers from as far afield as London and Leicester, to seek out more treasures whilst savouring an environment that is both sophisticated and friendly.

Despite the endless pressures to conform, thankfully each of us remains unique. Our combinations of preferences are very personal to us and it is for those very mixtures of wish and impulse that Nicholson's caters. For example, although it is clear from the first greeting and offer of help from the staff that they recognise the importance of decisions about bed-linen, shirts, a hat, a night-dress or cuff links, it is just as clear that they know that the pause from browsing to relax over coffee and cake may be equally memorable. As regular customers agree, it is just as rewarding to go to Nicholson's when one needs cheering up as it is when one needs advice on an outfit or a change of image. Small wonder so many sales are of small items- cards, tea towels- mementoes of yet another hour spent pleasantly, exactly when it was needed.

Nicholson's then is as unique as its patrons. Within its light, airy, deceptively spacious 125 year old premises the norm is to find 'the very thing' for which one has come, be that a pot of Earl Grey, a tomato, mozzarella and avocado salad, a bar of handmade soap, an antique writing desk, a Gaggia espresso machine, or a vase to set off the table linen one bought last time. With diplomatic honesty the staff will listen, comment and suggest. The truth works: satisfied customers return season after season to the profusion of delights under the one roof, to an experience one must sample for oneself.

USEFUL INFORMATION

OPEN: All year
CHILDREN: Welcome
CREDIT CARDS: All major cards
LICENSED: Yes

CAFE: Simple but delicious fare
WHEELCHAIR ACCESS: Not easy
PETS: No

THE OLD BARN
Cromer Road
West Runton
Norfolk
NR27 9QT

Tel: 01263 838285

North Norfolk Top
Guest House award 1996

If you were looking for an attractive Norfolk conservation village in which to stay, then West Runton would come high on the list and if you could top that with a stay at The Old Barn then you would have hit the jackpot! Here in this pretty village situated on the North Norfolk coast you have the perfect spot and The Old Barn is literally only five minutes away from the sea and the sand. From the Old Barn, apart from the beaches and the sand, there is so much else to do. You can ride, golf, sail, take interesting walks, visit The Broads and National Trust properties or perhaps spare time to explore the Victorian town of Cromer just two miles away. Here you will find one of the last remaining piers which still has its annual seaside show.

The Old Barn dates back to the 18th century and is one of the oldest barn conversions in which there is a stunning drawing room overlooking the pretty and secluded garden. Karen Elliott owns and runs this delightful, welcoming guest house. She is a lady who likes to get to know her guests; something that over the years has brought the majority of her guests back to The Old Barn time and time again. Many of them have become personal friends and it is the atmosphere that Karen and these friends create within The Old Barn which makes newcomers feel immediately a part of the way of life in the house. It is quite wonderful.

It goes without saying when you realise the high standard that Karen has achieved, that the bedrooms will be perfectly appointed with the most comfortable of beds. Each room has television and tea and coffee making facilities. The lounge is beautifully furnished and the dining room just the sort of room in which it is a pleasure to eat. Breakfast is a great meal only superseded in excellence by the home-cooked dinner available every evening when Cromer Crab frequently features as a starter, Lamb cutlets with fresh vegetables as a main course and delicious desserts like the old fashioned Sticky Toffee Pudding or a French Apple Tart finish a meal to be remembered.

USEFUL INFORMATION

OPEN; January to December
CHILDREN; From 10 years
CREDIT CARDS; None taken
LICENSED; No
ACCOMMODATION; Ensuite rooms
3 day breaks from end Oct-end March
£85,00 per person D.B.B.Daily rate from £19 pp-£22pp

DINING ROOM; Delicious, home-cooked
VEGETARIAN; Upon request
WHEELCHAIR ACCESS; Not suitable
GARDEN; Pretty garden with furniture
PETS; Yes

PAIGES
1-5 Shirehall Plain
Holt
Norfolk
NR25 6B9

Tel: 01263 713520
Fax: 01263 711148

Egon Ronay

Holt is an attractive Georgian market town with a lot of interesting buildings and a friendly, rural atmosphere. It is two miles inland from the coast where there is fishing, bird-watching, marshes and miles of sandy beaches. No one ever seems to be in a hurry here and that is true of Paiges, an attractive restaurant/cafe housed in a wonderful part 15th-16th century and part medieval building, originally the manor house and certainly the oldest building in Holt. The atmosphere is wonderful, enhanced by candle-light, flint walled, mullion windows, beautifully warm in winter and cool in summer, fully opening continental style folding doors opening onto a large, pamnent tiled seating area designed and restored in 1990, lovingly and carefully by Tony Saunders and from time to time visits from Prince Charles, who came to see how the work was progressing. The end result is charming and none of the old world style has been lost. The wooden/old pamnent floors, the beams and certainly the atmosphere are there to be enjoyed. Throughout Paiges there are fresh flowers and the scent lingers delightfully.

Owned by Pam and Tony Saunders, Paiges is run on oiled wheels - the mark of the professional. Nothing is too much trouble and everything seems to happen without effort! No member of staff will try to oust you from your table. You are encouraged to relax and simply enjoy the ambience and the excellent food. The chef, Ivano who is half Italian and half Ukranian, has all the Latin passion one would expect and creates dishes with a strong continental flavour. He is insistent on the use of fresh produce and vegetables of the highest quality. The end result is perfect food whether it be a starter, a main course, luscious desserts or irresistible home-made cakes, gateau and bread, all made by Sarah who is baker, manageress and head waitress. The restaurant seats thirty six to forty comfortably and you sit at solid wooden tables. There is a good wine list and for tea and coffee lovers, a comprehensive range. Open from 9am-9pm, Paiges is popular with local people who pop in for morning coffee and perhaps a warm, freshly baked scone, or to meet their friends at lunch-time. Whenever you go to Paiges and for whatever you choose to drink or eat, you will find it memorable.

USEFUL INFORMATION

OPEN: 9am-9pm
CHILDREN: Welcome
VEGETARIAN: Catered for
WHEELCHAIR ACCESS: Yes
GARDEN: Yes

RESTAURANT: Delicious fare. Home-cooked.
CREDIT CARDS: All major cards
LICENSED: Restaurant
PETS: Not in restaurant but in the yard

THE RED CAT HOTEL
Station Road
North Wootton
King's Lynn
Norfolk
PE30 3QH

Tel/Fax: 01553 631244

ETB 2* Approved Hotel

You will find the third generation of the Irwin family running the Red Cat Hotel today with just the same welcoming and informal approach to guests as their ancestors - you can see the actual 'Red Cat' displayed from the main pillar in the bar! The hotel, run in the manner of a traditional country style English hostelry, is famous for many things and especially for the excellent range of Real 'Ales + Cream Flow' Beers served from underground cellars. Built of traditional Carr Stone, the Red Cat is everything one could wish for. It is set in the rural village of North Wootton next to the once old Railway Station and just off the Wash Marshes and sits in its own lawn grounds with horse riding nearby and close to King's Lynn Golf Course. The historic medieval port of King's Lynn, the famous North West Norfolk Coast, Bird Reserves, Sandringham Royal Estate and numerous leisure facilities are only a few minutes away.

The friendly spacious bars are full of memorabilia and curios collected over the years by the Irwins. People come here from miles around to enjoy the fellowship, the hospitality and the general happy ambience of the Red Cat. Others come for the food, which is excellent value and offers a good choice at reasonable prices. For those on diets, this does not pose a problem. Many people come to stay for a while, whether on business or pleasure. They find the homely, caring atmosphere preferable to a bigger, more formal establishments. The eight bedrooms which boast some of the most comfortable beds in the county, are centrally heated and ensuite. Each room is attractively decorated with colour co-ordinated drapes and bedcovers. Every room has remote control television with teletext, hair drier and a generously supplied hospitality tray. One room is ideally suited for a family. Breakfast is a feast and will certainly set you up for the day whether it is to go to work or take off exploring the area. Special Break rates are available throughout the year.

USEFUL INFORMATION

OPEN: 12-2.00pm & 6.30-11pm
CHILDREN: Welcome
CREDIT CARDS: Yes. Not AMEX
LICENSED: Full On
ACCOMMODATION: 8 ensuite rooms
RATES: From £19pp Family room £48.00

BAR FOOD: Wide range, good value
VEGETARIAN: Yes + diets
WHEELCHAIR ACCESS: No
GARDEN: Yes, lawn
PETS: Yes (housetrained)

RUSSET HOUSE HOTEL
Vancouver Avenue
Goodwins Road
King's Lynn
Norfolk
PE30 5PE

Tel: 01553 773098

3 Crown Commended

As early as the 12th century King's Lynn was one of England's most important ports and this sense of seafaring history is still evident today. Late medieval merchants houses stretch back to the river between cobbled lanes and the Custom House still provides a landmark for Lynn's fishing fleet. West Norfolk around King's Lynn has large areas of outstanding natural beauty, providing the perfect habitat for many species of birds. Sandringham, the Norfolk home of the Royal Family, with its house, museum and magnificent gardens is only a few miles away. South and West of King's Lynn rivers and dikes divide the rich agricultural fens, reclaimed land and home to many species of birds, some very rare. With a thriving Arts Centre, Sports Centre and magnificent Corn Exchange Theatre, King's Lynn offers something for everyone.

The ideal place to stay in Lynn is Russet House, personally run by the Proprietors, John and Denise Stewart, which still has the welcoming homely feel it had when it was built as a private dwelling back in the 1890's. It became a hotel in the 1970's and enjoys a reputation for its friendly warmth as well as the comfort throughout and the excellence of its food. 1985 saw the addition of some ensuite bedrooms, a bar and a garden lounge, all carefully done to fit in with the character of the house. In 1996 it became necessary to remove the Victorian glass houses but the gardeners bothy was saved which still stands in a corner of the delightful garden. There are thirteen ensuite bedrooms in Russet House and each is beautifully furnished and appointed, Two or three bedrooms are suitable for families with extra beds or a cot available. Two rooms are on the ground floor with level access to the cosy bar, toilets, restaurant and lounge; one of these may be suitable for someone in a wheelchair. Russet House offers delicious fare on its menu and is a favourite venue for small parties who wish to stay over. Family, regimental and old school reunions tend to appreciate the comprehensive wine list and well stocked bar. Business men, tourists, lazy weekends, walkers and cyclists all regularly stop because the Russet House is perfectly situated for access to Coast, Country and Commerce .

USEFUL INFORMATION

OPEN: All year
CHILDREN: Well behaved welcome
CREDIT CARDS: All major cards
LICENSED: Yes
ACCOMMODATION: 13 ensuite rooms
RATES: From £48 dbl.
No smoking in restaurant, reading lounge
and four poster bedroom

RESTAURANT: Excellent menu
BAR FOOD: Home-made fare
VEGETARIAN: Catered for
WHEELCHAIR ACCESS: Yes
GARDEN: Yes
PETS: Yes

SHRUBLANDS FARM
Northrepps
Cromer
Norfolk
NR27 OAA

Tel/Fax: 01263 579297
E-Mail:www.broadland.com/shrublands

ETB 2 Crowns Highly Commended

This area of Norfolk is known as Poppyland, a name which was immortalised in the writings of Clement Scott who was a frequent visitor as were many when, at the end of the last century the railway brought visitors from London and the Midlands. It is a delightful area and at Northrepps, a small village just two and a half miles south east of Cromer is Shrublands Farm, owned and run by Peter and Ann Youngman. Shrublands itself is full of history with a legend that tells of the 'Shrieking Pits' referring to the ponds on the farm. It concerns a housemaid who worked at Shrublands in the late 18th century and had a doomed love affair with a neighbouring farmer. Cromer's hero is the much decorated lifeboat coxswain Henry Blogg. The town is noted for its lifeboat and pier and the latter has the last traditional end of the pier show in the country bringing people here to stay specifically to go to it.

The strictly non-smoking farmhouse is mainly Victorian/Edwardian in style although the original house dates back to the mid 18th century. Peter and Ann work together to make the guests feel welcome and at home. The atmosphere and ambience is that of a welcoming family home with guests being treated as friends. It is still a three hundred acre working arable farm which Ann's parents came to in 1930, and Ann was born here. Today Peter is helped on the farm by their son Jeremy and daughter Emma who lives nearby helps with the enterprise. Very much a family concern which is one of the reasons why it is such a great place to stay.

There are three guest bedrooms, one twin with a private bathroom, one double with a private bathroom and a twin room with shower ensuite. Furnished with furniture in keeping with the age of the house, the decor is traditional Laura Ashley/Sanderson. Quite charming and each room has radio alarm and a hostess tray. A delicious and generous farmhouse breakfast is served every day and in the evening an optional meal is available cooked by Ann using much local produce. Children over twelve years are very welcome but pets are only permitted if they sleep in the car.

USEFUL INFORMATION

OPEN: All year except Christmas   DINING ROOM: Good home-cooked
CHILDREN: Over 12 years   fare
CREDIT CARDS: None taken   VEGETARIAN: Upon request
LICENSED: No   WHEELCHAIR ACCESS: No
ACCOMMODATION:3 rooms all ensuite   GARDEN: Yes
RATES: From £20 pp B&B   PETS: Only if they sleep in car
STRICTLY NON-SMOKING HOUSE

STENSON
32 Overstrand Road
Cromer
Norfolk
NR27 0AJ

Tel: 01263 511308

Stenson stands out as a very special guest house amidst the many in the Cromer area. Built in 1897 for the sum of £800, as a holiday home for the rich, it stands detached with a half an acre of delightful gardens and stables, which house a Race horse, and many other pleasurable features. Seventy five chickens make sure that newly laid eggs are on the Breakfast menu every day. There are six self-catering chalets for those who prefer to be totally independent. If you enjoy horse racing you will soon discover the enthusiasm that the owners, Richard and Vivian Bateman have for the Sport of Kings. They organise days out at the races at Yarmouth and Fakenham for their guests which are great fun and add an extra spice to their stay. This is a paradise for children and the family pet is welcome as well providing you are staying in a chalet and not in the house.

This is a carefree, happy establishment in which to stay for people of all ages. The bedrooms are all comfortably furnished in keeping with the age of the house, they all have washbasins, television, hair dryers and a hostess tray. One bedroom is on the ground floor and has wheelchair access. The large lounge is a great meeting place and in cooler weather the open fire in the reception hall sends out a welcoming warmth. Two Labradors and two cats add to the contented, homely feeling that is the essence of Stenson. In the Dining Room you will be served an excellent breakfast with many choices including freshly poached apricots, prunes and figs with cinnamon or porridge. In addition to the traditional English Breakfast you may choose to have your eggs cooked in whichever way you prefer. Smoked Haddock is also on the menu as well as a delicious home-made Kedgeree. The evening meal, cooked by Vivian, who loves cooking, is a varied feast and will include Vegetarian or Special diet menus if required. There is always a fish dish and various salads, delectable desserts, a cheese board and a free bottle of wine.

Cromer offers a whole range of entertainment from the glorious beach to swimming, golf, tennis, riding, squash, putting greens, stunning walks along the cliff tops, a bowling green, go-karting for all ages, shire horse centre, cricket, National Trust properties, old churches, a pier and museums. A great place for a holiday and nowhere better to stay than Stenson.

USEFUL INFORMATION

OPEN: All year

DINING ROOM: Super, home-cooked fare

CHILDREN: Very welcome

VEGETARIAN: Yes + Special diets

CREDIT CARDS: None taken

WHEELCHAIR ACCESS: Yes

LICENSED: No

PETS: Welcome in Chalets only

GARDEN: 1/2 acre

ACCOMMODATION: Comfortable bedrooms.

RATES: From £20 B&B Children £10 BB+Evening Meal from £32

THE WELLINGTON HOTEL & FREEHOUSE
Garden Street
Cromer
Norfolk
NR27 9HP

Tel: 01263 511075
Fax: 01263 513750

In the town centre of Cromer and just above the old Victorian pier and beach is The Wellington Hotel and Freehouse, one of the most cheerful hostelries in the county and in which the landlord, Eric Hopwood and his wife Shelagh claim to be 'probably the cheapest pub in Britain'. Certainly they can claim to be a proper pub and they firmly tell you that what you see is what you get! It is a pub much loved by its regulars and if you go into the Victorian 'Locals Bar' with its lofty ceilings and large windows, you will probably meet up with members of one or other of the two Pool Teams, the two Football Teams, the Cricket Team and the three Darts Teams. This makes the bars busy throughout the year and produces endless fun, competition and cements friendly relations. It is a great place to visit and the stranger soon finds him or herself part of the fun and chatter.

The food served at the Wellington either in the small restaurant or in the bar is good home-cooked fare and is in no way pretentious. The home-made Steak and Guinness Pie and Cottage Pies are always popular, the steaks are tender and succulent and anything to do with fish is fresh and delicious as one would expect in Cromer. There are dishes for children and for Vegetarians. Daily Specials supplement the printed menu. You get substantial portions and the price is right. Breakfast, when you stay here is another great meal with a choice of either a full English fried breakfast, Scrambled Eggs and Bacon, Poached Eggs or Kippers with orange juice, cereal and plenty of toast and preserves as well as tea and coffee. The eight letting rooms, four of which are long term and the other four en-suite, are individually decorated and furnished. All the rooms have television, hospitality trays and hairdryers. The latter four rooms are not above the bar so you can be assured of quiet.

USEFUL INFORMATION

OPEN: All year
CHILDREN: Welcome
CREDIT CARDS: None taken money
VEGETARIAN: Always a choice
WHEELCHAIR ACCESS: Yes
ACCOMMODATION: 8 rooms 4 ensuite
RATES: £17.50 - £20.00 pppn B&B (£10 sgl supp)
Mid Week Breaks; Oct-Mar 4 nights for price of 3
Children upto 14 years half price, under 4 years quarter price

RESTAURANT: Good home-made fare
BAR MEALS: Wide range. Value for

LICENSED: Full On
GARDEN: Yes.
PETS: No

THE WHITE HOUSE
44 Hunstanton Road
Dersingham
King's Lynn
Norfolk
PE31 6HQ

Tel: 01485 541895
Fax: 01485 544880

B&B 2 Crowns Commended

Valerie Brundle shares her delightful Victorian house in Dersingham with her guests and makes them feel relaxed and at home. It is the friendly sort of house that is run apparently with the greatest of ease but one knows that underlying the informality is the hand of a lady skilled in the art of caring for people. You will find The White House in Dersingham half way between King's Lynn and Hunstanton on the A149. Less than a mile away is the Queen's Norfolk home, Sandringham, open to the public for most of the year, well worth a visit. King's Lynn is only ten minutes drive away and is full of historic interest., Nature Reserves abound around the coast and rare bird species arrive with regularity. Bircham Mill is a working mill and both Holkham Hall and Houghton Hall, two stately homes with magnificent gardens are there to be savoured. The former has a superb beach close by Burnham Market and the other Burnhams have historic links with Admiral Lord Nelson and are but a few of the villages waiting to be explored.. Valerie Brundle is a lady with a keen sense of humour and always willing to help you plan your day's excursion. Valerie is the step-mother of the Formula One racing driver, and Television commentator Martin Brundle. Her oak beamed dining room pays tribute to his exciting and challenging career

The White House is a late Victorian home, and has that spaciousness that the architecture of the era permitted. The rooms are all light and airy and still have much of the Victorian charm including the original Victorian lamps, chandeliers, brass door locks, porcelain door handles, original doors and mosaic tile entrance hall. The house is strictly non-smoking and no pets are taken. Children over five years old are welcomed. There are six guest rooms, mainly ensuite, the remainder are scheduled to be en-suite by the end of 1998. Each room is furnished with style and taste, with the emphasis on comfort. All rooms have had new beds this summer to meet with the latest Fire regulations and have well supplied hostess trays. Television is available in the Television Lounge. Valerie enjoys cooking as does the Chef, a former Chef on the luxury liner 'Canberra', which is apparent in the excellence of the freshly produced breakfast for your enjoyment. In addition to the Traditional English breakfast, vegetarian and Continental dishes are available on request. A superb three or four course evening meal is available by arrangement.

USEFUL INFORMATION

OPEN: All year	DINING ROOM: Excellent breakfast
CHILDREN: Over 5 years	VEGETARIAN: Upon request
CREDIT CARDS: None taken	WHEELCHAIR ACCESS: Restricted
LICENSED: No	GARDEN: Yes
ACCOMMODATION: 6 rooms	PETS: No. Non-smoking house
mainly ensuite (all ensuite by end of 1998)	Large off Street Car Parking
RATES: From £16-£2 5 per person	

THE WHITE HORSE INN
Fakenham Road,
East Barsham,
Fakenham,
Norfolk
NR21 0LH

EATB 3 Crowns

Tel:01328 820645

The 17th century White Horse is a pleasant long and low village inn, painted white on the outside it has the rich, red roof tiles, prevalent in Norfolk. Mr and Mrs Baines have been the landlords here for over eleven years and are clearly popular with locals who come in to enjoy the beer, chat over the news and village affairs or maybe play a game of darts. Many of the visitors who have found their way here over the years have become regulars whenever they are in this part of Norfolk. From here it is easy to reach the North Norfolk Coast and Sandringham. Norwich is twenty six miles away. Birdwatchers are bewitched by the number of birds and for walkers the countryside is ideal.

Recognised for the excellence of its interesting and varied menu, the non-smoking restaurant is always busy. You will find all sorts of interesting dishes available from traditional English to Asian and Thai. In the Bar the blackboard menu offers Daily Specials, frequently time-honoured favourites such as steak and kidney pie and also has a wide range of snacks from sandwiches to soup, Ploughman's to pate. Sunday Lunch is looked forward to and in the summer it is wise to book a table. Vegetarians are not forgotten and will always find a 'Dish of the Day' there especially for them. In summer people frequently choose to eat and drink in the attractive garden.

Staying here is a pleasure. There are three rooms, some with four-posters and a cottage The bedrooms are all ensuite and have television, tea and coffee facilities. The beds are supremely comfortable and breakfast is a delicious meal.

USEFUL INFORMATION

OPEN: 11-3pm & 6.30-11pm
CHILDREN: Welcome
CREDIT CARDS: Visa/Master. Euro/Switch.
LICENSED: Full On
ACCOMMODATION: 3ensuite
plus a cottage
RATES: From £25pp B&B

RESTAURANT: English, Asian & Thai
BAR FOOD: English home-cooked fare
VEGETARIAN: Yes
WHEELCHAIR ACCESS: Yes
GARDEN: Yes.
PETS: Outside only

BRAMLEY
Standard Road
Wells-next-the-Sea
Norfolk
NR23 1JU

Tel: 01328 710384
Mobile: 0410737451

Wells-next- the-Sea is one of Norfolk's charming seaside small towns where everyone seems to know everyone else and the visitor is especially welcome. It has a famous old stone quay and from here you can follow many pursuits including walking, fishing and bird-watching. There are several National Trust properties within easy reach and The Queen's home, Sandringham, is open when the family are not in residence. Looking for somewhere to stay you will do no better than Jean Popes' welcoming home, Bramley, which is only a short walk from the quay side. This is a warm and comfortable house, centrally heated throughout. The rooms are light and airy and well furnished with two double guest rooms with private bathroom and an ensuite twin-bedded room which has wheelchair access. A substantial full English breakfast is served every day. Evening meals are not available but Wells has a number of good eateries. Smoking is not permitted except in the Guest Lounge. There is private Car Parking behind locked gates.

USEFUL IN FORMATION

OPEN: All year
CHILDREN: Over 9 years
CREDIT CARDS: None taken
LICENSED: No
ACCOMMODATION: 2dbl with
private bathroom. 1tw ensuite
RATES: From £12pp pn B&B

DINING ROOM: Substantial full English breakfast. No evening meals
VEGETARIAN: Can be catered for
WHEELCHAIR ACCESS: Yes
GARDEN: Yes
PETS: Yes
SECURE PARKING

NELSON'S TEA & COFFEE SHOP
21 Staithe Street
Wells-Next-the-Sea
Norfolk
NR23 1HB

Tel: 01328 711650

A good tea and coffee shop is one of life's pleasures especially on holiday when you have time to enjoy cream teas, home-made cakes, home-made soups and a whole range of other delicious fare cooked in this instance by the owner of Nelson's Tea and Coffee Shop. Here is an old world shop with large bay windows and everywhere there is Nelson memorabilia. It is beautifully decorated and when you walk in you have the sense of stepping back in time. Nelson's has a great reputation with local people who regularly pop in for morning coffee or to meet their friends for lunch and afternoon tea. Visitors having once discovered its beautifully cooked and presented fare, tend to make it a home-from-home whilst they are staying in Wells. Staithe Street you will find two minutes from Wells' Victorian Stone Quay and from The Butlands, a large restful green, ringed by trees and elegant Georgian houses.

USEFUL INFORMATION

OPEN: 9-5pm except July-Aug 9-7.30pm
CHILDREN: Welcome
CREDIT CARDS: None taken
LICENSED: No

TEASHOP: Home-cooked fare
VEGETARIAN: Always available
WHEELCHAIR ACCESS: Yes

THE MALTINGS
The Street
Weybourne
Holt
Norfolk
NR25 7SY

Tel/Fax: 01263 588731

Built in the 16th century and still retaining many of the original features, The Maltings Hotel is a delightful place to stay in a glorious part of Norfolk. It is only twenty five miles from historic Norwich with its superb cathedral, within reach of four stately homes, a Military Museum, a Steam Railway and the beautiful Coastal Heritage Walk. You can fish from the beach, go coarse fishing, play golf on five major courses and still enjoy the peaceful, tranquillity of this rural setting. Owned by Andrew and Ross Mears, the hotel is run with the degree of professionalism that ensures the well-being of guests. The furniture and decor throughout are superb with some fine antique pieces. Eleven double, seven twin-bedded and two singles, all ensuite make up the twenty guest rooms. Each is well-appointed, comfortable and has television, direct dial telephone and a generously supplied hostess tray. The Restaurant has a delicious a la carte menu which includes many International dishes and in the well-stocked bar food is also served. Personal service, good food, extensive wine list, smiling staff, all make The Maltings Hotel a good place to be.

USEFUL INFORMATION

OPEN: All year. Rest:12-2.30pm & 7-9.30pm
CHILDREN: Welcome
BAR FOOD: Good choice
VEGETARIAN: Yes
ACCOMMODATION: 20 ensuite rooms
RATES: £32 sgl pppn £28 dbl. pppn. B&B

RESTAURANT: International Menu
CREDIT CARDS: All major cards
LICENSED: Yes. Extensive wine list
WHEELCHAIR ACCESS: No
GARDEN: Yes
PETS: Yes

ORCHARD HOUSE
Thornham, Hunstanton
Norfolk PE36 6LY
Tel: 01485 512259
2 Crown Commended

Thornham is a quiet coastal village within the Conservation Coast Area of Natural Beauty. It is an ideal spot for all country pursuits and for those who like exploring, you will unearth all manner of quaint inns, flint and chalk villages as well as golf links, sailing and two Bird Reserves. It is situated on the Coastal path looking onto empty sandy beaches and a natural harbour. For those looking for somewhere to stay in this undiscovered part of North West Norfolk, Orchard House is the perfect choice.
Set in two acres of mature grounds and south facing, it is a tranquil haven for anyone wanting to recharge their batteries. Owned by Mary and Bill Rutland who have lived in the village most of their lives, they have a wealth of local knowledge which they are happy to share with their guests. They rightly describe their charming, comfortable home as more a house that takes guests than a guest house. There are two ensuite bedrooms, one deluxe ensuite and one standard room. All of them are beautifully appointed and complete with hostess trays. The Deluxe suite can be either bed and breakfast or self-catering - it has a mini kitchen. A full Norfolk Breakfast with a selection of fresh fruit, bacon and home-made preserves is taken in the Conservatory overlooking the garden every morning.

USEFUL INFORMATION

OPEN: All year except Christmas Day.
CHILDREN: Over 8 years breakfast
VEGETARIAN: Upon request
WHEELCHAIR ACCESS: No
GARDEN: Mature garden
PETS: No

DINING ROOM:Full Norfolk
CREDIT CARDS: None taken
LICENSED: No
ACCOMMODATION: 3 ensuite 1 standard
RATES: From £20pp B&B

ORCHARD HOUSE IS STRICTLY NON-SMOKING

THE OSTRICH INN
Stocks Green
Castle Acre
King's Lynn
Norfolk
PE32 2AE

Tel/Fax: 01760 755398
Internet: ostrich.ray@aol.com.

The Ostrich Inn became well known in the 16th century as a coaching inn caring for travellers. It still retains much of its old world charm and certainly the happy atmosphere that has been generated over the centuries. Raymond Wakelen is the cheery landlord who, together with his staff, makes sure everyone who comes through the old doors is welcomed and cared for. The ale is well kept, the bar well-stocked including an extensive wine list - even a bottle or two from Greenland! Combine the good wine with the excellent International cuisine available here and you have a memorable meal. Vegetarian food is one of the specialities of the inn. Simpler food is served in the bar and can be anything from a sandwich to a full blown meal. There is a Beer Garden, much in use in the summer together with a small, aromatic herb garden. For those wanting to stay a night or two, comfortable bed and breakfast accommodation is available. The Ostrich is the only inn as you walk from south east Norfolk to north west, on the Pedlers Way and very popular with walkers who enjoy the carefree spirit of the inn.

USEFUL INFORMATION

OPEN: 12-3pm & 7-11pm
CHILDREN: Welcome
CREDIT CARDS: All major cards
LICENSED: Full On
ACCOMMODATION: B&B rooms
RATES: £15pp.pn B&B

RESTAURANT: International cuisine
BAR FOOD: Wide choice
VEGETARIAN: Speciality
WHEELCHAIR ACCESS: Yes
GARDEN: Beer & Herb garden
PETS: Yes on a lead

POPLAR FARM
Sisland
Loddon
Norfolk
NR14 6EF

Tel: 01508 520706

Sisland is a tiny hamlet close to Loddon, with a beautiful thatched church named as 'Norfolk Tourist Church of the year' in 1994 and parts of which date back to 1300. The hamlet has a wild flower centre and a an alpine nursery. It also has Poplar Farm a working, mainly arable farm but with pigs and a Charolais herd of cows with calves born between March and June. The River Chet runs through the farm on its way to Loddon. The farm is approximately ten miles south east of Norwich, close to the market towns of Beccles and Bungay and near the famous Norfolk Broads. It could not be a better place to have as a base for a holiday, a short break or a home from home if you are on business. James and Milly Hemmant are the owners and their friendly approach to guests is always appreciated. There are three bedrooms, a family room, a double and a twin all sharing a bathroom with plentiful hot water. Each room has tea making facilities and there is a private sitting room with television and video. For those who enjoy tennis, a well maintained court is there for your use. Breakfast is a hearty farmhouse meal which will set you up for the day.

USEFUL INFORMATION

OPEN: All year
CHILDREN: Welcome
CREDIT CARDS: None taken
WHEELCHAIR ACCESS: No LICENSED: No
PETS: Not in house
RATES: From £15pp B&B

DINING ROOM: Farmhouse breakfast
VEGETARIAN: Yes + Vegan if
requested
GARDEN: Yes. Try metal detecting!
ACCOMMODATION: 1dbl.1 fam. 1tw not ensuite

THE DYKE
CHRISTIAN HOTEL
5 St Nicholas Place
Sheringham
Norfolk
NR26 8LF

Tel: 01263 822053

Many people may recognise the name 'Keychange' in conjunction with the charity which is mainly concerned with Mums/Babies/Hostels/Care Homes/ Day Centre/ Nursing Homes all around England and Scotland. Here in Sheringham they have an evangelical interdenominational Christian Hotel. It offers the visitor a comfortable, friendly base from which to have a holiday or to work. Certainly it provides a tranquil and peaceful existence with a great deal of humour and fun as well as excellent home-made cooking both at breakfast and in the evening. There are sixteen attractively furnished bedrooms, six of which are ensuite and each room has a hostess tray and a Gideon Bible. The pretty dining room has 26-30 covers whilst the Lounge Hall is full of comfortable chairs. The Games Room also has television and Video. Daily informal morning and evening services are held throughout the summer which guests are welcome to attend if they wish. Run by a team of four, this is a happy contented establishment and ideally situated for the exploration of this stunning part of Norfolk.

USEFUL INFORMATION

OPEN: All year
CHILDREN: Welcome fare
VEGETARIAN: Upon request
WHEELCHAIR ACCESS: Yes. Ramp
GARDEN: 9 hole putting green Summer house
ACCOMMODATION: 16 rooms 6 ensuite
RATES: From £22 BB&EM Special out of season breaks

DINING ROOM: Excellent home-cooked

CREDIT CARDS: None taken
LICENSED: No
PETS: No

TWINSON LEE
109 Tennyson Road
King's Lynn
Norfolk
PE30 5PA
Tel: 01553 762900 Fax: 01553 769944

RAC Listed

Twinson Lee is a comfortable, friendly family home into which Susan and David Thomas welcome guests for bed and breakfast. It is just a pleasant ten minute walk to the centre of King's Lynn, through a lovely park. All sorts of people come to stay here and many of them to enjoy the excellent cycling which has become a major holiday feature because of the rural landscape. Others come to explore the historic town which boasts many architectural features including the resplendent Customs House, the Town Hall and the Corn Exchange. There are many other attractions close by including Sandringham, the Norfolk home of the Queen and her family. Within the house there are one single, one double and one family room. None of them are ensuite but the spacious bathroom has plenty of hot water and this does not cause a problem and each room has a wash basin as well as television. Breakfast is a super meal cooked by David who is known to be 'a Welsh Wizard at breakfasts' ! Evening meals on request are equally delicious.

USEFUL INFORMATION

OPEN: All year
CHILDREN: Welcome
CREDIT CARDS: None taken
LICENSED: No
ACCOMMODATION: 1sgl.1dbl 1fam
RATES: £17sgl £32dbl £36 family room

DINING ROOM: Great breakfast
Evening meal upon request
VEGETARIAN: By arrangement
WHEELCHAIR ACCESS: No
GARDEN: Yes
PETS: Yes

Selected venues in this chapter

' Go thy way, eat thy bread with joy,
and drink thy wine with a merry heart...'
Ecclesiastes

Chapter Two:
BROADS AND BEACHES
Great Yarmouth to Cromer

After the Dersingham tour, let's move south east across the county to our second base, Gorleston. Before we look at the town itself we'd better take a little time to get the general feel of its surroundings.

We can expect a mixed feast, which at its best is full of magic. Time and again, there will be that feeling of awe inspired by nature at its most powerful and dramatic. At its worst, on the other hand, we may catch the odd glimpse of the trash of modern neglect and of the brutality of cash conscious 'planning', not to mention the candy-floss flicker of mechanical holiday-making vulgarity. In short, it can be much like everywhere else. Variety, however, needs to be the main thread of life's rich pageant, so let's take it all in for future reference while we reflect upon that paradox of all paradoxes - human nature.

Geographically, the area falls into three sections. Firstly there is the coastal strip, made up of many parts that run from the sublime to the 'Oh, really!' Then there is 'Broadland', which in its own way has just as varied a range of possibilities. Finally, comes the more rural swathe running south from Cromer, via North Walsham to the outskirts of Norwich. This last is Norfolk's only city and county town which, although let down as a base by its traffic problems, would call for more than one visit to do justice to its history, culture and wide range of shopping facilities, and so will later have a chapter to itself.

Although **GORLESTON** is, on paper, part of Great Yarmouth, it has kept its distinctive, quieter character intact. This makes it better for our purpose than its ebullient neighbour which seems hooked on pumping out adrenalin right round the clock - fun for a while, but eventually far too exhausting. Centred on its SOUTH PIER, the town boasts a harbour, a large open-air swimming pool and a range of traditional seaside amusements. The ranks of colour-washed houses, typical of the old town, are best viewed from the pier, from which one can also look across to the disused lighthouse and south wards down the coast to Lowestoft. A town for quiet reflection over a meal at the end of the day's exploration, Gorleston also offers morning dips from the beach, provided one keeps clear of the stretch between the pier breakwater and the model yacht pond.

Three miles inland from our base, lies BURGH CASTLE, all that survives of the Roman fortress of Gariannonum. Built during the third century, its three hefty flint walls show the seriousness of its role as a 'Fort of the Saxon Shore', part of the chain of defence against ferocious raids by marauders from across the North Sea. Although today it is stranded, it would have had access to the sea 1500 years ago and may well have harboured a fleet of warships. Later in its history a Christian community was founded inside its walls. Later still a Norman motte, or defensive mound, - topped, probably, with a wooden fortress - was built. Whatever the nature of its past, the castle is worth a visit for the spectacular views from its unwalled west side across the top reaches of BREYDON WATER, which is also of interest as a feeding ground for wildfowl and wading birds. These can be observed from hides along the north bank, and there are also guided walks organised by the Yarmouth Naturalists, under the beady eyes of cormorants who use the posts, which are set up to mark the deep water channel, as points of vantage while they dry their wings.

There is one further short trip to be made from Gorleston before braving Yarmouth. A mile to the south-east of the town lies FRITTON LAKE [Enquiries - 01493 488208], a two mile long stretch of delightful water forming the main part of a county park, just south of the A143. Probably created as a result of peat cutting, the lake can be explored in a hired a boat - a good idea as there are many kinds of water fowl to be seen. Fritton's other attractions include an undercover falconry centre, heavy horses, golf and putting courses and fishing facilities.

Whatever one's reaction to the **GREAT YARMOUTH** [Information - 01493 846345] of today, there's no denying that its evolution has been a fascinating business. Nor can one deny that in its approach to 'The Holiday', it's gone for gold! As the beaches here get at least as much summer sun as any others in Britain, those catering for the inrush of visitors have done everything possible to be sure they make the most of it - one way or another! There wouldn't be space to reel off everything that's on offer as the list is far too long, from AMAZONIA [Enquiries - 01493 842202], a tropical flower and wildlife experience, to TREASURE WORLD [Enquiries - 01493 330444], showing through modern technology how treasures from the deep are recovered, and the SEALIFE CENTRE [Enquiries - 01493 330631], where one can discover some of the most dazzling displays of marine life ever seen in Britain.

All one can suggest is that if these sound appealing, then five minutes with the town guide book would generate enough ideas to fill your day many times over. Make no mistake, we're talking serious 'fun', here, from waxworks to Jurassic giants, boating lakes to amusement arcades and from the putting green to the circus, while there are more than a dozen different sport centres, including no less than three golf clubs. Fortunately for our purposes there is another side to Yarmouth, if we're ready to brave the minefield of 'attractions'. Away from the roistering seafront of the Leisure Centre and the roller-coastered pleasure beach lie museums, monuments, galleries and craft centres a'plenty - well, enough to justify driving through the outer wasteland of the town to discover the secrets at its heart, at any rate.

ANNA SEWELL HOUSE, a 16th century cottage nestling near the parish church, is the birthplace of the authoress of 'Black Beauty' - still one of the most widely read children's stories in the world and the sixth most popular book ever written in the English language. Now a restaurant, the cottage was more than two hundred years old when Anna was born, on the 30th March 1820. She died at Old Catton, Norwich, in 1878, six months after her famous book was first published.

On the South Quay near the Town Hall lies the ELIZABETHAN HOUSE MUSEUM. Built in 1596, its panelled rooms with period furniture house exhibitions or toys, games, china and civic plate. There is also a fascinatingly restored Victorian kitchen. The last remaining steam drifter, the 'LYDIA EVA', is moored by the quayside not far from the Elizabethan House. It gives a remarkable insight into life during the great days of the herring fishing industry, when steam drifters thronged the port. This exhibition is open daily between Easter and September from 10am to 4.30 pm and admission is free.

The NORTH WEST TOWER was built in 1334 as part of the town walls. It has been converted to a visitors centre where history can be relived through the story of 'Spray', one of the old trading wherries from the Broads. The tower is open between the end of July and the first of September, between 10am and 4pm, and is situated on the North Quay of the River Bure.

The Norfolk Museums Service has opened a MARITIME MUSEUM FOR EAST ANGLIA in a historic shipwrecked sailors home on Marine Parade Central. It contains a major display of models, paintings and other items showing local marine history including fisheries, life-saving, Nelson and the Norfolk Broads. Generally, it is open from Monday to Friday, and Sunday, between 10am and 5pm, although in the early part of April, Sunday opening is not until 2pm. From Monday to Saturday between 9.30am and 5.30pm, one can visit the MUSEUM EXHIBITION GALLERIES in the Central Library in Tolhouse Street. These are modern galleries with a changing programme of local and travelling exhibitions.

Another part of Yarmouth's history is brought to life by English Heritage, who have renovated three houses in ROW 111 as typical examples of the small town houses of the 17th century. They make an interesting contrast to the OLD MERCHANT'S HOUSE, another English Heritage monument, which shows some of the advantages enjoyed by the better off. Row 111, which also offers access to GREYFRIARS CLOISTERS, is open between April and September, Monday to Friday, 10am to 6pm, apart from the lunch break from 1pm to 2pm.

Before leaving this aspect of the town behind, one should look into the TOLHOUSE, an early medieval building once used as a courthouse and gaol. The original dungeons are still in existence and one can also visit its museum of local history. The BRASS RUBBING CENTRE, where a wide range of replica brasses is available, completes the visit. Opening times are similar to those for the Maritime Museum. Our final call will be to the CANDLEMAKER AND MODEL CENTRE

[Enquiries - 01493 750242], which lies near the Market Place, opposite the Boulevard Bus Terminus. Within the candle shop and workshop, where various stages of candle-making can be inspected, one will find England's largest variety of hand -crafted candles. In addition to touring the workshops one also has a chance to do some candle-dipping for oneself. A small entrance fee is charged, which includes the cost of the candle.

Having realised that much of Yarmouth's history still survives, it might be worth a pause to reflect before we head off northwards along the coast. The town's name comes from the River Yare, which joins with the River Waveney to the west of the town after winding through low-lying meadows east from Norwich. The Yare widens out into the spread of Breydon Water and then turns sharply south, creating the peninsula on which Yarmouth is built. The old town and port developed on the east bank of the river, ignoring the open sea, and then spread across to the west bank.

By 1086, Yarmouth was big enough to be included in the Domesday Book. It then grew steadily, as a harbour and centre for shipbuilding throughout the Middle Ages. Between the town wall - a good stretch of which still stands - and the river, houses were crammed together into 145 narrow lanes or 'Rows', one of them less than a single metre wide. We have seen something of the remaining examples, and have also recognised the town's good fortune in having the remarkable 13thcentury Tolhouse, one of England's oldest surviving municipal buildings.

For the Middle Ages to 1963, when the last drifter was sold, Yarmouth's fortunes waxed and waned with those of the herring industry. Surviving the early days of conflict, with first the Cinque Ports and then the Dutch, over North Sea fishing rights, the trade reached its heyday just before the First World War, when over 1100 drifters were based at Yarmouth. Overfishing led to a decline and once the last boat was sold it was North Sea oil and gas which saved the town from stagnation, following its selection as the first centre for oil and gas exploration. Meanwhile the Victorians had already discovered the seaside and Great Yarmouth seized this opportunity to extend its boundaries to include the miles of golden sand on the seaward side of the peninsula. It began to cater for holiday-makers as a major endeavour, so that today it is one of the best known resorts of its kind in Britain.

We'll leave Yarmouth by the A149, as planned, and eventually follow the coast north and drop in on the villages that lie behind its miles of dunes and beaches. To do this we need to turn on to the B1159, the coast road. Before turning off, it's worth pausing to wander a mile or two out of our way in the direction of CAISTER CASTLE, the first brick built castle in England and currently close to the home of the largest private collection of motor vehicles in Great Britain. Exhibits range from the first real motor car in the world with a full history, the 1893 Panhard et Levassor, to the first Ford Fiesta, and Jim Clark's Grand Prix F14 car, used in the film 'Chitty Chitty Bang Bang'. The castle itself is a magnificent, moated ruin, built in the 1430's by Sir John Fastolff

[1378 - 1459], who may well have been the model for Shakespeare's Falstaff - although the original Sir John was far from being the cowardly fat knight portrayed by the Bard.

Leaving the cars and the castle behind, we have to come to a decision. While we are exploring this part of the county in general, and the Broads in particular, we will want to see as many of the best known examples as possible - which means we can't miss Ormesby. Nor for that matter should we overlook Rollesby or Filby. In other words, we are marginally stumped by geography: there is no direct road from Caister Castle via the Broads back to the coast. So my choice has to be a deliberate detour - to head inland to the B1152, then turn right towards Martham, before turning right again along the A149 towards Rollesby and, eventually, back to Caister on Sea, where we can continue our coastal exploration. Quite a detour - but we're here to see the country, so let's press on. Of course, this being Norfolk [let's not forget] as soon as the decision's made an unexpected bonus appears on the horizon.

We'll find 'unexpected' is the understatement of the millenium at THRIGBY HALL WILDLIFE GARDENS [Enquiries - 01493 369477], which lies a short way down a left turn off the A1064, near the village of **FILBY**. On the other hand, if the essence of 'The Norfolk Experience' has become part of your life, you *might* see it as perfectly natural to come across rare tigers in the company of huge crocodiles, noisy gibbons and a great many other interesting creatures prowling around in the grounds of old Thrigby Hall. Surprised or otherwise, you'll find parking is free, and taking a picnic - weather permitting - is recommended as the best way of spending as much of the visit as possible where the animals actually are rather than thinking about them through the windows of a cafeteria. Open daily from 10am, Thrigby also offers among its other attractions a very useful gift shop.

The village of **ROLLESBY** is one mile north-west of the 200 hundred acre ROLLESBY BROAD, which is linked to the deep water ORMESBY and FILBY BROADS. That leads me to the plus side of our detour: the road from Rollesby to Ormesby offers some of the best views of typical Broadland to be found. There's an odd side to that too - over quite long stretches, the waterways are virtually invisible, since they're lower than the rest of the landscape. It's quite a surprise to find out just how near they are and suddenly come across sails that seem to be tacking across the middle of a field!

The Broads are Britain's outstanding Wetland and are protected as are all National Parks. Their attractions are astonishingly diverse: they're a paradise for wildlife, containing numerous species of fish, birds, plants and insects unique to the area. They are world famous for water activities from sailing to fishing. Perhaps one needs to explore them by boat to savour their full flavour - but that is by no means the only way of doing the job. Walking and cycling can be just as rewarding. The countryside is crossed and re-crossed by paths giving access to a very English way of life that is as out of the ordinary as it was more than a century ago, and as resistant as ever to the pressures of the 'modern-day world'. This is always assuming that one can, even partially, discount the arrival of the motor cruiser which, nowadays, has totally usurped the traditional wherry. This distinctive type of sailing vessel, with its huge main sail, plied the Broads in Victorian times. It offered the ideal way to transport life's necessities - timber, wheat, barley - along Norfolk's extensive waterway network, which in those days was vastly superior to the poor roads for this purpose. Because it was developed to cope with all the conditions likely to be met in this trade, it went everywhere. It drew surprisingly little water, which allowed it through the shallower stretches; it's easily lowered single mast and sail let it pass beneath the many low bridges. In a sense, it was a kind of symbol for the area as much as it was *the* means of access to the many villages and other communities. It's passing is symbolic too, for residents and visitors alike. Times *have* changed in this part of the world, just as they have everywhere else, despite the unexpectedly timeless *feelings* one notices so often as one travels around. The old buildings are to be seen on every hand; the traditions often seem unshakeable- but the changeover from wherry to motor-boat still represents more than a difference in power source.

Regardless of the changes Broadland, which covers a 200 square-mile area between Norwich and the coast, is still as intriguing as it is spectacular, as laid back as it is frantic, in high summer, when the popular parts seem like the M25 on water. The statistics tell part of the tale - 2000-plus boats for hire, at least 7000 other owner-driven craft and endless streams of water buses taking sightseers by the thousand along the rivers which serve as the region's arteries. If all those figures begin to sound like a peculiarly aquatic version of hell - and I suppose that's what it nearly became as the 70's wore into the 80's - don't panic. There could be light at the end of the tunnel. During the 90's 'Green' has become a buzz-word as most of us have begun to fall over backwards to cosset 'The Environment'. The motives don't matter - but the effects do, so that at the threshold of the 21st century, there is , as I say, a glimmer of hope. People are beginning to see areas such as the Broads as worth saving *in their own right*, as something more than exploitable assets. Of course, they're also noticing that improving the natural environment can make them even *more* exploitable - but we won't go into that. However we look at it , the impression is of one particular 'hell' which may only be temporary and, ultimately, totally avoidable, with the Broads equally able to offer peace for the peaceful - and the other thing for the ravers. I, for one, live in hope.

In any case, even today - with the enlightenment barely past its dawning - it's not all frenzy everywhere from June to September. That facet of Broadland's reputation is, I would suggest, as blinkered as it is prejudiced - and never mind the statistics. At this point I'm not about to support my suggestion by reeling off a list of the area's 'gems of tranquillity since that would almost certainly be self-defeating, with tens of thousands of readers all dropping everything to dash off and see for themselves. No, all of us must find our 'gems' for ourselves, [they *are* there, waiting to be found), and then keep very quiet about them.

From just a quick glance at the map, there would seem to be plenty of scope for choice. Depending on how small you're prepared to go - and some 'authorities' include reedy, weedy bits of water not much bigger than the back yard - there are between 30 and 50 true Broads. In any case, as the dividing line between 'real' water and 'real' land is so hard to pin down, such is the mixture of swamps, reed beds and boggy woodland surrounding many of them, 'true' size is all a bit relative. Perhaps, for us, it really doesn't matter much anyway. They're there, there should be enough to go round - and a careful search is almost bound to deliver the goods. In fact, I wouldn't be at all surprised if a pretty short detour from this chapter's chosen route turned out to do the trick.

We need to talk 'history' here, for a sentence or two - or twenty even - to explain the presence of these lakes in the first place. At first sight they're all a bit mystifying, and that's part of their charm, but their origins are not to be found in the glacial activities of the aftermath of the last Ice Age, as was believed for many years. Research over the last four or five decades has proved that the overwhelming majority of these shallow lakes are man-made, the upshot of many years of peat-digging, dating back to the early Middle Ages. Each Broad lies in a different parish and, in those days, provided its fuel and much of its prosperity. Taken together, there's no doubt that they played a key-role in the economy and the quality of life of what was a prosperous and, for those days, a densely populated area.

As the natural water levels changed in the 14th century, the workings became flooded. The process then expanded - no doubt with a little help from people who saw its potential advantages - as links with the nearby rivers were established, until the overall picture emerged that we see today as such an important part of Norfolk life. In those early days, of course, because of their origins, one could imagine that there were Broads wherever there were big enough groups of people with a need for fuel. When the workings flooded, however, and the 'new' fuel, coal, began to arrive by sea, population centres shifted somewhat. New industries emerged too, and populous areas in, say, the west of the county developed without a Broad in sight.

Nowadays the low-lying landscape runs inland from towns that have become the east coast's centres for both industry and holiday-making. This makes Broadland easily accessible from continental Europe, and doubtless contributes further to its international reputation. In the end though, as I've hinted already - and shall describe in more detail later - that reputation has more to do with the variety of lifestyles and the underlying elements of timelesness than it has to do with just being 'handy'. By global standards, perhaps, Broadland isn't that big, for all that it extends from Hickling Broad and Horsey Mere in the north, past the back of Great Yarmouth to Oulton Broad, just across the border in Suffolk, and westwards, to link up with Norwich, Coltishall and Wroxham - but it's got it all there, as they say. Whatever people do in or on the water can be done somewhere within those magical 200 square miles - apart from surfing, I suppose. But then nowhere's that perfect, thank God.

Which brings us back to **CAISTER ON SEA**. The name comes from the Latin 'castra', meaning a camp or fortress. Caister was founded in the 2nd century AD, as a fortified Roman town, having been one of the chief centres of Boadicea's Icenii, many years before. There are substantial remains from this period of its history, including part of the town wall, buildings of the main street and a section of broad, cobbled road with a drain down the middle. However many visitors are attracted by the archaeology, though, doubtless many more are drawn by the call of the seaside. Caister's wide sandy beach is reached by Beach Road, cut through the dunes and opening into a car park. Most of the bathing is safe, but some stretches shelve steeply and signs warn the visitor of the location of strong tides and deep water.

The road we take at this stage, the B1159, wriggles and wind northwards, never that far from the sea. Many of the villages and hamlets it links on its way to Cromer, its final goal, seem to survive these days thanks only to the income from the caravan sites and holiday camps that have mushroomed around them. Such places not being quite what we had in mind, and time being short, we shall aim to stop on our northerly course only where there's a little more to attract us. We might come back another time with the grandchildren, buckets and spades - but not just now!

On the other hand - and there is another hand - there is something about the landscape that *does* speak to the spirit. It doesn't hurt to stop the car close to the dunes for a few minutes, - if only to put the pressures of modern triviality, the endless worries about matters of no lasting importance, firmly in perspective. Faced with the view over miles of dour sea, over endless stretches of sand beset by tides that ebb and flow regardless of our pride, sorrows and flights of fancy, we can only marvel at the tenacity of human endeavour in its struggle with the implacable power of nature. Generations of farmers and fishermen - and their families - have hacked out a living here, have thrived and have seen fit to praise their God for his blessings in the churches whose towers etch exclamation marks against the sky. Wherever one looks, from north to west to south, it all seems truly miraculous. Yet, just as miraculous is the effect on the landscape of the change of seasons: in the grasp of winter the desolation is almost unbearable for those of us who have arrived from softer regions, where people seem more or less in control; in spring and summer one's spirit is lifted again and again by the clear light, the colourful fields and the clean, strong air as the land stirs from its slumbers. As I say, we need places like this to cut our troubles down to size.

Aside from all that, now we're on the B1159, this road has its own way with bends: they rush up a bit too quickly if you aren't ready for them. Away from the conventional [and avoidable] 'holiday- havens', there are more than a dozen other villages which, after the preparation of that earlier stroll on the dunes, will more than justify the price of the car park. Whilst **HEMSBY** and **CALIFORNIA** [named after the pub at the top of the beach path], offer safe swimming from their beaches, we shall pass on a bit further to **WINTERTON** and **WEST SOMERTON** before calling our first halts. Of the two, I find the latter more interesting and varied in its appeal. Once past

Winterton's church with its colossal, 132ft tower, there is only the beach, really, to arrest one's attention - and that can be a trap for the unwary, as bathing from the sands, especially between the markers is known to be dangerous. The church, though, is worth inspecting. Almost everything in it has spent time at sea: the cross was constructed from ships' timbers and items housed there include an anchor, ropes and a ship's lamp. So linked has the village been with the fortunes and misfortunes of seafarers that Daniel Defoe recorded in 1725 that no less than half of its houses were built using timber from wrecks.

West Somerton, on the other hand, offers a vastly different and intriguing experience. Being set at a distance of nearly two miles from the sea seems to have produced a mellowing effect and a wealth of local tales that are markedly less harrowing than many we have met. Best known, perhaps, are the smuggling stories from the 18th century. In those days, as the story goes, the landing of cargoes in Somerton Gap was controlled by signals from the windmill sails. Set at one angle they warned that the Revenue were about, while another simply meant 'Bring in a brandy!' This is a pretty village too: footpaths lead inland to MARTHAM BROAD and to the River Thurne's peaceful water meadows. Anglers are drawn to the weedy reaches at the end of the Bold, as many fine catches have been made there.

On the subject of angling, some readers may wonder why there's been so little - if any - mention of sea angling so far. After all, Norfolk has miles of accessible beaches, so what could possibly be the problem? In a word, 'weather' is the problem. The nature of the seabed, and other factors, are such that if it's summer fish you're seeking, you can more or less forget them - they aren't there to anything like the extent that they are around, say, the coasts of Devon and Cornwall. There's always the chance of some excitement off the piers - and local boatmen will oblige with a trip out into deeper water - but these are winter beaches, in the main, and the quarry are winter fish such as cod and whiting. I suspect that answers the question! Winter beaches - with winds screaming in across the North Sea unchecked since their last landfall somewhere inside the Arctic Circle! These visits of ours are supposed to be gently relaxing experiences where we meet nature in harmony, tranquillity, - and comfort! If your idea of fun is standing rigid at the water's edge with sleet driven through your cheek bones by a savage nor' easter, read another book - or volunteer for the SAS.

So if angling is your pleasure, if you love nothing better than those leisurely hours beside a lake or a meandering river, Norfolk is heaven with a rod and line. Let's take it in sequence, from King's Lynn around to Yarmouth. To start with, there is the River Great Ouse, which runs south of King's Lynn. It's said to offer 'good' coarse fishing. *Good?* When I was a lad, in the 'Home Counties', a day on the Great Ouse was a dream to die for! Round from there, eastwards, there's the River Bure at Blickling and Aylsham, with autumn coarse fishing after the weed has died back, or there's lake fishing at Gunton Park, four miles from Cromer. On again, and we come to the most varied areas: several Broads, including Salhouse, Oulton and Hickling, offer superb course fishing, away from the pleasure craft, with pike as one major quarry; the Rivers Bure, Thurne and Waveney are fine places for the float and ledger, with the possibility of a good mixed bag. There are trout in Breydon Water, as there are in several purpose-made fisheries around the county. Finally, to my favourite reaches, having left my Ouse-obsessed youth some way behind: the River Wensum above Norwich. In pleasant surroundings, the fishing here is full of surprises, ranging from roach, perch and dace to pike - and even grayling!

So, equip yourself for pitting skills against the stately bream or the more sprightly roach and rudd. If you're feeling mean - try the pike. But leave the beaches to the macho masochists. Remember, the real fishermen, who braved the seas in Norfolk's history and legends, did it for a living!

Back to Somerton. Sometimes enough is almost too much! Along the lane to Martham Broad, one passes the church of St Mary the Virgin, on the left. It's yet another of Norfolk's many imposing places of worship, with its around Norman tower surmounted by an octagonal belfry and the remains of a wall painting in the nave dating from the 14th century. Despite the charm and atmosphere of the building the main point of interest lies in the churchyard - and this you will barely believe. Standing on carved lions' paws is a huge sarcophagus - in itself, not that amazing as such things go - inside of which are the remains of The Norfolk Giant, who *was* amazing, by any standards. Robert Hales, born in the village in 1820, grew to be 7ft 8 inches tall [or nigh on 2.5 metres] and weighed in at 32 stone [or nearly 180 kilograms].

In his early manhood Robert travelled the country with his sister Mary, who was only a few inches shorter than he was. Such was the fame brought by his extraordinary size, that even the citizens of the USA paid over good dollars just for the chance to stand in awe before a man who weighed as much as three of them put together, on average. Back from America, in the 1850's, Robert became licensee of a London pub, had an audience with Queen Victoria and enjoyed popularity and success right up his death, at Great Yarmouth, in 1863.

Giants and windmill-watching smugglers? 'Whatever next?' I hear you say. Well, next is **HORSEY** - and here we have another of Norfolk's lightning changes. Horsey village itself is little more than a hamlet - although the familiar Norfolk cottages set off an unfamiliar Norfolk church . All Saints, hidden beneath the trees, has a thatched roof and is definitely not what we've come to expect. There are two routes to the beach: down the rough lanes and tracks across dunes, or along the lane in the village, following the 'By-road' signpost. One imagines these lanes were used by smugglers to bring their cargoes from the shore to the village for transport by wherry to Norwich.

Sadly, most people aren't that interested in the village as such [or in smuggling?] these days. They come in droves to take to the water on HORSEY MERE, in small boats, or to fish in the reed-lined bays around its fringes. For us, perhaps, high summer when the traffic is heaviest is a time to avoid. We haven't come this far to get stuck in a jam - water-borne, or otherwise. Spring or autumn - the latter, if one is an angler - those are the times. Oh yes, and don't forget the windmill: there are wide ranging views from its high gallery, across the sand dunes to the sea and round to the Broads, dotted with sails.

The mere, an offshoot of the Broads, is still pretty, despite its popularity. It's 120-acre stretch of water, now owned by the National Trust, is a breeding ground for wildfowl and marsh birds. It was also, according to local stories, the place where Nelson learned to sail - though why he should want to travel forty miles from his home in Burnham Thorpe for a sailing lesson is not exactly clear.

Continuing north, we come to **WAXHAM**. The dunes here are worth more than just a quick look. Behind the golden beach the wind-blown sand has been knitted together by tough marram grass into a virtual sea wall. In places, this is actually quite hilly, though even more interesting is the way that small trees have taken a hold, showing how vegetation can establish itself if these areas aren't disturbed. Again, it's another indication of how this amazing coast changes as nature adds a bit here and strips it away somewhere else.

After Waxham, the next stretch of beach and dunes we come to it is at **SEA PALLING**. This seems quite accessible as a lane from the village ends in a concrete ramp which gives good access to the wide sands. Swimming is worthwhile, and boats can be launched from the ramp at any state of the tide. It's time to turn inland again now, along the B1151 towards **STALHAM**. We have three interesting and very different calls to make before we head back towards the sea again - which we'll meet close to the atmospheric little village of Happisburgh.

SUTTON WINDMILL AND BROADS MUSEUM [Enquiries - 01692 581195], near Stalham, claims to offer something for everyone in its displays of 'the past at its best'. To start with, Britain's tallest windmill - a familiar Norfolk landmark - offers superb views of the surrounding countryside and coastline from its high gallery. There is even more at ground level, though. Built 200 hundred years ago, and still in use up to 1940, the historic corn mill was bought for restoration recently and a policy of traditional replacement is still being carried out, with the aim of making it productive once again. Meanwhile, it offers a chance to see some of the finest old corn-milling machinery in the area and to wander through an amazing range of collections, including old razors, kitchen implements, trade tricycles, bank notes and heaven knows what else by the time you come to read this. Nearby, in Church Road, **SUTTON**, is SUTTON [Windmill] POTTERY [Enquiries - 01692 580595]. The main attraction here is its large selection of hand thrown stoneware.

From the mill a brief wriggle or two through the lanes brings us to **HICKLING**. The real Norfolk-lover will tell you the only way to approach this village is by boat, arriving at the PLEASURE BOAT INN, whose 'staithe' - a Broadland word for 'landing stage' - is known to every regular boat man on these waters. True enough, I don't doubt - and maybe it would have been worth hiring a boat at Horsea, say, just for the purpose. But that would have meant the car was 'there' while we are still 'here'. Short of an awful lot of backtracking, that sounds just the kind of problem you bought this book to avoid!

All the same, it's worth noting that HICKLING BROAD is one of the widest stretches of water in Norfolk and that the Norfolk Naturalists Trust has set up several hides for observing the wildlife that still flourishes amongst all that tacking, jibing and keel-hauling, or whatever boat people do to relax.

The third call on this detour could be a 'one-off' rather than the kind of thing I'd usually recommend. It occurs to me that on our second tour we may have been a bit short of exercise compared with the Dersingham days, when we spent plenty of time stomping round nature reserves and country parks. Since we settled at Gorleston, we've been sitting in the car for hours - when we haven't been wining and dining - so maybe we could do with pepping up. STALHAM SPORTS HALL [Enquiries - 01692 580684] might offer a solution. It's worth a thought anyway, if a spot of tennis or badminton would fit the bill and tone one up for the next stage.

If we've read the map and the road signs correctly, we should be on our way now along the B1159. More to the point, we should be aiming at the sea. The world could be divided into two groups at this point: those who prefer Eccles on Sea, because it has a super beach and those who prefer Happisburgh for its eccentricities, its atmosphere - and to hell with more miles of sand! I imagine that I've given my position away already.

The price you pay at **ECCLES** is the approach . A ragged collection of beach chalets and holiday homes straddle an unmade road behind the dunes - but if you can handle that you'll be well rewarded. At Cart Gap, reached by the lane from Whimpwell Green, is the only proper car park between Sea Palling and Happisburgh. From there it's just a hop and a skip to gently sloping sands, protected by zig-zag wooden groynes. Provided the weather is calm, there's another bonus: a ramp suitable for launching small boats for a pleasant cruise along the coast is available.

HAPPISBURGH

The eccentricities of **HAPPISBURGH** start the moment you first see the name. The word is, that, said locals are so tired of trying to explain that it's really pronounced 'Hazeborough', that they've given up and decided to mispronounce it themselves. Being in Norfolk, of course, that's not the end of the story: the church guidebook says it should be 'Haisbro', which comes from the Old English name 'Haep'.

However you say the name, the look of the place will be enough for you to park the car and wander around to take in the sights. Originally, it was much larger but the sea has been hard at work and many of the old buildings have simply been washed away, along with part of the coast. Indeed, the village of Whimpwell, that used to adjoin Happisburgh, has vanished altogether. On the plus side - but only just, I imagine, if you actually live there - the glacial deposits to be seen in the cliff face are rather interesting. From time to time relics are exposed by further falls, the most dramatic of these ranging from the remains of the great fish, discovered in 1659, to a timber-framed wall, exposed in 1947.

There was a church in the village in 1086, according to the Domesday Survey, but it was given by William D'Albini, whom we first heard about at Castle Rising, along with the Lordship of the Manor to the Benedictine Priory at Wymondham, which he founded in 1101 as a cell of St Alban's Abbey. The church was rebuilt in the 14th and 15th centuries, and the magnificent west tower is the prime example of this later work. There is a great deal of such East Anglian 'perpendicular' construction elsewhere in the church, although lightning and fire required major repairs in 1822 and more work was done sixty years later to deal with the ravages of dilapidation and old age. Finally, in October 1940, German bombs destroyed the Old Rectory and blew out all the windows on the south side - although one assumes this onslaught was unlikely to have been deliberate. I mean, 'This week, Happisburgh - next week, London,' sounds a bit unlikely!

Today's church is a magnificent building, but it's in the churchyard, again, that one's emotions are really stirred. From its highest point one has sweeping views of the sea and, inland, of the rest of the pleasant unspoiled village. But if one starts to examine the tombstones, there isn't much that's 'pleasant' to be found. There are too many shipwrecked sailors buried there for that. The villain of the piece is Hazeborough Sands, which run parallel to the coast for nine miles, roughly seven miles offshore. There are literally scores of victims of this death trap taking their final rest in the shadow of the tower of St Mary the Virgin, from the 119 members of the crew of HMS 'Invincible', lost on 13th March 1801, to the crew of the barque 'Young England', which went down in 1876.

The strangest grave of all is that of Jonathan Ball, who at his own request was buried in 1846 with a plum cake, a Bible, a poker and a pair of tongs! Nobody seems to know why he chose these things, but the rumour is that he'd been such a villain during his life that he'd certainly need some way of controlling the flames where he was going. Prior to his death, he seems to have made a practice - rather like the Italian Borgias - of poisoning his drinking partners. Fate caught up with him in the end, though, as he appears to have died by mistake, having drunk a potion that was meant for somebody else.

On a quite different note, Happisburgh also has literary connections. Some believe that the poet William Cowper, who visited the village in his childhood and again towards the end of his life, watched a thunderstorm gather over the sea there and then wrote the lines: *'God moves in a mysterious way, his wonders to perform; He plants his footsteps in the sea and rides upon the storm.'* There is a Conan Doyle link as well: Sir Arthur stayed in the village while writing 'The Dancing Men' and this association is marked by a plaque on the wall of the house next to the pub.

Between Paston and Bacton, we move from echoes of past centuries slap bang into the present day. The formidably fenced off acres with their gas holders, pipes, control systems and other bits of brute technology come as that much of a shock. They are not what you'd expect on the fringe of otherwise mostly rural Norfolk. Clearly, such junk has to go somewhere if we are going to use undersea gas to roast the Sunday lunch, but one can't help feeling sorry for anyone living nearby.

HORSEY MERE

If we can bear to pause, however, there is another place of interest tucked away inland from the road and not too far off. So pause, if you will, for a moment or two and reflect on the ruins or BROMHOLM PRIORY. Founded in 1113, the Priory was well-known in the Middle Ages for possessing part of the 'True Cross'. This relic was believed to cure leprosy and to bring the dead back to life. Chaucer knew of it: in his 'Reeve's Tale', the Miller's wife asks for help on the 'hooly croys of Bromeholm'. Over a hundred years after that, the South Wales prophetess Mother Shipton said that 'Bacton Abbey shall be a farm' - she seems to have been right, once again.

There is a beach with protecting groyne and a concrete sea wall - but with the much more attractive Mundesley just up the road, we'll probably prefer to get well away from the North Sea plumbing, after our look round the Priory. As we approach

Mundesley we pass through the village of **PASTON**, where we ought to make a brief stop. St Margaret's Church has several monuments to the Paston family, writers of the famous 'Paston Letters', which gave a vivid account of Norfolk life during the turbulent Wars of the Roses. Sir Richard, a later Paston, built the superb long thatched barn beside the church, in 1581.

On again, and in a moment or two we enter **MUNDESLEY** itself [Information - 01263 721070], scene of the August MUNDESLEY FESTIVAL [Information 10263 720842]. This quiet holiday village has a spaciousness that welcomes and inspires us as we stroll along the old High Street, inland from the coast road, to COWPER BOUSE, a white-painted Georgian residence where the poet stayed at the time of his visits to Happisburgh. By contrast, concerning the immediate area, a respected authority informed me recently that the income from the gas pumped over to the Continent from the installation nearby actually exceeds the export earnings of the entire British car industry put together.

On a less alarming note, I'd like to draw your attention to one activity that has not been give a fair crack of the whip, so far (pun only just intended). We haven't talked too much about horse riding so far on our way round, so let's make up for that here. BRIDGE FARM STABLES [Enquiries - 01263 720028] are open all the year and mounts are available for beach exploration and hacking for between one and three hours along nearby tracks and country lanes. This facility is extended to small groups, while lessons, livery, stable-management, instruction and riding days are also on offer.

A ramp by the coastguard station gives access to the promenade and from there to a wide sandy beach, good for swimming. The water is shallow along this stretch yet, between Mundesley and **TRIMMINGHAM**, it has carved away whole sections or cliffs, fields, houses and even break-waters, over the last 100 years. A little to the south of the village is STOW MILL, an excellent example of the tower mill design, complete with sails. There are good views here from the hill, and an absorbing exhibition of milling pictures and documents.

Between Mundesley and Overstrand there is no access to the sea because of the dangerous state of the cliffs. Close to the water, near the cliff edge, nothing much in the way of buildings has stayed secure. Overstrand's first church fell into the sea in the 14th century. The present church of St Martin replaced it but has also had its problems. At **SIDESTRAND**, a mile further east, the 15th century church was in danger until 1881, when it was taken down and moved inland to its present site!

OVERSTRAND itself is large for a village and mostly modern, with a good sandy beach - provided one avoids the crumbling cliffs - which is protected by groynes. To reach it, you have to descend 100 ft from the cliff top car park by steps or by a steep track with a hairpin bend in the middle. Sounds a bit wearing? Don't worry: we're nearly at Cromer, for the second time, where we turn for home along a route that takes in a clutch of places guaranteed to revive any flagging spirits.

Actually, this time, we'll by-pass Cromer itself, and drop down the A149 - A140 towards Aylsham instead. In that way, we can make a bee line for ALBY CRAFTS [Enquiries - 01263 761226], at **ERPINGHAM**, one of the finest craft centres in the area. Open daily from 10 till 5, [except on Mondays], between March and December, Alby brings together a range of really high quality craft workshops, lace and bottle museums, a tea room and gardens. The stained glass shop and workroom owned by the extremely talented Sheila Nixon, offers the most magnificent hand made antique lamp shades. She will even make items to your own specifications for your home. The ceramics and furniture shops are worth a visit also - to say nothing of the four-acre Plantsman's Garden, with its ponds, trees and collections of unusual shrubs, plants and bulbs.

Having dragged ourselves away from the delights of Alby, we should move on without too much reluctance, as **AYLSHAM**, a few miles down the A140, has plenty to whet our appetites. Collectors will be drawn to the SALEROOMS [Enquiries - 01263 733195], where vast ranges of items are auctioned regularly as 'Antiques' [three weekly], 'Pictures' [bi-monthly] and 'Books and Collectables' [also bi-monthly]. Nor should AYLSHAM MARKET be overlooked if we're in town on a Monday: there is everything for sale here, somewhere, from poultry and rabbits to cars, furniture, china and, again, collectables.

BLICKLING HALL

Away from the town - but not far - and we are talking country houses. MANNINGTON HALL and WOLTERTON PARK [Information for both - 01263 584175] are well known and full of fascination; BLICKLING HALL [Information 01263 733084], owned by the National Trust, is famed as one of the greatest Jacobean houses in East Anglia. We'll go there first and then take one of our detours to visit the other two before returning to Aylsham. The B1354 is our road.

Blickling dates from the early 17th century and is really imposing as one approaches it. The Hall contains fine collections of furniture, pictures and tapestries including the colossal tapestry of Tsar Peter the Great, as well as a distinguished library with a special exhibition room. Outside there are delightful gardens, including a formal woodland wilderness garden and a large park with a lake and miles of walks. As with most National Trust houses, facilities also include a shop, a restaurant and a plant sales area.

On to Mannington and we find a moated medieval manor house which is still a Walpole family home. Although the Hall itself is only open by appointment - and for special interest groups - the outstanding gardens are a real feature, especially for the roses which are found everywhere in many different settings, and which flower throughout the seasons. Mannington garden shops are stocked with souvenirs and craft work as well as plants and a fine selection of roses in containers. Wolterton, north east of Mannington, near Erpingham, is another Walpole house, designed by Thomas Ripley for Horatio, brother of England's first prime minister, Sir Robert Walpole.

The House, abandoned after 1858 when the 4th Earl of Orford moved to Mannington, was restored at the turn of the century by the 5th Earl, and is undergoing further reorganisation and restoration at present. As a result, the interior is also out of bounds, generally speaking, unless one joins one of the parties taking a pre-booked guided tour. Nonetheless, the walks through Mannington and Wolterton estates offer a rare treat. Over twenty miles of waymarked footpaths link them with the Weavers Way and the Holt Circular Walk. Orchids are to be found, as are man-made lakes, a wildlife mere with observation hides, a fine 18th century barn and extensive views of the Grade 1 listed Halls and other buildings.

After taking a last look at Wolterton, we must slip back to the A140 for a while. We shall soon return taking a turn off left onto the B1145 and then head for **NORTH WALSHAM** [Information - 01692 407509].

NORTH WALSHAM TOWN CENTRE

This town has been a focal point for the surrounding rural area since the 14th century, when it became a centre for the booming wool trade. The wealth this trade produced is expressed in the quality of the large church standing in the town centre, near the famous Market Cross built to the order of the Bishop Thurlby, in 1549 and included, in 1930, by the Commissioners of Works in a list of Ancient Monuments of National Importance. Paston School, founded about the same time, provided Horatio Nelson's education immediately before he went to sea. Just outside the town is the scene of the battle in which Bishop Despenser ended the Norfolk Rising, a part of the 1381 Peasants' Revolt.

Away from historical insight seeing, the town has its own variety of more modern attractions, although in, say, the NORFOLK MOTORCYCLE MUSEUM [Enquiries 01692 406266], one is still tempted down memory lane. Not far away, THE CAT POTTERY [AND RAILWAY JUNKYARD] [Information - 01692 402962] offers a very specialised appeal to cat lovers as well as to collectors of railway memorabilia and other curiosities. Finally, there is a SPORTS CENTRE [Enquiries - 01692 402252], for anyone who didn't get enough exercise at Stalham, and a host of shops in the middle of the town to cater for most needs and interests.

Close to North Walsham is a small village whose name is far better known than that of its bigger neighbour - **WORSTEAD**. Having given that name to a type of fine woollen cloth, first made in the area, it seems to have retired, exhausted. It's a visual delight, make no mistake, with its great St Mary's Church dominating the remaining fine old buildings around its central square. It's all very photogenic - but where has all the rest gone? The church, as built in 1379, shows the size and wealth of a medieval town rather than of a village, and all of it seems to have been based on a profitable wool market. There was even access to a canal, opened in 1826, linking North Walsham with the River Ant - yet, again, all that is left is a name, an idea. Fashions changed presumably, trade slumped - either that or the empire died. Who knows? Still, St Mary's is one of the most magnificent of Norfolk's churches, with its fine 109 ft tower, its flying buttresses and it's beautiful rood screen. And the village is quite close to the main road; why not drop in and draw your own conclusions?

From Worstead we wander down the A149 to its meeting with the A1151 then take to the lanes again in search, this time, of **HORNING** - as part of yet another scenic detour. This is a village set in woodland where private houses have their own inlets from the River Bure which, together, form a kind of miniature Venice. Whilst these houses - and their gardens - are very attractive, it is the village's location, on the Bure, that gives it its importance. This is the river which, with its tributaries, threads most of the lakes together. SOUTHERN COMFORT [Enquiries - 01692 630262] caters for this facility, offering public guided cruises through the Broads, three times daily. BROADS TOURS [Enquiries 01692 630842] tends to the needs of more intrepid sailors who'd rather explore in a launch on their own.

HORNING

POTTER HEIGHAM, a few miles east on the A1062, offers similar services through MAYCRAFT BOATS [Enquiries - 670241] and PHOENIX BOATS [Enquiries - 01692 670460] but here the accent is on self drive as a way to explore the River Thurne, Hickling Broad and Horsey Mere. In fact, the whole village is about boats and boating, with shops, a supermarket and lines of sheds full of everything likely to be needed for a holiday afloat. Overseeing the entire production, in a sense, is the MUSEUM OF THE BROADS, a sizeable building housing the growing collection of boats and traditional tools of Broadland Industries, the whole making up the finest available chronicle of the relation between man and the Broads environment.

Time to own up to a minor failure: the general idea on these tours is 'Onward, ever onward', ideally around a circle - with *no back tracking*! After Potter Heigham, I'm actually forced to lead you back down the A1062 and through Horning, again. It can't be helped because we must take in the stretch of country above Norwich before we turn east, finally, for Gorleston. In any case, we need to see another side of Broadland, while the scenes of Horning, Hickling and the rest are still clearly in mind, in order to get the whole picture, you might say.

A moment of confession, too: this guide is all about a very personal view of East Anglia - I know, it shows! A balanced approach to the region would fail, I suspect, because no one *is* that balanced. The whole thing would lack conviction, rather like a bland catalogue of place names, more or less. So the backtrack after Potter Heigham isn't entirely a matter of chance - seen as part of 'the plan', it offers the only realistic route that leaves enough of the best part of this tour [in my view] to last, so we finish on a high point. By 'high point', as so often, I mean most over the top. As I see them **WROXHAM** and **HOVETON** are exactly that. In a sense they are absolutely extraordinary.

The two villages can almost be seen as a single community, separated by the River Bure, and standing as 'The Capital of the Broads'. Many people, once again, use this area as a starting point for Broadland exploration and BROADS TOURS [Enquiries - 01603 782207] or FINEWAY LAUNCH HIRE [Enquiries - 01603 782798] are well able to help out with choices from a variety of craft. Nothing unusual in that - all very sensible, in fact. Nice boat, lovely water - anything else? Oh, yes! Plenty.

For a start, in an age when motor cars have beaten the railways into the ground nearly everywhere, Hoveton has two stations. *Two*? In a *village*? Not only does one offer main line links to Norwich and the North Coast but the other is the terminus of the BURE VALLEY RAILWAY [Information - 01263 733858], fast becoming one of Norfolk's most popular attractions. The nine-mile route, built on the track bed of the historic East Norfolk Railway's Wroxham to Aylsham line, runs through some of the county's most scenic and unspoilt countryside. From Wroxham, the 15inch gauge track goes to Aylsham via Brampton, Buxton and Coltishall. A wide range of extra facilities and combination tickets - linking the train ride with other attractions - is readily available.

'Well,' you may say, 'we've seen rivers and done railways - what else is new?' The *combination,* of course, is new and it's to hand in a really intriguing setting. Put it this way - if Walt Disney, or any of his followers, had tried to create a 'Capital of the Broads', it would have been a disaster. We'd have been sold so much cute, phoney fantasy that we would have wanted our money back after five minutes. Wroxham/ Hoveton has nothing to do with any of that - it's utterly real, a skilful mixture of ancient and modern that still raises your eyebrows, without a Disney trick to be seen.

I nearly crashed the car the first time I drove into the villages' centre. I had read about the 'World's Largest Village Store', but even so the place itself stunned me. I can't imagine any village anywhere having anything quite like ROYS OF WROXHAM - indeed, there are probably quite a few cities with nothing to touch it, either. It is, simply, huge, especially in relation to its surroundings - but it fits. I suppose 'Heritage buffs' might take exception to a modern store in an old village, but that would be a mistake because it *does* add something that's worth having. Its style even echoes the other buildings nearby quite flatteringly. Anyway, seeing is believing - certainly, 'out of town shopping' is given a whole new meaning by the sight.

Let's not forget we're still in Norfolk, though, where surprise and sudden change is a way of life. One mile north of Wroxham Bridge lies HOVETON HALL [Enquiries - 01603b782798], a 19th century country house said to have been designed by Humphrey Repton and his son John - a view supported by its similarity to Sheringham Hall, another Repton design. The best view of the Hall is from the Lakeside Walk - after that one's eyes rarely stray from the gardens, the woods and surrounding parkland which are an endless delight with their rare rhododendrons, azaleas and water plants and the particular fascinations of the walled kitchen garden and herbaceous borders. Having absorbed the effects of this splendid combination of plants, trees and shrubs, refreshment in the tea room is most enjoyable, while selections from the plants and from the gardening books can only help to intensify one's own efforts.

If something of my enthusiasm for Wroxham is beginning to sink in - well, it's not over yet. Up the road from Hoveton Hall we come to another tour de force: WROXHAM BARNS [Information - 01603 783762] seems to me to be to craft centres what Roys is to village stores - the breathtaking ultimate! For a start, there are ten acres of it. That's ten acres of prime Norfolk countryside in which is set a fine collection of carefully restored 18th century barns where fourteen working craftsmen make decorative glass, hand-made children's clothes, stained glass, willow baskets, prints, jewellery, pottery, perfumes and oils. They also turn wood, build boats, sketch, do needlework, press apple juice and create floral works of art. Examples of the end products are all on sale in the gift shop and if you come away empty handed, I'll be astonished. If, somehow or other, the gift shop misses the mark, there is always the Gallery Collection of classic and casual clothing and knitwear, upstairs. And then there's the tea room, the animals in the 'Junior Farm', Williamson's Traditional Family Fair [with all its rides, some of which are nearly 100 years old].

'No more,' I hear you cry. Understandable - so we'll just pop around a couple of corners to have a look at the superb dried and silk flowers at WILLOW FARM [Enquiries - 01603 783588],while we get our breath back, - and remember to save its nature trail for another visit, perhaps? At the farm, in a 300-year old thatched barn, we'll find masses of colour, ideas and everything for flower arranging - including friendly advice. There are stunning arrangements on display too, while the staff will also make up 'specials' to your own requirements.

So many memories, such a full day - if the thought of the evening meal *seems* irresistible, it probably isn't. Time to stiffen our backbones, pull in our belts and make martyrs of ourselves again. Exhaustion is all in the mind - an attitude problem. Seriously, there is one more corner of Broadland we must visit before night falls -and since it has its own brand of magic, I hope the prospect won't send too many shock waves through your feelings of relief. The starting point for this last leg of the journey is FAIRHAVEN GARDEN TRUST [Enquiries - 01603 270449], where delightful natural woodland and water gardens are set in the heart of this landscape of rivers and lakes.

The Trust's water gardens line the side of the private SOUTH WALSHAM BROAD. A vintage style river boat runs trips every half-hour from within the gardens, on all open days - it would be nice to think that we are not too late for that. If we are, we can always enjoying strolling amongst the rhododendrons, primulas and azaleas and staring in amazement at the giant lilies, rare shrubs and the quite extraordinary nine hundred year old King Oak. During the year the Trust offers three special weeks of attractions focusing on primroses, primulas and autumn colours. At any time the wild flowers, in general, are worth a visit all to themselves.

A short cruise through the lanes from Fairhaven brings us to **ACLE**, a small town now by-passed, mercifully, by the main A47. It lies on the edge of the HALVERGATE MARSHES, in the centre of the Broads National Park and should be visited on a Thursday, if that suits, as that's the day for the weekly auction - which would add a trace of passion to the day-to-day pleasures of a tour round its attractive small shops. The moorings at ACLE BRIDGE and ACLE DYKE are popular with water-borne visitors, and the railway links are handy for both Norwich and Great Yarmouth. Incidentally, if you fancy taking to the water briefly, MERMAID CRUISES [Enquiries - 01493 728876] will sell you tickets for the M.V. 'Princess Elizabeth' - which could be as near as most of us will get to the Caribbean equivalent.

We'll leave Acle in a westerly direction and do a short zig-zag, at first, to take in the RSPB Reserve at **STRUMPSHAW**. Established in 1975, this mixture of marsh, woodland and meadow, covering more than 450 acres, includes the restored STRUMPSHAW BROAD. Several hides have been set up and are available for members of the public to observe the varied wildlife that frequents the area.

Thrusting onwards in a south-easterly direction from Strumpshaw, we come, by way of **BUCKENHAM** and **FREETHORPE** to **REEDHAM**, where the chain ferry provides the one crossing of the River Yare for vehicles between Norwich and Yarmouth. The detour that saves is food for thought. Whether or not one wants to press on further south - and we do, as it happens - in these days of Chunnels and roll-on/roll-off hydrofoils [or whatever] it's a real treat to slow down a little, park the car on the floating platform and relax while the diesel driven chain does the business - let the chain take the strain, so to speak. The ferry is not all that big, so be prepared for possible queues, but that can actually be turned to advantage as the village has its fair share of hostelries to justify nothing more earnest than sitting around watching other people work.

A few miles away in the direction of Halvergate Marshes to the north-east, BERNEY ARMS could be said to beckon, as its seventy foot high, late 19th century windmill operated drainage pump offers dramatic views of the marshland and, across Breydon Water, of Burgh Castle, which we visited earlier in the day. Since you can't get to the Mill by road - the nearest is all of two miles away - the ramblers amongst us may well choose to ramble. If, like me, you're just that little bit too lazy, I dare say you'd be welcome aboard the train for the short trip up the line to BERNEY ARMS HALT from either Reedham or Yarmouth.

The Marshes form yet another Nature Reserve, traversed by the Weavers Way long distance footpath, on its route from Halvergate to Yarmouth. Seats are provided at intervals for leg resting or just taking time to absorb the view out over the grazing marsh which floods during autumn, winter and spring. To show another aspect of the area, boat trips are available from Burgh Castle on the first Sunday of every month at 10am and 2pm.

Now is the time to take the ferry and head further south still, towards the Suffolk border. We'll go to the north-east of Raveningham, which we've already seen, to complete this loop past the edge of NORTON MARSHES, and then along a short stretch of the A143 before taking a right turn into the enclave around **BURGH ST PETER**. By now we're really close to the Suffolk attraction of OULTON BROAD, on a level with Lowestoft - but that belongs to a later chapter, so we won't dally, as the aim is to complete a picture rather than break completely new ground.

The River Waveney does a major meander here, before heading back up north to join the Yare in Breydon Water. In the last century, when the wherry was, in a sense, the key to the Broadlands economy, some Norwich businessmen, tired of the delays caused by having to unload all their cargoes in Yarmouth onto boats designed for local conditions, decided that the answer was to make the Yare navigable for ocean going ships, which might also use an alternative outlet through Lowestoft. We'll see later what was done at the seaward side of Oulton, but for now, as we finally turn to head for home, it's interesting to note where the two channels were dug to bring this about, linking not only the two rivers, but the Broad with the Waveney itself.

So there it is - by now we should be on the A143, with only the outskirts of Yarmouth between us and Norwich. I promise you some rare treats in this truly 'Fine City'.

THE ARK RESTAURANT WITH ROOMS
The Street
Erpingham
Norwich
Norfolk
NR11 7QB

Tel: 01263 761535

Good Food Guide, AA Best Restaurants,
Egon Ronay

This is a quite remarkable establishment which was started about fifteen years ago when Michael and Sheila Kidd moved into the area and decided that in order to survive they would open their own restaurant in their own premises. The premises had a lot of ground in which they kept pigs, poultry and goats and then lessened this activity as, through sheer hard work, The Ark - aptly named- came into being. The gardens are now beautiful, you can play croquet, look over the different breeds of fowl or just read in the shade.

Within the house well planned alterations have made The Ark a delightful place in which to eat. Sheila is an inspired, self taught cook, who has used her travels in Europe and Australia to bring exciting recipes to table. Her cooking reflects the fresh vegetables, seafood and game available locally. On the varied menu you are always going to find something to excite your palate. If you have a favourite dish ask Sheila to prepare it for you. If you give her enough notice and the ingredients are to be found locally and fresh, she will do her best to oblige. Vegetarians are well catered for and will enjoy an innovative menu. Freshness is always the keynote and your vegetables are likely to have been grown in the garden of The Ark, or in the gardens of the local estates.

The dining room is small and intimate with a maximum of thirty six covers. It is here you will find Michael in charge and he will encourage you to enjoy wine from his well chosen and interesting list.

The Ark has three double rooms. The Attic Room is a family room with a full ensuite bathroom. The Garden Room - which has its own private garden and is suitable for residents who have a dog, has an ensuite shower room. Lastly the Tulip Room has a shared bathroom. Guests have their own lounge and have access to the gardens. Breakfast is flexible - there is no menu so the choice is yours. The Ark is a great place no matter whether you come to eat or stay. It has many accolades including Egon Ronay's Cellnet Guide and the Best Restaurants in Britain. Somewhere to visit and remember with pleasure.

USEFUL INFORMATION

OPEN: Closed part of October   RESTAURANT: Delicious inspired menu
Other occasional short times   VEGETARIAN: Innovative menu
TUES-Sat 7pm until 9.30pm   DISABLED ACCESS: Ground floor
CREDIT CARDS: None taken room   GARDEN: Lovely grounds. Croquet
LICENSED: Yes   PETS: In ground floor room by arrangement
ACCOMMODATION: 2 ensuite 1dbl with shared bathroom
RATES: £125.00 p.n. for 2 people. DB&B

AYLSHAM HOUSE HOTEL
Norwich Road
Aylsham
Norfolk
NR11 6JH

Tel: 01263 734851

English Tourist Board
2 Crown Commended

Situated on the outskirts of Aylsham in peaceful countryside, the Aylsham House Hotel is an ideal central point for anyone wanting to explore North Norfolk, seek out all the historic pleasures of Norwich and take a look at the magic of The Broads. This attractively built complex has an extensive bar and A La Carte menu which can be enjoyed in the comfortable and well furnished bar or the cosier 'No smoking room'. It is an ideal place for families with a menu that has something for everyone. Children especially love the dishes prepared for them including jacket potatoes with a variety of fillings. The food is of a high standard and at a price that will fit most pockets. Whenever you come here you will find it friendly and welcoming and the staff more than ready to look after you.

There are fifteen bedrooms, all en suite with television, telephone and beverage trays. Each is comfortably furnished and every morning a full English breakfast is served or a healthy alternative if you would prefer it. Continental breakfasts can be served in your room. The large Function Room can cater for up to one hundred & fifty people. With splendid views of surrounding Norfolk countryside, its own private bar and dance floor, it is suitable for all family occasions, weddings, anniversaries, christenings or birthdays. For a wedding this is particularly nice with an adjoining garden available for photographs. Companies and businesses find the rooms excellent for meetings, seminars and conferences and frequently the suite is used for trade shows.

Many National Trust properties and attractions are within easy reach including Blickling Hall, Felbrigg Hall, Sheringham Park, the Thursford Collection, Wroxham Barns, the North Norfolk Steam Railway and many more. The historic city of Norwich, Cromer on the coast and many more picturesque towns and villages are all waiting to be explored.

USEFUL INFORMATION

OPEN; All year 11am-11pm
CHILDREN; Welcome
CREDIT CARDS; All major cards
LICENSED; Full On
GARDEN; Yes
RATES: 2 day breaks 120.00 D.B.B 2 people sharing

RESTAURANT; Wide ranging menu
BAR FOOD; Good selection, value for money
VEGETARIAN; Always a choice
DISABLED ACCESS; Yes. Facilities
ACCOMMODATION; 15 rooms ensuite

BLYTH HOUSE HOTEL
79/80 Marine Parade
Great Yarmouth
Norfolk
NR30 2DJ

Tel 01493 843329

Great Yarmouth is a place that provides fun and activity for all the family, whatever the age and on the sea front right opposite the famous Britannia Pier is Blyth House Hotel, just the place to stay for those who want a relaxed, informal holiday or break in an excellently run hotel. Within eight minutes walking distance of the hotel's front door is Sea World Pleasure beach, the Winter Gardens, Wellington Pier, the Town Centre and Market Place. The night life is lively and extensive throughout the week in the height of the season and on most weekends throughout the year. Close to Norfolk Broads and many other fascinating places to visit, Blyth House makes a good base for an inexpensive holiday.

Pat Rogers and Jackie Short own and run the hotel with other members of their family. It is very much a family concern with the youngest member of the team currently learning the ropes of running hotels from all aspects. They have certainly created a warm and happy atmosphere at Blyth House and never seem to mind how much they do for guests. There are twenty three comfortably furnished bedrooms, and all have tea making facilities. Downstairs there is a cosy bar, a lounge and a separate television and video lounge with an extensive library of videos. Everything has been thought of to ensure the welfare of guests including providing safe storage for fishing and diving equipment. The food is good, home-cooked fare and plenty of it. Breakfast is a substantial meal which will set you up for the day and the evening meal has a changing menu daily. Much emphasis is placed on the use of fresh and local produce. It is certainly value for money. Children are very welcome and under ten years they are half price. Pets are not permitted.

Guests tend to congregate in the bar for a drink before the evening meal or when they return later on. Here they can chat over the day that has gone and plan for tomorrow's adventure. The family are always on hand to help the plans if required. Between them they have a great deal of local knowledge. Open all the year, Blyth House is a happy house to stay in and the price is right.

USEFUL INFORMATION

OPEN: All year	DINING ROOM: Good home-cooked fare
CHILDREN: Welcome	VEGETARIAN: Upon request
CREDIT CARDS: Visa/Master	WHEELCHAIR ACCESS: No
LICENSED: Residential	PETS: Not permitted

ACCOMMODATION: 23 rooms not ensuite at present
RATES: From £17 pp BB & EM in low season
From £20pp BB & EM in High season - Under 10 half price

THE ELDERTON LODGE HOTEL & RESTAURANT
Gunton Park
Thorpe Market
NR. North Walsham
Norfolk
NR11 8TZ

Tel: 01263 833547
Fax: 01263 834673

ETB 3 Crowns Commended
AA 2 Star with Rosette for Food

Elderton Lodge standing in six acres of mature gardens has always been a discreet sanctuary far from the madding crowd. It was reputedly here that Lillie Langtry, the celebrated Victorian beauty, entertained Edward VII. Then, as Prince of Wales, he was a frequent visitor to the adjacent Gunton Hall, family home of the Earls of Suffield.

Built in the 18th century and Grade II Listed, it was originally the Shooting Lodge and Dower House to the Hall. To this day the hotel maintains that timeless grace that buildings of this period possess. Built of bricks made on the estate and faced with pebbles from the nearby coast, the walls are now wisteria clad and mellowed with age. Inside the house the period feel has been lovingly maintained with original panelling in the public rooms, open Victorian fires and a host of period features including stuffed birds, sporting pictures and prints, antlers, fishing rods - almost a Scottish Shooting Lodge in English surroundings!
The award winning, romantic candlelit restaurant majors on the wonderful local fresh produce that is readily available, fish and shellfish from the nearby coast and game in season from the neighbouring estates. Much use is made of other food from the wild such as elderberries, blackberries, field mushrooms, puff balls and other edible toadstools, and the local speciality, samphire. The whole makes for perfect meals cooked by the talented head chef and his dedicated team.

The Lounge Bar and Conservatory have magnificent views over the hundreds of acres of Gunton Park where the herds of deer graze peacefully and the sunsets are truly spectacular. Eleven beautifully appointed ensuite bedrooms with remote controlled televisions, direct dial telephones, and hospitality trays, complete the picture. Truly a wonderful place to stay, very tranquil, quiet and peaceful, blazing sunsets and wonderful starlit skies. A still largely undiscovered gem - what more could one want?

USEFUL INFORMATION

OPEN; 12 noon-2.30pm & 6-11pm
CHILDREN; Over 6 years
CREDIT CARDS; Visa/Master/
Switch & Delta
LICENSED; Full On
ACCOMMODATION;
11 ensuite rooms   Short breaks available
RATES: Single from £50 Double from £80

RESTAURANT; Elegant, romantic, candlelit

VEGETARIAN; Selection available
WHEELCHAIR ACCESS; Yes. One step
GARDEN; 6 acres mature gardens
PETS; Dogs 5.00 per night

THE FALGATE INN
Ludham Road
Potter Heigham
Gt Yarmouth
Norfolk
NR29 5HZ

Tel: 01692 670003

English Tourist Board
2 Crowns Commended

The Falgate Inn is renowned for providing the traditional hospitality of an English Inn. It is certainly the focal point of village life in Potter Heigham, a rural setting yet within easy reach of the outside world such as Great Yarmouth and Norwich, the sandy beaches of the Norfolk coast and the historic buildings which abound in the county. You will also find that the inn is only six hundred yards from Potter Heigham Staithes where boats can be hired to explore the Broadland rivers, or the exclusive nature reserves of Hickling Broad and Horsey Mere: a naturalist's dream, an angler's delight. Several traditional restored windmills are also to be found in the area.

Recently fully restored after a disastrous thatch fire (except for a new, safer, tiled roof), the Falgate was until 1836, a Toll House with facilities for changing horses on the Yarmouth-Norwich Mail Coach. It is a delightful place to visit whether you come here for the excellent food, the beer or wine or to stay a night or two. Malcolm Lines and Beryl Hill are the proprietors and it is Beryl who is innovative and responsible for encouraging their imaginative chef in his pursuit of excellence. Every day in the restaurant traditional meals are served with always something new and exciting, as well as two or more Sunday roasts, to encourage the most reluctant palate. In the bar the menu is wide ranging and offers everything from a simple sandwich to a basket meal. There is a splendidly relaxed and informal atmosphere about The Falgate and you are welcome to eat wherever you wish including a Family Room which seats twenty five.

Many people have discovered the comfort and fun to be had in staying at The Falgate which has five guest rooms. A double and twin room are ensuite and the other three, a single, a twin and a family room have wash basins. All the rooms have television and a hostess tray. An iron and a hairdryer are available if needed and if you happen to come back with wet clothes after hiking or fishing, there are drying facilities. The Inn is run on family lines, the staff are polite, cheerful and well trained both in inn-keeping and health and hygiene.

USEFUL INFORMATION

OPEN: Summer: 11-3 & 6-11pm — RESTAURANT; Good traditional fare
Winter:12-2pm & 7-11pm — CHILDREN: Welcome
Sundays:12-2.30pm &7-10.30pm all year — BAR FOOD: Wide range
CREDIT CARDS: Master/Visa/Delta/Switch — VEGETARIAN: min 4 dishes
LICENSED: Full On — WHEELCHAIR ACCESS: Pub & Rest
ACCOMMODATION: 5 rooms 2 ensuite — GARDEN: Yes
RATES: £17pp B&B £21 ensuite — PETS: On leads. Bar only

THE FUR AND FEATHERS
Slad Lane,
Woodbastwick, Norwich,
Norfolk NR13 6HQ

Tel: 01603 720003

This is a comparatively new pub, opened in 1992 which has rapidly gained a great reputation for its hospitality and especially for its beers. It is the Flagship of Woodfordes Norfolk Ales of which seven are on tap including two National Prize winning beers "Wherry Bitter" and "Norfolk Nog". The Brewery and Visitors Centre is located next door which makes the whole complex very interesting for visitors. Wisely the pub was built to encourage a slightly old-world atmosphere which it has done successfully and cleverly ensured that every nook and cranny has a table at which food can be served. The Fur and Feathers has a tremendous reputation for its food and has few equals in the inns of Norfolk. If one had to define its position in the market-place one would have to say that its main business comes from the tourists and from those who visit the Brewery complex rather than a pub for locals.

Inside the Fur and Feathers you will find a friendly welcome from the landlords Jean and John Marjoram who have been here since the day it opened together with most of their staff. It is a great location in the centre of the Norfolk Broads but only 6 miles from Norwich and 20 minutes walk to Salhouse Broad. The whole area is in fact a private estate and the rural feeling is enhanced by the small herd of British Old White cattle who graze in the meadow next to the pub. The garden attracts people in warm weather and there is ample parking space.

Great effort has been put into the compiling of a menu that suits all tastes and remains within sensible prices. There are starters and light meals which include a chilli dog which is a hot dog style topped with chilli or the more sophisticated devilled whitebait. salads, sandwiches freshly cut with Granary bread, stuffed jacket potatoes, Ploughman's and many other tasty bites. The main courses cover a wide range from burgers, pies, lasagne, ribs, meatloaf to a 10oz sirloin steak. Vegetarians are catered for.

USEFUL INFORMATION

OPEN; Winter: 12-2.30pm & 6-11pm
Summer: 11-3pm & 6-11pm
CHILDREN; Not in the bar
CREDIT CARDS; All major cards
LICENSED; Yes
PETS; Garden only
SMOKING; Bar only

RESTAURANT; Good, sensibly priced Food.
BAR FOOD; Wide range
VEGETARIAN; Catered for
DISABLED ACCESS; Yes + toilets
GARDEN; Yes

GROVE FARM
Repps-with-Bastwick
Gt Yarmouth
Norfolk
NR29 5JN

Tel: 01692 670205

Grove Farm is a working, two hundred acre farm owned today by Jennifer and Peter Pratt but it has been a Pratt family home for much longer and in the large, attractive redbrick and pantile farmhouse which dates back to 1736, you can feel the love and happiness which has gone on in previous generations. It stands amidst a large lawn and gardens in the quiet village of Repps-with-Bastwick as though it were out of this world, but in reality it is close to the Norfolk Broads and only five miles from the coast, making it an ideal base for people on holiday. Both Jennifer and Peter Pratt have a keen interest in art and antiques and this is very much reflected in the furnishing of the house in which they have created a relaxed, warm and friendly atmosphere. They are also bird watching, painting and history enthusiasts and can tell you a lot about the wildlife, the flora and fauna of the area as well as some of the history, the legends and myths of this part of Norfolk. If you enjoy walking, they will also point you in the right direction from which to get the most enjoyment.

All the pretty bedrooms, furnished with a happy mixture of antiques and modern, are ensuite. There is a spacious family room with a double bed and two singles, a double room with a king-size bed and a twin-bedded room. All the rooms have television and a plentifully supplied hostess tray - nothing like being able to make a drink whenever you wish. Breakfast is a feast and Jennifer uses free range eggs which she will cook in whatever way you wish. The full English breakfast is a true farmhouse meal but you can have a lighter Continental breakfast if you wish. There are no evening meals but Jennifer will advise you where to go. The large garden is there for your use and complete with children's swings and a tennis court. To while away a pleasant hour or two, there is a snooker table. Grove Farm is a strictly non-smoking house.

USEFUL INFORMATION

OPEN: All year
CHILDREN: Welcome breakfast
VEGETARIAN: Catered for
WHEELCHAIR ACCESS: No
GARDEN: Yes. Swings. Tennis court
ACCOMMODATION: 1fam 1dbl 1tw all ensuite
RATES: Low season £16 High season £18pp B&B - Children: £10

DINING ROOM: Great farmhouse

CREDIT CARDS: None taken
LICENSED: No
PETS: No
A NON-SMOKING HOUSE

HORSE AND GROOM MOTEL
Main Road
Rollesby
Great Yarmouth
Norfolk
NR29 5ER

Tel: 01493 740624
Fax: 01493 740022

3 Crown Commended. Les Routiers.
Disabled Rating Category 2

The Horse and Groom Motel is conveniently situated on the edge of the Norfolk Broads and close to the seaside resort of Great Yarmouth. The historic city of Norwich with its stunning cathedral is twenty minutes away by car. Ideal for anyone wanting to explore the North Norfolk Coast and to take a look at North Suffolk. Walkers find the area exhilarating, it entices Bird watchers, offers fishing, sailing, horse riding and the chance to look over Stately homes. And they are just some of the reasons for coming to stay in this area.

Guests using the Horse and Groom Motel always come back again if they get the opportunity. It is a modern, attractive place in which the needs and comfort of the guests are paramount. The extremely well trained staff are excellent. All the bedrooms which are comfortably and attractively furnished, sleep two or four people. They have satellite and terrestrial television, tea and coffee facilities, dial direct telephone and radio alarm. All the rooms have ensuite facilities of shower, wash basin and toilets. Family rooms are available, consisting of one double bed and two singles. Cots can be provided. A specially appointed disabled room is also there with bath, toilet and wash basin.

The excellence of the Horse and Groom Restaurant is known far and wide for its culinary fare. Meals are available every day of the week with seafood and steaks the house speciality. The chef takes a pride in using only the seasons freshest and finest produce. An equally well chosen wine list adds to the pleasure of dining here. Many people choose to eat in the uniquely designed bar which has a friendly atmosphere all of its own. The home cooked bar meals are enjoyed in comfortable surroundings, which, when combined with the large selection of beers, wines and spirits, make it a popular meeting place.

USEFUL INFORMATION

OPEN: All year. Mon-Sat 11-3pm & 6-11pm
Sun: 12-3pm & 7-10.30pm
CHILDREN: Welcome
CREDIT CARDS: All major cards
LICENSED: Yes
ACCOMMODATION: 20 ensuite rooms
RATES: From £36.95 Special 2 night break
£145 2 people sharing double room, DB&B

RESTAURANT; Superb food
BAR FOOD: Wide choice
VEGETARIAN: Always a choice
WHEELCHAIR ACCESS: Yes
PETS: Yes
GARDEN: Yes

THE HORSESHOES INN
Cromer Road
Nr Erpingham
Norwich
Norfolk
NR11 7QE

Tel/Fax: 01263 761378

The Horseshoes Inn is a traditional Norfolk Coaching Inn situated right beside Alby Craft Centre on the A140 road to Cromer. It is ideally situated for anyone wanting to explore Norwich, Cromer, North Walsham and the North Norfolk Coast. There are a plethora of historic houses, gardens, fishing lakes, leisure centres with swimming pools and indoor bowls, all within easy distance. Probably one of the things that makes this inn so popular is its retention of old values, charm and the look of the 1890's. Inside it is warm and comfortable and more often than not you will find locals playing some of the old traditional pub games that include the 'Old Bull Ring and Hook' and the Spinning Wheel game 'Twister'.

John Edwards owns and runs this Free house with the help of his friendly and efficient staff. Here you will get well kept ale with real ales which will include Woodfordes Wherry and Adams Broadside as well as several guest beers. There is also a well chosen wine list compiled by Adams of Southwold who have made sure it contains several interesting wines from around the world and all at sensible prices. Traditional fare is also one of the strong points of this hostelry. Everyday the menu has twenty home-cooked traditional meals as well as a good range of bar snacks and vegetarian choices. The restaurant is strictly non-smoking.

For those who want to stay there are two double ensuite rooms, one single and one family room, all of which have nice pieces of antique furniture and pretty decor. In addition there is a well equipped holiday flat in the grounds. Children are welcome and they thoroughly enjoy the swings and slides in a safely fenced area.

USEFUL INFORMATION

OPEN; 11.30-2.45 & 6.30-11
Sat and Sunday all day
CHILDREN; Welcome
CREDIT CARDS; Visa/Master Card
LICENSED; Full   toilets
GARDEN; Yes. Swings & slides
ACCOMMODATION; 2 dbl. ensuite
1sgl 1fam Holiday flat
RATES; High season 30.00 Low season 25.00

RESTAURANT; Good traditional fare
BAR FOOD; Wide range. Daily specials
VEGETARIAN; Always a choice
DISABLED ACCESS; Portable ramp +

PETS; Outside only
SMOKING; Not in restaurant

HOTEL WROXHAM
The Bridge
Wroxham
Norfolk
NR12 8AJ

Tel: 01603 782061 Fax: 01603 784279
Website:www.minotel.com

RAC 3 Star/4 Crowns Commended

The first thing that strikes you when you step through the double doors and into the well appointed foyer of the Hotel Wroxham is the stunning vista that draws one into the very heart of the hotel and its riverside setting. It takes only a few minutes, preferably with a glass of your favourite tipple, but relax into a comfortable armchair in the bar, lounge or restaurant and you will soon find the cares of the world drifting away with the tides. As the sun sets over the Waterside Terrace Bar and Restaurant you realise that indeed you could be anywhere and that you have felt this relaxed feeling before, but certainly it was long ago and you know that it is very seldom found.

The new proprietors of this lovely venue, were smitten in the same way and, such was the feeling that they were convinced to leave their high powered London jobs and invest in the Hotel Wroxham. Having spotted a winner, they are now applying their considerable marketing and customer service skills to ensure that their guests enjoy the very best that they have to offer. The eighteen luxury, fully equipped ensuite bedrooms, many with private riverside balconies have been refurbished in the last year and their clientele are fully catered for with a daily choice of full English breakfast, bar snacks, traditional carvery or a full a la carte menu which is changed twice yearly. For those that feel adventurous, day boats may be hired directly outside the hotel but one can arrive by boat and tie up for free if taking advantage of the variety of hospitality the hotel offers. There is also plenty of private car parking space available.

Situated at the centre of the Norfolk Broads and on the River Bure, Wroxham, the unofficial capital of The Broads, offers something for everyone, whether it is waterborne, enjoying the beach, or spotting the rare species of birds and butterflies. The historic cathedral city of Norwich is seven miles to the south and to the north and east is a long and varied coast line of salt marshes, cliffs, wide, deserted beaches and grassy dunes interrupted by small fishing villages and family resorts such as Great Yarmouth. Whatever your choice of pursuit, the Hotel Wroxham is the place to stay for a holiday or somewhere from which one can conduct business, hold meetings, banquets, weddings or simply....relax and enjoy.

USEFUL INFORMATION

OPEN: 11am-11pmdaily 12-10.30pmSun
CHILDREN: Welcome
CREDIT CARDS: All major cards
LICENSED: Yes
ACCOMMODATION: 18 luxury rooms
RATES: Sgl from £45 Dbl. £50 High Season
£35 & £40 Low Season

RESTAURANT: Delicious fare
BAR FOOD: Traditional menu
VEGETARIAN: Always available
GARDEN: Yes.Riverside Terrace
PETS: Not in rooms

THE KINGS ARMS
High Street
Ludham
NR Gt. Yarmouth
Norfolk
NR29 5QQ

Tel:01692 678386
Fax: 01692 678188

Ludham is a picturesque Norfolk village just twelve miles from Great Yarmouth. It is a quiet restful place and in its midst is the 18th century Georgian style building which houses the Kings Arms, a true village inn which has a good restaurant and its own fish and chip shop 'Planet Codwood' next door. It is a contented, friendly hostelry much loved by the locals who are regularly to be seen at its bar but it is also somewhere where people come from miles around to enjoy a quiet drink and sometimes in the case of Show business artistes working in Great Yarmouth, a retreat from their frenetic world. The pub is five minutes walk away from Womack Water, a peaceful, scenic tributary of the river, and mooring place of 'Wherry Albion' the last trading boat to tie up here. Ludham was also the location for the film 'Conflict of Wings'.

The Kings Arms is owned and run by Noel and Nicki Smith who use their wealth of experience in inn-keeping to great advantage here. Everything runs smoothly, the staff are well trained and the chef is an expert with a great knowledge of English and Continental cooking. His menus are highly rated and include such delicious fare as fillet of sole stuffed with prawns and mushrooms in white wine sauce. The menu in fact has something to suit everyone's taste and pocket. The Restaurant is strictly non-smoking. If you do not want a main meal there is a great choice of traditional bar food including some delicious, freshly cut sandwiches with a variety of fillings, or a Ploughman's, big enough to ensure you will not go away hungry. The Wine List has been carefully chosen to include a selection of Continental, Australian, Hungarian and German wines - all at sensible prices. If you have decided to eat some of Planet Codwood's Fish and Chips you are very welcome to sit at tables in the Beer garden and tuck in.

Ludham has a lot to see in its own right including Hunters Boatyard with its fleet of sailing craft. Catfield has a Nature Reserve, there is a Nautical Museum at Potter Heigham and the historic city of Norwich is only twelve miles away.

USEFUL INFORMATION

OPEN: 11am-11pm
CHILDREN: Welcome
CREDIT CARDS: Visa/Master/Debit Cards
LICENSED: Full On
GARDEN: Large Beer Garden. Play area

RESTAURANT: A la Carte. Chinese
BAR FOOD: Sandwiches to Fillet steaks
VEGETARIAN: Yes
WHEELCHAIR ACCESS: Yes
PETS: Yes - on lead

THE LIGHTHOUSE INN
Coast Road
Walcott
Norfolk
NR12 0PE

Tel/Fax: 01692 650371

Situated on the main coast road in Walcott, The Lighthouse Inn is a comfortable, friendly Free House - the only one in Walcott. It is renowned for the standard of its food and beer and has been in 'The Good Beer' and 'The Good Food Guide' for some years. Owned and run by Steve Bullimore aided by a friendly, efficient staff, the inn is a popular place not only for locals who enjoy the companionship and camaraderie of the bar, but also for others who come to Walcott especially to join in the fun and at the same time take the opportunity to have a meal or a snack chosen from a traditional English menu. The Lighthouse Inn prides itself in producing quality and value for money food, using fresh locally grown vegetables and quality meat, with which they make the daily pie-specials, using home-made pastry. Fresh fish is delivered daily and so the dishes vary. Home-made Daily Specials are on the Blackboard and more often than not have time honoured favourites. The menu always includes Children's Meals as well as a selection of dishes for Vegetarians. Pot Meals including a very tasty Smuggler's Pie are delicious, the steaks melt in the mouth and for those who like something less filling there is a variety of Bar Snacks including freshly prepared sandwiches and Toasted Sandwiches as well as Ploughman's Lunches. Salads are varied and in season may well include local crab for which the area is famous.

Walcott is easily approached either from Norwich, Stalham, North Walsham and Cromer, making a visit to the Lighthouse Inn a sensible and delightful option during a day's outing.

USEFUL INFORMATION

OPEN: All year except Dec 25th/26th
CHILDREN: Welcome in Family or Dining Rm
CREDIT CARDS: All major cards
LICENSED: Full On
WHEELCHAIR ACCESS: Yes

RESTAURANT: Good home-made fare
BAR FOOD: Wide choice
VEGETARIAN: Always a choice
GARDEN: Yes PETS: Yes

MOAT FARM
East Ruston Road
Lessingham
Norfolk
NR12 0DW

Tel: 01692 580535

Lessingham is situated within the Broadland area where boats can be hired, and sailing, fishing or Broad Tours and Nature Trails, are all within easy reach. Sandy beaches are two miles away, the historic Cathedral City of Norwich is only eighteen miles, the village itself boasts a nice pub and a fine church whilst the old market town of Stalham with plenty of eating places, shops and the Broads where you can hire craft, is just two miles. In fact it makes a great base for a holiday and to stay in the friendly comfort of Moat Farm is an added bonus.

This three century old Farm House became the home of Russell and Cossette Hart in 1981 and they have spent time and care in making it a special place. Russell is a retired builder and it is he who has converted the traditional Norfolk Farm buildings into spacious self-catering quality accommodation. There are six barns sleeping three to six persons. Within the house there is Bed and Breakfast accommodation with its own separate entrance. It comprises of a large, comfortable lounge/dining room complete with television, one large family bedroom with a cot, one large double room and a single room. All the rooms have television, vanity basins, hairdryers and hospitality trays. One bathroom is shared between the three rooms. A great traditional farmhouse, breakfast is served every morning and a vegetarian meal is available. No evening meals are served but there are plenty of good eateries within easy reach, to which the Harts will be happy to direct you. There is ample room for parking but regrettably pets cannot be accommodated. The gardens and grounds are pleasant places in which to stroll or perhaps try out your skill at Putting. For those who enjoy walking, Moat House Farm is an ideal starting place with many footpaths close by.

USEFUL INFORMATION

OPEN: All year
CHILDREN: Welcome
CREDIT CARDS: None taken
LICENSED: No
ACCOMMODATION:
1 Family, 1 Double, 1 Single Not ensuite
RATES: From £16.00 Children 1/2 price

DINING ROOM: Breakfast
VEGETARIAN: Yes
WHEELCHAIR ACCESS: No
GARDEN: Yes. Putting
PETS: No

PEBBLES COUNTRY INN & FREEHOUSE
Whimpwell Street
Happisburgh
Norfolk
NR12 0QD

Tel: 01692 651183

Built in 1774 Pebbles Country Inn and Freehouse is full of an old world atmosphere acquired over the years and enhanced today by Joanne Viner, the landlady and her family who all have the well being of their guests at heart whether it be drinking in the inn, dining in the charming restaurant, having a quick snack in the bar or staying in one of the two pleasant bedrooms furnished in farmhouse style. Both bedrooms have television and a hostess tray. The food is renowned in the area for its quality and affordable prices and married together with an extensive wine list, a meal becomes memorable. The menu includes all sorts of dishes including succulent steaks, fresh salmon, duck, Guinea fowl and much more. The emphasis is on the use of fresh local produce and vegetables and the result is simply delicious. In the Bar there is a wide range from which to make a choice. The setting of Pebbles is charming. You can take walks along the Cliff top, enjoy the beach, explore the old church and venture into the Lighthouse. Norwich with its fascinating streets and magnificent cathedral, is twenty miles away

USEFUL INFORMATION

OPEN: 11-3pm 7-11pm all year
CHILDREN: Yes & Menu
CREDIT CARDS: None taken
LICENSED: Full On
ACCOMMODATION: 2 rooms
RATES: £30 per room, per night

RESTAURANT: Extensive menu
BAR FOOD: Wide range of snacks
VEGETARIAN: Yes
WHEELCHAIR ACCESS: Bar only
GARDEN: Beer Garden
PETS: No

RED ROOF FARMHOUSE
Ludham Road
Potter Heigham
Great Yarmouth
Norfolk
NB29 5NB

Tel: 01692 670604
Fax: 01692 670065

Gordon and Molly Playford farm Red Roof Farm in the heart of a rural area but part of Potter Heigham and with a National Grid Ref TG4119 making it easy for visitors to find. This is a wonderful part of Norfolk and close to The Broads and Weavers Way making it the ideal holiday retreat for visitors who want to take to the water, walk peaceably in glorious countryside or simply explore The Broads. Bird-watchers find the area a paradise and for beach lovers, the seaside is only approximately six miles away. The historic cathedral city of Norwich is not far off with its wealth of architecture and a great shopping centre as well as theatres and museums. Children love staying at Red Roof Farm because there are so many animals to see including shire horses, sheep, chickens, pot bellied pig, ducks, peacocks, cats and dogs. They are invited to feed the lambs if they wish to. For adults the farm has its own private fishing and if you have your own horse, stabling is available.

The Playfords have created a delightfully warm and welcoming home into which their guests are soon made to feel at ease. The strictly non-smoking, modern house is furnished to a high standard but with a degree of informality that makes it simple to relax. The bedrooms are all light and airy and have pretty drapes and bedcovers. The furnishing is attractive and the beds especially comfortable. Each room has large washbasins, television, shaver point and a generously supplied hostess tray. It is wonderful sleeping in such a peaceful, restful place and every morning you wake to the sounds of the countryside and in the sure knowledge that when you come downstairs Molly will cook you a delicious and substantial breakfast which starts the day off splendidly. No evening meals are provided but the Playfords will willingly point you in the direction of the many good eateries within the vicinity.

USEFUL INFORMATION

OPEN: All year
CHILDREN: Welcome breakfast
CREDIT CARDS: None taken
LICENSED: No
PETS: Yes by arrangement

RATES: From £16pp B&B

DINING ROOM: Great farmhouse
VEGETARIAN: Catered for upon request
WHEELCHAIR ACCESS: No
GARDEN: Yes.
ACCOMMODATION: Comfortable
                         bedrooms not ensuite
STRICTLY NON SMOKING

REEDHAM FERRY INN
Reedham
Norwich
Norfolk
NR13 3HA

Tel: 01493 700429

Reedham Ferry Inn is a delightful 17th century riverside hostelry with the passenger and car ferry operating alongside from 8am-10pm, seven days a week. On a fine day it is fascinating to sit on the riverside patio, enjoying a drink, and watching the activity on the river. Equally pleasant is it to be inside the Reedham Ferry Inn absorbing the friendly atmosphere and listening to some of the banter of the locals standing around the bar. People of all walks of life and from all over the world visit the Inn and it is not unusual to hear several different languages spoken. If they could all be translated most of the words would have been in praise of the Inn, its landlord, David Archer, and his cherful, experienced staff.

There are three rooms in the Inn, including a Family Room, in which one can eat, two of which are non-smoking. The menu is traditional English fare and plenty of it. There are several starters and always a choice of main courses as well as some old-fashioned puddings on the dessert menu. Food is also served in the Bar where the Chef's Daily Specials are very popular. Sandwiches and salads also feature. On Sundays there is a traditional Sunday Roast Lunch with a choice of meats and poultry, Yorkshire Puddings, crisp roast potatoes, fresh vegetables and all the trimmings. Reedham Ferry Inn has an interesting wine list with wines from around the world, a large selection of Malt Whiskeys and some delicious Fruit Wines including Damson and Blackberry.

From Reedham Ferry Inn you can set out to explore all sorts of fascinating places including Bygones Village, Sealife at Great Yarmouth which is six miles away or the historic city of Norwich with its magnificent cathedral. There are two golf courses within fifteen miles, some splendid walks and of course, boating on the river. Whatever you decide to do you will find a visit to the Reedham Ferry Inn memorable.

USEFUL INFORMATION

OPEN: 11-3pm & 6.30-11pm
Sun 12-10.30pm. Food all day
CHILDREN: Welcome
CREDIT CARDS: All major cards
LICENSED: Full On
GARDEN: Riverside frontage. Patio

RESTAURANT: 3 rooms including
2 non-smoking.
BAR FOOD: Chef's Daily Specials
VEGETARIAN: Upon request
WHEELCHAIR ACCESS: Yes
PETS: Well behaved

THE SEAFARERS
North Gap
Eccles Beach
NR Lessingham
Norfolk
NR12 0SW

Tel: 01692 598218

Listed/Commended
Ordinance Survey Reference Landranger

Map No 134 Grid Ref. 4133288

This former 18th century Manor farmhouse opens its doors in a genuine welcome to the many guests who have found it a comfortable home-from-home over the years. Off the beaten track, it stands in a quarter of an acre and is adjacent to a sandy beach, enjoying wide rural views. It is a restful, tranquil spot, totally unspoiled and yet within a twenty mile radius of Norwich, Cromer and Great Yarmouth and within three miles of the Norfolk Broads. People stay here for many reasons including its ideal situation which offers beach fishing, bird watching, coastal and countryside walks, sailing and a little paradise for artists. The Norfolk Broads are unique and remain unchanged with the passing of time, historic Norwich is a delight and capped with the beauty and magnificence of its Cathedral.

Owned and run by Jean and John Murden, this welcoming house is comfortably furnished and much attention has been paid to detail to ensure that anyone who stays here has a memorable holiday. For example, for those spending a day on the beach, there is an outside toilet and changing facilities. The garden with its chairs also has Clock Golf and other games. The accommodation caters for up to six guests with two twin-bedded rooms, the second twin-bedded room shares a bathroom with an adjoining double room. All three bedrooms have pretty colour coordinated curtains and bed linen and the furniture throughout is period style cherry mahogany. They are all centrally heated, have radios, hostess trays and the twin ensuite has a television. The guest bathroom is spacious and contains bath with shower, toilet, wash basin, bidet and shaver point. Both the Dining Room and Lounge have television and video and French doors from the lounge open onto the garden.

A truly substantial and freshly cooked traditional English Breakfast is served every morning but a lighter Continental or Vegetarian meal is available. A free pick up service is offered to guests arriving by rail, air or coach at Norwich should they wish to stay a week or more. Timetables of services can be made available upon request.

USEFUL INFORMATION

OPEN: All year except Christmas
CHILDREN: Over 8 years
CREDIT CARDS: None taken
LICENSED: No
ACCOMMODATION: 2tw 1dbl
RATES: From £16pp low season

DINING ROOM: Breakfast only
VEGETARIAN: Yes
WHEELCHAIR ACCESS: No
GARDEN: Yes. Clock Golf & games
PETS: No

VILLAROSE
30/31 Princes Road,
Great Yarmouth,
Norfolk

Tel: 01493 844748

Great Yarmouth has always been a happy place for holidaymakers and it is the quality of the accommodation that has always been very important. Villarose in Princes Road, describes itself as a Guest House but with twenty three rooms, fourteen of which are ensuite, it could be deemed to be an hotel. Whatever the definition, it is a comfortable and friendly place in which to stay. Pat Housego is the owner and she is aided by her son who is the chef. Between them and a cheerful staff, they ensure the well being of everyone who stays here. Pat always likes to treat her guests in the way, she herself, would like to be treated when she is away from home.

Villarose was built in 1859 and is a gracious house with a big patio in the front. It is within two minutes of the sea and the shops and the many attractions that Great Yarmouth has to offer. People come here throughout the year and many find that an off season break is more enjoyable than the busy summer season. Later in the year, one can walk across the beach or along the promenade with complete ease. There is fun in Great Yarmouth at night with some good hostelries, three piers, on one of which is a theatre owned by Jim Davidson, and lots of other things to do.

The twenty three bedrooms are attractively and practically furnished and with the recently added luxury of a well supplied hostess tray. Breakfast is cooked freshly to order every morning and evening meals are available by arrangement. There is a bar for the use of residents only which is popular in the evening when they return from a day out and enjoy chatting it over with newly found friends.

USEFUL INFORMATION

OPEN: All year
CHILDREN: Welcome
CREDIT CARDS: None taken
LICENSED: Residential
ACCOMMODATION:23 rooms 14 ensuite
RATES: From £12.50pp.pn £17.50 in high season

DINING ROOM: Excellent breakfast
Evening meals by arrangement
VEGETARIAN: Yes
WHEELCHAIR ACCESS: Yes
GARDEN: No. Large Patio
PETS: By arrangement

THE WAVENEY INN
Staithe Road
Burgh St Peter
Norfolk
NR34 0BT

Tel:01502 677217/343
Fax: 01502 677566

Situated in the very heart of the attractive Waveney Valley at the southern end of the Norfolk Broads, the Waveney River Centre has everything to make a Broads holiday perfect and that includes The Waveney Inn, a traditional Broads Pub which is the social meeting point for visitors and local people. It draws its clientele from the various facets of the Waveney River Centre which is a family run Boating and Caravan Centre offering a traditional East Anglian welcome to all, whether day visiting, on a weekly Caravan Holiday or taking advantage of the permanent Boat Moorings or Holiday Caravan Site. The extensive facilities include a heated indoor swimming pool, sauna, spa bath and gym, a children's adventure area, boat hire by the day or hour, a fully stocked shop, free daytime public moorings, overnight public moorings with electric hook-up for private vessels, touring caravan and tenting site with electric hook-up, toilets and showers, attractive year round marina berths with electric hook-up, boat lift and winter storage, boat sales and service, luxury hire caravans in a secluded sun-trap area, a permanent holiday caravan site and last but by no means least, The Waveney Inn.

In the Inn you will find a happy, carefree atmosphere whether you are eating or drinking. One of the most pleasant things to do is to take a drink from the bar and wander outside to enjoy it and to watch the activity on the water. It is good fun and a great way to relax before going into the Restaurant which offers an excellent carvery with several different joints and poultry, a selection of crisp roast potatoes, Yorkshire puddings and fresh vegetables. There is also an extensive a la carte menu with something to tempt everyone's taste buds. International Theme Nights are held regularly and are very popular. In the Bars, the menu is simpler but includes the time-honoured favourites and a touch of the Oriental. The staff are a cheerful lot and carry out their duties with obvious enjoyment, finding time for a friendly greeting even when they are at their busiest.

USEFUL INFORMATION

OPEN: 12noon-11pm
CHILDREN: Welcome.
CREDIT CARDS: Visa/Master
LICENSED: FullOn
GARDEN: 16 acres
WHEELCHAIR ACCESS: Restaurant only

RESTAURANT: Excellent carvery
Extensive a la carte.
BAR FOOD: Traditional & Oriental
VEGETARIAN: Yes
PETS: Garden & Lobby only

THE WHERRY HOTEL
Bridge Road, Oulton Broad,
Lowestoft, Suffolk NR32 3LN
RAC***

Tel: 01502 516845
Fax: 01502 501350

The Wherry Hotel is the premiere hotel of the eastern Norfolk Broads and has acquired this accolade by having not only an outstanding location but a warmth of welcome and a well-trained, enthusiastic staff who clearly enjoy the reward for their efforts when they see contented guests. The Wherry is an imposing building, parts of which were built in 1836, but the whole is now a modern hotel, comfortable, elegant, stylish with its own traditional hospitality and charm. People come here for many reasons, sometimes as a family, sometimes as a couple taking a break and sometimes for business purposes. It suits everyone. You can sit in the hotel's lounge and enjoy a quiet drink or bar meal while you watch the boats bustle on the broad, going a little further afield, Lowestoft with its award winning beaches and water, is two miles away. From Monday to Thursday the hotel is totally peaceful and ideal for people wanting a break to recharge their batteries or to use the efficient, well planned conference facilities. Friday, Saturday and Sunday, The Wherry tends to be the haunt of the younger set who enjoy its night-club environment. However whenever you come to The Wherry you will appreciate its outstanding comfort and facilities.

At the heart of every good hotel is its restaurant and The Wherry Hotel is no exception to the rule with its elegant Mariners Restaurant offering Carvery, Table d'hôte and A La Carte. Acclaimed Chef Melmet Tuzemen and his team, prepare some of the region's finest international cuisine. With ingredients that range from a wide selection of fresh local fish, to exotic fruits and spices, grilled steaks and tender lamb, the only difficulty is making your choice. To complement your meal there is a carefully chosen and interesting collection of wines from around the world. It is an ideal place for an intimate dinner or a private party.

USEFUL INFORMATION

OPEN: All year Bar: 11-11pm Sun:12-10.30pm   RESTAURANT: Imaginative
CHILDREN: Welcome menu.   Talented chef
CREDIT CARDS: All major cards   BAR FOOD: Light snacks
LICENSED: Full On   VEGETARIAN: Yes
ACCOMMODATION:30 ensuite rooms 2 suites   WHEELCHAIR ACCESS: No
RATES: Sgl £46 dbl. £66 dbl./sgl occupancy £55 GARDEN: No
Executive Suite/Honeymoon £80 Weekend Bargain Breaks & Midweek Breaks
Conference & Function facilities   PETS: At Manager's discretion

ALLENS FARMHOUSE
Three Hammer Common
Neatishead, Norfolk
NR12 8XW
Tel: 01692 630080

When Jan and Jeremy Smerdon bought Allens Farmhouse in 1997 they discovered that the previous owners had run it for bed and breakfast and they decided they would continue. They both like people, enjoy cooking and are quite happy to share their attractive home which was built in the early 1700s although the interior was extensively and sympathetically modernised during the 1980s. It has a large walled garden which has been landscaped to create a beautiful lawn surrounded by flower beds with the added attraction of a well, pond and orchard. A sheltered corner of the garden with easy access from the front drive, is for the use of guests. A gas Barbecue and picnic equipment are available for any DIY outdoor meal enthusiasts. The Grade II Listed house with a wealth of old beams and mainly furnished with antiques, is warm and welcoming, relaxed and informal. The three bedrooms are situated around a gallery landing with the bathroom adjoining. A large drawing room with television and Video is available for guests. Breakfast is a delicious meal with several choices including kedgeree and kippers. A three course home-cooked dinner is available on request. Allens Farmhouse is ideally situated and is within easy walking distance of Alderfen Broad, a nature reserve and haven for many different species of wildfowl. It is also renowned for its collection of unusual and rare insects including the swallow tail butterfly.

USEFUL INFORMATION

OPEN: All year
CHILDREN: Welcome fare
CREDIT CARDS: None taken
LICENSED: No
PETS: Well behaved
RATES: From £16pp B&B Children free under 3

DINING ROOM: Delicious home-made
VEGETARIAN: Upon request
WHEELCHAIR ACCESS: No
GARDEN: Yes. Barbecue. Well & pond
ACCOMMODATION: 2dbl 1tw not ensuite

BIRCHDALE HOUSE,
Blickling Road,
Aylsham, Norfolk NR11 6ND

Tel/Fax: 01263 734827

This, charming, peaceful house is in a Conservation area and stands in half an acre of well kept gardens complete with a summer house in which afternoon tea is served when the weather is right. Jenni Cross is the owner and she is a natural born hostess who delights in looking after her guests, making sure of all their creature comforts, including cooking a delicious and very sustaining breakfast every morning complete with fruit, fruit juices, cereals, toast and preserves as well as freshly brewed coffee and piping hot tea. All sorts of diets can be catered for and packed lunches provided, if they are ordered in advance. There are no evening meals but with a number of very good pubs and restaurants in the vicinity , it poses no problem. Jenni has one ensuite twin bedroom, one double with a private bathroom and a single room. All of them are beautifully appointed and in addition to a hostess tray, television, hairdryers and radio alarms, there is always bottled water. Birchdale House makes an excellent base from which to discover this fascinating part of Norfolk. The National Trust properties of Blickling and Felbrigg Halls are just one mile and nine miles respectively. A narrow gauge railway connects to the Broads and boat trips. The coast is 10 miles and all around Birchdale House there are some excellent walks with many Waymarked paths, cycle tracks and bridle ways.

USEFUL INFORMATION

OPEN: All year
CHILDREN: Welcome
CREDIT CARDS: None taken
LICENSED: No
ACCOMMODATION: 1dbl. 1 tw 1 sgl
RATES: Tw £18 dbl. £17 sgl £17 pp B & B
Short breaks 3 nights or more £1pp reduction per night

DINING ROOM: Super breakfast
No evening meal
VEGETARIAN: Yes + diets
WHEELCHAIR ACCESS: No
GARDEN: Yes + summerhouse

THE BROADS HOTEL & RESTAURANT
Station Road, Wroxham
Norfolk   NR12 8UR
Tel: 01603 782869 Fax: 01603 784066

Conveniently situated only eight miles from the Historic City of Norwich is the family run Broads Hotel in the centre of the village of Wroxham and adjacent to boating, sailing, fishing and within easy reaches of Norfolk's vast beaches. Wroxham, the unofficial capital of the Norfolk Broads, is a charming place in its own right and from here one can easily visit some exciting places. Many people have found The Broads Hotel the best place to stay; somewhere that is both efficiently run and has a delightful touch of informality. It also has that personal service that only smaller hotels can provide. Over the years the owners, David and Helen Bales and their sons Andrew and Nigel have gained a well deserved reputation for the hotel and its restaurant. The latter known as The Rose Room Carvery and Restaurant, with a decor that echoes its name, is known for the high standard of cuisine both on the carvery and the a la carte menu. It is open seven days a week all the year round and is as popular with residents in the neighbourhood as it is with guests staying in the hotel. There is a well stocked bar, which is also much frequented by local people as well as visitors. The comfortable, centrally heated bedrooms are fully ensuite with direct dial telephones, tea and coffee making facilities, colour television . Immediately opposite the hotel is the beautifully renovated Broads Cottage with an additional seven rooms of de luxe standard, in great demand for both business and holiday use. Also under the management and ownership of the Bales family is Salhouse Lodge Country House, less than two miles from the hotel. Formerly a vicarage, it has been restored and extended to provide arguably the best eating and drinking venue in the district.

USEFUL INFORMATION

OPEN: All year	RESTAURANT: Carvery & a la carte
CHILDREN: Welcome	BAR FOOD: Yes
CREDIT CARDS: Visa/Master/AMEX/Diners	VEGETARIAN: Yes
LICENSED: Yes	WHEELCHAIR ACCESS: Yes
ACCOMMODATION: Ensuite rooms	GARDEN: No
RATES: From £26pp B&B Children: £10	PETS: Yes

THE GALLON POT
1-2 Market Place,
Gt. Yarmouth, Norfolk
Tel: 01493 842230

It was as far back as 1771, that Burroughs, in the somewhat eccentric hands of William Norton Burroughs, Mayor of the Borough of Gt. Yarmouth, became noted for the quality of its wines and spirits. It took German bombs in 1943 to put paid to this tradition but to-day, this town centre public house, now known as 'The Gallon Pot', with a cellar bar proudly bearing the name of 'Burroughs', has been refurbished superbly by Michael and Maria Spalding. It has the quality of a four-star hotel with its warm traditional furnishing, dark mahogany bar and comfortable seating. There is an intangible warmth and happiness in the atmosphere here. The pleasant and hospitable staff go out of their way to please. The one single lounge bar has split level eating areas which offer easy access for wheelchairs on the northern entrance. Downstairs in the basement is the Cellar Bar with full function facility and a family room. Maria's menu offers a super range from snacks, starters, main meals, pot meals, fish to freshly made sandwiches served in either wholemeal or white bread. In addition, you should look at the blackboard for details of the home-made daily and weekend specials. In the summer months, varied flavoured brewed teas can be savoured with a choice of delicious cakes and rich pastries. One of the better places to eat, from the plethora, that are available in the town, on the many occasions I have eaten here, the staff have been extremely efficient and friendly.

USEFUL INFORMATION

OPEN: All day every day	RESTAURANT: Excellent food
CHILDREN: Yes. Family room	sensible prices
CREDIT CARDS: All major cards	BAR FOOD: As restaurant
LICENSED: Full Licence	VEGETARIAN: 4 dishes + Daily
GARDEN: Outside picnic tables	Specials
on paved area	WHEELCHAIR ACCESS: Yes
PETS: Guide dogs only	

KENTFORD HOUSE
82 Marine Parade
Great Yarmouth
Norfolk NR30 2DJ

Tel: 01493 844888

The beach is just across the road from Kentford House at eighty two Marine Parade and the sound of the sea lapping the shore is the first thing you hear each morning when you stay in this comfortable, friendly guest house. Not only is it convenient for the beach but it is within walking distance of virtually all that Great Yarmouth has to offer the visitor. It is next to the Cinema, nearly opposite Britannia Pier, close to the theatres and the town centre shops as well as the Bowling Greens. An ideal place in which to stay for a break or a holiday. Most people when they come to Kentford House park their car in the ample parking space in front of the house and forget about driving for the duration of their stay. The owners, Peter and Ann Miasek, are friendly people who work hard to ensure that all their guests enjoy their stay. The house has a very definite home-from-home atmosphere. Ann is Thai and you can see her influence in the furnishings everywhere. It is charming and all the ten letting rooms, of which five are ensuite, are attractive and comfortable and have television and a hostess tray. For families there is a cot available. Breakfast is a delicious meal with generous portions. No evening meals are served but Great Yarmouth is full of good eateries, so that poses no problem. Kentford House has a Residential Licence and it is very pleasant to finish off the day with a night cap, perhaps chatting to your fellow guests about the day and swapping ideas for the following day.

USEFUL INFORMATION

OPEN: All year
CHILDREN: Welcome
CREDIT CARDS: None taken
LICENSED: Residential Licence
ACCOMMODATION: 10 rooms. 5 ensuite

DINING ROOM: Excellent breakfast
VEGETARIAN: Upon request
WHEELCHAIR ACCESS: No
PETS: No
RATES: From £14pp B&B
Children under 12 half price

LA CARROZZA
The Station, Wroxham
Norfolk NR12 8UT

Tel: 01603 783939

It would take imagination to take a dilapidated building at Wroxham and Hoveton train station and turn it into one of the most unusual restaurants in the county. This is exactly what Nando and Pauline have done. In the ten years since Nando first had this brain-wave, La Carrozza has gained a great reputation for good Italian food. One can imagine what the architect must have said to Nando when he was approached to carry out this radical idea! What has been achieved is charming and atmospheric. The railway theme has been continued and the restaurant is set out in the style of a railway carriage and with a bit of imagination one could suppose one was on a journey to Venice on the Orient Express - helped by murals depicting this journey. If one had to describe the food at La Carrozza succinctly, it would be to say that here one can sample Italian food at its best, with dishes created by the proprietors, Nando and Pauline. Nando's imagination did not stop when he visualised La Carrozza; he has gone on to create delicious dishes ever since, much to the pleasure of the regulars who come here and for newcomers who are excited by the venue in the first instance and then remember the delicious food for a long time. The preserved Bure Valley Railway is a short walk from La Carrozza, which offers a picturesque journey to the historic town of Aylsham and nearby Blickling Hall, former residence of one of Henry VIII's wives.

USEFUL INFORMATION

OPEN: February-December
CHILDREN: Welcome
CREDIT CARDS: Most major cards
LICENSED: Yes Supper license

RESTAURANT: Italian food at its best
VEGETARIAN: Yes
WHEELCHAIR ACCESS: Yes
PETS: No

OLD FARM COTTAGES
Old Farm, Tunstead
Norwich, Norfolk NR12 8HR

Tel: 01692 536612   Fax: 01692 536612

Situated in a delightful rural area not far distant from the historic city of Norwich and a number of stately homes, glorious gardens, museums, leisure craft centres and riverside inns, the six self-catering cottages belonging to Old Farm, are the perfect place for a country holiday at any time of the year. The coast with its sandy beaches at Happisburgh, Eccles and Sea Palling are also within easy reach.

The cottages have been converted from the original red brick farm buildings, including the stables, coach house and the granary. Each has a character of its own and they are all charmingly decorated and comfortably furnished. Equipped with every modern amenity that today's holidaymaker demands, the cottages are restful and the perfect place to stay, The Coach House and The Stables both sleep six. The Granary five and The Mast, Marlers Cottage and the Ostelry four. Each cottage retains original features such as beams, stable dividers and brickwork and each enjoys the private benefit of its own enclosed patio.

All guests are welcome to relax in the grounds of the farm, where they can play table tennis and pool in a games room in one of the barns or use the heated indoor swimming pool and gym. Pets are allowed under certain conditions by prior arrangement. Boats can be hired at Wroxham. Private fishing is available at Dilham.

USEFUL INFORMATION

OPEN: All year
CHILDREN: Welcome
CREDIT CARDS: All major cards
ACCOMMODATION: 6 self-catering
cottages

WHEELCHAIR ACCESS: Yes
GARDEN: Yes. Swimming pool
Games Room
PETS: By prior arrangement
RATES: Weekly lets from £260-£664

SLOLEY FARM
Sloley, Norwich
Norfolk   NR12 8H J
Tel: 01692 536281 Fax:: 01692 535162
Internet: sloley@farmhotel.u-net.com
2 Crowns Commended

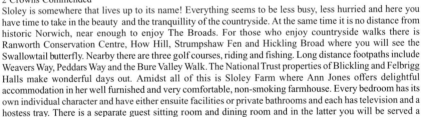

Sloley is somewhere that lives up to its name! Everything seems to be less busy, less hurried and here you have time to take in the beauty and the tranquillity of the countryside. At the same time it is no distance from historic Norwich, near enough to enjoy The Broads. For those who enjoy countryside walks there is Ranworth Conservation Centre, How Hill, Strumpshaw Fen and Hickling Broad where you will see the Swallowtail butterfly. Nearby there are three golf courses, riding and fishing. Long distance footpaths include Weavers Way, Peddars Way and the Bure Valley Walk. The National Trust properties of Blickling and Felbrigg Halls make wonderful days out. Amidst all of this is Sloley Farm where Ann Jones offers delightful accommodation in her well furnished and very comfortable, non-smoking farmhouse. Every bedroom has its own individual character and have either ensuite facilities or private bathrooms and each has television and a hostess tray. There is a separate guest sitting room and dining room and in the latter you will be served a delicious, substantial farmhouse breakfast with free range eggs and home-made preserves. The house is centrally heated. There is also a Campsite hidden from the house complete with everything the camper needs. Wheelchair access is possible. It is open from Easter to October.

USEFUL INFORMATION

OPEN: 2nd Jan-23rd Dec
Campsite Easter to October
CHILDREN: Welcome
CREDIT CARDS: None taken
LICENSED: No
ACCOMMODATION: 3 bedrooms ensuite
RATES: From £17.50 10% discount for 7 nights +
Children 10-14 years half price

DINING ROOM: Delicious breakfast
No evening meals
VEGETARIAN: Catered for
WHEELCHAIR ACCESS: On campsite
GARDEN: Yes
PETS: No
STRICTLY NON-SMOKING HOUSE

SQUIRREL'S NEST
71 Avondale Road
Gorleston-on-Sea
Norfolk NR31 6DJ
Tel/Fax: 01493 662746

Squirrel's Nest and Irene Squirrell, represented the whole of East Anglia and the West Midlands in the best Catering Establishment in 1996. A well deserved accolade for this perfectly run hotel which provides the perfect base for a holiday and where it is recognised that food is always a very important ingredient in the success of any vacation. During World War II, 71 Avondale Road was a billet for the forces and when Irene and her husband Don took it over, it was in urgent need of refurbishment. This they have done beautifully. It was completely redecorated and every bedroom was made ensuite. The furnishings throughout the house have been designed to highlight the Victorian era of the building. It is both tastefully and restfully done with an eye to the comfort of guests. There are nine bedrooms, all with matching Duvet Covers, Curtains and wallpaper. There are two Victorian four-posters amongst the rooms and five non-smoking rooms. Every room has several additional touches including television, a hostess tray complete with biscuits, trouser press, luggage rack, shampoos, showergel, handkerchiefs and cotton, needles etc. Irene is the chef and her meals are always eagerly awaited. The Bar and Dining Room have lace tablecloths and the cosy bar is decorated with unusual Plaques from Italy.

USEFUL INFORMATION

OPEN: All year
BAR: Mon-Sat 5.30-11.30 Sun: 12-4 7-11pm

Winter: Mon-Sat: 7pm -11.30pm Sun: 12-4pm
VEGETARIAN: a choice of 12 dishes
BAR FOOD: Snacks only
ACCOMMODATION: 9 ensuite
RATES: Low Season from£23pp B&B

RESTAURANT: Full A la Carte. Table
d'hôte changed daily from April-end October
CHILDREN: Welcome
CREDIT CARDS: All major cards
LICENSED: Residential & Rest.
WHEELCHAIR ACCESS: Yes
PETS: In some rooms £2 per day
GARDEN: Yes

High season From £30pp B&B Children only pay for meals when sharing parent's rooms

THE SWAN MOTEL
Gillingham, Beccles
Suffolk NR34 0LD
Tel: 01502 712055 Fax: 01502 711786
Info@Swan-motel.demon.co.uk

Luxurious is probably the best way to describe everything about The Swan Motel from its beautifully appointed rooms with all ensuite, direct dial telephones, and remote controlled televisions. All the accommodation is centrally heated and includes family rooms, honeymoon/executive suites with four poster beds and access and facilities for the disabled. People visit here for all sorts of reasons, not only to stay for a break, business or en route elsewhere but they come to enjoy the lively well-stocked bar and to relish the excellence of the cuisine which is imaginative, innovative and at the same time remembers that some people prefer simple, unadulterated traditional English dishes, which is reflected in their Daily Specials Board. In the Summer months, the bargain hunters amongst you will find a trove of treasure at their Sunday Car Boot Sales, and the tempting aroma in the air which is coming from their BBQ being held in their extensive well-appointed Beer Garden. All year round, the weekends, hold the very best in local music and live quality entertainment and the atmosphere is always second to none. Winners of The Topspot Gold Awards in 1997 and 1998, The Swan Motel is well situated for many purposes, whether it is exploring the Broads or the many other pleasures to be found around Norfolk and Suffolk.

USEFUL INFORMATION

OPEN: All year.
CHILDREN: Welcome Carte, Daily Specials
BAR FOOD: Good range + Afternoon Teas
CREDIT CARDS: Most major cards
LICENSED: Yes
ACCOMMODATION: 15 rooms ensuite
RATES: £39.50 sgl £49.50 dbl./tw
Honeymoon/Executive suite £60 with a Jacuzzi
Special weekend breaks: Prices on application

RESTAURANT: Table d'hôte, A la

VEGETARIAN: Extensive range
WHEELCHAIR ACCESS: Yes
GARDEN: Yes
PETS: No
CAR PARKING: Yes, Large facilities, no
charge

YE OLDE SADDLERY
Neatishead
Norwich
NR12 8AD

Tel:01692 630866

   In the main street of Neatishead and occupying a prominent position, is Ye Olde Saddlery. It could not be more conveniently situated; there is a shop and post office opposite, a good pub is nearby and it is only five hundred yards from staithe and river. The owner, Muriel Thompson, who lived in Zambia for thirty years and is a retired school teacher, was born in Neatishead. She has vivid memories of the past and is keenly interested in local history. Her friendly, welcoming attitude makes staying here a delight. When she acquired the property, she spent a considerable time refurbishing the house until she achieved the delightful and high standard that prevails today. The five guest rooms are charmingly appointed, two doubles are ensuite, and a third has a private bathroom - a cot or child's bed is available on request. The ground floor twin-bedded room has a toilet and shower facilities as does a single room. All the bedrooms have television and hostess trays. A delicious, sustaining breakfast is served every day. There is a guest sitting and dining room with a bar.

USEFUL INFORMATION

OPEN: All year
CHILDREN: Welcome
CREDIT CARDS: None taken
LICENSED: Residential
ACCOMMODATION: 5 ensuite rooms
RATES From £14pp low season £17pp high season
Reduction for children by arrangement

DINING ROOM: Great breakfast
VEGETARIAN: On request
WHEELCHAIR ACCESS: Yes
GARDEN: Yes
PETS: Yes

Selected Venues in this chapter

'Die I must, but let me die drinking in an Inn!.
Hold the wine cup to my lips sparkling from the bin!.
So when the angels flutter down to take me from this sin,
Ah, God have mercy on this slot , the Cherubs will begin...

Walter de Map

Chapter Three.
Norwich: a truly 'Fine City'
Norwich and Beyond

A thousand years of history have formed **NORWICH** [Information - 01603 666071] - 'The Truly English City'. Today it's full of contrasts: the timeless peace of the Cathedral Close and the stark modernity of Anglia Square; the ancient lanes below the Castle and the futuristic vision of the Castle Mall; the market that has been held since Norman times and the host of multiple stores in St Stephens.

The skyline is dominated by three structures: the 11th century Anglican Cathedral, the 19th century Roman Catholic Cathedral and the tower of the City Hall, overlooking the Market Place. These three, in a sense, say everything: it's that old, that diverse, and that important - although not perhaps as important as it was under William the Conqueror, when it was one of the largest cities in England.

It's funny how the MARKET keeps coming to mind and yet, as it's the biggest of its kind in England - and open six days a week - maybe it's not that surprising. Size isn't everything, but when it's coupled with a unique style in bustle and banter, it makes an unforgettable package. It forms the city's focus, along with the castle and the old cathedral, within the curve of the River Wensum. Everything else has grown from this fascinating maze of narrow streets, lanes and amenities.

NORWICH CATHEDRAL

We can approach the CATHEDRAL OF THE HOLY TRINITY [Information - 01603 764385], the See of the Bishop of Norwich, from any one of three equally pleasant routes. Whether we go via the mainly Georgian square of TOMBLAND, and through the 14th century ETHELBERT GATE, or through the 15th century ERPINGHAM GATE or from the east, by the River Wensum WATERGATE, makes no odds - the impact is just as great. Greater still is the effect of the soaring space that greets you the minute you enter the door. Quite simply, the Norman nave is superb - and at least as spectacular, in its own way, as the 15th-century spire which, at 315 ft, is second only to that of Salisbury amongst British cathedrals.

Fortunately for this Guide the Cathedral is much more than an exercise in architectural history and a walk round the interior of the building offers a series of contacts with the symbols of a faith that has been reaffirmed amongst worshippers over many generations. From the roofs with their thousand decorated bosses depicting events from the Old and New Testaments, to the ancient effigy near St Luke's Chapel, the paintings and carvings and, not least, the grandeur of the utterly majestic stone, the building is full of wonders. It is as much a testimony to the enduring nature of that faith as it is to the extraordinary skills of its masons.

Let's begin our tour at the West Doors, from where we can see the soaring height of the nave to best advantage and gaze upwards for a moment or two at those amazing bosses. Opening up before us is the setting for great services and for the normal Sunday Eucharist. There are ten altars in the Cathedral, each used in turn throughout the week for Holy Communion. The Pulpitum Screen divides the building into two parts: the Nave is open to all, whereas the Choir was reserved in the early days for the Benedictine monks who were responsible for the life and worship of the Cathedral. Nowadays the situation is quite different: the Choir, where the monks once gathered seven times a day for worship, is used twice daily by the clergy, choir and laypeople for Morning and Evening prayer, to which everyone is welcome.

Between the Pulpitum Screen and the Choir is the Chapel of the Holy Innocents, dedicated on 6th January as a place of quiet prayer in which to remember the innocent victims of cruelty and persecution. The building as a whole has a cross-shaped floor plan, with the intersection beneath the tower and spire. At the centre is the Lectern, where the Bible is read, and this is in the form of a pelican feeding her young with her own blood - an established symbol of Christ. Moving east from the Lectern, we come to the Tomb of the Founder Bishop Herbert de Losinga, who began the work on the building in 1096. At the top of the steps behind the High Altar is the Bishop's Throne. Beneath the wooden seat are two sections of carved stone which once formed the sides of an earlier throne brought to the Cathedral from another site, and these are at least 1200 years old.

If we walk back to the Crossing from the Tomb of the Founder and turn right into the North Transept we come to St Andrew's Chapel which has a fine 15th century painted panel behind its altar. From there we need to return again to the centre stalls and walk round the Ambulatory to the Reliquary Arch. The relics of the saints were kept here up to the Reformation but nowadays it houses an exhibition of silver from churches around the Diocese. All entry donations are given to charitable causes.

The Jesus Chapel, to the north east of the Bishop's Throne, is decorated with the kind of wall painting which may once have covered most of the interior of the building. The Chapel's Norman altar is an original. At the easternmost end of the Cathedral is St Savior's Chapel, which is dedicated to Christ as the Saviour of mankind. The original chapel, which was horseshoe shaped, was demolished in the 13th century but the Lady Chapel which replaced it fell down in the 17th century. The present chapel dates from this century and is a memorial to men of the Royal Norfolk Regiment who were killed on active service.

On our left as we leave the memorial is the ancient effigy which we've mentioned already and beyond it is St Luke's Chapel, which serves as the parish church for the people of the close. The magnificent front, carved with the Seven Sacraments, came from the church of St Mary in the Marsh when it was destroyed in the 16th century. The greatest art treasure of the Cathedral is located here: the altarpiece known as the Despenser Reredos, after the Bishop who commissioned it in the 14th century. The next Chapel, of Our Lady of Pity, was named after its donor, the monk Bauchon. It has a modern statue of the Virgin Mary by John Skelton, a painting by John Opie of Christ's Presentation in the Temple and a modern stained glass window depicting Benedictine saints. There is also a lovely 15th century reredos, by Martin Schwartz, of the Adoration of the Wise Men. The last Chapel is St Catherine's, in the South Transept. It has a glass door created in 1989 by Peace and Scott and is reserved for quiet prayer.

There are two areas outside the main building which should be visited, while we're here. Beyond the Prior's Door are the Cloisters, which are the largest in England. They were the hub of monastic life as the refectory, dormitory, infirmary and guest buildings all lead off from them and are linked by them to the body of the Cathedral. The library, exhibition area and choir rooms are housed above them today.

The Cathedral Close is also the largest space of its kind in the country. Here the community remembers the 'local hero', with a statue of Nelson near the King Edward VI School where he was once a pupil. More sombrely, nurse Edith Cavell, executed by the Germans in 1916 for helping Allied prisoners escape from Brussels, is buried near the South Door. Finally, a happier memory rests in the commemoration each year, on May 8th, of the 15th-century mystic Juliana of Norwich author of the first book in English to be written by a woman.

R.C. CATHEDRAL

Incidentally, if you found Holy Trinity impressive, it's worth crossing the City to the top of EARLHAM ROAD to spend time in its Roman Catholic counterpart, the CATHEDRAL OF ST JOHN THE BAPTIST [Information - 01603 624615]. On arrival, the first impression is reminiscent of a younger, scaled down Notre Dame. Inside, too, it loses little to its older neighbour. It may be smaller, but is in no way less arresting, from its glass to its powerful stonework and the Cathedral stands as a truly splendid 'Thanks offering to God', which was the declared intention of its benefactor, Henry Fitzalan Howard, 15th Duke of Norfolk.

In giving to the people of Norwich what was, at the outset, the largest parish church in England, the Duke was also responding to what he saw as a gap in its architectural heritage. The City had a wealth of medieval buildings, covering the period from the 11th century Norman to the 15th century perpendicular styles - but there was, he felt, no worthy example of the Early English period. 'Late' being better than 'never', in the circumstances - even though that meant looking back six hundred years - he appointed as architect George Gilbert Scott, son of Sir George Gilbert Scott, who had made such a massive contribution to the Gothic revival. He was chief architect until 1897, when ill health forced him to hand on the position to his brother, J.Oldrid Scott.

The foundation stone was laid in June 1884 and work continued until 1910, when the church was finally ready for opening. On December 8th of that year there was a private blessing of the church, followed by a Pontifical High Mass, sung by the Bishop of Northampton, Dr Keating, and marked by a personal message of thanks to the Duke from the Pope. As the Bishop put in his sermon: *'This is no ordinary church. Its magnificent proportions, the majesty of its architecture, the vastness of its spaces, the endless charm of mighty pillar, soaring arch and triumphant vault, grouping and regrouping themselves to the delighted eye, recall the masterpieces of the Ages of Faith, and challenge comparison with them.'*

As the numbers of catholics in the diocese grew over the next 25 years - to the point where 2000 people attended mass on one occasion - it was hoped that the vast diocese of Northampton, of which the parish was a part, would finally be split. The time turned out to be right on 13th March 1976, when Pope Paul VI announced the re-creation of the Diocese of East Anglia, with St John's designated as its cathedral. As a pleasing touch to the occasion, when Bishop Clark was installed by Cardinal Hume in the following June, among the many dignitaries who attended was the 17th Duke of Norfolk, a cousin of the founder.

GUILDHALL

The city's other best known - or most photographed - church is ST PETER MANCROFT. It stands at the opposite end of the Market Place from the GUILDHALL which, dating from the 15th century [and much restored four hundred years later], has amongst its prized possessions a Spanish admiral's sword which Nelson gave to the City after his triumph off Cape St Vincent. St Peter's is a fine piece of Perpendicular architecture and its bells are still the same ones that pealed out in 1588 to proclaim the defeat of the Armada.

By now you must have noticed quite a few of the qualities that make Norwich unique. I wonder if you picked this out, though - the 'Truly English City' is also the 'City of Churches'! Look around, from somewhere like MOUSEHOLD HEATH - a favourite haunt of the painter John Crome - and count the spires and bell towers of the flint-built churches. There are more than thirty! Many date from the Middle Ages; the total number is greater than that in the City of London, Bristol and York put together - or in any other City in Western Europe!

While we're up on the Heath we can look across the countryside to decide if we'd like to visit any of the little communities round about, to put the finishing touch to a second [or even a third] day in the City. To the south and east are several villages and hamlets that, even today, are still too individual to be called suburbs - praise the Lord! A tour through Surlingham, Stoke Holy Cross, with its weather-boarded mill which is now a restaurant, onto Caister St Edmund could be on the cards. First, however, on a point of purely personal obsession, I think I'd choose to make a quick phone call to 01603 813145.

A call to that number should produce a booking for - wait for it - a tour round the LOTUS CAR FACTORY at **HETHEL**. For anyone who shares my obsession, missing that opportunity, having travelled this far, would be all but sacrilege. If those who *don't* share it can barely stifle their yawns, they have my undying sympathy. On the other hand, even the sad people who've never been moved to tears by the sight of a British racing green Lotus Formula One leading the way around Silverstone, must accept that finding a state-of-the-art sports car factory near a Medieval Cathedral near an Iron Age settlement near a bird sanctuary near a craft centre near some of the best coarse fishing in England adds up to one very varied package - absolutely 'something for everyone', for once [and even that's not counting all the marvellous railway journeys].

As dreams fade back to reality, there's a chance for some more fresh air at **SURLINGHAM** which will bring back memories of our first tour along the north coast. CHURCH MARSH is an RSPB reserve where a circular route of one and a half or two miles, starting from the Church, offers sightings of a variety of wildlife - especially if you make use of the reed screen and hide that have been set up along the path. The TED ELLIS TRUST [Information - 01508 538036] at WHEATFEN BROAD, is a bit more specialised. Here the two mile footpath is set in 130 acres of marsh carr and woodland and includes a stretch over the last remaining tidal marshes on the River Yare.

Remembering that word or two about angling in the last chapter, TASWOOD LAKES [Information - 01508 470919] at FLORDON are worth a mention, while we are focused on Norwich. The five lakes are set in wooded, picturesque grounds - so peaceful that even the nesting herons stay nesting! That's my idea of fishing! The waters are stocked with a large variety of freshwater species including tench, roach, rudd, perch and carp - something for everyone all through the season.

CAISTER ST EDMUND appears to have Roman links that may be even more important than those we found at Caister on Sea. Its Church is inside the remains of another walled town, Venta Icenorum. Legend says it was previously part of Boadicea's capital. Sadly, however much she got around, there is no proof that this was any more than just one more town, in her eyes.

Leaving Caister, we nip smartly through the western outskirts of the City. This is an area prone to flooding, with little to see that's as quaint as some places in our recent memory. There is another insight into the wealth of Norwich's past, though. Count the manor houses, the country homes of families who grew rich on the City's trading strength. Look at the acres and acres of lush parkland. Well, we've seen serious beaches and serious 'fun'; this stretch is all about serious *money* No wonder Norwich has built up such a host of amenities - apparently there have always been plenty of people around who could afford to foot the bill.

At the start of our circle away westwards it's worth pointing out **COSTESSY**. visit in August would draw us strongly in this direction as it's here that we'll find the NORFOLK SHOWGROUND, scene of the annual ROYAL NORFOLK SHOW [Enquiries - 01603 748931]. This spectacular event must be one of the most important of its kind in the country, and you may be quite sure that anyone who is anyone from throughout the length and breadth of Norfolk will be there.

The circle can be completed by a spell of meandering around the lanes, away from the famous bits, just looking at life. Suppose we cut across country from the point we've reached on the A47 for a mile or two, to kick-start the process. We'll go about as far as **EAST TUDDENHAM**, before swinging away north. There's a rather nice gallery and showroom out that way, off to the left, about two and a half miles past the end of the dual carriageway. It's called BRIGHT SPARKS [Enquiries - 01603 880724] and is open most of the year apart from a spell after Christmas, and the whole of September. Located in a traditional Norfolk farmhouse, set in rural surroundings, the gallery has been set up to exhibit and market the work of artist blacksmiths. Alongside this main activity, other crafts are on display which complement the ironwork - and each other.

Time to move north now, so we'll cross the main road and drive down a lane or two to **LENWADE**. My main interest here is in taking a look at the upper reaches of the River Wensum - and in seeing if the fish are feeding. Just out of curiosity - no time to fiddle with fishing tackle. The Wensum has played such an important part in the geography and history of Norwich - where we first came across it - that it's quite absorbing to compare the 'young' river with the more mature version of the lower reaches.

A touch of left turn along the A1067, towards **BAWDESWELL**, and we're into deja vu, as the FOXLEY WOOD NATURE TRAIL, run by the Norfolk Naturalists Trust, reminds us of our experiences further north still, when we were staying at Dersingham. This Reserve, however, is the largest remaining block of ancient woodland in Norfolk. Wide rides between the trees encourage butterflies and the site, which is open all year from 10am to 5pm, except Thursdays, is carpeted in wildflowers in spring and summer.

There's another 'must see' waiting in the wings about now. Across country a bit from Foxley we'll find the NORFOLK WILDLIFE PARK at **GREAT WITCHINGHAM**

[Enquiries - 01603 872274], one of the higher points of this somewhat casual mini-tour. The Park's brochure claims it is *not* a zoo - or even a wildlife park, at least not in the accepted sense. After a few minutes relaxing in this particularly beautiful stretch of countryside, you see the point only too clearly. It's as though the aim is to encourage visitors to become *acquainted* with the animals rather than just to stand and gawp at them. True, some of the 'wilder' residents have their homes in broad, spacious enclosures, but by and large the general idea is that everything and everyone just roams around the place, enjoying the friendly encounters. There's also a large carp pool, a model farm and an extensive collection of rare and unusual trees and flowering shrubs to complete the picture - not to mention the familiar gift shop and cafe facilities.

Another mellow little Norfolk town is next on our list of briefer visits. A lane or two, a trace of the B1145, and we find ourselves easing into **REEPHAM**. There is the usual variety of shops around the small MARKET PLACE, to beguile us while we add to our collections, but the chief source of interest, as so often in the County, lies within the boundaries of the churchyard, which actually accommodates three churches. Reepham is the only Norfolk town that is blessed in this way, although one church is only a ruin and the other two have adjoining chancels.

Cruising more or less due east now, we skirt **CAWSTON,** cross the B1149 and A140 and take a wander down the Bure Valley, which had to be left out of our Wroxham encounter, owing to lack of time. Nowadays, RAF COLTISHALL is a bit too busy to make this stage of the circuit to be all that idyllic, but every river has its own special brand of enchantment - and the fish get on with life, regardless of air traffic. Of course, while we're in the area we might be lucky enough to see one of the steam trains puffing down the line from Aylsham, and we could do a lot worse than pause at **BRAMPTON**, **BUXTON** or **COLTISHALL**, if only to have a final look at one of the smaller stations.

Back on the B1150, and we're heading for Norwich again, via **SPIXWORTH -** and lets not forget that the City is still the raison d'etre for this chapter. We aren't going straight back, however, because in common with most similar sized cities in England, Norwich has an airport - and this airport has the potential for a final touch of *fun,* to turn today's rather lazy touring into something really memorable.

At APEX FLIGHT TRAINING [Enquiries 01603 414341], for only a small sum we can take to the air in a Cessna light aircraft and see the view with a vengeance. Even the shortest flight takes in the City, the Cathedral, the river and the Broads - so don't forget your camera, for holiday photographs such as you've never seen. As if that isn't enough, they even let you fly the thing for a while.

Well, now we've tucked the 'trains, boats and planes' routine under our belts - and we aren't even half way through *Norfolk* yet, never mind the rest of it - we'd better get back to the City. A word about the traffic first: it's not the sheer weight of numbers that's the problem - it's the mixture of history and geography that works against the touring motorist. Over the centuries, Norwich has grown organically, with street after street curving away from the focal points of the Castle, the Market and the Cathedral like some kind of urban spiral nebula. Ironically, not only are those central points the ones we're really looking for - they are also the most difficult to get at, unless you are a local.

NORWICH CASTLE

It safest to park somewhere off, say, ST GILES STREET, ST GEORGES STREET or near the Castle and then walk. Once you're parked, it's a great deal easier because so much of the really old part has been pedestrianised - mercifully - and that's where you'll find the kind of places that make shopping in Norwich such a delight. Take a map, however: you're entering a winding, intersecting street-maze in which things sometimes aren't where they seem to be - and you'll need to get *back* to the car, at some stage. I suppose you could take a taxi, but the map is much more fun. Mind you, I imagine you could be loaded down with 'must - haves' at the end of the day. That could suggest a cab. When you're collecting your map, there are a couple of other 'tourist needs' worth having. The 'Out and About Guide' is useful for keeping up to date with what's on and where, while the 'Evening News' and 'Eastern Daily Press' give even more current news of events.

Let's start with something really spectacular, shall we? You will be amazed by the treasures to be found in the City's nine hundred year old CASTLE. This museum's variety of collections, housed in the huge keep [one of the largest in the country], is enough to hold the visitor's interest for hours on end. It includes Egyptian mummies, Celtic gold, weapons, musical instruments, the world's largest collection of teapots and Lowestoft porcelain and many works by the Norwich School of painters.

Close by the Castle, you'll find BRIDEWELL ALLEY and the BRIDEWELL MUSEUM, dedicated to displays of Norfolk life, showing traditional activities such as fishing, weaving, flint-knapping and brewing. A short stroll brings you to Norwich's unique and delightful COLEMAN'S MUSTARD SHOP. Entering its doors is just like stepping back into Victorian times- and it even has its own MUSTARD MUSEUM at the back. Amongst the city's other museums is ST PETER HUNGATE, rebuilt in the early 15th century. It avoided demolition in 1902, fortunately, and now houses a fine collection of religious arts and crafts.

This could be a good moment to do some shopping for its own sake - and old mustards are just the beginning. We're close to ELM HILL, possibly the most atmospheric street in this 'City of Atmosphere', where cobbled paving runs between pastel coloured timber-framed buildings that house enough art galleries, antique shops and music shops to satisfy all of us - and still leave some to spare. Mind you by this point you've probably discovered TOMBLAND, PRINCES STREET, a pottery, the picture-framer's, the antiquarian bookshops and the BRASS-RUBBING CENTRE and ended up destitute, which would be a shame as, in a sense, we're still only in first gear. We haven't even been to the teddy-bear shop yet!

ANTIQUE SHOP

Around this part of Norwich, we're talking arcades - as well as alleys - and among them you'll find shops that are a match for any of the exclusive premises in Europe, never mind Knightsbridge, Bond Street or Kensington (or am I getting carried away here?). Of course, the prices are a match too, but who cares? Buy a bar of soap, or some bootlaces and let your imagination go into orbit!

We're still not finished. The flesh may be weak - but curiosity is a force to be reckoned with, even so. Surely the thing to do is to put the parcels and carrier bags in the boot, take a deep breath - and have another go. Don't forget, this is meant to be a *holiday*. You won't regret it.

STRANGERS HALL is an excellent breather - and it's only a stone's throw from where you've just been stocking up. This mansion, in CHARING CROSS, was given a shot in the arm when it was opened as a museum of domestic life. It's quite astonishing how it puts things in perspective, among the various styles of decoration of its rooms and in its exhibits, from Victorian underwear to tradesmen's signs and the 1898 Panhard et Levassor that originally belonged to the Honourable C S Rolls, himself. In fact we could have a small wager if you like: a fiver says the forerunners of almost everything we bought half an hour ago are in the Hall, somewhere (and I'm only just joking)! Strangers Hall is a 'must see.'

You won't have to go far to realise that Norwich is also the arts and entertainment capital of East Anglia. There are so many galleries, theatres and concert halls, so many minor events and attractions, that you can fill every evening of your stay as easily as the days, from just a quick flick through the local paper. For me the MADDERMARKET THEATRE [Information - 01603 620917] tops the bill. Its fame is international, for the quality of the productions staged in the uniquely intimate setting of its replica Elizabethan auditorium. There is a year-long programme which includes touring companies, celebrity nights and local professional presentations of the work of major British and international playwrights. The theatre is in ST JOHN'S ALLEY, signposted from the Market Square.

Round the corner, in a medieval merchant's house on St Andrew's Street is another of the nation's finest: CINEMA CITY [Information - 01603 622047], renowned as an art-house cinema. Throughout the year it shows a selection of British and American independents, foreign language and classic repertory films. Since it also offers excellent cafe, bar and restaurant facilities, it's ideal for 'making an evening of it'.

Amongst all the high profile presentations we must include THE SAINSBURY CENTRE FOR THE VISUAL ARTS [Information - 01603 593199] and the NORWICH GALLERY [Information - 01603 610561]. Fifteen minutes from the heart of the old City, the Robert and Lisa Sainsbury Collection is housed in a building at the University of East Anglia designed by Norman Foster. The contemporary works exhibited are another example of the familiar Norfolk contrast as they are worlds apart from the 14th century works in the Cathedral or the Cotmans and Cromes in the Castle that we saw only hours ago. And yet they are part of the pattern, of the kaleidoscope of images that have flooded our minds since we first set out. The Centre also displays non-Western art and runs a full programme of temporary exhibitions. It is open from 11am to 5pm, Tuesdays to Sundays.

Back to town, back to ST GEORGE'S STREET - and we are looking for the ART SCHOOL, which houses the Norwich Gallery. From July to September it hosts 'EAST INTERNATIONAL', [which also stages exhibitions at the Sainsbury and at the Norwich School of Art and Design]. 'East' is an annual exhibition of art by contemporary artists from around the world. As such, it is the largest presentation of its kind in Britain.

One more touch of culture - or perhaps three - before it's 'last-blast-at-the-shops' time. Culture? That depends on the individual I suppose, but they do say that, while THE WATERFRONT, with its gigs and club nights - whatever they are - is a bit racy for us, there are other clubs for the more discerning that are really quite pleasant, and definitely part of the local culture. The 'Norwich Arts and Entertainment Map' will doubtless put you in the picture - if you're up to it! Meanwhile, we shouldn't forget the smaller, more informal attractions of the NORWICH ART CENTRE [Information - 01603 660352] and the KING OF HEARTS [Information - 01603 766129]. The Centre is a small, lively music venue which also hosts comedy and theatre. The King of Hearts, a historic building in the centre of the City, presents exhibitions as well as musical and literary events, with light meals on the side, in the coffee shop or courtyard.

Have we left the brightest and best till last? Only you can judge - but you'll need to be in Norwich in October if you want to see and hear everything. At that time, the annual NORFOLK AND NORWICH FESTIVAL will arrive again, with a superb line-up of major symphony orchestras, ensembles, quartets, jazz and blues groups, dance bands, cabaret and other presentations. It's multimedia, international - and the biggest arts extravaganza of the year for the region. In fact, it's the oldest single city festival in Britain, dating from the late 18th century - and the scale is just as impressive, with more than one hundred and twenty events spread over the twelve days. Ticket and other enquiries should be made to the Ticket Shop at the Guildhall [01603 764764].Again on a smaller scale, Norwich also welcomes the LORD MAYOR'S WEEKEND CELEBRATIONS. These bring carnival time to the City centre, with floats, music and a grand firework finale to round it all off.

The last shopping, the only just remembered gift or souvenir, can often be tracked down among the wealth of specialist shops to be found elsewhere in, say, ST GILES, ST BENEDICTS, LONDON STREET, BEDFORD STREET or MAGDALEN STREET. These are a pleasure to discover in their own right, especially when seen as a colourful backcloth to the images we have only just taken in. Truly finally, if you really need *more* - and can live with your obsession - you will find all the major high street chain stores represented here, along with the local variety - Norwich's own department stores.

I think I'll take pity on you at this stage - it wears me out just thinking about all you've been through - and you must be on your knees. So, a random thought to ease the mind: there must be one or two readers who've heard of 'Norwich City'. The football team? No, of course you don't *follow* them - but you know the name. And you know the nickname: 'The Canaries'? In case you've ever wondered why, [I mean, it doesn't have quite the cutting edge of 'The Gunners, 'Spurs', 'The Hammers' - or even 'United' or 'The Dons', does it?] the story goes this way: when Dutch weavers settled in Norwich in the 16th century, it's said they brought their pet canaries along too. Well, even the Dutch wouldn't leave them behind! Having learnt land reclamation and architecture from the immigrants, the locals took to their pets as well and canary breeding became a hobby in the area. It was so successful that, by the eighteenth-century, the 'Norwich Canary' was recognised as a distinct breed, prized for its song and its colour. Hence 'City's' nickname - but can they *sing*? That's the question.

ABBEY HOTEL
16 Stracey Road
Off Thorpe Road
Norwich
Norfolk
NR1 1EZ

Tel: 01603 612915

1 Crown Commended EATB

The breakfasts in this comfortable hotel, in the centre of Norwich, have been described by International visitors as second to none - you only have to read the Visitors Book to have this confirmed. That is only one reason why one should stay in the Abbey Hotel, owned by Stephanie East who runs it with the help of her friendly, efficient staff. It is a warm, welcoming establishment where it is easy to relax and unwind after a day's exploration of Norwich, which has a tremendous history and will delight visitors with its superb Cathedral, fascinating old streets and a great shopping centre. Originally The Abbey Hotel was a large Victorian Town House with gracious, high ceiling rooms and plenty of light. The conversion has been carefully done and many of the original features retained. Stephanie has worked hard not to lose the Victorian ambience but at the same time she has also been aware of the needs of the modern day traveller.

Within the house there is an attractive dining room where you will be served a most enjoyable breakfast In the evening this room is available to guests who may wish to relax and watch television, although each bedroom is fitted with a colour set. For the comfort of all our guests this has been designated as a non-smoking room. There are seven prettily decorated bedrooms in which you may smoke, two of which are ensuite - one twin bedded and one family room, the remaining five rooms are standard rooms consisting of three singles, one twin-bedded and one family room. Stephanie does not serve evening meals but Norwich is full of good eateries to suit everyone's pocket and taste. Stephanie will happily recommend and direct you.

Norwich, one of the most complete medieval cities in England, is a wonderful base for anyone wanting to enjoy firstly the culture of the city and secondly the Norfolk Broads which are on its doorstep. Here you will find many outdoor pursuits including fishing, bird-watching, cycling and walking. A few minutes walk away from the hotel is Mousehold Heath, popular with walkers, orienteers and ramblers.

USEFUL INFORMATION

OPEN: All year. Xmas excepted   DINING ROOM: Renowned for its
CHILDREN: Over 2 years   great breakfast
CREDIT CARDS: None taken   VEGETARIAN: All diets with notice
LICENSED: No   WHEELCHAIR ACCESS: No
ACCOMMODATION: 7 rooms, 2 ensuite   PETS: No
RATES: From £19 pp standard B&B - £25 pp ensuite B&B

ADLARD'S
70 Upper St Giles Street
Norwich
NR2 1AB

Tel: 01603 633522

For the uninitiated the unobtrusive green-painted frontage of Adlard's would give no idea of the gastronomic experience to be found inside. Here David Adlard and his Head Chef Aiden Byrne, continue to prove that the food here is second to none. David and Aiden are accomplished chefs who base their cooking on classical French foundations with chef's licence which takes their inspired cooking into new realms. It is wise not to be in a hurry when you lunch or dine here for it would be the height of bad manners, if not sheer stupidity, not to give yourself time to appreciate the food set before you. How about a starter of soft boiled Quails' eggs on a mushroom tartlet draped with hollandaise and topped with diced Smoked Salmon and Chives?

Follow that with a Scallop mousse topped with Sea Bass and moistened with Fennel Nage with Mussels and Tomato Concasse. Finally, freshly cooked Pear Charlotte with Calvados ice, and you have had a delicious, well balanced lunch and not for one moment will you ever doubt it was value for money. If all this is too much for you at lunchtime you are perfectly welcome just to have one course. Dinner beggars description. Perhaps a starter of Red Mullet and Aubergine Puree with Bouillabaise Sauce followed by Guinea Fowl and Celeriac puree and Wild Mushrooms. For the sweet, Prune and Armagnac Souffle with Prune Ice-Cream or Tangerine Cheesecake Mousse with Caramelised Tangerine. These suggestions are as nothing to the rest of the menu which changes regularly.

After dinner you will find the coffee superb and acknowledge that the wine list is way above the ordinary. Here you will find 'bin beginnings' a wealth of halves and a full contingent of high-quality bottles from around the world. David Adlard never hides his light under a bushel and he is not ashamed of singing the praises of his house wines which, in his words, "are many streets ahead of 'plonk".

Right in the heart of historic Norwich, Adlard's should be the Mecca for any visitor as it is for the many regular afficionados.

USEFUL INFORMATION

OPEN; Lunch; Tuesday-Saturday
Dinner: Monday-Saturday. Closed Sunday
CHILDREN; Welcome
CREDIT CARDS; All major cards

RESTAURANT; Glorious food
VEGETARIAN; Always a choice
DISABLED ACCESS; Yes. Not to toilets
SMOKING; After the main course

THE ALMOND TREE HOTEL & RESTAURANT
441 Dereham Road
Costessey
Norwich
Norfolk
NR5 0SG

Tel: 01603 748798 Fax: 01603 749114
Internet cfoster@almondtree u-net.com

The Almond Tree Hotel is easily found on the main A1074 just a mile inside the A47 with its junction to the Longwater estate. An ideal situation for anyone who wants to discover the hidden secrets of Norwich, Norfolk and indeed, East Anglia. The beautiful and historic City of Norwich with its magnificent Cathedral is just ten minutes from the hotel.

Chris and Caroline Foster with the help of Caroline's mother, created this delightful hotel from a chalet bungalow and opened it complete with its excellent restaurant in 1987. It has never looked back and is one of the most popular hotels in the area. Each of the eight bedrooms has been individually designed and decorated and has ensuite facilities, direct dial telephone, colour teletext television and radio. A generously supplied hostess tray together with a room service menu completes the picture. The honeymoon suite boasts a sumptuous draped four poster bed and here, as everywhere in the hotel, the attention to detail is apparent. For those who need it there is a laundry service. Business men can use the fax and photocopying facility. It is an ideal venue for small conferences and meetings of up to twenty four people with a full range of equipment available.

The Restaurant, which is open to non-residents is one of the most restful places imaginable. Furnished elegantly and with a colour scheme that enhances the intimacy. The International theme of the menu, which is changed weekly, provides some exciting dishes. There are always six different starters followed by a delicious selection of main courses and home-made desserts which will tempt even the most strong-willed. The wine list is extensive, with wines from all around the world.

The immaculate and manicured gardens with an attractive terrace are lit by floodlights in the trees weaving a delicate and romantic pattern. Here one can sit at night, possibly enjoying a barbecue. It is equally attractive in the daytime and has proved very popular for private functions, weddings, birthdays and other occasions. Two night weekend-breaks, which must include Saturday, are on offer subject to availability. An oasis of comfort in a busy City, is the best way I would describe this hotel, having tried many others in Norwich, considerably more expensive.

USEFUL INFORMATION

OPEN: All year
CHILDREN: Welcome Wonderful food
CREDIT CARDS: All major cards
LICENSED: Full on. Fine wines
ACCOMMODATION: 8 ensuite rooms
RATES: High Season £45.00 sharing
£25.00 single supplement

RESTAURANT: International menu

BAR FOOD: Available lunch & evening
VEGETARIAN: Choices available
GARDEN: Yes & terrace. BBQ
WHEELCHAIR ACCESS: Yes + toilets

THE AQUARIUM
22 Tombland
Norwich
NR31 1RF

Tel:01603 630090 Fax: 01603 612195
Internet: Wildebeest:Arms@Virgin:Net

The Aquarium is one of Norwich's most exciting and individual newcomers, and the newest addition to a small group of privately owned bars and restaurants which includes the very highly acclaimed Wildebeest Arms. It is situated in the most picturesque part of the city, close to the magnificent Cathedral and within five minutes walk of the shops.

The Aquarium attracts a wide range of people, it has brought something totally different into the city incorporating an exciting, varied and in-expensive menu with a very unique, refreshing ambience. The overall atmosphere is one of sophistication which is enhanced by the aqua-green velvet chairs and bar, not forgetting the two very large, upright Aquaria.

At 5.00pm, Monday to Friday there is a 'Bolli Hour' with Champagne at half price and a bar menu is available day and evening. At lunch-times a special 'lunch menu' is on offer, priced at £10.50 for two courses. The main menu offers constantly changing, innovative dishes, together with daily specials, available every evening. Every dish is perfectly prepared, cooked and presented by a very talented, team of young chefs and can be seen from the open kitchen in one of the dining areas.

The restaurant itself is situated downstairs with smoking and non smoking rooms to either side of the entrance hall and the bar is unusually situated upstairs with wonderful large windows positioned to the front of the building, giving you views over the city. There is a side room adjoining the bar that is available for private parties and functions.

Examples of dishes available: A start of seared marinated wafers of Monkfish with cumin, coriander, lime, olive oil and tabbouleh. A main course of breast of chicken wrapped in pancetta with refried black beans, guacamole, tomato salsa and sour cream.

USEFUL INFORMATION

OPEN: Rest: Mon-Sat:12-2pm & 7-10pm
Bar:11.30-3pm & 5-11pm
CHILDREN: Yes (Restaurant only)
CREDIT CARDS: Master/Visa/Amex/Switch
LICENSED: Yes
WHEELCHAIR ACCESS: Yes

RESTAURANT; Wide selection
with emphasis on fresh fish and seafood
VEGETARIAN: Dishes available
GARDEN: No. Outside Terrace seating
to front of building. Weather permitting
PETS: No

THE BEECHES HOTEL & VICTORIAN GARDENS
4-6 Earlham Road
Norwich
Norfolk
NR2 3DB

Tel:01603 621167
Fax: 01603 620151
beeches. hotel.co.uk

3 Crown
Highly Commended.
AA 2**

Two listed and sympathetically restored Victorian houses together with a new annexe make up this enchanting hotel which stands in three acres of tranquil wooded grounds less than ten minutes stroll from the centre of Norwich. No one could walk through the front door and not recognise the love and care which has been applied to give it a relaxed and informal ambience. Each of the twenty seven attractive en-suite bedrooms has received an individual design; some are reserved for non-smokers, some overlook the famous Plantation Garden, designed in the mid 1800's by Henry Trevor. Sadly over the years the garden became neglected as the house passed through various owners. In 1980 the house and its 'secret garden' were rediscovered. Today it is restored to much of its former glory and guests are free to wander through the delights of this important reminder of our Victorian heritage, with its ornate Gothic fountain and Italianate terrace.

The restaurant offers an interesting menu with an Italian bias but using fresh local produce and cooked to order at modest prices. The restaurant is open to non-residents. A small conference room seats up to thirty people. Pets are not permitted in the hotel. A pearl in the heart of historic Norwich', and it is featured on the cover of this guide.

USEFUL INFORMATION

OPEN: 7am-10pm Closed Xmas
CHILDREN: High chairs. Cots
CREDIT CARDS: All major cards
LICENSED: Hotel & Restaurant
ACCOMMODATION: 27 ensuite rooms
RATES: From £65 dbl. & £50sgl Special breaks
GARDEN: Superb

RESTAURANT: Italian bias, fresh produce, reasonable prices
BAR FOOD: Not applicable
VEGETARIAN: Two dishes daily
WHEELCHAIR ACCESS: One special double room
PETS: No

DUNSTON HALL HOTEL & COUNTRY CLUB
Ipswich Road
Norwich
Norfolk
NR14 8PQ

Tel: 01508 470444
Fax: 01508 471499
Four Star.

Dunston Hall Hotel is a fine example of what careful and loving restoration can do to an old building dating back to 1859. Until 1992 it had a chequered history but in the hands of the present owners it has blossomed and is a delightful place to stay. All the gracious rooms have been beautifully furnished and decorated with a mixture of antique and modern marrying quite happily. The well trained staff do everything in their power to ensure that guests have a contented and memorable stay.

Within the hotel, the bedrooms are all ensuite and boast television, a hostess tray and many other little touches to add to your comfort. In the La Fontaine Restaurant, elegantly decorated and furnished with immaculate table linen, napery, gleaming silver and sparkling glass, the service is quiet and unobtrusive allowing you time to enjoy the delicious food at your leisure. The menu, prepared by talented chefs is imaginative and innovative with a good selection of starters and perfectly cooked dishes such as paupiette of pork - pork fillet rolled and filled with apricots and hazelnuts enhance with a port jus or a succulent saddle of English lamb. Fish and seafood also grace the menu with Dover sole a firm favourite or, as a treat, the superb fresh Sheringham lobster. For lovers of a good steak, the meat is tender and cooked to your requirements. Delectable desserts and a selection of English and Continental cheeses completes the meal. The wine list reflects the excellence of the food and offers wines from around the world. Dunston Hall is also well known for its superb Carvery and Grill Restaurant. If you prefer to eat in the Lounge Bar, the menu is simpler, wide ranging and excellent value for money. Here you may also enjoy morning coffee and afternoon tea.

Golf enthusiasts will be pleased with the course here and there are many sporting facilities offered in the Country Club. Whether you stay here because you have business in Norwich or have come to relax, Dunston Hall is perfectly situated no distance from the centre of historic Norwich with its magnificent Cathedral, its Castle and streets full of history.

USEFUL INFORMATION

OPEN: All year
CHILDREN: Welcome
CREDIT CARDS: All major cards
LICENSED: Full On
ACCOMMODATION: All ensuite rooms
RATES: Dbl. £89 prpn. Single £79.
Children sharing with adults £10 supp.
Breakfast is available as a separate cost.

RESTAURANT: La Fontaine
& Dunston Hall Carvery Rest
BAR FOOD: Lounge Bar Menu
including Morning Coffee &
Afternoon Tea

EARLHAM GUEST HOUSE
147 Earlham Road
Norwich
Norfolk
NR2 3RG

Tel/Fax: 01603 454169

AAQQQ Recommended
ETB 2 Crowns Commended

This elegant Victorian Guest House is a few minutes by bus or car to the centre of Norwich, a city just waiting to show off all its treasures to the first time visitor and to renew its acquaintance with those who have been before and found one visit simply not enough to absorb all it has to offer. If you prefer a gentle stroll into town, it will take you about twenty minutes. Earlham Guest House which provides one of the best breakfasts in Norwich, does not do evening meals but there are good, moderately priced eating places within a few minutes walk. It is a perfect place for the businessman or tourist to stay. Sufficiently far from the hustle and bustle of the centre but by no means isolated.

Susan and Derek Wright are the owners of this attractive house. They came here with their young son in 1991 and set about refurbishing Earlham Guest House with the objective of making it the sort of place that they themselves would like to stay. With great care and attention to detail and without destroying any of the Victorian airiness of the rooms, they have decorated with great taste, furnished with a style in keeping with the house and made the five twin or double bedrooms and two singles, some ensuite and some with king size beds, extremely comfortable in a non-smoking environment. Every room has colour television and a hostess tray with tea, coffee and chocolate drink. You will be served breakfast in a comfortable breakfast room. The Earlhams aim to provide quality foods and choices to suit all tastes. There is a range of cereals, a plentiful supply of toast and preserves, piping hot tea, freshly made coffee and a full English breakfast. A Continental meal is available if preferred. Vegetarian foods are also freshly served to order. You are very welcome to make use of the pretty patio garden and the small residential lounge. It is a friendly house, fully central heated and the welcome is genuine.

USEFUL INFORMATION

OPEN: All year except 6 nights at Christmas
CHILDREN: Welcome class breakfast.
CREDIT CARDS: All major cards
LICENSED: No
ACCOMMODATION: 5 rooms dbl. or tw 2 sgl
RATES: Sgl £21pp B&B Dbl. £38,50 B&B
Reductions for over 2 nights inc. a Saturday
excluding Public Holidays

BREAKFAST ROOM: First
No evening meal
VEGETARIAN: Yes
WHEELCHAIR ACCESS: No
GARDEN: Patio PETS: No

THE GEORGIAN HOUSE HOTEL
32-34 Unthank Road
Norwich
Norfolk
NR2 2RB

Tel: 01603 615655 Fax: 01603 765689

This distinguished early Victorian hotel stands a little back from one of the busy roads leading in to the centre of Norwich. It is literally a few minutes walk and you are in the heart of the shopping centre and close to the Cathedral. This makes The Georgian House one of the most popular hotels for visitors and people on business, n the whole of Norwich. It is large enough with twenty seven bedrooms to have the stature of an hotel but at the same time retains a feeling of a comfortable family home. Dee and Gerry Goodwin are the owners and their philosophy on the running of hotels is that high standards in every department together with a happy atmosphere and a warm welcome provide the ingredients for their guests being totally content. The hotel is run with a degree of professionalism that is impressive but at the same time they manage to make it appear informal. It is no wonder that many of their guests are regular visitors who in turn recommend it to others.

There are sixteen double bedrooms, eight single rooms and three spacious family rooms, some of which are designated non-smoking rooms. All the rooms are ensuite, attractively furnished in a modern style with comfortable beds and soft colour fabrics and decor. Each room has colour television, direct dial telephone, hairdryer and a generously supplied hospitality tray. Breakfast is a very satisfying meal with several choices including both a full English or a Continental. Vegetarians and Special diets are catered for. During the day it is possible to get bar snacks and at night dinner is served in the pretty dining room where the tables are nicely appointed and glisten with sparkling glass and well polished silver. The chef is talented and produces an eclectic mixture of English and French dishes; something to suit every palate. The wine list is comprehensive and well chosen with wines from all around the world, and at sensible prices.

Norwich has so much to offer the visitor that many people never get further away than the centre. The cathedral is magnificent and will provide hours of pleasure to those who love beauty and architecture. The narrow streets like Elm Hill with its attractive shops and houses, the pedestrianised shopping centre, Norwich Castle and of course 'The Canaries' Norwich's much loved football team, the Theatre, are all there for your entertainment and pleasure. If you want to go further afield then The Broads are within five miles, Gt. Yarmouth is about twenty miles. You can go ballooning - a rare experience in which to take a bird's eye view of the city, you can fish, there are golf courses and other sporting facilities.

USEFUL INFORMATION

OPEN: All year
CHILDREN: Welcome
CREDIT CARDS: All major cards
LICENSED: Full On
ACCOMMODATION: 27 ensuite rooms
RATES: From £42.50sgl & £55 dbl.
Weekend breaks £72.50

RESTAURANT: Excellent food
English with a French influence
BAR FOOD: Snacks
VEGETARIAN: Yes
WHEELCHAIR ACCESS: No
GARDEN: Yes, at the rear.
PETS: No

ITTERINGHAM MILL
Restaurant with Rooms
Itteringham,
Norwich, Norfolk

Tel: 01263 587688

Believe it or not you can see the Mill Race through the floor of this fascinating restaurant where you can also stay if you wish. Itteringham Mill was built in 1620 and indeed there is a mention of a Mill at Itteringham in the Doomsday Book. The Mill was still being used as a working Mill within living memory and was converted by Lord Walpole into a private house. During the Second World War flying officers from the nearby base at Mastlake were billeted at the Mill, the most famous of whom was the celebrated fighter pilot, Johnny Johnson, who we understand spent the night before his wedding at the Mill and who mentions Itteringham Mill in his autobiography. After the war Itteringham Mill had another famous occupier, Sir Carol Reid, who directed the film "The Third Man". We understand that his third son was born here and that somewhere in the garden is a stone engraved with the son's name and "The Third Man"!

Bryan and Lilian Webster with their daughters acquired the mill a few years ago and have turned it into a charming, welcoming restaurant in which the very reasonably priced menus change every day. Fresh produce is all important and that plays a significant part in what is available every day. It is difficult when one sees how efficiently and professionally Itteringham Mill is run, that Bryan and Lilian started it almost as a hobby!.

If you would like to stay in this welcoming happy home, there are five, beautifully appointed ensuite bedrooms each with television and tea/coffee making facilities. You will rapidly be absorbed into the lifestyle of this unusual venue and for sure you will go away unwillingly, looking forward to the opportunity to return.

USEFUL INFORMATION

OPEN; Restaurant; Wed-Sunday
CHILDREN; Welcome Non-smoking
CREDIT CARDS; Visa/Master/Diners/Switch
LICENSED; Yes
ACCOMMODATION; 5 ensuite rooms
RATES: From £40 double

RESTAURANT; Delicious food

VEGETARIAN; Catered for
DISABLED ACCESS; Yes + toilets
GARDEN; Yes for eating & drinking .
PETS; Not indoors
NON SMOKING: Throughout.

THE KINGS HEAD
Harts Lane, Bawburgh,
Norfolk, Norwich NR9 3LS

Tel: 01603 744977
Fax: 01603 744990

Good Pub Guide

There is a wonderful story told about The Kings Head in the 1750s when a Revenue officer came into the bar one day for a tankard of ale for which he was charged one penny. Believe it or not the landlord was summonsed for overcharging the man because the price should have been three farthings. The landlord suffered the heavy fine of five shillings! We cannot promise you that the prices are that low today but the inn is certainly value for money and you most definitely will not be overcharged. The Kings Head is only four miles from the centre of Norwich and just off the southern bypass but it can offer you five golf courses nearby, ten pin bowling, fishing, walking and its own four court Squash Club. The village of Bawburgh is truly rural and dates back to 800BC.

Owned and run by mother and son, Pamela and Anton Wimmer who hail from New Zealand, The Kings Head, which has a river side location, is a traditional 17th century inn complete with beams, an inglelook fireplace, roaring log fires and a warm welcoming atmosphere. You will not find gaming machines or juke boxes here, just genuine hospitality and the opportunity to enjoy your drink and food accompanied by good conversation. It is a recipe that works. People come out from Norwich regularly and it is a constant attraction to visitors. In the summer months you can take your drinks outside either to the pretty courtyard or to the beer garden.

The Wimmers enjoy good food and they make sure that the menu at the Kings Head is always exciting and innovative but never ignoring the fact that some people like simple, old-fashioned fare. They are fortunate in having a skilled French chef who with his brigade delights in providing excellent food for both the restaurant and the bars. The restaurant itself is non-smoking but you may smoke in the restaurant part of the bar, The Squash club is a very popular part of the Kings Head closely followed by the fact that Aromatherapy, Reflexology and Massage are also available. Many Norwich firms have found the Conference facilities for up to twenty five people very useful.

USEFUL INFORMATION

OPEN: 10.30am-11pm	RESTAURANT: Good, innovative food
CHILDREN: Welcome	BAR FOOD: Wide range
CREDIT CARDS: All major cards	VEGETARIAN: Catered for
LICENSED: Full On	DISABLED ACCESS: Yes. No toilets
PETS: Yes	GARDEN: Yes. Riverside

SQUASH CLUB: 4 courts Out door bowls. Courtyard. Beer garden

THE OLD INN
Marsham Road
Brampton
Norwich
Norfolk
NR10 5HN

Tel: 01603 279438

Dorothy and Rodney Galer are the proud owners of this charming house which is mainly Georgian although parts date back much earlier. Do not be fooled by the name. It was once the village pub but today is strictly a private residence into which the Galers are happy to welcome visitors. Brampton is steeped in history. Set in the Bure Valley it dates from Roman times and has a strong connection with the Sewell family of 'Black Beauty' fame. It has a round tower 11th century church.

The Bure Valley Narrow Gauge Railway stops at the village. Public footpaths and a riverside walk make it a splendid area for ramblers. The coast and the Norfolk Broads are not far off. Several historic houses are also within reach including Blickling and Felbrigg plus Redwings Horse Sanctuary. The old market town of Aylsham has a fascinating market and auction on Mondays. The Old Inn has three centrally heated, well appointed bedrooms complete with hostess trays. Not ensuite, but the public bathroom has plenty of hot water and a separate shower. There is a television Lounge and there is plentiful off road parking. Breakfast, served in the sunny Breakfast Room, is a full English meal with choices or a Continental breakfast if preferred.

USEFUL INFORMATION

OPEN: 1st January-30th November
CHILDREN: Welcome
CREDIT CARDS: None taken
LICENSED: No
ACCOMMODATION: 3 rooms not ensuite
RATES: From £16pp B&B

BREAKFAST ROOM: Traditional
English Breakfast
VEGETARIAN: Upon request
WHEELCHAIR ACCESS: No
GARDEN: Yes
PETS: No

THE QUEENS HEAD
High Street,
Foulsham
Dereham,
Norfolk
NR20 5AD

Tel: 01362 683339

Foulsham is an attractive place in its own right with a fine market place rebuilt after a devastating fire in 1771 and the village's imposing Georgian houses are dominated by the 15th century tower of Holy Innocents' Church. At its focal point is The Queens Head dating back in parts to the 17th century. The atmosphere is wonderful, full of character and somewhere that delights both locals who use its bars regularly and visitors who arrive as strangers and depart as friends. The owners Colin Rowe and his partner Dorothy Deadman have been at The Queens Head for fifteen years and have spent that time in making it a truly outstanding establishment. With great care and attention to detail they renovated skilfully ensuring that the old features were retained. The interior is charming with low beams, feature fireplaces and a pleasant clutter of antiques and knickknacks giving it a cosy and intriguing atmosphere.

In addition to the well kept ale the food is excellent. Everything is cooked using fresh local produce in a menu which has something for everyone. If you do not want a full meal then the range of freshly cut and well-filled sandwiches will tempt you. Steaks are a very popular item on the menu. The meat is tasty and tender and will be cooked whichever way you like it. Potty Meals (served in a pot) are also consistently popular. There are always Daily Specials and some interesting vegetarian dishes such as a tasty cauliflower cheese with a dash of white wine. Children have their own menu and whatever your choice you will find it value for money.

The large garden is always popular in good weather especially with children who are enchanted to see buxom turkeys trotting around. There is a bowling green for the grown ups, and every May Day, the pub plays host to an annual *Fun Run* - not to be missed! Recently Colin and Dorothy have refurbished an old stable block and made a super function room. The Queens Head is a true village pub, somewhere to be enjoyed by everyone.

USEFUL INFORMATION

OPEN: Normal pub hours	DINING ROOM: Wide range
CHILDREN: Welcome	BAR FOOD: Great choice
CREDIT CARDS: All major cards	VEGETARIAN: Dishes daily
LICENSED: Full On	WHEELCHAIR ACCESS: No
ACCOMMODATION: Not applicable	PETS: Yes

SPIXWORTH MOTEL
Crostwick Lane
Spixworth
Norwich
Norfolk NR10 3NQ

Tel: 01603 898288
Fax: 01603 897617

ETB 3 Crowns Commended
Business Travellers Research
4 Star Recommended

Just two miles outside Norwich off the B1150 North Walsham Road and conveniently set for those on holiday or business in this part of Norfolk, Spixworth Motel with its Restaurant and Bar is an ideal place in which to stay. The Norfolk Broads and Redwings Horse and Donkey Sanctuary are just down the road, the Norfolk coast from Cromer to Gt.Yarmouth, no more than twenty miles distance and the historic centre of Norwich City four and a half miles. The Motel, now more a Hotel, with popular Restaurant and Bar is family run with particular attention to cleanliness and comfort with quality beds and rooms well heated in winter. The evening restaurant with its extensive menu has something to tempt even the fussiest taste buds. A well stocked bar, adjacent to the restaurant, a favourite meeting place and always a great atmosphere.

The twenty two bedrooms at the Motel are all shower and WC ensuite, comfortably furnished and mostly on the ground floor. Each room has satellite television, direct dial phones and tea and coffee making facilities. There are a number deluxe rooms, bath and shower ensuite, king size bedded and larger screen teletext television. Many of the rooms are suitably equipped for family occupancy. The fact that most bedrooms, the restaurant and the bar are on the ground floor makes it easy for the disabled.

Leisure Guests return year after year and 'all year round' Company users tend to make the Spixworth Motel their base when in the Norfolk area. Spixworth is a village of some 1,500 dwellings and a range of shops and facilities with the Motel on the eastern green belt edge of the village and the Motel's own four acre meadow. There is no problem with parking in the large forty space car park.

You will find the Spixworth Motel just two miles North of Norwich off the B1150 North Walsham/Coltishall Road, a roundabout exit off the A140/A1042 ring road. The Motel runs a minicab service for the convenience of Guests.

USEFUL INFORMATION

OPEN: All year. Rest:6.30-9pm
CHILDREN: Welcome
CREDIT CARDS: All major cards
LICENSED: Residential & Restaurant
ACCOMMODATION: 22 ensuite rooms
RATES: B&B per room per night
£32.50-£47.50 with full English breakfast

RESTAURANT: Extensive menu
BAR FOOD: Always a choice
VEGETARIAN: Catered for
DISABLED: No special facilities
but rooms, restaurant, bar on ground floor
PETS: By prior arrangement

SPROWSTON MANOR HOTEL
Sprowston Park
Wroxham Road
Norwich
Norfolk
NR7 8RP

Tel:01603 410871
Fax: 01603 423911

AA****RAC

Sprowston Manor Hotel, one of the finest in East Anglia, incorporates La Fontana Health Spa and is a sister hotel to the prestigious Churchgate Manor at Old Harlow and to Belstead Brook Manor in Ipswich. The four star hotel is an elegant Victorian building set in ten acres of country parkland adjacent to the Sprowston Park Golf Course. It was originally the manor house of the Gurney family who had much to do with the fortunes of Barclays Bank. Every effort has been made to keep as much of the original features as possible and this is evident as you wander through the rooms and see the high ceiling rooms with their ornate plaster work. Throughout the hotel the furnishings are both charming and perfect for the setting. There are ninety four beautifully appointed bedrooms, each with its private bathroom. Every room has direct dial telephones, colour television, video, an honesty bar, a hospitality tray, trouser press, hair dryer and safe. The indoor swimming pool is just one of the many attributes of Sprowston Manor. Croquet is played on the immaculate lawns and Chess is there for anyone who wants to pit their brains against a worthy foe!

The two Restaurants, the Manor and the Orangery both serve superb cuisine in delightful settings. The ever changing menu includes dishes from around the world with emphasis on the very best traditional English. In the Gurney Bar food is also served and the menu there is unusual, exciting and delicious. A Vegetarian menu is available. Sprowston Manor's Conference facilities are renowned with nine Meeting Rooms, the larger can accommodate one hundred and fifty guests. They all have complete conference equipment and services. There is a helicopter landing area.

La Fontana Health Spa has a philosophy designed to balance the mind and the body and guests may choose from a unique range of therapeutic spa treatments, for revitalisation or relaxation. There are residential health and relaxation breaks but guests in the hotel may use the health spa from 8am-8pm daily. Due to its popularity it is advisable to book any additional treatments prior to arrival to avoid disappointment.

USEFUL INFORMATION

OPEN: All year
CHILDREN: Welcome
CREDIT CARDS: All major cards
LICENSED: Yes
ACCOMMODATION: 94 ensuite rooms
RATES: From £97 dbl. £91 sgl
Special Breaks from £74 p.n.

RESTAURANT: The Manor & The
Orangery both serving superb food
BAR FOOD: Upmarket menu
VEGETARIAN: Yes
GARDEN: 10 acres
PETS: At management's discretion

WILDEBEEST ARMS
Norwich Road
Stoke Holy Cross
Norfolk
NR14 8QJ

Tel: 01508 492497
Fax: 01603 612195
Internet:
Wildebeest:Arms@Virgin:Net

AA 2 Rosettes.
Good Food Guide

One does not expect to find something like the Wildebeest Arms in a quiet, picturesque village, amid beautiful countryside which is a haven for ramblers and nature lovers. In fact when the owners, Henry Watt and Andrew Wilkins first bought what was then the village pub, the Red Lion, people thought they were mad and predicted a disastrous failure. How wrong they were.

Today this exciting establishment has become the haunt not only for locals who still enjoy a drink at the bar but also people who have come from miles around to sample the excellent, award winning food and enjoy the warm, friendly atmosphere which has been created by the well trained young, enthusiastic and friendly staff.

The Wildebeest Arms has been totally refurbished, the bar is situated in the middle of the long restaurant area surrounded by unusually shaped tables, all made from a single oak tree together with high backed wicker chairs and pew bench seating round the edge of the room. At either end there is a large open fireplace and vibrant, flower arrangements add both colour and beauty. The decor is delightful, painted in warm, earthy colours and furnished with an African theme.

To the front and rear of the building, the gardens have been beautifully landscaped and there is extensive wooden bench seating for those wishing to eat or drink outside. There is also ample car parking available.

At lunch-times, in addition to the main menu a set three course 'Menu Du Jour' is available priced at £12 and in the evening Special dishes are always written on the blackboards. The dishes are all cooked to perfection and beautifully presented by the young team of talented chefs, visibly seen at work whilst you sit and enjoy your meal.

USEFUL INFORMATION

OPEN: Daily. Rest: 12-2pm & 7-10pm
Bar: 12-3pm & 6pm -11pm
CHILDREN: Welcome
CREDIT CARDS: All major cards
LICENSED: Yes
PARKING: Ample

RESTAURANT: Delicious award winning menus. Daily Specials
VEGETARIAN: Yes. Vegans on request
WHEELCHAIR ACCESS: Possible
GARDEN: Yes. Seating front & rear
PETS: No

THE WOODS END
Bar and Restaurant
Woods End,
Bramerton,
Norwich
NR 14 7ED

Tel: 01508 538899
Fax: 01508 538877

If you like river side walks or simply have a feel for the river, The Woods End is the place to visit. The picturesque free house, built in 1885, overlooks the deepest river in Norfolk - the River Yare. The Woods End Bar and Restaurant is situated just five miles east of Norwich on the southern bank of the River Yare. It takes just ten minutes to reach by car from Norwich City Centre. From window seating, or from one of the many outside picnic benches, the view across the river and farmland is superb.

The Woods End has, what can only be described as, a women's touch about it! The many hanging flower baskets and flower tubs make this one of the most picturesque river side bar restaurants in Norfolk. Inside, the walls are lined with brass trinkets and pictures. The plush armchair type seats are great for relaxing in after a long river side walk. Amanda Manley, the proprietor, and her staff, go out of their way to provide a warm and friendly atmosphere.

After a day out walking, fishing or boating, what better than to unwind in The Woods End bar with a pint of locally brewed ale. As for food, there is an extensive menu to choose from, including an imaginative vegetarian menu. During the summer months outside live music and barbecues are a regular feature at The Woods End.

USEFUL INFORMATION

OPEN: March to November 11-3pm   RESTURANT: Good English fare
Summer:11-11pm   BAR FOOD: Basket meals.
CHILDREN: Welcome. Play area   VEGETARIAN: Good variation
CREDIT CARDS: Visa/Master/Switch   WHEELCHAIR ACCESS: Yes
LICENSED: Full On/Off   GARDEN: Yes
PETS: Outside Only

BATTEE'S TEA ROOM
Point House, 5 High Street
Coltishall, Norfolk
NR12 7AA

Tel: 01603 736626

Point House is a Grade II Listed Building in the High Street of Coltishall, a picturesque village on the edge of the Norfolk Broads, just 3 miles from Wroxham, the unofficial capital of The Broads. It is surrounded by all sorts of interesting establishments including Antique shops for which the village is famous. Point House was once one of the grand residences in the village but now it houses four quality establishment and at one end of the house is Battee's Tea Room with a wonderful walled Tea Garden and surrounded by interesting old out-buildings. Matthew and Sarah Batterbee are the inspiration behind the Tea Room and Tea Garden and they provide delicious food in a comfortable and friendly atmosphere. Battee's is decorated with warm, bright colours with interesting pictures on the walls, colourful table cloths and real flowers on all the tables. Everything is home-made and you will see no packets of sugar, salt, jam or the like. A wide range of sandwiches, baguettes and jacket potatoes with various fillings feature largely but everyday there are home-made dishes which constantly change but never ignore firm, traditional favourites. The cakes and pastries, desserts and old fashioned puddings tempt everyone. Food is available all day and includes one of the best Afternoon Teas in Norfolk.

USEFUL INFORMATION

OPEN: All year. Closed Tues in winter
CHILDREN: Welcome
CREDIT CARDS: None taken
LICENSED: No
GARDEN: Yes. Walled Tea Garden

TEA ROOM: Everything home-made.
Wonderful afternoon teas
VEGETARIAN: Always on offer
WHEELCHAIR ACCESS: Yes. Ramp
PETS: In garden only

BIRDS PLACE FARM
Back Lane, Buxton, Norwich, Norfolk   NR10 5HD
Tel: 01603 279585

Birds Place Farm is a small family run farm in the Bure Valley and part of the peaceful village of Buxton. Surrounded by the beautiful Norfolk Broadland countryside, it is a tranquil place in which to stay whilst you enjoy a holiday exploring all this magical area has to offer. For those who like outdoor pursuits there is fishing, sailing, bird-watching, cycling, walking and much else. The historic city of Norwich is within easy distance, with its fabulous Cathedral, fascinating streets and a great shopping centre. The farmhouse dates back to the early sixteen hundreds and is full of character with its oak framed walls, old beams and a large open fireplace. The old walled garden, with its massive thick walls, is much older than the farmhouse. It is an ideal spot to sit and relax during the summer days enjoying a cup of tea or coffee, made with the farm's own spring water and at the same time indulging in home-made cakes and pastries. The atmosphere inside and outside the farmhouse is truly exceptional. Bill and Jenny Catchpole are the owners who moved back into the house after Bill's mothers death. They spent the next eighteen months renovating and uncovering many beams and woodwork. It is now comfortably furnished and has many fine antiques. There are three attractive bedrooms, one family and one double, both ensuite and one single with a private bathroom. All the rooms have television and a hostess tray. The cosy sitting room has an open fire with television for the use of guests. In the old world dining room you will be served an extensive and varied full English breakfast, dried and fresh fruit, home made jams and preserves. At night a home-cooked three course dinner by candlelight makes a fitting end to a super day. In winter a huge log fire burns to enhance the comfort. Home-made bread rolls and home grown produce is always served. Jenny and Bill enjoy good food and this is evident in the pride they take in cooking for their guests. Birds Place Farm is licensed so you can enjoy a bottle of wine to complete the excellent meal.

USEFUL INFORMATION

OPEN: All year
CHILDREN: Welcome fare
CREDIT CARDS: None taken
LICENSED: Residential
GARDEN: Lovely walled garden
PETS: No
RATES: £20 - £23 per night Children under 10 £15

DINING ROOM: Delicious, home-cooked
VEGETARIAN: Catered for upon request
WHEELCHAIR ACCESS: No
ACCOMMODATION: 1dbl 1fam. all ensuite
1 sgl with private bathroom downstairs
self-catering accommodation available late 1998

THE LODGE COUNTRY HOUSE
Vicarage Road
Salhouse
Norwich
NR13 6HD

Tel: 01603 782828
Fax: 01603 784066

The Lodge is a converted country house which has become an attractive and sought after place to eat by local people, those who like the drive out from Norwich and for the many tourists who come to this part of East Anglia. It is owned by the Bales family, who also own and run The Broads Hotel at Wroxham with the sons in charge here. A friendly, welcoming place, it is probably best described as an out of town restaurant with both pub and wine bar atmosphere. At lunch and in the early evening you will find it frequented by the over 45's and in the later evening by the younger element. The ale is well kept, there is a good, inexpensive wine list and the food on the A La Carte menu is wide ranging. There is also a Carvery. Extensive, well kept grounds, provide ample outside eating areas. An ideal place to go for those not wishing to fight the traffic of Norwich and Wroxham.

USEFUL INFORMATION

OPEN: 11-11pm
CHILDREN: Welcome evening.
CREDIT CARDS: All major cards
LICENSED: Yes
GARDEN: Large with play area for children
WHEELCHAIR ACCESS: Yes

RESTAURANT: Good menu, lunch &
A la Carte & Carvery
BAR FOOD: Good choice
VEGETARIAN: Yes
PETS: Not indoors

THE NORFOLK MEAD HOTEL
Coltishall. Norwich,
Norfolk NR12 7DN
Tel: 01603 737531 Fax: 01603 737521

The Norfolk Mead Hotel is a Georgian country house hotel owned and run by Jill and Don Fleming who have spent much time and care to make every room beautiful. Throughout the hotel you will find lovely antique furniture in a happy marriage with other pieces. The twelve acres of well-maintained and colourful gardens are a joy to stroll in and they have the addition of a swimming pool, a croquet lawn and an aromatic herb garden - much used in the delicious meals served every day. All sorts of people come here to stay, some for pleasure and some on business; Norfolk Mead is the sort of place to recharge your batteries at the end of a hectic day. There are ten pretty bedrooms, each one individually decorated and furnished. The sort of rooms which encourage relaxation and with beds that will ensure a good nights sleep. All the rooms have television and a hostess tray complete with coffee, tea and biscuits -a great boon to the traveller. Breakfast, served in the elegant dining room, is a sumptuous repast and certainly enough to set one up for the day. Dinner, chosen from the A la Carte menu based on traditional English fare with a Continental twist, is a great finish to a perfect day. With some one hundred wines on the list, there is something to suit everyone's palate and purse. During the summer months a light lunch is served in the Bar but through the year Lunch is available from 12-2pm and Dinner from 7-8.30pm. The hotel bars and restaurant is open to non-residents.

USEFUL INFORMATION

OPEN: All year
CHILDREN: No
CREDIT CARDS: All except Diners
LICENSED: Yes
ACCOMMODATION: 10 ensuite rooms
RATES: From £70 per room p.n.
GARDEN: 12 acres .Swimming Pool.

RESTAURANT: Delicious food.

BAR FOOD:Light lunches in summer
VEGETARIAN: Yes
WHEELCHAIR ACCESS: Not in
accommodation. Croquet
PETS: Yes

RATCATCHERS INN
Easton Way, Eastgate
NR Cawston, Norfolk
NR10 4HA
Tel: 01603 871430

If you are looking for a drinking haunt then the Ratchers Inn is not for you, for here we have one of the outstanding food inns in Norfolk, somewhere that people come from as far away as London especially to eat. Egon Ronay himself is a regular customer First mentioned in the census of 1861, the local ratcatcher would meet on the cross-roads outside and collect a penny a tail from the farmers, for the rats he had caught.. The Ratcatcher is definitely different in as much as the Bar is situated in the centre of the main room providing an interesting place for a drink before eating at one of the tables surrounding the bar. There is a capacity for sixty five covers and it is always busy. The menu is extensive and every dish is freshly cooked to order. Wherever possible they adopt a 'home-made' policy and freshness allied to quality and value are the benchmarks of the Ratcatchers philosophy. For example they bake their own bread on the premises' they make their own herb oils, chutney dishes, purees, stocks etc. and they pickle their own samphire. Sweets are a particular speciality of the Ratcatcher and they are all freshly made to their own specification. Jill and Eugene understand and appreciate the requirements of their vegetarian customers. There is not only an extensive vegetarian selection, it is imaginative and adaptable for vegan and special dietary needs.

USEFUL INFORMATION

OPEN; 12-2.30pm & 6-11pm
CHILDREN; Welcome
BAR FOOD; Wide range
LICENCE; Full
GARDEN; Beer Garden
SMOKING; Not encouraged.

RESTAURANT; High quality, home - cooked
CREDIT CARDS; Master/Visa/Switch
VEGETARIAN; Yes + vegan & other diets
DISABLED ACCESS; Yes + toilets

ROOKERY FARM
Thurning
Norfolk
NR24 2JP

Tel: 01263 860357

AA Listed

If you were able to read the Visitor's book of this delightful, three hundred year old farmhouse, you would not hesitate to book immediately. One quotation says 'We envy you your scenery, your roads, your beaches and your bacon...we never thought of trying anywhere else. This is our ninth visit'. There can be nothing better than that sort of recommendation especially when Rookery Farm lives up to it for everyone who stays. It is family run by Mrs Fisher, has a wonderful, homely atmosphere, is relaxed, informal and a thoroughly happy establishment. It is ideal as a base for walking, cycling and visiting the Norfolk Coast and Broads. It is a working farm , the house has Dutch gable ends and is set in a quiet rural community of some fifty people spread throughout farms and cottages. Visitors enjoy the pretty walled garden and eagerly await Mrs Fisher's great farmhouse breakfast. She provides an equally good evening meal by arrangement.

USEFUL INFORMATION

OPEN: All year except Christmas
CHILDREN: Welcome
CREDIT CARDS: None taken
LICENSED: No
ACCOMMODATION: Comfortable not ensuite
RATES: From £16pp B&B

DINING ROOM: Great farmhouse breakfast. Evening meal by arrangement
VEGETARIAN: On request
WHEELCHAIR ACCESS: No
GARDEN: Yes
PETS: No

THE MOAT HOUSE
Rectory Lane
Hethel
Norwich
Norfolk
NR14 8HD

Tel/Fax: 01508 570149

Open all the year, the elegant moated Georgian house is set amongst beautifully maintained grounds of six acres, providing a haven in the summer months for wild orchids, unusual flowers and shrubs. It also provides a haven for those wanting to beat a retreat from the busy world. The Moat House is as delightful inside as it is outside. The rooms are spacious and classically furnished. Old portraits hang in the welcoming hall while the walls of the comfortable sitting room are decorated with equestrian pictures and memorabilia reflecting the owners, Lesley and Colin Rudd, interest in eventing. Breakfast is a delicious, sustaining meal and dinner a feast. In winter you are encouraged to enjoy a glass of port after dinner in front of the large log fire. If you are weight conscious then a sauna can be waiting for you to help you shed a few pounds. There is a luxurious indoor swimming pool, and if you have been too energetic during the day, you can get rid of the aches and pains in the Jacuzzi. The ensuite bedrooms are superbly furnished and equipped with everything one could wish for.

USEFUL INFORMATION

OPEN: All year	DINING ROOM: Delicious breakfast
CHILDREN: Over 14 years	Dinner by arrangement
CREDIT CARDS: Yes	VEGETARIAN: By arrangement
LICENSED: Yes	WHEELCHAIR ACCESS: No
ACCOMMODATION : 2 double rooms ensuite	GARDEN: 6 acres
RATES: £30-£37.50 Sgl supplement £18.50	PETS: No

THE WALNUTS
8-12 New Street
Cawston, Norwich
NR10 4AL - Tel: 01603 871357
ETB 2 Star Highly Commended

Margaret Tubby has a visitors book full of complimentary remarks from the many visitors she has had over the years, many of whom come back quite regularly. You will read 'the best B&B I have stayed in, you certainly know how to make people welcome' and that really reflects every entry. Margaret is a warm, caring person who genuinely enjoys making her guests comfortable and contented. The Walnuts is situated in a quiet conservation area in half an acre of gardens complete with a swimming pool which is heated in summer. It is only nine miles north of Norwich airport, centrally located for the Norfolk Broads the coast and Norwich itself. Cawston is surrounded by lovely countryside and not far afield are National Trust properties, steam railways, parks, lakes, gardens, glass blowing and a hundred and one other things to do and see. Within the friendly walls of The Walnuts are three pretty guest rooms, one double with an ensuite bathroom, one twin ensuite with a shower and the third double has a private bathroom. All the bedrooms have television and a hostess tray. Breakfast is a freshly cooked meals with a good choice and although there are no evening meals, this is not a problem because there are restaurants and pubs within easy reach. A comfortable, well furnished lounge complete with television, books and games is there for the enjoyment of guests

USEFUL INFORMATION

OPEN; Open all year except Christmas and Boxing Day	DINING ROOM; Traditional breakfast
	VEGETARIAN;Yes
CHILDREN; Over 8 years	DISABLED ACCESS; Not suitable
CREDIT CARDS: None taken	SMOKING; Not permitted. Garden only
GARDEN; Yes with heated swimming pool	PETS; No
ACCOMMODATION: 3 rooms en suite	

PRICES; 22.00 per person High Season. 21.00 per person Low Season 9.00 single supplement
Short break: 1stOct-31st March 2 nights 40.00 per person. 1stApril-30th Sept 42.00 per person

Selected venues in this chapter

' God gave the grape,
good wine to make,
to cheer both great and small.
But little fools they drink too much,
and big ones - none at all '.

Anonymous

CHAPTER 4.:
NORFOLK -
WOODS, WATERWAYS AND WILDERNESS
All Points West of Norwich

I love the Brecks. This area of Norfolk has, for me, all the wonders of the true desert - with none of the drawbacks. It has the silence, emptiness, space - but not the fierce heat, aridity, sand - or the scorpions!, nothing life threatening at all, in fact.

Despite the growth of the towns at the corners of the rough rectangle that defines Breckland - where Wymondham, just up the road, for example, has all but doubled its population in the last thirty years - the stretch of heath and scrub and occasional oasis of woodland remains a wilderness, the last in England, and the country's least densely populated area. Yes, I love it for that.

Yet one of the charms of a wilderness comes when you leave it behind for a while, with your soul shrived, your mind cleared and your eyes set on far horizons - or in a good pub with fine ale and a roaring fire! Breckland handles that very well too. Its outposts of civilisation are extremely civilised when it comes to dealing with the traveller's needs, as I hope you'll soon find out. South Norfolk knows all about the 'inner man' and offers some of the best cuisine in the region.

There is more to South Norfolk than empty space. If anything, its history stretches back further than that of other parts of the region, for our primitive 'farming' ancestors found its dry soil easy to work, its deposits of flint useful for tools and weapons - while its abundance of streams and meres made for a reliable water supply. Reminders of those ancient days crop up all over the place, from burial mounds on a large scale to tiny flint arrow-heads just lying beside the path, discovered on a heathland walk.

Beyond the Brecks the history continues and is seen, dramatically, in the prosperous towns that flourished while the wool trade was a good earner. When it collapsed in the 19th century other sources of income had to be found - and these proved to be at least as varied as anywhere in England, from racing cars to electronics and tourism.

For our generation - just about - one stage in the area's history may never be forgotten: its role in World War II. This was 'bomber country' and even today the relics of that facet of wartime are found down almost every road. There are very few journeys that don't pass the remnants of an abandoned airfield where, when the moon is full you can still hear the old aircraft engines being run up, or catch the sounds of laughter and ghostly voices coming from some derelict building; or so they say. For me there's a personal interest, a family story, as my father and one of my uncles were stationed at Marham, east of Swaffham, for a while, and have tales to tell of the days when the bomber boys came off duty and went to town in rather a big way.

There is still a high concentration of operational air fields in the area because the terrain remains ideal for their construction. Not only that, but East Anglia is the most easterly part of the country and, in the days of the Cold War, that had a certain significance! Wartime experiences are commemorated in more tangible ways, too. At Thorpe Abbots and Seething Airfield are memorials to American airmen, based in the area in large numbers between 1943 and 1945, who took off on missions from which they never returned. These offer far more than a moving tribute to those who lost their lives: they also give us a chance to step back in time and see the conditions experienced by the servicemen as well as to understand the impact they had on the local population.

This won't just be a nostalgia trip though. There'll be quite a bit of it, but we're supposed to be on holiday and holidays are supposed to be enjoyable. So the things we like - the relaxing occupations, the wining and dining, the healthy walks and the leisurely expeditions to shops, galleries and so forth - will be kept high on the agenda. Possibly no better than equal first though, for this is a remarkable area in its own right, and deserves to be seen as much more than just a setting for our favourite pastimes. After all, let's face it, some of our pet indulgences are more than a tiny bit commercial - and we need a balance at all times, even on holiday.

Where shall we be based then? I must say I favour a return to Dersingham, partly for reasons of symmetry in route planning and partly to have the chance of sea air at journey's end. That's all very personal, but if you glance at the map, a roughly circular route to the south east from the coast, turning off to skirt Norwich and returning via East Dereham and Castle Acre looks rather good. It also helps to stick to the idea of using bases on the fringes of areas rather than right in the middle of them, where the experiences could add up to something rather overwhelming. That sort of change is good, when one's enjoying a break. It's the essence of the idea, in fact.

We leave, then, on the A149, signposted to King's Lynn, where we switch to the A10 and make for **DOWNHAM MARKET**, a mellow town lying on the Norfolk side of the Fens, with their wide skies and peaceful waterways. Fenland itself will have its own chapter later - for us, this town is a gateway to more southerly country, to the land that lies along the Norfolk - Suffolk border.

DOWNHAM MARKET CLOCK TOWER

The town centre, which features an interesting and very decorative clock tower and hosts a bustling Friday market, is a focus for the scattered Breckland / Fen-border villages to whom it offers a wide choice of shopping and other facilities. A mile's march to the south of the town, DENVER SLUICE marks the upper limit of the tidal reaches of the River Great Ouse. It's part of a drainage scheme of sluices designed in Charles I's time by a Dutch engineer, Vermuyden, to improve the land for agriculture and even create a basis for a new market town, called Charlmont. Repeated flooding wrecked the scheme but, thanks to modern techniques, the idea has been revived with some success. Perhaps visitors are less impressed by farming and find the sight of the yacht and dinghy masts, bobbing above the banks at Denver, rather more eye-catching. The nearby smock mill is also a popular attraction.

If we leave Downham Market by the A1122 and turn right at its junction with the A134, a drive of about twelve miles will bring us to **MUNDFORD** and to the edges of Breckland proper. Before we travel too far, though, we need to take a left turn off the main road at **STOKE FERRY** and head north to OXBURGH HALL [Information - 01366 328528]. This magnificent moated residence was built in 1482 by the Bedingfield family whose descendants still live there. The public rooms are particularly interesting in that they show the development of character as the Hall grew from its beginnings in the Middle Ages. The early style is quite Spartan; the Victorian parts reveal the taste for luxury and comfort that was a hallmark of the period. On show too is embroidery carried out by Mary Queen of Scots when she was held prisoner there.

One of Norfolk's finest medieval buildings, the Hall, whose dominant and dramatic exterior has become a well known landmark, reveals the strength and confidence of its origins. These qualities were further emphasised by the Tudor addition of an 80ft high Gatehouse. As so often with National Trust properties, the gardens are a treat in themselves. If one has an energy problem a stroll around the garden may be inspiring enough. Otherwise, there are delightful woodland walks through the estate, including the recently added two mile route through the Home Covert. Light lunches and teas are available in the hundred seat 'Old Kitchen', between 11am and 5 pm. Table licence is operated. A series of brass band concerts are among the events presented at the Hall, along with a range of garden Open Days. Programmes for these events are available on request.

By now we are running through a landscape that's quite unfamiliar after all we have seen to the north and east on the coast, and around the Broads. The Forestry Commission has changed the historic character of the countryside so, while we are well used to contrasts - we've even come to expect them - what's on offer here is something new again. One leaves the bustle of civilisation behind and starts to think 'Wilderness'. As the Commission's additions to the woodland - and their new plantations - are mainly conifers, an air of brooding mystery has been created where once the more ancient shading had held sway, with its ghosts and myth memories. Around Mundford one can see the point clearly: delightful stretches of more recent, enlightened, planting of beech, birch and lime are set off vividly by the striking darkness of dour walls of Scots pine.

We'll see more of this later - first we have to pass through a time warp in the form of GRIMES GRAVES. Let me reassure the faint-hearted straight away: we aren't about to enter a burial ground - and old bones certainly aren't on the menu, whatever the signpost suggests. Grimes Graves are named after the Anglo-Saxon god 'Grim', otherwise known as 'Wodin'. Hollows in the ground are all that is left of a site where, 4,000 years ago, neolithic miners sank shafts and crawled along tunnels to chip out the flint for their tools and weapons from the chalk beds twenty feet beneath the ground. It was much later that the invaders from Scandinavia, who would have known next to nothing of the New Stone Age, attributed the remains, already ancient by the time they got there, to divine activity - as they tended to do with anything they didn't understand. Modern archaeology, however, knows better. From the many finds made in the area, including such chalk carvings as that of a possible fertility goddess, valuable additions have been made to our knowledge of the lifestyle of those very early ancestors of ours.

As a rather pleasant footnote to the serious history, it's worth recording that the ancient skill of flint mining only died out as recently as the 1930's when one 'Pony'

Ashley passed away. For years he had worked single handed at Grimes Graves' Neolithic workings, using the same methods as the miners had used 4000 years before.

The vigorous post-war expansion that we mentioned earlier doesn't seem to have harmed the old town of **THETFORD** [Information - 01842 752599], whose traditions, presumably, are too strong to be upset by anything short of an earthquake. It's more than old - it's surprisingly ancient for, a thousand years ago, it was actually the capital of Danish East Anglia and is one of the few towns in Britain to have Saxon remains.

THOMAS PAINE - THETFORD

As with most similar places in Norfolk, the Middle Ages were good years for Thetford. We can see this from just a glance at the townscape's old buildings, at what's left of the two castles and at the various priory ruins. The remains of the Dukes of Norfolk were held here until they were moved to Framlingham in Suffolk, after the Dissolution of the Monasteries by Henry VIII. For a while, until 1091, Thetford was even the See of the Bishop of East Anglia. Everywhere, it seems, reminders of the past abound as do the interwoven threads of its religious heritage. In a way these features are enhanced even further by the local tales.

If we start with CASTLE HILL we find that, according to legend, it was once the site of a fabulous castle, full of treasures. All went well for years until the King was threatened by an attack on the castle that he was certain would overwhelm it. He decided, apparently, that the only thing to do was to bury the lot, so he ordered his men to raise an enormous mound over the castle, treasure and all. Even though a more reasonable assumption is that the mound was actually raised as a defensive measure, and that all that's ever likely to be dug up is a set of seven bells still missing from the Priory, I guess most of us would still prefer the legend.

Amongst the Priory stories there is much to amaze us too. For example, a local craftsman in the 13th century had a vision of the Virgin Mary who told him he would be cured of a disease if a chapel was built in her honour. A local woman also had a similar vision. In due course a stone Lady Chapel was constructed at the Priory, complete with a statue of the Virgin, transferred from the site of the old Thetford Cathedral. As might be expected, this statue was rather the worse for wear so the decision was made to re-decorate it. I suppose we shouldn't be too amazed to learn that, in the process of restoration, a hollow in the head was discovered, containing the relics of saints. Nor should one be totally stunned to hear that these relics had such miraculous powers of healing that, before long, Thetford became a centre for pilgrims from all over the country.

Perhaps two more tales will have to do for now, or else we'll be far too late for lunch. Firstly let's cast our minds back to Little Lord Dacre, who died at the age of seven at Nunnery Farm in Thetford, after a fall from his rocking horse. Foul play was suspected - it was bound to be because his ghost soon began to be seen, prancing up and down on a headless rocking horse.

Although whether the *child's* death was the murderer's intention rather than an unfortunate side-effect of a maniacal attack on the *horse*, is not totally clear. Whatever, the apparition became such a nuisance that it had to be laid by a member of the clergy. With only partial success, one surmises, as a century later people were still claiming that bloodstains could be seen on the wall where he fell.

For our final tale let's move from murder to treason, another favourite topic of the modern media - only this one is far from modern, and concerns one Tutt, a local shepherd, by all accounts. The story goes that when the Danes were attacking the Saxon town of Thetford they were somewhat stuck for a weak point in the town's defences. Full frontal assault having proved a fiasco, they thought they'd try a much more effective, time-honoured strategy - straight bribery. Honest Tutt was only too happy to oblige, it seems, and agreed to guide the Danes in along a secret way across the marshes, in return for a reward 'beyond his highest expectations'. Life being tough, and no game for suckers, he got just that - he was hanged on the mound that now bears his name. End of stories - back to the 'real' world, whatever that means.

Thetford evolved around the meeting of the Rivers Thet and Little Ouse at the crossing point for the Icknield Way, England's oldest trade route. This was guarded at first by Iron Age earthworks on Castle Hill, later developed and fortified by the Normans, who also added a second emplacement on another mound. Today the three way bridge over this junction gives access to a RIVERSIDE PROMENADE, with many of the town's better shops close at hand. The medieval boom in Thetford was not the only one, however - the Georgian buildings seen on almost every street in the older town suggest that times were prosperous then too.

By leisurely SPRING WALK lies a house built in 1880 to serve as a pump room, when an unsuccessful attempt was made to keep up with fashion and turn the town into a spa. Such an idea might have been greeted with a sneer by Thomas Paine, the radical writer born in Thetford in 1737 and author of 'The Rights of Man'. A strong supporter of the French and American revolutions, he is commemorated today in a gilded bronze statue that was erected outside the seventeenth century KING'S HOUSE in 1964.

Born in White Hart Street, Paine had a brief spell as an excise man before being sacked for agitating for a pay rise. He then went to America, where he published his first political pamphlet. He held several posts in the American government after that, and is seen as having quite an influence on the thinking behind the Declaration of Independence. In a sense that was only the start, as the ideas that pour from his great book were not only years ahead of their time but were, over the next 150 years, to lay the foundations for most of the social reforms that took place throughout Europe. Family allowances, education grants for the poor, graduated income tax and arms limitation treaties are among the many concepts that he pioneered and which are now part of our everyday life.

At the time, though, they weren't exactly welcome in an England where the squire and the parson ran most people's lives as though by an equal divine right. Paine was forced to flee to France in order to escape prosecution and soon got himself elected on to the Convention. Unfortunately, being a rebel to the end, he refused to go with the flow and chose instead to suggest to his fellow revolutionaries that maybe Louis XVI wasn't such a bad guy after all and ought to be let off. He nearly had his own head guillotined for that little number and had to take to the road again - in a hell of a hurry. Eventually, it was back to America - the last refuge in those days of streams of misfits - where he died in 1809, having increased his unpopularity even further with a strong attack on Christianity in his book 'The Age of Reason.'

Let's return to the town. With the collapse of the wool trade new directions had to be found for Thetford - and many other places - as we have already realised, if people weren't to starve. The BURRELL MUSEUM pays tribute to one such effort: the town was the base chosen by the firm of Charles Burrell, famous for building steam traction engines. To dot the i's and cross the t's, a visit to the MUSEUM OF LOCAL HISTORY, in the 15th century ANCIENT HOUSE would be welcome, as would one final call, at the CHURCH OF ST MARY THE LESS, which again is ancient, being part Saxon and part Norman.

While we're in the Museum, whatever else we do, we musn't miss examining the beautifully detailed replicas, made by Peter Shorter, of selected items from the hoard of late Roman gold and silver, known as the Thetford Treasure. The original finds, comparable in importance with others from Mildenhall and Sutton Hoo, are now on permanent display in the British Museum, but the exhibits in the Ancient House, and the story behind them, are still truly fascinating.

What makes the Thetford Treasure so vital to our understanding of Roman Britain is not just its obvious beauty but rather the picture it conveys, through the images depicted, of the life of those times, especially regarding the various religious beliefs. To study the pieces after time spent thinking about St Withburga and the rest, can easily double the impact. It is clear that this is one of the great archaeological finds of the century and that it includes some of the finest pieces of their kind ever found throughout the Roman Empire. Yet that is not all that is remarkable - believe it or not, the gold objects were never worn, indeed some of them weren't even finished.

It seems likely that the gold jewellery was all produced by the one workshop, either in Gaul - modern France- or in Britain, towards the end of the 4th century at a time when East Anglia was attracting more and more very unwelcome - and usually violent - interest from Saxon pirates. How easily one can see, in one's mind's eye, the picture of this terrified jeweller fleeing from the invaders with his entire stock in a bag on his back, suddenly realising that the only thing he could really do to keep it safe was to bury it until the troubles were over, then come back and dig it up again. Only he never made it. Perhaps he forgot. Perhaps he was killed, himself - or just died of natural causes. I suppose that, at that time, it's just possible that he even experienced some sort of religious conversion which led him to forsake material goods, in general, and those with rather too detailed pictures on them of Mars, Cupid, Venus and the rest, in particular. One more East Anglian mystery; one more unanswerable question.

You'll be relieved to note that I will not describe all of the wonderful objects, or to go into detail about the gold, the emeralds, garnets, amethysts and so forth. You'll like what you like and pass by the rest, but we might just ease off a moment to think about the people to whom it was all so significant - and not just because the materials themselves were worth a king's ransom.

One can say at the start that hiding the treasure on GALLOWS HILL, a shoulder of ground to the north of Thetford, was probably the best idea on offer at the time. The hill had been of strategic importance since prehistoric times, and one can imagine our mystery goldsmith thinking that if the Saxons even over-ran that stronghold he wouldn't have much to live for, anyway. As it happens he was not alone in the idea, as another major hoard, of Roman silver from about the same period, has been found nearby.

Together they tell us a tale of the Romans that sits rather strangely alongside the more familiar facts.

It seems that these people, who conquered half the world, who developed the most powerful fighting force that had ever been seen, who were superb architects and engineers and who enjoyed a quality of life on their days off that ran to central heating, steam baths, gourmet food and fine wines - not to mention sophisticated poetry, philosophy and literature - became utterly eccentric, when it came to religion. They appear to have had a god for virtually everything, from booze to bedtime, for a start, and some of these deities stretch credibility way beyond the acceptable limits of true faith, I would have thought.

I mean, it asks rather a lot of the modern mind to expect it to accept that a chap who had just had a tough week slaughtering Goths, or building colossal aqueducts - or even organising the politics and economics of the Empire - would feel anything meaningful was achieved by dressing up in a sheet and prancing around in a forest glade with ivy leaves in his hair. But he did, because he believed that was what Bacchus, or Faunus or something demanded of him, if life was to continue on an even keel. Yes, very strange - yet the Thetford Treasure tells us that such behaviour was all the rage in 4AD, down East Anglia way. No wonder that the Saxons walked all over them, fairly soon afterwards

Regardless of all that, the items are extremely beautiful in their own right and underline the claim of the Museum to a place in our itinerary. And next time you're in London, pop into the British Museum for a swift peep at the originals, along with the finds from Mildenhall and Water Newton.

Another touch of fresh air is on offer almost as soon as we leave the town, as long as another detour sounds inviting - just to stretch the legs, you understand. Remember, 'Onward, ever onward'? THETFORD FOREST, one of the largest forest areas in the country, stretches out north and west from the developed areas and down across the border into Suffolk. It offers walks and experiences that set off beautifully the urbanisation we've just left.

Having fortified ourselves with a stout lunch in town and walked off some of the excesses in the forest, it's time to meet the true BRECKLAND face to face, at EAST WRETHAM HEATH. All the qualities that make travel in this area such a haunting experience can be found within surprisingly few miles of the village. The word 'breck' or 'brake' simply means a tract of heathland broken up by intermittent areas of cultivation. Around FOWLMERE and DEVIL'S PUNCHBOWL cultivation is very intermittent. As with any wilderness, the Brecks can give the impression of an almost ghostly lack of substance. Just as the sands of the Sahara drift and change, the reed-fringed meres come and go - dry one season and deep and sombre the next, with trees sprouting out of their depths like the masts of yachts moored up on the Broads to the north.

RINGMERE is situated in a Nature Reserve operated by the NORFOLK NATURALISTS' TRUST, quite close to **EAST WRETHAM**. Fowlmere is a bit difficult to reach, as it's surrounded by wire, trees and nettles. Despite the name, Devils Punchbowl is almost cosy by comparison, even down to the picnic areas As a footnote to this brief sortie into the wild, it should be said that some care is needed. It's not a place in which to get lost - and the paths are there for a reason. To stray is to run the risk of wandering into a marsh or running up against a Ministry of Defence battle training ground which visitors are forbidden to enter - for fairly obvious reasons.

Now, if our last two sets of experiences have been as natural as possible, the next two are going to be totally artificial (contrast, again). You don't find steam trains - naturally - in the middle of a country park and squirrel monkeys aren't - naturally - free to roam around the trees in the middle of the East Anglian countryside. True enough, but they are *there,* all the same. BANHAM ZOO [Information - 01953 887773] is reached from Wretham via the A11, a stretch of country lane and a mile or two of the B1113. Considered by many to be Norfolk's premier wildlife attraction, it is set in twenty five acres of attractive parkland, where visitors and residents alike can meet in comparative freedom. Among its features are the 'Safari Walkway', the 'Woodland Walk' and 'Monkey Jungle Island'. A road train is available for an even more leisurely tour. The zoo is open daily from 10am.

On the way to the second artificial experience there's just time for another tall tale. It is focused on the little village of **QUIDENHAM**, over to the right as we head south from the Zoo, and can be told quite safely as we're travelling in broad daylight. It goes like this: apparently, a godless owner of Quiddenham Hall left directions that, when he died, his coffin should be carried to the church by twelve drunken men on the stroke of midnight. Accordingly, a dozen stout topers were gathered together to do the job and carry out his dying wish, but they seemed to lack the necessary co-ordination - which, one might suggest, the deceased should have realised - and weren't generally up to it. Eventually, as they reached the bridge near the churchyard, they lost control of the situation - and the coffin - and fell as one man into the river beneath, with predictable results. Right up to the present, at the right kind of midnight, the chilly air still carries their rowdy shouts and laughter to the ears of the intrepid spectator - to be followed by an enormous splash and a stream of ghastly cries. I agree, that's quite enough, for now!

Further down the B1113, with a touch of the A1065 thrown in for good measure, we come, as promised, to the second blast of the totally unexpected - BRESSINGHAM STEAM MUSEUM TRUST AND GARDENS [Information - 01379 687386]. Another attraction with 'something for everyone', its fame rests on its celebration of the power of steam in all its forms, from mainline locomotives to small, stationary engines. There's a fine collection of traction engines, a Victorian steam roundabout and three separate narrow gauge railway rides running for five miles around Bressingham's gardens, woods, meadows and lake. The steam story, though, is only half the appeal.

BRESSINGHAM

Once you've had enough nostalgia, you can recover in the six acres of glorious gardens. Alan Bloom, Bressingham's founder, has created the world famous DELL GARDEN as a worthy backdrop to his beloved engines and now it's a feature in its own right. With nearly 5,000 different plant varieties and 47 island beds of perennials slipping bands of colour between the lawns and the mature trees, there is every kind of fascination for the dedicated gardener. The whole picture is an unforgettable spectacle, where the sights, sounds and smells of the age of steam blend almost unnoticed into a garden of delights.

With our minds full of shrubs and tank engines, let's hope there's still room to take in the directions to Diss, our next goal. It's quite simple really: get on the A1066, eastwards, change up to top and ease down when you see the town sign (more about town signs, later. Some of them are quite special).

DISS [Information - 01379 - 650523] *is* an attractive town, known for its mixture of Tudor, Georgian and Victorian buildings, ranged up around the wide, six acre DISS MERE. Streets twist out from the head of the little market place like narrow veins, rather than impressive traffic arteries. The CHURCH of ST MARY'S looks down graciously upon all these goings-on - as it has done for centuries - towards MERE STREET, the main shopping area, and over the jumble of tiled roofs, yards and gardens that surround it. At the further end of the street MERE'S MOUTH opens out into a stretch of water where ducks and other wildfowl residents often gather.

The roads towards **BURSTON**, two miles to the north east, and **SHELFANGER**, two miles north, are especially attractive. Their rows of houses, like painted backcloths in a variety of styles, with their patches of coloured plaster, draw the eye out to the country beyond and to the ever changing skyscape. The town is at its busiest, by the way, on a Friday, market day. If your spirits are jaded - and you baulk at too much solitude then DISS MARKET is probably just the tonic you need. Either that, or a stroll by the Mere to 'people-watch' and feed the ducks.

The mere itself began to form about twelve thousand years ago, as the last Ice Age began to recede. In a hollow at the edge of the Waveney Valley, created by the collapse of the underlying chalk bedrock, water collected in a hole which is now up to sixty feet deep with as much as forty feet of mud at the bottom! It was once used by the town as a mixture of reservoir, wash bowl and drain - and also acted as a natural boundary which directed the pattern of urban growth. The more health conscious generations of recent times have wisely limited its functions to the purely recreational.

Having refreshed ourselves, we're back to our other favourite occupation - shopping, which, in Diss, is always interesting and enticing. We're mainly talking speciality shops in a rarely found combination, which has the variety found in many a City yet is laid out so compactly as to keep exhaustion to a minimum. The range of possibilities is amazing and includes shops specialising in decorated cakes, army surplus, needlecraft, health products and jewellery. Many of the shops are located in charming courtyards amongst streets whose architectural qualities are utterly fascinating. Worth a visit too, are NORFOLK HOUSE YARD, HALES YARD and COLES YARD - while not forgetting THE WAVENEY FISH FARM. In fact the local saying that 'you can buy anything in Diss' seems totally justified.

Friday is the day for the auction as well as for the market when the town seems to be bursting with colour, characters and unbelievable bargains. DISS AUCTION ROOMS [Information - 01379 650306] offer 2,500 lots each week, including antiques, fine art - and local produce! Viewing is on Thursdays between 2 and 8pm. Before leaving Diss, its award-winning MUSEUM [Information - 01379 650618] ought to be seen. Housed in the historic OLD SHAMBLES building, it presents visitors with a variety of changing displays highlighting local history and prehistory. As with so many Norfolk towns, the image most likely to stay in our minds long after we'd moved on to somewhere else, is this unbroken line of places and people stretching way, way back. So, as we pack our purchases into the boot, let's just pause for two very final glimpses of that amazing past

FAIR GREEN definitely fits the bill. One of two original town centres - the other being the area around ST NICHOLAS STREET - but only incorporated into the town proper this century, it now presents an idyllic village scene, with attractive groups of 17th and 18th century houses and cottages. The Fair itself was granted a Royal Charter in 1185, but was eventually closed for 'disorderly behaviour', along with many other fairs, by an Act of Parliament in 1872. Final call? Diss also has the last working corn market in the country - the CORN HALL AND FRIENDS' MEETING HOUSE. Built in 1854, by George Atkins, it has an impressive classical portico, recently restored along with the rest of the exterior.

We must press on now, so no more last glances, no more bargains. Our next extended halt is some miles away, up the A143 and we must arrive in good time, to do it justice. En route, as ever, there are one or two other places of interest that we really *ought* to see. We leave Diss along a country lane before cutting back to the main A140, as we ought to drop in to **BURSTON**, for our education. BURSTON STRIKE SCHOOL [Information - 01379 741565] set the scene for events that led to the longest strike in history, which went on for 48 years! The story is well documented, and has been seen on television. Each year there's a Labour rally on the village green and this same green still sports its old-fashioned maypole.

From Burston we return to the Norwich road, but turn away from the city southwards, pressing on to a commemoration of more recent history than is usual. At **THORPE ABBOTS**, near **DICKLEBURGH**, a short distance from the main road to the left, is the 100TH BOMB GROUP MEMORIAL MUSEUM [Information - 01379 740708]. I expect you'll find this tribute to those members of the American 8th Air Force who lost their lives in the Second World War to be a very moving experience. It's more than just a commemorative gesture - the visit will take you back for a moment or two to those grim, gallant days as you witness the conditions experienced by the servicemen and the effect that they had on the lives of the local population. The encounter may also encourage a touch of reflection on your own memories of that period, of the history of which we were actually a part.

Further up the road a few miles we ease off to the left and draw into the village of **HARLESTON,** an excellent centre for exploring one of the most delightful stretches of the River Waveney, that runs north east from the great 17th century red-brick SCOLE INN. There's good coarse fishing here, if there's time to snatch an hour or two, while for those who prefer to pause and just 'be', there are glorious sights to be seen when the valley is filled with blossom, in spring, or when the cottage gardens and rose nursery are ablaze with their summer finery. The village itself has some pleasing Georgian houses and a mellow old market place. Not to be missed either, is the MILLHOUSE [Information - 01379 852556], where a fine range of decorative English slipware, tin glaze, majolica and functional items for the house and garden is always available. Other speciality shops are also a local feature. There are hardware stores like something out of Ali Baba, designer fabric shops, various boutiques and more besides.

As we wander back to the main road, we can see how this area would have attracted artists, so it's no surprise to discover that Sir Alfred Munnings, a past President of the Royal Academy, was born in the pretty hillside village of Mendham, two miles away across the river and just inside Suffolk. We can't pass by **EARSHAM** without calling in, either, and this isn't some stage management trick to keep up the suspense. THE OTTER TRUST [Information - 01986 893470] really is the kind of place you can't possibly come across every day. Here is the largest conservation collection of otters in the country, bred for reintroduction into the wild, and a visit will be one more of those experiences you'll always be delighted to remember.

EARSHAM OTTERS

In this wonderland, just off the A143, you can watch these charming creatures in enclosures that are as completely natural as possible - and be completely won over by them at feeding time when they're at their most playful. Other attractions include a collection of water fowl, muntjac deer and - would you believe - wallabies.

Shortly after leaving the otters we need to strike off left from the A143. There's a cross country short cut that will save a few miles as we make our way to the 15th century Hales Hall and Raveningham before eventually arriving at Lodden. There has been a house at HALES HALL [Information - 01508 548395] since before Domesday [1086]. Formerly the great house of Sir James Hobart, Attorney General to Henry VII, the present Hall comprises the original Gatehouse and Steward's House, built in the 1480's, along with the largest brick built medieval barn in Britain. The Hall, which stands on the edge of the beautiful HALES GREEN, is also renowned today as the site of READS NURSERY, which houses the National Collection of Citrus Fruits together with other exotic species, including figs and climbing plants.

Since we share a wide variety of interests it's no surprise that, hot from the garden delights of Reads, our attention is soon rivetted on the antiques at THE RAVENINGHAM CENTRE [Information - 01508 548441], a short distance away, beyond the A146. The older furniture in the showrooms is not all that's on offer - it's contrasted skilfully with pieces in new pine. To delight the collector further there's also an opportunity for browsing in the art gallery and for examining the many examples of craft work. Raveningham operates a furniture making and restoration business, too.

There's hardly time to get into top gear along the A146, before we come to **LODDON** [Information - 01508 520690] and with it, back to Broadland. Today it's often linked with the neighbouring village of **CHEDGRAVE**, although the two grew up quite separately. Although Loddon is no longer a market town and was, in fact, more self sufficient in the 19th century than it is today, it retains an active community. Indeed, both the parishes hold great charm for residents and visitors alike, as they lie in one of the most pleasant and relaxing parts of the Broadland complex. The River Chet has boats for hire, public mooring and easy access to the River Yare.

Loddon HIGH STREET stretches from the WATERMILL and STAITHE to the wide, open space in front of HOLY TRINITY CHURCH, built in 1486. A corner of the churchyard has been set aside as a nature reserve, while the Staithe, at one time a landing place for water borne goods is now just a reminder, really, of the town's role in bygone days as a centre for trade and administration for South-East Norfolk. This role stemmed from its well established road and water links with Norwich, Yarmouth, Beccles, Bungay and Wroxham. The church was provided by James Hobart, the builder of Hales Hall. During the next three centuries the town expanded steadily and by the 1800's 'gentlemen's houses' were being built amongst the shops, farms, workshops and public houses of Loddon, as well as in the estates around it. The finest was Loddon House, but, in 1786, this became a 'private madhouse'.

The Proctor-Beauchamps were the main Chedgrove family, and they built an elegant mansion at Langley Hall, [later a public school] with landscaping by Capability Brown. They also installed a stained glass window from Rouen Cathedral in the village's All Saints Church. Methodism was also well supported in Loddon. John Wesley was a regular visiting preacher, and chapels for Wesleyans and 'Ranters' were established. In 1884 Sadd and Moore, seed merchants, millers and maltsters, moved to Loddon to become the main employers for more than fifty years. The town's importance, in these respects, has since ended and a 'Broads Information Board' is all that marks the site of the business where laden wherries once plied their trade.

This is also good country for exploration on foot, and three main walks are to be recommended. The first starts at Chedgrove Church and, in the course of two to five miles - depending on the choice of route - takes in HARDLEY FLOOD, a Site of Special Scientific Interest that is of international importance to migratory wading birds. It was formed by flooding in the 1920s and after endless failed attempts at drainage over the following decades was left as a permanently flooded woodland. At various times of the year a wide variety of birds is to be seen including herons, shovellers, pochard, common terns, kingfishers, snipe, hen harriers and reed and sedge warblers.

The TWO HALLS WALK runs for six and a half miles from the Church Plain car park. As the name suggests, its points of interest are focused on the Georgian LODDON HALL and on HALES HALL. Finally, a selection of shorter, circular walks may be enjoyed around the RIVERSIDE MEADOWS, taking in the PYES MILL picnic area and the orchard of old Norfolk apple varieties behind ASTON BOATS. The footpath between Holy Trinity and MILL ROAD is arched over by trees and is especially lovely in spring when it is a mass of blossom and wild flowers. Elsewhere, note should be taken that the grazing marsh is an Environmentally Sensitive Area, managed to preserve and encourage its flora and fauna.

From this final touch of Broadland, our tour takes us now across country, westwards once again, as we head for the next significant stopping place, Wymondham. Crossing the A146, we find ourselves on a lane that leads to the village of MUNDHAM and then to Seething airfield [Information - 01508 550288], where STATION 146 was home to 448 Bomb Group, Second Air Division, USAAF 8th Army Air Force during World War II. The exhibits that have been collected here, including unique photographs, wartime diaries and personal effects as well as the model aircraft room, inspire yet another pause for reflection.

Having found the B1332 soon after leaving the airfield and turned right a short way south through **WOODTON,** we find ourselves travelling west towards the A140, which we cross just south of **TASBURGH,** in search of the award-winning MUSEUM at **FORNCETT** [Information - 01508 488277]. This is another shrine for engineering buffs as it houses a remarkable collection of truly fascinating industrial stationery steam engines. There are many exhibits to stop us in our tracks - but pride of place must go, surely, to an engine once used to open Tower Bridge!

From Forncett it's really only a brief wriggle north and then west again [B1113 - B1135] before we slip past the A11 and into **WYMONDHAM** [Information - 01953 604721]. Confusingly pronounced 'Wind-um', the town is dominated even from a distance by its majestic, twin towered Abbey. It's a charming market town, that still retains a wealth of listed buildings despite the ravages of the Great Fire of 1615. It's also enjoying the relief provided by the new by-pass and the benefits of a recent town centre improvement scheme, both of which make it even more attractive for visitors and more efficient for the local farming community. Indeed, it's busy FRIDAY MARKET reminds us that it's still an active independent community which refuses to be overshadowed by Norwich, its big city neighbour.

While Wymondham has expanded considerably and changed with the times, it has maintained its traditional atmosphere. This, as we shall see, results from considerable skill in blending the old with the new in the most delightful way. If the 17th century MARKET CROSS has become the town's trademark, the ABBEY, dedicated to St Mary and St Thomas of Canterbury, will always be its piece de resistance. Founded in 1107 by William D'Albini, as we know from our previous travels, its church was built to serve both the Benedictine monks and the townspeople. As clear distinctions about the rights of each group were never made, the quarrels between them were endless. The problem was solved in 1445 when the people put up the great west tower - from then, until the Dissolution in 1538 the monks were said to own the nave, the north west tower and the north aisle while the town people used the remainder. After 1538 the Abbey Church was granted to the people as a whole for payment at valuation.

Wymondham is no stranger to adversity, disorder and revolution. The most famous incident was Ketts Rebellion in 1549, when the brothers Robert and William Kett led a revolt against the local landlords after the common pasture land was enclosed. The rebellion put the wind up the Government in London, and two military expeditions were sent to suppress it. The brothers were captured - Robert to be executed at Norwich Castle and William at Wymondham.

Three hundred years later another major feature of present day life was built in the town: the RAILWAY STATION. Opened originally to serve the Norwich - Ely line, and once employing more than a hundred people, it's still a part of the rail link between Norwich, London and the Midlands. However, the fully restored buildings offer much more besides. As winner of the 'Best Station in England' certificate, Wymondham now presents a truly broad 'railway experience'. From the Ross Jamieson Hornby Model Railway Collection to the 'Brief Encounter' refreshment room and the nostalgic exhibition of railway memorabilia there's everything here to waft one back on a major daydream of the Golden Age of Railway travel. From the free car park to the range of railway books, pictures and mugs, next to nothing has been overlooked in making this stretch of 'Memory Lane' well worth a visit.

The mid 19th century collapse of the wool industry brought great hardship to Wymondham. Between 1836 and 1845 the number of operating handlooms dropped from six hundred to sixty. As a the result the town became largely a backwater, missing out on much of the major Victorian urban development. Whilst remembering their predecessors suffering, for today's visitors that cloud was silver lined as it left the bulk of the town centre unspoiled and much as it was in the 17th century, after the fire. Aside from the historical perspective, there's much to appeal to us in other aspects of the town. The period streetscapes are the setting for a good selection of antique and second hand book shops. There's the market on Fridays, a HERITAGE MUSEUM in the BRIDEWELL, and delightful walks along a 'green corridor' through the town and out to the RIVER TIFFEY VALLEY WALK, where waterside footpaths provide fine views of typical Norfolk valley landscapes. There is even a modern LEISURE CENTRE for those of us who find riverside walks to lack a challenge. I suspect the rest of us, being somewhat saner, would rather return to the car and head off in search of what ever comes next!

'Next' is the pleasant medley of Georgian houses, bordering splendid greens, at **HINGHAM**. These fine buildings are grouped around two squares and are linked by narrow streets. The large 14th century ST ANDREW'S CHURCH contains a bust of Abraham Lincoln, a descendant of Samuel Lincoln, a local weaver, whose religious beliefs made him seek the greater tolerance of 'the colonies'. There he joined Robert Peck, an argumentative rector who, somewhat earlier, had also gone to seek 'freedom' in America. Peck founded the namesake town of Hingham, Massachusetts and a connection between the two is still maintained.

Hingham's town sign is the first example we have seen of a whole series of about a hundred produced for Norfolk towns by Harry Carter, the son of Sir Howard Carter, leader of the expedition which discovered the tomb of Tutankhamen in 1922. We shall see others later at Watton, Swaffham, Castle Acre and elsewhere. Our way now leads through Attleborough and Watton to our next main Norfolk centre, East Dereham. This will follow the A11, south west for about six miles, then either take the direct B1077 route or else continue as far as Snetterton for a glimpse of the motor-racing circuit, before taking the next right turn along the B1111. This may be a better idea, as it will give us a further look at the edge of the Brecks.

ATTLEBOROUGH always used to be famous for rearing turkeys, which had to make the journey to London's markets on foot - poor beasts! It also had quite a reputation for its cider. Today the PARISH CHURCH, once the heart of a much bigger building, is worth seeing, along with a number of familiar attractions elsewhere in the town, which is linked by rail to Thetford, Norwich and Cambridge.

While we're in this particular area another minor literary digression wouldn't come amiss. The roughly triangular stretch of land south of the Attleborough - Watton road has links with three writers whose work was more varied than one would expect, coming as it did from what could be seen as a comparatively sleepy backwater, around the turn of the century. Edward Fitzgerald [1808-1883], author and translator, died at the Rectory at **MERTON** in 1883, while on his annual visit to his friend George Crabbe, grandson of the poet Crabbe. Fitzgerald's translation of 'The Rubaiyat of Omar Khayyam' still remains, more than a hundred years later, one of the most widely read and frequently quoted works of its kind to be found in the Western world.

South east of Merton lies **GREAT HOCKHAM,** where the Breckland novelist Michael Home [1885-1973] was born in 1885. One of the nine children of a village tradesman, barber and pig-killer, he won a place to Thetford Grammar School and then went on to study modern languages at King's College, London. In fact, 'Michael Home' was the pen name under which the writer produced his exemplary works founded on local life, the first of which, 'God and the Rabbit', appeared in 1934. Under his own name, Christopher Bush, he wrote more than fifty detective novels, despite seeing service in two world wars. Eight more Breckland novels followed and the autobiographical works 'Autumn Fields', 'Spring Sowing' and 'Winter Harvest' make particularly vivid reading.

Across the B1111 at **SHROPHAM** we'll find the home of Mary E. Mann [1848-1929] who, though born in Norwich, spent most of her life in the village, where her husband Fairman Mann was a farmer. They lived at the Manor House until 1913, and were deeply engaged with all aspects of village life, from guardianship of the workhouse to organising school treats and visiting the sick. So moved was Mary Mann by these experiences that, almost inevitably, they became the background against which she wrote most of her novels.

The stories that created Mary Mann's claim to national recognition are a powerful evocation of the lives of Breckland labourers and their families during a time of great agricultural depression. Although she also wrote romances, 'The Fields of Dulditch' stories, reprinted in 1976, portray with a stark reality rarely found in novels of rural life, her characters' morality ,superstitions and, above all, the relentless poverty that often led so many of them to the workhouse. Now I know that these are not the kind of thoughts that one would choose whilst on holiday, and that much of the work of Mary Mann would be a disaster as a book at bedtime in one's hotel, nevertheless it is a fact that times have changed and it won't hurt us to remember that from time to time in the future.

On then, to Watton - but first we must have a look at the racetrack at **SNETTERTON**, for a whiff of nostalgia for the 'Golden Days' of British motor racing. In their heyday Lotus cars, produced by Colin Chapman's local firm, beat the world's best in the hands of drivers like Jim Clark and Graham Hill. If our humble saloon seems a bit dreary by comparison, let's be comforted by the knowledge that a Formula One brute would be useless for our needs. We'll take the B1111, followed by the A1075, north west, and leave the 'boys' toys' where they belong.

WATTON, a small town with an unusual clock tower dating from 1675, is known today for its WARTIME MUSEUM, which tells the story of RAF Watton, and of the town, from 1937 to '45. In yet another burst of contrast, it's also hard by WAYLAND WOOD, to the south, where the events of 'Babes in the Wood', as illustrated on the town sign, took place, according to local legend!

The ancient story goes back to a ballad, first published in Norwich in 1595. The story of 'The Babes' is, I imagine, too well known [even in the days of 'Star Trek' and Tellytubbies] to need re-telling, but it certainly has a strong root in the Watton area. Although no-one knows how the Wayland Wood connection started, it was so strong by Victorian times that, when the oak tree under which 'The Babes' were said to have sheltered was struck by lightning in 1879, people came from all over the country for souvenirs. More remarkably still, in a way, nearby Griston Hall Farm had acquired the reputation of being the home of the wicked uncle.

A swing in the road to the north-west, and we're on our way, now, to **EAST DEREHAM** [Information - 01362 698992], which lies at the heart of Norfolk and is a lively market town and shopping centre. There is a charming piece of local history linked with the little known Saxon saint, Withburga, who founded a nunnery here in the seventh century. The daughter of King Anna of East Anglia, she is commemorated on the town sign, which depicts the legend of two deer who arrived in answer to her prayers to give their milk to the nuns during a time of famine. This miracle is claimed to have given the town its name, and is heightened by a further incident in which a huntsman, who tried to set his dogs on the deer, met with divine retribution in the shape of a sudden fall from his horse - which killed him.

DEREHAM TOWN CENTRE

The part-Norman ST NICHOLAS'S CHURCH stands on the site of the nunnery. ST WITHBURGA'S TOMB is to be found in the churchyard, as is the grave of the poet William Cowper, whose tale we first heard up on the north coast. In earlier times, the tomb was venerated as a shrine, although the monks of Ely removed her relics in the 10th century to place alongside those of her sister, St Etheldreda. A spring burst from Withburga's empty tomb and this, having become famous as a healing well, may still be seen in the churchyard.

Seeing the fine stone monument to Cowper, one is driven to reflect for a moment or two on the life of this 'gentle and humane man', who suffered from the bouts of depression that seem to afflict so many people with such a temperament. He lived a retired life with his companion Mary Unwin and his pet hares and cats - a feature which is marked in the 'Cowper Window', erected in the Church to commemorate the centenary of his death, and which shows the poet in his morning cap with his pet hares at his feet.

Gentle he may have been, but that didn't prevent Cowper from taking the odd dig at contemporary life, in the form of several witty satires. He wrote hymns too, as we noted at Happisburgh, and many sonnets and verses. The ballad of 'John Gilpin' was a Cowper creation - but his contribution to our culture that is probably remembered [and quoted] more often than all the rest put together has to do with tea, which he had the inspiration to observe was *'the cup that cheers but does not inebriate.'*

As you may well soon discover, the area has a host of other strong literary associations, but we'll only look at one more before we move on. Augustus Jessopp [1824-1914] wrote a number of historical works centred on East Anglia. 'The Coming of the Friars' is his most popular book and gives a lively history of Medieval life in the region. He also produced a collection of essays under the title 'Arcady for Better or Worse', based on tales and reminiscences from his parishioners.

Strolling away from the churchyard of Cowper and Withburga, we find that the town centre is still very pleasant, with its mixture of old and new architecture. Nearby are BISHOP BONNER'S COTTAGES, named after a 16th century rector who went on to become Bishop of London, which are home to the MUSEUM of the DEREHAM ARCHAEOLOGICAL SOCIETY.

A small picnic site and car park at CHERRY LANE give good views of the 1836 WINDMILL, open between May and September, while, not far way, GRESSENHALL houses the NORFOLK RURAL LIFE MUSEUM and UNION FARM [Information - 01362 860563]. This former workhouse, complete with its working, restored period farm, offers a series of imaginative displays of rural life and Victorian cottages and gardens. Craftsmen's Row is a further attraction, whilst the riverside and woodland walks entice the casual stroller, if the weather is encouraging.

Sadly, with our departure from Dereham, our South Norfolk tour is nearing its end. So, it is fitting that one of our last encounters should be with **SWAFFHAM** [Information - 01760 722255], held by many to be Norfolk's most attractive market town. Yes, I've kept the best till last again! A thriving community, Swaffham lies on the northern edge of Breckland and the Thetford Forest, where the rolling landscape typical of North Norfolk meets the open plain of the southern part of the county. The geography gives us an opportunity to put all we've seen into perspective.

First-time visitors are invariably surprised by the extent of the triangular MARKET PLACE, with its 18th century MARKET CROSS (not a cross at all, but a rotunda, built by Horace Walpole, 4th Earl of Orford).

SWAFFHAM

The Market Place is surrounded by elegant Georgian buildings that date from Swaffham's days as a fashionable centre for Norfolk's gentry, who spent 'The Season' enjoying the great social and sporting functions that were a feature of the town. Every Saturday the normal scene of tranquillity is transformed by the OPEN AIR MARKET and AUCTION which attract thousands of people seeking to buy or sell and to keep up with the local news and gossip. Outstanding amid the period elegance surrounding the spectacle is MONTPELIER HOUSE which, in the 18th century, almost certainly accommodated Lady Nelson (Lord Nelson himself was a frequent visitor - as was Lady Hamilton)! The north aisle of the 15th century CHURCH OF SS PETER AND PAUL, one of the finest of East Anglia's many medieval churches, is associated with the tale - part fact, part fiction - of a local pedlar, John Chapman. It seems he went to London to seek his fortune and met a stranger who told him of a dream in which he had found a fortune under a pear tree in a garden in a country town. The pedlar recognised the description of his own garden, went home, found the fortune - and built the north aisle of the Church out of gratitude. He is depicted on a bench end in the Church, with his pack and his dog (another bench end is said to show his wife, leaning over the shop door, holding a string of beads). Incidentally, the 'Pedlar of Swaffham' is also commemorated in yet another town sign by Harry Carter.

One other 'treasure' of the Church deserves our attention. It is home to part of the library of rare books collected by Sir Henry Spelman, the distinguished historian, including his edition of 'Holinshed's Chronicle' and 'The Works of James I.' Sir Henry's grandfather was Sir John Spelman, a Justice of the King's Bench during the reign of Henry VIII. Typically for those times, the learned justice seems to have got rather more out of preparing the indictment that led to the beheading of Anne Boleyn - namely an estate of land at Narborough, to the north west - than he ever did out of attending her coronation. Sir Henry was buried at Westminster Abbey, but other monuments to the Spelman family can be seen at NARBOROUGH CHURCH.

Other local attractions extend from the TOWN MUSEUM [Information - 01760 721230] to CERES BOOKSHOP [Enquiries - 01760 722504], THE HAYES GALLERY [Enquiries - 01760 723755], with its numerous Victorian and 20th century paintings in oils and watercolours to ECOTECH, which is a new environmental attraction, featuring imaginative exhibitions and interactive displays in an innovative 'green' building.

Before we begin our final surging run for home, we really ought to nip out of the town towards the south for a look at the ICENII VILLAGE at **COCKLEY CLEY**. The village is a full-scale reconstruction on the original site of an Icenii encampment and shows in some detail how the tribe lived more than two thousand years ago. There is also an Elizabethan cottage which includes a museum, a Saxon church of around 630AD, a carriage, a vintage engine and an agricultural museum. If that's not enough, towards the end of a day such as we have enjoyed, there is a delightful nature trail to provide a trace of exercise should this be necessary, prior to driving off again.

As it happens, whilst we're wandering around Cockley Cley, it would be appropriate to take a brief look at Norfolk's first recorded 'personality'. Boadicea [or Boudicca, as the trendy element seems to prefer to call her these days] was the wife of Prasutagus, king of the Icenii [or Iceni , for the trendy], an Iron Age tribe who inhabited the Breckland area. Everything that we know about her comes from the writings of Roman historians who appear to have regarded her as quite a lady. A red-haired woman of immense stature, she wore a great gold necklace and a brightly coloured cloak and liked nothing better than hurtling round the landscape in her chariot beating up Romans - at which pastime, as history also relates, she was somewhat better than average.

After the death of her husband, the Romans tried to seize his territory - an idea which didn't go down too well with the locals. Under Boadicea's leadership, said locals did a bit of seizing on their own account and sacked the invaders' settlements at Colchester, St Albans and - would you believe - *London*. Some revolt, one would have said - and some lady, as we've already noted. Sadly [or not, if you were a Roman] her end game wasn't quite up to it, and she and her followers came to a shuddering halt in front of the Roman army, who cheated by being more disciplined than everybody else. The tribesmen were put to flight - and the sword, if they didn't run quickly enough - and so ended one of the earlier attempts to stand against the might of bureaucracy from

Europe. The Romans cribbed a lot of their best notions from the infinitely subtler Greeks - but 'bureaucracy' was all their own idea. True, they had great soldiers - but you should have seen their *filing* systems.

All that red hair of Boadicea's gives some idea of how she must have reacted to her defeat. A typically Titian tantrum, I would surmise (not one to give in gracefully, our Iron Age queen). Nor did the Romans have too much time for failures, so there is no further record of her in the histories. The word is that she topped herself - which would figure, if it had been a real *big* tantrum. At any rate, she vanished rather sharply from the scene, leaving very little behind to mark her passing except for *at least two* burial mounds that local legends absolutely *insist* are her last resting place.

Let's fast forward 1700 years and ease over to **HILBOROUGH**. This parish was the home of the Nelson family, from 1734 to 1806, a role which makes an interesting comparison with that of Montpelier House, which we have seen already. In those days, every local rector was a Nelson, including the Admiral's father, who only moved to Burnham Thorpe shortly before Horatio was born. It is possible they moved away for their health as two previous sons, born at Hilborough, died in infancy. Obviously, the noble lord bore the place no hard feelings, though, as he visited several times as a boy, to stay with his grandfather at the Rectory - and his grandmother at the Nunnery. Even more significantly, when he was granted his peerage, he adopted the title of 'Baron Nelson of the Nile *and Hilborough*'. Another link exists between the Admiral and the village as, after his death at Trafalgar in 1805, his brother William presented Hilborough with the magnificent Trafalgar Arms church plate.

As we drive away from the village, we aim ourselves back to base, by way of the A1065, the B1145 and a final right turn along the two minor roads that lead past Sandringham to the coast.

Once more, though, it isn't quite over - as you might have guessed! We haven't been to **CASTLE ACRE**, yet. A steep street leads into the village, and its 11th century CLUNIAC PRIORY. The extensive and well-maintained remains lie on the old PEDDARS' WAY, which, as we know, ran south from Holme next the Sea into Suffolk. They are set in farmland bordering the River Nar and, together with the remains of the CASTLE, are open to the public, making an ideal picnic site. The Priory was founded by William de Warenne, William the Conqueror's son-in-law, and first Earl of Surrey, who also built the Castle. The ragged remains, set in glorious scenery, clearly show the shape and size of the original Priory, whose west front has one of Britain's finest remaining tiers of Norman arcading.

Displays of medieval masonry, found during excavations, are housed in the few Priory rooms still intact while close by at PALES GREEN, CASTLE ACRE STUDIOS [Enquiries - 01760 755405], hand thrown porcelain and stone ware are for sale, along with paintings and prints. The workshop and showroom are usually open throughout the year, between 10am and 5pm.

The last miles of our route take us north, past Great and Little Massingham and then the Royal estate, and Dersingham.

Perhaps we'll have to make do with a symbolic gesture in the morning, before we progress westwards. Time, as ever, is always short, it seems. With this in mind, I'd suggest that a call at DERSINGHAM POTTERY AND DERSINGHAM GALLERY [Enquiries - 01485 540761] in CHAPEL STREET, would suit admirably. Displayed there, in converted stables, built from the local carrstone that, by now, we find so familiar, is an interesting collection of hand thrown stoneware by June Mullarkey as well as watercolours and oils by Ben Mullarkey. A gentle stroll around, followed by a purchase or two sounds like an excellent au-revoir to this delightful north coast area, and an ideal source of the inspiration we need to carry us on to our next base, Ely.

CHURCH FARM HOUSE
Church Road
North Lopham
NR Diss, Norfolk
IP22 2LP

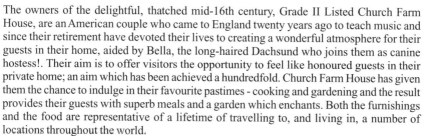

Tel/Fax: 01379 687270
Email: B&B@bassetts.demon.co.uk
Internet:
http://www.bassetts.demon.co.uk/cfhmain.htm

One Crown Highly Commended. Member of Wolsey Lodges &
'A Break with Tradition' Consortium

The owners of the delightful, thatched mid-16th century, Grade II Listed Church Farm House, are an American couple who came to England twenty years ago to teach music and since their retirement have devoted their lives to creating a wonderful atmosphere for their guests in their home, aided by Bella, the long-haired Dachsund who joins them as canine hostess!. Their aim is to offer visitors the opportunity to feel like honoured guests in their private home; an aim which has been achieved a hundredfold. Church Farm House has given them the chance to indulge in their favourite pastimes - cooking and gardening and the result provides their guests with superb meals and a garden which enchants. Both the furnishings and the food are representative of a lifetime of travelling to, and living in, a number of locations throughout the world.

Church Farm House has three ensuite guest rooms; one double with ensuite shower and a king-sized bed (American Queen-sized), one single room with ensuite shower and a twin room with ensuite bath. Breakfast is an Anglo-American feast and at night you dine by candlelight in the Dining Room at a table laid with shining family silver and a variety of crystal glassware and china. With delicious food, charming company and a memorable house, there is little more one can possibly need or want.

You will find Church Farm House directly across from the old village church in the agricultural village of North Lopham, near the market town of Diss. It is a house that has been lovingly restored to offer modern comfort and old world charm enhanced by a wealth of beams and all sorts of nooks and crannies which give the house great character. Church Farm House is ideally situated for people wanting to visit Bressingham Gardens and Steam Museum, five minutes away. Stately National Trust homes such as Ickworth House are a pleasant drive away. The historic and breathtakingly beautiful 'wool' village of Lavenham with its ancient timber-framed Guildhall, is close enough for an afternoon's outing. Cambridge, Norwich and Bury St Edmunds offer perfect venues for day trips.

USEFUL INFORMATION

OPEN: All year
CHILDREN: Over 14
CREDIT CARDS: None taken
LICENSED: Residential Licence
ACCOMMODATION: 3 ensuite rooms
RATES: £27PP B&B. 3 Course dinner £16.50
Special 2 night off-peak breaks for 2 people £155
inclusive of 2 Nights B&B and 2 dinners

DINING ROOM: Superb food
VEGETARIAN: By arrangement
WHEELCHAIR ACCESS: No
GARDEN: Mature & beautiful
PETS: Well behaved dogs by arrangement

STRICTLY NON-SMOKING HOUSE

THE CAT AND FIDDLE
Fakenham Road
East Rudham,
King's Lynn
Norfolk
PE318QZ

Tel:01485 528566

If you enjoy a true, traditional village pub then you will find The Cat and Fiddle the place to be. In the heart of East Rudham, it has been a hostelry for over a hundred years and originally commenced life as the bakery for a monastery taking on the name The Bakers Arms, appropriately enough, when it became a pub. In the 1970s it changed its name to The Cat and Fiddle which appealed more to the large RAF population working and living in the area. Today it is an interesting mixture of the old and the modern, very comfortable, informal and relaxed but retaining many reminders of the years gone by especially the open fireplace where the main bread oven used to be.

Beamed ceilings add to the atmosphere and so do the many jugs and old steins hanging from the ceiling as well as a yard of ale and much more memorabilia. The dark oak tables are pre-set with hunting scene mats, providing yet another feel of the past. Jonathan Hollister is the landlord who took on the license when his parents retired three years ago. He knows everyone in the village and his welcome for strangers is just as heart-warming as to his regulars. There is something very stable about the life of a village pub. There is a pool room and a games room where some heated battles take place - all in good spirit of course!

The Cat and Fiddle serves very good food, specialising in steaks and grills but offering several other choices as well including excellent home-made pies. The steaks are renowned for their succulence and there is a large variety. Friday night is known as 'Steak Night'. pork mixed grills are another speciality. There are always bar snacks including freshly cut sandwiches and salads. You must try one of the home-made pies which will not be equalled anywhere else in Norfolk. The Patio garden is popular during the summer months and it is delightful to sit out there in the comparative peace of this rural community.

USEFUL INFORMATION

OPEN: Weekdays except Wednesdays 12-3pm	RESTAURANT: No
Every day 6.30-11pm. All day Sat from 12 noon	CHILDREN: Welcome
CREDIT CARDS: None taken	BAR FOOD: Specialising in Steaks.
LICENSED: Full On	Traditional fare
VEGETARIAN: Good selection	GARDEN: Yes. Table tennis in summer
WHEELCHAIR ACCESS: Yes	PETS: Yes. Under supervision

GREENACRES FARM
Woodgreen
Long Stratton
Norfolk
NR15 2RR

Tel/Fax: 01508 530261

EATB 2 Crowns
Commended

Greenacres is a period 17th century farmhouse tucked away in the hamlet of Woodgreen. There are ancient ponds and woods, quiet woodland tracks and lanes where you may walk or cycle. It is a blissful retreat. It is only a mile and a half from Long Stratton Village (A140) This central location makes it ideal for discovering the beauty of Norfolk and Suffolk. The historic cathedral city of Norwich is twelve miles off.

Inside this comfortable farmhouse many of the original features still exist including an inglenook fireplace and a 60ft glass topped well in the Snooker Room. David and Joanna Douglas are the owners and the house is beautifully furnished throughout with a pleasing mixture of antique and other pieces. The three guest bedrooms, one double ensuite, one double with private bathroom and an ensuite twin-bedded room are charming. The beds are comfortable and the modern necessity, television, is in each room as well as a generously supplied hospitality tray. Breakfast is a satisfying, freshly cooked meal and at night, if you want an evening meal, a simple two course feast is available using local produce, vegetables and fruit from the garden when available. Fresh salmon is frequently on the menu as well as a variety of casseroles.

USEFUL INFORMATION

OPEN: All year
CHILDREN: Welcome
CREDIT CARDS: None taken
LICENSED: No
ACCOMMODATION: 3 ensuite rooms
RATES: From £18 pp on B&B

DINING ROOM: Excellent breakfast
2 course home-cooked evening meal
VEGETARIAN: Upon request
WHEELCHAIR ACCESS: No
GARDEN: Yes + tennis court
PETS: Yes

HOLMDENE FARM
Beeston
King's Lynn
Norfolk
PE32 2NJ

Tel/Fax: 01328 701284

Tourist Board Registered

The village of Beeston is set amid rolling farmland with a myriad of quiet lanes making it ideal for cycling and walking. A traditional village pub is the focal point of the community which is popular with locals and visitors. The fine Norman Church is another attraction well worth a visit. For the energetic golf, fishing and horse riding are available in neighbouring villages and there are several famous houses to visit within easy ach including Sandringham, Oxburgh, Felbrigg, Blickling and Holkham, as well as the stunning North Norfolk Coast.

With all this to see and do there can be no better, more relaxed place to stay than Holmdene Farm, which offers bed and breakfast accommodation and also has cottages for self-catering enthusiasts. Owned and run by Gaye Davidson who has a wealth of experience, whichever you decide is the place for you, will be delightful. In the 16th century farmhouse with its beamed ceilings and open log fires, there is one ensuite double room, one twin and two singles sharing a bathroom. Each of the rooms is attractively furnished, very cosy and comfortable. Breakfast is a feast as one would expect from Gaye who runs art, craft and cookery courses to which guests are cordially invited. Evening meals are available by arrangement and they are delicious. Gaye uses all the best ingredients, local produce and fresh vegetables. She is also happy to cater for Vegetarians and other dietary needs if she is forewarned.

The self-catering cottages, The stables and the oat store are both fully equipped, attractively furnished and decorated. The Stables which is suitable for wheelchairs, has an ensuite double, a twin and two single rooms with the addition of a double put-u-up Holmdene is a working farm with arable and livestock. Guests are welcome to help with feeding the calves, lambs, goats and chickens. There is a great atmosphere here, somewhere guests feel very welcome and comfortable.

USEFUL INFORMATION

OPEN: All year
CHILDREN: Welcome
VEGETARIAN: With prior warning
WHEELCHAIR ACCESS: In one cottage
GARDEN: Yes
ACCOMMODATION: 1 ensuite dbl. 1tw. 1sgl.
RATES: From £16 B&B
The Stables From £165-£405per week
The Oat Store From £135-275 per week

DINING ROOM: Excellent breakfast
Evening meal by arrangement
CREDIT CARDS: None taken
LICENSED: No
PETS: Yes

THE OLD SHOP
24 London Road,
Downham Market,
Norfolk PE38 9AW

Tel: 01366 382051

AA QQ

Downham Market has a wealth of history. It was once the site of the 19th century Horsefairs, it has some fine architecture and stands on the edge of the Fens. Great countryside to explore and full of interesting places to visit. June and Eric Roberts own The Old Shop which they run as a Guest House. The Old Shop was once the local general store and whatever alterations have been made to it have been done with loving care and with a determination to protect the character of the building. This has certainly been achieved and you will find the house is full of nooks and crannies, has crooked ceilings and sloping walls. The welcome within these walls is second to none. June and Eric both know exactly how to ensure their guests comfort and well being.

There are two attractively appointed double bedrooms both of which are ensuite and a family room with private bathroom, each has television, and a well-stocked hospitality tray. In the morning after a peaceful night's sleep you come downstairs to a pretty dining room where you will be served a delicious full English breakfast, freshly cooked . If you prefer something lighter you will find that there are fruit juices and cereals as well as plenty of toast, butter and preserves. There is a Guest Lounge with colour television and video.

The Old Shop is open throughout the year and as well as the warmth of the welcome, it is a great place to stay for a short break out of season. Business people who stay here find it relaxing after a days work and relish the home-from-home atmosphere created by June and Eric.

USEFUL INFORMATION

OPEN: All year
CHILDREN: Welcome
CREDIT CARDS: None taken
LICENSED: No
ACCOMMODATION: 2 ensuite rooms
1 family room with private bathroom
RATES: From £16pp B&B Children from £10.00

DINING ROOM: Great breakfast
Evening meal by prior arrangement
VEGETARIAN: Upon request
WHEELCHAIR ACCESS: No
PETS: Welcome

RAVENWOOD HALL COUNTRY
HOTEL & RESTAURANT,
Rougham,
Bury St Edmunds,
Suffolk
IP30 9JA

AA ***

Tel: 01359 270345
Fax: 01359 270788

Nestled within seven acres of its own lawns and woodland, featuring both wild flowers and formal borders, Revenwood Hall is in a tranquil world of its own offering seclusion, yet it is merely 3 miles from the ancient market town of Bury St Edmunds. Many pleasurable hours can be spent using the Hall's wide range of leisure facilities, including a hard tennis court, a croquet lawn and heated swimming pool. Locally there are golf courses, plentiful woodland walks and both hunting and shooting can be arranged.

The Hall's intriguing history began in the reign of Henry VIII and even now its ornately carved oak structure are rare 16th century wall paintings with an air of mystical Tudor charm. There are fourteen delightful bedrooms, all with private bathrooms and antique furniture. The Oak Room has a superb four-poster complemented by 16th century panelling. Modern requirements are there as well with television, direct dial telephones in every room as well as hairdryers and hostess trays. The Hall's fifty cover award winning restaurant is a cosy, intimate place in which to sample the finest of local ingredients with meats, fish and poultry smoked on the premises. Conference facilities are available in the Pavilion for up to two hundred delegates.

USEFUL INFORMATION

OPEN: All year
Bar 12-2pm &6.30-9.30. 10pm On Fri & Sat
Rest:12-2pm & 7.30-9.30. 10pm on Fri & Sat
CHILDREN: Welcome
CREDIT CARDS: All major cards
LICENSED: Full On
ACCOMMODATION: 14 ensuite rooms
RATES: From sgl£63 dbl. £83

RESTAURANT: Award winning
Classical/Modern menus
BAR FOOD: Light meals
VEGETARIAN: Choice available
WHEELCHAIR ACCESS: Yes
GARDEN: Yes. Tennis,
swimming, croquet
PETS: Yes

THE RED LION MOTEL
87 Market Place
Swaffham
Norfolk
PE37 7AQ

Tel/Fax: 01760 721022

AA 3 Q's Recommended

Right in the heart of historic Swaffham is the Red Lion Motel which has been there since the 17th century, and hundreds of years before the word 'Motel' came into the English language. It is one of the cosiest and most warm-hearted of establishments you could ever wish for, combining the atmosphere of a local pub frequented by regulars with the modern motel rooms providing the accommodation. George and Veronica Hoare are mine hosts - Veronica is known affectionately as Ronnie. They have the happy knack of making their regular customers and visitors feel at home and equally important to the well being of the pub.

People come to stay here for several reasons. It is a convenient base for the exploration of this part of Norfolk. It is ideal for the businessman and it has some fascinating history. The eleven ensuite bedrooms are all self-contained and around a courtyard, charmingly furnished and each has direct dial telephone, television and a well-filled hospitality tray. Breakfast every morning is freshly cooked to your order and is both delicious and sustaining. At night you return to a happy, contented atmosphere. The residents have their own bar if they do not wish to join in with the regulars and from here you can enjoy a drink whilst you take a look at the enticing menu of home-cooked dishes in which local produce is used where ever possible, as well as other exciting food. The same applies in the bar where the menu is varied and you can have anything from a daily special to a sandwich, a Ploughman's to a salad. The wine list matches the food and above all the price is right whether you are staying, eating or drinking.

USEFUL INFORMATION

OPEN: 10am-11pm all year
CHILDREN: Welcome
CREDIT CARDS: Yes
VEGETARIAN: Always some dishes
LICENSED: Full On
ACCOMMODATION: 11 ensuite rooms
RATES: From £22.50 sgl pp pn & £35 dbl. pn

RESTAURANT: Home-cooked fare
BAR FOOD: Wide range, value for money
GARDEN: No. Front Patio
WHEELCHAIR ACCESS: Yes
PETS: No

SHILLINGSTONE
Church Road
Old Beetley
NR. East Dereham
Norfolk
NR20 4AB

Tel: 01362 861099
Mobile: 0421 306 190

1 Crown Commended

Shillingstone, a large modern house, in a rural, quiet and very peaceful spot, on the edge of the village of Old Beetley and next door to the church, could not be better situated for anyone wanting to explore the small local towns , all of which have markets, in this exciting area of Norfolk. Each of these towns is of interest and then there is Sandringham and National Trust Properties such as Oxburgh Hall, Felbrigg and Blickling are near by. Gressenhall Rural Life Museum is in the next village and for those who enjoy sporting activities, Dereham Golf Course is two miles away and there is Fishing close by. Walkers will enjoy the many delightful, scenic walks and there is a swimming pool in Dereham

Jeanne Partridge owns Shillingstone and has a warm and genuine welcome for all guests to her home with its lovely, large, well-tended garden and Victorian Conservatory. In the summer you are welcome to enjoy the garden and relax on seats under the shade of sun umbrellas. Inside the comfortably furnished house has large, sunny double and twin bedrooms, all on the first floor with Hand basins, H&C water, Tea/Coffee making facilities and television in all rooms.

A Luxury Bathroom is also on the first floor. Guests have a Lounge with Colour television for their sole use with an entrance via French Windows into the garden. Guests also have their own Front Entrance to Shillingstone. The house is centrally heated and very cosy in winter. Every morning Jeanne provides an excellent breakfast served in the pretty Dining Room. There are no evening meals but the Village Inn serves bar meals, lunches and evening meals. The B1146 will lead you to Beetley and whether you are coming from the North or the South at Beetley you turn into High House Road then immediately left in front of the Methodist Chapel into Church Road. Shillingstone is the house next to the Church.

USEFUL INFORMATION

OPEN: All year
CHILDREN: Welcome breakfast
CREDIT CARDS: None taken
LICENSED: No
ACCOMMODATION: Double & twin rms
RATES: From £16 pp B&B

DINING ROOM: Full traditional

VEGETARIAN: Yes + other diets
WHEELCHAIR ACCESS: No
GARDEN: Yes with furniture
PETS: Yes £10 per visit

STARSTON HALL
Starston
Norfolk
IP20 2PU

Tel: 01379 854252
Fax: 01379 851966

'Top 20 in country'
Which Magazine
Highly Commended ETB

Starston Hall, set in the middle of a 2000 acre farm estate, twelve miles south of the historic cathedral city of Norwich, is quite rightly included in the top twenty Country House Guest Houses by Which Magazine.

This Elizabethan house is full of atmosphere enhanced by antiques and luxurious interiors. The 4 acres of gardens are complete with a moat and resident ducks. There are facilities for riding, fishing, golfing, cycling and walking for the energetic. Scenic churches with round towers, American airfields from World War II, and the great architecture of Norwich with its quaint lanes, boutiques and historic cathedral beckon nearby. The Norfolk broads to the North and the Suffolk coast are only twenty minutes away.

This is the home of Christine Baxter. She thoroughly enjoys spoiling guests in her delightful home. Every room has its own special ambience, with unspoiled views over open countryside. There are two very well appointed bedrooms in the main house both with their own ensuite facilities, colour television, radio and Christina's excellent attention to detail. Additionally a converted barn offers a suite for two with its own cosy sitting room.

The food enhances your break far from the madding crowd. Early morning tea delivered to your door precedes breakfast in the sunny breakfast room. Freshly squeezed orange juice, cereals, home-made muesli with fresh fruit, yoghurts, full traditional English breakfast including not only free range eggs but also croissants and baked beans which are home-made. In the evening dinner, a four course table d'hôte feast is served in the elegant candle lit dining room. Christina does her utmost to indulge guests with varied menus and specials in innovative vegetarian cooking. You are invited to ask your friends to join you for aperitifs and dinner.

USEFUL INFORMATION

OPEN: All year
CHILDREN: Over 12 years
CREDIT CARDS: None taken
LICENSED: No
ACCOMMODATION: 3 rooms ensuite
RATES:£35pp pn Dinner £25pp

DINING ROOM; Delicious home-cooked
VEGETARIAN: Innovative meals
WHEELCHAIR ACCESS: Limited
GARDEN: 4 acres with moat
PETS: No

STRENNETH
Airfield Road
Fersfield
NR Diss
Norfolk
IP22 2BP

Tel: 01379 688182
Fax: 01379 688260
ken@mainline.co.uk

Ken and Brenda Webb own and run Strenneth, a 17th century house with a 20th century address :- Airfield Road. It stands in its own grounds on the edge of the little village of Fersfield and close to the busy, market town of Diss. It is surrounded by delightful countryside which encourages guests to take walks.

Strenneth is one of those comfortably furnished, informal houses in which you immediately feel relaxed. Whilst it is well-furnished, it nonetheless has that 'lived-in' feel about it. Ken and Brenda are friendly people who work hard to ensure that their guests have an enjoyable and memorable stay. There are seven attractively appointed guest rooms, all ensuite. Each room is individually decorated and furnished, the beds, with high quality bed linen, are very comfortable. There are double rooms, twin-bedded and single, most of which are non-smoking and on the ground floor. In one room there is a splendid and very romantic four-poster. All the rooms have television and a generously supplied hostess tray.

When you come down in the morning after a peaceful night's sleep, you will smell the fresh coffee brewing. Breakfast is a delicious meal with plenty of cereals, fruit juice , and a choice of a traditional full English breakfast. Plenty of toast and preserves and tea and coffee complete a meal that is both substantial and memorable. There are no evening meals served here but Ken and Brenda will happily point you in the right direction for the many good eateries within easy distance.

USEFUL INFORMATION

OPEN: All year
CHILDREN: Welcome
CREDIT CARDS: All major cards
LICENSED: Yes
ACCOMMODATION: 7 ensuite rooms
RATES: £22.50 pppn Four-poster £30 pppn B&B

DINING ROOM: Delicious breakfast
VEGETARIAN: Upon request
WHEELCHAIR ACCESS: Yes
GARDEN: Yes
PETS: Yes

YAXHAM MILL,
Freehouse & Restaurant
Norwich Road,
Yaxham,
Dereham,
Norfolk

Tel: 01362 693144
Fax: 01362 858556

Standing on the historic site of a Norfolk tower windmill dating from 1860, the present complex is the result of careful, loving use of old buildings and melding them with the present time. Former mill cottages have become individually designed self-catering accommodation, beautifully equipped, warm and comfortable. For example The Baker's shop, Stables, Blacksmith's and Forge Cottages were all part of the original hamlet.

You will find Yaxham Mill in open Countryside approximately two miles from the market town of Dereham in the heart of Norfolk. A wonderful area to visit, it is rich in history, superbly scenic and has a plethora of wonderful places to visit whether it is taking off for the Broads, going to the coast or exploring the villages and market towns and gazing with awe at the beauty Of some of the National Trust properties and gardens.

The owner, Eileen Leveridge, is an established breeder of Norfolk Ducklings but she nonetheless finds time to personally supervise the running of Yaxham Mill, in which she is ably assisted by a cheerful and very efficient staff. Her chef, Charles Newcombe, is a wizard with food with a preference for Italian cooking but he insists on there being a wide range of English and foreign dishes always available. This is a man who has created meals for Princess Margaret and Lady Thatcher and many other celebrities. He considers catering for 900 people at a Coldstream Guards charity event to be the pinnacle of his career- so far! The menu is always exciting and you dine in the superb forty four seat restaurant at tables laid with pretty linen cloths, cutlery that gleams and glass that sparkles. Bar snacks are available in a separate bar. For those who possibly have a wedding or a corporate function in mind you will find Yaxham Mill ideal. The organisation is perfect, marquees can be set up in the grounds and live entertainment is readily available.

USEFUL INFORMATION

OPEN: All year. 11-3pm & 6.30-11pm   RESTUARANT: Excellent, interesting fare
Weekends: All day   Including Italian dishes. Booking
CHILDREN: Welcome   advisable Especially for Sunday Lunch
CREDIT CARDS: Visa/Mastercard   BAR SNACKS: Wide Range
LICENSED: Yes   VEGETARIAN: Catered for
DISABLED ACCESS: Yes. Ramp.Toilets   ACCOMMODATION: Self-catering
GARDEN: Beer garden   cottages
Overnight caravan park - Short breaks. Overnight £37.50 double £25.00 single. ·

THE WALPOLE ARMS
The Common
Itteringham
Aylsham
Norfolk
NR11 7AR

Recc: Camra,
Which Guide to Country Pubs
Egon Ronay, the Good Pub Guide.
Award for Wine Quality

This attractive old inn just oozes character and atmosphere and at the same time is one of the most welcoming inns in the county. It is definitely an inn with a difference. Paul and Maggie Simmons are mine hosts and it is their love of life that spreads such a happy feeling everywhere. Paul was once a professional drummer and Maggie an Art Director in the Music Business and it is perhaps their knowledge of show business which lends the extra ingredient to the Walpole Arms. All sorts of things happen at the Walpole. For example, they regularly have theatre groups performing either in the rear garden or in the restaurant. Special food evenings have become very popular and eagerly awaited. It might be Italian or Norfolk Seafood, Oriental or Mediterranean Seafood. Every Bank Holiday the inn accommodates the Norfolk Craft Fair for three days during which it is nothing to see five thousand people enjoying the spectacle.

Every day the bar, with its original oak beams, low ceilings, huge log fire and traditional furniture attracts locals and visitors. The Restaurant is in a restored barn and here also the original beams have been kept. It is non-smoking and a great place to eat. The food is delicious with everything freshly cooked and using local and organic produce as much as possible. The Walpole has its own Smokehouse and produces wonderful smoked salmon, smoked sausages and cheeses which appear on the restaurant menu and also in the bar. The Walpole's success comes from the excellent team work of the owners and the staff. Each of them has something special to offer, whether it is an extensive knowledge of world wines or the nuances of perfect dishes. No one can fault the welcome and it is simply a very happy place to visit.

You will find the Walpole Arms on the edge of the village and close to the River Bure. Don't miss it.

USEFUL INFORMATION

OPEN: Mon-Sat 12-3pm & 6-11pm	RESTAURANT: Exciting food
Sun: 12-3pm & 7-10.30pm	BAR FOOD: Wide choice
CHILDREN: Welcome	VEGETARIAN: Yes
CREDIT CARDS: All major cards	WHEELCHAIR ACCESS: Yes
Credit Cards 5% Debit Cards 50p	GARDEN: Yes
LICENSED: Yes. Full On	PETS: Dogs on leads but not
	during eating hours

BELL BARN
Lime Kiln Road
West Dereham, King's Lynn
Norfolk   PE33 9RT
Tel/Fax: 01366 500762

ETB 2 Crown Commended

Christina and Philip Wood are the owners of this delightful, skilfully converted 18th century Norfolk Barn. They have managed to retain its character and you see exposed flint walls and a plethora of old beams. It is relaxed and informal, full of atmosphere and the first thing that strikes you on arrival is the imposing Entrance Hall which is in the old threshing area. The Wood's have a great eye for colour and design and Bell Barn with its traditional furnishings, stripped pine and antique furniture and co-ordinated decor, reflects their taste everywhere, providing the guest with one of the most attractive places to stay in Norfolk. There are two large guest bedrooms, each with a single bed and one is ensuite with a shower room and the other has a private bathroom. No evening meals but a delicious traditional English breakfast is served in the large south facing dining room every day. There is also a Guest Lounge with television. West Dereham is to be found between the small market towns of Swaffham and Downham Market - ideal for exploring the Fens and Breckland. Perfect for walking and enjoying the un-crowded waterways offering excellent opportunities for boating and observing the special Fen habitats.

USEFUL INFORMATION

OPEN: All year
CHILDREN: Welcome
CREDIT CARDS: None taken
LICENSED: No
ACCOMMODATION: 2 large bedrooms ensuite
RATES: From £18pp B&B Children under 12 half price, 3 nights 10% reduction

DINING ROOM: Excellent breakfast
VEGETARIAN: Upon request
WHEELCHAIR ACCESS: No
GARDEN: Yes. Swings

BROOM HALL
Richmond Road, Saham Toney,
Thetford, Norfolk IP25 7EX
AA** 68% Johansens Recommended

Tel/Fax: 01953 882125

Set in fifteen acres of parkland and approached via a winding drive, Broom Hall is an elegant Victorian residence. Staying here is much being part of a country house party. Warm, friendly and comfortable, it is situated in the quiet and friendly Norfolk village of Saham Toney with its 15th century church, attractive thirteen acre mere and a full eighteen hole golf course. The owners, Angela and Nigel Rowling, have a keen eye for beauty and colour and the furnishing of the house throughout reflects this. The eight ensuite bedrooms each have their own warm personal character providing colour television and tea/coffee making facilities. Guests enjoy a perfectly cooked, substantial traditional English breakfast and at night there is the option of a home cooked three course evening meal in the dining room overlooking the garden. The large lounge with an open fire is for the exclusive use of guests and also available is the use of a full size snooker table. An unexpected bonus is the indoor swimming pool. Broom Hall has a residential licence. A delicious cream tea with home made cakes is available and one can order a snack from the bar. Smoking is permitted only in the Bar and Snooker room.

USEFUL INFORMATION

OPEN: 5th Janu-23rd December
CHILDREN: Welcome
CREDIT CARDS: None taken
LICENSED: Residential
ACCOMMODATION: 8 ensuite rooms
RATES: From £28 pp B&B Children from £10 B&B

DINING ROOM: Excellent breakfast
Three course evening meal optional
BAR FOOD: Snacks. Cream teas
VEGETARIAN: Always a choice
WHEELCHAIR ACCESS: Yes

CARYSFORT & CARYSFORT TOO
Self Catering Holiday Cottages
Stratton Farm
West Drove North
Walton Highway,
Norfolk   PE14 7DP
Tel: 01945 880162

4 Keys Highly Commended

These two attractive self-catering cottages are set on Stratton Farm adjoining the owners' home. It is an idyllic spot, peaceful, tranquil with only bird song to wake you in the mornings. Here you can fish for carp and other coarse fish in the lake or swim in the heated swimming pool which is available from May 1st- 30th September. The two cottages are beautifully appointed. There are two bedrooms in each cottage. Carysfort has two twin rooms with zip and link to make two 6ft doubles. Carysfoot Too has one twin with zip and link and one twin room. All the bedrooms have ensuite bathrooms; two with bath and shower and two with shower. The kitchens are fully equipped and include microwave, refrigerator freezer, washer/dryer etc. All the linen and towels are provided. Deep comfort everywhere is the hallmark of these cottages, aimed at making you feel at peace with the world and yourself. Derek and Sue King are the owners and they run the farm and the holiday accommodation between them. The farm has pedigree Shorthorn cattle. The Kings will be happy to show you around.

USEFUL INFORMATION

OPEN: All year
CHILDREN: Over 8 years
CREDIT CARDS: None taken
LICENSED: No
ACCOMMODATION: 2 cottages
both with 2 bedrooms. Fully equipped
RATES: £370 for two bedrooms. pw. 25% reduction for the single bed cottage.

WHEELCHAIR ACCESS: In one cottage
GARDEN: Yes. Coarse fishing in lake &
heated swimming pool May 1 - Sept 30
PETS: No
NON-SMOKERS ONLY

CASTLEGATE RESTAURANT
Stocks Green
Castle Acre
King's Lynn
Norfolk
PE32 2AE

Tel: 01460 755340
Fax: 01460 755473

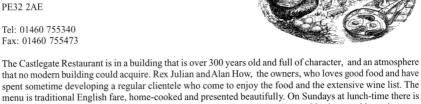

The Castlegate Restaurant is in a building that is over 300 years old and full of character, and an atmosphere that no modern building could acquire. Rex Julian and Alan How, the owners, who loves good food and have spent sometime developing a regular clientele who come to enjoy the food and the extensive wine list. The menu is traditional English fare, home-cooked and presented beautifully. On Sundays at lunch-time there is always a choice of roast meats and poultry, as well as a vegetarian dish. Plenty of fresh vegetables, crisp roast potatoes and the traditional Yorkshire Pudding, make it a meal to remember - and it is not expensive. In the evening a full a la carte menu is available.. Food is served throughout the day and is served in the evenings from Wednesday to Saturday. The Castlegate Restaurant has a devoted band of regulars who are local but you will also see many visitors who have been taking a look at the historic priory and castle situated in the village. The shop next door and attached to the Restaurant offers delicious home-made pies and pastries.

USEFUL INFORMATION

OPEN: All year. All day + Wed to Sat eve.
CHILDREN: Welcome
CREDIT CARDS: All major cards
LICENSED: Yes. Fine wine list
GARDEN: No

RESTAURANT: Home-made
English fare
VEGETARIAN: Always a choice
WHEELCHAIR ACCESS: Yes
PETS: No

CROSS KEYS INN
11-13 Market Place
Wymondham
Norfolk
NR18 0AQ
Tel: 01953 602152

East Anglia Tourist Board Approved

There are many attractive old inns in Norfolk but one of the warmest welcomes to be found anywhere is at the Cross Keys Inn in Wymondham. Built in 1617, it is full of character and an atmosphere built up over the centuries that is carried on today by Eddie and Anne Nelson, the landlords. Two cheery people with a wealth of experience in looking after, and keeping happy, all manner of customers. They have their regulars because the Inn is one of the focal points in the town, but they make complete strangers feel at home. Wymondham is an attractive place with a splendid 12th century abbey and a fine market cross. There are seven guest rooms, some of which are ensuite. They are all warm and comfortable, attractively furnished and complete with television and hostess trays. The food in the Cross Keys both in the restaurant with its forty six covers and the bar, has a great reputation. It is all home-cooked and the emphasis is on traditional fare. Vegetarian and special diets are catered for. A happy place to visit whether simply for a drink or a meal or to stay.

USEFUL INFORMATION

OPEN: 10.30am-11pm
CHILDREN: Welcome
CREDIT CARDS: All except Diners
LICENSED: Full On
ACCOMMODATION:2dbl 3tw 3fam 1sgl
RATES: With shower £20 sgl £35 dbl.
Without showers £17.50 sgl £30 dbl.

RESTAURANT; Good, traditional fare
BAR FOOD: Good choice. Good prices
VEGETARIAN: Yes
WHEELCHAIR ACCESS: Ramps
GARDEN: Patio
PETS: No

CROSSKEYS RIVERSIDE HOTEL
Bridge Street
Hilgay, NR Downham Market
Norfolk   PE38 0LD
Tel: 01366 387777
Tourist Board 3 Crown Commended

Formerly a coaching inn and farm complex Crosskeys Riverside Hotel is now a delightful small country hotel set in its own grounds beside the tranquil River Wissey. Everything about it is restful from the large riverside garden which offers coarse fishing from the hotel frontage to gentle row boating, bird-watching to country walks. Inside the renovations to the 17th century building have been done with careful attention to preserving the original Olde England character, with exposed beams and inglenook fireplace. The delightful rustic bar is a meeting place for visitors and from it leads the restaurant and a small lounge for non-smokers. Christine and Alan Bulmer are the proprietors and they have created a relaxed, pleasant atmosphere for the guests and hence, if you look at the visitor's book, you will see a high proportion of return visits. The food is excellent whether a fixed price, three course   Table de hote menu or the A La Carte Menu, both complemented by a comprehensive and well chosen wine list. There are five guest bedrooms, all ensuite with two four-poster beds 'Queen Size', two twins and one family suite. Two of the rooms including the family suite are on the ground floor.

USEFUL INFORMATION

OPEN: 1st Feb-mid-November
CHILDREN: Welcome
CREDIT CARDS: Visa/Master
LICENSED: Residential/Diners
ACCOMMODATION: 5 ensuite rooms
RATES: £27 B & B   PETS: Yes (£3.50 payment)
Children under12 1/2 price

DINING ROOM: Delicious food
both Table d'hôte & A La Carte
VEGETARIAN: With advanced notice
WHEELCHAIR ACCESS: Yes
GARDEN: Yes to river frontage

CHESTNUT FARMHOUSE & MARGARET'S TEA ROOMS
The Street, Baconsthorpe
NR Holt, Norfolk
NR25 6AB
Tel: 01263 577614

Roger Bacon a Furniture Maker, and his wife are two charming and enterprising people who between them have created an excellent bed and breakfast opportunity for guests at Chestnut Farmhouse and in addition Margaret's Tea Rooms for which she won the coveted 'Tea Council Award of Excellence in the Top Tea Place of the Year Awards. The old farmhouse built around the middle of the 17th century is a fascinating house in which there are two large ensuite guest rooms with easy chairs and colour television and a hostess tray. A full English breakfast is served in the Strawberry Parlor. Guests are invited to help themselves to a selection of fresh fruits, fruit juices, cereals, yogurts and Margaret's own home made bread. The hot course is served on platters to each table. Special needs are catered for wherever possible.
Margaret's Tea Rooms, recommended by Egon Ronay's Guides, serve Morning Coffee, Light Lunches and Afternoon Teas and are open from Good Friday until the end of October Tuesday to Sunday. Closed on Mondays except Bank Holidays. Baconsthorpe is a small rural village three miles south east of the Georgian town of Holt and five miles from the North Norfolk coast. The National Trust properties of Blickling Hall, Felbrigg Hall and Sheringham Park as well as the Norfolk Wildlife Trust at Cley Marshes are a short drive away.

USEFUL INFORMATION

OPEN: B &B All the year round	DINING ROOM; Excellent breakfast
Tea Rooms: 10.30-5pm	Good Friday Tea Rooms: Home-made fare
to end October Tuesday-Sunday	VEGETARIAN: Catered for
Closed Mondays except Bank Holidays	WHEELCHAIR ACCESS: Not suitable
CHILDREN: Well behaved	PETS: No
CREDIT CARDS: None taken	LICENSED: No
ACCOMMODATION: 2 ensuite rooms	NO SMOKING
1 night Double £55 7 nights £48	

EARSHAM PARK FARM,
Harleston Road, Earsham, Bungay,
Suffolk NR35 2AQ
2 Crown Highly Commended. AA QQQQ Selected
Tel/Fax: 01986 892180

Earsham Park Farm probably dates back to Earl Bigod in the 12th century although the farmhouse is relatively modern, Victorian in fact. Its situation is idyllic, facing south and overlooking the beautiful Waveney Valley. It is the home of the Watchorn family who welcome guests in a truly Suffolk hospitable manner. A network of farm walks with a wealth of wildlife runs through the farm and very close to the 'Otter Trust'. Earsham is only half an hour from the coast and Norwich. You can bring your own horse with you. Bobbie Watchorn cares magnificently for her guests in the most relaxed and informal manner. She insists that people treat the house as a home and not feel it is an impersonal hotel. The non-smoking house is elegant, comfortable and warm, the three ensuite bedrooms are charmingly furnished with antiques, one has a four poster. Each room has television, radios and a welcome hostess tray. Breakfast is a traditional farmhouse meal with home-made muesli, fresh fruit, dried fruit compote, fruit juices and yoghurts. The cooked breakfast will include the farm's own sausages, bacon and eggs as well as potato cakes, mushrooms and tomatoes. Home-made, award winning bread and locally produced preserves. In a beautiful dining room, overlooking the valley, you sit at a large farmhouse table, furnished with Portmeirion china to enjoy one of the best breakfasts in Suffolk.

USEFUL INFORMATION

OPEN: All year	DINING ROOM: Delicious breakfast
CHILDREN: Well behaved welcome	VEGETARIAN: Yes
CREDIT CARDS: None taken	WHEELCHAIR ACCESS: Not suitable
LICENSED: No	GARDEN: Yes
ACCOMMODATION: 3 ensuite rooms	PETS: Overnight in car only
RATES: From £20 pp Rates per child £10	
Strictly non-smoking	

THE JOHN H STRACEY
West End, Briston, Melton Constable
Norfolk   NR24 2SA
Tel: 01263 860891
Les Routiers (1997 Award for Casserole) Award of Merit

This nice Freehouse and Restaurant actually dates back to the 1500's when it was a well-known resting and shoeing place for horses en-route from Wells to Norwich. Until twenty years or so ago it was named The Three Horseshoes and it was at that time the stables were converted into a cosy restaurant comfortably seating forty people. For over thirteen years Ray and Hilary Fox have been mine hosts here and they have enhanced the reputation enormously helped by their right hand Sarah who has been with them almost as long and a number of other friendly, willing and efficient staff. It is the sort of place that brings people back regularly whether it is weekly, monthly or annually. They are always remembered and if it happens to be a special occasion such as a family birthday, they are especially cared for. Inside the Inn is full of character with a huge, real log fire in the bar throwing up its welcoming heat and light onto a lustrous copper canopy. There are all sorts of fascinating displays of copper pieces, the ceilings are low, the beams old and the atmosphere is warm and cosy. The restaurant has a wide, varied menu with something to suit every one and there are bar meals as well. In the bar you may well be tempted to enjoy a very good home-made steak and ale pie in a bowl with separate vegetables or perhaps a lasagne, fish or steak. There is a pretty ensuite double guest room as well as a double and a twin with a shared bathroom. The rooms are attractively appointed and very comfortable. Television and tea making facilities are in each room. You will be served a great English breakfast which will set you up for exploring the area. The coast is a quarter of an hour away with Wells the local port, Blakeney the 'boat harbour' and Sheringham or Cromer in the opposite direction. Holt, a quaint country town is just four miles away. Thursford offers its steam museum down the road. The National Trust properties of Blickling and Felbrigg Hall can be visited, as well as Langham Glass and the North Norfolk Railway. The cathedral city of Norwich is sixteen miles.

USEFUL INFORMATION

OPEN; 11.30-2.30 & 6.30-11pm
CHILDREN; Restaurant only
BAR FOOD; Great variety home-made specials
CREDIT CARDS; Visa/Master
DISABLED ACCESS; Easy steps
ACCOMMODATION;3rooms,1ensuite
RATES: £18.50 pppn (No Sgl Supplement)

RESTAURANT; Wide range home-made fare
VEGETARIAN; Catered for
LICENSED; Yes
GARDEN; Yes for drinks & food in summer

KESMARK HOUSE BED & BREAKFAST
Gooseberry Hill, Swanton Morley,
NR Dereham, Norfolk NR20 4PA
Tel: 01362 637663

This beautiful listed Georgian house, stands in large, well maintained grounds in delightful countryside. From Kesmark House you can enjoy some stunning walks, fish if the mood takes you, or seek out some of the interesting local hostelries. You will also find that the pretty Market town of Dereham is just a five minutes drive. It is fun to explore, has some excellent shops and many, very good eateries. Inside the house there are still many of the original features including a fine mahogany staircase, large spacious windows which look out over the countryside and two and a half acres of garden. It is warm, relaxed, comfortable house in which your hostess, Carol Pastor goes out of her way to ensure you have a memorable stay. The bedrooms are very well appointed and each attractive in its own right but the very large peach coloured double room which has a large French maple wood bed and armoire, and its own bathroom, is particularly appealing. There are two other, well furnished, double rooms which share a bathroom and a very pretty single room. All the rooms have colour television with remote control and a hostess tray. Carol is a cookery writer with a great love of food and her breakfasts are very special; home-made preserves, country breads, locally produced sausages and bacon from a farm shop and fresh eggs. There is good coffee and a selection of 'real' leaf teas. Ask Carol to recommend tea-rooms they are her passion.

USEFUL INFORMATION

OPEN: All year
CHILDREN: Welcome
CREDIT CARDS: None taken
ACCOMMODATION: 3dbl, 1sgl
RATES: Double £39 Single £25

DINING ROOM: First class fare
VEGETARIAN: If ordered the night before
WHEELCHAIR ACCESS: No
PARKING: Off road parking
PETS: Yes

KOLIBA
8 Louie's Lane
Diss, Norfolk   IP22 3LR

Tel: (+44) (0) 1379 650046 Fax: (+ 44 (0) 1379 650046
Internet/E.Mail:Olgakoliba@aol.com

The quaint town of Diss has a history that dates back through many centuries. Diss Mere the centrepiece helped shape the town. It has a fine church and has been awarded the Best Kept Town in Norfolk. Diss is also very conveniently situated for anyone wanting to explore this part of Norfolk with all it has to offer. Built in 1988 Koliba is a charming, modern, centrally heated, family home owned by Olga and Joe Burke who delight in having guests staying and do everything in their power to ensure their stay is comfortable and happy. Koliba means a dwelling in the land in Serbo-Croation and Romanian languages and it is from Yugoslavia that Olga hails, of Romanian ancestry. There are three guest rooms, one twin, one double, sharing a private bathroom and a single, on the ground floor, with shower. All the bedrooms are with remote control television, Clock/Radio, Tea/coffee making facilities with the addition of herbal teas, drinking chocolate and fresh whole, semi or skimmed milk or Soya milk plus home made biscuits and fresh fruit. There is also the use of an iron and ironing board and a trouser press if required. Breakfast is a delicious meal and Dinner when available is of International cuisine including vegetarian.

USEFUL INFORMATION

OPEN: 28th Dec-24th Dec
CHILDREN: Over 12 unless in family group.
CREDIT CARDS: None taken
LICENSED: No
ACCOMMODATION: 1tw 1dbl 1sgl
RATES: From £18 pp B&B

DINING ROOM: Excellent breakfast
Dinner by arrangement
VEGETARIAN: Catered for
WHEELCHAIR ACCESS: No
GARDEN: Yes
PETS: No

POPLAR FARM
Fersfield Road
Bressingham
Norfolk   IP22 2AP
Tel: 01379 687261
EATB One Crown

Rita Soar owns and runs the 16th century Poplar Farmhouse, a lovely old house with exposed beams, inglenook fireplaces and a great deal of character. It is a working, arable farm positioned in quiet surroundings but only a ten minute walk from the world famous Blooms Steam Museum and Gardens and also a local pub where you can get a good evening meal. Rita thoroughly enjoys having guests in her home and that is apparent when you experience the warm, friendly welcome which makes you feel at home immediately. There is a Sun Lounge and a sitting room for the use of guests and Breakfast is served in the sunny dining room - a meal to remember, freshly cooked and using both farm and local produce. There are five guest rooms, a twin-bedded ensuite, two single and two doubles as well as two bathrooms with plenty of hot water, each room has a wash basin. All the rooms have television and a hostess tray. From Poplar Farm it is easy to reach the coast, Norwich, Ipswich and Bury St Edmunds are all within 25-30 mile radius. There are pleasant walks with the Anglesway Walk nearby. You can take river cruises through Norwich and the Broadlands. The National Trust Ickworth House and others are within easy distance.

USEFUL INFORMATION

OPEN: All year
CHILDREN: Welcome breakfast.
CREDIT CARDS: None taken
LICENSED: No
ACCOMMODATION: 5 rooms 1 ensuite
RATES: from £16 pppn B&B

DINING ROOM: Good farmhouse
No evening meal
VEGETRIAN: Upon request
WHEELCHAIR ACCESS: Not suitable
GARDEN: Yes
PETS:No

No smoking in bedrooms

SALISBURY HOUSE
Victoria Road
Diss, Norfolk
IP22 3JG

Tel / Fax: 01379 644738

Sir John Betjeman described the old town of Diss as 'the perfect market town'; an apt description, and in its midst is the equally perfect Salisbury House set in delightful gardens in which there is a south facing walled patio, a croquet lawn with a fully furnished summer house, and a large lawn area full of beautiful trees, shrubs and flowers with many unusual varieties, and a duck pond graced with a weeping willow. Once inside you are in the welcoming environment created by the owners, Sue and Barry Davies. The Victorian decor and furnishing provide an elegant background to the lounges and the two restaurants. The five bedrooms are comfortably furnished and tastefully decorated with all the facilities expected of a country house hotel - private bathroom, hairdryer, radio, colour television, drinks tray, games and books. Salisbury House has established a reputation for an interesting and varied menu, and an extensive wine list of 250 bins, comprising many French wines from £7.95 for house wine to £120 a bottle. One can dine in the elegant restaurant from a delicious a la carte menu or less formally in the Bistro. Barry Davies is responsible for the kitchen and is acknowledged for his skilful and individual style of cooking. Only the finest raw ingredients are used and produce is obtained locally where possible. The green room may be used for business conferences or as a private dining room for up to fourteen people.

USEFUL INFORMATION

OPEN: All year
CHILDREN: Welcome
CREDIT CARDS: All major cards
LICENSED: Full On
ACCOMMODATION: 5 ensuite rooms
RATES: Sgl from £45 Dbl. from £70

RESTAURANT: English & Continental
BISTRO: Wide menu, delicious food
VEGETARIAN: Upon request
WHEELCHAIR ACCESS: Yes
GARDEN: Yes. Croquet, garden chess

SCARNING DALE,
Dale Road,
Scarning, Dereham,
Norfolk NR19 2QN
Tel: 01362 687269
Fax: 01362 687378

You will find that Scarning Dale is nothing like the run of the mill establishments in which one frequently stays. This is a very special house, heavily timbered with inglenook fireplaces that date way back to the 17th century. You come to it at the end of a long drive flanked by beech hedges. In the grounds are the remains of what is reputed to be part of the Abbey of Wendling, founded by Sir William de Wendling in 1267. Apart from anything else Scarning Dale is ideally located for visiting the many attractions of Norfolk and Suffolk. The sitting room with its heavily timbered ceiling and wonderful fire place in which a log fire burns in winter, is a very restful place. For exercise you can use the heated swimming pool, play a quiet game of snooker or table tennis. The accommodation in the house is for just six people which creates a delightful family atmosphere. For those who prefer it there is a range of self-catering facilities, each with their own garden. You are welcome to bring your pets here and equally welcome to take breakfast in the main house if you wish. The Magraths who own Scarning Dale can arrange private dinner parties in the house for up to sixteen people and are equally skilled at arranging business meetings, large parties and wedding receptions in a charmingly converted barn.

USEFUL INFORMATION

OPEN; All year
CHILDREN; Welcome
CREDIT CARDS; None taken
LICENSED; Yes
ACCOMMODATION; Ensuite rooms
PRICE; £35-£45.00 per night per person

DINING ROOM; Delicious home-cooked
VEGETARIAN; Catered for
DISABLED ACCESS; Not really
GARDEN; Yes. Heated indoor pool
PETS; In self-catering accommodation

THE MALT HOUSE
Denmark Hill
Palgrave, NR Diss
Norfolk   IP22 1AE

Tel: 01378 642107 Fax: 01379 640315
malthouse@mainline.co.uk
Two Crowns De Luxe

Located on Palgrave village green, the 17th century converted Malt House, just one mile from Diss and two miles from the world famous Bressingham Gardens, is a delightful, tranquil and restful house, the home of Phil and Marj Morgan. Furnished tastefully throughout, one especially notices the colour and beauty of the drapes and bedcovers and the interesting collection of pieces that the Morgan's have brought back from the East; they lived in Hong Kong for many years. The mature landscaped garden with a pond is the scene one sees from the bedroom windows with the peaceful countryside beyond. Strictly a non-smoking house, there are three ensuite guest rooms which have king size or twin beds and a roll out bed can be provided for a child over Two years of age. Breakfast is a delicious, freshly cooked meal with a choice of a traditional English breakfast or maybe Kippers. Plenty of fruit juice, fresh fruit, cereals, toast and preserves as well as freshly made tea and coffee gives one a substantial start to a days exploration. No evening meals but there are several good eateries within easy distance to which Phil and Marj will point you.

USEFUL INFORMATION

OPEN: All year
CHILDREN: Over 2 years
CREDIT CARDS: Visa/Diners/Euro
LICENSED: No
ACCOMMODATION: 3 ensuite rooms
RATES: £35pn.pp B&B sgl £60 dbl.
Children £10 for roll away bed

DINING ROOM: Delicious, substantial
breakfast. No evening meal
VEGETARIAN: Upon request
WHEELCHAIR ACCESS: No
GARDEN: Landscaped
PETS: No
STRICTLY NON-SMOKING HOUSE

WESTON HOUSE FARM
Mendham, Harleston
Norfolk   IP20 0PB

Tel: 01986 782206 Fax: 01986 782414

ETB 2 Crowns Commended. AA Recommended QQQ

Weston House Farm is a 17th century Grade II Listed Farmhouse set in an acre of garden overlooking pasture land on a 300 acre mixed farm. It is supremely peaceful in a rural area with extensive views across and beyond the Waveney Valley. The farm is just outside the village of Mendham, the birthplace of Sir Alfred Munnings. It is within easy reach of the Suffolk Heritage Coast with Minsmere Bird Sanctuary, Southwold, Dunwich and Aldeburgh well worth a visit. Nearby is the Otter Sanctuary at Earsham. Also within easy reach are the Norfolk Broads and the historic city of Norwich. The three pretty guest rooms, two double and one twin, are all ensuite and have recently been refurbished. Each has a hostess tray and clock radio. The Lounge is elegantly and traditionally furnished, warm and comfortable with log fires, a piano and reading matter. Breakfast, served in the bright Dining Room, is a farmhouse feast and if you dine here at night, a three course dinner is served using all fresh produce including locally caught fish and home reared beef. It is a happy, friendly house and you will be given a great welcome. Weston House is strictly non-smoking throughout.

USEFUL INFORMATION

OPEN: From March-November
CHILDREN: Welcome
CREDIT CARDS: AMEX
LICENSED: No
ACCOMMODATION: 2dbl. 1tw all ensuite
RATES: £16-£25 pppn Children £10.50-£13.00
Dinner £11. Children £7.50

DINING ROOM: Delicious home-cooked
fare
VEGETARIAN: Upon request
WHEELCHAIR ACCESS: Yes
GARDEN: Yes
PETS: Dogs by arrangement

VERE LODGE
South Raynham,
Fakenham, Norfolk NR21 7HE
**** Highly Commended ETB

Tel:01328 838261 Fax: 01328 383300

Vere Lodge is for those who demand the very best in self-catering. Every one of the charmingly named cottages, Apple, Possums, Plump, Dove, Doll's House, Garden Wing, Honeysuckle, Rowan, Dahlia. Thyme, Lavender, Robins Nest, Rose and Secret Garden, is perfect for a holiday or a short break. It is very difficult to do justice to Vere Lodge without actually seeing it but Bryn Frank states in his Good Holiday Cottage Guide: 'There is magic in this beautiful place which even the most detailed and colourful Brochure fails to capture.' It changes with the seasons and really is a place for all seasons. In the Winter the cottages form an oasis of warmth and peace. Winter and Summer there is plenty to do, and lots of space in which to do it. People who have discovered Vere Lodge enthuse about it and return whenever possible. Every cottage is fully equipped with everything one could wish for. They are there to be enjoyed. The cottages are varying in size and sleep anything from three to seven people. You can come here on a short break which can start from any day of the week.

USEFUL INFORMATION

OPEN: All year
PETS: Yes
CHILDREN: Yes
CREDIT CARDS: Mastercard/Visa
RATES: As the rates are so varied, and change with the seasons, please telephone Vere Lodge directly, for a brochure.

GARDEN: Yes
CENTRAL HEATING: Yes
LICENSED: In season only
WHEELCHAIR ACCESS: Yes

Selected venues in this chapter

When I demanded of my friend what viands he preferred,
he quoth ' A large cold bottle and a small hot bird'
Eugene Field.

✱✱✱✱✱✱✱✱✱✱✱✱✱✱✱✱✱✱✱

' It is very poor consolation to be told that a man who has given one bad dinner,
or poor wine, is irreproachable in private life.
Even the cardinal virtues cannot atone for half cold entrees'

Oscar Wilde

✱✱✱✱✱✱✱✱✱✱✱✱✱✱✱✱✱✱✱✱

' Artichokes. These things are just plain annoying...
after all the trouble you go to, you get as much actual 'food'
out of eating an artichoke as you would from licking 30 or 40 postage stamps.
Have the shrimp cocktail instead'.

Miss Piggy.

CHAPTER 5.:
Town or Gown or City or Town?
Cambridge & Ely

We're now going to change our base and our county. The plan is to move over to the west, to acquaint you with Cambridgeshire - and that's not as simple as it may appear. I knew a fair bit about Norfolk even before guiding you around the county: I'd seen pictures of the Broads; 'Norwich' sounded familiar and was likely to be everything I would expect of a county town and cathedral City - and the coast was, well, Yarmouth and sand and bits of solitude. But to move from the Broads to the Fens, then to Cambridge itself, there were no 'pictures' in my mind, so you travel with an enthusiastic novice.

To commence, from the north and west, to know precisely where you are is to say the least confusing. I will try to justify this remark. Question: where is Peterborough, Huntingdon, St Neots, Grafham Water?, you may say Huntingdonshire or Rutland, you like I, would be geographically incorrect!, they're *all* in Cambridgeshire these days. Very surprised ?, when I drove along the A14 from Kettering and found an entire county - and a thousand years of history - had been simply 'signed away', by the Boundaries Commission, I most definitely was.

Mind you, a certain ex-Prime Minister is still MP for Huntingdon. I wonder if *he's* noticed. That it's gone, I mean; the whole county for which his constituency used to be the county town. I wonder if it matters to him. Maybe, if it doesn't, we should take a lead from our ex-leader, and just get on with it. But I still find driving through a non-existent county decidedly odd. What if a similar boundary change happened on the M1? One hundred miles of motorway and 100,000 cars could cease to exist.

That's not all: it gets even stranger. The *real* Cambridgeshire - as opposed to all the boundary change additions - has two focal points: Ely and Cambridge. Now everyone knows about Cambridge, from Berlin to Bangkok to Botswana, they *know*, but what of Ely?'

Ely is 1300 years old; Cambridge 1500. Ely is a city, *with* a cathedral, of course; Cambridge, a town, with *no* cathedral! Now, isn't that surprising? Sort of terribly English, somehow, as in: 'Towns are for gentlemen; cities are for tradesmen'. Something like that. Populations? Cambridge is at least ten times the size of Ely, and growing, probably, thanks to Bill Gates.

Cambridge isn't famous just because it's *bigger*, since it isn't *that* big. Stockport, Stoke-on-Trent and Stockton on Tees are all roughly the same size, but it's not the size it's 'The Varsity', my dears. The good old Alma Mater. But that isn't an ultimate answer, either. It only leads to another question: why build it *there*?

In the fifth century, Cambridge was a Saxon market town; in the ninth it was a Danish army base and in the 11th a Norman military stronghold. Two hundred years later, the students started to arrive. Isn't that strange? What could possibly have attracted them to a community with no cathedral, no learned minds, no sacred shrines, no culture - nothing? With just a bunch of red-necked Norman militia for company, who were usually terribly busy jousting, sloshing down the mead and beating up the locals. Sounds quite a place to start a university, with books and Pythagoras and St Augustine and stuff. A rather worse idea than building a new University of Hampshire in the middle of Aldershot, one would have thought. Not a bit of it - that's what they did, the rest is history.

By the way, the rejection of Ely had nothing to do with lack of space around the Cathedral, in case that's what you're thinking. At the start, no-one could have had the slightest idea that the first college would breed, so to speak, until there were dozens of them! For what they had in mind at the time, I'm sure a corner of the Cathedral Close would have been quite enough. I see the Ely of that time simply hiding itself on its island in the midst of the misty Fens and pretending not to notice. It would have stayed there too, if some 17th century bureaucrat hadn't had the bright idea of doing away with marshes, and starting by draining the Fens! When this happened Ely came out of the mist and onto dry land.

Our first day in Cambridgeshire is going to be a change from the pattern of the routine thus far, instead of leaving the hotel and driving into the country side, we will devote the day to exploring Ely, hence giving the driver, poor thing, a deserved rest.

Since **ELY** [Information - 01353 662062], is not so well known as its neighbouring city, perhaps how it got its name would be a ideal place to start. 'Eels'. were common in the fenland that surrounded the island where it all started, so it became known as 'Eel Island'. eels, So, it was 'Eel Island', otherwise 'Elge' or 'Elig', eventually, tongues slipped from 'Elig' to 'Ely', and that is the origin of the name of this City.

Which makes me wonder about the lady who got the show on the road in the first place: St Ethelreda. It could be expected that after two failed marriages, she'd look for somewhere to hide, somewhere a bit cut off, away from it all. Perfectly natural. And she wouldn't have been the first woman to run away from her husband and enter a nunnery, especially in those days (we're talking seventh century AD here). But she didn't look at what was on offer and pick the most promising. She set up her *own* operation on a site she chose *herself.* On an island in the middle of a sea of *eels*! How many divorcees do you know who'd do that?

In my experience women don't like live eels. I remember taking my former wife fishing on one occasion - during a holiday not a million miles from Ely, lovely day, sunshine, gentle breeze, lapping water and a clear sky. In short, an utterly hopeless escapade, fish hide on such days. They feel safer in the rain, when most sensible *people* stay indoors. Very quiet, it was. For hours my wife, bored and amazed by my pig-headed determination to sit it out, stripped off to the bikini she chanced to be wearing and, after a few minutes sunbathing, fell asleep. Half an hour passed. Then it happened. My float dipped to what turned out to be the only bite of the day. Just as you would expect - I make no apologies - in my hysteria, I over-did everything. I struck far too fast and far too hard. The very tiny fish on the end of the line came out of the water like a miniature Polaris missile and followed a curved path over my head. Over my head towards my wife's naked back, where she lay, totally out of it, in the full heat of the sun. I had time to see that I'd hooked a small eel, fully eight inches long. I did *not* have time to shout a warning. The first she knew about any of it was when this frantic, ice-cold, wriggling little beast hit the small of her very hot back at about 180 miles an hour.(and it wasn't even winded, judging from the way it went on thrashing). I'm told her screams shattered pint mugs in the beer garden of the pub a mile down the lane. Certainly, great flocks of wading birds took up from the reed beds and returned in disgust to Scandinavia. I learned several words I didn't think ladies knew. Now, had I hooked a pike - or even a carp - of a decent size, I'm sure the story would have ended quite differently. But an *eel*! So, you see, women and eels *really* don't mix, and it could be why this poor lady is no longer my wife.

Which leads to more of the questions that could fill this chapter. For example, having wondered why they started 'The Varsity' at Cambridge, I'm now wondering why this seemingly saintly lady picked this particular island at all. As a penance, perhaps? Mortification of the senses?

Of course, walking along THE GALLERY towards THE CATHEDRAL, one has to be glad she took the trouble. The 'Lantern of the Fens' deserves every bit of its reputation as a masterpiece of medieval engineering and architecture. The present building dates from 1081, a year which marks the end of Ely's first troubled phase during which the Danes ransacked Ethelreda's original hilltop religious community and Hereward the Wake used the island as a centre of Anglo-Saxon resistance against the Normans. It took the efforts of William the Conqueror himself to quell the rebels, but once peace had been enforced, everyone went straight back to the important business of making money.

Not surprisingly, the Abbey that had been re-established in the 10th century by Benedictine monks went with the flow and soon became one of the major monastic houses in England. It's easy to see just how 'major' from the scale of the Cathedral: it has one of the longest naves in the country, its wooden ceiling is all of 72ft above the ground and its overall magnificence dominates the countryside for miles around. Credit for the original concept goes to Simeon, Abbot of Ely, and a Norman, who was given his post by the King. Later additions were just as noteworthy, not least being the 14th century central octagonal tower, conceived by Alan of Walsingham, one of the monks, as a replacement for the original, which had collapsed. Coming forward five hundred years, the painted ceiling undertaken by H.L.Styleman-L'Estrange and T.Gambier-

Parry is another of those superb examples of Victorian creativity which are a special feature of the region.

We don't know exactly what Henry VIII thought about eels - although it's unlikely that he ate as many as the Saxons seem to have done - but there must have been something about Ely that got to him. It was let off pretty lightly during the Dissolution of the Monasteries and suffered a lot less damage than many similar places. You can see that at a glance, as soon as you start to look around the collection of monastic buildings beside the Cathedral that are still in daily use. As a group, there can't be many to touch them anywhere else in England. Which is only fitting, when you think how much of the monastery's wealth was spent on painting and decorating!

Apart from the history this area also has a tremendous appeal as a work of art, as a huge piece of live-in sculpture, and it's good to see that both these aspects of the city's heritage are recognised locally. Several guided tours are available, each one focusing on a particular theme. You can, for example, take the TOWN TRAIL, which offers a fairly general look at the architectural attractions. Then there's a CATHEDRAL TOUR which, obviously, concentrates on the masterpiece itself. Or there's a DRAMA TOUR, a GHOST TOUR, a PHOTOGRAPHIC TOUR - and so it goes on. The TOURIST INFORMATION CENTRE has details of everything in this line and will even, I gather, tailor specialised tours to suit particular interests and requirements. As a taste of what you can expect let me pick out a few particular delights.

If we start at a gateway, which seems reasonable enough, we could be faced with something a bit special straight away. The ELY PORTA, or Walpole's Gate, dates from the 14th century and was the entrance to the monastery used by important guests. It has now been incorporated into the KING'S SCHOOL, which has a claim to be one of the oldest schools in England. Turn left through the gate and you come almost at once to PRIOR CRAUDEN'S CHAPEL, also 14th century. Here you'll find remains of wall paintings and a marvellous medieval tiled floor which includes a panel showing Adam and Eve with the Serpent.

Beyond the Chapel lies the 13th century GREAT HALL of the Monastery, now the BISHOP'S RESIDENCE. One of the finest views of the Cathedral can be seen from its gateway, while across The Gallery, the 15th century BISHOP'S PALACE, which gives a further insight into the lifestyle of those early days, is now a Sue Ryder Home. There are nigh on a dozen more treats of a similar nature - as I say, I've only given a taster here. All in all, they amount to an extremely pleasant way of spending the best part of one's first day in the City.

After the culture, I suspect our collector's urge will need attention, and Ely has plenty for us here, too, to round off the afternoon. There are four main shopping streets which run parallel and to the north of the Cathedral's main axis: HIGH STREET, MARKET STREET, MARKET PLACE and FOREHILL. Here you will find a range of premises offering craft, gift and curio items, much as you would expect. But Ely is also a market centre for the area so, on Thursdays, there is a GENERAL MARKET, in the Market Place and, more to our liking, a CRAFT, COLLECTABLES AND CURIOSITIES MARKET, on Saturdays, in the same venue.

Talk of collectables leads me to suggest moving a bit further afield, down Forehill and WATERSIDE to the banks of the River Ouse. That's where you'll find RIVERSIDE WALK, WATERSIDE ANTIQUES [Enquiries - 01353 667066] and THE MALTINGS [Enquiries - 01353 662633], once Ebenezer William Harlock's brewery building and now converted into a public hall, conference centre and - in case you thought I'd forgotten - a restaurant! Also a coffee shop, if you're dieting, or a tea room for an afternoon break.

THE MALTINGS

Now we've spread our wings somewhat and left the hub of it all, we could look at some more extended excursions. I have come across half a dozen that fit the bill, I think, and they are so varied that hardly anyone could be disappointed.

The three mile NATURE TRAIL, naturally focuses on the wildlife of the immediate area, taking in ROSSWELL PITS and the surrounding countryside. FEN RIVERS WAY, on the other hand, is more ambitious and takes the visitor to Cambridge along the river banks. It's an out and back ramble, unless you make a major detour for the return, so that needs bearing in mind if the car's still in the hotel car park! Whilst we're in a mood to cover the miles, BISHOP'S WAY is worth considering. It's an appealing circular route out to the north and west of the City, covering more than seven miles of medieval lanes and passing the site of the former BISHOP'S COUNTRY PALACE. Nearer to base, the TOWN TRAIL combines odds and ends of the tours we did at the start with more historic buildings and some time along the riverside.

The other two trails do need the car. The DOROTHY L SAYERS TRAIL visits the towns and villages mentioned in her well-known novel, 'The Nine Taylors'. The CROMWELL TRAIL addresses itself to the 'rich legacy of buildings and places associated with Oliver Cromwell'. Which brings me to another brief snatch of local history.

The TOURIST INFORMATION CENTRE is located just around the corner from the Cathedral, in the former family home of the 'Lord Protector of England'. Of course, for much of the time he actually *lived* there he was just plain O. Cromwell, farmer, and nothing to do with 'Lord' of anything. He moved to the City in 1636, but his ideas can't have been seriously affected by its history or origins as one of the first things he did when he started running the short-lived 'republic' was to close the Cathedral itself. No hard feelings on the part of the good people of Ely, though: normality having been resumed with the return of Charles II, Cromwell's house has been restored and now presents a vivid and imaginative reconstruction of 17th century life. This has been extended recently to include a Civil War Exhibition, a Portrait Room and a Haunted Bedroom, complete with ghost! A video on Cromwell and the period gives a further insight into the domestic life and character of the man, while another on Fens Drainage, which was first achieved successfully during his term of office, completes the visit.

CROMWELL'S HOUSE

There are other museums in the City, of course. The STAINED GLASS MUSEUM [Enquiries - 01353 667735] in the Cathedral has superb examples of stained glass from the 14th to the 20th century on display, including a panel from the Royal Collection which shows a 1793 portrait of George III by Sir Joshua Reynolds. Meanwhile, the story of Ely from the Ice Age to the present is told in the old BISHOP'S GAOL MUSEUM, in Market Street [Enquiries - 01353 666655]. The displays here range from geology to military history and from archaeology to tableaux of the Debtors' and Condemned cells.

Two further attractions on offer in Ely deserve a mention before we move down the road. Firstly, it's a good place for eating out: the restaurants, pubs and cafes provide a wide range of choices for meals and snacks. To freshen up after a touch of self-indulgence, there's nothing to beat messing about in a boat and the ANNESDALE MARINA, at the RIVERSIDE BOATYARD [Enquiries - 01353 665420] can fit you out with something suitable on a short term or daily hire basis.

RIVERSIDE

As you moor up at the end of your short cruise which, really, marks the end of the visit, I trust you will find yourself reflecting on a host of pleasant memories drawn from your experiences in the 'City of the Fens'. For two reasons: firstly, we can all use good memories and secondly, I've a feeling you'll need something to cushion your psyche against the manic mind machine down the A10, which is our next port of call.

CAMBRIDGE [Information - 01223 322640] is rather *intense*, I find. Although I've always thought of myself as a 'Light Blue' man (based on nothing more meaningful, I confess, than my childhood's partisan approach to the Boat Race - especially if the Cambridge eight were ahead at Hammersmith Bridge) my first encounter with the reality of the place was all but terminal. Oxford, which I knew, and Cambridge, the two great rivals, couldn't be more different - even though both have become the focal point of the bustling communities that surround them. Where Oxford has 'dreaming spires', Cambridge boasts 'soaring pinnacles'; Oxford drips antiquity amidst its echoing quadrangles, wide streets and beautiful buildings; Cambridge has merged its own antiquity (and it's only slightly younger) with 'the cutting edge' and all that implies, in a frenzy of research, analysis and scientific speculation that seethes through its often narrow streets in search of expression. In short, Cambridge is a 'happening place', while Oxford, though far from resting on its laurels, prefers to assert, quietly, that the more things change the more its permanence as a great centre of European learning will endure.

The first true Cambridge college, PETERHOUSE, was founded by the Bishop of Ely (of *Ely*? Isn't *that* odd?) in 1284, in a town that was already a busy commercial centre. The students, as we have seen, were already there, lodging in groups around the spiritual and secular teachers whose ideas seemed most inspiring. As we've seen, too, the reason why any of them chose to go there at all is shrouded in ancient mystery. Even if Cambridge *was* commercially successful, Ely was quite wealthy enough to cater for the idea and the Cathedral, as a storehouse of religious and other learning, should have been an irresistible magnet - but it wasn't. Sod's law, I suppose; the 'who'd have thought it' factor again.

Today the town's prosperity is founded on a wide spread of industries, from radio and electronics to cement making, from flour milling to printing and the design and manufacture of scientific instruments - and Microsoft, maybe, which would be Mr Gates' first sortie away from his US homeland (speaks volumes, that does). The actual University is where 'the cutting edge' is sharpest, though, as it has become a big league player in the world of scientific research. Rutherford first split the atom at its Cavendish Laboratory and created the science of nuclear physics; the Observatories, Scott Polar Research Institute and the University Chemical Laboratory have spread the gospel from there.

Presumably, if you set up something like that within a landscape of listed buildings, the only way to create the 'modern' image necessary for 'modern' studies (and funding) is in the people, rather than the buildings. The Americans solve the problem the other way around, I believe: their science needs high-tech buildings to strike a balance with its comparatively conservative academics.

This 'image notion' could explain everything, even - or especially - the contrast in the two universities' cycling sub-cultures. In both places, anyone who is anyone gets on a bike as a way of life, or at the drop of a hat. There the similarity stamps on the disc brakes. Oxford cyclists appear to float by and around traffic-jammmed motorists; pedestrians are similarly able to progress among flying gowns and whirring wheels without let or hindrance. Cambridge? It's back to Boadicea's war-chariots again, and the rest of us expect any minute to be sliced off at the knees. Somehow, life is so much more *urgent* beside the Cam than it ever was between the Thames/Isis and the Cherwell.

Cambridge, in short, is to me an attitude of mind that seems to have been encouraged to flourish in recent years *despite* its historic setting; Oxford is a mellow fusion of attitude *and* setting to the benefit of both. On the other hand, this *is* supposed to be a Tourist Guide and I *am* supposed to offer a million reasons why you really shouldn't miss a single place I mention! Can I do it for Cambridge? I mean, is that a *challenge*? Nothing of the kind. Even if it stunned me to begin with I came to love the place - but for reasons that would never have occurred to me if all I'd had to go on were photographs of students in punts and 'King's College Chapel at Sunset'. If 'the cutting edge' isn't exciting, what on earth *is*?

We'll talk about the architecture first. The colleges are magnificent, from Peterhouse, the earliest, by way of KING'S, renowned for the glories of its CHAPEL (one of the supreme achievements of Gothic architecture) right up to the really good modern buildings of the post-war era. By all means absorb as much as you can of the past, but don't miss the ERASMUS BUILDING in QUEENS (1961), the NEW HALL for women (1954), FITZWILLIAM COLLEGE (1963) and the HISTORY FACULTY BUILDING (1968).

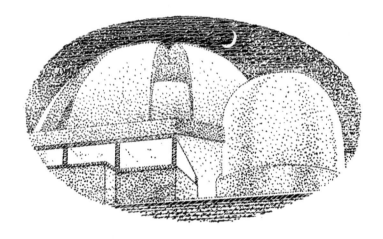

NEW HALL

Mind you, an unguided tour of the Colleges, aiming to soak up as much architectural heritage as possible, needs to be planned carefully in advance - with the aid of a good street map. Don't be put off by the prospect - you won't regret any of it and you'll be moved again and again by the splendours that present themselves. During vacations, visitors can go into college courtyards, chapels, dining halls and certain gardens at most times - so that's not a problem. Nor is getting lost, really: it's not a maze. But if you want to see it all without back tracking or going round in circles - and then don't pre-plan with a map - it's more than a problem, it's an exhausting certainty.

With planning, the whole treat of an experience unfolds like the scenes of a great play. See as much as time allows, but in addition to the buildings already mentioned, be sure not to miss RUBENS 'ADORATION OF THE MAGI', in King's College Chapel, the OLD COURT of CORPUS CHRISTIE, the PRESIDENT'S LODGE of QUEENS' and the WREN LIBRARY of TRINITY. Then get a good night's rest, because on day two....

On 'Day Two' it's museums and galleries - the 'alternative Cambridge', if you like. At its heart as far as I'm concerned, is one of the world's greatest museums: THE FITZWILLIAM, on TRUMPINGTON STREET, founded in 1816 by Viscount Fitzwilliam, from whom it received a hundred thousand pounds plus his own library and art collection. Since the days of the good Viscount there has been a fair flow of other benefactors, but the Coutrauld family must be near the top of the list.

What I like about the place is the range of exhibits as much as their superb quality. There are major Egyptian, Greek and Roman collections, while the range of illuminated manuscripts is balanced by an incredibly comprehensive display of English pottery and porcelain. The collection of paintings is no less impressive, with representative works from significant European movements spanning the last five hundred years. Amongst the stars in this galaxy are pictures by Titian, Rembrandt, Gainsborough, Hogarth and Turner.

Still on the alternative Cambridge theme, we'll leave the glory of the Fitzwilliam 'Old Masters' and wander along Trumpington Street to KING'S PARADE and GREAT ST. MARY'S CHURCH, the official University Church, which is 15th century with a 17th century tower. We can climb the tower if we choose, to enjoy the panoramic views it offers out across the spires and rooftops of the town to the countryside beyond - we may even hear the chimes, whose tune was specially written in 1793, and later copied for Big Ben.

GREAT ST MARY'S CHURCH

In front of the Church is the square where THE MARKET is held three times a week. Apart from our insatiable interest in such matters, the feature itself serves another purpose that might easily have been overlooked while we were traipsing around amongst the opulence and grandeur: it reminds us that Cambridge was a market town for more than a thousand years *before* the University was established. In other words, it was a trading centre on that scale for almost twice as long as it's been an academic centre! Stand among the choir stalls in King's Chapel, with the Rubens behind you, you know that you are in England, nowhere else in World can even begin to create the same ambience.

If it feels like we have returned to the 'Onward, ever onward', that's right. With the Fitzwilliam and the Market in our minds now, we must press on to BRIDGE STREET, with just a quick look at the ROUND CHURCH, one of the few circular churches in England, before crossing the River Cam and heading along MAGDALAN STREET to the left turn into NORTHAMPTON STREET. We need to reach our next destination before those last two memories have a chance to fade.

You know how I am about contrasts? Well I've got one in mind, now. We've just been wallowing in priceless masterpieces in the midst of an academic centre that grew up around an even more ancient Saxon market, for some reason. In FOLK MUSEUM, where the everyday life of Cambridgeshire over the last six hundred years is faithfully recorded, we'll see the other half of the story. It's told in a series of rooms, each showing a particular facet, from domestic life to trades and occupations, from children stories to the general rural lifestyle. The unique character of the Fens is also highlighted with examples of the range of equipment that evolved to help people cope with its more extreme qualities - including (wait for it!) a series of traps and spears used for *eel catching*! Of course! What else? The 'town and gown' relationship between the citizens and the dons and students is also featured in a display that includes the standard weights and measures used by the University to check up on local traders.

Right next door to the Museum, KETTLE'S YARD ART GALLERY [Enquiries - 01223 352124] bounces the contrast straight back again as we return from day-to-day affairs to the creativity of great art. The origins of the Gallery go back to the days in the 1950's when Jim Ede opened up his own home to show his personal art collection to students and others who might be interested. That building, and its extension, now house the Gallery's permanent collection of works by masters of 20th century English Modernism. A new unit was built at the front of the house in the 1970s, to which additions were made in the 80s and 90s. It is here that one finds an ever changing series of exhibitions of contemporary and 20th century art. These may range from, say, 'English Stone Sculpture of the Period 1910 to 1937', to exhibitions of paintings and photographs. In addition, there are events and activities including holiday workshops, drawing courses and seminars and symposiums. Finally there is an extensive education service offering courses of short or long duration. Deservedly, in its own way, Kettle's is fast becoming as big an attraction to artists as the laboratories were to the likes of Newton and Rutherford.

Talk of Newton sparks off more thoughts of contrast: a representative list of past graduates makes interesting reading. On the one hand, we have Wordsworth, Pepys, Milton, the Elizabethan dramatists Marlow and Fletcher, Francis Bacon, Byron, Thackeray, Tennyson and Macaulay; on the other we have a let's say, the 'realists' - men who were mainly interested in how the 'real' world worked or in how to make it work better. Such a group would include Isaac Newton, Oliver Cromwell, William Wilberforce and Lord Palmerston. That such great men should have studied at various times at one of England's great universities is not remarkable - but the variety of the interests certainly is. What a range! From metaphysics to anti-slavery, from the laws of physics to republicanism, from the liberal tradition to romantic poetry. Nor should one forget the creator of one of the world's best known diaries (after Mrs Dale, of course, if you can admit to remembering that pearl of the Home Service).

Seriously, such a range of thinking - from Milton to Newton to Wilberforce - can hardly have been surpassed that often within a single institution. It is, in a sense, more impressive as a record of human achievement than are the buildings in which it was inspired. It points, too, to the way the world has changed. For all its reputation, the

University today - with its thirty colleges established over seven hundred years - is just one among many. There are more universities in Britain than there are colleges in Cambridge, and more specialisation. The likelihood of the emergence of a modern counterpart to this single galaxy of talent that blazed with such individual brilliance between the 17th and early 20th centuries, is practically zero. Everything is more spread around these days - and, elsewhere certainly, much less class conscious. It's a far cry from 'Eton and Oxbridge' to 'Anytown Comprehensive and Reading'. Or Leicester. Or Keele. One cannot, perhaps should not, attempt to compare the two phenomena, but it's worth noting the difference - even if Cambridge, in the lifestyle of its students, still seems from time to time to be on a different planet from Cardiff, despite everything!

By the way, while we're still up to our necks in culture, I'm reminded again of the general observations I made at the beginning of the chapter: this neck of the words poses more questions than it answers and nothing is ever quite as it seems. We've been talking Tennyson and Byron and Thackeray; we've touched on the Eton and Oxbridge route to the hallowed halls of 'The Establishment' - while remembering Cambridge's current reputation for *scientific* excellence. All definite, factual stuff, agreed? How on earth, then, in the 'Swinging Sixties' did this package give birth to 'The Cambridge Footlights Review' (which breathed a gale of new life into political satire throughout the media), and which begat 'Beyond the Fringe', 'Private Eye', 'That Was the Week That Was', David Frost, Peter Cook, Jonathan Miller and all the rest? How could it *happen*? *Why* it did it happen, on the banks of the Cam, rather than in downtown Birmingham, Newcastle or Glasgow? What encouraged this particular bunch of students to turn on their class and snarl at every tradition they could find? If that's not amazing, I'm the King of Siam! In fact, I'd suggest it's even more amazing than finding a priceless Rubens on a wall behind a chapel altar - certainly it's even more food for thought.

The mention of food, as ever, brings us once again to our familiar other enthusiasms: eating out and, by association (or telepathy) shopping. Cambridge caters superbly for both these needs, much as you would expect given its sophistication in other respects. The main shopping areas run south east to north west and include Trumpington Street, King's Parade, Magdalen Street, Sydney Street and Regent Street. But Cambridge is also a town of narrow side streets and alleyways and it is there that we'll find the old book, antique and art shops that are our main quarry. LION YARD SHOPPING CENTRE, on the other hand, is the Cambridge version of the modern 'all-things-to-all- people' experience that most towns and cities see as a necessity. It's located between Sydney Street and King's Parade, not far from the GUILDHALL and LIBRARY.

Approaching the end of our 'Light Blue' phase, is there anything we've missed? Bound to be, I should say, but in closing this chapter, let me draw your thoughts to two final aspects of 'town and gown' life.

The first footnote, as it were, concerns some more on museums. At times, Cambridge seems to have a museum for everything, be it geology, archaeology, classical archaeology, science, ethnology and so on. Whatever your own enthusiasm, you would expect to find it stimulated somewhere between JESUS GREEN, PARKER'S PIECE and THE BACKS. The Backs? That's where lawns and gardens sweep down to the west bank of the Cam, to the setting for those leisurely punt excursions that seem to be an essential part of student life: 'If you're stuck for an idea, go pole a punt!'

PUNTING ON THE CAM

One is also led to believe that serious punting is the perfect antidote to a previous night's excesses. These tend to be very excessive at regular intervals, as 'town and gown' pitch into RAG WEEK (February), the MID-SUMMER FAIR (June), the ARTS FESTIVAL (July), the FOLK FESTIVAL (July) and the JAZZ FESTIVAL (the late Summer Bank Holiday). There is also a motley FESTIVAL OF MUSIC, DANCE, SPEECH AND DRAMA; the LENT BUMPS, which is a rowing contest held in February and possibly the most widely known event of the lot: MAY WEEK, with its riot of wining, dining and dancing that runs for ten days from the end of May.

Obviously, this little list could influence the timing of your visit, depending on whether your main interest is the history, your collections - or the lifestyle. To me, it's just a bit of fun - as long as it doesn't last too long, and as long as there's a quiet, welcoming hotel awaiting my return, and Cambridge has a wealth of hotels to suit every taste and pocket, or there are the usual delightful places to stay just outside of the town.

ARBURY LODGE
82 Arbury Road
Cambridge
Cambridgeshire
CB4 2JG

Tel: 01223 364319
Fax: 01223 566988

ETB Listed Commended.
RAC Listed AA 3Q's Recommended

Just one and a half miles and a pleasant twenty minute walk from the heart of Cambridge, is Arbury Lodge Guest House. It is a house built in the 1930s, roomy and comfortable and essentially a home from home which is something that Anita and Carlo Celentano work hard at, and they certainly succeed. You feel welcome from the moment you step through the front door and nothing seems to be too much trouble for them. It is an immaculately run house, spotlessly clean and with fresh decor. It is run as a family home in which their guests are invited to be a part but at the same time not being intrusive. The house is open all the year round and it pleasantly warm throughout. There are five guest rooms, all attractively furnished and with comfortable beds. Each room has television and a hostess tray which includes tea, coffee, drinking chocolate and biscuits. A delicious breakfast is served every morning starting with fruit juices and cereals on a help yourself basis, followed by a traditional full English breakfast, plenty of toast butter and preserves complete the meal. No one could every leave the table hungry! Continental Breakfasts are available if required and special diets can be catered for given notice.

Cambridge will enchant anyone who visits it. With a wealth of beautiful, old buildings, the Backs, the narrow streets and the bustle of a University City, it will give you hours of pleasure. There are a profusion of antique and book shops as well as some clothes shop which will tempt. With a number of quaint hostelries, many restaurants and take away, there is always something to please the most difficult eater, although after such a big breakfast you probably will not want to eat until the evening. You can take a gently stroll along the banks of the River Cam, look in at King's College's glorious church and listen to the fantastic sound of the choir, or perhaps take to the water in a boat. Cambridge is always lovely but sometimes one gets the best from it in the off season. There are less people about and it gives one the time to stand and stare. Milton Country Park with its lovely walks round lakes, play area, picnic area and with bird-watching as well as fishing, it is a pleasure. The American Cemetery is at Coton and the excellent Duxford War Museum at Duxford is only a short way off.

USEFUL INFORMATION

OPEN: All year
CHILDREN: Welcome
CREDIT CARDS: None taken
LICENSED: No
ACCOMMODATION: 5 rooms, 2 en-suite
RATES: Dbl./tw from £20pppn sgl from £19pppn

DINING ROOM: Great breakfast
VEGETARIAN: Yes + special diets
WHEELCHAIR ACCESS: No
GARDEN: Yes
PETS: No

NO SMOKING THROUGHOUT EXCEPT SINGLE BEDROOM

THE BLACK HOSTELRY
The College, Firmary Lane
Ely
Cambridgeshire
CB7 4DL

Tel: 01353 662612
Fax: 01353 665658

ETB Listed Commended

This most surely be one of the most unusual bed and breakfast venues in the whole of England! The Black Hostelry is so called because the Black Monks (Benedictine) who wore black habits, used to hostel here when part of the Monastery, but since the Dissolution of the Monastery in 1539 it became a Canon's house and still is today. It is the home of the Vice Dean of Ely Cathedral and his wife and it is Mrs Green who looks after the guests. It is a unique experience staying in a Cathedral House which offers very private accommodation to the individual guests and access to a memorable visit to Ely Cathedral and its surroundings. It is surrounded by parkland and is very quiet.

The Black Hostelry offers a spacious apartment consisting of a sitting room, bedroom and bathroom with television and a hostess tray. The toilet for this suite, although for the private use of guests, is separate and involves a few steps. There is also a spacious double room with adjoining private bathroom, and these guests have breakfast in a medieval undercroft whilst the apartment guests breakfast in the sitting room. Canon and Mrs Green describe the accommodation as 'clean, comfortable, old fashioned, but warm and relaxing'. They understate the case - it is one of the most charming and welcoming places one could wish to stay in.

Apart from the uplifting pleasure of being so much part of Ely Cathedral when you stay here, it is also very convenient for Cambridge and for exploring the many picturesque and unusual villages and small towns in this part of the country. In Ely itself, apart from the cathedral, there is much to see including Oliver Cromwell's House, The Old Gaol Museum and the Stained Glass Museum in the Cathedral. There is a bustling market on Thursday and Saturday, plenty of good restaurants and much more. A little further afield is Peterborough, King's Lynn and the fabulous county of Norfolk with historic Norwich and the Norfolk Broads.

USEFUL INFORMATION

OPEN: All year except Christmas
CHILDREN: Welcome
CREDIT CARDS: None taken
LICENSED: No
ACCOMMODATION: 1 Apartment with private bathroom 1 dbl. room with private bathroom
RATES: £24.50 pp B&B £10 for 3rd person sharing room
Children: 3-10 years £7.50

DINING ROOM: Excellent breakfast
VEGETARIAN: Cater for all diets
WHEELCHAIR ACCESS: No
GARDEN: Yes
PETS: By arrangement

CAMBRIDGESHIRE MOAT HOUSE
Bar Hill, Cambridge CB3 8EU
***

Tel: 01954 249988
Fax: 01954 780010

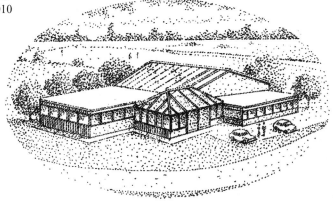

Set in one hundred and thirty four acre Country Park, The Cambridgeshire Moat House is just six miles from the historic centre of Cambridge. It is a modern building, beautifully equipped with all that the modern day traveller could wish for. There are ninety nine en-suite bedrooms. All the rooms have Television, Direct Dial Telephones, Guest Information Channel, Radio and a generously supplied Hospitality Tray.

Fifty per cent of the bedrooms are strictly non-smoking. The well-stocked bar is a popular meeting place for people and the restaurant has an excellent table d'hôte and a la carte menu encompassing English and Continental dishes. Light snacks and meals are also obtainable in the Bar or Lounge. Very popular with business people during the course of the week, the weekends are a chance to enjoy the Special Classic Weekend which offers a minimum of two nights accommodation, dinner in the restaurant to the value of £17.50 per person, a full National Breakfast, use of the Hotels Sports facilities and reduced rate Green fees on the Golf Course. The current tariff is £50 inclusive of Breakfast or £64 inclusive of Dinner and Breakfast. Children sharing parents room have discounts according to age. Golfing Breaks are another great offer with two days of golf, use of the Leisure Club and dinner in the restaurant as well as full National breakfast. The price £160 per person. There is a swimming pool and tennis courts.

USEFUL INFORMATION

OPEN: All year
CHILDREN: Welcome
CREDIT CARDS : All major cards
LICENSED: Yes
ACCOMMODATION: 99 en-suite rooms ground floor rooms
RATES: Sgl from £40 Dbl. £90 room only
Golf Special Breaks inc.
Classic weekend & Golf course

RESTAURANT: English/Continental
BAR FOOD: Light snacks, sandwiches
VEGETARIAN: Always a choice
WHEELCHAIR ACCESS: Yes. 50
GARDEN: Yes.
PETS: Yes

QUARTERWAY HOUSE
Ely Road
Little Thetford
Cambridgeshire
CB9 3HP

Tel:01353 648964

2 Crown Commended.
Which Magazine,
AA 3Q RAC Listed
East Anglia Tourist Board

Quarterway House is only four years old but built in a traditional style. In such a short time it has acquired a welcoming atmosphere largely created by the owner Valerie Beckum who enjoys sharing her home with guests and ensures that everyone who stays here feels at ease and relaxed. A big, well maintained and remarkably mature garden adds to the pleasure of staying here complete with its pond, stables and orchard. Situated just two miles from the enchanting cathedral city of Ely and thirteen miles from Cambridge with its university and fine buildings and half a mile from King's Lynn, it is ideal for people either on business or enjoying a leisure break. For the energetic there is an eighteen hole golf course just one mile away, there is fishing on the River Ouse, Riding and great walks. Bird watchers find the area rewarding, clay pigeon shooting is available within three miles and for those who enjoy the sport of Kings, Newmarket with its two race courses and National Horse Race Museum is close by.

Valerie serves her delicious meals in a farmhouse kitchen with a large colonial wax pine table. She enjoys cooking and uses her own fruit and vegetables as well as free range eggs to enhance her dishes. Breakfast is a feast with a wide choice including kippers and her evening meal is always eagerly looked forward to by her guests. Packed lunches and early breakfasts can be cheerfully arranged, and Vegetarians and Vegans are equally well catered for. There are three delightful bedrooms furnished in a traditional manner and decorated in restful colours with pretty drapes and bedcovers. The two double rooms, one with a king size bed, are ensuite and the twin room has a private bathroom. Each room has television with teletext, hairdryers, fruit and biscuits as well as a hostess tray and has adjustable central heating. Whether you come here for pleasure or on business you will leave refreshed and with the firm intention of making a beeline for Quarterway House whenever you are in the area.

USEFUL INFORMATION

OPEN: All year
CHILDREN: Welcome fare
VEGETARIAN: Upon request
WHEELCHAIR ACCESS: No
GARDEN: Large and beautiful
Barbecue and picnic table available for use
ACCOMMODATION: 3 ensuite
RATES: From £35 dbl. £25sgl

FARMHOUSE KITCHEN: Delicious

CREDIT CARDS: Most major cards
LICENSED: No
PETS: By arrangement
NON-SMOKING HOUSE

UNIVERSITY ARMS HOTEL
Regent Street,
Cambridge CB2 1AD
****

Tel:01223 351241
Fax: 01223 461319
devere.unicams@airtime.co.uk

The University Arms is one of Cambridge's largest city centre hotels with over one hundred and sixty years of service and experience to offer guests. Close to all the historic sights of Cambridge, it provides the visitor with a superb base not only to enjoy the beauty of the river and the Backs, the Colleges and their stunning gardens, the excellent shopping and much else, it is also within easy reach of so many interesting and fascinating places to visit. Within walking distance of twenty five historical Colleges including Jesus, Emanuel and the famous King's chapel. You can enjoy a chauffeured punt along the River Cam, try a guided tour on an open bus to show you the historic sites, take a trip along the Cam to Ely on a pleasure cruiser. Duxford Air Museum, where you will find Europe's largest collection of historic aircraft, and the American War Cemetery are within easy reach. For those who love the Sport of Kings, Newmarket will provide you with a wonderful day at the races.

Within this elegant and impeccably run hotel there are one hundred & fifteen luxury bedrooms all superbly appointed with direct dial telephone, television, video and a hospitality tray. Forty rooms have facsimiles. There is twenty four hour room service and parking for one hundred cars. Many of the rooms look out over twenty five acres of parkland called Parker's Piece. In addition the hotel has six unique conference suites available for meetings, ranging from 2-300 people theatre style (three suites have the capacity for two hundred people theatre style). The Conference Co-ordinators do everything in their power to ensure the event is a resounding success.

The majestic oak panelled restaurant with spectacular stained glass windows which depict many of Cambridge's college crests, offers delicious traditional cuisine and is a favourite place to dine for many local people and those who live not too far away. The elegant Octagon Lounge tempts one to sit and relax and Parker's Bar is quite delightful,

USEFUL INFORMATION

OPEN: All year	RESTAURANT: Superb traditional cuisine
CHILDREN: Welcome	PARKER'S BAR: Sandwiches and snacks
CREDIT CARDS: All major cards	VEGETARIAN: Options available
LICENSED: Full On	WHEELCHAIR ACCESS: Yes. Ramp
ACCOMMODATION:115 luxury rooms	GARDEN: Yes
RATES: From £105 Leisure & Activity Breaks available	PETS: Yes. £5

AYLESBURY LODGE
5 Mowbray Road
Cambridge
CB1 4SR
Tel/Fax: 01223 240089

ETB 2Crown Commended
AA QQQQ RAC Acclaimed

With easy access to the M11 and just one and a half miles from the city of Cambridge with its many colleges, fine architecture, the River Cam, the Backs and excellent shopping, Aylesbury Lodge Guest House is an ideal place to stay. Guests who have stayed here in the home of Tracey and David Parkins, will tell you that they have found the house very comfortable, extremely clean and attractively furnished and decorated. In addition, the Parkins are too modest to say how much their friendly, caring attitude is appreciated. All the bedrooms are ensuite and two rooms have four posters. They all have television with Sky Movie Channel, direct dial telephone, a hostess tray, hairdryer, and a complimentary bathroom pack. Breakfast is a wholesome home-cooked English Breakfast which starts off with cereals and fruit juices and with plenty of toast and preserves as well as freshly brewed coffee and piping hot tea. No evening meals are served but Cambridge has an abundance of eateries of all kinds to suit all tastes and pockets. The Parkins will be happy to point you in the right direction, as indeed they are happy to help you plan your day, if you wish. Smoking is only permitted in the Guest Lounge.

USEFUL INFORMATION

OPEN: All year	DINING ROOM: Excellent English
CHILDREN: Welcome breakfast	
VEGETARIAN: Upon request	CREDIT CARDS: All major cards
WHEELCHAIR ACCESS: 1 ground floor room	LICENSED: No
ACCOMMODATION: All en suite rooms	GARDEN: Yes
RATES: From £30-50 per room	PETS: No

CAMBRIDGE GARDEN MOAT HOUSE
Granta Place, Mill Lane, Cambridge
CB2 1RT
Tel: 01223 259988
Fax: 01223 316605
****

If you want fun with the family, or peace and tranquillity, take a break at Cambridge Garden Moat House. Set in three acres of private gardens on the banks of the River Cam, it is just a stone's throw from the historic centre of Cambridge. It has everything to offer the visitor including a swimming pool, gymnasium and a beauty salon. The one hundred & seventeen ensuite bedrooms are all charmingly furnished with pretty drapes and bed covers. Each room has television, direct dial telephone, an honesty bar, trouser press and a hostess tray. The non-smoking restaurant has an all encompassing menu offering dishes from around the world. Children are always given great consideration and they have their own Noble Nosh-Up menu. The Lounge and Bar are welcoming places and all disabled people, who are very welcome, can be offered the minicom service in the bedrooms. The Club Motivation health and fitness club is open to residents with its modern gym, indoor swimming pool, spa bath, solarium and beauty treatment rooms. Right in the heart of Cambridge, the Cambridge Garden Moat House is a superb base for business or pleasure. This is my favourite hotel in Cambridge, if I could afford to live here permanently, I would stop investing in the Lottery.

USEFUL INFORMATION

OPEN: All year	RESTAURANT: A la carte menu
CHILDREN: Welcome. Own menu	BAR FOOD: Light snacks, sandwiches
CREDIT CARDS: All major cards	VEGETARIAN: Always options
LICENSED: Full On	WHEELCHAIR ACCESS: Yes
ACCOMMODATION:117 suites	GARDEN: Yes & Fitness Club
RATES: B&B Sgl £74 Dbl. £90 weekends only	PETS: No
Weekdays Sgl £120 Dbl. £150 room only	

CAMBRIDGE LODGE HOTEL
139 Huntingdon Road
Cambridge
CB3 0DQ
Tel:01223 352833
Fax: 01223 855166
RAC 'Best Small Hotel Eastern Region 1997' ETB

Situated within minutes of the historic city of Cambridge, the Hotel is an ideal base from which to explore the sights and delights of Cambridge with its old colleges, impressive architecture, narrow winding streets, punting on the river and a host of museums and galleries. Ely, famous for its cathedral, is less than fifteen miles away. This Mock-Tudor House has an aura of quiet elegance reminiscent of more genteel times. The owners, Sheila Hipwell and Darren Chamberlain, ensure that guests are made to feel totally at home. The Cambridge Lodge has twelve double and one single ensuite rooms. Each has television, direct-dial telephone, tea and coffee making facilities. The Bridal Suite is quite enchanting. Reflecting the ambience of the Hotel, the restaurant combines intimate surroundings with excellence. The varied menu of French and English cuisine served with friendly efficiency make it a popular choice for guests and non-residents alike. The public lounge is relaxed and comfortable, providing an informal, cosy atmosphere in which to have a pre-dinner drink or afternoon tea. Cambridge Lodge is also well known for its small conference facilities and for the care and attention it pays to wedding receptions and other functions.

USEFUL INFORMATION

OPEN: All year	RESTAURANT: Open to non-residents
CHILDREN: Welcome	Classic French & English cuisine
CREDIT CARDS: All major cards	VEGETARIAN: Always a choice
LICENSED: Yes	WHEELCHAIR ACCESS: Yes
ACCOMMODATION: 12dbl 1sgl all ensuite	GARDEN: Yes
RATES: Dble. £72.50 prpn. Sgl. £58.	
Inclusive of Breakfast & Vat.	PETS: By prior arrangement

GRAFTON HOTEL & RESTAURANT
619 Newmarket Road
Cambridge
Cambridgeshire
CB5 8PA

Tel: 01223 241387
Fax: 01223 412321

The Grafton Hotel is quietly situated close to the centre of Cambridge and is set back from the Newmarket Road . The Hotel has extensive car parking facilities. People have been coming to The Grafton for years because it is so comfortable and is entirely suitable for anyone wanting to enjoy Cambridge and explore further afield, as well as those on business. One of its advantages is the closeness to major road links which makes it simple for over night visitors. Cath and Gerry Cross own the Hotel and their welcoming presence makes all their guests feel rapidly at home. The elegant restaurant and cosy lounge bar are open to residents and non residents alike and can offer everything from a quiet drink and snack to a sumptuous a la carte meal. All the rooms are en-suite with direct dial telephones, remote control colour television, radio alarms and tea/coffee making facilities. There is room service, hairdryers and irons are available on request.

USELESS INFORMATION

OPEN: All year	RESTAURANT: Wide choice. Open to
CHILDREN: Welcome	non-residents
CREDIT CARDS: All major cards	BAR FOOD: Snacks available
LICENSED: Yes	VEGETARIAN: Always a choice
ACCOMMODATION: 5sgl,6dbl,6tw all en-suite	GARDEN: Yes
RATES: From £35-£45sgl B&B & £45-£60dbl	PETS: YEs

THE PANOS HOTEL & RESTAURANT
154-156 Hills Road
Cambridge
CB23 2PB

Tel:01223 212958
Fax: 01223 210980

Johansen's Recommended Les Routiers

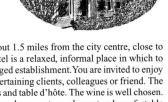

This small intimate hotel, personally run by the owner Genevieve Kretz, comprises six comfortable and well appointed bedrooms with remote control television, cable television, tea and coffee making facilities, mini-bar and radio alarm. Genevieve does everything possible to make her guests feel welcome, ensuring a friendly, personal service, unparalleled in Cambridge. The restaurant, opened in 1979 has gained an excellent reputation for its cuisine's and is one of Cambridge's premier restaurants. In addition to the superb food, the wine list features many fine wines to enhance and complement the menu. The Panos is within easy walking distance of the City centre and all amenities. Close by are the famous Cambridge Botanical Gardens and the charming and historical 'Backs' of the colleges. From the conveniently situated Railway Station, Ely and its beautiful Cathedral are just twenty minutes away and London is a forty five minute drive along the M11. There is a Car Park at the rear of the Hotel.

USEFUL INFORMATION

OPEN: All year
CHILDREN: Welcome
CREDIT CARDS: All major cards
LICENSED: Yes
ACCOMMODATION: 6 en-suite rooms
RATES: Sgl £50 Dbl £70   Special rates for long staying guests

RESTAURANT: Excellent cuisine
VEGETARIAN: Always a choice
WHEELCHAIR ACCESS: Yes
GARDEN: No
PETS: No

THE SORRENTO HOTEL
196 Cherry Hinton Road
Cambridge
CB1 4AN
Tel: 01223 243533
Fax: 01223 213463

AA Listed ETB****

Situated on the south side of Cambridge in a residential area, about 1.5 miles from the city centre, close to Addenbrookes Hospital and the M11 motorway, the Sorrento Hotel is a relaxed, informal place in which to stay, where you will be warm and comfortable. It is a family managed establishment.You are invited to enjoy an aperitif or a continental beverage in the licensed bar before entertaining clients, colleagues or friend. The restaurant has a superb menu of Italian and French a la carte dishes and table d'hôte. The wine is well chosen. The individually designed bedrooms offer the necessary luxuries to make your stay a pleasant and comfortable one. Each room has ensuite facilities, hair dryer, colour remote control television with satellite viewing, direct dial telephone and suitable writing facilities to enable guests to continue their studies or business in the comfort and privacy of their bedroom. Conference facilities are available ranging from a one to one interview to a full delegate package of up to sixty delegates. All the modern equipment for meetings is available.

USEFUL INFORMATION

OPEN: All year
CHILDREN: Welcome carte menu.
CREDIT CARDS: All major cards
LICENSED: Yes
ACCOMMODATION: En suite rooms
RATES: Sgl £54.50 tw £86.00 Treble £97.50

RESTAURANT: Italian/French a la

BAR FOOD: Not applicable
VEGETARIAN: Always a choice
GARDEN: No
PETS: By arrangement

THE BRIDGE
151 Hills Road
Cambridge
CB2 2RJ

Tel: 01223 247942   Fax: 01223 416585

Three Crowns

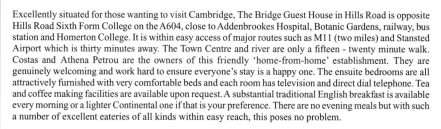

Excellently situated for those wanting to visit Cambridge, The Bridge Guest House in Hills Road is opposite Hills Road Sixth Form College on the A604, close to Addenbrookes Hospital, Botanic Gardens, railway, bus station and Homerton College. It is within easy access of major routes such as M11 (two miles) and Stansted Airport which is thirty minutes away. The Town Centre and river are only a fifteen - twenty minute walk. Costas and Athena Petrou are the owners of this friendly 'home-from-home' establishment. They are genuinely welcoming and work hard to ensure everyone's stay is a happy one. The ensuite bedrooms are all attractively furnished with very comfortable beds and each room has television and direct dial telephone. Tea and coffee making facilities are available upon request. A substantial traditional English breakfast is available every morning or a lighter Continental one if that is your preference. There are no evening meals but with such a number of excellent eateries of all kinds within easy reach, this poses no problem.

USEFUL INFORMATION

OPEN: Jan2nd-Dec 20th
CHILDREN: Welcome
CREDIT CARDS: All major cards
LICENSED: No
ACCOMMODATION: En suite rooms
RATES: £28sgl. £45dbl. £60-75 Family rooms

DINING ROOM: Excellent breakfast
VEGETARIAN: Upon request
WHEELCHAIR ACCESS: Yes
3 ground floor rooms
GARDEN: Yes
PETS: By arrangement

St. IVES

IAN PETHERS

Selected venues in this chapter.

' I went on a diet, swore off drinking and heavy eating,
and in fourteen days I lost two weeks'
Joe E. Lewis

CHAPTER SIX:
Wetland Wanderings.
Huntingdon to Chatteris & South Cambridgeshire

There aren't many parts of the world, I imagine, that can claim to offer all things to all men (or women). If you're still game for it, after all the time we've spent together - and the miles we've covered - we could be near to agreeing that East Anglia has as good a chance as anywhere of justifying a place near the head of the list. All right, there are a few things missing: it's short on Alps, tropical rain forest and blistering heat, but they are probably over-rated, anyway, if you don't ski and you sweat easily (skiing is OK, it's the apres ski - beastly phrase - that I find so noisily, expensively and tediously phoney). None of that in Norfolk, nor in any of the rest of it, as far as we've seen. It's all very real: real history, real cathedrals and churches - and real nature, in its vastness and power, its peace and loveliness, and last but not least genuine friendly and welcoming local people, whom given a choice would not choose to live anywhere else.

So, we've seen the signs of the sea's untamable strength, we've felt the silence of the empty Brecks and we've shed a tear or two at the sight of the springtime blossom in the river valleys. On the other hand, we might have been struck most of all by the relationship between the people and their surroundings, the simple honesty of communities that, by and large, have been at one with their environment throughout a long, long history. We've seen some examples, too, of places where the relationship has been fouled up by unaware planning - or the lack of any planning at all - but these things are everywhere. Fortunately we've learned to look the other way while we rush on to somewhere better.

As we gaze out toward the Fens from our base in Ely, we're about to discover another side of the region's character that's just as extreme as its beauty, its drama, its history and its solitude. What's more, it's as fundamental to this watery landscape as the churches seemed to be in Norwich - at least, it is in the eyes of virtually anyone who has ever written about it, or taken note of the underlying reality in the course of a journey from, say, the outskirts of Cambridge to Wisbech or Spalding. According to one writer, it seems to be a recognised fact that the longer you linger in Cambridgeshire, the more characteristics you find to be very definitely on the odd side.

Take the Church at March, for example. It is said that when the people started the building work the devil pulled it all down, on the grounds that the Fens belonged to him. Apparently, this process continued until someone had the bright idea of erecting a cross to bar his way. St Wendreda's Church bears witness today to the success of the scheme, as does the cross itself, which is still standing between the Church and the market - between God and Mammon.

Mysterious tales of the Fens proper must run into three figures or more. Typically, lone travellers are warned to beware the Jack O' Lanterns which are said to appear at the dead of night to lure the unwary to a boggy death. Another reputed trap for the over confident is found at Spinney Abbey, Wicken, where mysterious lights and ghostly singing monks rattle the nerves more than somewhat. Worse still actually occurred at Warboys, not that far away: having been the scene of one of the most important witchcraft trials in English history, it still enjoys a certain notoriety for strange goings on, from time to time, that seem to be better documented than is usual.

Escape all of this, and you might just find yourself seeking solace in, say, Whittlesey. Fine - only why are the townspeople dancing through the streets in parade in *January* behind a Straw *Bear*? A fertility rite, you say? Again, fine: it seems to work, as the area is renowned for its regular abundance. All the same, at a time when we are being told that genetic engineering is agriculture's *real* way forward, it's a bit *abnormal*!

Go to St Ives (a mite further away), on the other hand, and you may well witness the selection of six boys and six girls who are to be given bibles on 'Whit Sunday' - according to the role of the *dice*! While we're at it, why do the stout residents of Stilton waste perfectly good cheese by rolling it down the High Street every May? What baleful deity could possibly get a kick out of *that*? Especially as said cheese was never made in Stilton in the first place, and only picked up the name by accident, more or less, folklore is fun.

As we gird ourselves up for this excursion we could be forgiven for feeling a brief shiver of apprehension. Of course, most of us are too long in the tooth to be truly *frightened*, we tell ourselves. I mean, we've seen it all. What can it be like, this land of ghosts and mad cheese-rollers? Perhaps we'd do best to see the next tour as a bit of a challenge, and as a chance for an attitude change. It could be just that - in more ways than one.

Fenland has its towns, villages and smaller communities that relate to each other in much the same way as those in the rest of the region. Obviously it also has interesting shops, markets, auctions, craft centres, garden centres, museums, art galleries, theatres, wildlife parks, and a truly magnificent flower show in the bulb season, you can not help but be impressed with the trillions of daffodils that abound in the hedgerows etc. Thus far, we've found such places totally magnetic; we've turned off dual carriageways and travelled down lanes at the first sight of any 'brown sign' showing the slightest chance of picking up just one more 'must have'. All of which has been extremely pleasurable, we have purchased the inevitable gift and 'bits and pieces' to remind us of this enchanting journey. All part of the big holiday picture. It also gives a living to a great many very decent East Anglians, which is as it should be.

The trouble is, as soon as we move away from Ely we're going to need to look at life in a very different way. The shops, the centres and so forth are all so easily available, while the markets are truly out of this world - but if we spend too much time browsing and not enough studying the landscape and absorbing the atmosphere, we'll miss most of the point of it all. Believe you me, this place is special - strange, definitely - but absolutely special. In a sense, it has an aspect that is almost Biblical, at times. I hope the notion won't cause offence, unlike some of the other bits of casual malice I might have dropped in your laps!

Really - Fenland can seem to be one of those parts of the globe, which most of us rarely see where, on the Third Day, God over-rode the idea of gathering the waters together and the earth together, separately. Between Cambridge and the sea, he was content just to let them mingle a bit - and see what we made of it all, in due course. As you're about to find out, we didn't make an awful lot, for centuries - and, when we did, we missed one rather basic point that nearly sent the entire effort down the drain. Literally! Delusions of grandeur? Not in Fenland, not if you know what's good for you. They simply wouldn't hold water - like a lot of other things around the region.

A fairly swift sortie down the A142 by way of Stuntney brings us, in time, to our first call, at the village of Soham. As we amble along, we begin to take more notice of the countryside that is going to become very familiar over the next day or two. We also notice from the map that certain words, or parts of words, turn up too frequently for coincidence in the place names. We may wonder, perhaps, if they have any special meaning. Well, they do - so we'd better take a quick look at some of the more common ones. As, by and large, they tend to reflect the features of the landscape round about, we'll also need a closer look at that, before we get down to cases.

It will probably come as a big surprise, as you look out at the enormous, flat fields of the Fens, to find out that most of the area - which today has few trees - was covered with huge forests, thousands of years ago. In the course of tending the great fields, which change so markedly during the year, depending on the crop - flowers, sugar beet, grain, potatoes or cabbages - farmers still plough up trunks of the ancient trees that used to flourish here. These warped and twisted remains are known as 'bog oak', although they could just as well have come from any other tree.

These days, the most widely held belief is that it was the formation of the peat that choked the trees. At a later date the low lying land was flooded and turned into one enormous bog - for a while. Later still there must have been some kind of colossal subsidence, which left islands in the marsh, such as the one on which Ely itself was established. Man intervened some time after that; we shall see later the effects of the various attempts to reclaim the marsh for farming. But, for the moment, it is enough to notice that the islands are islands no more, only humps and hummocks above the fields, and that the general level of the ground has continued to fall, dramatically, over the centuries. So, to place names.

Towns and villages on the humps and hummocks often have the suffix 'ea' or 'ey' - from the Old English for 'island'. Examples of this pattern include places such as Ramsey, Thorney and Whittlesey. In other uses of Old English, we find ' mere' meaning 'lake'; 'lode', a navigable waterway that's been cut through the swamp; 'drove', which is also a cut and 'hythe', which we would call a 'quay'. So now we know - and we'll know a lot more by the end of the day.

A thousand years ago or more, **SOHAM** was best known for its monastery, founded by Felix of Burgundy. Like many others in the area it caught the eyes of some rampaging Danes who didn't like the religion, loved the gold and silver church plate and did what Danes usually did in the circumstances - destroyed the monastery and left the country in rather a hurry, with the loot in the back of the boat. It would seem that this wanton violence caused such a shock, locally, that not a lot happened for several hundred years afterwards. Eventually work was begun in the 12th century on a *new* Church which still stands today, having had many additions over the years. Its huge tower, complete with a peal of ten bells, is very much a local landmark.

DOWNFIELD WINDMILL (Enquiries - 01353 720333) is a popular attraction, that is well worth looking over while we're in the area. If we happen to have picked the 'Merry Month' for our visit, it's also a good idea to take in the VILLAGE COLLEGE FESTIVAL, held in May every year, with exhibitions, discussions, music and dancing. Finally, I should put in a word for the PUMPKIN FAIR, which is a classic village fete - with a unique difference - and really great fun for September visitors.

The countryside south of Soham, next on our itinerary, is one of the most intriguing stretches from our point of view, and is certain to take up a large part of this stage of the tour. Bounded to the west by the River Cam, and elsewhere by three 'A' roads, we'll find an area where architecture, engineering and wildlife conservation have all produced experiences that could be talking points amongst us for years. So, leaving behind the Fair, the Festival or the Windmill - depending on the month - let's take a slow circuit away from Soham and see what we can find, amidst the fields of flowers, golden grain - or even cold, dark cabbages. What a variable picture life can paint for us around here, to be sure!

Almost at once we are off down a right turn, along the A1123 to WICKEN FEN (Enquiries - 01353 720274) for a close encounter of the marshy kind. Wicken is open all year from dawn to dusk, except on Christmas Day, and is a National Nature Reserve, run by the National Trust, covering more than 800 acres.

WICKEN FEN WINDPUMP

It is Britain's oldest nature reserve, too, presenting a unique fragment of the wilderness that once covered East Anglia. A haven for birds, plants and animals alike, the Fen can be explored by traditional wide droves and lush green parks as well as by means of a board walk nature trail - all giving access to a variety of hides. The William Thorpe Visitor Centre was originally built as a field centre, but now houses displays, a shop, refreshment facilities and an information point.

The two trails, the hides and the extensive, less formal walks - stretching out more than ten miles - lead into the heartland of this very special place. Fen meadows, alive with colour, are crossed and re-crossed by water ways that all but seethe with wildlife which can be seen to great advantage from the hides. The three quarter mile board walk trail gives reasonably easy access throughout the year; the two and a quarter mile nature trail takes the more experienced walker deep into the wilderness proper. To get a real feel for the Fens of former times we can do no better than begin at Wicken where we can see, at first hand, the kind of landscape and drainage systems that were typical of the area up to the 19th century.

It takes careful husbandry to conserve this kind of heritage, with its native flora and fauna, and visitors are obviously delighted by the work to date. Not least among the evidence of this care is the way in which the last of the wind pumps, once used exclusively for drainage, has been preserved on the site in its entirety to become, perhaps, its most typical landmark. Alongside the mill, the harvesting of sedge and reeds by the wardens gives a further insight into the rigours of life in days gone by.

Following our first Fen interlude we'll try the adventurous option and travel on along the A1123, before turning left down a minor road leading to Upware, Reach and - if we're in luck - to **BURWELL,** where we'll have plenty to see. A village of quaint, traditional Fenland cottages, Burwell has two main features amongst its obvious charms, apart from its connections with THE TOWERS TRAIL, a circular, fifty five mile route from Ely, that takes the motoring tourist south of the City on a day's exploration of locations landmarked, in the main, by their remarkable water pump windmills. Although the real business, these days, uses electric pumps, in days gone by there were wind pumps by the hundred bordering every water course, as the local people strove to keep the land dried out enough to be worked effectively.

So, here we have Burwell, where the MUSEUM that we have come to see lies at the village centre, next to STEVEN'S WINDMILL - what shall we make of it all? The museum was opened in 1992 and includes a timber framed 18th century barn, a blacksmith's forge and wheelwright's shop and a nissen hut, housing war memorabilia. In addition, there is a purpose built exhibition building in traditional stone and wood cladding, incorporating a range of open wagon sheds. The displays reflect the life of a bygone age as experienced by the villagers who lived and worked in the Fens. The museum, which is open Sundays, Thursdays and Bank Holiday Mondays, from 2pm to 5pm, also has an interesting shop. Steven's Mill - worth a visit to itself - is maintained and opened on certain occasions.

By now we're heading more or less south towards Cambridge again, and the B1102 will serve as well as anything to take us down in the general direction of the city's outskirts and the A11. **SWAFFHAM PRIOR** is the next village along our way. 'Swaffham?' I hear you say. 'We've met that name before, haven't we?' Indeed we have, and not that far away, across Breckland, in West Norfolk. I hope we share a similar memory of it as one of the prettiest of the county's market towns - and one of the richest in terms of history, folklore and tall tales! But is there a connection?

Indeed there is! Remembering we're still in East Anglia, there are, as there would be, conflicting views on the origins of the name. In fact, there's an opportunity for any visitors who feel intrepid - as well as discerning - to follow in the steps of Cadfael, the medieval monk turned detective, as seen on television, and try to get to the root of it all. I'm sure the staff of the Museum at Swaffham, in Norfolk, would be as interested in the outcome as any of us (they dared me to say that)! For the moment, all I can do is present the two cases.

The first has it that the name, shared by the Norfolk town and the Cambridgeshire villages, comes from a bunch of rather coarse Germans, brought over by the Romans to help keep order amongst those followers of Boadicea who might still have had a taste for a punch up. The Romans did quite a lot of this policing, throughout their empire, using a bunch of thugs from one country that they'd 'colonised' to suppress other thugs (or patriots?) in a region more recently brought into the Imperial fold. One such gang was the 'Swabian' people, from somewhere in Saxony, and the idea is that they gave their name to settlements they established once they had sorted things on Rome's behalf. It is said that the name 'Swabian' could very easily have become 'Swaffham ', over the years.

The other story - and it is the one I prefer - sees these communities as being set up much later, after the Saxons had taken over from the Romans. The connection here is with the 'Swaefas', a powerful Germanic tribe, who arrived as part of the general invasion. Today the link is commemorated in SWAEFAS WAY, one of the many pleasant walks established around the Norfolk town. Perhaps, in Cambridgeshire, they prefer to keep their memories less tangible.

Right, having settled that, let's look around the place. The first thing that strikes us is the sight of two churches in the churchyard. They're there because of a parish amalgamation, in 1667. ST CYRIAC'S was virtually derelict twenty years or more ago with, sadly, little more to offer than a view through empty windows of a mess of rubble and largely dry and dead creepers. Times have changed for the better in this case, as I'm pleased to report that matters have been taken in hand in more recent years, so that the building, whilst not used for services, is being cared for properly again, and is open to visitors. ST MARY'S, on the other hand, which is in full and regular use, has been admirably restored and is as rewarding to visit as many of the churches which we've already seen.

Not far away is FOSTER'S WINDMILL (Enquiries - 01638 741009), a fine example of the tower mill style, built in 1858 by the millwrights Fyson and Son. Much of the machinery is intact, but the mill's main interest to us is that it represents the peak of development in the use of wind power in this area. It is open only by appointment, and donations are preferred instead of a fixed admission charge. Health buffs will be delighted to hear that there is stoneground flour on sale!

Having visited Wicken and Burwell - not to mention all the driving in between - we can see that the drainage, begun in earnest in the 17th century and undertaken to make the incredibly fertile peat available for agriculture, has meant that true Fen conditions are preserved today in only a few isolated areas - almost entirely as Nature Reserves. We'll look at the engineering feats involved in the drainage process a little later in the chapter, but for the moment, having had a brief introduction to the wildlife and plants, let's look in more detail at that aspect.

What *is* a Fen? Basically it's a waterlogged place, as we've seen, where reeds and other plants grow in patches of standing water. East Anglia has fenland of two types: there are peat beds on the landward side of the region and marine silts on the seaward side, around the edge of The Wash. This fen country is very different in its vegetation from other peat bogs or non-peaty marshes because Fenland peat has been saturated with lime. Consequently, when it is drained, it is extremely suitable for the production of crops which could not tolerate the acidity that is normally found in other marshy areas.

The humps and hummocks that we've already noticed where the villages and towns have been built are isolated outcrops of Jurassic boulder clay, more than 136 million years old. This clay underlies the bulk of the Fens and is often at such a great depth that it rarely, if ever, reaches the surface.

Once some degree of drainage had proved successful - from the end of the 17th century onwards - flax, hemp, oats and wheat were grown, while the freshly gained pastures were soon providing grazing that could fatten up cattle from the north as they made their way to the markets in London. This new found pastoral idyll did not last long, however, as nobody had quite thought about what might happen when the peat dried out after drainage and the land began to shrink. The area nearest the sea, because it was based on silt rather than peat, was barely affected but, in the rest of Fenland, the ground level gradually sank below that of the so-called drainage channels and it was very much a case of back to the drawing board! Natural water flows having proved unpredictable, it was decided that if pumps were put to work all might not be lost. The story of the pumping methods and machinery is almost worth a chapter in itself - but, in a book of this kind, the best it can hope for is a paragraph or two, which will come later!

Today, East Anglia's Fenland is respected as one of Britain's most prolific farming regions, where potatoes, sugar beet, wheat and corn, celery, peas, carrots and fruit crop very heavily. To the man in the street the main association, I suspect, is with bulbs, particularly daffodils and tulips. We have seen what a naturalist's paradise it can be already, at Wicken. Even if we were unable to identify all the pond weeds, milfoils, duckweeds, great yellow cress, water violets and species of water lily, it was obvious that there was a variety of plants living here that one could expect to encounter only rarely. The waters edges make their own contribution, with masses of bull rushes, sedges, and reed grasses, which, from the wardens at Wicken, we know are still cut and used for thatching and basketry.

Other vegetation varies according to local enthusiasm for the reed cutting business, but clumps of trees and shrubs often develop, with willows, alders and green-winged orchids along the verges of the drainage channels. In all, at least 267 different plants have been recorded at Wicken alone. Nature being what it is, where there are plants on which to feed there are usually plenty of beasties to feed on them - or on each other. The range is enormous: naturalists have discovered 72 species of mollusc at Wicken and 212 different kinds of spider. At the other end of the spectrum, we learn that coypus and otters are seen from time to time, whilst anglers report astonishing catches of roach, rudd, bream, perch, tench, pike and carp.

And then there are the birds! Again, it's all down to food supply and this splendid agricultural land provides plenty to attract lapwings, redshanks, snipe, reed and sedge warblers, reed bunting as well as many kinds of duck which nest on the Ouse Washes. In addition, bird watchers report sightings of ruffs, black terns and the rare black-tailed godwit. In fact, the winter floods bring thousands of waders and ducks to the Fens along with the largest flock of the Bewick's swans in Britain.

Three miles south west, beyond Lode, ANGLESEY ABBEY (Enquiries - 01223 811200) is a 13th century Augustinian foundation, now operated by the National Trust, that was absorbed into a beautiful Tudor country house early in the 17th century. It contains the famous Fairhaven collection of paintings and furniture and is surrounded by an outstanding, ninety nine acre landscaped garden and arboretum, with wonderful statues, a display of hyacinths in spring, and magnificent herbaceous borders and dahlia gardens in summer.

ANGLESEY ABBEY

The 18th century LODE WATER MILL, which still grinds corn, is sited in the grounds and may be seen working on the first Saturday of each month - although flour seems to be on sale during most times of opening - which should be checked by phone before the visit is arranged.

If we head down the A14 from Lode, we should find ourselves taking the easiest route to the next village on our list, Fulbourn, with the minimum of road rage - ours or anyone else's! We turn right, along the main road, as though we were heading for the middle of Cambridge and then take a left, before the airport, to reach the next goal - where we'll have a chance to scale the County's dizziest heights, which are all of three hundred feet above sea level!

As a village **FULBOURN** is almost as significant as a hub for radiating footpaths as it is for its own, innate attraction. One walk leads to the three mile long FLEAM DYKE, a massive earthwork, built in the 7th century to defend East Anglia against the Mercians. To the north east, another path takes the rambler to Great Wilbraham, while a third, to Little Wilbraham, is landmarked by a gleaming windmill that has been converted to domestic use.

FENLAND FOOTPATH

A little way off to the south-west, the GOG MAGOG HILLS offer fine views of the towers and spires of Cambridge from their 300 ft high summit. One can see WORT'S CAUSEWAY, off the road to Great Abington, which is crossed by the Roman Via Devana, running parallel with the main road and offering a rewarding nine mile walk south east to Horseheath. Just south of the Hills there are other footpaths which lead from the Roman road to WANDLEBURY CAMP, which the Icenii rebuilt from the ruins of an earlier Iron Age fort. The whole area now provides a focus for weekend recreation for people from the City.

To recover from our exertions I'd recommend a leisurely sprint south east, across the A11 to **BALSHAM,** which will be a prelude to a couple of visits that sound like an excellent distraction from the more earnest experiences of the last few hours. As we catch our breath, having parked the car, what are the landmarks of the village, we find ourselves wondering? Immediately, our eyes are drawn to the church, with its fine 13th century tower, but when we go inside, it is the choir stalls, I suppose, which mainly hold our attention. These are decorated with carvings of animals and men - at least, that is the first impression, as a closer examination suggests that their hideous grins are more in keeping with demons than with the righteous! Another point of interest is found by the south door. The old instruments kept in a glass case are souvenirs of those days, one hundred and fifty or so years ago, when the church had its own band.

Midway between Balsham and Linton lies CHILFORD HALL (Enquiries - 01223 892641) where I hope we'll find time not only to explore the buildings but to enjoy a modest taste of the vineyard's fine English wines. *Very* modest, for the driver! I suppose the rest of us could indulge, as long as that didn't spark off an argument lasting the rest of the day! The Hall is open every day from Good Friday to the 1st of November, between 11am and 5.30 pm, and a tour includes not only the ancient building, which houses the winery but, possibly, even an introduction to the local ghost! Outdoors, one can make a journey to see the south facing vines and the beautiful grounds which are home to a permanent display of sculpture by international artists as well as other exhibitions throughout the season. A touch of refreshment - apart from the wine - might be taken at the Vinery Cafe before we press on.

Having pressed a bit, we should find ourselves a little further down the road at Cambridgeshire's Wildlife Breeding Centre at LINTON ZOO (Enquiries - 01223 891308). As we stroll through the beautiful gardens we are able to enjoy encounters with wildlife from all over the world, including such rare and exotic creatures as a Grevy's Zebra, snow leopards and giant tortoises - not to mention binturongs and tarantula spiders. Throughout the sixteen acre site, the emphasis is very much on conservation and education - although there are plenty of picnic areas and all the usual facilities. The Zoo is open every day throughout the year, except for Christmas Day, from 10am to 6pm, in the summer, and from 10am to dusk, in the winter months. The last admission is 45 minutes before closing time - and one should note that the cafeteria is open only during the busy season.

There is about to be another major burst of 'contrast' - I can feel it in my bones - a veritable kaleidoscope of multi-coloured impressions, ending up with something as far removed from animals in zoos as we could get. There may well be the odd time warp thrown in to keep us firing on all six. First we must leave Linton, to trot along the A1037, in a north westerly direction and then, rather neatly ease between Great and Little Abington. At the interchange, where we meet the A11, we find ourselves in close contact with the remains of a stretch of Roman road for a while.

From my earlier jottings, you will probably have gathered that I prefer the Greeks to the Romans, because I can never find much that's as subtle about the descendants of Romulus and Remus. Of course the Renaissance change all that very dramatically, when Rome - and the rest - rediscovered classical Greece and, by and large, went ballistic. What would we possibly have become without that little bit of history, I wonder? My guess is that next to none of our culture would have got far past Morris dancing! There is one thing about the Romans, though, that I really respect: their attitude to the business of road building. Just look at it, for a moment, as we whizz down this admittedly very short stretch.

If a Roman governor wanted a road built, he didn't pussyfoot about as we do today. There were no 'Public Enquiry' PR exercises in the first and second centuries

AD. There were no committees demanding bore holes and engineers reports, no time taken up with feasibility studies - indeed, there you could say there was none of the bureaucracy that they seemed to revel in everywhere else. Basically, one would have to say that they'd cracked it! Their approach was beautifully straightforward. If the governor in question needed to go fifty leagues in a direction where no road existed - he just had his minions build one! A straight one. Immediately. If anything got in the way - anything like a marsh, a river or a hill - they still went straight on. Across it, over it, up and down it - regardless. Very impressive. Possibly very boring, too. Rather like the Romans themselves, at their worst - which they usually were - I suppose. Of course it would be *very* boring, if we did it today. Probably *terminally* boring. Imagine going all the way from London to Glasgow in the family Mondeo, in a dead straight line, down the middle lane at seventy, what a tedious thought. I digress - again. I hope you see what I mean by kaleidoscopic images, though: one minute it's snow leopards, the next it's Roman engineers. Amazing.

Meanwhile it's time to take a quick look at **WHITTLESFORD,** four miles west of Great Abington. Sealed off in a cul-de-sac by a white railing, beside the Old Red Lion Inn, is DUXFORD CHAPEL, which was founded early in the 13th century as a hospital. From the 14th century onwards it had a very varied history: it was a 'free chapel' until dissolved by Edward VI, then a toll house for the bridge before being converted into a barn for the inn.

SAWSTON HALL, a mile north east of Whittlesford, has always been in the hands of the Roman Catholic Harleston family, since it was built in the mid 16th century. This connection probably lay behind Mary Tudor's decision to shelter there when her claim to the throne - and her life - were at risk at the hands of the supporters of Lady Jane Grey. It would have been a good choice in another sense, as it has many secret chambers. The first Village College was founded at Sawston in 1930. Its aim was to offer advanced education for children, with particular reference to the rural environment, and also to provide adult further education, in those days the village had thirteen public houses, learning is thirsty work after all.

We are on the A505 now, having left Sawston, and should be making for Junction 10 of the M11 so as to reach **DUXFORD,** whose branch of the IMPERIAL WAR MUSEUM (Enquiries - 01223 835000) will take the contrast theme into orbit, almost literally. A preserved wartime fighter airfield, Duxford is *the* aviation museum in Europe. Among the 150 historic aircraft on show are biplanes, Spitfires, Gulf War jets and one of the Concordes. The wartime atmosphere is retained and, as many of the aircraft can still fly, we might be lucky enough to see one take to the air. Tanks and artillery are also on show, displayed in a series of dramatic battlefield scenes through which the visitors can walk. Finally the remarkable - and award-winning - American Air Museum presents aircraft suspended as though in flight.

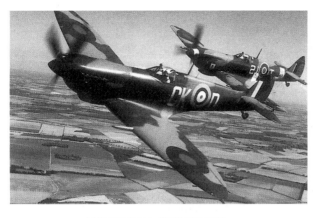

DUXFORD SPITFIRES

Duxford is open throughout the year, apart from the 24th to the 26th December, from 10am to 6pm in summer, and from 10am to 4pm in winter. It is also worth noting that air shows are staged several times during the year, details of which can be obtained by phone.

There's another familiar sounding name on the right as we carry on down the A505: FOWL MERE. The other one was actually FOWLMERE - ONE WORD - north of Thetford - and there's another Nature Reserve to be found here, which could be useful for a bit of a stroll, to help clear away the cobwebs of World War II memories.

Round Royston, to the north, and (surprise, surprise) a right turn brings us onto the modernised version of *another* Roman road, a *real* one, one of the all time greats, even: ERMINE STREET. I have a feeling, by the way, that we might have strayed, for a minute or two, into Hertfordshire, somewhere back there - for which I beg forgiveness. It can't be helped, as we want to reach Wimpole from Duxford, and this is the only route that not only makes sense but is actually a touch of *fun*!

Once we've passed the A603 on our right at Croydon it's but a stone's throw, as they say, to Arrington, and that's where we need to leave Ermine Street for our next visit, to WIMPOLE HALL (Enquiries - 01223 207257). This immensely imposing mansion dates back some three hundred years and its attractions are clear enough at the outset, for not only is it the biggest of its kind in Cambridgeshire but it has a setting in the grand style in an extensive wooded park as well as an extraordinary pedigree.

The interior features work by Gibbs, Flitcroft and Soan and is in keeping with the high parliamentary office held by some of its owners over the years (others, however, were so extravagant that they went bankrupt). Of particular interest are the library, the state rooms - and even the plunge bath! Standards are definitely kept up outside too, as the park - landscaped by Bridgeman, Brown and Repton - is complete with a grand folly, a Chinese bridge and a number of lakes. There is also a series of spectacular avenues and extensive walks through the grounds and colourful garden. Wimpole's HOME FARM, part of the estate, is nearby and there one can meet rare breeds of farm animals including long horn cattle, Soay sheep and Tamworth pigs. The whole complex is operated by the National Trust, who have provided a restaurant and shop amongst other facilities. Again, as opening times vary throughout the year, a telephone call helps make a visit less frustrating.

We are obliged to face a brief touch of overkill now: would you believe, there is even *more* Roman road! Some kaleidoscope, wouldn't you say? Anyway, we want to reach Grantchester and the A603 seems to be the preferred route.

Having noted the Radio Astronomy Laboratory on our left, (State of the art meets antiquity?) we slip across the M11, and there we are: **GRANTCHESTER**, adored by so many generations of tutors and students that one can hardly imagine Cambridge without it. Today the little village still manages to retain the serenity of its past in a setting of plaster, timber and thatch. The poet Rupert Brooke lived and wrote at the Old Vicarage, before the First World War. On the Trumpington Road, just outside the village, a signpost points to BYRON'S POOL, where, as eager undergraduates, presumably, not only Byron but earlier writers such as Spenser, Milton and Dryden sat by the water awaiting their muse. It's probably less attractive than it was in their day, although the paths leading to it are pleasant enough as they wind through the spinneys that rustle with the sounds of busy squirrels.

In the CHURCH of SS MARY AND MICHAEL, at **TRUMPINGTON** can be found a brass dated 1289, of Sir Roger de Trumpington. It is the second oldest in Britain, after that of Sir John D'Abernon which is in the Church at Stoke D'Abernon, in Surrey, and dates from 1277. After Grantchester, if I may pander to my obsession with 'contrast' again, I'd like to suggest giving the dreaming lanes routine a skip for while, and letting the motor have its head down the somewhat faster A428, to **ST NEOTS**. This time we're visiting a town - the first we've seen today, as it happens - and that points up the contrast idea even further.

St Neots is quite a pleasant market town, although it does not have as much to do with the Fens proper as some, in reality. Furthermore, as far as I can tell it used to be part of long lost Huntingdonshire, in the golden days of our youth. So, despite its history, it is now one of those boundary change additions of Cambridgeshire that I touched on briefly, before we started out. St. Neots is a delightfully interesting town, the square itself is positively huge, and backs onto the River Ouse. Another major point of interest in the town is the 15th century Perpendicular church tower which rises splendidly beyond the square. Inside the church are wonderfully rich carvings of angels, birds and animals that should not be missed.

While we're wandering around the square it might be a good time to think about the importance of markets in this part of the world. As we've seen, Fenland is unrivalled for the fertility of its rich soil and for its abundant variety of crops. If we want to see how varied and how abundant, we have only to drop in on market day. A feast for the eyes - and the palate - will be there to greet us.

Wherever we go in the Fens we will find different *ranges* of fruit, flower and vegetable crops being grown, to suit variations in the local soil and conditions. In short, while other areas we have seen have spoken to our aesthetic sense, with their craft centres and galleries, the message here goes straight to the 'inner man' and I, for one, find it irresistible. Whether we're looking at apples, soft fruit and strawberries around Wisbech, or fresh cabbages, cauliflowers and Brussel sprouts around Boston, or carrots and celery from the peaty soils near Chatteris and Ely - the words they bring to mind are quite simple. 'Eat me,' they're saying. 'Eat me.' Over and over again.

With so much Fen produce being used to supply the country's shops and supermarkets, it's mildly astonishing that there's any left over, locally. There is, though - masses of it. Wherever we find ourselves we'll see fresh, local fruit and vegetables on display in high street shops, on market stalls, at auctions and in farm shops. As if that isn't enough, there'll be countless roadside stalls also offering tempting produce for us to buy. All of which tends to suggest to me that, of the many opportunities available, Market Day is the one that we really can't miss - if only because it's there that the choices will be greatest and the experience itself most unforgettable. Of course, the roadside stalls will have their own special charm and novelty - but 'The Market' - that's the thing.

Leaving St Neots and following the line of the Ouse along its east bank, we're led through Great Paxton, Offord D'Arcy and Offord Cluny towards something of a conurbation, focused on Huntingdon. Together they mark the turning point of this tour. After just one little side track in search of butterflies we shall turn north and west along roads that should bring us back to Ely by nightfall.

In the days of the Romans two of their major (wonderful?) roads crossed at what is now the town of **GODMANCHESTER**. The Via Devana ran from Colchester to Chester, and Ermine Street - which we've sampled - linked London with York. The town retained its importance and became one of England's earliest boroughs, having been granted its charter in 1215. However, local politics - and economics - being much the same then as now, it was decided that Godmanchester should be combined into one borough with neighbouring Huntingdon. The 300 acre meadow of PAUL HOLME lies between them, on one side of the causeway that dates from the 17th century, with WEST SIDE COMMON on the other. Both open stretches are replete with criss-crossing footpaths and little feeder streams running into the Great Ouse.

Before moving on to take in Huntingdon itself, a digression a short way to the west will have to be made for a visit to HINCHINBROOKE HOUSE, the only real stately home in the county. It is believed that the sculpted gatehouse, which was originally part of Ramsey Abbey, was brought across in the 16th century - today it can be reached by an under-pass from the main road. The mansion itself was built by Oliver Cromwell's wealthy great grandfather, Sir Richard Cromwell, around the remains of a nunnery. The 1st Earl of Sandwich added to the west side of the court after the Restoration but unfortunately a serious fire in 1830 caused extensive damage. The house was restored extremely carefully, however, and it is now a school open to the public at certain times during the summer holidays.

Having made this detour, we could justify it on two counts, while we're at it, as there is another attraction in nearby **BRAMPTON**. There we will find the 15th century farmhouse which was the family home of Samuel Pepys. If we want to look over it though, we shall have to make an appointment, as it appears not to be kept open which was rather disappointing.

There are many fine old buildings in **HUNTINGDON**, showing a variety of gable designs and window styles, and finished in a range of colour washes. Best known of these perhaps, is the ELIZABETHAN GRAMMAR SCHOOL. Although this was once the county town - when there *was* a county - it is more cramped than Godmanchester. Fortunately, sufficient unspoiled corners are still left to justify our visit.

Oliver Cromwell was born in a house close to Ermine Street and its site is marked by a plaque on what is now the Huntingdon Research Centre. He was baptised in the part 11th century ALL SAINTS CHURCH, where his father is buried. About 1610, the young Oliver attended the Old Grammar School which, although a Tudor Foundation, was accommodated in what is basically a Norman building. Samuel Pepys was also a pupil. Nowadays the former school houses THE CROMWELL MUSEUM, which was opened in 1962 by the then Speaker of the House of Commons.

There are very reasonable opportunities for shopping in either Godmanchester or Huntingdon, but the most vivid memory for me has nothing to do with shops. THE GEORGE INN, once the property of Cromwell's grandfather, is nowadays the setting for some excellent drama productions. It has an inner courtyard, overlooked by a gallery, where the plays of William Shakespeare are regularly staged.

Now for the butterflies! They are going to take us out *right* out of our way - the little dears - but as they are creatures who don't feature that often in the course of our tours, I insist that, on their occasional appearances, they should be given their heads. With this in mind, we must travel up the A14 and the Great North Road - now labelled so very boringly as the A1 - towards Peterborough, until we find, after three or four miles, a turning to WOOD WALTON FEN on our right. The Large Copper butterfly, which takes its name from the copper bands on its wings, is found there, and is a protected species. The butterfly was brought to England from Holland in 1927 to replace the native British species, which had been extinct since 1848. Should we be lucky enough to spot one we can tell if it's male or female as the male has twice as much copper colouring on its upper wings as the female.

Returning to the tour, we need the B1090 now, followed by the A141, to skirt round the south side of Huntingdon so that we can take a loop via the A14 to call at **HEMINGFORD GREY,** en route to our next town. This is a delightful village of mellow brick, timber and thatch with a stout walled 12th century manor house which is still occupied. Its appearance has changed little since the 18th century, apart from the 'modifications' brought about by the weather of 1741 which brought down the top part of the steeple of ST JAMES'S CHURCH, which still stands beside the Great Ouse in its truncated form. The local rumour is that the remains of the upper part are still lying on the river bed. The village is commonly linked with **HEMMINGFORD ABBOTS**, which is also worth a visit, in order to see its two attractive meres.

A right turn after the villages, along the main road, brings us shortly to **ST IVES**, the most easterly community in the group. It, too, is a market town and was originally called Slepe, until the name was changed when a priory dedicated to St Ivo was built there in 1050. Amongst the first features to catch our attention is the 15th century bridge, which has a chapel in its centre bay. Oliver Cromwell had a farm close by and is commemorated in the market place, where a statue shows him booted and wearing a most unlikely choice of rather dashing hat.

The NORRIS MUSEUM in St Ives is well endowed with a range of aspects of local history, including a number of paintings and a primitive ice skate to remind visitors that there was a time when the Great Ouse used to freeze regularly in winter. While we're here it's worth pointing out that, time permitting, the river journey from St Ives to Huntingdon shows many of the lovelier aspects of the area that cannot be seen, or tend to be overlooked, when travelling by car.

So much for urban sophistication, for a while. Now, with the odd false start, triggered by side tracks that are just too inviting, we're going to go for the big one, so to speak, and take on Fenland in macrocosm - in other words, nearly all of it! As we travel, we shall be weaving our way through a weird landscape of straight roads, even straighter drainage channels, sluices and washes, all of which seem to be obsessed with a south west / north east axis, making travel in any other direction erratic, to put it mildly.

Then there are the fields! Because hedges are rare, and their boundaries are often hidden ditches, they seem enormous, even compared with those in Norfolk that we learnt to take in our stride, more or less. No book or picture can really prepare anyone for this first meeting. What with the far distant horizons and the utterly endless sky, I felt like a Lilliputian the first time I drove out this way, along one of those roads from Chatteris I think it was, towards March or Wisbech. Or, put another way, I drank in the view, for a moment, then, like Alice in Wonderland, down I went. Utterly overwhelmed. One can be too literary, I suppose, but that's the way it was.

To prepare ourselves for the experience we'll take it gently for a while and browse through a few words about the engineering side of the long battle to drain the Fens. As we've seen already, before any attempts were made at drainage this was a very different world, of misty marshes and bogs, of small islands inhabited by strangely independent people, whose livelihood was almost totally focused on the fish and wildfowl of this eerie, watery area. Not only are there legends that we've met of ghosts and witchcraft - there are even older stories in which for example, the belief is expressed that Fenland people were generally web-footed!

The landscape we see today is largely the result of man's ingenious uses of his developing technology and his constant desire to tame the wet wilderness and create more farmland. The story seems to begin in the Bronze Age and spans the centuries from Roman and Saxon times, when the inhabitants were restricted to the isolated islands and the wide silt ridge which formed around The Wash. Reclamation of land took place gradually between Domesday and the 13th century and owed much to the interests of the great land owning monasteries as various banks were built out from the surrounding uplands to provide a degree of flood protection.

FENLAND NARROWBOAT

While the Dark Ages saw a halt to reclamation, by the early 17th century - as the economy recovered - the attention of speculators was drawn to draining the peat fens in the south and the remaining areas of silt fens further north. These speculators - or

'Adventurers' - under the guidance of the 4th Earl of Bedford, started work on a systematic drainage programme. Not all the schemes were successful despite the fact that experienced engineers were commissioned, such as the Dutchman, Cornelius Vermuyden whose first attempts at Denver - as we saw in a recent chapter - were not wholly successful. Nothing daunted, the greatest attempt of all was undertaken, involving the construction of the Old and New Bedford Rivers between Earith and Denver. Elsewhere other engineers such as Sir Philibert Vernatti were carrying out work to drain the South Lincolnshire Fens. As a reminder of those days, one still comes across evidence of the major influence of the Dutch on the architecture and the place-names of Fenland - which is another parallel with parts of Norfolk that we've seen. Local opposition was intense because the systematic drainage of the area was seen as a threat to the traditional fishing and wildfowling rights of the Fen dwellers. Their fierce resistance and destruction of drainage works earned them the name 'Fen Tigers'.

Drainage schemes continued, but as has already been pointed out, the thought that the land might shrink as the soil dried out had not quite occurred to anyone. In fact, shrinkage took place at an alarming rate and, as the level of land dropped, water could no longer drain into the rivers which were by then higher than the fields. At that point, wind-driven pumps were introduced to remove the water from the land and back into the rivers. Unfortunately their reliance upon strong enough winds limited their usefulness and, as the land continued to shrink, the task became more and more difficult.

It was not until steam power was introduced in the 1820s that it became possible to drain the Fens effectively. In more recent times, first diesel then electric pumps have been introduced, and these are capable of raising thousands of gallons of water a minute. Today the Fens have a sophisticated network of drains, embankments and pumps to protect the land from the ever present threats of rain and tide. Alongside the sophistication there are many reminders of a very different past, of a time when the fine balance between the power of nature and the skill of man must have made the lives of Fenlanders seem something of a nightmare.

As we start to seek out some of these sites for ourselves, it might be best to take things gently with some features of the area that are rather less awe inspiring. With this in mind, the A11203 will take us to the charming cottages of **EARITH** that are as much of a comfort to the visitor as they must have been to the villagers who have lived in them for so many years. Then, staying with the main road, we move on to **HADDENHAM**, scene of an annual STEAM ENGINE RALLY. It is also where we will find HADDENHAM GREAT MILL, a four sail mill built in 1803 for Daniel Cockle. One of two mills that are sited at the village, it overlooks the Fens and countryside, is complete with three sets of stones and is open by appointment and on special open days only.

Turning south at **WILBURTON** onto the B1149, we cross the Ouse again and then take a left turn along a minor road, crossing CAP DYKE - with SMITHEY FEN away to the right - before turning left at the edge of **COTTENHAM** and heading for **WATERBEACH**. If we make use of a touch of the A10 northwards, it's not long before we're parking the car in the grounds of DENNY ABBEY AND FARMLANDS MUSEUM (Enquiries - 01223 860988). The Abbey is a superb English Heritage Grade One building and joins the farmyard in an attractive fen edge setting. As a religious building its fortunes followed the history of the monks, Knights Templars and Poor Clare nuns who lived there over the years. After the Dissolution of the Monasteries the Abbey itself survived only by being adapted into a farmhouse.

As the land has been an agricultural estate since medieval times the old farm buildings are an ideal setting for a museum which tells the story of Cambridgeshire farming and village life. A variety of activities is on offer, together with refreshment facilities and a shop and picnic area, the estate being open from 12 noon to 5pm daily between March and the end of October.

We now move north up to **STRETHAM** - along the A10, Ely road, again - and over the Ouse for the umpteenth time, to reach this village, where an old pumping engine is the major attraction. STRETHAM OLD ENGINE, the sole surviving beam pumping engine, was built at Stretham in 1831 by the Butterley Company of Derbyshire. Its massive horizontal steel beam, pushed up and down like a seesaw by steam power, drove the flywheel beneath it to which it was linked. That, in turn, was connected to a 37ft diameter scoop wheel which would lift water at a phenomenal rate for those times: 124 tons a minute could be lifted a height of twelve feet into a dyke.

STRETHAM OLD ENGINE

A diesel engine took over in 1924, although the old steam engine has since been called on to play its part in emergencies, from time to time. It is maintained in perfect working order by the Stretham Engine Preservation Trust and is open to inspection by the public. Incidentally, the engine house also accommodates, on its upper level, a collection of samples of peat and bog oak, and Roman pottery fragments which have been dug from the Fens. The site is open at weekends and bank holidays from 11:30am to 5pm, and advance booking is required of all groups.

Approaching **LITTLE THETFORD**, still on the A10 - and wishing we were out of the traffic - we find our prayers answered by a lane to the left, which ought to take us, if anything is that certain, to **WITCHFORD**. From there its only another short spin westwards before we arrive at **SUTTON**, where the village's ST ANDREW'S CHURCH gives us our first ecclesiastical experience since before lunch - unlike Norfolk, where they cropped up every five minutes.

We're aiming for Chatteris, which lies beyond Horsley and Longwood Fens, but we should take in **MEPAL**, where the OUTDOOR CENTRE (Enquiries - 01354 692251) offers watersports and other forms of exertion that could help us to loosen up our tense muscles after so many hours in the car. The Centre also has a multi-purpose sports arena with the usual range of facilities, including badminton courts.

Taken together, the NEW BEDFORD RIVER - or Hundred Foot Drain - and its surroundings are an extraordinary eye-catcher as we leave Mepal. There it is, to the right and left of us, this enormous ditch that is as straight as an arrow, for the most part, absolutely vital to the economy - and absolutely hideous. I suppose we must forgive it, as it's not even *trying* to be a tripper trap - the area's soil is so productive that the local economy appears to be totally autonomous, avoiding the need to attract the tourist like ourselves and hopefully you the reader. Furthermore, 'horses for courses' is as good a rule in tourism as it is in many other things and there is more to life than sugar coated scenery. It doesn't hurt to drop in on the grittier bits, the bits that actually produce the food, the raw materials and the tools to sustain life - any kind of life - with or without holidays. So, let's look around and see how they do it up here - while we thank the Lord they do, so the rest of us don't have to starve, and admire their way of life.

More miles on the A14 bring us to **CHATTERIS**, with its MARKET and its annual FESTIVAL. This typical Fenland town is popular with anglers while bird watchers are attracted to the surrounding wetland areas. It also has a MUSEUM which tells the local story.

Now our weaving down by-ways is really becoming a task for the poor driver, if we're to complete the rest of our itinerary - but no-one would expect a six lane motorway across an ancient Marsh. Or would they? Remember the Romans. So it's south, to start with, down the A141 to **WARBOYS**, then north west up the B1040 until we come to a halt at **RAMSEY**.

The remnants of a former Benedictine monastery, built on an island in the Fens are found at the site known as RAMSEY ABBEY GATEHOUSE (Enquiries - 01263 733471). This National Trust property has as its main feature the late 15th century gatehouse of the monastery and is open daily from 1st April to the end of October, from 10am to 5pm.

It's been a while since we looked at the natural aspects of Fenland, at the reserves and conservation so, as we leave Ramsey, we'll make a bee-line - I'm joking, of course; I meant a series of winding roads - around **WIMBLINGTON**, to spend time exploring the wetlands proper at **WELNEY**, a famous nature reserve on the Ouse Washes. The WILDFOWL AND WETLANDS TRUST, WELNEY is one of the best known wetland nature reserves in the country. Recently featured on the BBC TV programme 'Heading South', it offers year round bird watching with viewing from modern hides. The heated observatory also leads the field amongst comparable facilities. Covering an area of 1,000 acres on the Ouse Washes, the Reserve is managed traditionally with summer cattle grazing producing ideal feeding conditions for wintering wildfowl, in addition to its attractions for waders during the summer. It is also one of the most important sites in Europe for wintering Bewick's Swans and Whooper Swans and facilities have been made available for viewing the birds under floodlights. An additional feature at Welney is the ARTS AND CRAFTS facility which organises workshops, activities, and exhibitions for adults and children. Also on offer are exhibition and retail spaces, refreshments and demonstrations.

As the light is now fading, there is perhaps sufficient time to have a welcoming cup of coffee before the last leg of the trip. We'll go back over the Hundred Foot Washes, down to Littleport, and then make a last detour to Prickwillow before slipping back into Ely at day's end. **LITTLEPORT** is a pleasant town to explore, despite its fame as the scene of the 19th century 'Littleport Riots'. In a similar way to CHATTERIS, it grew from a small island community as a range of agricultural improvements took off, following the drainage of so much of the Fens. It now lies between a loop of the A10/A1101 and the River Ouse, looking out over the SOUTH LEVEL. It is a pleasant place for a touch of shopping, even at the end of a long day such as we have experienced, and if you have the time do call at The Black Horse in Sandhill Street, there you will be welcomed, fed and watered by two charming hosts, who will also be able to show you a pictorial history of the area.

Well, there's just the one more call, to the north west of Littleport at Prickwillow, which we reach by passing BURNT FEN on the left, before turning right for a short distance along the B1382 to find the site of the museum. PRICKWILLOW DRAINAGE ENGINE MUSEUM (Enquiries - 01353 688360) features various working examples of drainage engines which make an interesting comparison, at this end of our tour, with the many old windmill driven pumps that we've seen - and heard about - earlier on. In addition to the engines there are examples of other associated equipment and displays relating to the history of Fenland drainage in general. Centre-piece of the collection is a 1923 Mirrless, Bickerton and Day unit that is a wonderful example of the engineering skills in which Britain led the world at that time. Throughout the summer engines are run on certain days and the entire static display is open from 10am to 5pm between April and October, and 11am to 4pm at weekends only, from November to March.

At the start I said that this experience would be different, strange and more about the landscape and atmosphere than about architecture and artefacts - and that's just how it's turned out. You have seen the South of Cambridgeshire, the inland Fens and seen that they are rural, rich and rumbustious - while keeping ever on the alert lest nature tries to get its own back. Tomorrow we move further afield, westwards and northwards to areas where urban landscapes and 'culture', and more 'gentle' arts and crafts slip back into the limelight. If all goes to plan we shall see another cathedral City, some fine churches and many more craft and garden centres along the borders with Norfolk and Lincolnshire, which we'll visit a little later still. Again, there may well be surprises, but nothing too terrifying - just a few bits of food for thought, linking the varied experiences that are beginning to accumulate as we wander on. I hope the idea has a certain appeal - actually, after today, I'd like to think we can hardly wait to get started!

THE CROWN AND PUNCHBOWL
Horningsea,
Cambridgeshire
CB5 9JG

3 Crown Commended

Tel: 01223 860643
Fax: 01223 441814

Horningsea is a pretty rural village just 4 miles from Cambridge and close to the River Cam. At its heart is the 17th century Crown and Punchbowl Inn, much loved by local people and with an ever widening reputation since it became part of the Excalibur Group of Inns in July 1997. The atmosphere is delightful and the management and staff have a happy knack of making everyone feel at home from the moment they arrive in the bar.

The Crown and Punchbowl has been superbly refurbished and has several rooms in which one can dine. There is a spacious elegant restaurant, two delightful conservatories and two bar areas. It is one of these bar areas that always brings comments from newcomers to the Inn; it has an original pulpit! In fact there is great attention to detail throughout the Inn with nice antiques, unusual curios and works of art. A boat theme runs through the conservatories and with antique rugs, stags heads, log fires and dining by candlelight, the atmosphere is both relaxed and at the same time vibrant. The large garden is very popular in the warmer weather.

Food like at The Crown and Punchbowl at Fordham and The Red Lion at Icklingham, is always fresh, fish is the speciality of the house and a daily blackboard offers a range of tasty dishes. Five en-suite bedrooms, recently refurbished and with television, direct dial telephones and hostess trays, make staying here a pleasure and well situated for exploring Cambridgeshire and East Anglia with all it has to offer.

USEFUL INFORMATION

OPEN:12-3pm & 6-11pm	RESTAURANT: Fish a speciality
CHILDREN: Welcome	BAR FOOD: Wide range
CREDIT CARDS: Visa/Mastercard	VEGETARIAN: Always a choice
LICENSED: Full On	WHEELCHAIR ACCESS: Yes
ACCOMMODATION: 5 en-suite double rooms	GARDEN: Yes
RATES: £35pp.pn B&B	PETS: No
£43.50 single room occupancy	

GROVE COTTAGE
Malting Lane
Ellington
Huntingdon,
Cambridgeshire
PE18 0AA

Tel/Fax: 01480 890167
hugh.silver@dial.pipex.com

Grove Cottage sits peacefully in the rural village of Ellington, five miles west of Huntingdon. Grafham Water, with its water sports, fishing and nature reserve is three miles away and, together with Huntingdon itself, the historical sites of Cambridge, Ely, Peterborough, Ramsey and St Ives are all within easy reach from the village. Also within easy reach are the Hamerton Wildlife Park and the Raptor Foundation.

A charming, thatched, timber-framed Grade II Listed part 11th and part 17th century building, Grove Cottage is an entrancing, typical country cottage with its own small garden. One end of the cottage has been turned into a self-contained unit comprising one bedroom, full bathroom and lounge to be used by guests. There is also a small annexe to the bedroom which could be used as a bedroom for one child. The suite has television, hi-fi, a hostess tray and hairdryer. A healthy, substantial continental breakfast is served in the dining room. Grove Cottage has been the home of Hugh Silver for over ten years and has been sympathetically improved during that time. The improvements include the installation of central heating and double glazing throughout the property. Hugh is a friendly, hospitable man who enjoys his guests and works hard to ensure they have a happy and memorable stay.

For guests staying more than one night, the kitchen is available should they wish to prepare their own light microwave evening meal. For tourists, especially from abroad, and by prior arrangement, transportation is available and can include transfers from airports, local and day-long sight-seeing tours. This is a strictly non-smoking establishment.

USEFUL INFORMATION

OPEN: All year
CHILDREN: Welcome
CREDIT CARDS: None taken
LICENSED: No
ACCOMMODATION: Self-contained
unit, 1 doub bedroom, 1 child's room

DINING ROOM: Substantial, healthy
Continental breakfast
VEGETARIAN: Upon request
WHEELCHAIR ACCESS: No
GARDEN: Yes
PETS: By arrangement only

RATES: £25 p.m. sgl occupancy £35 double. STRICTLY NON-SMOKING HOUSE
£10 for child or 3rd person, Surcharge of £5 for one night only occupancy

THE HORSE SHOE INN
90 High Street
Offord D'Arcy
Cambridgeshire

Tel: 01480 473081

This wonderful old pub is a traditional English hostelry dating back to 1626 and still complete with many of its original features. The ceilings are low, old beams abound and the atmosphere has been built up over the centuries, nurtured now by the cheerful, friendly landlords, Raymond and Anne Stringer. They are the sort of people who seem to make the running of a pub effortless but in fact, it is their sheer professionalism which makes it seem as if it runs that way. No one comes here without feeling welcome and it is frequented by people from all walks of life. Ideal for the fisherman, the river offers great sport. Walkers enjoy the long and short walks that abound in the area. Walkers and Ramblers will find a Public Right of Way by the pub. Boats can be hired from the Marina. It stands in the centre of the Cambridgeshire village of Offord D'Arcy just three miles from St Neots and Huntingdon.

The Horse Shoe is very much family orientated. In fact the two most modern things about it are its excellent two acre Beer Garden where there is a Bouncy Castle for children and the large 100 space car park for cars.

You can eat either in the Restaurant area or at the bar. The food, freshly cooked is good, traditional pub fare with the emphasis on perfectly cooked, succulent steaks. Sunday Lunch, which is very popular, has a choice of roast meats, always with all the trimmings like Yorkshire Pudding, Horseradish, Apple Sauce, Mint Sauce as well as crisp roast potatoes and plenty of fresh vegetables. The Bar menu offers a range of tasty snacks including Jacket Potatoes with a variety of fillings, freshly cut, well filled sandwiches and Ploughman's. The menu changes daily and always has a number of Blackboard specials. Well kept Real Ale, a well-stocked bar and a carefully chosen wine list are there for your enjoyment.

USEFUL INFORMATION

OPEN: 12-11pm 7 days a week
CHILDREN: Welcome. Bouncy Castle
CREDIT CARDS: None taken Specials
LICENSED: Full On
GARDEN: 2 acre Beer Garden. Play area
PETS: Yes

RESTAURANT: Traditional pub fare
BAR FOOD: Wide choice. Daily

VEGETARIAN: Always a choice
WHEELCHAIR ACCESS: Yes

THE ICKLETON LION
Abbey Street,
Ickleton
Cambridgeshire
CB10 1SS

Tel/Fax: 01799 530269.

The only pub in the 12th century village of Ickleton, The Ickleton Lion, is very much the focal point of village life. Built in the 17th century it is the epitome of the English traditional hostelry.Beloved by the locals it is also, because of its proximity to Saffron Walden just six minutes away, and Cambridge fifteen minutes, a favourite place for people to come, enjoy a relaxed drink before eating some of the delectable dishes on the a la carte menu available all the week and the Table d'hôte on Friday and Saturday. The food in the restaurant has a strong French and Italian influence whilst the Bar menu offers more traditional fare which can be anything from home-made fish cakes to a simple sandwich. This is great walking country and special lunches are available for Walkers. Fishing is available on the local river. The 12th century church is full of interest. Tony and Mary Mertz are the proprietors and it is the combination of their skills and interests which has made the Ickleton Lion so popular since their arrival two years ago. Tony has a keen interest in food and wine and it is he with his very able chef who plan the menus. Mary is Irish and has the natural friendliness of her country which makes her very popular with people who come to the pub whether locals or strangers.

USEFUL INFORMATION

OPEN: Normal pub hours
CHILDREN: Yes. Play area within 1 minute
CREDIT CARDS: All except AMEX & Diners
BAR FOOD: Wide choice
LICENSED: Full On
GARDEN: Yes & for outside eating
PETS: Yes. Not in restaurant

RESTAURANT: Emphasis on
French and Italian food

VEGETARIAN: Yes
WHEELCHAIR ACCESS: With
    assistance

THE NEW SUN INN
20-22 High St,
Kimbolton,
Huntingdon,
Cambridgeshire
PE18 0HA

Good Pub Guide

Tel: 01480 860052

Kimbolton only has one thousand five hundred inhabitants and is a very friendly place. This sense of friendship and welcome is the hallmark of The New Sun Inn to be found in the elegant Georgian High Street with Kimbolton Castle opposite. This awe inspiring building, open to the Public on Bank Holidays, was once the home of the Dukes of Manchester but is now a Public School. Catherine of Aragon is said to have stayed in Kimbolton Castle before her death and haunts the Avenue of Trees. She probably wants to join in the fun of the Statty Fair (Statue Fair) held on the third Wednesday in September when the whole High Street becomes a fairground for twenty four hours.

The New Sun Inn is a typical village pub with a lot of atmosphere and a regular clientele who will tell you how much they enjoy the well kept ale, the chatter and the company of the cheerful landlords, Stephen and Elaine Rogers. The Bar is at the back of the Inn and to reach it you walk through the comfortable lounge which also leads to the restaurant. The stone floors, the mass of beams and a large fireplace give the bar a great deal of character and with a pleasing old world decor, it is a popular place. From it leads a conservatory and a small patio - much in use in warm weather.

Food at The New Sun Inn is good pub fare, well cooked and plenty of it, which you can eat in the conservatory, the lounge or on the patio. One can recommend the excellent steak and kidney pudding, or the liver and bacon and but whatever you choose will be tasty. The twenty four cover a la carte restaurant offers racks of lamb, fresh Dover sole and other interesting dishes. There is a Daily Specials board with time-honoured favourites available every day. Bar Food is equally sustaining with a variety of doorstep sandwiches, jacket potatoes with many fillings and many other things. Everything is value for money and will not hurt the wallet. A genuine pub.

USEFUL INFORMATION

OPEN: Mon-Sat 11-2.30pm & 6-11pm
Sun: All day 12-10.30pm
CREDIT CARDS: Visa/Master/Switch
CHILDREN: Not in Bar
LICENSED: Full On
PETS: Yes

RESTAURANT: A la Carte
BAR FOOD: Wide range.Good value
VEGETARIAN: Always 2 dishes
WHEELCHAIR ACCESS: Yes
GARDEN: Yes. Patio

THREE HORSESHOES & STABLE RESTAURANT
23 High St,
Graveley, Huntingdon
Cambridgeshire PE18 9PW

Heartbeat Award for 7yrs.
Cleanest pub in Cambridgeshire

Tel: 01480 830992
Fax: 01480 831649

Graveley might be a small village surrounded by 6 other villages of a similar size but it has never been dull and if you stand in the bar of the Threehorse Shoes you may well hear some of the things that have happened here. RAF Graveley was one of the Pathfinder Airfields during World War II and cinema heartthrob Clark Gable flew from the airfield. The pub was used as a home from home for air and ground crews during the war and even today reunions of these veterans still take place. The fact that the owners Robert Moss and Terry Vass were both in the RAF and have a keen interest in the force adds to the pleasure of the many ex-service men and women who come here. After the war when the airfield closed one of the Bunkers was used for nefarious gain - the Great Train Robbers stached and counted their ill-gotten gains there.

Today, apart from the continuing service interest, the Three Horseshoes is very popular with walkers using the many public footpaths and bridleways which run close to the pub. Others are fascinated by the small Maze, one of only six in the UK, which is close by. One of the great pleasures in the bar is the absence of a juke box, dart board and pool table. Background music, quietly played, is the only intrusion on the lively conversation. The Public Bar is an attractive and well lit place seating 40 people comfortably. It is decorated in country life style and the walls display the work of local artists. There are also 'History' walls dedicated to RAF Graveley and to local history depicting the life of the village in days gone by.

The Stables Restaurant is non-smoking and a popular place, colour co-ordinated with crisp napery. The a la carte menu offers a wide choice with anything from a succulent rack of lamb to a vast mixed grill. Between the restaurant and the bar there are some thirty dishes on offer, each perfectly cooked and presented and at prices that will not hurt the pocket. The carefully chosen wine list complements the food. During the day the restaurant is frequently used for meetings and seminars. During the summer months Cream Teas are served daily. It would be hard not to enjoy this friendly and lively hostelry - try it.

USEFUL INFORMATION

OPEN: Mon-Sat 11-3pm 6.30-11pm
Sun: 12-3pm & 7-10.30pm
CHILDREN: Welcome
CREDIT CARDS: All except AMEX
LICENSED: Full On
PETS: Yes

RESTAURANT: Delicious food
BAR FOOD: Wide choice
VEGETARIAN: Many choices
WHEELCHAIR ACCESS: Yes
GARDEN: Small patio

WALLIS FARM
98 Main Street,
Hardwick,
Cambridge
CB3 7QU
2 Crowns Highly Commended

Tel: 01954 210347
Fax: 01954 210988

Hardwick is a pretty village seven miles from the centre of the University City of Cambridge. In its midst is Wallis Farm with a delightful late Georgian farmhouse set in large gardens looking out onto the farmland and woodlands in which guests can walk, including a bridleway which leads the National Trust property, Wimpole Hall. In the next village, two miles away there is the Meridian Golf Club with eighteen holes. It is a great area for cycling to other delightful villages including Rupert Brooke's Granchester which is on the River Cam, or going on the cycleway into Cambridge. On a Sunday morning you will hear the church bells summoning the faithful to church after which a short walk to the village shop to collect the Sunday papers.

Peter and Linda Sadler farm the three hundred acres here, mainly arable but amongst the animals you will find two donkeys, Tessa and Pepper, a goat called Safi and a few rare sheep. Linda looks after the guests although Peter has been known to be the 'waitress' if he is not too busy on the farm and at weekends their daughter Hannah helps with breakfast. There is a charming, family atmosphere in the house where one immediately feels comfortable and at home. Nothing is too much trouble for Linda in caring for her guests.

A barn has been converted to provide four perfectly appointed en suite bedrooms, all on the ground floor. They are all decorated differently, have stripped pine furniture - some specially handmade - exposed beams making the rooms very spacious and restful Laura Ashley drapes and bedcovers. Each room is centrally heated, has colour television, clock radio and a well-supplied hostess tray. A fifth room at the end of the farmhouse is a large suite with its own patio and garden furniture. It has a double and single bed, en-suite bathroom, a sitting area, television, two chesterfield sofas and hostess tray. Breakfast is served in the farmhouse and looks out onto the garden which includes a fish pond. In summer the patio doors are opened so guests can eat in the garden if warm enough. Otherwise you sit round a stripped pine eight foot dining table enjoying a delicious meal. The Blue Lion, a few steps from Wallis Farmhouse serves excellent lunches and evening meals.

USEFUL INFORMATION

OPEN: All year
CHILDREN: Welcome
CREDIT CARDS: None taken
LICENSED: No
ACCOMMODATION:
5 en-suite ground floor rooms
RATES: Sgl £35. Dbl. £46

DINING ROOM: Delicious breakfast
VEGETARIAN: Upon request
WHEELCHAIR ACCESS: Yes
GARDEN: Yes & Patio
PETS: By arrangement
NON-SMOKING HOUSE

THE WHITE HORSE
118 High Street,
Barton,.
NR Cambridge,
CB3 7BG

Tel/Fax: 01223 262327

The White Horse is a traditional country pub, the focal point of the attractive village of Barton, very close to Cambridge and with easy access from M11 Motorway (Junc 12). It is a family run pub with Lynda and Richard Ellis at the helm, mainly assisted by their two sons, Steven and Paul and daughter Joanne. They are a close and contented family and this comes over in the welcoming atmosphere and the pleasure they all take in making sure that everyone feels at ease. The furnishing throughout is attractive and comfortable creating just the right environment in which to enjoy the well kept ale.

Home-cooked food by an able chef ensures that anyone who eats here will enjoy their food. Every day, in addition to the regular menu, there are tasty Specials, which may well include time-honoured favourites like an excellent steak and kidney pie or maybe something more unusual. Vegetarians are catered for with a variety of bakes and pasta. The restaurant is strictly non-smoking. The well kept garden tempts people outside to eat and drink in the warmer weather and it has a children's play area. An enclosed patio completes the picture.

USEFUL INFORMATION

OPEN: 11.30-3.30pm & 5-11pm   RESTAURANT: Traditional English
CHILDREN: Welcome. Play area   BAR FOOD: Yes + Daily Specials
CREDIT CARDS: None taken   VEGETARIAN: Always a choice
LICENSED: Full On   WHEELCHAIR ACCESS: Yes + toilets
GARDEN: Yes. Enclosed Patio   PETS: Yes

THE WHITE PHEASANT
Market Street,
Fordham,
NR Ely,
Cambridgeshire
CB7 5LQ

Tel: 01638 720414
Fax: 01638 720447

Excalibur Inns have several very good hostelries in the Cambridgeshire area and The White Pheasant is a good example of the standard in which these pubs are run. The White Pheasant has been welcoming travellers since the 17th century and is as hospitable as it has always been. You can feel the atmosphere of the centuries as you walk through the welcoming doors. This Inn stands at the gateway to the Fens, marvellous territory for those wanting to explore this magical part of East Anglia. Ely with its magnificent Cathedral and a spire that can be seen for miles across the fens, is nearby and so are many other interesting places.

The White Pheasant has recently been refurbished with antique rugs everywhere, suits of armour, books and paintings heightening the ambience. It is pleasant simply to sit in the friendly bar enjoying a drink and even better to have a meal chosen from the daily changing blackboard on which you will always find a wide variety of fresh fish. Freshly cooked in many different ways, either simply grilled or with a sauce, the taste is wonderful. There are many other dishes to choose from including succulent steaks cooked just the way you like them. venison steak, Suffolk back bacon chops, pan fried chicken breast and baby corn are just some of the dishes on the a la carte menu. The bar food menu in addition to sandwiches, ploughman's, tasty, time honoured daily specials has delicious things like Barnsley lamb chops, lamb's liver, bacon and onion gravy are all there for your enjoyment and all at sensible prices.

The Crown and Punchbowl at Horningsea and The Red Lion at Icklingham are part of the group and both have the same high standards.

USEFUL INFORMATION

OPEN: 12-3pm & 6-11pm
CHILDREN: Welcome standard.
CREDIT CARDS: Visa/Mastercard
LICENSED: Full On
GARDEN: Yes
PETS: Well behaved on leads

RESTAURANT: A la Carte. High
Fresh fish daily
BAR FOOD: Excellent choice
VEGETARIAN: Always a choice
WHEELCHAIR ACCESS: Yes

NORMANTON PARK
Rutland Water South Shore
Edith Weston,
Oakham
Rutland
LE15 8RP

Tel: 01780 720315
Fax: 01780 721086

Normanton Park is very special, something that is acknowledged by those who visit this lakeside hotel whilst exploring Rutland Water or those who come to stay either on business or pleasure. It stands 50 yards from scenic Rutland Water, England's second largest man-made reservoir. It is an unusual hotel building in a fine Goergian stable block that once was part of the estate of the demolished Normanton Park manor house. The interior is stylish and furnished in a light airy fashion which seems to enhance the stunning views one gets over the lake. The formal Orangery Restaurant has an exciting menu which includes local produce such as venison, pheasant and Rutland Water trout. The vaulted Sailing Bar, with canvas sails strung out across the rafters, is in effect a stylish pub open to all comers. There are delightful bedrooms in a new extension with swish modern furnishings, including a plump sofa-bed or armchair, and with glorious lake views. Quainter rooms around the courtyard have undeniably bright and cheerful design schemes. The staff are all young and friendly and it is a pleasure to stay here. Close by ,The Normanton Park's sister hotel, Barnsdale Lodge is equally good.

USEFUL INFORMATION

OPEN: All year
CHILDREN: Welcome
CREDIT CARDS :All major cards
LICENSED: Full On
VEGETARIAN: Always a choice
ACCOMMODATION: 23 en-suite rms
PETS: Not in restaurant.
In bedrooms £10 surcharge
RATES: Please telephone for details

RESTAURANT: Excellent menu using
local produce
BAR FOOD: Sailing Bar menu-
wide range
WHEELCHAIR ACCESS: Yes
GARDEN: Grounds down to Rutland
Water

THE ANCHOR
Sutton Gault, Sutton,
Ely, Cambridgeshire CB6 2BD
UK 'Inn of the Year' Les Routiers 1995.
Les Routiers Gold Key Award 1998
Good Pub Guide Star Rating.
ETB 3 Crowns Highly Commended
Tel: 01353 778537 01353 776180

The Anchor Inn is an ancient Fenland riverside Inn with an award winning restaurant. It was built around 1650 in the shelter of the bank of the New Bedford River or 'The Hundred Foot Drain' as it is also called, to provide lodgings and sustenance for the men who had been conscripted to dig the new rivers. The Inn is full of character with a cosy atmosphere enhanced by scrubbed pine tables and undulating old floors, antique prints, log fires and lit by the glow of gas light. The food, for which The Anchor is renowned, is traditionally British but also includes more exotic recipes from other parts of Europe and the Far East. The menu is reprinted daily to accommodate the emphasis on fresh food. The A La Carte menu is available at lunch-time and in the evening every day and has an extensive selection of starters and main courses. The delicious home-made puddings and the unusual British Farmhouse Cheeses make a fitting finish to an excellent meal. There is also a great value fixed price lunch menu. The Anchor has two en-suite guest rooms, one is a suite with a double bedroom and sitting room. The sitting room has a sofa bed making it possible for the suite to sleep three. The other is a delightful twin bedded room, newly furnished and decorated with views across the river and the Ouse Washes.

USEFUL INFORMATION

OPEN: All year
CHILDREN: Welcome
CREDIT CARDS: All major cards
VEGETARIAN: Always a choice
LICENSED: Full On
ACCOMMODATION: 1 suite 1twin bedded room
RATES: From £29.75-£79.50

RESTAURANT: Award winning
BAR FOOD: Great value fixed price
lunch
WHEELCHAIR ACCESS: Yes
GARDEN: Yes
PETS: No

DUXFORD LODGE HOTEL AND RESTAURANT
Ickleton Road,
Duxford, Cambridgeshire CB2 4PP
AA***RAC ETB. Two AA Rosettes.
Tel: 01223 836444   Fax: 01223 832271

Situated one mile from J10 M11 and five minutes from Duxford War Museum and set in its own beautiful grounds, Duxford Lodge Hotel, a fine historic red brick house has an interesting history. It has been home to 19th Fighter Squadron RAF in World War II and the famous including amongst others, Winston Churchill, Douglas Bader and Bing Crosby. Today in the efficient, friendly hands of Sue and Ron Craddock it offers a warm and friendly welcome to all who come across the threshold. The whole house is furnished stylishly with the emphasis on colour and comfort. There are fifteen bedrooms all individually styled with full en-suite facilities plus direct dial telephone, remote controlled colour television, clock/radio alarms and tea and coffee making facilities, trouser press and hair dryer. There is a choice of outside garden rooms (some with four poster beds) opening onto the lawns and flower beds, while to the top of the house are spacious attic rooms, two of which are executive. The award winning Le Paradis and Le Petit Paradis Restaurants are renowned for their cuisine. Good food and fine wines are at the very heart of Duxford Lodge, both restaurants boast two AA Rosettes and are an oasis of culinary flair, good service and comfort. Duxford Lodge has two conference rooms, one of which can seat twenty delegates board room style and up to thirty theatre style. The smaller room is more suited to informal one-to-one meetings or interviews.

USEFUL INFORMATION

OPEN: 2nd January-24th December inc.
CHILDREN: Welcome restaurants.
CREDIT CARDS: Visa/Master/AMEX/Switch
LICENSED: Yes. Fine wines
ACCOMMODATION: 15 en-suite rooms
RATES: Midweek from £73 sgl & £93 dbl.
Weekend: from £45 sgl & £80dbl

RESTAURANT: 2 award winning
Superb cuisine
VEGETARIAN: Yes & most diets
WHEELCHAIR ACCESS: Restricted
GARDEN: Acre of tended gardens
PETS: Yes

THE GREEN MAN
Dunsbridge Turnpike,
Shepreth, Hertfordshire SG8 6RA

Tel:01763 261921

Eight miles from Cambridge and three miles from Royston, Dunsbridge Turnpike is in a quiet position on the old A10 which is now a 'no through road'. In its midst is The Green Man, a 17th century inn, a friendly family run pub with Alan and Wendy Hardiman at the helm. It has an exceptionally nice atmosphere and is furnished in a stylish but comfortable manner. Everyone who comes here remarks on its relaxed atmosphere and congenial company. Pub games are played quite seriously sometimes but you are always welcome to join in a game of darts, crib, dominoes or petangue in the garden. The very large garden is extremely popular in the warm weather and it is a place which is totally safe for children with a play area of their own. There are Summer and Winter menus with many choices and best described as good home-cooked fare which is value for money. Every Sunday there is a traditional two course roast lunch. The Beer is well kept with Real Abbot Ale plus quarterly guest ales. A wine list is also available.

USEFUL INFORMATION

OPEN: Mon-Sat 11.30-11pm
Sun: 12-3pm &7-10.30
CHILDREN: Welcome
BAR FOOD: Great choice
and great value
PETS: Outside on a leash only
WHEELCHAIR ACCESS: Yes

RESTAURANT: Good
home-cooked pub fare
CREDIT CARDS: Mastercard/Visa
LICENSED: Full On
GARDEN: Yes. Play area. Petangue
VEGETARIAN: Several options

HILL HOUSE FARM,
9 Main Street, Coveney,
Ely, Cambridgeshire CB6 2DJ
ETB 2 Crown
Highly Commended AA 4 Q's Selected.
Farm Holiday Bureau

Tel/Fax: 01353 778369

There have been families of Nix living in Coveney since 1640 and today Hilary Nix runs Hill House Farm, a spacious Victorian farmhouse, three miles west of Ely with its glorious Cathedral, in which she welcomes guests. This is a working three hundred acre farm and everything about it is friendly. Inside the house the three tastefully furnished and decorated, en-suite bedrooms all have television, tea and coffee making facilities, clock radio, hairdryer etc. and their own entrance, with open views of the surrounding countryside. One of the double bedrooms is on the ground floor. A comfortable guests lounge and traditional dining room, where a first class breakfast is served. There is also a pleasant, peaceful garden where guests can relax in the warmer weather. Easy access to Cambridge, Newmarket, Huntingdon and Peterborough makes Hill House Farm ideally placed for touring the counties of Cambridgeshire, Norfolk and Suffolk. Wicken Fen and Welney Wildfowl Trust are nearby. There are Stately Homes, Museums, the National Stud and the Horse Racing Museum at Newmarket and many more places easily reached. This is a strictly Non-Smoking house.

USEFUL INFORMATION

OPEN: All year except Christmas	DINING ROOM: Excellent food
CHILDREN: Over 12 years	VEGETARIAN: Upon request
CREDIT CARDS: None taken	WHEELCHAIR ACCESS: No
LICENSED: No	GARDEN: Yes
ACCOMMODATION: 2bl, 1 tw all en-suite	PETS: No
RATES: Dbl. £44 per room B&B	STRICTLY NON-SMOKING HOUSE

MANOR HOUSE
Owlend,
Gt Stukeley,
Huntingdon,
Cambridgeshire PE17 5AQ

Tel: 01480 458967

This fine old house was built about 1650 with a timber frame and later, probably between 1750 and 1800, the roof was changed to a Mansard roof. It is as delightful inside as it is out. The rooms have all the character one would expect in a house this age. The living room has exposed ceiling timbers and there is an inglenook fireplace in the dining room with a wood burner. The atmosphere in the Manor House is one of warmth, friendliness and genuinely welcoming. The house stands in an acre of garden with a field behind and to one side. Every one who stays here comments on the tranquillity surrounding the house. Blissfully quiet at night and yet Stukeley is only two miles north of Huntingdon. There are three, non-smoking guest rooms, a single, a twin-bedded room and a family room. Each room is attractively furnished and has colour television and a hostess tray. Breakfast is a feast and an evening meal is available. The food, all home-cooked and using local produce and fresh vegetables, is delicious. Lots of casseroles, roasts, chicken as the main course and delectable sweets make a memorable meal.

USEFUL INFORMATION

OPEN: All year	DINING ROOM: Home-cooked fare
CHILDREN: Welcome	VEGETARIAN: Yes
CREDIT CARDS: None taken	WHEELCHAIR ACCESS: No
LICENSED: No	GARDEN: Yes
ACCOMMODATION: 1sbl 1tw 1fam	PETS: By prior arrangement
RATES: £17.50sgl £30dbl £35-45 family room	

THE PHEASANT INN
Keyston,
Cambridgeshire
PE18 0RE

Tel: 01832 710241
Fax: 01832 710340

Thatched village pubs always have a special attraction and The Pheasant Inn at Keyston is no exception. Full of atmosphere, it is part of the Huntsbridge Group who own the Three Horseshoes at Madingley and the White Hart at Great Yeldham, it is the most welcoming and informal place. The same wide-ranging menu is available throughout the building and you eat what you like wherever you like. Just drop in or book a table, either is totally acceptable. Martin Lee, the chef and a director of Huntsbridge, serves fashionable British food with strong Mediterranean leanings. The menu is extensive and can be anything from wild boar sausages with mashed potatoes, seared scallops or ravioli with provencale vegetables. Fish and vegetable dishes account for a good portion of the menu. Its wine list is tremendous, chosen for all three pubs by one of the directors who is a Master of Wine. He has taken care to choose selectively and with a determination to produce good wines for as little as £12 a bottle as well as the more expensive classics. The Pheasant like The Three Horseshoes and the White Hart should be a must on everyone's visiting list.

USEFUL INFORMATION

OPEN: 7 days except Dec25 &26.
Normal drinking hours
CHILDREN: Yes. Children's helpings
CREDIT CARDS: All major cards
LICENSED: Full On. Superb wine list
GARDEN: Yes 38 seats outside
PETS: No

RESTAURANT: Does not apply
you may eat where you wish on the
same menu. Wide range British food
with strong Mediterranean influence
VEGETARIAN: Always a choice
WHEELCHAIR ACCESS: Yes

THE PINK GERANIUM,
Station Road,
Melbourne,
Royston,
Hertfordshire
SG8 6DX

Tel: 01763 260215
Fax: 01763 262110

For the last twenty five years The Pink Geranium has been an internationally acclaimed British Restaurant. In the 70's it attracted attention when Prince Charles named it his favourite restaurant. When Sally and Steven Saunders took over in 1987 they were amazed to be entertaining many celebrities like Rod Stewart, Barbara Cartland, Alison Moyet, Pierce Brosnan and Ruby Wax. The Restaurant is a beautiful thatched cottage built circa 1500, Egon Ronay quotes it as 'One of Britain's Prettiest Restaurants' . Steven Saunders is Savoy trained and one of Britain's leading chefs, He also adds the role of Author, Cookery, Journalist, Television Presenter and tutor to his workload. The A la Carte menu is revised seasonally using the finest and freshest ingredients. Dining here is an unbeatable gourmet experience. Sally and Steven also own the beautiful 17th century Sheene Mill Hotel and Brasserie, two hundred yards from The Pink Geranium, which offers stylish food at affordable prices accompanied by gentle piano playing most nights.

USEFUL INFORMATION

OPEN: Lunch: Tues-Fri
Dinner Tues-Sat
CHILDREN: Welcome
CREDIT CARDS: All major cards
LICENSED: Yes

RESTAURANT: A gastronomic
feast
WHEELCHAIR ACCESS: Yes
GARDEN: Yes
PETS: No

CAMBRIDGE QUY MILL HOTEL
Newmarket Road,
Stow-cum-Quy
Cambridge CB5 9AG
AA***
Tel: 01223 293383 Fax: 01223 293770

The Cambridge Quy Mill Hotel is a Victorian Grade II listed Water Mill and Millers House which has been tastefully converted into a quality Hotel. It is set in eleven acres of pastures and water meadows overlooking Quy Water and situated on the Cambridge Northern fringe conveniently off the A14, ten minutes away from the Newmarket Racecourse and the M11 trunk road with ample free car parking and helipad facilities. You can wander through the gardens, where wildlife abounds, see the Peacocks, take a leisurely stroll along the riverbanks, try trout fishing or archery or even Clay Pigeon Shooting. The hotel prides itself in being able to offer both corporate and leisure-break customers, quality, style and charm at competitive rates. Many of the old features have been retained within the hotel which is stylishly and comfortably furnished. There are twenty one en-suite bedrooms, even the single rooms have double beds and the superior four-poster bedrooms feature double Jacuzzi baths. You can enjoy Haute cuisine or country-inn charm. There is informal dining in the Quy Mill Inn or alternatively dine in the Water Mill a la carte restaurant where you will be served excellent cuisine in the delightful surroundings of the Victorian water wheel. After which retire to the Lounge with its deep chairs and log stove to enjoy coffee and perhaps a Remy XO.

USEFUL INFORMATION

OPEN: All year except Christmas
CHILDREN: Welcome. Family rooms
CREDIT CARDS: All major cards
LICENSED: Full On
ACCOMMODATION: 21 en-suite rooms
RATES: Sgl room only £65 Dbl. £85 Executive £95

RESTAURANT: Excellent cuisine
QUY MILL INN: Great bar food
VEGETARIAN: Always a choice
WHEELCHAIR ACCESS: Yes
GARDEN: 11 acres
PETS: Yes with notice

THE RISING DRAGON
12-14 Chequers Court,
Huntingdon,
Cambridgeshire
PE19 6LJ

Tel: 01480 454674
Fax: 01480 414888

Huntingdon is a quiet, dignified town made famous by the ex Prime Minister John Major, whose home and constancy it is. It is a very pleasant place to visit with good architecture, shops and a number of fascinating hostelries and eateries. In the latter category comes the excellent Rising Dragon where polite and charming staff make sure everyone is given a warm welcome. You will find The Rising Dragon just off the busy High Street and once you enter its doors you come into a restful room, decorated in pretty warm colours. Everything about The Rising Dragon is of a very high standard and it is the ideal place to come for lunch or for an intimate dinner. The choice on the menu demonstrates thirty years experience in Peking style cuisine. If you are not familiar with 'Chinese Cuisine' leave the choice to Tony Hui and his assistants and you will have a feast of selected dishes spread before you including chef's favourites which might not appear on the menu.

USEFUL INFORMATION

OPEN: Mon-Sat 12-2pm &6-11.30pm
Closed Sundays
CREDIT CARDS: All major cards
LICENSED: Full On

RESTAURANT: Superb Szechuan
             and Peking cuisine
VEGETARIAN: Yes
WHEELCHAIR ACCESS: Yes

SHEENE MILL HOTEL AND BRASSERIE
Melbourn, NR Royston,
Hertfordshire
SG8 6DX

Tel: 01763 261393

Sheene Mill is in an idyllic spot that overlooks the Millpond and the River Mel, which actually runs beneath it. The Mill is a fully restored 17th-century Watermill, the original having been listed in the Domesday Book. Just two minutes from the A10 and fifteen minutes from the M11, it is ideal for anyone wanting a break. There are eight charming en-suite guest rooms, all of which, plus the Brasserie, overlook the river. The delightful, large conservatory offers the sight of the ducks antics on the river, with glimpses of kingfishers or mink, and squirrels darting about amongst the trees. In the summer you can have drinks or coffee on the terrace surrounded by all this beauty. Sheene Mill, which is in the same ownership of the internationally famous Pink Geranium Restaurant just two hundred yards away, has an excellent Brasserie of its own serving superb cuisine throughout the week. Most nights one dines to the sound of a softly played piano. There is an excellent traditional Sunday Lunch. Monday to Friday one can have Lite Bites in the Conservatory and Country Room or an a la carte meal in the Brasserie. In the summer there are Lite Bites and Barbecues on Sundays. The Bar is open to non-diners except Saturdays and Sunday Lunch.

USEFUL INFORMATION

OPEN: 7 days a week lunch and dinner
CHILDREN: Welcome
CREDIT CARDS: All major cards
LICENSED: Full On
ACCOMMODATION: 8 en-suite rooms
PETS: No

BRASSERIE: A la carte menu
CONSERVATORY: Lite Bites
VEGETARIAN: Always a choice
WHEELCHAIR ACCESS: Yes
GARDEN: Yes. Terrace
(Please apply for prices)

SWALLOW HOTEL
Kingfisher Way,
Hinchingbrooke Business Park,
Huntingdon, Cambridgeshire PE18 8FL

Tel: 01480 446000 Fax: 01480 451111
Central Reservations 0645404 404 Fax: 01914 151777
Email: info@swallowhotels,com.

In May 1998 Swallow Hotels opened a new luxury 4 star hotel extremely well situated on the A14 in the heart of the national roadwork network, convenient for the A1 and M11 with good access to M1 and M6. It has everything that the modern traveller requires whether on pleasure or business. There are one hundred and fifty bedrooms with private bathroom, air-conditioning, radio, satellite TV, direct dial telephone, tax/modem point, tea and coffee making facilities, hairdryer, trouser press, iron and ironing board. There are specially adapted bedrooms for disabled guests and for families. The restaurant and lounge are attractively appointed and the food is delicious with the emphasis on fish and prime cuts of meat, served with or without sauces and accompanied by vegetables that are fresh and just cooked. The well-stocked bar is a friendly meeting place. There are conference facilities seating up to two hundred and fifty delegates. Free Car parking. The Swallow Leisure Club with heated indoor swimming pool, fitness room, steam room and spa bath is available to hotel guests as well as non-residents.

USEFUL INFORMATION

OPEN: All year
CHILDREN: Welcome
CREDIT CARDS: All major cards
LICENSED: Full On
ACCOMMODATION: 150 rooms
RATES :From £110sgl & £130 dbl.
SPECIAL BREAKS

RESTAURANT: A la carte.
BAR FOOD: Light meals and snacks
VEGETARIAN: Always a choice
WHEELCHAIR ACCESS: Yes
specially adapted rooms
GARDEN: No
PETS: Yes in bedrooms

SYCAMORE HOUSE RESTAURANT
1 CHURCH Street,
Little Shelford,
Cambridgeshire CB2 5HG

Good Food Guide & Michelin Guide

Tel: 01223 843396

Little Shelford is an attractive, peaceful village approximately five miles from the city of Cambridge. It is a short drive away from the Imperial War Museum at Duxford and from the lovely medieval town of Saffron Walden. In Church Street you find Sycamore House Restaurant in a three hundred year old building set in a beautiful garden. It was a pub for many years and then in 1993 Michael and Susan Sharpe converted it into one of the nicest restaurants for miles around. The pretty, non-smoking dining room offers a short fixed priced menu which changes monthly and always reflects seasonal availability of fresh produce, fish and game. The food is cooked perfectly, the dishes quietly inspired and delicate use is made of fresh herbs. A vegetarian option is always available. The well chosen wine list is generously priced and contains seventy wines from many regions of the world. Not open for lunch, it is open for Dinner from Tuesday to Saturday inclusive. It is non-smoking throughout.

USEFUL INFORMATION

OPEN: Tues.-Sat from 7.30pm
CHILDREN: Over 12 years
CREDIT CARDS: Visa/Master/Switch
LICENSED: Full On
GARDEN. No

DINING ROOM: Delicious inspired
English fare reflecting seasonal produce
VEGETARIAN: Options available
WHEELCHAIR ACCESS: Yes 2 steps
PETS: No

NON-SMOKING THROUGHOUT

THE HARDWICKE ARMS HOTEL
Ermine Way,
Arrington,
NR Royston,
Hertfordshire SG8 0AH

Tel:01223 208802 Fax: 01223 208885

The Hardwicke Arms is an old coaching inn on a site which has evidence of an Inn at least since the 13th century. It has a tremendous history and has always been very much part of the village of Arrington. This hotel is conveniently located for visits to Cambridge, the Imperial War Museum at Duxford, racing at Newmarket, going into London via the M.II, or visiting Suffolk, Norfolk and Cambridgeshire. Jochen Julius the current owner has refurbished the hotel attractively. He created a new car park, the original car park was on the opposite side of the road (see the hotel sign) and so the back of the hotel became the front! Nothing else about this hotel is back to front. There are two restaurants and a Sunday Carvery, and two well-stocked bars. There are rooms for functions and weddings and outside catering for every kind of occasion is a speciality.. The twelve en-suite guest rooms, double, twin, single and a family rooms, are comfortable, well equipped with direct dial telephones, television and hostess trays.

USEFUL INFORMATION

OPEN: All year
CHILDREN: Yes
CREDIT CARDS: All major cards
LICENSED: Full On
ACCOMMODATION: 12 en-suite rooms
RATES: Sgl £32.50-36 Dbl. £48-55
2/3 day weekend breaks

RESTAURANT: 2 very good
restaurants. A la Carte
BAR FOOD: Large selection
VEGETARIAN: Always a choice
WHEELCHAIR ACCESS: Yes
GARDEN: Yes
PETS: No

THE OLD BRIDGE HOTEL
1 High Street,
Huntingdon,
Cambridgeshire PE18 6TZ

4 Crowns Highly Commended
Tel: 01480 452681 Fax: 01480 411017

The Old Bridge Hotel is an elegant town centre hotel, known far and wide for its excellent standards and for its two distinctive restaurants serving modern food and with an exceptionally fine wine list. It belongs to Huntsbridge Limited, a partnership of Chefs, each creating food of the highest possible quality within the relaxed and informal atmosphere of the traditional English inn. The combination provided of great food, wine and ale, beautiful buildings and convivial service is irresistible. Visit The Old Bridge and you will demand to know the names of the others in the group. One menu is offered throughout the building and you are encouraged to eat as much or as little as you like. The Terrace has a very relaxed atmosphere and service, and a stunning hand-painted mural, while The Restaurant is slightly more formal and is strictly non-smoking. There are twenty five en-suite non-smoking bedrooms. The Premium rooms have air conditioning and CD players. All rooms have direct dial telephones and television.

USEFUL INFORMATION

OPEN: All year 11am-11pm Sun 12-10.30pm
CHILDREN: Welcome
CREDIT CARDS: All major cards
LICENSED: Yes
ACCOMMODATION: 25 en-suite rms. 1 ground floor rm
RATES: Sgl from £79.50 Dbl./tw from £89.50
Premium dbl. from £120
WEEKEND BREAKS FROM £67.50 pp

RESTAURANT: A la carte
THE TERRACE: As above, less formal
VEGETARIAN: Always a choice
WHEELCHAIR ACCESS: Yes. Ramp

GARDEN: Yes
PETS: Yes

THE PRINCE OF WALES
Potton Road, Hilton,
Huntingdon, Cambridgeshire PE18 9NG
3 Crown Commended
Tel/Fax: 01480 830257

The Prince of Wales is a traditional two bar village inn right in the centre of the picturesque village of Hinton. Set in the heart of rural Cambridgeshire it is only a short drive from the regional centres of Cambridge, Peterborough and Huntingdon making it an ideal place to stay for business travellers and visitors alike. You can enjoy a pint or two of excellent real ale while you play a game of pool or darts in the cosy public bar. The more spacious lounge bar has a blazing log fire on cold nights and is a comfortable place in which to enjoy a drink, a freshly prepared three course meal or a simple bar snack chosen from the comprehensive and well priced menu. In the summer months one can enjoy 'Al Fresco' on the secluded Patio, where occasional barbecues are held throughout the season. Robin and Judith Doughty are mine hosts. He is a life long 'Real Ale' fan and it shows!! The four well appointed bedrooms all have their own en-suite shower and toilet and are equipped with remote control television, hairdryer, tea and coffee making facilities, radio alarm clock and direct dial telephone.

USEFUL INFORMATION

OPEN: Mon:6-11pm
Tues-Fri 11-2.30pm & 6-11pm
Sat & Sun: 12-3pm & 7-10.30pm
CHILDREN: Over 5 years
CREDIT CARDS: All major cards except Diners
LICENSED: Full On
ACCOMMODATION: 1dbl 1tw 2sgl all en-suite
RATES: Sgl from £27.50 Dbl. from £37.
Short breaks special prices including dinner

BAR FOOD: Comprehensive menu
VEGETARIAN: Yes
WHEELCHAIR ACCESS: Yes
GARDEN: Patio. BBQ
PETS: Yes by prior arrangement.£25
                                                    deposit

THE RED LION HOTEL
Station Road East
Whittlesford, Cambridge CB2 4NL
Three Crowns

Tel: 01223 832047
Fax: 01223 837576

Built in 1290 as a monastery for the Order of Carmelites, The Red Lion is full of atmosphere and character with exquisite carved beams and fireplaces, the work of the monks. The buildings included a hall and chamber with buttery and bakehouse. A popular rest for travellers over the centuries, King James the 1st stayed when he was taken ill on a journey from Newmarket in 1619. Over the years there have been many changes but always carefully done to protect its charm. Whittlesford is a small village one mile from the Imperial War Museum at Duxford, seven miles south of Cambridge, Newmarket twelve miles and Stansted Airport twenty miles. First class accommodation is provided in the twenty-one en-suite bedrooms. Each room is beautifully furnished and provided with colour television and facilities for making hot drinks. Traditional English fare is served every day in the bar and the a la carte restaurant. The Public Bar is a lively place used by locals. The Banqueting and Function Room is well equipped for wedding receptions, birthday celebrations, company dinners and private parties. With seating for one hundred and forty or two hundred people for a buffet, it is a popular place.

USEFUL INFORMATION

OPEN:11am-11pm
CHILDREN: Welcome
CREDIT CARDS: AMEX/Visa/Switch/Connect
LICENSED: Full On + Entertainment
ACCOMMODATION. 21 en-suite bedrooms
RATES: £39sgl £54dbl Child £5 Breakfast only

RESTAURANT: Traditional English fare
BAR FOOD: Wide choice
VEGETARIAN: Yes
WHEELCHAIR ACCESS: limited
GARDEN: Yes
PETS: No

THE THREE HORSESHOES
High Street,
Madingley, Cambridgeshire
CB3 8AB

2 Rosettes. All major Guides.
Egon Ronay Food Recommended

Tel: 01954 210221 Fax: 01954 212043

This busy lively inn in the High Street, Madingley, is one of the most popular in this part of Cambridgeshire, largely because of the efficient, friendly and cheerful manner in which the proprietor, John Hoskins runs it. It has a tremendous reputation for its food which tends to be traditional English with a Continental influence and always includes time honoured favourites. The same menu is on offer in both the bar and the restaurant. On Sundays the menu has the addition of roast leg of spring lamb with rosemary and garlic, olive oil braised leeks and potato and olive gratin. The beer is well kept and the staff, both well mannered and attentive. The aim of the Wine List is to have around one hundred of the most interesting wines John can lay his hands on, offering a full spread through the price range. 'Interesting' means with character, individual, intriguing - not necessarily classic. So please be prepared to try something you've never heard of - you won't regret it.

USEFUL INFORMATION

OPEN:11.30-2.30pm & 6-11pm
CHILDREN: Welcome
CREDIT CARDS: All major cards
LICENSED: Full On
GARDEN: Yes

RESTAURANT: Delicious, varied menu
BAR FOOD: As restaurant menu
VEGETARIAN: Always a choice
WHEELCHAIR ACCESS: Yes
PETS: Yes on leads. Not in restaurant

THE THREE PICKERELS
Mepal, Ely,
Cambridgeshire CB6 2AR
AA Recommended

Tel: 01353 777777
Fax: 01353 777891

The Three Pickerels is a delightful, Edwardian, riverside inn, set in the centre of the picturesque village of Mepal, close to the Cathedral City of Ely. The proprietors Stuart and Margaret Hammond are welcoming, informal and friendly, without losing one iota of the high professional standards they set for themselves and their equally friendly staff. It is very much a traditional village pub used by locals whose cheerful banter at the bar helps to create the contented atmosphere. The ale is well kept, and the food, either in the restaurant or the bar, is imaginative and delicious. If one had to describe it succinctly one would say the menu was English, Mediterranean and Oriental with a great emphasis on fresh fish. The choice offers something for every palate and is definitely value for money. The Three Pickerels has three guest rooms, individually and comfortably furnished with a shared bathroom. Ideal place to stay for pleasure or business. It is easily accessible to Cambridge and Ely, you can shoot, fish and follow many country pursuits.

USEFUL INFORMATION

OPEN: 11.45-2.30pm & 6.30-11pm
Sunday evening: 7-10.30pm
CREDIT CARDS: Visa/Master
CHILDREN: Over 5 years
LICENSED: Full On
ACCOMMODATION: 3 rooms shared bathroom
RATES: £30 twin £22 single

RESTAURANTANT: Wide choice
English, Mediterranean, Oriental
BAR FOOD: Extensive. Value for money
VEGETARIAN: Always a choice
WHEELCHAIR ACCESS: Yes
GARDEN: Yes
PETS: No

THE EXHIBITION
2-5 London Road,
Godmanchester, Huntingdon
Cambridgeshire PE18 8NZ

Tel: 01480 459134

This is an intriguing hostelry which one might describe as a fusion between a pub, a wine bar and a bistro. The result is a delightful place to visit, where the welcome is great and the proprietors William and Maggie Middlemiss with their staff do everything in their power to make your visit memorable. There are two areas in The Exhibition. One is elegantly Georgian and the other Victorian. Both have been decorated in a stylish manner in keeping with the period. Skilful use of colour, fabric and furnishing provides a pleasing atmosphere in which to eat and drink. The Exhibition is close to the river and has a large Beer Garden which is extremely popular in warm weather. One can walk along the banks of the River Ouse, play golf close by or take a look at Godmanchester's famous Steam Engines. In all there are eighty covers and one can eat a whole range of delicious food from the regularly changing menu which may include Mussels in White Wine, perfectly cooked Halibut Steak and seasonal fare. If one does not want a full meal then there are a variety of lighter dishes available including a simple sandwich. The wine list is carefully chosen and there are fourteen wines which you may have by the glass. Open every day of the week, it is especially busy on Friday, Saturday and Sundays when it is open all day.

USEFUL INFORMATION

OPEN: Mon-Thurs 11.30-3pm & 5.30-11pm
Fri,Sat,Sun: 11.30-11pm
CHILDREN: Yes
CREDIT CARDS: All major cards
LICENSED: Full On
GARDEN: Beer Garden. Car Park

RESTAURANT: A la carte
Delicious. Reasonable prices
BAR FOOD: Light meals etc.
VEGETARIAN: Good choice
WHEELCHAIR ACCESS: Yes
PETS: Guide dogs only

Selected venues in this chapter

' Now spurs the lated traveller apace.
To gain the timely Inn'

William Shakespeare

CHAPTER 7:
Around & About the Environment City
Peterborough and The Fens

It's breakfast time on a delicately beautiful May morning. As you sit over coffee and something more healthy than the over-filling, classic 'English breakfast', you're gazing out across the Fens from your window seat in the hotel dining-room in Ely, more or less convinced that you have seen it all, Fenland. You've driven every which way from Huntingdon to somewhere you've temporarily forgotten. Now, near the end of your stay in this delightful Cathedral city, you feel that you really *know* the place: you've seen its windmills, its wildfowl, its water-ways and its wetlands. You've seen the markets, a mansion or two and the highly informative museums. To cap it all, you've pored over the fascinating facts and gossip of its history and listened to its tales and legends. That must be all there is to see, do and visit, any more must be the gift-wrapping on the parcel.

Well, not exactly, when did you last have a round of golf? Come to that, when did you last even *see* a golf course? Then, what about boats? We've *seen* them, dozens of them, and been backwards and forwards across the rivers and drains - but hasn't it struck you as odd that, apart from that short trip up from St Ives to Huntingdon, we haven't actually set sail yet? And if you went as far as to strap a couple of bikes on the car before you left (on the advice of a well-meaning neighbour who only remembered East Anglia as flat) you're probably wondering when you're ever going to use them - while you curse the neighbour's interference.

"What's going on?" you demand, "when do we unstrap the bikes, get on a boat or take out the drivers and irons?" Glad you asked those questions, because a large part of this chapter is going to give the answers. If I may enlarge a little, (sorry, but it must be done) I've left all these activities out quite intentionally, because I didn't want them to detract from our many meetings with the essential Fens. I thought it would have been very clumsy, even laughable, to suggest rushing away from a hide at Welney, after an hour or two watching the waders in total peace, for a quick eighteen holes before cocktails! After half a day browsing through the Market at St Neots, how would you have responded to a command to "Get on your bike!" with half a ton of fruit and veg in your carrier bags. I doubt whether you'd have been *mad* keen.

Boating? Well we could have chugged along the Hundred Foot Washes in a dead straight line for a few miles - but that would hardly have been much fun. The old course of the River Nene is far more the thing - and that's the idea I've been keeping up my sleeve, in a manner of speaking. Of course, we *could* have taken to the water on the Ouse, east of St Ives, but there were other things to do over there, that *had* to be done - Wicken and Welney, for two. So the Nene wins, on account of the time factor, if nothing else.

I said a large part of this chapter will be about these more energetic pastimes, but not *all* of it. Most of the rest will be Peterborough. Now that's an interesting city. Thirty years ago, I knew even less about it than I did about Ely - and you know how little I knew about that. I barely knew where Peterborough was, or why! Something about a factory making diesel engines, and that was it. What an admission (or omission, even). Modern Peterborough slapped me hard on the wrist when I arrived, for thinking and acting like a dumb Southerner. I stopped myself (mentally, of course) when I started to explore and first set eyes on the Cathedral That was just the beginning as you'll find out in the following pages.

So, it sounds like another busy time. We must get started - no more last cups of anything - and take to the A10 out of Ely to begin our final Cambridgeshire tour. There's no direct route to our first call: a flying crow could go straight over the Old and New Bedford Rivers, but we can't and the only bridges are either side of the goal, at about the same distance from it. So, toss a coin - it's heads and we go north (rather closer to familiar Welney than I'd have liked) with the B1411 as our road, to the left, a short way out of the City.

To start with, the sense of direction is a bit awry as we swing from one compass point to another. Then, when the place we're aiming for is almost within hailing distance (but across *both* rivers) we turn hard right, towards the north east and drive in a straight line away from it! We would, of course, because this is a very *odd* place. Having passed Little Downham and Pymoor on the chicane before the straight, we should have our eyes open for a sharp left turn in our road, followed by the river crossings, somewhere near Welney. A few more wriggles then, just after Tip's End, another left brings us on to the B1093 sign-posted, if we're lucky, to **MANEA**, which is almost where the story really begins.

FENLAND WILDFOWL

It *actually* begins at **WELCHES DAM**, where the RSPB and the Wildlife Trust for Cambridgeshire run the 1000 hectare OUSE WASHES NATURE RESERVE (Enquiries - 01354 680212). All that wet grassland seems to be a paradise for dragonflies and damselflies, not to mention native plants, of which more than three hundred species have already been recorded. The reserve in general and the grassland in particular have two quite distinct characters, according to the season: in summer, at their driest, they attract many breeds of waders and ducks, along with Redshanks, Snipe and Lapwings; in winter the Washes flood and become transformed into one of Britain's most important locations for wildfowl. Incidentally, to make the most of a summer visit it's quite a good idea to book a place on one of the boat trips that are available at Bank Holidays. The car park, hides and toilets are open at all times throughout the year and admission is free - even to the visitors' centre, which is open daily between 9.00a.m. and 5.00p.m.

Having left Manea and wiped the mud off our wellies, we have another choice, this time between going directly to our next destination or taking the scenic route, which is a bit of a dog-leg affair. As we're 'touring' we wouldn't expect to go 'directly' anywhere - what would be the point? So we'll turn right along the B1098 and run parallel to the Sixteen Foot Drain for a while, just to see what happens.

As not a lot usually happens, hopefully we can turn left at the B1099 junction with barely a furrow in our brows, and ease into **MARCH**. We'll be in and around the town for a while, so we might as well park up and give the engine a rest while we survey the scene. We can see at once that the place we've come to is busy enough, especially on market-days. Originally a port, in the Tudor period, it boomed in the 19th century with the arrival of the railway, as did so many of the towns we've seen already, especially in North and West Norfolk.

Without a doubt the river front is March's most appealing feature and it has often been spoken of as "a Thames-side town in miniature". As we stroll along by the River Nene, we can certainly see the point, as the many attractive cottages and other buildings have their own special charm in good measure. Of course, if we ever get out on the *water* - or even go so far as to hire a *boat* for a touch of *cruising* - the full picture will really come to light. For now, as more or less humble pedestrians, the mercies aren't so small that it's hard to be grateful.

At the southern end of the town lies ST WENDREDA'S CHURCH, scene of the minor war between the Devil and the builders that we spoke about earlier. One can't help feeling pleased that the builders won as they, and their successors, have left us some spectacular architecture. In particular, the double hammer beam roof is a real tour de force with something like two hundred angels carved in the oak, their wings being open in flight rather than folded back, as is more usual in 'angel' roofs.

Someone once told me that they thought March was a straggly sort of a place. I have to say that I think that misses the point as, for me, it just wanders around, in its own pattern of natural development. Anyway, you must judge for yourselves - but try to do so on Wednesday as this is not only one of the market days, but also the *only* day for visiting some of the other attractions I have in mind, just a stones throw away up various roads leading out of the town. They're all 'outdoor places' - and peaceful by and large - so they'll make a wonderful antidote to the tensions of bustling around amongst the crowds and the stalls.

The first 'antidote' could well be DUNHAMS WOOD (Enquiries - 01354 652134), a delightful four acre touch of eccentricity in the middle of the flat Fen landscape. Uniquely, it is an oasis of woodland in a terrain where clumps of trees are actually rarer than hens' teeth, and the resident wildlife absolutely love it. A well-spent quid allows the visitor to join a guided walk led by Arthur Dunham himself and offers a perfect way to relax and unwind whilst strolling amongst the trees and looking at unusual pieces of outdoor sculpture - as well as the model railway.

The Wood lies two miles east from March off the B1099 that would take one, eventually, to Upwell. It's open on Bank Holiday Sundays and Mondays, plus every Sunday during August - and you see the problem straight away: we shan't be anywhere near the place at those times. We're more likely to be in Aviemore or Llanelli, knowing our luck - not to mention the map-reading! Wednesday is March day, we've decided, so what is to be done? Look at the small print on Mr Dunham's publicity, that's what. I quote; "Other dates for groups by arrangement." There you have it - if Dunhams Wood sounds like essential viewing, find some friends, form a group - and *arrange* it!

Across town from the sculptures and trees we could, if we chose, stretch our legs a little further at GAULT WOOD (Enquiries - 01354 652527), which is almost in March's suburbs. It's on a slightly larger scale than our last call, with sixteen acres of newly-planted trees - more than 10,000 of them - paths and a pond. It *is* more than a stroll, and an eventual decision could be down to the time factor. I suppose, on a car based tour, we owe it to our bodies to snatch every chance for some fresh air and exercise - and it's not much of an excuse to mutter something about wasting good shopping time. Have a look, and act on impulse? Could be - or even let the weather decide, eh?

Back in the car, whatever we chose, we badly need the B1101 now, as it will take us to two more outdoor attractions and then into Wisbech, where we'll certainly want to linger for quite a while. So, we head north from Gault Wood back into the centre of March, and then north again as our chosen route leads us first to the NORWOOD ROAD NATURE RESERVE (Enquiries - 01223 846363).

Norwood is more familiar than the last two, as it has something of a 'proper' Fenland feel to it. That's not to *detract* from the others - there's room for a variety of approaches just as long as these reserves continue to be created and maintained. Here we're looking at the establishment of a six and a half acre mixture of wildlife habitats based on abandoned gravel pits, and very attractive it is too. What's more, it's manageable for jet-setting tourists like ourselves who need to cram in everything and still pitch our tents half a county away by nightfall.

That said - and done - we'd better get on with it; next stop STAGS HOLT FARM PARK AND STUD (Enquires - 01354 652406) which, with its ancient parkland and Victorian farm buildings, offers yet another total change of experience, and a dramatic one at that. I have to tell you that while the overall presentation is as fascinating as one could wish, it's the heavy horses that are the star turn. The centre is especially committed to the protection and rearing of the Suffolk Punch breed, and the great beasts are as endearing as they are impressive. How often have we picked out one attraction from a range offered to us at a particular site and said "That's worthy of a trip all to itself?" Five minutes with the Suffolk Punches and we'll all be saying it again! Stags Holt does actually offer more, with other farm animals, carts and wagons, farm implements and country bygones all to be seen. A harness room, a nature trail and a picnic area are further delights - not to mention the tea room for a touch of recovery at the end of it all. This tailor-made "day in the country" is open from 10.30a.m. to 5.00p.m. on Sundays, Bank Holidays and School holidays between Easter and the end of September at an adult admission fee of £2.50.

Easing away from the Farm, I could well imagine the odd grumble surfacing from the back seats about how we've just been through a whole town without going into a single *shop*! True enough, and we'll agree not to mention the Market, I suppose. Alright, *markets* aren't *shops* but the idea's much the same surely; you go there with money and carrying nothing much else; ideally you come away loaded down to the ground - and broke! We won't argue the point; there'll be shopping enough before we see Ely again - shopping enough and to spare. At the moment there's one more decision about walking (or not walking) to be made; do we do the WOODMAN'S WAY or don't we?

We're looking at a six and a half mile circular walk, most of which lies to the south east of the town. It could fill in a number of gaps in our experience, as it takes us around March and Wimblington and reveals their one time island characteristics from the days before all the drainage took place. Or it could take up time that certain people would rather spend at the helm, doing their Nelson bit. As author, I suppose, I have the casting vote and vote that it's time to keep a promise and talk about boats - more precisely, about the pleasures of cruising in the Fens.

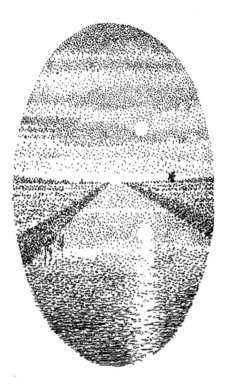

WATERSCAPE OF PEACE

To people in the know about inland waterways, it seems this is absolutely the place to be. The Broads have the high profile image, the razzmatazz, but talk of the Great Ouse, the Nene Ouse Navigation Link and you'll see eyes moisten amongst the strong men of the boating fraternity. Here they find an ever present sense of tranquillity and contentment. "Where else," they ask, "can you guarantee waking up to nothing more raucous than the lapping of the water and the rustle of a moorhen stirring amongst the rushes?" I take their point: I'm sure I'd rather come to with the soft murmurings of Nature in my ears than with the Radio 1 reveille howling from somebody's ghetto blaster.

After a leisurely breakfast, one is free to embark on a day of relaxation, moving at one's own pace through the unfolding Fen landscape. Soon, the high point of the boating day approaches, its entire raison d'etre: lunchtime! Now those freshwater mariners may be seen to weep openly at their memories of waterside pubs, good food and real, local ale. Having spliced that particular main brace, the day continues until the sun begins to sink past the yard arm, which means it's time to moor up for the night, to knock back a cocktail or two on the poop deck and think seriously about dinner - and is that really the tower of Ely silhouetted against the sunset? And so on.

The choice is simple: Fenland is to boating what a road in Southern Ireland is to motoring, whereas Broadland is more like the Monte Carlo Rally. If we *must* compare them - but perhaps that's futile, perhaps it makes more sense to stick to the fact that they're very different and to suggest that, if it's a pretty, peaceful potter that you want then FOX BOATS (Enquiries - 01354 652770) of March should be able to help with the decision. They can also offer traditional narrow boats available to hire for short breaks, weekends or by the week.

As I've suggested taking to the water at this point in our travels, let me tell you a bit more about what's on offer. March itself lies a little over halfway along the Nene Ouse Navigation Link which runs from Stanground Lock, near Peterborough, to the little village of Salters Lode, near Denver Sluice. From Denver the waterway links into the River Great Ouse with access to Ely, Bedford and Cambridge. At the Peterborough end there's a link with the River Nene from where it's possible to join up with the Grand Union Canal and the entire waterway network of England and Wales- only we won't be doing that over a weekend, fairly obviously!

Since we're at the midpoint, we can choose to go in either direction, up or down stream as it were. It depends on the kind of environment you'd prefer, I suppose, as the link combines stretches of the old course of the River Nene with fairly extensive cruising along some of the great drainage channels that were created, as we have seen, to reclaim the Fenland for farming. One could easily justify either choice: the river has the traditional appeal; the drainage channels are more out of the ordinary, more of a naval experience. Whichever one appeals, I'm sure you'll find the experience thoroughly memorable, for all the best reasons. Upstream you'd be looking at Whittlesey Dyke and later King's Dyke, with a couple of locks to negotiate to punctuate the otherwise tranquil cruising with just a touch of excitement. There are moorings at Whittlesey, so it's quite possible to stop and explore the town - although the plan is to visit it by road, later in our tour.

Downstream - which would be my choice - the river widens as it flows north east towards the villages of Upwell and Outwell. Next comes Marmout Priory Lock, where, amidst the activity, there could still be a chance to snatch a breather and enjoy the rural views extending across wide, open arable fields to the south, and orchards to the north.

The stretch of river that takes us to the end of the link at Salters Lode is known as Well Creek. It flows through the middle of a clutch of villages and hamlets which are often likened to Dutch canal villages, a similarity which extends to some of their names. Pleasant period houses flank the river and various moorings are available with those at Outwell Basin being particularly useful. From Outwell towards Nardelph (Dutch?), the route crosses the Mullicart Aqueduct which is an example of a feature not often found on East Anglian waterways.

If the boating urge has not been satisfied at this point, there's more on offer, as I said earlier, if you're prepared to brave the locks at Salters Lock and Denver Sluice. You can continue from Denver onto the River Great Ouse and sail away into the sunset accompanied by Beethoven's Pastoral, if that's your style, and why not? Be mildly warned though, the first stretch of the Ouse that you meet is tidal and can only be negotiated around two hours either side of high-water. Beethoven stuck in the mud lacks a touch of romance, I imagine!

After a last, swift look at the river, and at the gorgeous great horses as we whizz past Stags Holt we continue northwards on the B1101. It's a winding old way along this stretch, past Coldham, Friday Bridge and Elm to the junction with the A1101, where we turn left. Along that way, the mind homes in on those gentlemen who set out borders and boundaries and on the very strange results of their thinking. Some boundary lines are obvious: one look and it's plain that they couldn't be anywhere else. Others are merely vague: "Why should Norfolk become Cambridgeshire just *here*, exactly? Does it *matter*?" There's a third category which crops up all over this area: "This is crazy! 'over there' is more like 'over here' than anywhere else *on earth*. It gets worse if one's meant to be travelling around *within* a particular county because there are quite a few times when one isn't, or might be - or who cares, anyway? An odd business, but at least it gets us into **WISBECH** (Information - 01945 583263).

We have arrived at a town which is the prosperous heart of a rich flower and fruit-growing area. That would suggest that spring is the best season for a visit when the bulb fields are ablaze and the orchards, swimming with blossom, are at their loveliest. If that sounds convincing, I should sew a touch of indecision by pointing out that July is the month for the WISBECH ROSE FAIR. an annual and spectacular celebration of the flower growing history and traditions of Fenland. Not only is it one of *the* high points of the local year, it is also a major attraction for visitors from all over Britain and further afield, such is the quality of the dazzling and dramatic displays.

The architecture of Wisbech makes it one of the region's most distinguished towns outside of Cambridge. It has some of the finest streets of Georgian houses, and other buildings, in the country, which can be seen to very good effect at the North and South Brinks and Museum Square.

PECKOVER HOUSE (Information - 01945 583463), owned by the National Trust, is perfectly positioned at the centre of North Brink. A classic Georgian town house, it was built around 1722 by Jonathan Peckover, the Quaker founder of a bank that was later incorporated into Barclays. It is best known for its excellent plaster and wood rococo decoration, but the garden has at least an equal claim on our interest. Put simply, it is a superb Victorian creation, with its orangery, summer houses, roses, herbaceous borders, fernery, croquet lawn and reed barn, the whole extending over two acres. Couple that with fine views out over the River Nene and we have a treat that must be high on our list.

PECKOVER HOUSE, WISBECH

Right across the road from Peckover is another Wisbech landmark: the newly restored OCTAVIA HILL BIRTHPLACE MUSEUM (Enquiries - 01945 476358). The Museum charts the course of Miss Hill's career as a housing reformer and includes a section on her work as a founder of the National Trust. Both the Museum and Peckover are open at similar times, between 28 March and 1st November. As the pattern is slightly complicated, a preliminary phone call would be a good idea, to match the visits to the rest of one's programme.

In the middle of the town, the quite delightful Crescent, Union Place and Ely Place all but cuddle the Castle in a close-knit grouping. Although the latter building is now a private residence, it has incorporated elements of a number of castles built on the site over the centuries since the Norman version first saw the light of day. For example in the 17th century it was home to John Thurloe who was Cromwell's Secretary of State during the Commonwealth and the equivalent to a modern day chief of secret police. Quite a history!

Talk of history leads as night follows day to thoughts of museums - and Wisbech has one of those, naturally. It lies close to the Castle and is home to a wide selection of Fenland relics from all periods of the town's history. Whilst we're browsing, we might well be reminded of one local boy who made good. Nicholas Breakspear, who died in 1159 and is said to have been curate of Tydd St Giles, five miles north of Wisbech, was the only Englishman ever to have become Pope, as Adrian IV.

We'll do some shopping in a minute, but before that let's move back up to North Brink, above the River Nene, with its grand perfection of Georgian houses, each a gem of individuality yet all combining in classic harmony. Sited here, too, is the two hundred year old ELGOODS BREWERY, which is open for guided tours and set in a large, nature garden where visitors are always welcome.

Now for the shopping. Wisbech has, all in all, preserved its English Market town atmosphere very successfully. Market day is Thursday, which tends to suggest that this area needs even more careful planning for a stay that lasts long enough to take in a boat cruise, several different markets on several different days - and a bevy of Nature Reserve route marches, to boot. It's all going to make for a very busy break and then we'll *all* be able to go home for a holiday.

Nothing daunted, we must do a brief tour of the Wisbech shops; if only to assuage my forebodings about your reactions to a wholly different game that's waiting down the road ahead of us. My problem will be that if you love *this* too much I'll be tempted to hide the other one away, in a manner of speaking, whereas if it's the other one that excites you I'll have to hide myself away, literally, as I and my readers will obviously have nothing *important* in common. You've heard of Catch 22? Well, I'm living it. Now. On the other hand it is *my* problem and you didn't part with something like seven pounds to purchase this guide, just for a nose-dive into the author's psyche - not in a *travel* book, you didn't, even if this one did set out to be the 'War and Peace' of guidebooks. "And *failed*!" did I hear you snort?

The shops in Wisbech cover the range you would expect from a flourishing country town, but the tour de force is its collection of family owned businesses, where local specialities abound as do streams of temptations for the itinerant kleptomaniac. If I counsel moderation here, its only because we're still at an early part of the day and the boot is half full of fruit and veg from March market already. Yes, moderation - and an eye on the clock. Just as you'd expect, there's a good theatre in Wisbech, THE ANGLES CENTRE, where a wide variety of productions come to the stage throughout the year. The Centre has all the facilities that one would expect and would deserve more space to itself were we planning to be based in the town for any length of time. As it is, we're clock watching already and are unlikely to be around in the evening to take in a performance anyway, such is the nature of our necessarily hurried progress through the region. Let's just include it in our list of places that deserve a return visit, and press on, shall we?

The next spell of motoring should be rather swifter than usual, as we're taking the A47 south and then west and it's not a bad road, by and large. At **GUYHIM** (sounds Dutch, again, doesn't it?) it swings away to the right and would take us straight into Peterborough, if we wanted. Actually, we don't want; we have calls to make elsewhere, and the first will be at **THORNEY**.

The heart of this village, with its serene, ochre coloured houses has the distinct feel of a cathedral close, and that may have something to do with one aspect of its history. Mind you, it wasn't all 'peace' at Thorney in the early days, far from it. The Danes came across the original 7th century monastic church one day, and did their usual ravaging number, to such effect that it took the Normans a fair while to rebuild the ruins, once order had been re-established. The church we can see today, which was restored in the 17th Century, actually incorporates part of the abbey that remained after the Dissolution - but, as we've seen more than once before it is in the churchyard that we'll find evidence of what may well be Thorney's most interesting tale.

The French King, Louis XIV, developed a rather nasty paranoid thing about Huguenots back in the 17th century, and set about persecuting them to pieces. Many fled to East Anglia as refugees, and of them a significant number fetched up at Thorney, where their plight reached the sympathetic ear of the then Duke of Bedford, who offered generous help, by the standards of those days, and assisted in the setting up of a community for them in the village The French names and epitaphs on numerous gravestones tell their story and commemorate the generosity of their benefactor.

There is a further feature of interest in the area - again, if we feel there's time to do it justice - and that's up the Crowland Road at the THORNEY HERITAGE CENTRE, where more facets of the local scene are brought to mind along with relics of the periods of its history. Pause or add it to the list -the choice is yours. After all, you're paying!

From Thorney, a moderate fizz down the B1040 southwards across the River Nene brings us to **WHITTLESEY,** which sits between the original tidal river, the railway and the newer Whittlesey Drain. Sounds attractive, doesn't it? Actually it is well established as an industrial and market town, seems to be 'doing quite nicely, thank you' and can't be blamed for preferring its own view of reality to some froth and tinsel tripper's fantasy. Personally, as I've implied many times throughout the past chapters, I don't find that such a bad idea: half the fun of travelling, to me, is seeing other lifestyles *as they are lived* - and you don't get that in 'theme parks', however they're promoted.

As you might expect, there's an odd tale with a moral here, too. Until the Victorians got heavily into the drainage idea, Whittlesey Mere, a lake of 1900 acres, was very much a local feature for both the human and wildlife residents, particularly the waterfowl. In winter the floods expanded the area of water very dramatically and then, with the severe frosts so typical of East Anglia, the whole lot froze hard to become a mecca for ice-skaters from miles around. What the average duck thought as it came in for a landing and skidded beak first into the bank is not recorded! At the time, skating was a major Fenland activity and not just as a sport: it was actually the fastest and most sensible way of getting around the place in winter. So, along came the engineers and, in a major feat of taking the short-term view, and not leaving well alone, installed a massive centrifugal pump in 1851 and emptied the lot. Just like that. Naturally, the wildlife emigrated in something of a huff while the waterfowl wondered how much of a mixed blessing it might have been, since there weren't too many ducks to be seen with their beaks - or any other part - in splints, from the next winter onwards. From that winter too, I suppose, the local boredom level rose as skating had become a thing of the past and alternatives were not too apparent. Whittlesey was left to its brickworks and their forest like rows of chimneys, while life ticked on by, rather more sombrely than hitherto. There *was* a plus side, I have to say: the winter agues and the rheumatics that had plagued the local fen dwellers all but vanished at a stroke.

Today, Whittlesey has been somewhat redeemed in the eyes of itinerant wildfowl followers, by the creation of **LATTERSEY NATURE RESERVE** (Enquiries -01223 846363) which lies near the Whittlesey Dyke to the south of the town, off the B1093. Here 28 acres of grassland and ponds have been set aside and maintained, offering an excellent point of vantage for observing the descendants of the denizens of the former Mere, presumably. Alternatively, if one's ornithological aspirations turn rather rampant, the RSPB's **NENEWASHES** site (Enquiries - 011354 52134) provides even more excellent points for meeting one's needs.

By the time you've become familiar with a number of sites like these - never forgetting Wicken and Welney, either - it's clear that the havens for waterbirds that have been developed, enhanced and created are a major regional and national asset. Of course, the Ouse Washes are more than that and their significance, especially in winter, is truly international when thousands of birds, including the rare Bewick Swans, congregate there. There are many facets of life in modern Britain which are so easy to knock - and so in need of *being* knocked - that one can very easily be bored with the sport. When one encounters the results of all this work in East Anglia, by the RSPB and others, it's a positive relief actually to be able to applaud, without any 'ifs', 'buts' or 'if onlys'!

As we're about to plunge face first into the nearby metropolis proper, this could be the time to invigorate ourselves in preparation for the onslaught with as much outdoor activity - and even outdoor imaginings - as possible, back home - we could reflect a little on the 'outdoors' (without losing our concentration on the job in had, of course).

If we can claim to have thoroughly enjoyed boating and bird-watching to the nth degree, what's left? Absolutely mind boggling oodles as it happens, from angling to cycling to - yes, well, *golf,* now you mention it. If you *do* mention it, I can only say; "Be patient". The answer's only just up the road. As an antidote to the urban dream! As a prize! As something to do with the best things in life are worth waiting for, etc.

Angling. I don't actually fish any more. It used to be my second - or, occasionally, first - obsession But then I had to give it up, (remember my poor wife at Ely), along with eating meat and a few things of that order. I have no intention of preaching about the matter at this stage, and having let myself get drawn into a ferocious argument on local radio, with the angling editor of a provincial newspaper, I shan't be offering any arguments, either. You see, having fished enthusiastically for years, I *know* why people *do* it, and I also know that the 'popular' view of the angler as some kind of zombie who sits, motionless, beside a river because he can't do very much else is as ludicrous as it is pitiably ill informed. If it isn't a *moral* problem for you - and that's entirely up to the individual - then it's one of the most marvellous ways of involving oneself with the natural world that I can think of. To be a successful angler you have to study (and practise) for years until you can see the world through the eyes of your quarry, so to speak, and think like they think. That is an enormously difficult process to master, but if you manage it the rewards are extraordinarily gratifying. The water's edge is usually a very lovely and peace generating place to be. The fish, from tiny minnows to monstrous pike and carp, are actually very beautiful creatures in their own right and, finally, wherever one chooses to fish - on the bank of a lake, or thigh deep in a rushing, moorland stream -one is never truly alone, as there are usually a great many other residents of the area going about their business which the angler can observe better than most people, because he has learned to be still and quiet. Nor must we forget that favourite fishing times - dawn and dusk - are often the best times to be outdoors for all kinds of reasons, not least being that then is when the bustle of the day is at its lowest ebb and one can enjoy the quietness of just 'being' That's not bad 'Angling PR' from a non-angler.! Especially one who lost his wife mainly due to the sport.

To be informative rather than merely lyrical, Cambridgeshire, like Norfolk, is laced with a much higher share of waterways than average as, throughout its more recent history, man has added extensively to what Nature had left there in the first place. The Rivers Nene, Great Ouse and Cam have a tradition for excellent coarse fishing that goes back decades. As an alternative, the drains offer something that is even more spectacular, potentially. I have never fished these man made waters but I know others who imply by their exploits that some stretches are all but packed solid with fish - never mind the water - so big are the catches recorded there, with 'bags' of bream, for instance, frequently exceeding a hundred pounds per angler. So, as with Norfolk, if the rod and line are your delight, this will be just your kind of area. Which excess of mental side tracking should have brought us right into the middle of PETERBOROUGH (Enquiries - 01733 452336) if not bonnet first into the back wall of the car park!

Prior to my first visit to the City, as I may have implied somewhat leadenly earlier, I knew even less about it than I later found that it deserved. Peterborough? Never mind the diesel engines etc, even if I dug deep into my brain cells all I could come up with was a connection with a "Soke" (whatever that was). A football team? Possibly - but not in the same league (ouch!) as Man Utd, the Gunners - or even "my" lads at Crystal Palace. At that point the record struck. So, on one unforgettable day - whenever it was - I braved the unknown, drove further up the A1 than I'd ever dared drive before in my entire life, turned right and duly arrived. At which point the City stopped me dead in my tracks while my prejudices fell in a heap at my feet. I saw what the place was really about and, having started to make amends at the Cathedral, it wasn't long before, full of contrition, I had to stop for a coffee and come to terms with the limitations of a life lived for too long south of the Thames. It was only later, I suppose, that with the writing of this chapter, I was given the chance to square my account adequately, so to speak, and redeem some of the blatant ignorance of my formative years - which lasted past the age of fifty, I'm led to believe. Undoubtedly, Peterborough has flourished throughout the last few decades. It has grown and prospered as new investment has arrived and unemployment has dropped, and today, it feels thoroughly vigorous and alert. Nonetheless, the ancient heritage hasn't been forgotten, in a process where the very old and the very new have rubbed off each other's rough edges and learned to live more or less in harmony. The pleasing outcome is that Peterborough is an excellent example of co-existence: the 'cutting edge' with tradition, the urban with the rural and the industrial with the agricultural. So successful has this evolution been that Peterborough has been awarded the accolade of 'Environment City', an honour granted to only four cities in the whole of Britain

Let's start with a brief over-view, for the sake of context. Within the many diverse elements in the character and history of the City, unique combinations of activities, sights and sensations surface over and over again until they become some kind of norm for the enthusiastic visitor. It is the way these experiences *combine* that is the unique feature: there are other cities with cathedrals - but have they such a range of other absorbing features, from the antique to the 'shape of things to come', within such a short radius of its West Front? Have they five sports centres, on one hand, down the road from a futuristic shopping centre on another - with a Victorian park and a nearby prehistoric site thrown in for good measure? Moreover, as one 'sightsees' one's way around, one is impressed by how manageable it all is, as though the positive compactness was actually planned with visitors in mind.

The most famous feature in the city is, of course, the Cathedral of St Peter, begun by the Normans and from which Peterborough has got its name. The visual impact of the huge arches of the West Front is totally stunning, as is the painted wooden ceiling whose history goes back to the early 13 century. Katherine of Aragon was buried here permanently; Mary Queen of Scots dallied for a while and then was taken elsewhere as we shall see.

To move directly from St Peter's to the award-winning Queensgate Shopping Centre could turn a time warp into a terminal culture shock - so we won't do that. We'll just sidle up to it gradually to see for ourselves why this part of the modern city is a place where holiday makers want to spend so much time. That gradual sidle could well be by way of the ancient City Market, for a bit of bustle, or via an antiques centre for a familiar touch of self-indulgence.

Our tour of the City will be largely done on foot, having parked the car centrally to begin with. The route will follow a sort of outward spiral from the centre, to take in as much as possible before we need our wheels again to move even further out into the 'suburbs', where we'll find another, quite different spectrum of attractions. In one direction there's a steam railway, for example: in another we move back in time to absorb the atmosphere of a three thousand year old Bronze Age Settlement. How often do *any* of us get the chance to find out what a house that old actually looked like when it was new? How many of us have ever inspected weapons and jewellery that were already ten centuries old when Christ was born? Further afield still, there's a chance for a stroll in the Nene Valley or a more energetic hike, or even some of that cycling that some of us keep on about.

If we choose to stop over - and with this amount to see we're almost bound to do so - we'll find there's a vast choice of entertainment to fill our evening. People who get withdrawal symptoms if they can't jump up and down somewhere every few hours, can do it to music, in the water, on the tennis court or at the ten pin bowling centre. More sensitive souls such as ourselves, prone to seek academic or intellectual experiences, can visit the theatre, the cinema or attend a concert in the Cathedral. After that preliminary gesture *all* of us can get back to normal and indulge ourselves witless in restaurants of a very high standard, offering typically British menus to the typically British and more exotic or even ethnic food to those of us who still have taste buds.

Fine; now we have the 'feel' of the city, let's mix a metaphor and flesh out the skeleton, so to speak. Where better to start than right in the middle? There has been a place of Christian worship on the site now occupied by ST PETER'S CATHEDRAL (Information 01733 343342) since 655 A.D. The early church was sacked (not again!) by the unlikely combination of Hereward the Wake (who wasn't known for it) and a bunch of aggressive Danes (who very definitely *were*). Why they thought that beating up a church would help them defeat William the Conqueror isn't exactly clear, but he took a dim enough view of the business to turn up personally and flatten them, as we've read elsewhere, so they obviously had a problem with their tactics or logistics or whatever Danes did. Having won, the Normans opted to put the whole lot back with a vengeance and the stunning building we see today shows clearly the extent that they got carried away with the whole idea. Peterborough Cathedral is magnificent, from its massive columns of local Barnack Stone rising to the roof with its finely painted ceiling to the 15th century apse where the fan tracery of the vaulting is an object lesson in the artistry of the stone mason's work. The true glory, the part that no-one ever forgets, is that triple arched West Front that I mentioned in the introduction to the City. Architecture -good architecture - comes in all shapes, sizes and materials, it dates from many different periods (except the 1950's, which were disgusting across the board) - but I know we'd be hard pushed to find anything more moving than the sight of those great arches caught by a softish sunset. Stunning! There's no other word. But the story doesn't stop there: we're still in East Anglia, so there's bound to be a twist, somewhere. It's found in one of the epitaphs.

Robert Scarlett, so the inscription goes, was the local gravedigger who put the corpses of Katherine of Aragon and Mary Queen of Scots away tidily, in a manner of speaking. Mary didn't stay that long as her son, James 1, thought Peterborough was a bit down market and had her remains transferred to Westminster Abbey for re-burial. That's not the twist, though. According to the Epitaph, digger Scarlett interred, in his day, twice as many people as the entire population of Peterborough! *That's* the twist.

PETERBOROUGH CATHEDRAL

The Royalist - Roundhead conflict of those times, while touched on in the Cathedral, has other spin offs around the area. Outside Old Fletton, now one of the City's southern suburbs, one can find remains of Civil War fortifications; in gardens which were once the market place, stands Peterborough's market cross - complete with an upper chamber, added in 1671 to celebrate the Restoration. I hope you'll note the elegance with which that little snippet leads us away from the Cathedral to our next feature of note. Having crossed Midgate, and moved a little way north, we come to Northminster where we find THE CITY MARKET (Enquiries - 01733 343358), next to the multi-storey car park.

This is one stop shopping (with a vengeance) of the traditional kind where more than 150 stalls - including a modern foodhall - combine in an attempt to meet *everyone's* needs. There are dozens of different traders to be found here offering everything from fresh local produce to fish from Grimsby. The Market is open five days a week from 8.30a.m. to 4.00p.m. but is closed on Sundays and Mondays.

Continuing with the 'traditional' idea, our next step or two take us west, across Broadway, to Fitzwilliam Street and to a Centre that is unique to Peterborough. The premises occupied by FITZWILLIAM ANTIQUES (Enquiries - 01733 565415/566346) have been owned by the Stafford family since 1900, before which the building's fascinating history stretches back several centuries. Opened as an antiques centre in 1991, it has a spacious showroom situated on the ground floor where once there was a cobbled courtyard and an ancient smithy. An extensive range of furniture from early Georgian to Deco is on display in mahogany, oak, walnut and pine. Whilst in no way wishing to diminish the impact or quality of these items, for me, it is the rest of the range of the Centre's displays, activities and services which stick in the memory.

The variety of items offered by the many dealers who use the centre is truly staggering: collectibles are set out beside still more furniture; there are linens, books, memorabilia, pictures, mirrors, dolls, coins, cards, medals and so many other delights from porcelain to jewellery that it seems beyond belief that any of us will ever tear ourselves away from the place. Then there are the specialist services. These include repair and renovation of antique furniture and porcelain repairs and restoration. For once, the cliché 'something for everyone' seems about right.

The centre is open six days a week, from Monday to Saturday, between 10.00a.m. and 5.00p.m. - but that's not all. To be even more helpful, it seems they're even prepared to open up on a Sunday - in response to a phone call! There's even one *final* bonus for those who seem about to fill up the entire back of the car at this one shop: there's on street car parking, or the Queensgate Car Parks just three minutes away. How very thoughtful!

Since our next encounter could turn out to approximate to 'the big one' as far as this trip goes I counsel caution, again, and an oblique approach. Preferably after we've unloaded everything into the car and had a very stout tea or coffee in the tea room at CENTRAL PARK (Enquiries - 01733 454423) to revive ourselves or gird up our loins or whatever seems best in the circumstances. Peterborough's delightfully classic Victorian Park is just fifteen minutes walk from the heart of the city and offers a touch of sanctuary from modern day shop and business bustle. It incorporates several features to meet our need for revival: in addition to the tea rooms there are gardens and an aviary. On the other side of the coin, the presence of a children's play area, sandpit and paddling pool could contribute to a major relapse so care needs to be taken, in the usual Scrooge like way, of course.

Rested? Revived? Excellent. If the car is in the Queensgate multi-storey by now after picking up all those antiques and collectibles, so much the better. At least we know which way to run, if the next bit threatens to overcome us. And the next bit is QUEENSGATE SHOPPING CENTRE (Enquires -01733 311666). The operators claim that the Centre provides 'the ultimate shopping experience for all the family'. 'Ultimate' in the sense of 'final', or 'last', would that be? The *last* shopping experience (what the blazes *is* a 'shopping experience')? After this one need never do it again? After this one just - er - *died*? That 'ultimate'? Who knows?

I'm sure that the top retailers who have taken spaces in the Centre mean as well as they ever did, but the logic is a bit lacking. Why close down perfectly good shops in *existing* city centres in order to pile the same shops on top of one another somewhere else? I suppose it's more convenient to park your car in the same building where you can buy everything from a camera to a shirt to an electric kettle to a book - to a bottle of paracetamol to get rid of the headache that built up by buying a camera, a shirt, etc. Please don't misunderstand me: I'm not downgrading Queensgate as such. As far as centres of this kind go, I'm sure it's amongst the very best with its 80 stores, cafes, restaurants, and 2,400 parking spaces. No, it's not the place itself - it's the effect. Two steps inside the first 'mall' (another horrible word) and I start to feel very, very old, as I remember when Sainsbury's sold butter loose and the assistant beat your pat into shape with wooden paddles, or when the assistant in the Co-op put your money in a metal pot, clipped it into a carrier above his head and sent it whizzing across the shop to the cashier's till for your change. Very old. To put it another way, I know that shopping has become Britain's most popular participant leisure activity, but why do they *all* have to do it *here*, right in front of *me*? *Now*?

"Unfair! Unfair!" I can hear some of you cry. It's *progress*, regretfully I am of the age of the corner shop era, and miss the personal service and having my groceries delivered, sorry.

To recover, to re-establish contact with the broader view, it's but a step southwards, across Cowgate to Priestgate and the PETERBOROUGH MUSEUM and ART GALLERY (Enquiries - 01733 343329). All aspects of the story of the City are touched on in its displays, ranging from depictions of prehistoric monsters to exhibits of Roman Christian silverware, to a range of articles made by French prisoners during the Napoleonic war. The Art Gallery, for its part, draws the mind away from the mundane, with an exciting programme of exhibitions and events throughout the whole year. Very refreshing; and an excellent antidote to rampant consumerism, I always find. Both facilities are open from Tuesday - Saturdays, from 10am to 5pm (except for New Years Day, Good Friday and Christmas Week) and admission is free.

Whilst we are on the culture trail, a modest trek across the southern part of the City towards the river could prove rewarding. As we probably *will* want to 'over night' in the area, an eye could well be kept on what might be available by way of entertainment. THE KEY THEATRE (Enquiries - 01733 452336) is situated on the embankment of the Nene and presents a wide range of productions in its delightfully intimate setting. Its facilities include the Riverside Bar and the Key Coffee Shop, so it might be useful to call in now for a snack or a drink to get the measure of what's on offer for the evening. Alternatively, the theatre's newspaper - 'The Key Times' - is published on the first Tuesday of every month, and a free copy would bring one up to date after a few minutes browsing.

We need to cross the river, now - possibly by way of the London Road bridge - to reach our next destination, which lies a little further out to the South West of the City. RAILWORLD (Information - 01733 344240), coming between a trip to the theatre and an excursion to a Bronze Age site, shows the extent and variety of possible interests for which a modern city can be expected to cater in the context of tourist attractions. It also reinforces our own awareness of the ever present contrasts that are a key feature of the East Anglian experience.

Railworld has a great deal to say about modern rail travel and about the issues that focus on it. In displays that range from Britain's hover train via a large model railway layout to aspects of modern rail travel from this country and around the world, a very detailed and informative picture has been created. Beyond that, the 'Age of Steam' exhibits cater for our nostalgia while the highlighting of environmental issues is food for our consciences. Yes, a well thought out package, and at a couple of quid a throw it is certainly value for money, right down to the 'hands-on' displays - and the *flower beds*? Railworld is open daily from 11.00am to 4.00pm from March to October and closed on Saturdays and Sundays between November and February.

A moment ago I mentioned the Bronze Age (we all do, from time to time, I suppose, life going the way it does) and now we are off to visit the time-warp that is FLAG FEN (Information - 01733 313414). Three thousand years ago, the people of prehistoric Peterborough chose the site to the east of where the modern city lies for the construction of a huge timber platform, bigger than Wembley Stadium (sounds like everyone wanted to host the World Cup, even in those days). The smart money backs the idea that the platform - and the nearby kilometre long alignment of posts running across the fen - was used for religious purposes, for nigh on five centuries. Thanks to the preservative qualities of the peaty mud in which it has been lying ever since, archaeologists have been able to recreate much of the original settlement and add to that reconstruction of Bronze Age and later, Roman, buildings.

FLAG FEN

It's an extraordinary sensation to drive out of 20th Century Peterborough to the site in a fairly modern car and then, in a matter of minutes, to encounter conditions that were the norm three millenia ago. To add factual back-up to this emotional experience, there's a fully informative museum that stands close to the excavations and reconstructions. Other facilities include a visitors centre, a shop and provision for refreshments. Flag Fen is open seven days a week, from 11.00am to 5.00pm and the admission charge is £3.50.

Upstream along the River Nene, on the other side of the City from Flag Fen, Ferry Meadows, the heart of NENE PARK (Enquiries - 01733 234443) provides unrivalled opportunities for leisure activities - and golf! ORTON MEADOWS GOLF COURSE (Enquiries 01733 237478) - I'll bet you are grabbing for your mobile already -has an 18 hole 'pay and play' course, as does THORPE WOOD GOLF COURSE (Enquiries - 01733 267701), plus pitch and putt facilities, and they bring to an end the terrible sense of depression that's been grumbling away for two whole chapters or more. We are not talking championship standards here, but the setting is delightful and if your card is not quite as you would like it at the end of the game, the rest of the Park makes a very pleasant place in which to relax and recover.

The Nene Park Trust have done an excellent job at this location for those of us for whom 'relaxation' has all but become a religion. In addition to the Meadows - and the golf - there are lakes and woods for pleasant walks, coarse fishing and bird watching. If you need to be more active to unwind, the WATERSPORTS CENTRE has dinghy and board sailing available. Others of us with a leaning towards sophistication (!) can opt out of all of it, head for one of the cafes and just sit back and think of England while we enjoy the scenery and watch the people, yet again. Admission to the Park as a whole is free, but there is a charge for parking at weekends and Bank Holidays, from Easter to October. Given the scope of the place, it's also worth noting that the facilities for the disabled include wheelchairs and batricars.

Whilst in Ferry Meadows, we may well have noticed a phenomenon that slammed nostalgia into top gear: a plume of smoke, a whistle-blast - in short, a steam train, no less! All of which directs us, unerringly, to our next visit: THE NENE VALLEY RAILWAY (Enquiries - 01780 780444). This preserved steam line has seven and a half miles of track and features locomotives from Europe in general, and the UK in particular. Its period style station at Wandford incorporates all the appropriate facilities, including a booking office, a shop, and a cafeteria. In fact, the 'static' part of the display can take up as much time as the actual travelling, as the Museum and the Exhibition Engine Shed are both worthy of serious attention from railway buffs. The active side has the piece de resistance, though: 'Driver Experience' is offered, as well as the more usual 'seat in a carriage' - all of which makes for a rather good little outing. The Railway runs throughout the year and operates at a range of different ticket prices. It is best to phone to check details and to consult the 'Talking Timetable' (01780 784440) before planning one's visit.

We're reaching the final stages of our Peterborough sojourn and I plan to go out on a high with a swift, but delightful, last touch of shopping. First there's the question of exercise to be considered. The golfers can ignore this bit as they're probably prostrate on the sun-lounger by now, knocking back a gin and wondering why they keep on pushing themselves so hard. Exercise. Residents and visitors to Peterborough can make use of an astonishing variety of sport and recreational activities at the five SPORTS CENTRES and SWIMMING POOLS within the city. Individual leaflets on all the services are obtainable from the City Council or a phone call to 01733 455532 could get things sorted.

As I say, looking through the range is exhausting enough in itself; *doing* some of them sounds virtually terminal. However, if jumping around violently helps your soul and psyche, this is the time for you, your true quality time. The list we have been staring at - transfixed with horror at what some people put themselves through - starts with football and ends up with weight training. On the way it includes martial arts, hockey, badminton, netball, cricket, tennis, squash, trampolining, aerobics, table tennis, jogging and .... see what I mean? Tucked in there somewhere was one that really spoke to me: 'soft play'! Now, that could hold promise. It certainly sounds a lot less sweaty, red-faced and violent then most, whatever it is. Or you could follow me down to the Regional Pool (Enquiries 01733 551474) for a really energetic sauna and Turkish Steam bath in a luxurious health suite after a very brief dip in the pool! Don't all rush at once.

Fancy some shopping? Just to end the day and fill up the last couple of cubic feet in the boot. CATHEDRAL SQUARE is a really attractive environment for the only kind of shopping that seems to me to be remotely enjoyable. As one wanders around one catches sight of the Cathedral itself, from time to time, and the old GUILDHALL and almshouses are also eye-catching. Its all so very human - as opposed to 'corporate', you know? Small shops, instant accord with shop staff and a variety of wares, produce, curios and 'must haves' within a dozen doorways. What more could we want?

A good curtain call for a full day, I hope you'll agree - as you'll also agree that it's time we weren't here. We're half a county away from where we need to be by the time dinner is served and we don't want to miss the odd cocktail (lager, alcohol free liebfraumilch, prune juice or whatever sparks up your palate) before hand.

At this point in a more romantic publication than our guidebook could ever hope to be, the leader would jump up, scream "To horse! To horse!" and everyone would thunder off in the general direction of the nearest horizon. Such is the nature of progress (?) that our version is something to do with 'clunk-click', turn the key and engage cruise control, while we die of boredom. Never mind, the horizon is where we need to be right now, so lets do it. The end must justify the means, on this occasion.

Because we are in East Anglia, where nothing is quite as it seems, (and because of my personal peculiarities as a guide-book author) we're going to rush back to Ely for dinner by starting off in the opposite direction. The man *is* nuts, of course. Seriously, we can't come this far and miss out on PEAKIRK WATERFOWL GARDENS (Enquiries 01733 252271) which are to be found off the A15, seven miles north of the City. From there, we'll career away west and then south to do a bit of a sweep of the Cambridgeshire border country as a purely scenic experience and then we'll head for home in a thoroughly meaningful fashion.

So: Peakirk. Its billed as an "all round attraction for all the family", and that is exactly what it is. Cynics might sneer and say it's 'virtual ornithology', nothing to do with the real thing, but I'd definitely argue the point. Where is it written in stone that a thing can't be done properly unless you suffer while you're doing it? Or is that notion just peculiar to Northern European Protestantism? Come on: the whole point of bird watching should be to watch birds, not to get some kind of perverse pleasure from watching your fingers turn blue while you trousers saturate themselves from too long an immersion in a ditch and the first traces of gangrene appear in limbs kept immobile for hours. In short, Peakirk is mainly about the pleasures of ornithology - if you are into the miseries of it all you had better go somewhere else.

The site's twenty acres of woodland, water, grassy glades and formal gardens are 'home' to ducks, geese, swans and flamingoes as well as many other species, adding up to a total of 137, from every continent. Nature walks and trails circle the grounds, taking visitors to points of observation amongst the lakes and ponds. Picnic areas and a cafe have been provided, along with a very useful visitors centre. Admission details require a phone call, but in general terms the gardens are open daily between 9.30am and 5.30pm (or an hour before dusk in winter). Christmas Eve, and Christmas Day are the only days they're closed.

Rubbing down the wellies again, I think we can truly claim to be going home, even if it doesn't look like it. We turn left along the B1443, making a mental note to add TOLETHORPE HALL to our list of 'next-times', for a touch of Summer Shakespeare, then swoop round, as I mentioned, along a curve of minor roads towards the A1, where we've been more than once before, I seem to recall. On our way we notice more typical villages, including **BARNACK**, home of the Cathedral's stone, and **HELPSTON**, home of the poet, John Clare.

No time for any more of it, though: we're tired and hungry and still have two more calls to make. 'Onward ever onward' seems to work, as usual, and we find ourselves at the SACREWELL FARM AND COUNTRY CENTRE (Enquiries 01780 782254) at **THORNHAUGH** a jolly sight more quickly than we had any right to expect. Surrounding the working water mill, here, there are more attractions to delight us, even at this stage of the day. There's the farm, of course, but it has been combined with a bygones collection, a range of gardens and Nature and general interest trails. To complete the pleasure of even a brief visit, we'll find a gift shop and the Miller's Kitchen, where light refreshments are available. The centre is open around the year between 9.30am and 5.30pm, and it will cost us £3.00 to sample it all.

RIVER NENE, WANSFORD

To make a short break from the thundering main road we'll dog-leg off to the right at **WANSFORD** where pretty, traditional cottages nestle by the river, and trot down the B671 and along the A605 to the right for a breather - and a *short* breather - until we reach the nearby A1 which takes us quickly enough to **STILTON**, our next (and last) stopping off point for the day. Again, it's all rather strange. Situated at the edge of the Fens, this village can boast of what may well be the second best known name in the region after Cambridge. So? So it's well known because of *the* cheese. The cheese that's never actually been made there! That kind of strange! Nothing daunted, every May the villagers ruin wagon-loads of the delicacy by rolling it around in the street, as I mentioned in the introduction. I suppose psychologists would see that as a natural reaction to years of suppressed misapprehension - me, I just find it very, very odd. Unless I'm the one that's odd for preferring to find my stilton on a plate with some crackers , beside a glass of vintage port rather than ground into the dust at the wayside at the end of a day's frivolity.

The reason for the confusion is not that hard to find, if you have a nose for that kind of thing. Back in the impenetrable darkness of 17th century England, the Bell Inn at Stilton was a major staging post beside what was then the Great North Road. Leicestershire farmers used to take their produce there for collection and onward transmission to the flesh pots of London - and you can imagine how the rest of it went. To the average Londoner of those days, there was nowhere north of Barnet. The fact that cheese came down the Great North Road from time to time was all a bit mysterious - too mysterious to warrant further investigation. It had to have a name, and as 'Stilton' (where it had been picked up - fact) was easier to pronounce that 'Leicestershire' (where it was said to have been made - rumour) the choice was obvious, and to hell with veracity! And the next? I just wish they'd stop rolling the wonderful stuff around so much.

I think the vision of all that horrible waste just tipped the balance. I think I've had enough for today, I'm sure you the reader will be looking forward to a rest, my base is in Ely. Should you prefer to stay in Peterborough, like Cambridge there are many hotels of every description to suit whatever taste or pocket, the Newark Hotel in Eastfield Road is very pleasant and economical, the staff are most helpful and the food enjoyable.

The route to Ely is easy enough, you'll be pleased to know - although it does touch on familiar ground from time to time. In a nutshell, it's left along the B660 south of Stilton; the B1040 from Ramsey St Mary's to Pidney; bear left past Somersham to Earith; A1123 to Stretham (very familiar) and the A10, then north into the city.

THE BLACK HORSE
1 Sandhill Road,
Littleport,
Ely,
Cambridgeshire
CB6 1NL

Tel: 01353 860328

The Black Horse is a freehouse enjoying a great reputation amongst local people and attracting visitors from much further afield. You will find it on the Junction of the A10 with the A1101 adjacent to Sandhill Bridge on the banks of the Great Ouse. Ducks and Grepe frequent the large garden which has its own moorings and children's play area with its own attendant. There are some delightful walks from the pub to the Littleport Boat Yards where boats can be hired by the hour or the day. Or even from the pub direct. Statham Steam Engine Museum is within easy reach. Two annual fetes are well worth visiting. Littleport has its in July and Mildenhall Air Fete is in May. One can visit The Welney Wildfowl Centre, home of the Golden Oriole, seek out all the beauty of Ely Cathedral or spend time in Littleport itself which stems from 673AD.

Bob and Christine Meadows are the welcoming hosts; two people who have years of experience behind them and who thoroughly enjoy meeting people and making them feel at home. It is a busy place where the Public Bar is much like a club, its members being local regulars. The attractive thirty cover restaurant, most evenings, serves a wide range of delicious food with an Italian influence, cooked by an imaginative chef who also produces a range of food for the bar every day. It is great value for money. What is so nice about the restaurant is its intimacy and the feeling of well-being engendered by nice tablecloths, fresh flowers and linen napkins. Just the atmosphere in which to enjoy a delicious meal. Occasionally there is live entertainment - Bob was part of the entertainment world for many years. This is a thoroughly nice pub to visit in an area rich with history. The Lady of the house is ex-public relations, so you will appreciate the expertise between this couple, we wish them every success.

USEFUL INFORMATION

OPEN: Mon-Sat 12-11pm
Sun: 12-3pm & 7-10pm
CHILDREN: Welcome. Play area
CREDIT CARDS: All major cards
LICENSED: Full On
GARDEN: Large. Attended play area.
Moorings.

RESTAURANT: Delicious food with an
Italian influence
BAR FOOD: Wide range. Great value
VEGETARIAN: Always a choice
WHEELCHAIR ACCESS: Yes
PETS:Public bar only
 or Garden on lead

THE LAMB AND FLAG INN
Main Street,
Welney,
NR Wisbech,
Cambridgeshire
PE14 9RB
ETB 2 Crowns Recommended

Tel: 01354 610242 Fax: 01354 610469
CHRISTINEWILD@COMPUSERVE.COM

On the very edge of the Norfolk/Cambridgeshire border, some eight miles from the historic town of Ely and close to Downham Market, The Boston Creeper covered, 16th century Lamb and Flag Inn is pleasantly situated in the small village of Welney, adjacent to the world famous Welney Wildfowl Trust and well known for its fishing and bird watching. It is surrounded by miles of excellent angling waters and in the heart of very rich farming land.

Visitors coming here for the first time are thrilled with the atmosphere within the inn which was originally a coaching house and where today there are still low, beamed ceilings in the bars and dining room. It is a pub much loved by local people who come here to enjoy the well kept ale and the food. They are a friendly, cheerful lot who make visitors feel welcome. The Lounge Bar is particularly attractive and in the winter has a roaring log fire making it very cosy. In the oak beamed, non-smoking, dining room, which is frequently used for private parties, there is a very good a la carte menu which Gary Wild, the proprietor helped by his kitchen staff, produces using fish and meat bought locally, and never frozen. There are always great stews and casseroles, pies and curries, various lasagnes and bakes and usually at least six fresh fish dishes available and four types of steak. The Bar Food is equally delicious and can be anything from a simple, freshly cut sandwich to a tempting stew. Vegetarian dishes are available and cooked to order. Sunday lunch is one of the most popular meals of the week and children eat free!

The Lamb and Flag has five bedrooms, all recently decorated in a cottage style, with washbasins and new furniture, television and a hostess tray. Breakfast every morning is a hearty meal, in keeping with the high standard of the rest of the food one enjoys in the Inn. People come here to stay frequently on business as well as pleasure and they all find the cheerful, happy atmosphere of The Lamb and Flag refreshing.

USEFUL INFORMATION

OPEN: 12-3pm & 6-11pm
CHILDREN: Welcome
CREDIT CARDS: All major cards
LICENSED: Full On
ACCOMMODATION: 5 rooms
RATES: Sgl £24.50 Dbl. £34.50

DINING ROOM: Home-cooked fare
BAR FOOD: Wide choice
VEGETARIAN: To order
WHEELCHAIR ACCESS: Yes
GARDEN: Yes. Beer Garden
PETS: Yes

NEWARK HOTEL
239-241 Eastfield Road,
Peterborough
PE1 4BH

Tel: 01733 569811
Fax: 01733 312550

This comfortable hotel is within fifteen minutes walk of the city centre and is a popular venue for visitors coming to Peterborough either on business or pleasure. If one had to describe Peterborough one would say it was a city with two faces. Much business is done here and at the same time more and more people are discovering it makes an ideal touring base for Cambridge and East Anglia. It caters for all interests whether they are sporting or directed towards historical places.

Newark Hotel is a commercial town hotel caring for business people working in the city or coming for meetings. At the same time it still retains the friendly family atmosphere and opens its welcoming doors to many visitors from all over the world. If you asked those who have stayed here previously they would tell you that the main virtue of the Newark is its welcome, its comfort, its informal relaxed air and by no means least its good food. Conference facilities are available and they receive the same attention to detail that the owners, Paul and Viv Weatherhead give to the running of every department in the hotel.

The Restaurant is open in the evening although Business Lunches can be arranged. There is a three course Table d'hôte Menu with several choices and an A La Carte Menu which encompasses six starters followed by main courses which might be Duck a la Orange, Veal Dijonaise, Grilled Dover Sole or succulent grilled steaks cooked to your requirement with or without Sauces. There are always several vegetarian dishes and if you have room, the Sweet Trolley or Cheese Board are always tempting. The wine list is well chosen and the price is right! The Newark Hotel has nineteen rooms en-suite and fourteen not en-suite. Attractively and comfortably furnished each room has television, video and a hostess tray. Having stayed at this hotel I can fully recommend the friendliness of the staff.

USEFUL INFORMATION

OPEN: All year

RESTAURANT: A La Carte & Table d'hôte

CHILDREN: Welcome

CREDIT CARDS: All major cards

BAR FOOD: No

LICENSED: Full On

VEGETARIAN: Always a choice

ACCOMMODATION: 19 en-suite 14 not

WHEELCHAIR ACCESS: Yes

RATES: From £25pp.pn Children £5

GARDEN: Yes

PETS: Yes

BENNETTS RESTAURANT & THE WHITE HART
Bythorn,
Huntingdon
Cambridgeshire
PE18 0QN

Tel: 01832 710226

This is a pub which in the 1990's has been skilfully refurbished by the larger than life character, proprietor Bill Bennett: an excellent publican and also, a first class chef. The White Hart, originally built in 1736, is timber-framed in keeping with buildings of the time, and filled with whattle and daub. Most of the old beams have been exposed to add character to the public area. The pub is charming and has almost the feel of a country house with comfortable cane furniture in the large public bar area. Bennett's Restaurant, although part of the building, has an identity of its own. You enter it directly from the ample car park and find yourself in a comfortable lounge where you can enjoy a drink whilst studying the menu.

Bennett's unlike most establishments, provides a four-course dinner for an all in price both at dinner and lunch. It is marvellous value with a choice of six starters, soup, half a dozen main courses and a selection of sweets. The food is excellent, the menu changes regularly, and it is accompanied by a well chosen wine list with bottles from around the world.

There is a nice story told about the White Hart. Two highwaymen robbed a coach in Kettering and stopped at the pub to spend some of their ill-gotten gains. They were arrested whilst in the bar but by then they had hidden their catch somewhere on the premises. To this day it has not been found. All ideas to its whereabouts please contact Bill Bennett!

USEFUL INFORMATION

Open: 10-3PM & 6-midnight
Closed Sun p.m. & All day Monday
CHILDREN: Welcome
CREDIT CARDS: All major cards
LICENSED: Free House. Full On
GARDEN: Patio with seats and tables.

RESTAURANT: Traditional. First class
cuisine. Old fashioned values.
BAR FOOD: Available from £3.95
VEGETARIAN: Yes, always a choice
WHEELCHAIR ACCESS: Yes
PETS: Not in Restaurant

THE BLACK HORSE INN
2 Fotheringay Road,
Nassinton,
Cambridgeshire
PE20 1SK

Tel: 01780 782324

This Listed 15th century coaching inn is a must for anyone's visiting list. Full of atmosphere, warm and welcoming, low ceilings, beams, a historical fireplace from the 16th century said to be from Fotheringay Castle where Mary, Queen of Scots spent her last days, you would be hard pressed to find anything more delightful in the area. The village of Nassington itself is beautiful with lots of walks round and about, the river not far off. The food is excellent and cooked to perfection from a menu which includes warm chicken and bacon salad, steaks with special sauces, a simple Spaghetti Bolognese and a super Smoked Salmon Salad. The sweets are delectable, all home-made with a rich moist chocolate cake and double chocolate sauce, high on the list of favourites. Theme evenings are very popular here and can be anything from Spanish to Thai to old English. The pretty garden beckons customers in the summer months both to eat and drink. The beer is well kept, the food is good, the wines come from around the world, the service is friendly, and the price is right - what more can one want.

USEFUL INFORMATION

OPEN: 12-11pm	RESTAURANT: English & Continental
CHILDREN: Welcome	BAR FOOD: Wide menu
CREDIT CARDS: All major cards	VEGETARIAN: To order
LICENSED: Full On	WHEELCHAIR ACCESS: Yes
GARDEN: Yes	PETS: Garden only

BLACKSMITHS ARMS
Elm High Road,
Elm,
Wisbech,
Cambridgeshire
PE14 0DH

CAMRA Good Beer Guide

Tel: 01945 466422

The friendly, welcoming Blacksmiths Arms on the edge of the village of Elm to the south of Wisbech, has a host of stories to tell. It is an old pub but for some years was closed and reopened in 1995 in the capable hands of Joan and Colin Hill. To start with if you are in the garden you are in Elm, Cambridgeshire and when you are in the pub you are in Emneth, West Norfolk! The garden is part of the old Wisbech Canal which forms the county boundary but is now filled in. The Wisbech-Outwell Tramway,(the inspiration for the late Rev Audrey's 'Thomas Tank Engine' stories) used to cross the road immediately in front of the pub and locals will tell you of days, when following an accident, the original bar was used as a temporary mortuary! And that is only one of the stories.

Comfortably and attractively furnished with a well-stocked bar, it is no wonder the pub is popular. You will be well fed here on good pub fare and regaled not only with well kept ale but stories to boot! Robert Crofts the village blacksmith was the original licensee in the 1800's and it adjoined the blacksmiths shop. That has gone but the building of the adjacent carpenters shop is still owned by a member of the family. Robert's wife, Caroline was the blacksmith's 'Striker' and she was such a large lady that all the pub doors had to be widened to allow her access. The stories go on forever - definitely a pub to enjoy.

USEFUL INFORMATION

OPEN: Normal pub hours
CHILDREN: If well behaved
CREDIT CARDS: Visa/Master/Delta
LICENSED: Full On
PETS: Garden only

RESTAURANT: A la Carte evenings
BAR FOOD: Good pub fare lunch-times
VEGETARIAN: On request
GARDEN: Yes
WHEELCHAIR ACCESS: Yes

BOYALL'S HOTEL
19-24 Norfolk Street
Wisbech,
Cambridgeshire
PE13 2LF

Tel: 01945 474677
Fax: 01945 585590

This comfortable, modern hotel, established in 1936 is just five minutes walk from the centre of Wisbech, close to the A1101 Wisbech-Downham Market Road. Christopher Boyall, the owner, has furnished the hotel throughout with period pieces and a restful, attractive decor. It is a popular and busy establishment with a restaurant that has one hundred covers. The A la Carte English menu covers a wide range of food and has an excellent Carvery which is brought to your table. The eight fresh fish dishes are prepared daily with or without sauces. Bar Food is also available and can be anything from a sandwich to a full-blown meal. Sunday Lunch is one of the most popular meals of the week with roast sirloin of beef and Yorkshire pudding, roast leg of lamb or roast chicken, all served with fresh Fenland vegetables and roast potatoes. The nine bedrooms are all en-suite, individually furnished and decorated. In one there is a four poster and one room has a cot. All the rooms have direct dial telephones, television, trouser presses and hostess trays. Conference Facilities are available. Boyall's has a name for comfort, good service, good food and it lives up to that reputation.

USEFUL INFORMATION

OPEN: 11-3pm & 5-11pm
CHILDREN: Welcome
CREDIT CARDS: All major cards
LICENSED: Full On
ACCOMMODATION: 9 en-suite rooms
RATES: From: sgl £40 tw/dbl. £60
Suite £70 2 night minimum stay from £40pp

RESTAURANT: Good English Fare
with Carvery
BAR FOOD: A wide choice
VEGETARIAN: Always a choice
WHEELCHAIR ACCESS: Yes
GARDEN: No. Balcony
PETS: Yes

THE DAIRY FARM
Cranford,
Kettering
Northamptonshire
NN14 4AQ

Tel:01536 330273

The Dairy Farm is a thatched, early 17th century manor house in a very pretty village. It is surrounded by a disused Norman church, fine Georgian mansions, a medieval dovecote and lush meadows where sheep graze peacefully. Part of the farms three hundred and fifty acres surround it. It is the home of Audrey and John Clarke and they have created a delightful atmosphere into which they welcome guests. The sitting room is comfortably furnished and the dining room has an antique dresser and some fascinating ceremonial swords and muskets. The bedrooms are furnished with a happy mix of Victorian and more modern pieces, in one room there is a large four-poster. All the rooms have private facilities although from one room one has to walk down the corridor to the bathroom. Every room has television and a hairdryer. Breakfast is a true farmhouse affair, delicious and substantial. Audrey prepares traditional three-course dinners on request although there is a pub a couple of hundred yards down the road which serves good food. Children are very welcome and Audrey will happily baby-sit as well as provide early suppers.

USEFUL INFORMATION

OPEN: All year except Dec25-Jan1 inc.
CHILDREN: Welcome.
Early suppers baby listening.
VEGETARIAN: Upon request
LICENSED: No
ACCOMMODATION: 1tw.1dbl. 1 4poster
RATES: Sgl from £25 dbl. £45

DINING ROOM: Delicious
Breakfast. Dinner optional
CREDIT CARDS: None accepted
WHEELCHAIR ACCESS: Yes
GARDEN: Yes. Croquet
PETS: By arrangement
NO SMOKING

DALWHINNIE LODGE HOTEL
31-33 Burghley Road,
Peterborough PE1 2QA

Three Crowns Commended
RAC Highly Acclaimed

Tel: 01733 565968
Fax: 01733 890838

This City Centre Hotel is sufficiently small to offer a personal service to its clients and is run with pride by polite, well trained staff offering individual attention, where the accent is on comfort and cleanliness. It is well located within the city centre of Peterborough with train and bus stations being a five to ten minute walk. Peterborough with its historic cathedral and splendid Queensgate shopping centre is a pleasant place to be in its own right. A short drive will take you to a choice of four eighteen hole golf courses, Ferry Meadows Leisure Park and Nene Valley railway. It is a hotel which is popular with both business people and tourists. Every centrally heated bedroom has en-suite or private facilities, direct dial telephone, TV with movie channel, clock radio and complimentary tea and coffee. The Honeymoon Suite has a four-poster bed. In the friendly restaurant a comprehensive selection of dishes and a seasonal change of menu is available. The good traditional English Breakfast is designed for those with good appetites! Adjacent to Dalwhinnie Lodge is Burghley Guest House, in the same ownership, probably the best of its kind in Peterborough for price, location and comfort. Guests have full use of hotel amenities.

USEFUL INFORMATION

OPEN: All year	RESTAURANT: Comprehensive menu
CHILDREN: Welcome	VEGETARIAN: Catered for
CREDIT CARDS: All major cards	WHEELCHAIR ACCESS: limited
LICENSED: Yes	GARDEN: No
ACCOMMODATION: En-suite rooms	PETS: No

RATES: Dalwhinnie sgl from £34 dbl./tw £24.67 pp B&B
Burghley Guest House: sgl from £18.50 tw/dbl. £18pp B&B

HAMBLETON HALL
Hambleton,
Oakham
Rutland
LE15 8TH

County Hotel of the Year

Tel: 01572 756991
Fax: 01572 724721

Standing on a peninsula poking into Rutland Water, Hambleton Hall's position is magical. Surrounded by mature cedars the great Victorian house is one of the finest of Britain's top-flight country-house hotels. The owners Stefa and Tim Hart have achieved an intimate feeling throughout and furnished it with style, an eye for colour and a sense of the dramatic. The whole is totally pleasing and relaxed. Fires roar within exquisite marble fireplaces in winter, there are superb flower displays everywhere. Guests are looked after with the greatest care by an efficient, unobtrusive staff. The highly individual bedrooms, all have ensue facilities. Qazvin, for example, has hand-painted, seventeenth-century Persian panels, there are expensively stencilled walls. Whether you stay in the most expensive room or something less exotic you will still find features such as grand half-tester beds and slick bathrooms. Hambleton Hall is famous for its food. The chef is inspired and is known for his elaborate seasonal creations as well as his cuisine on a set three-course, no choice menu, which is excellent value and will not break the bank.

USEFUL INFORMATION

OPEN: All year
CHILDREN: Over 10 years
CREDIT CARDS: All major cards
LICENSED: Yes. Fine wines
ACCOMMODATION: En suite rooms
with 4 posters and half-testers
RATES: Sgl from £145 Dbl./Tw from £195 PRPN B&B

DINING ROOM: Inspired menu
VEGETARIAN: Always a choice
WHEELCHAIR ACCESS: Yes
GARDEN: Beautiful grounds

PETS: Yes

THE GORDON ARMS
527 Oundle Road,
Peterborough,
Cambridgeshire
PE2 0DH

Tel: 01733 231374

Two miles from the City centre, this lively hostelry with a good restaurant, is situated off Junction A1 close to the Ferry Meadow Nature Reserve, a good golf course, a caravan park, the East of England Showground and not far from Peterborough Cathedral and the Nene Valley Railway Steam Trains. Built in the early 1800's by Orton Hall, one mile down the road, the structure was moved to its present site, lock, stock and barrel by the tenth Marquis of Huntley. It is a friendly welcoming place where families can enjoy eating in the informal family dining room and the children can be let loose in the Children's Funky Forest Play Room. Business people eat here regularly appreciative of the good food and the fast service. The Gordon Arms really is somewhere for all ages. The menu includes All Day Breakfasts, succulent rump steaks cooked as you like them, vast Mixed Grills, Lasagne, Scampi and Red Thai Curry and much more.

USEFUL INFORMATION

OPEN: All year 11am-11pm	RESTAURANT: Steaks, Fish, Curries
CHILDREN: Welcome	BAR FOOD: Light or full meals
CREDIT CARDS: All major cards	VEGETARIAN: Always a choice
LICENSED: Full On	WHEELCHAIR ACCESS: Yes
GARDEN: Yes. Beer Garden	PETS: No

LAKE ISLE
16 High Street East,
Uppingham,
Rutland
LE15 9PZ

Tel/Fax: 01572 822951

Lake Isle was once a barber's shop; something impossible to contemplate now when you enter the doors of this charming, sophisticated yet relaxed restaurant. Claire and David Whitfield are the owners and they gave the restaurant its name because of their love for the poetry of Yeats from which the name is taken. Although Lake Isle has 12 pretty bedrooms, all en-suite, the emphasis is on the restaurant where serious, predominantly French cuisine is served. It has an unpretentious background with panelled walls, bare tables, a pine dresser and a fine collection of scales. You dine on three to five course dinners. The menu is exciting. David is the chef and he is adventurous. You might start on quail's eggs wrapped in smoked salmon served with a sundried-tomato hollandaise, followed by loin of venison served with apple rosti in a damson and juniper sauce. You will find Lake Isle much bigger than it looks from the high street, much of it is concealed in a Georgian extension and in cottages converted into suites. The bedrooms are stylishly feminine and have nice touches for your comfort like a bowl of fruit, sherry and home-made biscuits. as well as television, hairdryers and direct dial telephones. Smoking discouraged in public rooms.

USEFUL INFORMATION

OPEN: All year. Rest closed Monday.
CHILDREN: Yes
CREDIT CARDS: All major cards
LICENSED: Yes
ACCOMMODATION: 12 en-suite rooms
RATES: Sgl from £45 Dbl. £60 Family £75
Special breaks available - Conference facilities

RESTAURANT: French cuisine at its best
VEGETARIAN: Always a choice
WHEELCHAIR ACCESS: No
GARDEN: Yes
PETS: No

LOCH FYNE SEAFOOD
RESTAURANT AND SHOP
The Old Dairy,
Elton,
NR. Peterborough,
Cambridgeshire
PE8 6SH

Tel: 01832 280298
Fax: 01832 280170

Renowned for the excellence of its oysters and seafood both in the restaurant and the shop, there is a happy relaxed atmosphere in the Old Dairy, with its simple furnishings, attractive decor and friendly, helpful staff. There are several branches of Loch Fyne Oyster Bars, each with a very high standard. This one is to be found in Elton village just three miles west of the A1 Peterborough/Northampton interchange on the Oundle/Northampton road (A605) and is just 10 miles from city centre Peterborough. Fresh produce is delivered to each Oyster Bar over night and the secret of success is to serve the freshest raw materials in a simple manner. Fresh oysters on the half shell have all the zest of the Loch but they are equally enjoyed cooked in various ways. The lobster, langoustine and crab platters are spectacular. The variety of salmon coming from the company's own Smokehouse is widely popular particularly Bradan Rost - salmon smoked in a hot kiln. The wine list has been carefully chosen to go well with seafood and favours smaller growers who follow traditional organic methods of viticulture using no artificial fertilisers or pesticides. Notable among these is Leon Boullault from Nantes whose Gros Plant under the Loch Fyne label is fresh, crisp and dry with a clean, grape flavour - ideal with oysters.

USEFUL INFORMATION

OPEN: Mon-Sun 9am-9pm
CHILDREN: Welcome
CREDIT CARDS: All major cards
WHEELCHAIR ACCESS: Yes
PETS: In courtyard area only

RESTAURANT: Seafood specialists.
SHOP: Selling all types of shell fish etc.
LICENSED: Yes
VEGETARIAN: 2 dishes

PETERBOROUGH MOAT HOUSE
Thorpe Wood,
Peterborough,
Cambridgeshire
PE3 6SG

Tel:01733 289988
Fax: 01733 262737

As with all the Moat Houses, Peterborough Moat House is outstanding in its comfort and care of its guests. Standing in five hundred acres of parkland with an adjacent eighteen hole golf course, Peterborough Moat House is well appointed throughout with one hundred and twenty five en-suite bedrooms, all equipped and furnished to very high standard including direct dial telephone, television, mini-bars and hostess tray. From the moment you arrive you will be welcomed by a friendly, efficient staff who worked hard, throughout the hotel to see that your every need is met. Whether you choose to eat in the elegant restaurant where the menu is International and prepared by talented chefs, or have a light snack in one of the two well-stocked bars, you will find the food delicious and imaginative. The hotel is a popular place for conferences and meetings and has excellent facilities with sixteen rooms designed for this purpose with a maximum capacity of four hundred. These rooms are ideal also for private dinners, wedding receptions and other occasions.

USEFUL INFORMATION

OPEN: All year
CHILDREN: Welcome
CREDIT CARDS: All major cards
LICENSED: Full On
ACCOMMODATION: 125 en-suite rooms
Conference facilities
RATES: Sgl from £38 - £90   Dbl. from £76 - £105
Further details Tel 01708 766677

RESTAURANT: International menu
BAR FOOD: Wide range
VEGETARIAN: Always a choice
WHEELCHAIR ACCESS: Yes
GARDEN: 500 Acres parkland
PETS: Yes

THE PLATE AND PORTER
210 Station Road,
March,
Cambridgeshire
PE15 8SQ

Tel/Fax: 660322

This unusually named restaurant stands adjacent to the station in March, a busy little market town which came to prominence this century because of the railway, before that it was the hamlet of Doddington on the archipelago in the fens which includes the Cathedral City of Ely. In spite of the station and the ensuing noise, the interior of The Plate and Porter is a haven of tranquillity, decorated in restful colours with tables attractively set with cream linen. There are two restaurants either side of the reception area with lounge and bar. One can sit here, sipping a drink whilst perusing the exciting and imaginative a la carte restaurant. The atmosphere is relaxed and friendly and the staff quietly attentive.

From a list of starters one might choose Thai style fish cakes on a bed of stir fried vegetables, with a red curry and coconut sauce or a stew of Wood mushrooms. The main courses offer everything from fresh fish cooked with or without sauces, succulent steaks, poultry, game in season and much more. There are Pasta dishes and salads. The home-made Sweets are irresistible from a Summer fruit pudding, a glazed Citrus tart with lemon, lime and orange served with lime sorbet to Dark Chocolate Mousse or a Trio of Chocolate Pots. The wine list is sensibly priced and well chosen with good house wines - one might be tempted to try a glass of sweet Muscat de Bemmes de Venise with a dessert. Sunday Lunch is traditional.

USEFUL INFORMATION

OPEN: Tues.-Sat evenings from 7pm
Sunday Lunch from 12 noon
CHILDREN: Yes
CREDIT CARDS: Master/Visa/Switch/Delta
LICENSED: Yes. Supper Licence

RESTAURANT: A la carte menu
imaginative cuisine
VEGETARIAN: Always a choice
WHEELCHAIR ACCESS: Yes
PETS: No

QUEENS GATE HOTEL
5 Fletton Avenue,
Peterborough,
Cambridgeshire
PE2 8AX

ETB ***

Tel: 01733 62572/53181
Fax: 01733 558982

The Queensgate Hotel is a welcoming, friendly place less than ten minutes walk from the centre of Peterborough - a city that combines historic interest with the commercial drive of one of Britain's fastest growing cities. The Queensgate Hotel offers the charm, comfort and personal service of a country hotel - but with the most modern facilities and superb furnishings in the heart of this thriving area - making it ideal for business visits or leisurely weekends and holidays. The en-suite bedrooms are all individually designed to a very high standard, every room has satellite television, tea and coffee making facilities and a well stocked mini-bar. And for sheer convenience the rooms are hard to match with a neatly housed iron, ironing board, trouser press and hair dryer.

A direct-dial telephone, fax point and radio alarm ensure that you can keep in touch with business or friends - as well as setting your own early morning call. The restaurant with its Oriental surroundings, has an imaginative a la carte menu and a fine table d'hôte. The reasonably priced wine list has been well selected. A Continental Breakfast can be served in your room, otherwise a Full English or Continental breakfast is served in the restaurant. There are excellent facilities for conference and meeting rooms, ideal for the smaller wedding party.

USEFUL INFORMATION

OPEN: All year
CHILDREN: Welcome
CREDIT CARDS: All major cards
LICENSED: Full On
ACCOMMODATION: En-suite rooms
RATES: Sgl£59.50 Dbl. £69.50 Tw £75 B&B
Special weekend rates

RESTAURANT: Imaginative a la carte and table d'hôte
VEGETARIAN: Catered for
WHEELCHAIR ACCESS: Yes
GARDEN: No
PETS: No

RAM JAM INN
Great North Road,
Stretton,
Oakham,
Rutland
LE15 7QX

Tel: 01780 410776
Fax: 01780 410361

The Ram Jam Inn owes its name from a brew concocted by an 18th century landlord but that is its only resemblance to a true inn. You should come here if only for the experience. It is the epitome of all that is good in the field of highway motels and fast food establishment. Its owner runs the efficient and top notch Hambleton Hall nearby and the standards from there have been incorporated into the Ram Jam Inn, if in a totally different way. The focal point of the Inn is the open-plan, quarry-tiled dining area.

You can see the hard and fast working chefs producing the food in the exposed kitchen and bustling, efficient waiters ensuring that the dishes appear in next to no time. The food is simple but creative and can include such offerings as carrot and sweet-potato soup, spicy lamb, grilled salmon and local sausages and mash. There is a children's menu, home-made ice creams and a scrumptious cream tea. Breakfast is available to residents and non-residents. Although the inn stands right by the A1, all but one of the bedrooms are totally peaceful, looking out over an orchard. They are furnished in a bright, modern style and have spacious bathrooms. The price is right!

USEFUL INFORMATION

OPEN: All year
CHILDREN: Yes. Special menu
CREDIT CARDS: All major cards
LICENSED: Full On
ACCOMMODATION: Spacious en suite bedrooms

RESTAURANT: Creative fare
VEGETARIAN: Always a choice
WHEELCHAIR ACCESS: Yes
GARDEN: Yes
PETS: By arrangement

THE BELL INN,
Stilton, Peterborough,
Cambridgeshire PE7 3RA
Tourist Board Highly Commended
RAC***AA + Rosette

Tel: 01733 241066
Fax: 01733 245173

This historical inn which has stories to tell of a famous cheese, a highwayman and a famous horseman, is set in the quiet, but easily accessible village of Stilton, just off the A1 and close to Peterborough. Mine host, Liam McGivern has high standards and his great wish is to make The Bell Inn justify Samuel Johnson's sentiment 'There is nothing which has yet been contrived by man, by which so much happiness is produced by a good tavern or inn'. That he has achieved his wish is evident by the thriving, welcoming atmosphere of The Bell which stems from Liam and his efficient, friendly staff. There is a village bar, a residents bar and the award winning Galleried Restaurant where James Trevor and his Brigade of Chefs take full advantage of The Fen countryside and only use the very best of the local suppliers to achieve the highest standard of freshness and quality possible. There are nineteen ensue rooms, Deluxe and Four Posters retaining the olde worlde charm but with the modern requirements of direct dial telephone, television, video and a hostess tray. An excellent hotel recommended by all whom stay there.

USEFUL INFORMATION

OPEN: 12-2.30pm & 6-11pm
CHILDREN: Welcome menu
CREDIT CARDS: All major cards
LICENSED: Full On
ACCOMMODATION: 19 en suite rooms
RATES: Sgl from £45 Dbl. £59 weekends
Sgl £64. Dbl. £79 weekdays

RESTAURANT: Excellent Table d'hôte

BAR FOOD: Quality food. Value for money
VEGETARIAN: Wide range
WHEELCHAIR ACCESS: Yes
PETS: No
GARDEN: Yes

THE HAYCOCK HOTEL
Wansford-in-England
Peterborough, Cambs PE8 6JA
AA***RAC 4 Crowns 1 AA Rosette
Tel: 01789 782223
Fax: 01780 783508

Set in five acres of garden and parkland, on the banks of the River Nene and in the pretty village of Wansford, is The Haycock Hotel, a 16th century coaching inn which has a remarkable and eventful past. Mary, Queen of Scots and the young Queen Victoria were both visitors. More dramatically it is said that the Hotel once changed hands over a game of cards! Today it retains its character and charm, is friendly and welcoming and an ideal place for anyone to stay whether on business or pleasure. For the energetic, it is good walking countryside, you can go horse riding, fish, try your hand at clay pigeon shooting or play cricket. The magnificent Burghley House is nearby and so too is Peterborough Cathedral and the majestic man-made Rutland Water. Within the Hotel which is charmingly and comfortably furnished, there are fifty individually decorated rooms in a cottage style with pretty fabrics. Every room has direct dial telephone, satellite television and a hostess tray. With a great reputation for the standard and quality of its food, The Haycock offers an a la carte menu with many choices in the restaurant and an equally attractive menu in Orchards Brasserie. Petangue can be played in the garden.

USEFUL INFORMATION

OPEN: All year
CHILDREN: Welcome
CREDIT CARDS: All major cards
LICENSED: Yes
ACCOMMODATION: 50 en-suite rooms floor rooms
RATES: Room only sgl £85 dbl. £120
Time Away Breaks DB&B £139 pp for
2nights, 2 people sharing

RESTAURANT: Excellent a la carte menu
ORCHARDS BRASSERIE: Wide choice
VEGETARIAN: Always a choice
WHEELCHAIR ACCESS: Yes. Ground

GARDEN: 5 acres Petanque
PETS: Yes

THE KING OF HEARTS
1, School Road
West Walton
Wisbech
Cambridgeshire
PE14 7ES

Tel/Fax: 01945 584785

Two centuries ago church records show that the choir of the old church used The King of Hearts for refreshments after choir practice, today the inn is still dispensing hospitality to an appreciative clientele. The King of Hearts is the only pub and restaurant in the small village of West Walton, on the borders of Cambridgeshire and Norfolk. Entering the pub through the main entrance from the car park brings you into the servery. There is a carvery which has two choices of meats and all accompanying vegetables, which is open on Saturday evening and Sunday lunch-time and Sunday evenings. During the week from Monday to Friday the carfare becomes a hot, self service buffet with traditional food and then from June to August it changes to a cold buffet. There is an excellent salad bar and some delectable desserts. John and Helen Lusher are mine hosts with John the inspirational main chef. There are two dining rooms, one of which is non-smoking and children are welcome. The other seats twenty two and here customers may smoke but children are not allowed. A beautiful, raised, semi circular garden with seating is a popular haunt in the warm weather.

USEFUL INFORMATION

OPEN: 11.30-2.30pm & 7-11pm
CHILDREN: To eat but not in bar
CREDIT CARDS: All major cards
LICENSED: Full On
GARDEN: Delightful, raised, semi circular

DINING ROOM: 2 rooms, one non-
smoking. Carvery. Buffet
BAR FOOD: Traditional. Good value
VEGETARIAN: Always a choice
PETS: In garden only

SWALLOW HOTEL
Lynch Wood, Alwalton,
Peterborough PE2 6GB
Tel: 01733 371 111   Fax: 01733 236 725
Info@swallowhotels,com
Central Reservations 0645 404404
Fax: 0191 415 1777

This hotel is a perfect base for discovering a host of gorgeous villages and lovely open countryside. The Swallow is just a ten minute drive from the town centre of Peterborough, which has a great Norman Cathedral, good shops and the ambience of a well preserved old market town. You can visit Burghley House, Nene Valley Railway, Rutland Water with its water sports, and Ferry Meadows Country Park. The hotel can also book you a round of golf at a choice of three local courses. Ask about special Breakaways around the Burghley Horse Trials and the many other good value special breaks. The hotel boasts an eye-opening reception area with stone flagged walls and marble floors. There are one hundred and sixty three en-suite rooms, all with direct dial telephone, television, and hostess trays. The restaurant serves delicious food, Modern English, Continental and with a taste of the Orient. The well-stocked bar is a great meeting place and the whole ambience of the hotel is restful and caring. The Swallow Leisure Club is the perfect place to relax and unwind and enjoy the new fifteen metre pool.

USEFUL INFORMATION

OPEN: All year
CHILDREN: Welcome
CREDIT CARDS: All major cards
LICENSED: Full On
ACCOMMODATION: 163 en-suite rooms
RATES: From£105sgl £115 dbl.
SPECIAL BREAKS

RESTAURANT; A la carte
BAR FOOD: Light meals & snacks
VEGETARIAN: Always a choice
WHEELCHAIR ACCESS: Yes
GARDEN: 11 acres
PETS: Bedrooms only

THE MALTINGS
Main Street,
Aldwincle, Oundle NN14 3EP
Northamptonshire

Tel: 01832 720233
Fax: 01832 720326

 This is one of the most interesting, the most friendly and the most comfortable Bed and Breakfasts in the country. Owned and run by two gregarious and fun people, Margaret and Nigel Faulkner, guests are primarily accommodated in a beautiful barn conversion of an outhouse granary. The light, airy guest sitting room is equipped with TV, a wide assortment of local literature and the wherewithal to make tea or coffee from an assortment of flavours. The milk is fresh and there is a full tub of biscuits. French windows open on to the perfectly maintained garden. Upstairs there are two attractive bedrooms with pretty patchwork quilts and both rooms always have fresh flowers. Two luxurious bathrooms complete with bathrobes are there for guests use. A thoughtful pair, the Faulkners provide you with an umbrella in case it is raining whilst you cross the few yards to the house for your breakfast which, incidentally is served enfamille round the kitchen table if you are on your own, but more formally in the dining room if there is a full house. Within the house there is another charming bedroom with a super bathroom. This is a strictly non smoking house.

USEFUL INFORMATION

OPEN: All year
CHILDREN: Not under 10 years
CREDIT CARDS: Yes
LICENSED: No
ACCOMMODATION: 3 tw en-suite
RATES: Sgl £33-£35 Dbl. £45-47

DINING ROOM: Excellent breakfast
VEGETARIAN: Upon request
WHEELCHAIR ACCESS: Yes
GARDEN: Yes. Croquet
PETS: No
STRICTLY NON-SMOKING

BOSTON

IAN PETHERS

Selected venues in this chapter

'A man hath no better thing to do under the sun,
than to eat, and to drink, and to be merry'.
Ecclesiastes.

****

' Seeing is deceiving,
It's eating that's believing'
James Thurber

Chapter 8:
Holland in England - and Further Afield
Boston to Grantham & The Wash

The last time we sat over breakfast in our hotel in Ely, we looked out across the Fens and felt our pulses quicken as the morning mist lifted from the scene of our next journey. This morning is different: we are leaving early before the day has broken, as there are many miles to travel to our first stop.

Can you imagine the complaints last night at Ovaltine time: "How many miles does he think we can *do*, tomorrow? We'll have to be off before *dawn*. What's with a *dawn* start, on *holiday*?" And so on. Well, the dawn start notion wasn't my idea, but reason prevailed, there were no serious complaints, after all we were going into Lincolnshire, but why *Lincolnshire?*.

Good question; why indeed? Let me take a moment here to tell you about 'East Anglia' and the way it relates to the land to the north of the official border.. In the East the Fens do not end somewhere north of Wisbech. They go on - for miles - and they are *the* main feature. The crops around Spalding and Downham Market may be different, but the skills and the history aren't. So, while there may be minor differences to justify a *county* line at some stage, there's nothing important enough to think of a change of *region*. In the west, it's more about the absorption of Cambridge and the ad hoc borders *that* created. In simple terms, Grantham and Stamford have more in common with Ely, Peterborough and Huntingdon than they ever do with Skegness and Scunthorpe.

Firstly, another question: how can you get to Holland without the use of a plane, a ship or even the Chunel? Answer: you *drive* north east from Ely - and there you are. You remember how we felt, driving through parts of Norfolk, say, or Cambridgeshire, and seeing all the Dutch influences on the landscape, towns and villages? Someone, probably me, said we half expected to wake up and find ourselves in a farmyard on the outskirts of Amsterdam, what with all the windmills, pantiles an gable ends. Well, up around Spalding and Holbeach it's *official* - and they have the South Holland Spring Festival and the South Holland Centre to prove it. Intrigued?

Not intrigued enough to resist querying the idea of combining the flat, fenland South Holland bit with the fenless, undulating, western Grantham bit, it seems. In one chapter. Well, let me reassure you. In reaching the decision I weighed matters of geography, topography and geology very carefully. I carried out research into folklore, patterns of employment, social trends and demography. When I drew all these threads together carefully one thing emerged very clearly: they had absolutely *nothing* to do with it! What had *everything* to do with it was far more important and, in the end, carried the day: if I'd split South Lincs in two it would have meant writing *thirteen* chapters instead of *twelve*! Nobody writes a book with *thirteen* chapters!

331

I'd like to think that the admin is finished for the day, following that declaration, to see the reddening light of dawn on yon far Eastern hummocks was quite inspiring. We were on our way, although there *was* another bit of admin, even then. A member of our group questioned why we didn't just shift our base to Spalding or somewhere, instead of doing the long distance, out and back routine. If that sounded reasonable - it actually revealed a total lack of perception of the realities of Grand Tours like ours. One major reality is: always plan ahead. Ahead, in our case, is Suffolk. Suffolk is south of Norfolk, and more or less to the south of Cambridge, definitely south of Lincolnshire. So we move our tons of gear from Ely all the way up to Spalding today - and move them all the way back tomorrow, or the day after, *past* Ely and a long way down south to Bury St Edmunds, end of administration problems with our reasoning team member.

Once we *are* out of the car park the first leg is pretty straight forward, if a touch over familiar. In a nutshell, it's a case of the A142 via Sutton to Chatteris; the A141 via March to Gayhim and then the A47, followed by the A15, round Peterborough and over the county line. As I say, simple but bordering on the boring by now, so best accomplished with minimal delay. We cross the River Welland just before the intersection with the A16, and there we are: South West Lincolnshire - the gateway to England's largest county which we shall link a little later with South East Lincolnshire (South Holland) to save us tempting fate.

Once again, we've arrived in what we'll discover is some seriously rich country where miles of rolling parkland are the setting for quite astonishing historic houses and stately homes that would be thought of as *palaces* anywhere else. All in all, it is a magnificently rural landscape, embracing ancient woodland, fenland, stone villages and historic market towns within an area of 946 square kilometres that rejoices - justifiably - in the name of South Kesteven.

No sooner are we over the river than we make our first contact. Clustered along the banks of the Welland is a group of communities - a town and several villages - known as the Deepings. Chief of these is **MARKET DEEPING**, a small low lying market town whose triangular centre is the focus of a number of fine buildings, built mainly of Barnack ragstone. The Deepings almost certainly date back to prehistoric times and local excavations have unearthed artefacts and other objects of Bronze and Iron Age origins. Market Deeping, specifically, was an important stagecoach centre although it must have prospered for many years before that as its CHURCH, dedicated to St.Guthlack, an Anglo-Saxon hermit who came to Crowland around 669 AD, was in use as a centre of worship as long ago as 1240.

Market day is Wednesday, and this is a good time to look around for bargains. Whilst in full cry, we should also make a point of calling in at the MARKET DEEPING ANTIQUES AND CRAFT CENTRE, which is open seven days a week for visitors to browse amongst more than sixty stands displaying antiques, collectibles and also reproduction furniture. Individual shops in the town, which include a curiosity shop, are centred on MARKET STREET and to the east of the HIGH STREET, with further shops in MARKETGATE and the RAINBOW CENTER, and for a cup of tea etc., try the Market Deeping Stage hotel, owned and managed by a convivial lady host, and an expert of south Lincolnshire.

The Deeping villages are a delight in themselves; so that to choose one in preference to another is difficult to justify. Nonetheless, as time is pressing, one it has to be, so I suggest **DEEPING ST JAMES**, as it is quite close to the town and lies in a convenient direction for the next stage of the tour.

DEEPING ST JAMES

The River Welland used to be an important link for the villages when boats and barges were used to transport goods from area to area. Deeping St James is one such village and its waterside location has a strong effect on its great charm. It grew up around its church, as so many did, the PRIORY CHURCH OF ST JAMES having been founded in 1139 as part of a Benedictine Priory that was a cell of Thorney Abbey. Behind the Church is the priory farmhouse, an early 17th century structure believed to have been built with stones from the original Priory.

The village has a classified ancient monument too. In its centre we will find the CROSS, a small, square listed building which, in 1819, was converted for use as a lock-up for the village drunks. If we peer through the bars in the door, we'll see the semicircular stone seats and chains which are still there. Today, the local people tend to regard it with rather less respect, as the most unusual lamp post in Lincolnshire.

The Deepings, and particularly Market Deeping, have strong associations with our next destination, as we shall see after a wriggle down the B1166 to the Cambridgeshire border, followed by a controlled sprint along a straighter stretch to the town of **CROWLAND**, "the monastic heart of the Fens". Thirteen centuries ago when, as we know from earlier chapters, the immensely fertile arable land of the Fen country was still one bog, surrounding a number of bleak, isolated little islands, a small church and hermitage was set up on one of them, known as Croyland.

The early history of the Abbey, as it became, is hard to unravel because so many documents turn out to be more recent forgeries produced by Monks to back up decidedly dodgy land claims. The traditional view, although it's never been confirmed, is that the hermit Guthlac, after whom Market Deeping church is named, arrived in the area about 669 AD. He became a friend of King Aethelbald of Mercia, and it was the King who set up the first monastery, in 716. It was refounded around 950, after a bad Viking experience, then rebuilt again and later extended almost continuously into the 15th century.

Eventually the great Abbey, now the Parish Church, became one of the finest churches of the Fens, surpassed, perhaps, only by Ely Cathedral. Having existed well before the Norman Conquest, it was still the only monastery in Lincolnshire in 1066 and, by Domesday, was recorded as owning wide estates donated by pious benefactors. It stood throughout the Middle Ages as one of the largest and most important abbeys in the county, which was how it remained; its wealth growing from reclaiming and farming the surrounding Fenland and its huge, cathedral-sized church, until Henry VII had his 'Big Idea'. Soon after the Reformation Croyland followed the pattern of all the monasteries in England and was reduced to a heap of rubble.

The second of Crowland's ancient monuments could well be unique. Its triangular TRINITY BRIDGE once stood over three streams, before the draining of the Fens, when most of the main streets were waterways and the River Welland was split into two courses. Built between 1360 and 1390, the Bridge has three intersecting arches and one over arching super structure - hence the name. It seems to have replaced an earlier wooden structure mentioned in the Charter of King Aethelbald in 716 AD. As the drainage programme continued, the routes of the watercourses changed - today Trinity Bridge stands on dry land in the middle of the town! Nevertheless, the antiquarian Richard Gough, has said that it was *"the greatest curiosity in Britain, if not in Europe"*. Presumably the present absence of water makes that claim even stronger! *Very* curious!

TRINITY BRIDGE

While we're in Crowland and thinking about the River Welland, it's worth pointing out to any anglers who don't know this part of the world that we're in first class coarse fishing country. Further details can be found in leaflets from the SPALDING TOURIST INFORMATION CENTRE (Enquiries - 01775 725468) while permits are available from PETERBOROUGH ANGLING CLUB (Enquiries - 01733 67952) Tight lines!

The town has other attractions, too. The Friday Market, recently reinstated, has been held intermittently for centuries and now takes place at a site in NORTH STREET - which is as wide as it is because the river once flowed between the rows of cottages. There's another oddity there, too: many of the thatched houses in Crowland all date from the same thirty year period at the beginning of the 18th century. It occurs to me, at this point, that we could be forgiven for wondering if there's a connection between these oddities - not to mention the waterless Trinity Bridge - and the existence of *thirty four* pubs in the town in the 'good old days'! At present there are only five - obviously life has become a very different business in more recent times. Mind you, it's hard to decide whether vast quantities of alcoholic refreshment was essential just to cope with the hardship in those days, or whether modern man is far too busy to find time for a pint. Actually, it could be neither, now I think about it. It's more likely to be the lack of shelves full of cans of lager in the Georgian equivalent of Tesco's!

Having looked over the Abbey ruins and explored the shops one might turn to the outskirts of the town for a last look before leaving. On the way, it's worth taking on the MANSE, which dates from 1775 and used to be the Methodist preacher's house, and the 17th century MANOR HOUSE, where it is said the Normans locked up Hereward the Wake's mother in an earlier manor on the site. SNOWDEN FIELD lies beyond the TENNIS COURTS and offers fine views of the Abbey as we stroll across it. More to the point it's the location in June each year for the CROWLAND SHOW.

So, as we stand gazing at this old town and at the ruins of what was once its claim to fame, it's time to plan the next stage of the journey and to think of collecting the car and making tracks. The idea is to cut across county at first, using the B1166, partly to get the feel of the area - but mainly so I can keep a promise with a little surprise treat for some of you.

We take the 'B' road along a fairly obvious bit as far as **HOLBEACH DROVE,** then keep to the right as far as **GEDNEY HILL,** by-passing a windmill, - and there it is! GEDNEY HILL GOLF COURSE (Enquiries - 01406 330183). Apart from the fact that the promise just had to be kept, the Course is a must for the golfing fanatics, as it has one of the longest holes in the country, at 693 yards. Visitors are very welcome and either before or after their game have access to the snooker room, the restaurant and the services of the resident professional.

All very pleasant. So pleasant, as it happens, that I predict that by the time the golf fraternity have surrendered to the joys of the 19th hole, I'll hardly have enough readers left to make the rest of the trip viable. I can feel one of my moments of foreboding coming on. Action definitely being vital right now, it has to be time to leave the car park in a spray of gravel and a cloud of tyre smoke before we lose anyone else. No sooner said than we're travelling back towards the B1168 - or more accurately, until the first horrendous bend in the road brings us back to reality, panic! , where are we?

We're heading north, miraculously still on the B1168 and making our more serene way towards a collection of Whaplodes, in general terms, and towards **WHAPLODE ST CATHERINE** in particular. This village's second source of fascination - after its quite extraordinary name - is found residing in THE MUSEUM OF ENTERTAINMENT (Enquiries - 01406 540379), where the story of show business in terms of mechanical music is told in absorbing detail. True, there's more than a touch of deja entendu in it all, as this is the third museum of the kind that we've seen, but I *never* feel one can have too much of a good thing. This 'good thing' is the blast of nostalgia that it creates, which I find makes a wonderful antidote to the super cool so called perfection of today's utterly soulless plastic boxfuls of electronics.

Seriously, with every conceivable machine and instrument to hand, from the fairground pipe organ to the pianola and the gramophone, there's a chance to wallow in the romance of rose-tinted memories for hours on end. We haven't *got* hours on end, so we'll have to do the best we can with a conducted tour and the odd demonstration or two on a selection from the many treasures in the Museum's collection. If we're *very* lucky, our visit might even coincide with one of the regular concerts on the Rodgers Organs that are given throughout the year. We can't hang around, though: time is going to be pressing all day - and most of the night, at this rate, - until we rest the weary bones some time in the small hours, back in Ely. Having met with a clutch of Whaplodes - after a clutch of Deepings - we are about to find ourselves in the midst of Gedney' clutches, 'Sutton' clutches and 'Holbeach' clutches. This is terrific countryside, with the Wash to north for all the bird watchers and the ancient city of Lincoln to the east, who really would want to live elsewhere. Idyllic if you have a love of serenity, travelling in this beautiful area makes one think that God is in Heaven and all is right with the your world. There are many first class attractions in the area, such as the BUTTERFLY AND FALCONRY PARK (Enquiries - 01406 363833) at **LONG SUTTON**, where, for a touch over four pounds, you will have a great day out.

While we're on the way - it's really not far - there does appear to be an explanation for the 'clutch syndrome' that actually makes sense. As with nearly everything around here, it's to do with land reclamation, and Holbeach makes the point particularly clearly, I think. Holbeach was established as a village in Anglo Saxon times - when great tracts of its surroundings were almost permanently under water. Land reclamation in the Middle Ages led to some of its good citizens moving out to set up home - or shop - on the new ground where they could spread themselves a little. What more natural than that their *new* village should doff its cap to the old, to 'home', to 'roots', so to speak? As the new village grew, in the time honoured way, around its church, so Holbeach's emigrants eventually found themselves giving Holbeach *St Mark's* or Holbeach *St Matthew's* as their address. Obviously, Holbeach *Bank* is where the 'groat millionaires' settled! You *know* it makes sense. More to the point, it gets us to the Butterfly Park.

Here we have one of the largest tropical butterfly houses in Britain - and, in this case, 'big' is *definitely* beautiful, too. There's something about butterflies, y'know? There can't be many utterly harmless creatures in the cosmos that look so attractive as a bonus. I know that their caterpillars can have *very* horrid habits - we've all seen our cabbages looking like umbrellas after a hurricane, with nothing left but the spokes and we've cursed the wriggling little perishers - but the adult insects, even the humble Cabbage Whites, are surely something else, although I suspect you'd have to be rather thick skinned to mention that particular variety in the exotic setting of Long Sutton!

Exotic barely describes the place. Some of the world's most colourful butterflies and moths live here, floating around freely in droves amongst tropical, Mediterranean and temperate flowers whose foliage is set around ponds, pools, streams and waterfalls in the nearest thing on earth to the Garden of Eden, I imagine. If a sight of the world's largest moth isn't enough, then the dazzling array of other little beasties should charm any visitor to *pieces*!

Elsewhere in the complex there are ants, bees, leaf-cutters - and spiders and scorpions, for anyone who gets withdrawals if deprived of a daily dose of revulsion. Actually, I *like* spiders - not sure about scorpions, though. Their habits are *incredibly* horrid, I find. Then there's REPTILE LAND, where there just *had* to be a pair of crocodiles called 'Snap' and 'Crackle' - *and* a Burmese python more or less answering to the name of Cynthia! Then there are the birds: Long Sutton is also home to the LINCOLNSHIRE BIRDS OF PREY CENTRE where residents include examples of the world's largest owl and fastest bird of prey - at the start of a range that extends a long way from there, to 'stars' like 'Liberty', the American Bald Eagle and 'Fred' the Turkey Vulture, who seems to be the only trained vulture in the East of England. Do we need to know where the *untrained* ones hang out, I wonder. Amongst the other attractions are Snowy Owls, African Spotted Owls, Peregrine Falcons, Harris Hawks, Buzzards and Merlins. They don't just sit there, either - at least, not all of them. In the delightful setting of the Centre's Park, the resident falconer presents daily displays of the birds' prowess every day, at 12.00noon and 3.00pm. At which point we may well take up an invitation to adopt one of these amazing creatures by signing up for the scheme which makes a vital contribution towards each bird's care and also provides for breeding programmes here and abroad.

Finally, to make the most of Long Sutton, it would be worth writing or phoning in advance for a leaflet giving details of the Centre's SPECIAL EVENTS that are arranged at intervals throughout the year. We might decide to pass on 'Exotic Pets Day' in May, when we'd get a chance to hold a tarantula or a giant hissing cockroach, but 'Barn Owl Sunday' in July could be enthralling, as could 'In Search of King John's Jewels' between April and October, or 'Butterflies, Bramleys & Plums', in the Autumn.

If that was 'finally', the rest must be 'foot notes', namely, a host of other items from the FARM MUSEUM to the ANIMAL CENTRE to PHEASANT WORLD to the HONEY FARM to the award-winning LICENSED TEA ROOMS and TEA GARDEN, where I've been relaxing, in this attractively converted former stables, waiting for the rest of you to catch up. If you *must* call in the GIFT SHOP, that's fine - only make it a very *quick* call.

Before we commence to travel up the A17, there's a call to be made at GARNSGATE ROAD, Long Sutton - always assuming we can make an appointment at such short notice. Deryck Gilham has some excellent contemporary furniture in his SHOWROOM AND WORKSHOP (Enquiries - 01406 362538) which blend modern concepts with the ideals of traditional furniture making. If there's nothing there that is *quite* right for the visitor's requirements, Deryck also works to commission. Now we really must *go*! **HOLBEACH** is calling to us - and we actually need to *be* there.

After five or six miles, we *are* there and we find ourselves in a town with two distinctions: not only is it the second largest town in South Holland, it is also one of the largest parishes in the whole of England. Located, nowadays, in the midst of the bulb growing district, it used to be less than a couple of miles from the sea - until the 19th century reclamation work changed all that, creating miles of fertile farmland between Holbeach and the present day sea defences where once there was only marsh, water and oozing mud. The impressive 14th century CHURCH OF ALL SAINTS, with its magnificent 180ft broach spire, stands at the centre of the town and is home to an intriguing exhibition which tells the area's story in well judged detail. There is also a major contribution to the annual FLOWER FESTIVAL, mounted here during the last week in April and the first week in May when just about all the churches in South

Holland participate in the floral celebrations that have Spalding as their focal point. All Saints offers an interesting programme of displays and demonstrations over the two weeks of the Festival, ranging from craft work to calligraphy, and there is also a service of choral evensong on the final Friday.

A series of paths and lanes radiates out from Holbeach itself to the villages that lie closer to the sea, beyond HOLBEACH MARSH. There is even a pleasant walk to be had along the sea bank - but don't even try to go for a paddle. The sea shore proper is far away across a stretch of mud and marsh that is treacherous in the extreme. A safer digression might be to **GEDNEY**. Not Gedney anything - just plain Gedney, where another splendid Church, with a 14th century porch and a 15th century nave is to be found. In any case, this part of the Fen landscape is renowned for easy but fascinating walking so we should enjoy a stretch or two, perhaps for no other reason than the sheer pleasure of *doing* it.

So: Holbeach (and the Gedney clutches) - what now? With so many miles to cover, one thing there won't be is one of those 'pauses for reflection' that have cropped up elsewhere when there doesn't seem to be too much to say about the stretch of 'real world' that's actually in front of our eyes. We're too busy, far too busy, for any of that. Take now, for instance. We should be on the A151 on our way from Holbeach to Whaplode (as a matter of fact, I think we probably *are*) and that will bring us to some fairly intricate map reading while we negotiate something of a route-finder's nightmare in trying to cram everything in - from craft centres to museums to heaven knows what. Prepare yourselves for some enormous zig-zags from hell - and hold on very tightly. Can you really imagine a bout of philosophising on an obscure bit of East Anglian culture in the middle of something like *that*? I can - but I've decided to keep quiet, for once!

WHAPLODE. Let's get *on* with it!. Off to the left in **MOULTON**, Mo Teeuw, an accomplished and highly regarded artist, has a workshop and studio at 20 HIGH STREET where works in water colour, oil and pastel are on display and for sale. An appointment is necessary, so one can only hope that a phone call (01406 370012) from Holbeach, say - or even from Ely before setting out, if any of us can plan that far ahead in the state we're in - will give enough notice. Close by, Carol Parker and Kate White run MISH MASH (Enquiries - 01406 370191) a craft practice that specialises in papier mache work. The two artists create bowls, platters, mirrors, picture frames, fantasy animals and mobiles from this material in a variety of paint and collage finishes. Carol and Kate also take commissions and offer demonstrations.

This is where the story really begins. The obvious route now would be directly into the middle of Spalding, probably with an enormous sigh of relief. As it happens, we're having none of that! Far too easy - and far too many missed opportunities. We're going to take the B1357, off to the right, which looks like it's aiming for Boston - only we aren't going *there* either. Where we *are* going is to a little place called **SUTTERTON**

DOWDYKE, that isn't even on the map (of course - where else). With a name like that it ought to be near **SUTTERTON** - which *is* on the map - so we *should* be able to find it, given time. First off we need the A417, and a bit of the heavy right foot to make up for all those long minutes - or hours, even - that we have wasted chatting.

The A417 takes us in double quick time over the River Welland, where it opens into its rather skinny Estuary, before skirting the village of **FOSDYKE** and arriving at an intersection with the A16. We stay with the 417 and carry on to the north west, which puts Sutterton on our right - and leaves us looking for a phone box. While we're scratching around for some change - or the phone card - we *could* take a quick look at the village. It is dominated by its beautiful parish church, whose crenellated spire can be seen for many miles around. Although the church contains fragmentary elements that are Saxon and date from the 9th century, the tower was built as late as 1787. The thatched roofs of the village houses are an unusual sight in this part of the world and there is an extensive village green. While the sea seems miles away, recent archaeological excavations have confirmed that Sutterton was actually a port in Roman times.

Since CHERRY HOLT STUDIO (Enquiries 01205 460404) is (a) self evidently on the phone and (b) not far away, within minutes we should find ourselves looking over the exhibits in a working studio and gallery where traditional art by fourteen local artists is on display. There's everything here that might be suggested by the notion of 'tradition': wildlife, landscapes, seascapes and many others. As visitors to the area, it's unlikely that there'd be much of an opportunity for us to achieve a great deal from the studio's demonstration, in the time that we can honestly spare. But there are plenty of works on sale and commissions are undertaken - so we should be able to justify the visit easily enough. Cherry Holt Studio is open from Wednesday to Sunday, between 10.00am and 5.00pm.

Now we're going to **BOSTON** (Information - 01205 356656) by way of the B1397, although anyone who finds this minor road too slow and is impatient to get 'there' (whichever 'there' one happens to be talking about at any given time) can feel absolutely free to cut down any one of the side roads to the right, to join the A16 - and spend a long time in a car park waiting for the rest of us to arrive. We, meanwhile, will enjoy a more sedate journey while we recall to mind a few facts, figures and bits of history to set the scene for our arrival.

We're approaching an ancient town which was Britain's most important port, in Medieval times, when links with the Continent were almost all that 'foreign trade' actually meant. Unfortunately, nothing lasts for ever and this phase of Boston's prosperity collapsed under a double body blow: firstly, as explorers came upon parts of the world that had never heard of Europe, merchants realised that these discoveries created a grand chance to coin a quick buck - or even thousands of quick bucks. With that realisation, trade shifted from the East - North Sea - coast to the West - everywhere else - coast in double quick time and ports like Boston and King's Lynn took a bit of a nose dive. Secondly, ships were getting bigger - while the Wash just went on silting up, as it seems to have done for ever. These bigger ships, created by new technology and the need for more space for bigger cargoes and longer voyages, soon couldn't get into the shallower harbours and that, for a while, was that. Everyone pottered along, or went back to fishing and hoped for the best.

The River Witham has played a major part in all these ups and downs. Along with the silting up of the Wash, there were recurrent bouts of flooding, so in many ways the waxing and waning of Boston's fortunes have closely matched the state of affairs in the natural world around the town - never mind the impact of Colonialism, from the 17th century onwards. If you look across the Witham towards PACK HOUSE QUAY, the legacy of fine waterside buildings tends to suggest that the waxing had more effect, overall, than the other thing - especially as the North Sea and the Baltic are back in business, and the 'new' port, built on a site down river has obvious advantages over the old one. Boston also has a fishing fleet, with colourful boats heading out to the Wash at high tide. On their return they are to be seen at the moorings and quay alongside the HIGH STREET.

For a change, I'm going to leave the history to one side for a while and look first, instead, at what we can actually *do* in and around this amazing town, in the 'here and now'. To make this break with 'tradition' even more spectacular, why don't we pitch straight into 'Sport and Leisure'? No, I'm not still trying to appease the golfers. After all, Boston seems to have facilities that cater for practically everything.

The GEOFF MOULDER LEISURE COMPLEX (Information 01205 363483) has a splendid swimming pool, a toddler pool and a 45 metre flume slide. With the toddlers toddling and the older ones 'fluming' there should be plenty of room for the rest of us to put in a few lengths to tone up the muscles. If they aren't tuned up enough by all that, there's also a Fitness Suite (otherwise known as the Punishment Block, if you're as out of condition as I am) and relaxing Solarium in which to recover from the whole process. As an alternative, if you'd rather get a bit more violent with it all, THE PETER PAINE SPORTS CENTRE (Information - 01205 350222) has a wide range of masochistic pastimes on offer, including badminton and squash.

With that out of the way, I shall be able to appease the golfers, in case Gedney wasn't quite enough. The Borough has first class facilities for devotees of the driver, iron and putter. BOSTON GOLF CLUB (Enquiries - 01205 367526) has a highly esteemed eighteen hole course. There are nine hole courses at BOSTON WEST GOLF CENTRE (Enquiries - 01205 290670) and at KIRTON HOLMES (Enquiries - 01205 290669), both of which are a little way out of the town, off the A52. At Boston West there is also a Driving Range and a Pro Shop. Tennis is very much an institution in the area, too. There are superb facilities at the BOSTON TENNIS CENTRE (Enquiries - 01205 360821), where visitors are very welcome, and private courts at FRAMPTON and ROCHFORD TOWER. Throughout the Borough there are plenty of municipal courts, including several at CENTRAL PARK, which are open to the public.

I suppose we really can't get this close to the River Witham without talking angling, which is one of *the* most popular participant sports in this part of the world (after shopping)? The River itself frequently yields up huge catches of bream, perch and pike. Coarse fishing is also very successful in the man made canals (or 'drains', as they're known locally) with some of the best spots being found in the SIBSEY TRADER, HOBHOLE and SOUTH FORTY FOOT drains.

As we've seen elsewhere on this tour, South Lincolnshire, generally, is excellent cycling country - and the area around Boston is at least as good as anywhere, with no steep hills to speed up the ageing process and miles of all but traffic free lanes to explore in peace. A free cycling leaflet is available from the Tourist Information Centre (Phone - 01205 356656). Finally, one activity that barely gets a look in with these pages is horse riding. To restore that balance the Horse Riding Centres around Boston should be given their due, as should the network of specialist bridle trails. As I've worn myself out just writing all this down, I imagine that the rest of you could well be totally jaded. It's time common sense prevailed. Enough of all this physical torture; let's revert to type and go look for something gentler, preferably with a touch of healthy self indulgence to follow.

The Boston skyline is completely dominated by the tower of the beautiful 14th century ST BOTOLPH'S CHURCH - known practically everywhere as 'THE BOSTON STUMP'. That England's tallest parish church, whose tower can be seen up to twenty miles away, should be graced with such an inappropriate nickname seems odd - but as we keep on noticing, East Anglia's capacity to surprise has no limit. Now if 'Stump' just referred to the actual octagonal top section, they could have something.

BOSTON STUMP & ASSEMBLY ROOMS

The 'lantern' tower used to be lit at night as a navigation guide for sailors - a feature we've come across more than once in the coastal churches of Norfolk and elsewhere. Today, it's possible to climb part of the way up and enjoy the most extraordinary views that extend as far as Lincoln Cathedral, 32 miles away to the North, and Sandringham in Norfolk. The statistics don't stop there, however, the 'Stump' has a more lurid tale to tell, until recently it was used by unfortunate souls who could not face life any longer. Such was the popularity of the 'Stump' for this purpose, that netting was erected to prevent people reaching the top of the building. Hopefully you will not be tempted.

Equally stunning is the nave of the church. With a length of 282 feet, a height of 65 feet and a floor area of more than 20,000 square feet it could well be the largest church in the country. The interior of the church also has a magnificent roof, some fine carvings and an amusing set of misericords that date from 1390. There are also memorials in the church to the five local men who became governors of Massachusetts as well as to George Bass and Joseph Banks who sailed to Australia with Captain Cook. Outside is a statue of Herbert Ingrams who founded the 'Illustrated London News'.

Another well known landmark in Boston's 'built environment' is the MAUD FOSTER WINDMILL (Details - 01205 352188) which is England's tallest working windmill - the perfect counterfoil, one might say, to 'The Stump' itself. It is sited just beyond BARGATE GREEN, alongside the MAUD FOSTER 'DRAIN' and is also unusual in that it has five sails - or 'sweeps' - instead of the more usual four, to power the internal machinery.

The mill was built in 1809 to grind corn brought along the 'Drain' by barge and is still producing stoneground flour today. At weekends and on Wednesdays it is possible to climb to the top and see the workings of the machinery - and, as you can imagine, there are fine views from the platform outside. There is a small admission fee and refreshments are available.

No description of Boston, with its history so caught up with the river and the sea and with its present so involved with the new found opportunities for the life of its port, would be complete without a look at the lighter side of time spent afloat. The town has an attractive MARINA (Details 01205 364420) as well, which is located beside the GRAND SLUICE, upriver from 'The Stump'. You see, *everything* in Boston is related to - or measured from - the famous tower. I cant think of anywhere else where the inter-action is so much a part of everyday matters.

The Marina is open to leisure craft and motor cruisers but, of more interest to us, you can also hire a boat to explore the River Witham. On the other hand, you might fancy a down-river cruise with MARITIME LEISURE CRUISES (Enquiries - 01205 46595) who specialise in showing visitors the fascinating sights of THE HAVEN, the stretch of water lying between the town and the Wash. The cruise will take you right through the centre of the town, where a whole range of features will hold your interest, such as the PORT itself and the PILGRIM MEMORIAL at SCOTIA CREEK, out to the salt flats near WYBERTON MARSH close to the seaward end of the Haven. The mixture of seashore, sand dunes and salt marshes which go to make up the coast near Boston present an abundance of wild life. There are NATURE RESERVES at FRAMPTON MARSH, near Wyberton, while the adjacent GIBRALTAR POINT is recognised internationally as an excellent station for spotting migrating birds.

If we're looking for a taste of more conventional 'culture' by now, if *these* withdrawals are about to set in, then Boston is well equipped to come to our aid in this respect, too. In fact, few towns of a similar size can have such a rich and varied assortment of arts venues and outlets - so much so that the area where most of them are concentrated has come to be known as the 'CULTURAL QUARTER'. This phenomenon, has in its turn become so successful that further expansion is expected with a major new development during the course of 1998.

The Cultural Quarter is to be found just south of the MARKET PLACE - and that's another treat in store for us - beside the River Witham. The first building to grab our attention is the spectacular SHODFRIARS HALL, whose half-timbered construction and overhanging gables are particularly eye-catching. Once we've passed the old CUSTOM HOUSE, our next point of reference is SPAIN LANE and it's there that we find the BLACKFRIARS ARTS CENTRE (Enquiries - 01205 363108). In this remarkably well restored 13th century building a marvellous range of artistic activities is presented throughout the year. These extend from live concerts to drama productions and from film shows to exhibitions and performing arts workshops.

Opposite the 15th century GUILDHALL MUSEUM (Enquiries - 01205 365954) - of which more anon - is the SAM NEWSOM MUSIC CENTRE. This used to be a seed warehouse but has been sensitively converted for use by the MUSIC DEPARTMENT OF BOSTON COLLEGE. Concerts are held in the splendid recital hall throughout the year.

Finally, we come to FYDELL HOUSE (Enquiries - 01205 351520) which stands next to the Guildhall and is one of Boston's finest buildings. The 18th century house is owned by the Boston Preservation Trust and contains the 'AMERICAN ROOM', which was opened by Joseph Kennedy, the then American ambassador, in 1938. This splendid example of the architecture of the period is open to visitors on certain weekdays by prior arrangement. Having left Fydell House to find ourselves strolling in the street outside the Guildhall, there's only one place left to go before we leave the Cultural Quarter and turn our attention to some other facet of local life - some facet such as *shopping,* perhaps! I think we've *all* been incredibly patient, in the circumstances. Few buildings have had such a varied or significant role as Boston's Guildhall which is now seeing service as the Town's MUSEUM (Enquiries - 01205 365954). Over the years since it was built in 1450, it has been used as a Religious Guild, Town Hall, Courtroom, Banqueting Hall, Gaol, Council Chamber, Soup Kitchen - and a 'British Restaurant'.

The Guild of St Mary was founded in 1260; the current building was meant as their Hall, but after Boston was granted a Civic Charter, it became the Town Hall. The majority of today's visitors come to see the Court Room where the 'original' Pilgrim Fathers were tried. Before these Puritan leaders were taken to Lincoln for a further trial they were held in cells directly below the Court which are reached by a spiral staircase. If you're that way inclined, you can sit inside the actual cells yourself and see what it feels like to be locked up. Another fascinating - and very popular - feature is the 17th century kitchen, complete with its ancient fireplaces. One of its most unusual sets of equipment are the spits which, ingeniously, were turned by hot air. Amongst the amazing range of other exhibits are archaeological discoveries, costume and ceramic displays, the famous portrait of Joseph Banks and paintings by William Etty. There is a small admission charge for the Guildhall, which is open from Monday to Saturday between 10.00a.m. and 5.00p.m. throughout the year. It is also open on Sundays in summer between 1.00p.m. and 5.00p.m.

As I seem to be picking up the odd rumble of frustration all of a sudden, this seems to be the moment to see what Boston has to offer as a shopping centre. The answer, I suspect, will be enough to satisfy the current craving - for the moment, at any rate. To begin with, Lincolnshire's biggest MARKET is held in the town's MARKET PLACE every Wednesday and Saturday throughout the year. The vast open space, a stone's throw from 'The Stump', is packed with stalls at these times and crowds of visitors from all over the county bustle about in search of bargains - or just stocking up with produce from the surrounding farms and much further afield.

Among these crowds there will be many people who are visiting Boston for the first time and are finding, to their amazement, that its shops and stores are at least the equal, in terms of quality and variety, of those in any other town in the country - regardless of size. Around the Market Place and STRAIT BARGATE areas are found all the well known high street names and chain stores, together with an impressive department store. But that is only the beginning, as Boston also has an extraordinarily varied range of specialist shops some of which are tucked away in the narrow medieval lanes that radiate from the town centre.

Not to be missed are DOLPHIN LANE, a quaint passage which runs from the Market Place to PUMP SQUARE and picturesque WORMGATE, a cobbled street behind 'The Stump' which leads down to a small sweet factory and also to RED LION STREET. WIDE BARGATE should be high on our list, too. Not only does it have an enticing range of shops and restaurants but it is also the location of the weekly AUCTION on the GREEN CAR PARK. Held on Wednesday mornings, this event seems to be very much 'our kind of thing' - even if we will have to come early to catch the bargains. Off Wide Bargate is PEN STREET, a charming road which is especially attractive in summer when it is full of outdoor floral displays.

If we cross the TOWN BRIDGE we'll come to another narrow passageway called EMERY LANE. This leads us on into Boston's WEST END shopping area where there are numerous specialist shops selling everything from jewellery to toys and from music to electrical goods. The West End is also home to many of the town's best known restaurants where food from Italy, India and China features amongst many alternatives from nearer to home. Finally, while we're still in 'shopping mode', I must also recommend a visit to the impressive 15th century PESCOD HALL. This has been quite sensitively converted and is now used as a department of a local store.

As you might expect of a town that respects its ancient heritage, Boston is one place that is best explored on foot. So, after a touch of lunch, let's do just that and go out and about for a wander. We could pick up a free leaflet from the Tourist Information Centre to help us on our way, which describes three town centre walks in detail and is full of snippets of gossip, history and local anecdotes. For the moment, though, I'll just give you a 'taster' of what you can expect.

We have some idea of the wealth of treasures lying in wait around the town's many corners already: we've 'done' the Market Place, 'The Stump' and the 'Cultural Quarter' and we've seen Pescod Hall, Dolphin Lane and Wide Bargate. Believe me, these are just the tip of the iceberg! If we were impressed by Pescod Hall, for example, then SHODFRIARS needs examining in more detail: if we revelled in Dolphin Lane then we certainly shouldn't overlook EMERY LANE - and so on.

Nor is local history confined to ancient churches and houses: BLACK SLUICE and GRAND SLUICE speak silently of Boston's industrial and agricultural history as we examine the machinery used to keep the water under control and ensure the safety of the fertile countryside. In contrast, there's a plaque in the HIGH STREET to commemorate George Bass, a native of the town, after whom the Bass Straits were named, who lived there for some years. Joseph Banks, whose statue we saw outside 'The Stump' was the Boston Recorder - as well as a member of Captain Cook's party of explorers.

Many more names could be mentioned, of course, but I'd like to pick out one set that seem to typify the town's range of experiences and rich variety of characteristics. John Fox, who wrote the renowned 'Book of Martyrs' and Jean Ingelow, the great 19th century poet, both have their origins in Boston. But, at the furthest possible extreme, so do 'Old Mother Riley' and 'Mother Goose'! Need I say more?

Now that we're loaded down with history, culture and lunch - while the car is equally loaded with fruit, vegetables, antique music boxes, oil paintings, hand-made pots, hand-knitted sweaters and something rather unusual for the lady next door who promised to feed the cat while we were away - why don't we just *stop*? Over there, I seem to think, is CENTRAL PARK, just beyond Wide Bargate - so, come on, the sun is shining, the air is balmy and it's time we went and sat on a bench for a while.

A few minutes relaxation is the perfect epilogue to our day in this vibrant, historic treasure house of a town, I would have thought. It may well be the ideal place for a game of tennis or cricket, it may well host the BOSTON SHOW and many other events throughout the year but for the moment let's pretend it just hosts *us* - and 'us' is going to have a somewhat extended snooze before climbing back into the car and roaring off on the 'fresh fields' routine again.

Our way out of Boston will take us past Hubberts Bridge again - where we hope not to be delayed by any golfers begging for a last blast on the driving range - and down the A52 to SWINESHEAD, where, according to the old stories, King John tried to pull himself together after losing his jewels in the Wash in 1216. The old stocks and buttercross are a reminder of the place's former market town status, as is the handsome church with its fine tower, capped with a 'lantern' and a short spire. For all the many charms of the present day village, however, we're not really here for the sightseeing - we have a more precise mission.

Our 'more precise mission' *is*: FORESTERS COURT GALLERIES (Enquiries - 01205 820014) in the HIGH STREET. Open daily from 9.00a.m. to 5.30p.m. - with summer Sunday opening from 1.00p.m. to 4.00p.m. - the Galleries display the best work of a number of Lincolnshire artists in a number of exhibitions throughout the year together with various 'themed showings'. The atmosphere is friendly and down to earth, admission is free, so all I can say, if you're looking for a special picture for a special place, is: go for it!

'Go' is beginning to be the word of the moment, as far as we're concerned. While you've been staring transfixed at the pictures, I've been checking the map - and it terrifies me! We seem to have even further to travel than usual at this stage of a tour - so 'go' it definitely has to be. Time and discerning tourist guides can't afford to wait for anyone. From Swineshead we go down another short stretch of the A52 to **DONINGTON**, where we turn left on to the A152 for **GOSBERTON** and **PINCHBECK**, our next target.

THE PINCHBECK ENGINE (Information - 01775 725468) at WEST MARSH ROAD, is a unique survivor of the steam-powered pumping stations that transformed the drainage situation in the Fens during the early 19th century. Built in 1833, it continued to work for all but 120 years and has now been restored to the condition of its heyday. It is 'run up' for demonstration purposes from time to time and is the point of the DRAINAGE MUSEUM complex where graphic illustrations are presented to tell the often incredible story of the trials and tribulations involved in the process of keeping the water off the land. The Engine is owned by the Welland and Deeping Internal Drainage Board and the Museum is jointly managed by the South Holland District Council. Both attractions can be seen daily between Easter and November.

'Contract' being one of the main (and more polite) names of our particular game, we leave the *Drainage* Museum and head, right away, for a *bulb* museum, in fact, for *the* SPALDING BULB MUSEUM & HORTICULTURAL CENTRE at **BIRCHGROVE** (Enquiries - 01775 680490) which is next to no distance away ('bulbs' as in 'tulips', that is, - *not* 'bulbs' as in 100 watts.)

Bulbs and the SPALDING FENS have been synonymous for nigh on a hundred years. Although the town was once a great potato growing centre, times have definitely changed so that, nowadays, more daffodils are grown in South Holland than anywhere else in Britain. In fact, half the country's entire bulb output comes from these huge, local fields. Amazingly, the industry was only introduced into the region in the years before the First World War, by the Dutch. In the course of this century it's grown to the point where tens of thousands of visitors come every year to drive among the tulip fields, in April and May, and stare in astonishment at the riotously colourful acres where millions of blooms stand in formally ordered ranks. All of this is commemorated and recorded at the Museum - and there's a GARDEN CENTRE as well! The Museum is open seven days a week, from April to the end of October, and features everything from a fifteen minute slide show, in the GARDENERS THEATRE, on the history of the industry, to tours round a blacksmith's shop, a bulb sterilising unit and equipment for cleaning, weighing and 'sacking up' the products. In addition, the story is related at every stage to the lives of the people who did the work and on whose ingenuity the whole process depended.

Moving on to the Garden Centre, we find another pleasing spread of delights dear to the hearts of gardeners featuring a great range of top quality plants at affordable prices. 'Plants', in this case, doesn't just mean bulbs: there's something of everything; beyond plants there are gifts, furniture, barbecues and books. More to the point, as far as I'm concerned at this stage, there's a COFFEE SHOP where snacks, lunches and best of all, Lincolnshire cream teas, are available daily.

Time for **SPALDING** (Information - 01775 725468) I feel. A few more urban pleasures sound like a good idea after all the tulips and pumps and things. The River Welland flows through the middle of this splendid old market town. The areas on the east and west banks were linked by seven bridges when I first saw the place back in the 70s; at the last count there were nine - by the time you get to the end of the page there'll probably be three more, such is the pace of modern living!

The essence of the town is its harmonious mixture of old and new buildings and old and new lifestyles, while out from its suburbs are radiating links to a minor galaxy of activities all firmly focused on the 'Flower Centre of the Fens'. Amongst the oldest buildings, to strike a by now familiar note, is the splendid 13th century CHURCH OF SS MARY AND NICHOLAS, which is unusual for having double aisles, but much of the central area of the town is a conservation area which has been declared 'outstanding' by the Secretary of State for the Environment. Obviously, the presence of the river creates an additional attraction in a waterfront of great architectural merit, with the added bonus of some pleasant riverside walks. Again, as we look around - and with the floral reputation very much in mind - it's no surprise to learn that throughout the 90s Spalding has been a regular winner of the title of 'East Midlands Best Town' in the 'Britain in Bloom' competition.

AYSCOUGHFEE HALL, SPALDING

Not far from the church, we'll find another of the town's main claims to fame: AYSCOUGHFEE HALL (Enquiries - 01755 725468) in CHURCHGATE. This restored Manor House on the bank of the river is now a MUSEUM containing ten galleries dedicated to the history of Fenland, its people and its places of interest. The building itself is one of the finest and best preserved medieval buildings in Lincolnshire, and stands in delightful gardens with yew hedge that date from the 17th century. As if that isn't enough, the contents are quite riveting with galleries on everything from fishing to fen skating. A permanent display tells the story of Matthew Flinders RN who achieved fame for charting the coast of Australia while, nearby, are the ASHLEY MAPLES COLLECTION OF BRITISH BIRDS - on loan from the Spalding Gentlemen's Society - and the magnificently panelled library, furnished to recreate the appearance of a gentleman's library from the 19th century. Finally - but this is really only a selection - there is an ART GALLERY, known as the GEEST GALLERY in acknowledgement of its sponsor's generosity, where regular exhibitions from local artists and photographers are presented along with items from local societies and travelling exhibitions from other museums. Ayscoughfee Hall is open from Monday to Thursday between 10.00a.m. and 5.00p.m. and on Friday from 10.00a.m. to 9.30p.m. On Saturday between March and October it opens from 10.00a.m. to 5.00p.m. and on Sundays and Bank Holidays from 11.00a.m. to 5.00p.m.

I've hinted at other delights beyond Spalding's 'suburbs' and these include the amazing ROSE COTTAGE WATER GARDEN CENTRE and TROPICAL PLANT HOUSE (Enquiries - 01775 710882) at GLENSIDE NORTH - an almost unbelievable experience of a tropical environment even in the midst of an English winter - and the GORDON BOSWELL ROMANY MUSEUM (Enquiries - 01775 710599) where a real insight is given into Romany life through exhibits of caravans, carts and harnesses and photographs and sketches covering 150 years of Romany history.

Nevertheless, in Spalding it has to be flowers, flowers and more flowers - you can't really get away from them for more than an hour or two. As if anyone would actually *want* to! Which brings me, happily enough, to the town's main claims to fame in today's world, in the form of a Festival and a garden centre.

The SOUTH HOLLAND SPRING FESTIVAL (Enquiries - 01775 725468) reaches out into the whole area, especially to the Churches, to celebrate the largesse of Nature throughout all the acres of flower and bulb fields. It focuses largely on Spalding, where four days of festivities include funfairs, street markets and special events - and the entire spectrum of concerts, workshops, plays and exhibitions that make up the fortnight-long SOUTH HOLLAND ARTS FESTIVAL which surround the day of the SPALDING FLOWER PARADE, the high point of the entire riot.

The entire town is totally involved in this amazing extravaganza, which attracts thousands of visitors to the district each year. The carnival floats alone are decorated with eight million tulip heads - with a thousand needed to cover each square yard - and every street has a part to play, as far as one can tell. Certain events are more firmly located, either in the 25 acre SPRINGFIELD GARDENS (Information - 01775 724843) or in the splendid SOUTH HOLLAND CENTRE (Information - 01775 725031), the town's major focus for arts events throughout the year, from drama to dance, jazz to folk and from comedy to children's shows. As I say, it's a riot, a glorious riot whose popularity should be ensured as long as people rejoice in gardens and flowers.

Those who do - rejoice, that is - may never be persuaded to leave our next port of call. Rather like to golfers at Gedney! We're moving a little way out of the town, to the east for a while, along the A151, to visit the BAYTREE NURSERIES AND GARDEN CENTRE (Enquiries - 01406 370242) at HIGH ROAD, **WESTON**. As soon as we park the car, we know we're into something very special here - and we *are*! This is more, much more than just another garden centre and nursery; it's the Versailles of garden centres. It's a way of life.

To start with, it's absolutely *huge*. The whole complex is the size of a small town and covers more than thirty acres. Within that space there are more than twenty separate elements, covering literally everything from the rose garden to the water garden, seed potatoes to lawn mowers, bulbs (inevitably) to indoor plants and from garden furniture to greenhouses. But it doesn't even *begin* to slow down there - never mind stop! If you want more, you can always browse through the books, or buy a bouquet of fresh flowers or pick up the odd stone ornament - and *then* go on to examine the garden tools, the gifts, ranges of plant food, seeds and watering systems.

If you don't actually *like* gardening, but are only playing chauffeur, you could spend a very pleasant hour in the craft centre choosing a unique or precious gift for the home or for a friend from the range of work on display created by 32 top British artists. After *that* (if the gardener of the family is still lost among the conservatories or climbing plants) you could always pop over to the OWL CENTRE to contemplate the residents - who'll almost certainly contemplate right back at you. Have you ever tried to out stare an owl? I know someone who tried it - eventually they had to treat him for rigor mortis.

Baytree. I'd like to think that this extraordinary (that word again, somehow it's always cropping up around this area) concept - which has snowballed from a modest smallholding to one of Britain's top garden centres in a quarter of a century - would be a real high point for you in this particular tour. Let me know when you've seen it all - you'll find me in the HORIN RESTAURANT, listening to the birds in the aviary, where I've been for the last couple of hours, sampling the country food specialities and soaking up the atmosphere. Fancy a quick cuppa yourself - before we move on?

A little later we discover that 'on', in this case, means a leisurely cruise back from Weston, a touch of the A151 around Spalding - and a modest thrash down some more of it until we get to **BOURNE**.

BOURNE EAU

This red-brick market town, lying at the foot of Kesteven's limestone hills, is one of my adolescent Meccas that I never quite found time to visit. To car fanatics like myself, it's one of *those* places, that bring a misty film to the glazed eye, that recurrently bring a lump to the throat. What Malvern is to Morgans, Bourne is to ERA and BRM. If anyone says anything like "ER-what?" or "BR - who?" I could easily scream. Life-long motorists like us must surely remember the days when racing cars had their engines *in front* of the drivers and when the brutal projectiles only stayed on the road because the driver's skill kept them there. They must also remember when British Racing Green or Italian red *meant* something; when cars aroused more than a touch of patriotism. In short the long in the tooth crowd remember when racing cars had individuality and *actually* raced - instead of flying round the track on the back of a lot of very expensive technology in a performance that is unimaginable to the average driver and comes down to little more than a high speed chase between a bunch of look alike motorised adverts. Oh dear! Prejudice again, I fear.

Bourne is where they came from, if you're still wondering. The British Racing Green ERAs and BRMs were built here and they were the cars that brought Britain back to somewhere near the head of the starting grid. The rest is history - Lotus, Williams, McLaren and the rest - Bourne began it and the others just followed along. In my humble (?) view. Of course, there is rather more to the town than a bunch of adolescent day dreams - a lot more. To begin with, it seems to fall naturally into two areas for our consideration: there's the town, itself - and there's the people who lived there.

The ABBEY CHURCH OF SS PETER, close to the WELL HEAD, is the oldest building in Bourne. It was founded in 1138 as one of five English houses connected to the Arrouasian congregation who were part of the Augustinian Order. The Order was suppressed during the Reformation and most of the Abbey was wrecked. Only the nave arcade from this period still remains and additions to the Church date from the 13th, 15th and 19th centuries.

Another fine building, in a town that seems to have its fair share of them, is REDHALL. Standing near the centre of the town, this fine Elizabethan mansion was a private house until 1860 when it was bought by the Bourne and Essendine Railway Company to become part of the town's new railway station. A hundred years passed. Then some bureaucrat decided the best thing to do to update the railway network was to get rid of half of it. The Bourne line was closed and now everyone goes by car. As far as the next traffic jam! And that is about the only remaining certainty in 'modern' transport - even if it's twenty miles away, there's *always* another snarl up sooner or later!

Back to Bourne - or more accurately, to its sons and daughters - and here we find another amazing spectrum of characteristics. At one extreme we find that William Cecil, the 1st Lord Burghley was born where the Burghley Arms now stands in the centre of the town, in 1520. He went on to become Lord Treasurer to Queen Elizabeth I and to build Burghley House near Stamford, one of the palatial stately homes that I mentioned at the start of the chapter (and of which more anon).

If we want to stretch the spectrum even more, we could go back almost another six hundred years to find that Bourne was also the birthplace of a local roughneck who seems to turn up everywhere. William the Conqueror's pet nightmare, Hereward the Wake (another local boy who preferred making himself a nuisance to making 'good') was born in the town - having, as it seems, done something or other in nearly every other town and village in Fenland.

If we chose to conjure up a vocation as far removed from 'Resistance Leader' or 'Courtier' as possible, I suppose we *might* just come up with the occupation of another of Bourne's most famous sons. Charles Frederick Worth (that's right - *the* Worth, as in the telly ads) was born at Wake House in 1825. He became a fashion designer and parfumier - as most of us know - and that's *nothing like* a resistance leader. His designs and perfumes had a huge impact on the world of French fashions transforming the business into the global industry it has become today.

Coming right up to date, let me drop the name of Antonio Berardi. Born in Billingborough, near the town, Berardi is one of *the* new names in fashion today. Thus far he has had four collections and four shows and is not a bit shy about having top models such as Helena Christensen, Jodie Kidd and Naomi Campbell wearing his designs on the catwalk. Talk of fashion - or, I suppose, of practically anything on earth, where we're concerned - brings us rather smartly to the subject of shopping.

Bourne is a small town - but it is an attractive town, the kind that draws attractive shops to itself. As a result it has a variety of well known, high street name outlets backed up and balanced by larger local retailers and established family businesses. If we couple that array with thoughts of its Thursday and Saturday MARKETS - not to mention ANGEL PRECINCT, a shopping centre on NORTH STREET - Bourne sounds the kind of town in which many of us would like to bury ourselves, having thrown away the car. Many of us - apart from *me*. My car is so much an integral part of my life that I'm convinced I'll drive myself to my funeral.

Thus Bourne, then. Nice place, very nice place. Shame to leave, really - but orders are orders. And I'm under orders to see you sleep in beds every night, rather than in the back of the car. The *beds* are in Ely; *we* are somewhere north of Peterborough. It's "Onward, ever onward" again. *Further* north - well, north west to GRIMSTHORPE CASTLE (Enquiries - 01778 591205) on the A151.

GRIMSTHORPE CASTLE

This is the first of more than half a dozen stately homes that are open to us in what's left of this tour, and they're amazing places, down to the last drape and door knob, every one of them. In the main, despite the local variations, they all follow the same theme: They are statements, and some of us have rather mixed feelings about the wording of those statements. Didn't they all say something like this, at the time when they were built: "I have arrived, I am stinking rich. I am going to spend an awful lot of money, making sure that everybody knows about it - from a distance, apart from other stinking rich buddies of mine who can come to visit - provided they invite me back for the grouse shooting or the summer ball or their daughter's coming out!" Everyone else *did* keep away, for centuries, until the incumbents ran out of cash. Now the peasantry are more than welcome - at five pounds a head!

Sour grapes? I think not. Envy? Not at all. Would *you* envy anyone who *needed* a £200,000 McLaren F1 to prove he'd arrived? Or a £10 million palace to tell the rest of us he'd succeeded? Would you? I doubt it, not if you're reading a sensible book like this, you wouldn't. Then there is the question of *how* the very rich *became* quite so bizarrely rich, even. That is a question that's best not *asked* - never mind answered. Get into that number and most of our so-called 'heritage' becomes some what tawdry. So we'll leave it there, I think, all of it, to nestle down under the mists of tradition. I must say though, as far as this guide actually goes, I'm not mad keen on reeling off a load of statistics as we stagger from one exaggerated pile to the next. Time for a touch of independence, I'd say. This is not a guided tour of other people's self indulgences. So why don't we look at them en masse, so to speak, and save everyone some grief? In any case, if you choose to visit Stamford or Grantham, you can pick up any number of leaflets that are packed with details of Burghley House, or Woolsthorpe Manor or Harlaxton Manor, so we'll serve no purpose duplicating it all.

The other side of this rather vitriolic outburst is the acknowledgement that each Hall, Manor, House, Palace or whatever you choose to call it, is a stunning amalgamation of everything that extravagance can combine. On every hand, from Grimsthorpe to Belton House to Fulbeck Hall, there is architecture to die for; be it 15th, 17th, 18th or even 19th century; by and large if you've travelled these lanes you've seen the *best*. That's just the outside; the elevations, the views from across the Park. The Park is usually a tour de force in its own right, as is the garden, with invariably some of the finest landscaping and horticultural artistry to be found anywhere in the country. Then you go indoors.

At which point you don't know whether to weep or to have a brainstorm. There are ballrooms, drawing rooms, libraries, dining rooms, bedrooms - and they are simply *dripping* with every expression of opulence you can imagine, which just happen to include some of the finest tapestries, paintings, fabrics and furniture that you'll ever see, anywhere, in your entire life! They are, in a word - beautiful! Except they're *not* - not really. True beauty, of any kind, in any quarter, should evoke 'love' as a response. None of this looks terribly *loved* I'd say. It's just sort of *there*, to make an effect to fill up a hole, or a blank space on the wall.

There's too much of it on the whole, too many chairs or carpets, or 'Old Masters' jostling with too many Chippendales, Sheratons and things that Louis XIV gave to someone for Christmas. In fact (dare I even *breathe* this suggestion) there is the *odd* occasion when the collection, as a whole, goes right over the top to border on the - er - 'vulgar'. But don't miss it - really, take in as much of it as time and budget will allow. There can't be many areas of the country with as many stunning examples of the art form per acre as this stretch of Lincolnshire. Don't miss it, because you owe it to yourself to see the very finest examples of English architecture - and here is where they are, at their most accessible. We must move on.

We'll sweep up a long way north now, almost too far for our brief, in a sense, but we want to get the feel of the countryside and there are a couple of places that we ought to absorb. So, it's up the A15, past **ASLACKBY** for starters to a village renowned as a coaching centre in days long gone. **FOLKINGHAM** has another attraction, specific to our particular group, as we'll see in a moment, but it's interesting to see the visual reminder of its past role. The ancient - and splendid - GREYHOUND INN, which has a very prominent position in the village, overlooking the MARKET SQUARE, is believed to date from the early 17th century. It must have been of some importance to stagecoach operators needing a halt before the haul up to Lincoln, although it seems to have been transformed into its present state by some late 18th century restoration.

In a way that seems characteristic of village life in those days; having got the Inn, the local population then built a COURT HOUSE on one end of it. The Sessions were held there until 1828, and guilty parties were either sentenced and taken to the FOLKINGHAM HOUSE OF CORRECTION - or else deported. The House of Correction was actually part of what had once been FOLKINGHAM CASTLE - and is in fact all that's left of the old place now, apart from some earth mounds. "All very interesting," you may grumble, "but what's in it for *us*? Where's the so-called specific attraction?" Actually, it's right there in front of you, the Greyhound is now an inn with a difference - it accommodates a rather splendid ANTIQUE AND CRAFTS CENTRE behind its imposing elevation. Forty dealers operate from fifty different stalls, offering a range of crafts from dried flowers to wrought iron to pottery and woodwork. Antiques, collectibles and bric-a-brac are also on sale.

On again from Folkingham, across the A52 - but staying with the A15 - and we come to **SLEAFORD**, another very old town whose wealth originally seems to have had strong agricultural connections. Even today the tradition is maintained in the seed trade and the maltings, and Market Day - Monday - is a big event for people from the surrounding farmlands. As ever, it is the 12th century parish Church that catches the attention at first with a 144ft stone spire, which is one of the oldest in the country. Another major source of interest is the west front, which is famed for its rich and elaborate decoration. The church dwarfs the buildings in the MARKET PLACE, as it does most of the town centre. At one time, many years ago, it's effect might have been challenged by the Castle, also 12th century; where in 1216 King John was taken with a fatal fever. All that remains of the Monarch's place of demise today are a few mounds beside the CASTLE CAUSEWAY.

From Sleaford we swing south westwards and then south down the A607 past a number of other delightful villages to add to our list. We enter **GRANTHAM** (Information - 01476 566444) by way of BELTON HOUSE - and a couple of golf courses that could generate the odd yearning feeling. If they do, feel free to pop back out whilst the rest of us are touring the town. BELTON PARK COURSE (Enquiries - 01476 567399) has its own membership scheme but welcomes visitors - so that should fit the bill. The ancient town of Grantham is the largest in South West Lincolnshire. It suffered for years from the effects of traffic grinding through along the Great North Road until a by-pass, built in the 1960s, put an end to the problem. Now that the traffic and the dust have cleared, what we see is quite impressive, with some find old coaching inns and an attractive MARKET SQUARE.

At the heart of the town lies the superb PARISH CHURCH OF ST WULFRAM, with its soaring 282 ft, 14th century spire rising above the red brick town and forming a landmark that's visible for miles around. Architecturally, this is one of the most important town churches in England, with origins in the days of the Anglo Saxons. The Church, as built in 720AD, was dedicated to Wulfram who was a 7th century missionary. Some work was done in Norman times but only six pillars from that period still remain and the bulk of the church is, in fact, of 14th and 15th century construction. Together, the various elements blend into a structure that Sir George Gilbert Scott claimed was "second only to Salisbury in beauty".

The town grew up around the Church - the weekly market took place in the area in front of the West Front - but latterly the emphasis has shifted a little. For example, MARKET DAY is still an important weekly event but it has been shifted to WESTGATE, where it is held on a Saturday. Nevertheless, close to St. Wulfram's, we still find a cluster of interesting buildings, including GRANTHAM HOUSE, now a National Trust Property, which dates back to the late 14th century and grabs at our attention for its delightful acres of landscaped gardens that sweep down to the banks of the River Witham.

On ST PETER'S HILL we'll find a statue of Sir Isaac Newton, the great scientist and mathematician, who was born just outside the town, at WOOLSTHORPE BY COLSTERWORTH, in 1642. Newton, remembered by every schoolboy for his apple problem, was himself the most famous pupil (in due course) of the KING'S SCHOOL, a 15th century grammar school, where his initials are to be seen to this day, engraved in the cement on one of the window sills.

Behind the Newton statue, we come to the GUILDHALL, a grand, ornate Victorian edifice, with roofs in the French style. It dates back to 1867-69 and, at one time, incorporated the old town gaol, civic accommodation and the Sessions Hall. The building has a less ominous function today, as it is now an ARTS CENTRE and the location for the Tourist Information Centre.

Talk of 'shopping' in the context of Grantham has a curious effect on some of us. On NORTH PARADE is found what could have been the most famous shop in England, for a while. I refer to the grocer's shop which was the home - and source of income - of *the* Thatcher family. Nowadays it's a chiropractic clinic! The times they are *certainly* a 'changing'! There are many other shops to delight us - and not too many of us had a *grocer's* in mind during this trip, anyway. The town's main shopping areas are located in the modern, but stylish, Georgian design shopping centre and in two smaller sets of streets around BLUE COURT and KINGS WALK.

Drawing our stay in Grantham to a close, let's return briefly to its history and visit the town's MUSEUM, which stands beside the Guildhall. Here we'll find many examples of the excellent displays that are a feature of the area, relating to everything from archaeological discoveries to local industries. Pride of place amongst the permanent displays, however, are exhibitions with very strong local connections. There are tributes to Sir Isaac Newton, whom we've mentioned already, and to Baroness Thatcher. Alongside them is a tribute to the Dam Busters, that commemorates the role of Lincolnshire in the Second World War as the location of numerous bomber bases, notably those that sent out aircraft on the famous raids to destroy the German dams.

We leave the Museum with plenty of food for thought - but nothing like enough food for the rest of us. Yet again, we've reached the stage where nothing much seems to be able to get between us and the prospect of our evening meal. 'Best till last' wins again, however, and there's a real gem waiting for us mid-way - more or less - between Grantham and that bar - and restaurant - in Ely. As the day is drawing on, and 'rush hour' is underway, we'll pass up the A1, for safety's sake, and use the B1176 instead to take our part in the evening 'hare-and-tortoise routine' that will bring us, in time, to **STAMFORD** (Information - 01780 755611).

This town is held by many to be one of England's masterpieces with its many ancient buildings of mellowed local stone. Through history, it seems, everyone tended to agree: the Romans had a camp here, which the Saxons developed, and the Danes made it the capital of the Fens. Later still, the Normans changed all that, drove the Danes out - and the ruins of the result, a castle, can still be seen on the site of the Danish stronghold.

BARN HILL, STAMFORD

Wool made Stamford prosperous during the 12th century and 'Stamford Cloth' became known and respected throughout Europe. As the wealth accumulated, so did the buildings so that, by the 16th century there had been sufficient prosperity to trigger off an architectural boom that resulted in a delightful mixture of Georgian Mansions, Queen Anne houses and Tudor homes - in short, we have a 'high'! Stamford is a lovely town.

Looking at the CHURCHES first, as is our custom, we find that ST MARY'S is a 13th century structure with a remarkably fine 14th century spire with four stone evangelists, while ALL SAINTS has a 13th century nave and chancel and a separate tower and spire which were added in the 15th century - it also contains some remarkably fine brasses. An open church, acclaimed for its lovely stained glass, the 15th century work represents extensive rebuilding by John and William Browne, well known wool merchants, who were also responsible for the construction of BROWNE'S HOSPITAL, in BROAD STREET. Not far from All Saints is the CHURCH OF ST JOHN, a small 15th century church, built all of a piece. Of particular note here is the beautiful Lincolnshire style screenwork and the angel carvings in the roof.

Visiting all these churches - and there are two more in the town - our attention is often drawn to the jagged skyline created by their spires and towers that is such a characteristic feature of the place. Furthermore, amongst the more than six hundred listed buildings within the boundaries, there are also a 12th century priory and a now ruined 7th century chapel.

Today, winding roads and cobbled pathways lead around areas that one can easily understand Sir Walter Scott proclaiming as "the finest scene between London and Edinburgh". It was even attractive enough to Turner to come and convey his own impressions on canvas. Chance - and common sense - have contributed equally to this happy state of affairs. Stamford was lucky to escape the ravages of the industrial revolution and the more insidious, but just as hideous, effects of so-called 'modernisation' in the 20th century. Common sense then intervened and it was declared England's first conservation area in 1967.

As we've noted, the Great North Road *was* a problem for years, but present day travellers are spared even that intrusion - even if some locals acknowledge that 'The Road' did bring trade to the town in its time. In the light of that confession, one can see that Edward Brownings triple arched bridge, opened in 1849, which rid the town of a medieval bottle-neck said to be "the narrowest, most dangerous nuisance between London and Edinburgh", was a godsend, for the time being. A medieval street pattern formed the basis for Stamford's development, with thoroughfares lined with elegant Georgian buildings, embellished with wrought iron railings and decorated signs.

Against that townscape as a backdrop, we have a pageant of activities and interests whose scope has been unsurpassed anywhere throughout this tour. On the one hand there are THE MEADOWS of Stamford, an area of open parkland that is perfect for walking, relaxing and enjoying picnics; on the other there is the good natured urban bustle of the streets themselves, with their fine shops, hotels, inns and restaurants. The HIGH STREET and IRONMONGER STREET are pedestrianised shopping areas while ST MICHAEL'S CHURCH, which we spoke about recently, has actually been converted into a small shopping centre surrounded by boutiques, cafes and wine bars.

Antiques shops abound throughout the town, and two are well worthy of mention - although most of the others have their own fascination. THE ANTIQUES CENTRE on BROAD STREET is a permanent indoor centre, housed in the former STAMFORD EXCHANGE HALL. It is open seven days a week and has more than 85 stalls. ST MARTIN'S ANTIQUE CENTRE is slightly larger, with over fifty dealers specialising in a wide range of antiques from large items of furniture to jewellery. It is also open seven days a week.

To complete the shopping spectacular, one must never forget the MARKETS which have been a major feature of the town's life over the centuries. Market days are Friday, in BROAD STREET, and Saturday, in RED LION SQUARE. We'll close our visit to Stamford with a final salute to its artistic qualities. On ST MARY'S STREET we'll find the STAMFORD ARTS CENTRE, which stands as a remarkable and sympathetic restoration of an earlier theatre, built in 1766, which was one of the oldest provincial theatres in England. Following the restoration the Centre now hosts performances that cover the whole spectrum of the art - and even includes its own cinema.

One last thought, while we're talking drama and the arts: outside Stamford, only five minutes away from the A1, is TOLETHORPE HALL (Enquiries - 01780 754381) regarded by many as "the finest open air theatre in Europe". This complex incorporates not only the theatre, but also a restaurant and a bar within the historic Elizabethan Hall itself. One can assess the standard of this attraction by its having been awarded the accolade of MIDDLE ENGLAND VISITOR ATTRACTION OF THE YEAR in 1992, by the East Midlands Tourist Board.

And there you have it: South Lincolnshire. If not all of it, certainly most of the really wondrous bits - but you were absolutely right. It has been a very long day. Let's hope Stamford to Ely is not as far subjectively as it looks on the map to our weary eyes at this time in the evening. A1 (*very* careful), then A14 to Huntingdon, followed by the A1123 and the A10 back into Ely itself.

THE BLACK SWAN RESTAURANT
Hillside
Beckingham
Lincolnshire
LN5 0RQ

Tel: 01636 626474

At the end of the pretty village of Beckingham on the old main road which is now a dead end, is The Black Swan Restaurant, an old riverside country building previously used for many years as a public house. At the Black Swan every dish is home-cooked, using as much fresh local produce and ingredients as possible. The menu, mostly English with Continental influences, changes regularly and seasonally. You might start your meals with a twice baked cheese souffle served with mushroom sauce, grilled red mullet salad served with saffron vinaigrette and toasted almonds or maybe seasonal Melon served with fresh fruits with an Orange and Cardamon syrup. Follow this with Roast Magret duck breast served on a forest fruits compote with a casis sauce, Rack of Lamb with poached minted pears on a rosemary sauce or a Marinated Salmon salad served with Tiger prawns and a smoked Trout mousse on a green peppercorn sauce. The desserts are equally tempting and the selection of English cheese will delight a cheese buff. Sunday Lunch is a memorable meal. Children have their own menu and also one child per adult, under eleven years eats free. A vegetarian selection is always available. The wide ranging wine list is well chosen and sensibly priced.

USEFUL INFORMATION

OPEN: All year
CHILDREN: Welcome
CREDIT CARDS: Visa/Delta/Switch
LICENSED: Full On. Supper Licence
GARDEN: No

RESTAURANT: Mostly English
with Continental influence
VEGETARIAN: Always a choice
WHEELCHAIR ACCESS: Yes
PETS: No

THE CHEQUERS INN
Main Street
Gedney Dyke
Lincolnshire
Tel: 01406 362666

Good Food Guide and many others

This highly popular Fenland free house is known far and wide for its friendly hospitality, its well kept beer, its sound wine list, but especially for the high standard of its food. In the Main Bar you will almost always find local people enjoying a drink and nattering about current issues. They are a friendly crowd and always make strangers feel at ease. In the non-smoking restaurant the menu is wide ranging but the emphasis is on fresh fish such as Cromer crab, dabs with chips and halibut with a green peppercorn sauce. Seasonal game is much in evidence. Traditional favourites are also on the menu and the steak and kidney puddings are the best in Lincolnshire. Lincoln Red Beef is another favourite producing super roasts and tender, succulent steaks. The Bar menu has a wide choice with specials every day, sandwiches and many other things one would expect. It is great value and you can get a substantial meal for under £5. The pretty patio is used for dining in balmy weather, creating a delightful romantic ambience. Gedney Dyke is of historic interest and has much around it that is worth discovering including the Falconry Park two miles away.

USEFUL INFORMATION

OPEN: Normal Hours Food: 12-2pm 7-9.30pm
CHILDREN: Welcome menu.
CREDIT CARDS: All major cards
LICENSED: Full On
GARDEN: Patio

RESTAURANT: Exciting
Fresh fish a speciality
BAR FOOD: Traditional favourites
VEGETARIAN: Always a choice
WHEELCHAIR ACCESS: Yes
PETS: Guide dogs only

THE CROSS SWORDS INN
The Square
Skillington
Grantham
Lincolnshire
NG33 5HB

Tel/Fax: 01476 861132
harold@xswords.demon.co.uk

The quiet country village of Skillington dates back approximately to the 12th century and is full of interest. It is just off the Viking Way enjoyed by walkers, has a very old church in the village with a stained glass window depicting the attempt of one of the vicars to climb the Matterhorn; he succeeded but died on the descent. From here one can visit the Gliding Club, go horse riding or visit the many historical places, including National Trust properties, within easy distance. At the cross-roads of the village is the 19th century Cross Swords Inn, very much the focal point of village life. Its warm, friendly and cheerful atmosphere is created to a great extent by the landlords Mr and Mrs Wood who run it with the help of their family. Its busy restaurant has twenty eight covers and the food, all home-cooked, is generous in portion and great value for money. You will not find a pool table, a juke Box or a television here, just quiet piped music, good food and conversation.

USEFUL INFORMATION

OPEN: 12-2pm & 7-11pm
CHILDREN: Lunch-time only
CREDIT CARDS: All major cards
LICENSED: Full On
GARDEN: Yes

RESTAURANT: Good pub fare
BAR FOOD: Always a choice
VEGETARIAN: With notice
WHEELCHAIR ACCESS: Yes
PETS: No

THE FIVE BELLS
Edenham,
Nr Bourne,
Lincolnshire
PE10 0LL

Tel: 01778 591235

The Five Bells is at Edenham on the A151 just three miles from Bourne and one and a half miles from Grimsthorpe. Paul Stark and his wife Mary have been the landlords here for twenty one years and are well known and liked in the neighbourhood, They run it with help from family members and other long term staff and the objective for all of them is to ensure that customers enjoy their visit to the Five Bells. It is a cheerful, friendly hostelry much used by locals but it also enjoys a great reputation for its functions including dinner dances, wedding receptions and other special occasions. These functions are given the same keen attention to detail that is apparent throughout the inn. Nothing is left to chance, the beer is well kept and the food excellent. The everyday menu includes all the time honoured favourites as well as some interesting Continental and Oriental dishes. Bar snacks are always popular and cover all manner of dishes including freshly cut sandwiches, ploughman's and daily specials. Above all the Five Bells is value for money.

USEFUL INFORMATION

OPEN: All year except Christmas & Boxing Day
11-3pm & 6.30-11pm
CHILDREN: Welcome
CREDIT CARDS: Visa/Switch/Master
LICENSED: Full On + special hours to 2am
GARDEN: Yes

RESTAURANT: Good
　　　　　　　traditional fare
BAR FOOD: Wide range
VEGETARIAN: Always a choice
WHEELCHAIR ACCESS: Yes
PETS: No

THE GARDEN HOUSE HOTEL
St Martins. Stamford
Lincolnshire   PE9 2LP

Tel: 01780 763359   - Fax: 01780 763339

RAC***AA 4   Crowns Commended

On June 11th 1813 The Garden House Hotel was described in the Stamford Mercury as being of modern design with two kitchens, breakfast, eating and drawing rooms, with nine bedrooms above. Today the paper would need to say that this charming 18th century house is a beautiful twenty room hotel offering modern comforts and traditional service. It is delightful, situated close to the centre of Stamford, England's finest stone built town. It is within easy reach of Burgley House, Stamford Steam Brewery Museum, the Nene Valley Steam Railway, the cathedral city of Peterborough, Rutland Waters and Tallington Lakes as well as some excellent golf courses. The twenty bedrooms are tastefully decorated and furnished with television, direct dial telephone and hostess trays. In the elegant Dining Room where the walls are hung with original Belgian tapestries and each table has its own candle lamp, the emphasis is on home cooking and value for money, something appreciated by both locals and the traveller. The Bar and Conservatory both overlook the tranquil one acre garden at the back of the Hotel. Morning coffee and afternoon tea are served as required and the bar menu is available at both lunch-time and all evening. Conference facilities are also available.

USEFUL INFORMATION

OPEN:7am-11pm	DINING ROOM: Home cooking.
CHILDREN: Welcome Value for money	
BAR FOOD: Available at lunch and all evening	VEGETARIAN:Yes
CREDIT CARDS: AMEX/Visa/Master/Switch	LICENSED: Full On
WHEELCHAIR ACCESS: Yes	GARDEN: 1 acre
ACCOMMODATION: 20 en-suite rooms	
RATES: From £35 sgl & £70 dbl. Sgl surcharge £10 Four-poster £15	

THE GEORGE OF STAMFORD
71 St Martins, Stamford
Lincolnshire   PE9 2LB
Tel: 01780 750750
Fax: 01780 750701
Email:georgehotelofstamford@btinternet.com
Internet:www.georgehotelofstamford.com/
***

The 16th century coaching Inn, the George of Stamford's exact age is not known, but historians have referred to it as 'A very ancient hostelry, once belonging to the Abbots of Croyland' so it is possible that it was standing in 947AD. At that time it would have been comparatively small but today it is much increased in size, has retained much of the earlier features and has a tremendous atmosphere, and at the same time offers today's guests every modern comfort. It is warm, welcoming, hospitable and a pleasure to stay in with its log fires, oak-panelled restaurant, with a walled monastery garden, a cobbled courtyard decorated with hanging baskets - all in keeping with the style of Stamford. The hotel is both for business and pleasure, attached to the hotel is a Conference Centre incorporating all modern facilities. The A La Carte Restaurant offers both the highest standard of cuisine and service, the style is essentially traditional - the sirloin beef carved at your table is just one example - but utilises modern and international ideas. The Garden Lounge is less formal, serving food from 7.00am until 11pm, or alternatively in the summer months enjoy the picturesque courtyard. The internationally acclaimed wine list is not only to be admired but enjoyed at your leisure.

USEFUL INFORMATION

OPEN: All year	RESTAURANT: Traditional English
CHILDREN: Welcome & Continental	
CREDIT CARDS: All major cards	BAR FOOD: Wide choice
LICENSED: Full On	VEGETARIAN: Always a choice
ACCOMMODATION: 47 en-suite rooms	GARDEN: Courtyard. Monastery
RATES: Sgl from £78 Dbl. from £100	PETS: Yes

GUY WELLS
Eastgate
Whaplode
Spalding
Lincolnshire
PE12 6TZ
Tel: 01406 422239

This surely must be one of the most relaxed and restful guest houses in the Fens. Guy Wells is a creeper-covered Queen Anne farmhouse with a vast garden and fields beyond. There are greenhouses filled with daffodils, lilies and tulips which the owners Anne and Richard Thompson, grow commercially, and Richard is happy to show guests around the farm. Inside the house is full of flowers, as one would expect, and they marry, in complete harmony, with the fabrics and pictures.

There are eye catching displays of fine china in the cosy, beamed sitting room and dining room which come from Anne's grandparents' shop in nearby Spalding. The pretty bedrooms, mainly en-suite, have lacy and candlewick bedspreads and are furnished with Victorian antiques, providing an air of homely comfort. Anne is a good cook and provides delicious dinners using home-grown vegetables and at breakfast free-range eggs from their own hens add to the excellence of the substantial breakfast. Guy Wells is the sort of place that having once discovered, you will want to return, like many others.

USEFUL INFORMATION

OPEN: All year. Closed Christmas
CHILDREN: Not under 10 years
CREDIT CARDS: None taken
LICENSED: No
ACCOMMODATION: En suite rooms
RATES: Sgl £20-29 Dbl. £50 B&B Special breaks

DINING ROOM: Delicious home-cooked fare
VEGETARIAN: Upon request
WHEELCHAIR ACCESS: Yes
GARDEN: Lovely garden

THE MAGPIES
71-75 East Street,
Horncastle,
Lincolnshire
LN9 6AA
Good Food Guide 4
Michelin 2XX AA**
Tel: 01507 527004
Fax: 01507 524064

Horncastle is renowned world-wide as a thriving market town where the emphasis is on antiques. On the outskirts, in East Street, is The Magpies, a charming restaurant created out of three former cottages. It is a stylish but intimate place with attractively appointed tables with crystal glass and crisp white linen. It is run by the Lee family who put the well-being of their customers above everything and have devised an ever changing menu which tempts the most critical palate.
The best description of the food on offer is Modern English with a Continental influence. The wine list is reputed to be the most comprehensive in Lincolnshire with bottles from all the major wine producing nations from £10 to over £100 a bottle. Esoteric and unusual wines are a speciality. The Lees know a great deal about wine and are very happy to help you choose a wine to complement the delicious food. It is a restaurant that once visited will stay in your mind for a long time and you will want to return as do the many regular clients The Magpies has from a wide area around Horncastle.

USEFUL INFORMATION

OPEN: All year. Tuesday-Saturday
CHILDREN: Welcome
CREDIT CARDS: Visa/Mastercard
LICENSED: Restaurant

RESTAURANT: Delicious Modern
English and Continental fare
VEGETARIAN: Always a choice
WHEELCHAIR ACCESS: Yes

NEW SARACENS HEAD INN
Washway Road
Saracens Head
Spalding
Lincolnshire PE12 8AY
Tel: 01406 490339
Mobile 0802 296950

This is an 18th century village Inn covenant for the A17 trunk road. It has the bonus of having a small and friendly, well run caravan site behind the Inn which is open from March to November with electric hook-ups and showers. There is excellent wheelchair access. In the Inn which is open all year long, there is a warm and welcoming atmosphere enhanced by the cheerful open fires in season. The oak beamed dining area with thirty two covers offers a full menu from Thursday to Tuesday. The Inn is closed on Wednesday at lunch-time and no food is available on Wednesday evening. The traditional Sunday Lunch is very popular with succulent meat, crisp roast potatoes, fresh vegetables and all the trimmings. The wide ranging menu has something to appeal to everyone and the price is right. The Bar is a friendly place where the locals are happy to include visitors in whatever is going on, whether it is darts, dominoes, pool or just lively conversation. No juke box!

USEFUL INFORMATION

OPEN: 11-3pm & 7-11pm
Sunday 12-3pm & 7-10.30pm
Thurs-Tues & Sunday Lunch Closed Wed.
Lunch. No food Wed eve
CARAVAN SITE: Mar-Nov inc.
WHEELCHAIR ACCESS: Yes
PETS: Yes. Not in dining area
CREDIT CARDS: None taken
RATES: Standard £6 per night for caravans

RESTAURANT: Wide range
food
VEGETARIAN: Always a choice
BAR FOOD: Home-cooked
GARDEN: Yes s. Play area
CHILDREN: Welcome
LICENSED: Full On

THE OLDE SHIP
89, London Road,
Long Sutton,
Lincolnshire
PE12 9EE
Tel: 01406 362930
Fax: 01406 365241

In a semi-rural setting on the outskirts of Long Sutton with a large common pond next to the inn with ducks and geese, and close to Sutton Bridge, the historical swing bridge over the River Nene, The Olde Ship Inn has been a much loved hostelry for a long time. The main bar areas are 17th century and believed once to have been two cottages with very low ceilings and original beams which still exist. The atmosphere is wonderful and the hospitality tremendous. Ian and Joy Day are mine hosts and their cheerful, friendly approach is appreciated by everyone who comes here. They are keen animal lovers and have two goats. Winnie and George who live at the back of the inn and two miniature horses, Ben and Barney who reside in the close by Butterfly and Falconry Centre. The two bars are small and homely with polished copper bars and the twenty four cover dining room with its relaxed and informal atmosphere is a popular place to eat. The food, prepared and cooked by Joy is well known for its high standard and she insists on using only the best and freshest of vegetables and ingredients. Vegetarians are catered for and Joy will happily cater for special diets given short notice.

USEFUL INFORMATION

OPEN: Mon-Thurs:11.30-3pm & 5.30-11pm
Fri/Sat: All day Sun:12-3pm & 7-10.30pm
CHILDREN: Not under 14 years
CREDIT CARDS: Visa/Delta/Switch/JCB
LICENSED: Full On
GARDEN: Yes

DINING ROOM: Home-cooked
fare
BAR FOOD: Wide range
VEGETARIAN: Yes + other diets
WHEELCHAIR ACCESS: Yes
PETS: Guide dogs only

THE ANGEL HOTEL
Market Place
Bourne, Lincolnshire   PE10 9AE
Tel: 01778 422346
Fax: 01778 426113
AA**RAC ETB***

Bourne, a busy market town, has been settled since Roman times and is full of interest for the visitor. In the Market Place is The Angel Hotel, dating back to the 18th century when it was initially called the Nags Head, changing its name in the 1800s. It is full of character as one might expect an old coaching inn to be. Gone are the livery stables as such, but they have become part of the Hotel. The Angel has long been involved in many important local events, the least popular was its 'registration' in 1808, as a excise office. A central point for local merchants to pay their duties. It is a very popular Hotel today for all sorts of reasons, not the least because it is within easy reach of a number of fascinating places to visit like Burghley House, the preservation town of Stamford, Rutland Water and much else. It still retains a lot of original character, with most of the original oak beams still in evidence. There are fourteen en-suite, tastefully furnished bedrooms with direct dial telephone, colour television, alarm radio and beverage facilities. Two superior bedrooms have four poster beds and one also has a whirlpool bath and bidet. In the thirty two cover restaurant there is an informal choice of dining from the daily menu. The Angel also serves tasty bar meals, morning coffee and afternoon tea. The Copperfield Suite is available for conferences & functions

USEFUL INFORMATION

OPEN: All year Mon-Sat 12-2pm
&7-9.30 Sun: 12-3pm
CHILDREN: Welcome
CREDIT CARDS: All major cards
LICENSED: Full On
ACCOMMODATION: 14 en-suite rooms
RATES: Sgl from £40 B&B dbl./tw £50 4 Poster £60

RESTAURANT; Excellent menu
Table d'hôte at night only
BAR FOOD: Tasty snacks, morning
coffee, afternoon tea
VEGETARIAN: Always a choice
WHEELCHAIR ACCESS: No
GARDEN: No
PETS: By arrangement

THE DEEPING STAGE
16 Market Place, Market Deeping
Peterborough, Cambridgeshire
PE6 8EA

Tel: 01778 343234
Fax: 01778 343576

For travellers in the last century, The New Inn, now The Deeping Stage, was the first overnight stop on the Lincoln to London run. The hostelry was abundant with good food and fine drink and offered a warm place to stay. The Deeping Stage is rich in history; something one feels as you enter its welcoming portals. Supposedly an ostler walks the hallway at night, the early morning wake up at 4am and a coach and four clattering its way to the stables at midnight all help to enrich the great atmosphere. Today the accommodation is warm and comfortable, the rooms attractively decorated and appointed with ten en-suite rooms and two standard rooms. Every room has television, direct dial telephone and a hostess tray. In the restaurant there is a varied menu with something to appeal to everyone and at a reasonable cost. Food at the bar can be a freshly cut sandwich or a light meal. Vegetarians always have a choice. There is a pleasant garden, popular with everyone in the summer. A special 'low cost' Sunday menu is on offer for regular clients. All sorts of social activities take place including Karaoke, Quiz Nights and Supper Dances. A firm favourite of mine when in South Lincolnshire.

USEFUL INFORMATION

OPEN: All year. All day
CHILDREN: Welcome Reasonable prices
CREDIT CARDS: All major cards
LICENSED: Full On
ACCOMMODATION: 10 en-suite 2
RATES: £49 sgl £69 dbl.

RESTAURANT: Varied menu.
BAR FOOD: Wide choice
VEGETARIAN: Always a choice
WHEELCHAIR ACCESS: Yes
GARDEN: Yes   standard
PETS: By arrangement

GRIFFIN INN
Bulby Road,
Irnham, Grantham,
Lincolnshire

Tel/Fax: 01476 550201

Irnham is a picturesque Conservation village with a medieval setting. In its midst is the charming Griffin Inn which is the focal point of the village. Come here and you will soon discover all about what goes on in the community. It is somewhere to stay and recharge your batteries before taking on once more the pressures of modern day life. There are four comfortable bedrooms, attractively furnished with shared guest bathrooms. Each room has television and a hostess tray. Breakfast every morning is a delicious, substantial meal which will set you up for a day's exploration of this beautiful part of Lincolnshire with its great walks, and splendid scenery. Every day food is served in the bar from a wide ranging menu which changes regularly. The beer is well kept and the whole atmosphere of this quaint inn is delightful, welcoming and friendly.

USEFUL INFORMATION

OPEN: Winter 7-11pm Sat/Sun12-3pm & 7-11pm
Summer: All day
CHILDREN: Welcome
CREDIT CARDS: None taken
LICENSED: Full On
ACCOMMODATION: 4 guest rooms shared bathroom
RATES: £30double

BAR FOOD: Wide range
VEGETARIAN: 4 Variations
WHEELCHAIR ACCESS: Yes
GARDEN: Yes
PETS: Yes

THE HARE & HOUNDS COUNTRY INN
The Green, Fulbeck
Grantham, Lincolnshire   NG32 3JJ
Tel: 01400 272090 Fax: 01400 273663
Three Crowns

Combining the past harmoniously with the present, The Hare and Hounds is a delightful country inn located in the picturesque village of Fulbeck. Originally built in 1648 it still has many original features which retain its character and atmosphere but it also offers 20th century amenities of central heating, en-suite rooms and a charming refurbished bar and restaurant. The Inn has a beautiful patio garden which is very popular in warm weather tempting people outside to drink and eat and perhaps play a game of Petanque. It is adjacent to the historic Fulbeck Hall and only twelve miles from the majestic Cathedral City of Lincoln. It is a rural location with great walks and there are golf courses nearby. With an talented chef who has an excellent local reputation, the Inn is now making a name for itself as the venue for splendid Elizabethan Banquets which are held four times a year. The eight en-suite bedrooms have traditional country decor and overlook the mews garden. All the rooms have television and hostess trays. Two function rooms are much in use for small conferences, wedding receptions and other occasions. David and Alison Nicholas are the owners, who with their well-trained, friendly staff, make sure everyone enjoys visiting The Hare and Hounds.

USEFUL INFORMATION

OPEN:11.30-2.30pm & 5-11pm Mon-Fri
All day Sat & Sun
BAR FOOD: Comprehensive menu
VEGETARIAN: Several options
CREDIT CARDS: Master/Visa/Switch.
ACCOMMODATION: 8 en-suite rooms
RATES: Sgl £35. Dbl. £45 Triple Room £55

RESTAURANT:
English/Continental
CHILDREN: Welcome
WHEELCHAIR ACCESS: Yes
4 ground floor rooms
LICENSED: Full On
GARDEN: Yes. Patio & Petanque
PETS: By arrangement

THE JOLLY SCOTCHMAN
Holdingham,
Sleaford,
Lincolnshire
NG34 8NP

Tel: 01529 304864

The Jolly Scotchman is a traditional public house in a rural location just one mile from the busy market town of Sleaford. It is a good base if you want to have a drink and a meal before exploring places like Cranwell, the home of the Red Arrows, or the Six Sail working windmill in the village of Heckington about six miles away. It is called The Scotchman because there used to be a toll gate and they 'scotched' the wheels whilst tolls were being paid, a custom that dates back, like the pub, to the 16th century. The pub has a large garden which is popular with visitors and beloved by children because of its aviary, its chipmunks, rabbits and a large adventure playground. The large conservatory restaurant seats seventy comfortably and offers a wide ranging menu with an International flavour. You can choose from the a la carte menu or from the daily specials which are usually time honoured favourites. Bar Food is also available with anything from a sandwich to fish, chicken or vegetarian options.

USEFUL INFORMATION

OPEN: 11-3pm & 6.30-11pm
CHILDREN: Welcome. Play area
CREDIT CARDS: Visa/Delta/AMEX/Diners/Master
LICENSED: Full On
GARDEN: Large. Aviary, rabbits, chipmunks

RESTAURANT: International menu
BAR FOOD: Wide range
VEGETARIAN: Yes
WHEELCHAIR ACCESS: Yes
PETS: Outside only

THE OLD MILL
Mill Lane, Tallington
Stamford, Lincolnshire

Tel: 01780 740815 Fax: 01780 740280

Four miles east of the historic stone town of Stamford with its multitude of mellow buildings, on the original Great North Road, is Tallington, a quiet place. In its midst is The Old Mill, written about in the Doomsday Book, although the current building dates from 1682. Surrounded by lush water meadows and farmland, it is the epitome of peace and ideal for anyone wanting to find relaxation and quiet. The Old Mill has been renovated to provide spacious and comfortable accommodation with six pretty en-suite bedrooms. All the rooms have panoramic views overlooking a footbridge spanning the River Welland to the mill pond and water meadows beyond. These teem with wildlife and are a bird watcher's paradise. Many of the original features remain including the heavy exposed beams and the huge mill workings in the attractive and cosy dining room. Here a delicious and substantial breakfast is served and dinner is available by arrangement. There are many places of interest close by including Stamford, the ancient market towns of Oakham, Oundle and Uppingham. Majestic cathedrals at Lincoln and Peterborough, Burghley House, the Fens and Rutland Water. Golf and fishing. It would be hard to find a more idyllic place to stay and one that is excellent value for money.

USEFUL INFORMATION

OPEN: All year
CHILDREN: Over 10 years
CREDIT CARDS: None taken
WHEELCHAIR ACCESS: Limited1 ground floor room
ACCOMMODATION: 6 en-suite rooms
RATES: £24 pp.pn B&B

DINING ROOM: Excellent breakfast
Dinner by arrangement
VEGETARIAN: Upon request
LICENSED: No
GARDEN: Yes
PETS: By arrangement

THE PRIORY
Ketton, Stamford
Lincolnshire
Tel: 01780 720215 Fax: 01780 721881
priory.a0504924@infortrade.co.uk

AAQQQQ Selected Johansen's Recommended ETB***

This large historic house dating from the 16th century has been meticulously restored in recent years. Now a family home offering a number of rooms for guests, 'The Priory', described in Pevsner's Buildings of England, was in fact not a Priory but a prebendal manor house up until 1725, at which time it became a private residence. The exterior is a delight from any angle. It looks south over the large gardens and frontage to the River Chater. To the north the house turns its back on the street and the overwhelming presence of the very large 12th century church. The gardens are wonderful with formal rose beds, large manicured lawns and a charming riverside terrace. One can enjoy the gardens from the spacious conservatory where breakfast and dinner can be served. There is also a feature dining room and two lounges. Most guest rooms overlook the gardens. They have individually designed en-suite facilities. Bedrooms are large with luxury king-size beds, panelled walls, working shutters and designer fabrics. All have colour television, tea and coffee making facilities, radio, direct dial phones and central heating. The food and the wine live up to the exceptional standards of the house. It could not be a more enchanting and peaceful place to stay.

USEFUL INFORMATION

OPEN: All year
CHILDREN: Yes breakfast. Freshly
VEGETARIAN: By arrangement
WHEELCHAIR ACCESS: Yes
ACCOMMODATION. Large, en suite rooms
Facilities for meetings (Please apply for prices)

DINING ROOM: Excellent prepared evening meals.
CREDIT CARDS: All major cards
LICENSED: Yes
GARDEN: Yes - a delight
PETS. By arrangement

THE ROYAL OAK INN
Swayfield, Grantham
Lincolnshire   NG33 4LL
Tel: 01476 550247 Fax: 01476 550996
ETB Listed Commended. 'CAMRA' B&BGuide

The Royal Oak is in the midst of the thriving picturesque village of Swayfield in rural Lincolnshire. The quiet location is wonderful for anyone wanting to escape from the busy world and recharge their batteries in a friendly hostelry which has been dispensing hospitality since the middle of the 17th century. From The Royal Oak you walk, go mountain biking or pony trekking. There are National Trust properties, Burghley House, Grimsthorpe Castle, Belton House and Belvoir Castle being the most popular. Rutland Water is close by for sailing, fishing and walking. The Inn is welcoming, warm and friendly in the capable hands of David and Juliette Cooke who are happy when they see their customers enjoyment. Many people come to stay once and then return again and again. The food is excellent whether it is in the restaurant or the bar. The A la Carte menu, always displayed on the Blackboard has ten starters and twenty five main courses always changing. The Bar offers everything from sandwiches and burgers to £5 Table d' hote and a la carte. All the five en-suite bedrooms are new conversion of an old stone barn, spacious and pine furnished. New for Autumn 1998 is a luxurious Executive Suite with five foot four poster and double Jacuzzi. Whilst The Royal Oak has a wealth of beam ceilings and oak panelling, it is thoroughly modern and comfortably fitted for discerning guests.

USEFUL INFORMATION

OPEN: 10.30-3.00pm & 6-11pm

CHILDREN: Welcome
CREDIT CARDS: Visa/AMEX
LICENSED: Full On
ACCOMMODATION: 5 en-suite rooms
RATES: Sgl £33 Dbl. £44 Family Room £55

RESTAURANT: Blackboard Closed Christmas Night
displayed menu with 10 Starters & 25 main courses
BAR FOOD: Wide range. Value for money
VEGETARIAN: Always a choice
WHEELCHAIR ACCESS: Yes. Ramp
GARDEN: Yes
PETS: Yes

THE SNOOTY FOX & PARKERS RESTAURANT
Dozen's Bank,
West Pinchbeck,
Spalding,
Lincolnshire
PE11 3NF
Tel: 01775 640020
Fax: 01775 640176

The Snooty Fox which once used to be The Bridge Inn is to be found on the A151 Spalding-Bourne Road, on the banks of the River Glen, some 3 miles from Spalding famous for its Bulb Festivals. It is the friendliest of hostelries and the welcome given to customers by Jo and John Parker and Scott Donaldson, who have recently acquired The Snooty Fox, is second to none. Very much a family affair, Jo looks after Parker's Restaurant, John does all the cooking and Scott, Jo's son, runs the bar. Since their arrival they have spent much time and money upgrading the restaurant which now has super crockery, cutlery and glassware. Relaxed and pleasantly informal, the restaurant offers delicious food, beautifully presented. With an ever growing number of regular customers who have discovered how good The Snooty Fox is under its new ownership, there is no doubt that Jo, John and Scott have quickly achieved a successful beginning to their enterprise which leans far more towards styling themselves as a restaurant with a pub, not vice versa. More and more people will beat a path to this friendly establishment. Having talked to these people we wish them every success in their efforts to create an eating house to be proud of..

USEFUL INFORMATION

OPEN: 11-3pm & 6.30-11pm
CHILDREN: Welcome
CREDIT CARDS: None taken at present
LICENSED: Full On
PETS: Yes

RESTAURANT: Modern
'International' fare.
VEGETARIAN: Always a choice
WHEELCHAIR ACCESS: Yes
GARDEN: Riverbank pathway

Selected venues in this chapter

'...And must I wholly banish hence
These red and golden juices,
And pay my vows to Abstinence,
That pallidest of Muses?'....
William Watson

✶✶✶✶✶✶✶✶✶✶✶✶✶✶

' If there's an end
On which I'd spend
My last remaining cash,
It's sausage , my friend,
It's sausage, my friend,
It's sausage, friend, and mash'.
A. P. Herbert

CHAPTER 9:
'Shrine of a King, Cradle of the Law?'
Bury St Edmunds to Newmarket & further afield

The ancient Kingdom of East Anglia used to be made up of the North Folk (Norfolk) and the South Folk (Suffolk). Now we live in one, more or less United Kingdom that distinction has lost most of it's influence. A further bit of boundary blurring over more recent years has led to the two originals being joined by Essex (East Saxons?) and Cambridgeshire, in most people's minds. Others, like us, don't stop there and add in a bit of South Lincolnshire, in the name of logic. Beyond that, there are other 'authorities', I gather, who would like to see Hertfordshire and Bedfordshire drawn in as well. Is there no end? Can we look forward to the day when everywhere east of a vertical line from Brighton to Bradford is merged into one, vast hyper region? Very likely I'd have thought, along the lines of 'The Federation of Eastern Counties' - to parallel 'The Federation of European States', perhaps. Of course, history never stands still - it swings like a pendulum - so the next, mid millennial phase will be a reversion to local autonomy when the stout folk of St Neots can be expected to leap upon barricades sometime in 2063, with cries of "Independence for Huntingdon!" Soon after that, with a bit of bureaucratic huffing and puffing, we'll all go back to square one, while we do a head count of all the new millionaires who made a packet out of all the upheaval.

They don't worry about things like that in Suffolk. As far as I can make out, they don't worry about anything, much. You only have to look at their environment for a few minutes and it's quite obvious what underlies this total lack of *fuss*. Suffolk is *beautiful*! Devotees of East Anglia as a whole call it the Real England. If that's the case, Suffolk is more real than real. Put another way, it's the sort of reality that the majority of people actually *need*, as opposed to what they've actually *got*, around Milton Keynes, Dartford or Toxteth.

On the Suffolk coast, for example, you'll find some of the most picturesque, untouched villages in England, nestling on the cliff edge. Drays from the local brewery, still drawn by horses, deliver beer to the pubs and hotels in the gracious and uncommercialised little town of Southwold, while, over the river at Walberswick, artists, sailors and naturalists are attracted to a thousand acre nature reserve. Aldburgh too seems untroubled by the passage of time, as fishermen sell their catches from tarred huts on the beach and children sail their model yachts on the pond. Its 'official', too, for the local councillors themselves still hold their meetings in the quaint, half timbered Moot Hall - that dates from the *16th century*!

The pointer to the success of Suffolk, in my eyes, is summed up in that last fact: the Moot Hall is delightful, its very old - and *its still in use*! No-one has bought it to turn it into a tarted up tripper trap, its facade has not been grafted onto the front of a shedful of virtual reality at ten quid a ticket. No, it's a Moot hall - and four hundred years after it was built, local people look for no more from life than to go on 'mooting' in it. Excellent, wouldn't you say?

Further down the coast at Felixstowe, there's been a head on collision between the demands of the container ship business - this is one of the busiest ports of its kind in the country - and the expression of a more traditional role as a holiday resort with a distinctly pre-war flavour. Elsewhere one would have expected the jack boots of modernity to clump about flattening everything, but not in Suffolk - although Felixstowe is only just 'in'. Beyond the Stour/Orwell estuary lies Harwich, definitely in Essex and nothing to do with us for now.

The Northern extremity of this sublime coast is found at Lowestoft, where the fishing business rubs shoulders cheerily with holiday makers of all shapes and sizes and everybody makes a living. Here too Broadland, traditionally a feature of Norfolk life, cocks a snook at tradition - and boundaries - and appears as a Suffolk version only a short distance inland from the busy inner harbour.

Away from the A12 Suffolk is expansive and unspoilt, as a whole, but has pronounced local variations that mean it's best considered in three areas; West Suffolk, the lands between Bury St Edmunds, Newmarket and Long Melford; Mid Suffolk, 'Constable Country', the lands between Lavenham and the River Stour and East Suffolk, the Coastal strip from north to south that runs as far inland as Stowmarket. That idea suggests three Chapters to cover the county, and so it will be.

Wasting no more time, let's pack the bags, load up the car and say our last Goodbyes to Ely, before heading away south and east to our next base. Usually, I try to leave the best till last in these chapters, to end on a 'high', and so forth. Fine - only this time it's different, because the 'high' has a lot to do with universal responses to stimuli and so, maybe, we all have to go with the flow. What on earth am I talking about? Try this, by way of an answer: approach the population to a typically English town such as Widnes with the question: "What do you think of first when you think of Suffolk?" Ninety nine point three per cent won't know what you mean; five will get you ten that the remainder - both of them - will give a knee-jerk reaction and mutter 'Constable.' That's the way it is: plenty of brilliant minds, noble heroes and the like may well have drawn their first breaths in the county, but no-one quite seems to remember who they were. Constable, though, well, that's *very* different. Suffolk *is* Constable Country, everyone ought to know that. So, to pretend it isn't, to waffle on about the finer points of life in Framlingham, or the antique trade in Walsham le Willows with the major claim to fame tapping its toe in the wings would be too perverse for comfort. Or it could be the flash of inspiration, or originality needed to kick-start this bit of the book away from the knee deep footprints of those who went before us, lemming like, down the tourist trail by the hundreds of thousands - and never got further into Suffolk than East Bergholt. That's where *he* was *born*, you know. *Constable*!)

The more I think about it, the more I like it: we *will* leave the banks of the Stour, and all that goes with them, as a final touch of icing for the cake. Our mission will be 'to boldly go' somewhere else - up and around West Suffolk, for example. Why not? Fine, start the motor before I have time to change my mind. We're off to **BURY ST EDMUNDS** (Information - 01284 757084).

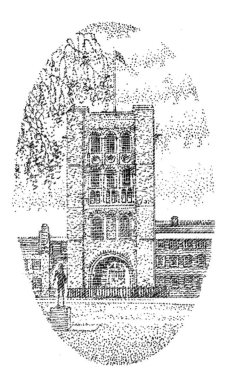

NORMAN TOWER, BURY ST EDMUNDS

Although this busy and beautiful market town in East Anglia's heartland retains many visible links with it's rich Christian heritage, it's still hard to realise the true extent of its influence. Our focus has shifted, over the centuries, and the idea that *anywhere* could be "one of the most powerful monasteries in medieval Europe" sounds alien and leads to responses like: "Really? and just *how* powerful would *that* be?" In modern terms, the Benedictine Abbey of St Edmunds was as powerful as they come. Within its area of interest, it could stand against anyone and did for nearly five hundred years. The Dissolution finished it, in 1539, when the Abbot, Prior and 42 monks signed a deed of surrender. Recycling then took over, as everything valuable was stripped, down to the stonework. That, in turn, was used - as an impromptu quarry - and today, we can see that many buildings nearby still have bits of the old Abbey incorporated into their structure.

The Abbey was built on the site of a 7th century monastery set up at the settlement of Beodricksworth by the Saxon King Seigbercht. For just over two hundred years learning and the Church flourished in the area in spite of being attacked by the Vikings, as a way of life. In 869AD, King Edmund lost his head - literally - in trying to defeat the invaders. Having suffered this unpleasant end, he went on to a far more successful 'after-life', it seems. According to the legend, his head was found in a wood, being guarded by a wolf, and 33 years later, during the reign of Alfred the Great, as the rest of his remains were achieving such a reputation for their miraculous powers they were all collected together at Beodricksworth - where they went on being miraculous. This situation has two (not unrelated) spin-offs; Beodricksworth became bigger and richer, thanks to the stream of pilgrims coming to pay homage to Edmund's relics; and Edmund became canonised as the patron saint of England. By the time of the Conquest, the Abbey had already been renamed St Edmundsbury and was under a French Abbot, Baldwin, who was responsible for laying out the town along the grid pattern that is so familiar today.

The next five centuries were a roller-coaster for the town and the Abbey: it is believed that a preliminary to Magna Carta was a meeting of 25 barons who swore an oath at the High Altar to force King John to accept the Charter of Liberties. This event, coupled with the role of King Edmund, gave the town its ancient motto; 'Shrine of a King, Cradle of Law'. Little more than a hundred years later, 3,000 townspeople rioted against the rule of the Abbey and monks actually attacked a parish church. When the Black Death arrived shortly afterwards, the delicate power balance became even shakier and there were more waves of revolt and retribution in 1380 and 1381.

The next hundred years saw much rebuilding in an atmosphere of renewed vigour, but the relationship between the town and the Abbey was far from stable. St Mary's Church was finished in 1427, while Henry VI was a frequent visitor to the Abbey, which continued to grow, despite the fire of 1465 that actually caused damage to St Edmund's shrine. The rebuilding was so sumptuous that Henry VIII's antiquary, John Leyland, wrote after a visit in 1538 that it was more like a city. Right up to the 1560s the Abbey's power remained unchallenged in any meaningful way. Thomas Cromwell sent a hit squad up to East Anglia to try to find evidence of misconduct but they failed and went away empty handed. The lull didn't last long after that and in 1538 the keeper of the King's Jewels found a pretext to remove gold, silver and church plate. The writing, as they say, was in the cloisters: one year more and it was all over, torn apart. Nine centuries of monastic traditions vanished at the stroke of a pen.

Of course, while the Abbey had become a thing of the past, life in all other respects went on regardless. Or even more dynamically. The town might have lost its monks, but it still had a superb church where Henry VII - an oddball to the end - had actually had his sister, Mary Rose, buried. While he gloated over the potential up the road for 'Plan B', presumably! There was also another church along the road, St James, that was much older and that was to have quite a future in the fullness of time.

In not much more than half a century the town survived a fire, in 1603, and was incorporated, in 1608, by James I, who also granted it a crest. The extensive period of building and refurbishment that followed in the 17th and 18th centuries gave Bury St Edmunds much of the character we see today, particularly as it was lucky enough to escape most of the worst excesses with which the Victorians chose to proclaim their prosperity elsewhere. On the other hand, those same Victorians had a fixation on anything old, in general, and medieval and romantic in particular, so the town has something to thank them for, in the form of a revival of interest in the Abbey and its surroundings.

A new diocese was created in 1913 and St James' Church was chosen to be the new cathedral because it was sited within sufficient space for the expansion that would need to follow. Once the two World Wars were over - and most of the Yanks *had* gone home - the town began a phase of controlled expansion which set up high-tech industries on the outskirts to supplement the centuries old occupations of brewing and agriculture. It seems to have worked extremely well, although when push comes to shove, each individual has to make a personal decision. Certainly, the traditional characteristics of a quiet market town, of a town with charm and assurance are very evident - and positive enough to justify every minute of the time we shall spend exploring its buildings, streets, gardens - *and* antique auctions, markets, craft centres and shops, I imagine.

Before we start our walkabout, which will probably be at the Corn Exchange (have you *seen* that place? Worthy of Manchester at the peak of its civic pride, that is!) we need to see Bury as something more than just another town with a Cathedral. It's the hub of a network whose roads, like radiating spokes, reach out to the furthest extremes of the Borough of St. Edmundsbury and beyond, to Cambridge, Norwich, London and the new style, East coast ports with their highly developed access to the Continent. Incidentally, that could be another reason for starting at the Corn Exchange: it's a symbol of the Bury that *is*. While I *love* Cathedrals (as you may or may not have noticed) we could do ourselves - and everyone else - a favour by setting out to avoid being overwhelmed, here, by that mighty Christian heritage, that ever present memory of monastic bureaucracy that has the potential to stifle everything else.

BEATING THE RETREAT, BURY ST EDMUNDS

As that same hub is the focal point of the Borough, in more ways than one, it's worth homing in on this aspect of community life in the area. St. Edmundsbury seems to me to be to Bury what Greater London used to be to the City: more than a set of suburbs, an entity, an environment with many subtle ties with *its* hub, and a complex that was seen to be more than the sum of its parts. I used to think it was unique, now I'm not so sure. The relationships - spatial and cultural - between St James' Cathedral and, say Haverhill, have a definite resemblance to those between St Paul's and Croydon.

Because of that relationship, because of the duality of 'The Town' and 'The Borough', the fact that large stretches of the countryside around Bury are still unspoilt in their beauty has a bearing on one's view of the town. They are *its* back-garden, *its* lungs and *its* space - not 'somewhere else', down a country lane. While they maintain this awareness of nature for visitors and residents alike, chiefly they sustain the intense effect that the countryside, with its wide spaces and huge skies, has had on the local character of 'South Folk', who respond positively to the serenity and solitude that can arouse fear in the hearts of many 'outsiders'.

Moreover, South Folk aren't restricted to idyllic villages across the fields in the middle of nowhere, they aren't kept in a reservation - they're all around us, on the streets of Bury. They have much to teach us - not least about the 'Borough' way of life as a model for all kinds of things. Of the town itself, Daniel Defoe wrote that it was "famed for its pleasant situation and wholesome air, the Montpellier of Suffolk and perhaps of England." Charles Dickens, years later, agreed: in 'Pickwick Papers' he says it is "a handsome little town of thriving and cleanly appearance." It's still growing, too. In the early 70s the population was 27,000 or so, ten years later the figure stood at 29,000 - in the 1992 Census that number had increased, yet again, to over 33,000.

So it's old, it's 'wholesome', 'handsome', 'thriving' and of 'cleanly appearance' - and it's expanding. I also heard on the grapevine that I'm not the only one who finds it a shoppers' delight! Which does sound better than the 'Ultimate shopping experience', doesn't it? I'd rather have a delight than an experience, any day of the year. So what are we waiting for? Let's do it.

As they take pedestrians very seriously in Bury St Edmunds, we'll park the car and join the infantry. Off street parking is the best idea and if we aim for the area off ST ANDREWS STREET, north of KING'S ROAD, we should find somewhere suitable. Next thing, after a short stroll, we find ourselves in front of the CORN EXCHANGE (Enquiries - 01284 757065), as stunning a Victorian municipal classical frontage as you could ever wish to see. More to the point, they still use it *properly* on Wednesdays, but not for 'exchanging', exactly - not in the way that Aldeburgh's moot hall is still used for 'mooting', if you remember. No, this is where the year round craft market is held, with dozens of different stalls selling everything from bags to aromatherapy oils. Food, we've started well - but what have we *here*?

Hot on the heels of the temple to trade syndrome come 'The Arts', as soon as there's enough *trade* to pay for them. It's no surprise then, to find among the Exchange's neighbours THE BURY ST EDMUNDS ART GALLERY (01284 762081), housed in another architectural stunner called MARKET CROSS, which just happens to be Robert Adam's only public building in East Anglia. I *like* this place! It's got *confidence*. Would you believe they aren't content with a facade to kill for, either - they *use* this one as well, and fill it with exhibitions throughout the year. They also have a *shop*! It's a treasure trove of beautiful and eccentric items, many made locally.

Looking at other people's *paintings* can fire the enthusiasm to pick up something to add to one's *own* collection. Something with a *slightly* lower price tag, perhaps! To satisfy *this* need elsewhere, we have only to amble across to CHURCHGATE STREET and there before us is the GUILDHALL GALLERY (Enquiries - 01284 762366) which should be able to sort the problem, as long as the emphasis is on '*slightly* lower', I surmise. Specialising in conservation, restoration and framing, the Gallery also buys and sells 18th and 19th century paintings and makes a point of always keeping a selection of the work of East Anglian artists in stock.

From now on, I think we'll follow an outward spiral path out of the town centre, which worked so well in Peterborough. It makes for a more varied day apart from anything else, instead of 'doing' all the shops, then all the galleries and so on. On that basis, the next stop looks like being THE GUILDHALL (Enquiries - 01284 757080), one of the town's medieval buildings that has managed to avoid being hidden behind an elegant 17th or 18th century facade. Built in the 15th century, around an existing 13th century gateway, it has a central tower which is a minor landmark in the area.

Moving north along GUILDHALL STREET we can reach an even older building, still in daily use. Of course! Aren't they all? The splendid - and unique - MOYE'S HALL, beyond CORNHILL, in the BUTTERMARKET, was built in 1180 and is claimed to be the oldest surviving Norman house in East Anglia, never mind Bury. It is now a MUSEUM (Enquiries - 01284 757488) and contains an eccentrically wonderful collection of artefacts from every period of note in the Town's history, as well as archaeological exhibits of national significance, including Bronze Age weapons and a 13th century monk's chronicle.

Feel like jumping through six centuries? Fine - let's do it, down Buttermarket and back to Churchgate Street, again - but a bit further along. All but six hundred years after Moyse's opened its door, the UNITED MEETING HOUSE was built in 1711, as one of the finest Presbyterian chapels in Suffolk. Following its recent restoration, one can see clearly just what they meant.

Looking up Churchgate Street we have a fine view of the 12th century NORMAN TOWER of the Abbey, the oldest of its buildings to have survived intact. Originally known as Cemetery Gate, it once led directly to the west door of the Abbey. For us, now, it's a landmark to guide the way to our next visit: THE ATHENAEUM (Enquiries - 01284 757080) - and how many English cities, apart from London, do we know with the *style* to boast one of *those*? It's another piece of 18th century magnificence, having been opened in 1714 as an Assembly Room, which is now most notable for its splendid ballroom, available for hire, and for its year round programme of wide ranging cultural events.

Our route now requires a stroll down CROWN STREET to take in two more features of Bury's secular side before we take to THE ABBEY TRAIL. At the far end of the street we come to the THEATRE ROYAL (Enquiries - 01284 769505) a beautifully restored Georgian building and the first purpose built theatre of its kind in England. It offers professional drama, dance, music and opera productions from many of the country's best touring companies.

Talk of the theatre brings us rather neatly to the highlight of the town's arts calendar; the annual seventeen day BURY ST EDMUNDS FESTIVAL (Booking Office - 01284 757099). Held in May, it offers music and entertainment to suit all tastes with a coverage that extends from concerts and plays to films, exhibitions, street theatre, walks and talks. Beginning with the 'Beating the Retreat' ceremony on ANGEL HILL and an evening of free music, the Festival fills the town with life and colour from start to finish as audiences delight in the performances of some of the world's finest artists. The final day extends from an open air flower market and a concert in the Abbey Gardens to fireworks over the Abbey Ruins.

I've mentioned the ABBEY TRAIL and, with thoughts of the Festival and rockets over the ruins in our mind, it must be the moment to wander back up CROWN STREET and get to grips with it. Although the Abbey was huge, by abbey standards, the delightful - even stunning - gardens are modest in area when put alongside, say, Holkham Nature Reserve, so this will be one trail that won't leave us bent double from exhaustion.

We enter the grounds by the NORMAN TOWER that we spotted earlier and soon find ourselves eyeballing a statue of St. Edmund, dating from 1974, that is the work of Elizabeth Frink, who was born and educated in Suffolk. From there it makes sense to stride across the sward towards the River Lark to find the ABBEY VISITOR CENTRE (Enquires 01284 763110), housed in SAMPSON'S TOWER and incorporated into the West Front, to prime ourselves with useful facts before pressing on. The ruins that still remain consist largely of foundations and part of the walls. 'Walkman' tour facilities are available but, for even more fun, at certain times of the year one can be led round, as a member of a group, by a costumed interpreter of the medieval chronicler, Brother Jocelin de Brakeland.

Surrounding the ruins are the prize-winning ABBEY GARDENS, whose stunning displays are open to the public throughout the year. Their main impact is felt in May and September, when bedding plant spectaculars set the tone for the annual 'Bury in Bloom' competition. The gardens also feature armadas of ducks, a children's play area, tennis courts and bowling green. More significantly - apart from the ducks - there is also a pleasant tea shop and a riverside walk to take us, if we choose, to a local nature reserve known as NO MAN'S MEADOWS. North of the gardens we find ABBOT'S BRIDGE, built around 1211 to carry the precinct wall over the River Lark, in all probability. This would have been needed when the Abbey acquired a vineyard on the far side.

To complete the Trail, we follow the curve of ANGEL HILL back past the ABBEY GATE, destroyed in the 1327 uprising and rebuilt in 1353, to the entrance to the CATHEDRAL CHURCH OF ST JAMES (Enquiries - 01284 754933), otherwise known at St Edmundsbury Cathedral The original 16th century structure is believed to have been designed by John Wastell, the architect of King's College, Cambridge. Made a cathedral in 1914, Suffolk's mother church was splendidly enlarged by Stephen Dykes Bower during the present century. In 1997, the cathedral was granted Millennium funding to erect the tower that had been conspicuously lacking hitherto. Amongst the many points of interest is the display of a thousand kneelers, which features some delightful embroidery. Admission is free - although donations are invited - and there are facilities for guided tours, a shop and a refectory available. On leaving the Cathedral, we continue down Crown Street to pass the Norman Tower, again, and the GREAT CHURCHYARD on our left, which was probably created between 1120 and 1148 and has many interesting vaults and tombstones. Just at the end of the churchyard we come to ST MARY'S CHURCH, where Henry VIII's sister is buried, you remember. Like the Cathedral, this 15th century building is part of the Abbey complex. It has a superb interior whose most magnificent feature is undoubtedly the roof of the nave which is of the hammer-beam type, decorated, as so often, with angels.

Across HONEY HILL from the Church we'll find the MANOR HOUSE MUSEUM (Enquiries - 012284 757072), a Georgian mansion that was built by the Herveys of Ickworth House and has been restored to its 18th century glory. It is home to a wide range of collections of horology, costumes and fine and decorative arts, backed up by interactive computer screens to bring knowledge to one's finger tips. The museum offers a continuing programme of exhibitions, workshops and lectures throughout the year, along with living history weeks and special events for school groups and for the public. Incidentally, on the subject of horology, there's another outstanding collection of clocks and watches - one of the largest in Britain - to be seen in Bury. THE GERSHOM-PARKINGTON COLLECTION is to be found in ANGEL CORNER, a Queen Anne mansion on the north side of Angel Hill.

Back down at the other end of Crown Street, though, our attention has been drawn to a building which testifies to another time honoured occupation in Bury: brewing. GREENE KING'S WESTGATE BREWERY (Enquiries - 0284 763222) was built in 1799 and fine beer has been produced there ever since. The Brewery forms one of the focal points in the Town and is a monument to the evolution of the industry. It is open for tours by arrangement. While we're on the subject of beer, readers familiar with Bury may wonder why I've said nothing so far about THE NUTSHELL and its claim to be the smallest pub in Britain, if not in the world. It may well be in the Guinness Book of Records, but the word is that the claim is being challenged. Until the dispute is settled, the writer, obsessed with veracity (!) offers no comment. It's certainly small - but we'll have to leave it at that for the moment. And please don't write any letters!

Aside from the architectural and other artistic aspects of its heritage, Bury has - you'll be relieved to hear - some excellent shopping facilities, as befits a 'shopper's delight'! I mentioned them briefly a while ago, but now, at last, is the time to look at them in more detail. Bargain hunting is best done on Wednesdays and Saturdays - market days - when the town centre becomes a seething arena for wheeling and dealing in everything from collectibles to cauliflowers. Whichever way you turn there are brightly coloured stalls offering fresh local produce - and not so fresh antiques. It's that rare situation where family run shops, high street name stores and informal stalls function amicably, cheek by jowl, to the mutual benefit of the proprietors and the punters. And there are even *auctions*, as well!

It may be a bit unfair to single out individuals from this flourishing horde - certainly one wouldn't choose to diminish anyone's contribution - but the odd name or two might help to prove the point, to give an idea of the kind of range we're talking about. THE BURY BOOKSHOP (Enquiries - 01284 7073107) stocks a range that extends from hardbacks through second hand books to maps and guides in its premises in HATTER STREET. In OUTWESTGATE, TALISMAN 2 (Enquiries - 01284 725712) buys and sells antiques, anything old - and eclectic clutter! At the more up to date end of the spectrum, BUR'D TREASURE (Enquiries - 01284 723158) tucked away in the centre of the Town, in HIGHER BEXTER STREET has a host of gift ideas for any occasion you may have in mind.

Other shopping areas in Bury are focused on CORNHILL, ABBEYGATE STREET and BUTTERMARKET and the by-ways in between. Given the variety of goods available, the compactness of the area and the freedom from traffic, I'm sure you'll share my conclusion at the end of it all, as we stagger back to the car park, loaded down to the ground: Bury makes shopping a real pleasure. Were it the shape of things to come, I'd rest easier than I might elsewhere, when faced with the kind of marketing that brings on one of my senile turns!

Right at this moment, there's an idea forming in my mind that it's time our outward spiral became more seriously outward. It takes a real effort of self-discipline to wrench oneself away, but it must be done. We're almost half way through the chapter and we haven't seen a mile of country lane, a field or a farm house, not to mention a single one of the scores of idyllic villages for which Suffolk is so highly regarded! It's time we were away into the hinterland - time and the end of a chapter wait for no man, woman or anything else.

Where are we going? Don't ask me, I'm just the author and, being utterly spoiled for choice, I haven't a clue. Toss a coin, again. Heads: that means 'up the map'. Toss it again. Tails: that means 'left hand down a bit'. Steady! Steady! Got it: the A1101 to Mildenhall and points northwest. A fine choice, if I may say so. Don't worry, we'll be going back to Bury. I can feel it in my bones - which , after all the rushing around, seem older that St. Edmund's.

By the by, notice any *more* perversity in the choice? It's there! Remember how we deliberately picked Bury in preference to the most famous stretch of Suffolk - Constable Country - for our starting point? The *second* most famous place is Newmarket - so we won't be rushing straight off there, either. Of course we'll get to it, eventually, as we will to East Bergholt, but let's run this tour our way and continue to avoid following the crowd.

The A1101 also has the advantage of a hidden agenda: it passes through **FORNHAM ALL SAINTS.** If you're wondering what that's got to do with the price of petrol, may I add that FORNHAM PARK GOLF COURSE (Enquiries - 01284 706777) is still the only eighteen hole pay and play course in St.Edmundsbury. See you on the way back? BURY ST EDMUNDS GOLF CLUB (Enquiries - 01284 755978) is a bit to the south, 500 yards from the A14 on the B1106. It *does* welcome visitors, so it may be worth a call - but I suspect Farnham's informality may mesh in better with our nomadic lifestyle, these days.

It's hardly any distance at all from Farnham to our next call, the village of **WEST STOW** - in fact, if you got a good drive in the wrong direction from, say, the last couple of tees, you could drop the ball in an empty Moorhen's nest on the lake at WEST STOW COUNTRY PARK (Information - 01284 728718) and send a few ornithologists totally berserk.

ANGLO SAXON VILLAGE, WEST STOW

This, by the way, is a Country Park with a difference. The 'difference' is that it has a reconstructed Anglo Saxon Village in the middle of it - complete with a "portable cassette playing 'time machine' to help re-create the whole Anglo Saxon experience". Interesting! Otherwise, it's mainly birds (120 different species), animals (25 species) and 125 acres of heath and woodland, bordered by the River Lark (I *love* that name). This may sound familiar, but then so are rainbows, sunsets, fresh coffee and chocolate - and one can't have too much of *any* of them. A large area of the park is a Site of Special Scientific Interest; *all* of it is a site of special interest to lovers of beautiful countryside. Preferably *without* a portable cassette playing machine to re-create anything). At the heart of the Park, the Visitor Centre uses displays to help realise the full potential of the site during a day out. There are special events too, which are publicised well in advance. A nature trail links the heathland nature reserve with the woods; river and lake and picnic sites have been established in a number of areas. Admission to all these outdoor delights is, amazingly, free and the Park is open everyday from 8.00a.m. to 8.00p.m. in summer and 8.00a.m. to 5.00p.m. in winter. The Village is open all the year round from 10.00a.m. to 5.00p.m. and an admission fee is charged, with a special rate for families.

To move on from West Stow, we take a loop which gets involved with part of the B1106 as it swings round to the east to meet the A134 Thetford road. Having turned left at the T-junction and headed north for a few miles, we take a right turn, through Barnham, to EUSTON HALL (Enquiries - 01842 766366) The home of the Duke of Grafton, the Hall was built in the 17th century and contains portraits of Charles II, his family and court, along with works by Van Dyck, Lely and Stubbs.

Within the boundaries of the extensive Estate one comes upon Pleasure Grounds, designed by John Evelyn and a Park and Temple which were the work of William Kent. The 17th century estate church is another interesting feature and one can cap one's visit with a call at the Craft Shop and a pause for some tea in the Old Kitchen. The Hall is open between 2.30p.m. and 5.00p.m. every Thursday from June 4th to September 24th and on Sundays from June 28th to September 6th.

After visiting Euston we retrace our route back to the A134, which we cross, before heading for Elvedon and our next major call, **BRANDON** (Information 01842 814955). This market town is set on the western edge of the Theford Forest, beside the charming Little Ouse, and is just about as far north as we can go and still be in Suffolk. The bridge over the river has been an important crossing point for hundreds of years and the excavation of a Middle Saxon town, complete with an early church confirms its role.

This is flint country, in a big way, and we recall the details of Grimes Graves - so very far away, across the 'countryline' in Norfolk, which we visited in an earlier chapter. Flint has played a major role in Brandon's history and its fame, to a great extent, rests on its being the last home in Britain of the industry that made flints for guns. This business brought in a substantial income until the invention of the percussion cap in the 19th century. At its height, during the Napoleonic Wars, a good 'knapper' would be turning out 15,000 gun flints *per week*! In short, the town is built *on* flint, *of* flint - to a great extent - and was mainly financed *by* flint! The arrival of the new invention didn't kill off England's oldest industry completely, however: recently, demand for gun flints from Africa and from American enthusiasts for old fashioned muzzle loaders has revived the trade to such an extent that the business had to move to bigger premises some years ago. The town's HERITAGE CENTRE, in George Street, tells the story of this and other traditional industry in the area.

From the land of flint and forest we drop down the A1065 for a short distance before turning right, across Wangford fen and then turning left onto the B1126 to reach our next destination. The scream of jet engines may well give us a clue to what's in store when we arrive.

LAKENHEATH is a sizeable village that is known to the nation, primarily, for its role as home to a USAF airfield. Some of us who worry about aliens, UFOs and the isolation (or otherwise) of man in the Universe, also know it is as the site of one of the most extraordinary encounters in British 'ufology'. According to the 'experts' in these matters, some American airmen claim to have come across an alien spacecraft that had actually landed in the woods near the base. Second opinions were sought and these airmen saw 'it' as well as 'its' smoke and flashing lights. The next day, 'it' had gone and all that was left was some burnt ground where 'it' had been standing. Dubious? Check it out, while you're there - and notice that the base itself was also *used* in the latest James Bond movie, 'Tomorrow Never Dies'

The centre of the village is a conservation area with many fine buildings, definitely worthy of a stroll of inspection. You'll see some delightful houses, built of a mixture of flint, brick, chalk and clunch, before the way takes you to the splendid church, with its magnificent cambered tie-beam roof. Inside, the 15th century carved benches catch the eye, as does the elaborately carved 13th century font. Finally, in the churchyard can be found the graves of relatives of Lord Kitchener.

Having spent some time pottering around Lakenheath, it's time to turn away in a more or less southerly direction towards Mildenhall. With a lingering, nostalgic look over the shoulder towards the Brecks, therefore, we must address ourselves to the serious business of the B12112 and the right fork that will take us, via the A1101 for a minute or two, to our destination.

MILDENHALL, ten miles north east of Newmarket, stands on the River Lark and has as its two focal points, the MARKET PLACE with the market cross and pump, and ST MARY'S CHURCH, which retains many features that date back to the 12th and 13th centuries. It has beautifully carved hammer beams in its aisled ceiling and tower which, typically for Fenland, can be seen for miles, so distant is the skyline as one approaches the town. The fame of the place is nothing to do with its aesthetics or its townscape: for most of us, 'Mildenhall' means treasure, the MILDENHALL TREASURE, a hoard of 34 pieces of 4th century Roman silverware that were ploughed up at nearby THISLEY GREEN in 1942, and are now exhibited in the British Museum. The town MUSEUM, in KING STREET, contains information about 'The Treasure' as well as many collections of local interest.

There's a local tale which catches at the imagination, too. In 1780, so the story goes, the then Lord of the Manor, Sir Thomas Bunbury, tossed a coin with Lord Derby to decide whose name should be given to a horse race to be run at the Epsom meeting. If Sir Thomas had won, we'd be having a flutter on 'The Bunbury' instead of 'The Derby' - which might have amused Oscar Wilde ('The Importance of Being Ernest'?) but might have lacked the style of the name we've got. Another thing: I can't imagine the fans of Everton and Liverpool FCs giving a major 'thumbs up' to the idea of their teams playing a local *Bunbury*!

Back to the church: the north porch is the largest in Suffolk - which is worth a thought, I suppose. Worth *more* of a thought, is the fact that arrowheads and small bits of lead shot, fired off by the supporters of General Cromwell during England's only successful revolution, have been found around the place, particularly in the woodwork of the *nave roof*! Now isn't *that* odd? I mean, can you picture those chaps of his, all dressed up in tin like walking sardine cans (complete with *helmets*) and known for their hatred of anything to do with *fun*, wandering up and down the aisles of St. Mary's, loosing off with their pistols, muskets and bows and arrows - at the *roof*? Why did they *do* it? Were they *drunk*? Surely, as good Puritans, they were never supposed to *be* drunk. As I say, very odd indeed!

To the north west of the town RAF MILDENHALL is one of the United States Airforce's most important bases in Europe. I suppose that status could have been under threat when 'The Wall' came down and the so-called Cold War so-called ended - but the fates were merciful and a better use has been found, I'm glad to tell you. The base is currently the venue for the MILDENHALL AIR FETE, at the end of May, when upwards of 300,000 people come to watch "the largest air display organised by the military anywhere in the world". Bully for them, I'd say - this is one occasion when 'virtual reality' beats the genuine article, all ends up, as dummy bombing runs with dummy bombs give most of the fun of the fair - without the blood and slaughter.

So much for Mildenhall (and my unwanted show of prejudice). Where do we go from here? I think we hit the A11 and head off for **NEWMARKET** - which has little to do with 'boys' toys' or the modern day world, praise the Lord! We're about to confront the other thing people know about Suffolk, apart from the paintings: horses - or, more accurately, horse-*racing*. As it's still East Anglia, though, it's still odd: most of them think the thing they know about is in *Cambridgeshire*! They could, of course, be readily forgiven. Apart from a vague idea that one of the races in the Newmarket calendar is know as the 'Cambridgeshire Handicap' (or something of the sort) there's also the map. Have you *looked* at it? Newmarket *should* be in Cambridgeshire - just about, at the very Easternmost edge, but definitely *in*. Instead there's this grotesque bulge, this salient, this *growth* on Suffolk's western border that absorbs the Town, the Heath, the important bits - and then stops dead (when it should have stopped dead before it even got to the Town's eastern suburbs - and stayed there). Again, very odd - but it gives us more to talk about, so life isn't all bad. *Planners*, though? Now, they *are* odd.

Newmarket is everything to do with 'the Sport of Kings'. It's reputation is world-wide in every part of the business from racing to breeding, training and sales. The involvement spreads out from the course into the town and beyond, to the surrounding heathland where strings of horses can enjoy ideal conditions for exercise and practise. That image, of the lines of glorious creatures easing through the street of Newmarket in the morning mist, is every bit as evocative as Flatford Mill - especially the Flatford Mill that we'll discover a little later.

There are *two* race-courses at Newmarket: the Rowley Mile, named after Charles II's hack 'Old Rowley', where the main classic races take place, and the July course. Rowley's meetings, from April to October, are National - even international events, not just for the events on the course, but also for the social whirl that revolves around them.

There are training premises and stud farms almost everywhere you look all around the town and in the surrounding villages as well. Of these, clearly the most famous is the NATIONAL STUD (Enquiries - 01638 666789), situated on the Heath, which is open for 75 minute conducted tours from the beginning of March to the end of August and on race days in September and October. Booking is essential - and one can easily see the reason. This place really is unique: where else might one see a Prince, a banker, an Arab Sheikh weep over a newborn foal - that bids fair to be worth *millions* if it wins a few big races! Don't give me that National Lottery stuff. We're taking *real* money, here. Mercifully, there are also plenty of people who actually love the horses themselves, if 'love' isn't putting it too mildly. They adore them, they revere them, they revel in all the mystique surrounding them - they get up in the dark and stay awake nights caring for them, worrying about them and obsessing themselves with every minor detail of their well-being. Such behaviour I would suggest, is *not* odd. Go to Newmarket, do the tour and see for yourselves. Go to the eight horse Stallion Unit, which is part of the tour, and see some of the successors to the great Mill Reef. Investments they may be - if that's how some people's minds work - but *perfection* is what they're actually about. Simply, in this part of her output, Nature can do no better. Horses are part of how we are and there's no point denying it. And they are utterly beautiful, which is more than you can say about some parts of our 'Heritage', those monuments to self-indulgence whose size is only exceeded by their vulgarity. Incidentally, the smug looks on the faces of some of the stallions isn't *all* to do with past triumphs on the world's greatest courses - there are up to a hundred mares and foals around the place, too.

A visitor centre, dedicated to the history of Newmarket, is planned for PALACE HOUSE, a 17th century building that was being restored at the time of writing and may well be finished by the time you visit the town. The House, which incorporates the remains of Charles II's palace, has accommodated several members of the monarchy over the years, including William and Mary. Much later, when Samuel Golding saved part of it as PALACE HOUSE MANSION, it saw service as the racing headquarters of the Rothschild family and was visited frequently by King Edward VII. The town benefited from these visits as the king persuaded numerous aristocratic friends and acquaintances to build racing establishments of their own in the vicinity.

On a totally different tack, on the outskirts of Newmarket is situated THE ANIMAL HEALTH TRUST, the only charitable institution in Britain with a full time commitment to the diagnosis, prevention and cure of animal diseases. Based at LANWADES HALL, the Trust currently has plans on the stocks for a new visitor centre at LANWADES STABLES. There is more, TATTERSALLS, off THE AVENUE, is the home of another 'international best' to be found in the town: the auctions. Horses have been bought and sold here since 1870, and the general public are freely admitted to all the sales which take place between April and December. Remember, though: don't nod, wink or scratch your head. You can't afford any of it and a bid by accident could leave you and your family destitute forever. This is telephone number money like you wouldn't believe.

One of Newmarket's most impressive structures - and institutions - is found in the HIGH STREET. In a listed building, dating from 1772 and rebuilt in the 1930s in the neo-Georgian style, we'll find THE JOCKEY CLUB, which makes and administers the rules of racing. Next door is a real must, even for those of us who'd go a long way to avoid the embarrassment of falling out of a saddle. THE NATIONAL HORSERACING MUSEUM (Enquiries - 01638 667333) offers a fascinating insight into every aspect of the sport in a way that gets every one of my votes.

You can forget 'virtual reality', 'walkman tours', 'ultimate experiences' and all the rest of the sales pitch - at this Museum you get as close as you could ever hope to the starting tape without any of the danger. While we're joking, though, let's not forget that it *is* dangerous. It's not *all* about the odds and the exchange of huge wads of cash. Under the guidance of retired jockeys and trainers, visitors to the museum are shown how to tack up, are dressed in silks and then let loose on the very horse simulator that professional jockeys use for training and winter practice.

If they survive that experience - and if the ex-jocks don't die laughing - there are minibus tours out to meet stable and stud staff with their horses. Finally, for those who are insatiable, there's the HALL OF FAME, which charts the history of the sport in this country over the four hundred years from its royal origins to the present day, the whole production being peppered liberally with tall tales and bits of gossip about the colourful characters - on two legs and four - who've been involved with it. To sum up: throughout the book, 'this is not to be missed' is a phrase that can come to mind with a *slight* lack of justification; at Newmarket I *mean* it! So much so, that I'd add it to the very short list of East Anglian features that ought to be compulsory viewing for anyone who fondly imagines he, or she, is British and *hasn't* seen them. New there's a topic for the bar, later: what would be on *your* list? Holkham, Norwich Cathedral, Wroxham, Ely and the Valley of the Stour? What about Blakeney? Or Happisburgh? Holt, perhaps? We could be up drinking - and disputing - all night. At *this* moment, however, we have to press on. What about the heavy horses at Stag's Holt? The Abbey Gardens at Bury St. Edmunds? I wish I hadn't started this. Press on, I said. Let's do it.

Hang on, we've lost someone - and I bet I know where they've gone. Newmarket, being the way it is, can give a most unusual gloss to our shopping obsession, so that's where we'd better look. I only hope the absentee is a *true* horse person and not just taking kleptomania to laughable extremes.

Not that far from the Museum is GIBSON SADDLERS LTD (Enquiries - 01638 662330) one of the country's oldest established firms in this business, who can probably measure up to anyone's requirements in their particular line. I wonder if our missing 'discerning visitor' is looking for a saddle to hang over the fireplace or a set of jockey silks to wow some friends at next week's party. Both are readily available at Gibson's. All seems to be well - some tack for a grand-daughter, apparently. Quite a relief. So *now* can we get on?

On the way back to the car, someone just asked about auctions - some comment or other that they'd overheard at Tattersalls. A good point, this, as SOTHEBY'S East Anglian office is in Newmarket and VOST'S, the fine art auctioneers and valuers, hold auctions throughout the year at Tattersalls - when it isn't full of horses, presumably. All of which reminds me, while we're on the subject, that we could do with a few more words about antiques, when the time's right - maybe at Long Melford? We are in 'Lovejoy Country' (as much as 'Constable Country', these days) let's not forget. Surely there can't be any *more* delays. There can't. Fine. So, d'you see that minor road over there, the one that's signposted to Molton? Shall we drive down it? Now - or, once again, I won't be answerable if we end the day in the dark, lost and screaming for our dinner. Suffolk has a reputation for picturesque villages that is nearly as well established as the fame of its painters, its horses - and even its painters of horses - so we can expect to find charming streets, delightful houses and historic churches wherever we go, more or less. To prove the point, the next leg of our journey, in a southerly direction back towards the Stour, gives us a chance to drop in on a clutch of them.

First off is **MOULTON**, which is nothing to do with any of that. Although it's little more than a hamlet, it's renowned for its landmark, a 15th century packhorse bridge that is so narrow and hump-backed that traffic has to follow the by-road and cope with a ford that can be as dry as a bone or awash with flood water. Moulton is linked with **DALHAM**, which we come to next down the B1085, by the River Kennet which flows parallel to the Cambridgeshire border in these parts. This village is famous for its thatched cottages, its five storey smock windmill, maltings and DALHAM HALL, where the Duke of Wellington lived for some years. Cecil Rhodes bought the Hall many years later for his retirement - but didn't manage to live long enough to retire.

The route now swings past **LIDGATE**, as we bear left on to the B1063 before turning right on the A143, which should be signposted to Haverhill - although that doesn't matter at this stage, since we're only taking it as far as a left turn onto the B1061 to bring us to **KEDINGTON**. We may well pause at Kedington, another charming little piece of Suffolk village scenery, to admire its location on the banks of the Stour. If we do, we should make a point of visiting the Church which is magnificently Medieval in its testimony to the great days of wool, and has exceptionally fine woodwork. After that it's heigh ho for **HAVERHILL**, very close by, for a cup of tea etc., try the Haverhill hotel absolutely excellent.

A fire in 1665 destroyed most of the older buildings in the town, although ANNE OF CLEVES' HOUSE - once part of the dower of the Queen Consort of England - has been completely renovated. Haverhill holds our attention mainly for the quality of its Victorian architecture, its local history collection and TOWN HALL on the HIGH STREET. This building, with its imposing brick and stone facade, now incorporates the ARTS CENTRES (Enquiries - 01440 714140) and the HISTORY CENTRE. The fire also damaged the 13th century church severely so that what we see now is largely a 19th century restoration. In terms of recreation, Haverhill has a wide spread of possibilities ranging from informal countryside activities in EAST TOWN PARK to the full programme of events presented at the Arts Centre throughout the year.

As with so many of East Anglia's towns life has handed Haverhill its share of ups and downs. When its traditional weaving, textile and agricultural businesses slumped in the 1860s the town declined economically and times were very hard for a decade or so. The trend was then reversed, thanks to the efforts of the Gurteen family whose own textile firm had been founded in 1748 and who were able to lead enough of a revival to build the Town Hall and donate land for a recreation ground. As we can see from its buildings, the town went on growing for the next thirty or forty years until textiles slumped again after the First World War. Nothing much happened, then, until the 50s and 60s when Haverhill joined in the Greater London Councils' overspill scheme and started to grow again quite rapidly. Today, this history is to be seen, as each period has left evidence of its presence in the architecture of the time, in an overall mix of old and new.

To stay in Suffolk, which seems to be the general idea, we need to wriggle down a lane or two, north of the A12092, before joining it at **STOKE BY CLARE**, our next call. The village is remarkably pretty, with its traditional cottages and lovely 15th century church, but in our eyes it is more remarkable as the home of BOYTON END VINEYARD (Enquiries - 01440 61893), which is open daily for tours and tastings from April to October. By the way, the Tudor tower on the village street which looks like a gate-house is actually a dovecote!

Following the main road east - with a touch of north - our tour brings us shortly to **CLARE** itself, a market town that could have been designed especially for us - it is renowned for all those aspect of urban life that give it its sparkle, namely antique shops, art galleries, coffee houses and pubs. We could be staying here a bit longer than average, I imagine! The history of the town is interesting enough to pay it some attention before we get down to the serious business. It was 'given' by William the Conqueror (which seems a questionable notion - how was it *his* to give, one wonders) to his relative Richard de Vierfait, the first Earl of Clare (nepotism rules, OK).

Members of this family played a significant role in England's history, particularly in the drawing up of Magna Carta and in calling the first popular parliament after that. Moreover, they were also more than a little involved with Cambridge University in its early days: Clare College was named after the family and Elizabeth de Burgh, sister of the 10th Earl, gave money to help refound it in the 14th century.

Reminders of this noble past tend to focus on what's left of CLARE CASTLE - but there's a wry comment on life in a tale of its latter days. Local indignation flared up when the railway arrived and a station was built that cut into the castle remains; today the railway has been abandoned and was as much ruin as the old keep that stands over it until the growth of tourism when the building came to be regarded as a point of interest for visitors.

The 16th century saw expansions in wealth and population in the town and many of its other fine buildings bear witness to the fact. Chief amongst these, perhaps, is the parish church of SS PETER AND PAUL, which has remained more or less as it was four hundred years ago. Clare's streets are meant for strolling not driving, so let's walk along and see what we find. A touch more history comes in the form of the 15th century PRIEST'S HOUSE at the churchyard corner, which is eye-catching for its amazing flourish of pargeting - highly decorated plaster-work - that is one of Suffolk's trademarks. After that digression, we're into our main interest with real gusto.

BREAKAWAY CRAFTS (Enquiries - 01787 277646) is located in FAY'S in WELL LANE and is one of those Aladdin's Cave places that are always a source of delight. Here we'll find a whole range of gift ideas and all kinds of craft products along with a selection of clothes and cards. Not far away, as a second call, we'll soon see why SUFFOLK SALES draw crowds of antiques enthusiasts to Clare year after year - and why the ANTIQUES WAREHOUSE is so popular. On a different tack, the NETHERGATE BREWERY (Enquiries - 01787 277244) in the HIGH STREET, could appeal to another side of our nature. Finally, lets not forget the MARKET and all that implies - we're experienced in East Anglian market matters by now, and should find Clare's example worthy of close inspection.

The former ancestral village of the Dukes of Devonshire, **CAVENDISH** sticks in the mind for its admirably restored pink washed thatched cottages clustered around the 14th century tower of ST MARY'S CHURCH. The perfect picture postcard English village is the ideal built environment to set off this stretch of the Stour Valley which is, in itself, extraordinarily lovely.

CAVENDISH

There are, of course, tales a'plenty to be told - some of them more gory than you'd imagine, as you shed a tear over the views. A son of the then Chief Justice, Sir John Cavendish, was the chap who stabbed Wat Tyler in the midst of a so-called parlez at Smithfield in 1381. The peasantry didn't take too kindly to that and came down on Sir John at Cavendish, crying for revenge. Sir John hid his valuables in the church belfry (curious priorities) and *then* fled. The delay may well have cost him his life as he was caught up on the road, at Lakenheath - and killed there instead. Sounds like a tale with more than one moral, to me.

Two features of today's village should hold our interest for a while: THE CAVENDISH MANOR VINEYARD (Enquiries - 01787 280252) is open all the year for a visit which includes a touch of wine tasting while the SUE RYDER FOUNDATION MUSEUM tells the life story of its founder and the history of the organisation she created in 1953 as a 'Living Memorial' to the millions who died in the two World Wars and to those who are still suffering and dying now as a result of persecution. It is an international charity which seeks to extend relief, regardless of race, religion or age whenever people are sick, homeless or destitute. Sue Ryder's work has been recognised widely: she has been decorated by the Polish and Yugoslav governments, was awarded an OBE in 1957 and appointed a Commander of the Order of St.Michael and St.George in 1976. She was created a life peer in 1978 and sits on the Cross benches in the House of Lords as Baroness Ryder of Warsaw. It is gratifying to see work like hers gaining recognition, not least to restore some balance within the general insanity! The Foundation Museum is open all year and further information is available from 01787 280252.

At this point, we move out of the Borough of St.Edmundsbury again whilst staying *in* Suffolk by the narrowest of margins. Another short stretch of the A1092 - and an even shorter stretch of the B1064, to the right - brings us into **LONG MELFORD,** which I'm inclined to leave totally to the antique collectors among you, while I hide in a coffee shop. Stop the car a minute and look at it, will you? Long Melford's HIGH STREET: about a mile in length - with *twenty* antique shops? We'll never, ever get away! And there's an ANTIQUES FAIR as well, on at least two days each month at the OLD SCHOOL. And regular book markets. I've a sneaking feeling that this single moment will justify everything that's gone into the production, distribution and sale of the entire Guidebook! All we need, now, is a couple of removal vans!

HOLY TRINITY CHURCH, LONG MELFORD

While you busy yourselves, I shall think about other, more serene aspects of the village. For a start, we must agree that the High Street is probably the most impressive single thoroughfare in Suffolk - long and spacious with dignified houses and some charming shop premises. As if that isn't enough, HOLY TRINITY CHURCH has the finest proportions of all the Suffolk churches and features a form of decorated flintwork - known as 'flushwork', that is unequalled. In fact, one could go further: What we are admiring may well be the most spectacular parish church *in the country?* Amidst the magnificence we might find a homely touch: there used to be a child's multiplication tables on one wall as a memento of the church's days as a school, between 1669 and 1880. Is it still there, I wonder? If it is, it's in the LADY CHAPEL, a cool and elegant space, admirable for contemplation and recovery from the day's many frenzies.

All around the village there are swathes of broad parkland and in their midst lie two great manor houses which are open to the public. MELFORD HALL (Enquiries 01787 880286) is one of East Anglia's most well known Elizabethan houses. It has changed very little externally since 1578, and still has an original panelled banqueting hall. Further areas of interest range from the Regency library to the Victorian bedrooms and fine collections of furniture, porcelain, Dutch and naval pictures and Beatrix Potter memorabilia. Outside, the garden contains some spectacular specimen trees and a delightful summerhouse. Finally, to stretch our legs, there is a very pleasant walk through the park to round off the visit. Opening hours vary with the seasons so it is best to phone before a visit to check the details.

The other mansion we would visit while we're in the area is also Tudor: the moated KENTWELL HALL (Enquiries - 01787 310207) was built a little earlier than Melford Hall, in 1564. The claim is that Kentwell is "where the sixteenth century comes to life" and, from the moment you begin your approach along its avenue, you can really believe it! The atmospheric red brick building is still a family home - but with a difference. All the main rooms and service areas have been set up and equipped in the style of four hundred years ago, while over selected weekends and Bank Holidays, award winning re-creations of the life of the times are presented.

Beyond the Hall other attractions include extensive gardens and woodlands, a mosaic Tudor Rose maze, and a RARE BREEDS FARM, where Suffolk Punch horses are much in evidence. Our addiction to refreshment is catered for in fine style in the tea room and a gift shop gives us a chance to add a commemorative item or two to the growing pile in the boot of the car. Opening times, basically are from 12noon to 5.00p.m. on Sundays between 8th March and 7 June; daily between 8th July and 6th September and Wednesdays, Thursdays and Sundays only between 7th September and 25th October. For details of the 'Re-creations' it's advisable to telephone in advance.

With the spectacle of Long Melford and it's antique shops, firmly in our mind's eye - from the mansions to the ambience of yesteryear and much more - we could hardly have a better moment to turn for home. Something about "Quit while you're winning"? Our last call should turn 'winning' into a triumph - it *has* to be one of the most extraordinary houses in England - and is close enough to Bury for the last few miles to be a doddle. Fine, so - if we're agreed - we'll make our way up the A134, before doing a zig-zag through the lanes to the left to arrive at **HORRINGER.**

The eccentric Earl of Bristol created the equally (or even more) eccentric ICKWORTH HOUSE (Enquiries - 01284 735270/735151) with its spectacular rotunda, its semi-circular wings and its curved corridors in 1795 to show off his collections. The paintings alone are a major attraction and include works by Titian, Gainsborough and Velasquez - but there's a superb collection of Georgian silver as well. The House, which is a National Trust property - as is Melford Hall - is set in an Italianate garden surrounded by a Capability Brown park with woodland walks, a vineyard, a deer enclosure, a Georgian summer house, a church, a canal - and a 'lake' Did any of those chaps *ever* do *anything* by halves? Again, the House has so many events and variations in its annual calendar that a prior phone call is a must to make certain of avoiding disappointment. In general, though, it is open most days between May and September: at other times it's worth a call.

THE ROTUNDA, ICKWORTH HOUSE

And there you have it: a tour of West Suffolk, from the halls, to the history, to the horses. I must say I love it, and agree with the claim that it's "more English than England". Certainly, there are other villages in other counties that can take your breath away - but only as *equals* to Cavendish, Dalham and Long Melford. Maybe there's little that's dramatic in the scenery, but when you look up at the sky where the East Anglian speciality of light, shade and vast cloudscapes offers drama in the extreme, there seems no point in quibbling.

THE AFFLECK ARMS
1, Brookside,
Dalham,
Newmarket,
Suffolk
CB8 8TG

Tel: 01638 500306
Fax: 01638 500106

This busy pub built in the 15th or 16th century is bursting with atmosphere and attracts people of all ages. In addition to its warm and welcoming bars, its fifty cover restaurant, it has a vast garden which is home to a mini zoo with tropical birds and coy carp which creates great interest. It is in the centre of Dalham and from here a five church circular walk takes place which ends once again at the pub. The walk needless to say creates great thirsts and the well kept ale and other drinks are eagerly sought.

There are two separate rooms for food, one of which is non-smoking. The menu has a wide range of dishes from all around the world, as well as traditional ones. Caribbean theme nights are always popular. In the Bar at lunch time, Basket Meals are very popular in addition to the time honoured favourites. Every day there are Daily Specials which are both value for money and very tasty. Eating alfresco in the garden in warm weather is very popular and has a regular following. The Affleck Arms is well situated for anyone wanting to go to the Newmarket Races or take a look at the National Racehorse Museum. Cambridge is not too far away.

USEFUL INFORMATION

OPEN: 12-2.30pm & 7-10.30pm All day Sun.   RESTAURANT: Wide ranging
CHILDREN: Welcome menu
CREDIT CARDS: All major cards   BAR FOOD: Basket Meals
LICENSED: Full On   VEGETARIAN: Yes
GARDEN: Yes & for eating alfresco   WHEELCHAIR ACCESS: Yes
PETS: Guide dogs only

THE ANGEL HOTEL
Bury St Edmunds,
Suffolk
IP33 1LT

ETB**** RAC***+
Merit Awards HC & R
AA*** 2 Rosettes 68%

Tel: 01284 753926
Fax: 01284 750092

Steeped in history and situated in one of the finest Georgian squares in England, The Angel Hotel in Bury St Edmunds is everything a visitor could wish for. From the management to the kitchen porter, the staff are unfailingly courteous and attentive, welcoming and determined that you will enjoy your visit, much as, one expects, travellers coming to the inn when it first opened in 1452, would have relished the hospitality. It is an hotel which exudes well being and one is in no doubt that it is loved by its owners, the Gough family who also own The Marlborough in Ipswich.

There are flowers and log fires in the public rooms. The bedrooms are individually furnished and decorated and all have en-suite bathrooms. Every room has television, hairdryers, hostess trays and many other touches for your comfort. The 'fine room' where Mr Pickwick stayed has been preserved today exactly as it was more than a century ago. In the elegant dining room, overlooking the ancient abbey, the award winning food is delicious. English classic cuisine at its best includes local speciality dishes and succulent roasts. The accompanying wine list is extensive and well chosen. The hotel is within an hour of east coast ferry ports and forty five minutes from Stansted Airport. There are several golf courses within easy reach and there is racing at Newmarket.

USEFUL INFORMATION

OPEN: All year	RESTAURANT: Superb Classic English
CHILDREN: Welcome	BAR FOOD: Light snacks
CREDIT CARDS: All major cards	VEGETARIAN: Yes
LICENSED: Full On	WHEELCHAIR ACCESS: No
ACCOMMODATION: 42 En suite rooms	GARDEN: Yes
RATES: Sgl £65 Dbl. £85-125 Tw £85-95	PETS: No

BRIGHTHOUSE FARM
Melford Road,
Lawshall,
NR Bury St Edmunds,
Suffolk
IP29 4PX

B&B 2 Crowns Commended.
S/C Flats 1 Key Commended
S/C Cottage 4 Key Highly Commended

Tel/Fax: 01284 830385

This lovely old Georgian farmhouse with later additions is part of a working four hundred acre farm complete with its own Farm Trail for the exclusive use of guests. It stands in a rural position in the heart of East Anglia and within easy reach of many places of interest such as the old Wool town of Lavenham renowned for its unspoilt beauty, Melford with its Antique shops. Bury St Edmunds itself is full of historic interest dominated by its magnificent Abbey. Sudbury is the birthplace of the painter, Thomas Gainsborough and Constable Country is at hand as well. Brighthouse Farm has been the home of the Truin family since 1963 at which time the house, garden and farm were badly neglected. They set about restoring it all and the successful result is what you see today. The garden is a delight. There is still tree planting taking place and other projects - farming never stands still. The Truin family have farmed locally for five generations and now it is John, Roberta and Odell who carry the flag and make sure their guests have a happy and memorable stay. They are friendly, outgoing people who have just the right knack of making you feel at home and at ease.

Brighthouse Farm is beautifully furnished with a mixture of antiques and other pieces, interesting picture and many other items of interest. Stylishly decorated, every room is pleasing to the eye and very comfortable. The Guest Sitting Room with a wood burning fire has television and wonderful aerial views of the farm. In the delightful Conservatory Dining Room you will be served a delicious breakfast with a changing menu every day. For example one day might be Juice, Cereal, home-made potato cakes, sausages, bacon, mushrooms, tomato, as well as plenty of toast, butter and preserves. The tea is piping hot and the coffee freshly made. Vegetarian breakfasts are also catered for. All the well furnished bedrooms are en-suite and some have their own sitting room. The comfortable orthopaedic beds have Dorma bedding. Every room has television and a hostess tray.

Brighthouse Farm also offers a self-catering, three bed-roomed cottage and a Caravan and Camping Site complete with toilets, showers and electric hook ups.

USEFUL IN FORMATION

OPEN: All year
CHILDREN: Welcome
CREDIT CARDS: None taken
LICENSED: No
ACCOMMODATION: En suite
S/C 3 bed-roomed cottage
Caravan & Camping site
RATES: B&B From £20 pp.pn

CONSERVATORY DINING ROOM: Great breakfast with changing menu. No evening meal
VEGETARIAN: Catered for
WHEELCHAIR ACCESS: No
GARDEN: Beautiful. Farm Trail
PETS: No

THE PLOUGH
Brockley Green,
Hundon,
Sudbury,
Suffolk
CO10 8DT

ETB 4 Crown Recommended

Tel: 01440 786789
Fax: 01440 786710

Delightfully tucked away in the quiet hamlet of Brockley Green between the rural villages of Hendon and Kedington, The Plough Inn, is a rewarding experience as many people have found who have discovered its excellence. We suggest you approach it from either Haverhill, to the south west, or Clare, to the south east. You will find the Inn on a hilltop, set in five acres of grounds and with stunning views over the Stour Valley. A marvellous place to stay for a holiday or break, it is located in the heart of East Anglia and only thirty minutes drive from Cambridge, Newmarket, Bury St Edmunds, Lavenham and 'Constable Country'.

Originally a small country pub, The Plough has been skilfully and lovingly extended using original oak beams and soft red bricks to retain a country inn ambience. It has never forgotten its origins and the Inn remains today a traditional country hostelry offering traditional pleasures. David and Marian Rowlinson are mine hosts, two charming people with a gift for making their customers feel at ease and at home. David's grandfather used to farm nearby and when he retired in 1957, David's father moved the family into The Plough. David took over from his father in 1982 and since then many advantageous developments have taken place.

In the bar with its wealth of beams, red bricks and country style furniture, you will find a contented group of local people who come here to enjoy the beer, the banter and the friendly atmosphere which spills over to encompass newcomers. The Bar menu is good and has 'Daily Specials' every day. Simms restaurant also has a bar. It is an attractive place, much like the bar in furnishing but with upholstered antique style seating. The tables are elegantly laid with crisp linen table covers and napkins, crystal glass and silver-plated cutlery. It is here you can dine on delicious English food with a French influence, beautifully presented, accompanied by a well chosen wine list. For those who want to stay in this idyllic setting, there are eight en-suite guest rooms, comfortably and attractively furnished. Each room has television, teletext, direct dial telephone and a hospitality tray. The Plough Inn is ideal for small conferences; its peaceful setting, comfortable rooms, good food and a willing staff are all conducive to a great working environment. Take time out to discover this very special Inn for yourselves - you won't regret it.

USEFUL INFORMATION

OPEN: 11-2.30pm & 5-11pm
Winter: 12-2.30pm & 6-11pm
CHILDREN: Welcome
CREDIT CARDS: Visa/Master/Switch/AMEX
LICENSED: Full On
ACCOMMODATION: 4dbl. 3tw 1 fam
RATES: From £70 double

RESTAURANT: English fare with a
French influence
BAR FOOD: Good choice. Daily Specials
VEGETARIAN: Yes
WHEELCHAIR ACCESS: Yes
GARDEN: 5 acres
PETS: Yes

THE RED LION
The Street,
Icklingham,
Suffolk
IP286PS

Tel: 01638 717802
Fax: 01638 515702

There are some pubs to which one is drawn immediately and the 16th-century Red Lion, just three miles from the historic Saxon village of Icklingham, is one of them. It has just about everything: a thatched roof, vast log burning fires, low ceilings with exposed beams, two comfortable bars and a charming thirty cover restaurant. The pub stands back from the road and has a large expanse of lawn in the front which, in summer, is a magnet for people who love sitting at the tables, surrounded by shrubs and trees, enjoying a drink or a snack.

It would be a wonderful venue for a wedding reception and Ian Hubbert and Jonathan Gates, the owners, say they can offer reception facilities for up to one hundred and fifty covers. Many devotees of the Red Lion come from Bury St Edmunds 6 miles away and Mildenhall which is just five miles away. It goes without saying that a pub of this stature serves good food. There is a full A La Carte menu in the restaurant which is made up of freshly cooked traditional English fare, including vegetables that are cooked to perfection. Bar meals include steaks, steak and kidney pies, and whole host of other traditional pub dishes. There are well filled sandwiches, Ploughman's with a variety of meats or cheeses, and daily specials. The prices are fair and the atmosphere superb.

USEFUL INFORMATION

OPEN: Mon-Sun 11-3pm & 6-11pm
CHILDREN: Yes. Children's menu
CREDIT CARDS: Visa/Master
LICENSED: Full On Licence
GARDEN: Front lawn with tables
PETS: Not in restaurant

RESTAURANT: Fresh, traditional
local meats, poultry, game, fish
BAR FOOD: Wide, interesting range
VEGETARIAN: Several dishes
WHEELCHAIR ACCESS: No

RIVERSIDE HOTEL & RESTAURANT
Mill Street,
Mildenhall,
Suffolk
IP28 7AP

3xxx AA & RAC 4 Crowns ETB.
Hospitality Award *AA Rosette for Food

Tel: 01638 717274
Fax: 01638 715997

As one might guess from its name, Riverside Hotel is a country house standing in its own grounds on the banks of the River Lark and just on the edge of the old market town of Mildenhall. Owned and run by two sisters and their husbands, Carolyn and John Child and Alison and Keith Lardner, this is one of the most charming and delightful places in Suffolk. The sort of place that radiates its welcome. Built in 1720, the Georgian house is gracious and beautifully proportioned. The public rooms have the air of a private country house, with their large windows, high ceilings, elegant drapes, a plethora of fine paintings and a wealth of books for those who enjoy curling up in a deep, comfortable armchair, shut off from the workaday world. Fresh flowers grace every room and their scent lingers in the air. The house is perfectly set off by mature trees and spacious lawns which sweep down to the river.

The gracious and restored Terrace Restaurant looks out over the gardens to the river making a perfect setting in which to enjoy good food. Riverside is well known for the standard and excellence of its fare and has won awards. Local game, fowl and fish are a regular feature of the menu as is venison in season. The hotel is open to non-residents and enjoys an excellent bar trade from local people as well as visitors. The bar menu offers a full range from sandwiches and Ploughman's to Curries and Stews. Riverside has a growing reputation for the manner in which they deal with wedding receptions, conference and private functions. The attention to detail added to the warmth of the welcome ensures that these occasions are a great success and for wedding photographs what could be better than the lawns with the river as a backdrop.

Riverside has twenty one en-suite bedrooms, all furnished individually and with great taste. Each room has television, direct dial telephone, clock radio and a hostess tray. A good place to stay at any time of the year, and keen anglers can also fish in the hotel's own private stretch of river. Riverside is the Suffolk venue for the Pudding Club, indeed they have a license which allows them to hold their meetings. This is great fun and if you would like to take part, a Pudding Club Meeting can be incorporated into a Getaway Break weekend.

USEFUL INFORMATION

OPEN: All year
CHILDREN: Welcome
CREDIT CARDS: All major cards
LICENSED: Full On
ACCOMMODATION: 21 en-suite rooms
RATES: £41 pppn B&B 2 nights DB&B £106pp

RESTAURANT: Delicious food
BAR FOOD: Wide range
VEGETARIAN: Yes
WHEELCHAIR ACCESS: Not really
GARDEN: Lawns down to river

WORLINGTON HALL HOTEL
Worlington,
Suffolk
IP28 8RX

Tel:01638 712237
Fax: 01638 712631

Worlington Hall was built in 1580 and today its mature red stone work , tall chimneys and tiled roof present a charming picture as one comes up the drive. The hotel stands in seven acres of beautifully maintained grounds which are a pleasure to sit in, play a round of miniature golf or walk around before returning indoors to enjoy a drink before dinner, or indeed at anytime. Much of the past remains in the atmosphere of the house no doubt reinforced by the fact that Worlington Hall can boast a Priest's Hole where monks used to hide at the time of the Dissolution. It is also apparent in the height and spaciousness of the rooms with their decorated ceilings. It is essentially a comfortable place to stay with the feel of a country house party about it rather than a formal hotel. The staff are welcoming, friendly and unobtrusively efficient.

There are eight guest rooms, all en-suite, each with direct dial telephone, television, trouser press, hostess tray and mini bar. In all the rooms you will also find a complimentary decanter of sherry and fresh fruit. In addition to these rooms is the Coaching House which sleeps 2-4 people. The chefs at Worlington Hall are renowned for the innovative and imaginative menus. They use as much local produce as possible and everything is fresh. All tastes are catered for with a mixture of traditional English dishes and several enticing Continental ones. Open to non-residents, Worlington Hall is frequently a popular venue for weddings and other functions as well as business meetings, seminars and conferences. Great attention to detail is always paid to these functions which is why they have such a good reputation.

This is a great area in which to stay. One can fish, walk, play golf, actually drive tanks. Within easy distance there are many places of interest including the many World War II air bases such as Mildenhall.

USEFUL INFORMATION

OPEN: All year
CHILDREN: Welcome
CREDIT CARDS: All major cards
LICENSED: Full On
ACCOMMODATION: 8 en-suite house + coaching sleeping 2-4
RATES: Sgl £50pp.pn B&B Dbl. £65
Coach House £85
Special Offers. Weekend Breaks

RESTAURANT: Innovative & imaginative menus both A la Carte & Table d'hôte
BAR FOOD: Always available
VEGETARIAN: Always a choice
WHEELCHAIR ACCESS: Restaurant only
GARDEN: 7 acres
PETS: Yes

39 WELL STREET
Bury St Edmunds,
Suffolk
IP33 1EQ

Listed East Anglian Tourist Board

Tel: 01284 768986
Fax: 01284 765511

Built in 1820, 39 Well Street is part of a fine Georgian terrace in the town centre of Bury St Edmunds. Five minutes from the A14 and a short walk from the coach and railway stations, the B&B is in the heart of the historic town centre. The theatre, cinema, shops, pubs and restaurants are all within easy walking distance. Bury is a thriving market town with a fascinating history and it is also the ideal jumping-off point for Cambridge, Norwich, Aldeburgh and the Suffolk and Norfolk Coast. We take pleasure in including you as part of our big family.

You'll receive a warm and friendly welcome and, as so many guests from around the world have discovered, you'll most probably want to come back. We have two double or twin-bedded rooms and one single, each elegantly furnished, charmingly decorated and with hand basin, TV, and hostess tray. Treat yourself to a memorable feast with a full traditional English breakfast or a lighter Continental one if you prefer. A wonderful place to stay, where even the cat and the dog are welcoming. Having been a guest at this establishment, and tied to re-book unsuccessfully, you will not be disappointed with the service.

USEFUL INFORMATION

OPEN: All year	DINING ROOM: First class breakfast
CHILDREN: Welcome. No cots	VEGETARIAN: Upon request
CREDIT CARDS: None taken	WHEELCHAIR ACCESS: Yes
LICENSED: No	GARDEN: Yes
ACCOMMODATION: 1dbl/tw en-suite	PETS: No
2 rooms not en-suite	SMOKING IN BEDROOMS ONLY
RATES: Sgl £20 Dbl. £36 En-suite £48.	

THE WHITE HORSE
Rede Road,
Whepstead,
Bury St Edmunds,
Suffolk
IP29 4SS

Tel: 01284 735542

The White Horse was built in the 15th century when it was a farm house which dispensed drinks. It retains much of the past today with a great atmosphere, open fireplaces and exposed beams. The village is a friendly place involved in 'Bury in Bloom' every year and you will find many gardens are open to visitors. The beauty and colour generated by the flowers is stunning. Bury St Edmunds is close by and with its fascinating history, great architecture and superb Abbey, it attracts many visitors and whilst the town has many hostelries many people still prefer to take the short drive out to Whepstead to enjoy the hospitality of The White Horse.

Rosemary Woolf is the sole proprietor since her husband died in 1996 and she carries on the tradition of hospitality they both created. The bar is a friendly place and much frequented by locals who enjoy the well kept beer and the cheerful banter that goes on at the bar. Visitors are always made welcome and quickly get drawn into conversation if they wish to. Rosemary hails from Mauritius and this is evident is some of the delicious Mauritian dishes that are part of the menu which changes daily. This is a lady who enjoys cooking and as well as traditional dishes you will find that Chinese, Thai, Indian - Baltis for example - as well as Mexican food appear regularly. At lunch-time the Bar food is popular with a good range of sandwiches, baguettes, Ploughman's and salads. On Sundays there is a set menu which includes the traditional Sunday Roast Dinner with all the trimmings. Delicious and great value.

The attractive Beer Garden which is large, is a popular place in warm weather and if you enjoy a game of Pool or Darts you will find both in the comfortable Public Bar.
This is an unpretentious pub but one which should not be missed.

USEFUL INFORMATION

OPEN: 11.30-3pm & 6.30-11.30pm
CHILDREN: At landlord's discretion
& over 5 years
CREDIT CARDS: None taken
LICENSED: Full On
GARDEN: Beer garden

RESTAURANT: Not applicable
BAR FOOD: Good range. Exotic
dishes from Mauritius & elsewhere
VEGETARIAN: 2 dishes daily
WHEELCHAIR ACCESS: Yes
PETS: Outside only

MASONS ARMS
14 Whiting Street,
Bury St Edmunds,
Suffolk
IP33 1NX

Egon Ronay Good Beer Guide

Tel:01284 753955

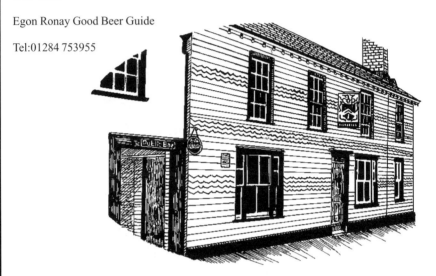

In the heart of Bury St Edmunds, a town that is renowned for its superb, historic buildings, the Masons Arms stands out because of its distinctive Essex weather-boarding exterior; the only pub to have this feature in Suffolk. Inside is equally interesting with old beams and traditional furnishing. Early 20th century 'Froth Blowers Club' memorabilia adorns the walls of the Lounge Bar complete with the rules as well as a number of press cuttings featuring the Masons in days gone by.

The pub is noted in Bury for its extremely friendly atmosphere in which regulars and strangers feel equally at home. It is the sort of place in which women on their own are comfortable. The Masons Arms has a picturesque old high walled garden which is popular for eating and drinking in summer and especially when there is a Barbecue. The good pub fare is mainly home-cooked and the menu has dishes that will appeal to everyone, sometimes English and sometimes Continental. Fresh fish is a feature and for vegetarians there is always a choice including stuffed mushrooms and an excellent vegetable curry. This pub is now under new management, do try it out, there are radical changes.

USEFUL INFORMATION

OPEN: 11-3pm & 5.30-11pm   RESTAURANT: Not applicable
food: 12-2pm & 7-9.30pm   BAR FOOD: Wide range
CHILDREN: Welcome   VEGETARIAN: Always a choice
CREDIT CARDS: None taken   WHEELCHAIR ACCESS: Yes
LICENSED: Full On   GARDEN: Yes. Seats 64. BBQ
PETS: No

OUNCE HOUSE
Northgate Street,
Bury St Edmunds,
Suffolk
IP33 1HP

Tel: 01284 761779
Fax: 01284 768315

This elegant town house is the home of Jenny and Simon Pott and must be one of the most interesting conversions in Bury St Edmunds - it was once a school. Today it exudes well-being from its immaculate facade to the spacious rooms inside. It has all the graciousness of a Victorian building with high ceiling rooms and tall windows. The Potts have furnished it with loving care and in keeping with the age of the house. Every room has choice antiques, the windows are draped with swagged curtains.

The immaculate bedrooms vary in size but no matter which one you choose, it will be full of character. Each room has television, hair dryer, direct-dial telephone and room service is available. The breakfast is memorable with everything cooked to order. There are several fruit juices, plenty of cereals, fresh toast, preserves and coffee and tea. The choice with the traditional breakfast is yours; your eggs can be scrambled, poached, fried or simply boiled. At night Jenny offers evening meals only by arrangement and they are a communal affair served in the dining room overlooking the garden There are early suppers for children, a friendly bar in the library and facilities for small conferences and meetings. Smoking is permitted in the bar/library only.

USEFUL INFORMATION

OPEN: All year
CHILDREN: Yes. Early suppers
CREDIT CARDS: Yes
LICENSED: Yes. Residential
ACCOMMODATION: 4 en-suite rooms
RATES: Sgl from £35 Dbl. from £60
Special Breaks available

DINING ROOM: Sumptuous breakfast
Dinner by arrangement
VEGETARIAN: By arrangement
WHEELCHAIR ACCESS: Yes
GARDEN: Yes
PETS: No

THE ROSE AND CROWN
82 Holmsey Green,
Beck Row,
Mildenhall,
Suffolk
IP29 8AP

Tel: 01628 713407

Derrick Marshall and Pauline Watts have only recently become the proprietors of The Rose and Crown but they have already been accepted by the locals and are rapidly acquiring a reputation for the friendly, welcoming atmosphere that they have created. It is the sort of pub, set in a rural area, which is suitable for any age. Children have a play area and a big field in which to run about in safety and there is a Horseshoe pit for anyone who fancies a game. The field is also used for basic camping and caravanning.

Barbecues are planned for the summer, you can sit on the patio or in the landscaped garden quietly enjoying a drink. Enjoy the local chatter in the bar, perhaps listening to a customer playing the piano. The beer is well kept and the food is a nice mixture of tried and tested pub favourites including the Rose and Crown Burger which is something special. Bar snacks are always available including sandwiches and Ploughman's. The Sunday Roast is delicious and excellent value. Children and Vegetarians are catered for. The accommodation consists of one double and two twin rooms all comfortably furnished and with television, hairdryers and a hostess tray.

USEFUL INFORMATION

OPEN: Mon-Sat 11-3pm & 7-11pm
Sun: 12-3 & 7-10.30pm
CHILDREN: Welcome
CREDIT CARDS: None taken
LICENSED: Full On
ACCOMMODATION: 1dbl 1tw not en-suite
RATES: £18 pp.pn B&B
PETS: Yes

RESTAURANT: Good value English
fare
BAR FOOD: Wide range
VEGETARIAN: Yes
WHEELCHAIR ACCESS: Yes
GARDEN: Yes +Field
for basic camping & caravanning

THE STAR INN
The Street,
Lidgate,
Suffolk
CB8 9PP

Tel: 01638 500275

Maria-Teresa Axon is a Catalan - there cannot be many of them cooking in East Anglia, but this is what this colourful lady does in her charming hostelry, The Star Inn in the centre of Lidgate. There is a warm, relaxed atmosphere on the whole but just occasionally one is aware of drama when Maria Teresa is cooking something special for her clients. Many have become regulars over the years and know that no better Mediterranean fish soup will be found anywhere. Then there are the prawns malaguena, which come with a lovely strong garlicky flavoured sauce and a finger bowl. Navarin of lamb cooked in red wine, lamb's kidneys cooked in sherry, real paella with both chicken and seafood, and a handful of French dishes. With such a gourmet choice it is no wonder that The Star Inn is firmly on the gastronomic map of Suffolk. There is no special Bar menu, it is the same as the restaurant but you do not have to eat a full meal. Vegetarians are catered for and there are special helpings for children. The restaurant has thirty five covers and there is seating outside for another twenty five. Private parties can be catered for. The wine list is well chosen and the House French wine is excellent as well as reasonably priced.

USEFUL INFORMATION

OPEN: All week. Lunch 12.30-2pm
Dinner: 7.30-10pm
CHILDREN: Yes. Children's helpings
CREDIT CARDS: All major cards
LICENSED: Full On
PETS: No

RESTAURANT: Exciting Catalan cooking
BAR FOOD: As Restaurant
VEGETARIAN: Yes
WHEELCHAIR ACCESS: No
GARDEN: Tables outside

THE BELL HOTEL
Market Hill,
Clare, Suffolk CO10 8NN

Tel: 01787 277741
Fax: 01787 278474

The village of Clare lies on the Essex/Suffolk border in Constable country. A fascinating place with its Norman Castle and country park and splendid walks as well as the Nethergate Brewery which supplies the beautiful half-timbered 16th century old coaching inn, The Bell Hotel on Market Hill. Beautiful inside and out it provides warm hospitality to all who go there whether for a meal in either the attractive Tudor Restaurant or the Garden Room Restaurant or to stay in one of over twenty bedrooms with en-suite facilities. The food is renowned way beyond Clare and offers English and Continental dishes, Chef's Specials and a Vegetarian Selection. The bedrooms are individual in character with every facility you could wish for. For that special occasion you can celebrate in style with an antique four-poster bed and whirlspa bath. The Bell Hotel has conference and banqueting facilities such as overhead projector, fax, telephone, television and video. Nearby are the historic towns of Lavenham and Long Melford. Further afield are Bury St Edmunds and Newmarket, the home of British horse racing and the university city of Cambridge. Stansted Airport is only half an hour away.

USEFUL INFORMATION

OPEN: All year
CHILDREN: Welcome
CREDIT CARDS: All major cards
LICENSED: Full On
ACCOMMODATION: 20+ en-suite rooms
RATES: Sgl £50 Dbl. £60 Fam £75 4 Poster £75
Honeymoon Suite £75 B&B

RESTAURANT: English & Continental
VEGETARIAN: Always a selection
WHEELCHAIR ACCESS: Difficult
GARDEN: Yes
PETS: By arrangement

THE DOWER HOUSE
By Bailey's Pool,
Pakenham, Bury St Edmunds,
Suffolk IP31 2LX

Tel: 01359 230670

The Dower House occupies such a pretty rural location beside a small river, which tumbles under a quaint bridge to Bailey's Pool. This is an 18th century house in which there are many exposed beams and an open fire in the drawing room adding to the feeling of well-being one gets as you cross the threshold. There is a short staircase leading up to the comfortable bedrooms, one of which has a king size bed with en-suite bathroom. This is the perfect place for anyone wanting to escape from the world and totally relax or maybe write a book or paint a picture. Canade geese fly overhead, ponies graze in the field opposite. Strictly non-smoking, this charming family home is very welcoming. Mrs Stephen Gurteen is your hostess and you can be assured of some first class, imaginative meals both at breakfast and dinner, which is optional and not available on Sunday evenings. To find The Dower House take the A143 out of Bury St Edmunds towards Ixworth. Ignore all Pakenham signs until Mill Road, Pakenham, then turn right, take left fork - the house is pink with white gates, on the left.

USEFUL INFORMATION

OPEN: All year except Christmas
CHILDREN: Not under 8 years
CREDIT CARDS: None taken
LICENSED: No
ACCOMMODATION: 1tw 1D or tw

DINING ROOM: Imaginative cooking
VEGETARIAN: Upon request
WHEELCHAIR ACCESS: No
GARDEN: Lovely grounds
PETS: No

HILL FARM
Kirtling, NR Newmarket,
Suffolk CB85 11Q

Tel: 01638 730253

Four and a half miles from Newmarket, famed for its two race courses, Hill Farm is in the small village of Kirtling, a peaceful situation surrounded by beautiful countryside. There is much else to do including some beautiful walks, racing and golf. The Broads are not far off, Cambridge is sixteen miles away and Ely Cathedral not much further. Hill Farm is four hundred years old and the house is full of nooks and crannies, low ceilings and a wealth of atmosphere built over the centuries. You will find a great welcome here. There are three rooms, two double and one single, all en-suite and each with television, telephone and a well-supplied hostess tray. The rooms are attractively furnished and the beds comfortable. Breakfast is a memorable feast, freshly cooked to your order. Dinner is available if you book in advance. This is a friendly, relaxed house to stay in and one to which, having stayed once, you will want to return.

USEFUL INFORMATION

OPEN: All year
CHILDREN: Welcome
CREDIT CARDS: None taken
LICENSED: No
ACCOMMODATION: 2dbl 1sgl en-suite
RATES: £45dbl per room £25sgl

DINING ROOM: Excellent food
Evening meal if ordered
VEGETARIAN: Upon request
WHEELCHAIR ACCESS: No
GARDEN: Yes
PETS: No

TWELVE ANGEL HILL
12, Angel Hill, Bury St Edmunds,
Suffolk IP33 1UZ

RAC Highly Acclaimed, AA QQQQQ Premier Selected
Which? County Hotel of the Year 1996. BTA Jewel of Britain 1998
Tel: 01284 704088 Fax: 01284 725549

In the delightful medieval town of Bury St Edmunds you will find a rather nice and very special Hotel. Twelve Angel Hill has won just about every accolade and lives up to its awards. It is richly furnished to an exacting standard with many antiques. The house was built in the 19th century, but some parts date back to the 1500's, many of the original features still remain. This totally non-smoking, warm, comfortable and centrally heated house is owned and excellently run by Bernie and John Clarke, who extend a friendly welcome to all their guests. There are six bedrooms, all en-suite with either bath or shower, TV, radio, trouser press, hair dryer, telephone and tea and coffee making facilities. The rooms are opulently decorated with matching soft furnishings and are all named after a French wine. One room has a magnificent dark wood four poster bed. Breakfast is served in the lovely dining room, where you are treated to a first class meal. For your evening meal Bernie and John will gladly book a table for you at one of the many restaurants in the town. The Hotel is centrally positioned close to the Cathedral, 14th century Abbey remains and gardens and the shops. Being a market town there is a lively Street Market on Wednesdays and Saturdays.

USEFUL INFORMATION

OPEN: All year except January
CHILDREN: No
CREDIT CARDS: All major cards
LICENSED: Yes
ACCOMMODATION 6 en-suite rooms
RATES: Dbl/Twin £75 prpn. Sgl. £50. Dbl. Single Occupancy £5. Supp.
Suite or Four-poster £80. Sgl occ. £60. All include Bkfst. & Vat.

DINING ROOM: Traditional English
breakfast. No evening meal
VEGETARIAN: Catered for
WHEELCHAIR ACCESS: No
GARDEN: Yes PETS: No

IAN PETHERS

KERSEY

Selected venues in this chapter

' Tis not the eating,
Nor 'tis not the drinking that is to be blamed, but the excess'.
John Seldon

CHAPTER 10:
ROMANCE AND REALITY
Bardwell to Stowmarket, Lavenham, & East Bergholt

I tried hard to keep this chapter until last, to follow the 'finish on a high' routine. I failed. Call it impatience if you will, but surely no-one can keep the Valley of the Stour waiting indefinitely. In any case, having started at Bury, it would really ruin the logistics to rush across the county to the coast, visit Lowestoft - and then travel all the way back again. So, on both counts, Constable comes next and there's nothing much for it but to go with the flow and follow the lemmings to his stamping grounds.

When Essex and East Anglia were separate kingdoms, in the days of the Anglo Saxons, the River Stour formed a natural barrier between them, as it flowed through chalky, low lying land to its estuary at Seafield Bay and its meeting with the Orwell off Horwich. Today there's next to no warfare between the counties, unless Colchester or Southend face Ipswich or Norwich in the FA Cup. Meanwhile, poplars and willows - and the occasional elms that still survive - stand beside the paths and ditches that cross the water meadows, and north and south of the river are linked many times by the pleasant, unspoiled bridges that span the waters between Sudbury and Flatford.

John Constable - of whom much more anon - was born in a house that overlooked this valley at East Bergholt, one of the most attractive villages in the area. It was a prosperous area as well as an idyllic one, that prosperity having been firmly based on the boom in the wool trade that started in the 14th century. By the time the trade collapsed, a little over a century ago, there were innumerable pointers to that wealth in the splendid architecture, especially churches, in towns and villages which seem to us today to be too small to justify such grandeur. Of course, it was the tidal waters of the Orwell and Stour that were as much responsible for the boom as any other factor. They became busy waterways, thronged with ships sailing to and from the continent and Ipswich, in particular, grew rich from the trade in cloth - while the knock-on effect spread up the valleys and the entire Suffolk/Essex border region felt the benefits.

In other chapters, after some sort of introduction, we have tended to launch into the day's tour with directions to the first port of call and a eulogy or two of its peculiar attractions. In this chapter we need a very different approach because I believe that the way we actually see the countryside of the Stour has been shaped to a huge degree by the vision and the work of one man, John Constable. He taught us a whole language of rural symbols and images, of light and shade so that most of us, to some extent, are unable to see 'his' country except through 'his' eyes - which is why Flatford Mill, for example, is the most famous mill in the country: we've all seen it, in the 'flesh', or in the picture and in both cases, our eyes have been directed by his. To that extent we need to know the man before we get to know the countryside. We also need to start this tour from his birthplace, if only to keep it neat!

EAST BERGHOLT, as we've observed, was once a centre of the woollen industry - but nobody remembers that. What they do remember is that Constable was born there, in 1776. It may well have a fine church and attractive architecture - but all that matters for most of us is that its roads and buildings were the setting for his emergence as one of England's most famous artists. As we're still in Suffolk, even that simple fact is not without a curious spin-off. Ask anyone to name the three best known painters that this country has produced and it's a virtual certainty that the same names will crop up again and again: Gainsborough, Constable and Turner - you know it! Here's the curiosity: all three were Romantics - Turner and Constable were born within a year of each other - but two of the three, Constable and Gainsborough, were born in the 18th century, in Suffolk and into communities that are less than a dozen miles apart! That fact has to be the strangest thing, don't you think? It confirms, too, that the countryside and the quality of light along the Suffolk/Essex border, the valley of the River Stour, are of a quite remarkable quality which can stimulate the creativity of men and women to an extent that is hardly equalled anywhere else in England.

When Hugh Constable, the artist's great grandfather, crossed the river from Essex to make his first home in Suffolk there is no way he could have imagined the consequences of his move. Eventually, his grandson - John's father - became miller of the actual Flatford Mill and Willy Lot, whose cottage was the subject of one of the best loved paintings, became the painter's boyhood friend. As a youngster, Constable spent endless enchanting hours on the banks of the Stour and grew to love the scenery of the riverside to such an extent that, ever afterwards, he was emphatic that they were what made him a painter.

At the age of 23, in 1799, he enrolled as a student at the Royal Academy in London, but went back to the Stour over and over again to make sketches for his full blown landscape paintings. These views of his native Suffolk, including 'The Haywain' (1820) and 'Dedham Vale' (1828) are among the most familiar paintings of their kind ever to have been produced - the more so, as subsequent generations of card and calendar makers have chosen them, along with the paintings of Flatford Mill, Dedham Mill and Willy Lot's cottage, as representing all that is best loved in the rural England of our daydreams.

Interestingly, in relation to impressions we've formed elsewhere in our travels, there's a touch of a Dutch connection here, too. Constable's concern with the changing patterns of light, the movement of trees in the breeze and the other effects of wind and sun, drew inspiration not just from the land of the Stour, but from the landscapes of Peter Paul Rubens (1577-1640) whose brilliant draughtsmanship, dazzling colour and vigorous compositions had a vital influence on the art of the whole of Europe. Given the influence of Constable's work and the extent of his output, given the streams of cards and calendars that have poured out for decade after decade, it is little wonder that the name 'Constable Country' has stuck so firmly. What else could it be called? So, what is it like today?

FLATFORD MILL, a watermill one mile south of East Bergholt, is now run as a residential field centre. Just upstream, FLATFORD BRIDGE COTTAGE (enquiries 01206 299193) has been restored by the National Trust and houses a display about the painter. In addition to a tea garden, shop and boat hire facilities there is an information centre and access by foot to Trust land in DEDHAM VALE. "Tea-gardens?" you wonder, audibly. "Boat-hire?" These are not what 'the man' chose to paint. "Are we going to like this?" Fair questions. Frankly speaking, Flatford is a tourist target. Where Willy and John wandered down leafy lanes in their boyhood, there are one way systems, car parking and shops full of souvenirs - none of which featured in the famous landscapes, fairly obviously. Indeed, had their counterparts figured in the Flatford of 1800, one can imagine any self respecting artist rushing off to Ipswich to paint something that was, at least, genuine. They weren't and he didn't - so what can one say? Exactly. I'll think of something. Just give me a minute.

Look at it this way: Constable had an extraordinary talent and this was his place; all along the Valley of the Stour was his place. To come to Suffolk and avoid it, whatever it's like, would be a bit like going to Salzburg and making a point of avoiding anything to do with Mozart - because of the crowds. Or like going to Florence and turning one's back on the churches and galleries - because of the queues. Very superior, very purist - but culturally crass, don't you think? I know that, by now, every gift shop east of Bury St Edmunds is delightfully stocked with 'Constable Curios' - right down to the Flatford toothpick and the Dedham loo roll holder, all there for you to buy as a memory of your visit to this ancient area. The man himself said: *"all that lies on the banks of the Stour; those scenes made me a painter."* So, there's the Stour, and it's banks, for you conjure up what inspired this great artist. With me you can focus on the cottages, the steeples, the trees, the water and the sky in the way that his paintings urge us to do. We can, at least, try to see as he saw and understand how he felt when he said: *"As long as I am able to hold a brush, I shall never cease to paint them."* All we need to see is the reality beyond the cafe, the car parks, the crowds and the clutter, which is still there despite all the hype that has grown up around it. I think I ought to take something for this tendency to get ecstatic every time I trip over a cultural classic. Back to the facts - and back to East Bergholt, briefly.

The reason for the return is fairly simple. On some of our trips we're indulging ourselves: we eat fine meals, we lounge around in the sunshine, we wallow in kleptomania. On others we touch on the fascination of the wildlife, from the everyday to the exotic, in reserves, country parks and zoos, even. Yet other visits delight us with the built environment, the finer points of streetscapes, of great houses and of ancient churches. And so on. East Bergholt is different in so far as it is the start of a minor pilgrimage to discover more about ourselves from the clues it gives us to the workings of the mind of a very English artist.

So, as we stand in the middle of the village we're looking at the place where his journey began. We know already that he believed emphatically that the valley formed his future as a painter, inspired him and, in short, made him what he was. Now his work is found in galleries throughout the country, in the Tate, the National, the Victoria and Albert Museum, the Minaries Gallery in Colchester and the Christchurch Mansion House in Ipswich. More to the point, there can hardly be a household in the country that hasn't had at least one of 'those' cards or calendars around at some time or other.

In terms of the artist's own experiences, he didn't just bury himself in East Bergholt and paint what he saw from his window. He travelled, finding subjects in the Lake District, at Salisbury, Brighton and Hampstead, where he lived during the latter part of his life and where he is buried, in the churchyard of St John's Church. Nevertheless he was bound, utterly, to the landscape of his childhood, to the banks of the Stour.

So I think there are two aspects of that little tale that we could keep in mind as we wander along the valley, two questions whose answers could be worth rather more than the cash value of the collectibles currently filling the boot. Remember that it's the Stour pictures that have had the impact, that have been reproduced over and over again. We know of - and respect - the others, but we aren't obsessed with them.

First question: do these pictures show us an ideal environment, almost a fantasy setting, where we'd all like to live out our lives? This is a question about a very deep level of our being that's generally hidden under layers of so called reality: the supermarket, the office desk, the housing estate, the holidays in the Seychelles are where we seem to think we have to -or want to - be. Are they? Are they really? Wouldn't all of us rather be in East Bergholt? Or Stoke by Nayland? Or in what we imagine such places to have been like once, judging from the pictures? Or do we really love the 'ultimate shopping experience', the M25 and the time share apartment? I'm convinced that Constable asks us those questions, just as I'm convinced that a stroll beside the Stour could throw up an answer or two (and that's why we're here).

Second question: Constable's lifelong love affair with the valley, I think, may parallel our own experiences (and set up a rather nice conflict, as we'll see). He could not break from his roots. He may well have chosen to justify this pattern by writing endless hymns of praise to their beauty, they may well have been that beautiful - indeed, they almost certainly were - but, regardless of any of it, the fact is that they had him by the throat, forever, wherever he put himself. The paintings of Lakeland, of Salisbury, of Hampstead Heath are fine work - but he isn't there - he's still somewhere around Dedham, all the time. Whilst I'm not sure that's a fault (or even a weakness) I'm very sure that it's interesting enough to put the second question: can Constable or, more to the point, anyone at all, ever break from their roots? Think about it: aren't all of us trying, deny it as we will, to recreate our own version of the familiarity, the security and the comfort that we found in our young days? Aren't we trying to recreate a rose coloured version of that familiar place - only bigger, or more successful, or cleaner or with the warts surgically removed? Now you can see the conflict: maybe one part of us is trying to cling on while another part is trying to drive us towards the 'perfect English village', albeit with a disco in the former market hall and an Indian take-away where the alms houses used to be! We claim to be discerning as a way of life. Where is it written in stone that a vacation is meant to be a limited period of brain death? Let's leave the birthplace, follow the line of the valley - and, as I say, think about it.

A tributary of the Stour flows under the bridge at **HIGHAM**, a small village with a triangular green and half-timbered houses - from there our way climbs to a quite respectable ridge. Not all East Anglia is pancake flat, whatever the armchair experts tell you! The charming Suffolk lanes wind prettily enough whenever we meet them but undulations - ascents, even - like this make them all but intoxicating. In fact, travel-writers by the score have said as much many times - so, originality for its own sake being pointless, I'll join the chorus and ring the praises: it is gorgeous around here! There are views in several directions, including down to the estuary with distant churches standing firm against the sky, as they did in Norfolk, although the Suffolk version has a more gentle resolve.

The next village we meet - **STOKE BY NAYLAND** - sits on top of it all at the crest of the ridge. This dominance is in turn dominated by the 120 ft high brick tower of the parish church, another one of Constables's favourite subjects. It's not just the architecture that attracts enthusiasts, as the church is also home to some splendid brasses. One of them is dedicated to Lady Katherine Howard, grandmother of Anne Boleyn and Katherine Howard who were among the wives of the insatiable Henry VIII. The setting for the church is pleasant, too - at least, it is to photographers who waft around in front of the row of houses like butterflies on buddleia.

I don't know what the Anglo Saxon (or Old English) would be for 'mañana' - but I'll bet they remember it in South Suffolk. Even the metaphors are in a dream: 'bees round a honeypot' would be far too frantic, too urgent for Stoke by Nayland. Everything drifts - and so do we, this time just the short way down the B1087 to **NAYLAND**. Here, hard by the STOUR VALLEY PATH (Walks Pack - 01473 583176) is another medieval village that can thank the boom in cloth making for much of its excellent architecture - although the church, which dates from around 1400, came close to a serious demise in 1884, from an earth tremor! Or was that a seismic wave generated by another UFO landing at Lakenheath? Whatever - and I must return to aliens in a moment - the original spire was found to be unsafe in 1834 and was removed. Fifty years later the remaining tower seems to have been affected by the tremor. Not to worry: eighty years after that a replica spire was put up during reconstruction in 1963.

While we're at Nayland Church, we should pop inside (we probably would, anyway) to see one of Constable's only two religious paintings, which hangs above the altar - and must be worth a fortune. Some 'authorities' claim the man did three ecclesiastical pictures - all agree on Nayland and St Michael's, Brantham but some want to suggest that he did a third for Manningtree which was later moved over to

Feering. I shan't comment as both the latter places are in Essex, which is still a couple of chapters away (I may know, by then).

The country around Nayland is usually regarded as the upstream boundary of true 'Constable Country', while purists tend to focus, even more narrowly, on Dedham Vale and the estuary beyond it. As tourists rather than purists, I suggest we dismiss such limitations and carry on up the Stour, so to speak, with our heads high and the ever-present hope of an antique shop or a splendid meal for motivation. You'll gather we have exhausted culture, pro tem!

It seems you can't ever get away entirely from Dedham in this neck of the woods. No sooner have we arrived at **BURES**, a pleasant township that straddles the Stour and the county line, when someone sees the bikes on the car and tells us there's a dedicated cycle route nearby that should be just the job. Fine, except - you've guessed it - we're talking about the Dedham/Bures Circular Cycle Route - and we're off again. Only we're not - not in that sense, anyway. We're off to the next call shortly and the bikes can stay very firmly put.

It was at Bures that Constable's great grandfather first arrived in Suffolk - but the place had had a touch of limelight long before that. The ill-fated Edmund (who was more successful as a corpse, remember) was crowned in a chapel above the town in AD855, when he was only fifteen. The chapel was consecrated more than 350 years later by Archbishop Langton, although, in typical East Anglian fashion, it's not to be found on ST EDMUND'S HILL but rather on a crest, half a mile out of Bures on the Boxford road.

Having exhausted culture, we could say the same of villages too, for a while, so I'm in favour, at this juncture, of a swift sprint to **SUDBURY** (Information - 01787 881320) for a minor riot of urban indulgence. Although the town's medieval origins are less obvious than elsewhere - possibly because of its expansion over the years - it flourished with the cloth trade as did most of the rest of the county. It has all the classic signs, if we look for them: ALL SAINTS CHURCH dominates the area around the broad and impressive MARKET HILL where those of us not glutted with the business can wander among the stalls and fill a few more carrier bags on a Thursday or a Saturday, when the whole area positively seethes.

There are further signs of prosperity in the architecture, none more imposing than GAINSBOROUGH'S HOUSE (Information - 01787 372958) in the street of the same name. The artist was born here in 1727, half a century before 'the other chap' and only a few miles from East Bergholt - as we may have flogged to death already. There, to my mind, the similarity slams on the anchors. Gainsborough made his name painting portraits of the rich and famous, in Ipswich, London and Bath. From his writings, though, one can get the idea that landscape painting was his real love - if less profitable could one imagine? Whatever the truth, he can't keep the scenery completely out of his work and many of his human subjects are posed against a background of recognisable local scenes. He goes further and tells recurrently of his longing to return to the landscape painting of his youth. Back to his roots, you see? Despite his inner conflicts, the work he produced gained him a massive reputation, and the house, with its fine Georgian front, displays more of his work than any other gallery. To keep it company, there are also displays of 18th century furniture and memorabilia. Alongside that a varied programme of exhibitions of contemporary work, chiefly by East Anglian artists, is arranged throughout the year. As opening times vary, a prior call is, as so often, a good idea. Admission will cost us £2.80 a head.

GAINSBOROUGH HOUSE

The paintings are inspiring in themselves, but for us, still reeling from the East Bergholt experience, they have more to say. Gainsborough was almost fifty when Constable was born and was an established figure in the art world and in 'society' as a whole. One would have said there was no way the younger man could have avoided seeing his work, especially after the Stour Valley had 'spoken' to him and directed his own future as a painter. If it was 'after'. There's a nice little mystery to think about, here. It is said that Gainsborough's early works *'influenced John Constable in the gradual evolution of his style as he distilled the essence of English lowland landscape'*. Interesting. I can't imagine that Constable could have done his stint at the Royal Academy without poring over a good few Gainsboroughs, which may well have 'influenced the evolution'. But had he never seen a Gainsborough before then? As I say, there's a mystery here - I wonder if one can solve it by looking at the pictures in Gainsborough House a bit more carefully. Could we then choose between these alternative scenarios: Constable wanders up and down the river bank, revelling in the beauty of the country around him, and decides, spontaneously, to put his impressions on paper and canvas; or does he wander up and down etc. until he sees what

Gainsborough made of it all, until he sees one of the older man's paintings, at which point he recognises an outlet for his own reactions, a response that's appropriate for an individual like him in a place like that. I have no idea of the answer, as yet, but I'm working on it as the broader issue is surely whether painting and drawing is an instinctive or a learned activity? Truly fascinating. Well, I think it is. Or would you rather have another stoneware pot?

Back to reality: whatever the truth of the relationship between the two painters, the people of Sudbury are justifiably proud of the local boy and have erected a statue of him near the Church and looking out across the market. There are two aspects of Sudbury life that are tailor-made for us at this moment: physical exercise and a retail outlet (not exactly a shop, I'm afraid) that's unique in our experience so far. Let's do the exercise first, to recover from the brain strain, liven up our circulation after too much driving (again) - and work up an appetite for lunch. There are three ways of doing this: if you want your exercise to be on the gentle side, then a stroll through GREAT CORNARD COUNTRY PARK, near the southeast corner of the town, off the B1508, should suit very well. A rung or two up the exertion ladder might suggest SUDBURY BOATHOUSE HOTEL (Enquiries - 01787 379090) where you can hire a rowing boat for a touch of crab catching on the River Stour - or how good an oars-person are you? Maximum agony (and therefore maximum benefit, on the 'no pain - no gain' theory) is on offer at the KINGFISHER LEISURE CENTRE (Enquiries - 01787 375656) which seems to provide a wide enough range for most of us to find an appropriate measure of suffering.

Refreshed, revitalised - or worn out - we'll find the glint coming back to our eyes at the next destination, I promise you. Sudbury's involvement with the cloth trade in its yesteryears has one significant descendant, these days: VANNERS SILK WEAVERS (Information - 01787 313933). This long established silk weaving company has a factory outlet, which could be another source of joy if we feel that one, at least, of our obsessions has been sorely neglected, so far today. I take the point: since we didn't purchase any 'Constable Curios' we haven't bought anything since yesterday afternoon, in Bury St Edmunds. Unforgivable, on my part, of course. Let me make amends at Vanners. The outlet sells an array of silk fabrics, designer seconds, ties, scarfs and gifts, in a variety of styles. For once 'something for everyone' seems about right - and silk is so desirable, so luxurious, so right, somehow. Me, I fancy a scarf - sort of Ronald Coleman, y'know?

If you're more concerned with fabrics for furnishings, then the GAINSBOROUGH SILK WEAVING CO. LTD., in ALEXAMDRA ROAD (Enquiries – 01787 3720181) may be of greater interest. Established towards the end of the 19th Century, the company moved to its present premises in the 1920s and was incorporated in 1926. As well as buying some fabric – which is such a high standard that the company has been granted a Royal Warrant – we might enjoy a 'silk weaving tour', which includes a chance to look over some of the earliest powered Jacquard looms, and a visit to the small SILK

MUSEUM. As we make our way round, it would be good to remember that woven fabrics from this corner of the Suffolk have graced many palaces and stately homes.

While we have Vanners and the Gainsborough Company in mind – and there are other silk weavers in the area – it's good to see how the cloth weaving trade that built up the town in the first place has re-surfaced, albeit in a more exotic form. It's also good to recognise their success in such an activity, here in this mainly rural county at a time when too many people seem convinced that 'progress', 'high-tech' and 'mass production are synonymous.

Feeling somewhat sleeker from that brief brush with sophistication, we can now take to the road with revived enthusiasm. The road in question has to be the A134 to start with, as it curves southwards, apparently back to the Stour. Don't be fooled: we aren't going back; we try to avoid 'going back' at all costs - and this is no exception. After a mile or two we take a left turn and ease along the A1071, signposted to Boxford and Hadleigh.

In the interests of our tight schedule, not to mention the irresistible claims of the former Viking Royal Town up the road (and lunch) we'll have to give **BOXFORD** little more than a glance as we rush past, I'm afraid - but no-one ever said that life in the form of a travel guide was fair or free of prejudice. With a trace of luck our feeling of guilt should fizzle out within minutes of our parking the car, such is the diversity of delights awaiting us - I think.

HADLEIGH (Information - 01473 823824) is steeped in history (yes - again) and offers every kind of Suffolk domestic architecture for inspection in a stroll down its long HIGH STREET. As with everywhere else around here, it rose to prosperity on the back of the wool trade but it seems, even at first glance, to have done rather better for itself than the average. Perhaps the finest group of buildings - a clear statement of its position as one of the wealthiest towns in the country in the 14th and 15th centuries - consists of the CHURCH, the GUILDHALL and the DEANERY TOWER. On the other hand OVERALL HOUSE, named after Bishop John Overall, one of the men responsible for the translation of the bible, as the Authorised Version for James I, can't be called second rate. The Guildhall, a fine timber framed building, is open to the public for guided tours; the Deanery Tower is actually a gateway and is all that remains of the original deanery. The St Edmund legend has another commemoration in Hadleigh Church. A 14th century bench end depicts the wolf that is said to have guarded the head after the saint's martyrdom and decapitation, holding the gory object in its jaws by the hair! Another story had it that Guthrum the Dane was buried below the south aisle - but closer inspection of the canopy of the tomb dates it much later.

If the smell of death is getting to be a bit of a problem, don't panic - the great outdoors around the outskirts of the town is reasonably great, very outdoors and good for a break, at this stage. In the circumstances, we may wish to pass on ALDHAM

COMMON (where the Protestant Vicar of Hadleigh, Dr Rowland Taylor, was burnt at the stake in 1555, having fallen foul of one of 'Bloody' Mary Tudor's purges) and trot off to FRIARS HALL FARM instead, to wander round the hay meadows and soak up a view or two across the countryside and towards the town. As an alternative, WOLVES WOOD (Information - 01255 886043) might sound more intriguing. This is an area of mixed woodland with waymarked paths, a hide and an information hut amongst the normal range of RSPB facilities.

Having made the break with the urban whirl somewhat casually (no tears, no last glances, no fanfares etc.) we could well make the most of it and head for the horizon, or more accurately for Kersey and Lindsey, which are hidden away down a side road, to the left of the B1070 that's about to take us to our next major call, Lavenham. **KERSEY** is another one of Suffolk's prettiest villages. Whichever way one comes upon its main street, one cannot avoid crossing a watersplash to reach the houses, with their dark timbers and pastel hued infilling. As there is all this water around, the village goes down well amongst the ducks, who behave as though they know that cars come a very poor second when it comes to who goes first. Like **LINDSAY**, not so far away, the village's name was given to a type of woollen cloth that was produced here, as a cottage craft, for centuries.

KERSEY

Nowadays, the main products, as far as we're concerned, are found at KERSEY POTTERY (Enquiries - 01473 822092) in THE STREET. Handmade stoneware pottery by Fred Bramham and Dorothy Gorst is on display and for sale as are etchings by Glynn Thomas. The pottery is open between Easter and Christmas from Tuesday to Saturday between 9.30am and 5.30pm and on Sunday from 11.00am to 5.00pm. Between Christmas and Easter it is open only at weekends. All of which brings us, as night follows day, to **LAVENHAM**, (Information - 01787 248207), known far and wide as the most complete of the medieval wool towns in the area. True, it's *so* perfect one keeps on pinching oneself whilst wondering if it's really a film set - but no, it's genuine, all of it. It's the Aldeburgh 'moot hall for mooting' syndrome multiplied by a hundred.

LAVENHAM

The town is, as more than one authority has remarked, 'resplendent' with possibly more medieval timber houses per square foot than anywhere else in England. Nonetheless, remembering Aldeburgh again, we shouldn't be surprised to find that it is actually a vigorous community in its own right in the late 20th century. "Spoilt for choice, spoilt for choice", one keeps on muttering as one stumbles from the car to the MARKET PLACE. Where, amidst all this clamour for attention, does anyone actually start? At times like these, we adopt the un-emotional, ruthlessly analytical scientific approach - and toss a coin! It comes down heads (again) which directs us to THE GUILDHALL OF CORPUS CHRISTIE (Enquiries - 01787 247646) while we mull over what we've just done, and its implications for the future. We are told that actual money - especially coins - will soon be a thing of the past, as we all go plastic and telephone banking. Fine. Only how will anyone make a really difficult decision - or start a Cup Final, or even a Test Match? Toss a credit card? Have you ever tried? In the middle of January, in a howling gale? Isn't it amazing how the decision makers who plague our every waking moment usually manage to forget the really important issues? Back to Lavenham.

The Guildhall is a late 15th century timber framed building, now owned by the National Trust, that overlooks and dominates the town's market place. Inside this major local landmark are exhibitions on local history, farming and industry, along with a display focused on the medieval wool trade. Outside, an attractively walled garden has a dye plant area adjoining the 19th century lock up and mortuary. Open from 28th March to 1st November, daily from 11.00am to 5.00pm (except Good Friday), the building is also used occasionally for community purposes, when parts ,or all of it, may be closed. Clearly this is another occasion for a preliminary phone call. Admission, for us, is £2.80 a head and gives us access to the displays and exhibitions as well as to the usual National Trust facilities. Incidentally, as one wanders from place to place within the ancient structure, it's also worth remembering that it's been a prison, a workhouse and an almshouse in its day, not just a dignified expression of the civic pride of the middle ages!

In the Market Place itself we'll find the LITTLE HALL, a private house for nearly six hundred years. The 14th century section had a hall and other additions in the 15th century, was 'modernised' in the 16th century and extended in the 17th century before being converted into tenements which occupied it for the next two hundred years. The Little Hall was restored in the 1920s and 30s by the Gayer-Anderson brothers, whose furniture, with its Egyptian connections, is on show from Easter to 25th October. Hours of opening on Wednesdays, Thursdays, Saturdays, Sundays and Bank Holidays are from 2.00pm to 5.30pm and entry will set us back £1.50.

Even the CHURCH at Lavenham is a treasure. With its noble tower and splendid, 15th century perpendicular design it is a fitting tribute to the generosity of two major benefactors, whatever the sub text. John de Vere, 13th Earl of Oxford, seems to have been reasonably straightforward in bestowing his largesse; Thomas Spring, a rich clothier, might have had other, more subtle motives: it is recorded that he actually asked Henry VII for forgiveness for having made *"usurious covenants, illicit sales and deceptions in measuring cloth."* In other words, our Thomas was a born loser, Kingdom of Heavenwise! Elsewhere in the church there are many more wonders. The richly carved screens are, almost literally (and appropriately) out of this world, as are the misericords, while the glass is also quite breathtaking. The building is open to visitors between 8.30am and 5.30pm in summer and is closed at 3.30pm in winter. Shopping is also high on the agenda in Lavenham (don't all rush at once). There is a wide variety of possibilities to cater for most tastes and needs around the area of the Market but the town specialities should generate particular interest. Here you'll find imaginative jewellery and craft outlets and several shops selling toys, doll's house furniture and miniatures. Best of all, perhaps, would be a visit just before Christmas when Lavenham holds its street fair.

With that festive, convivial image in mind, we'd best gird ourselves up more than somewhat as our trip through the lanes to our next destination is about to introduce a major scene shift, the nearer we get to the A45. We have a couple of pleasing calls to make first - but be warned: Suffolk is not all Stour Valley, cosy cottages and gentle, wooded hills. While it still *is*, just about, let's pop into **MONKS ELEIGH** and possibly **CHELSWORTH**, if the time allows.

CORN CRAFT (Enquiries - 01449 740456) at Monks Eleigh is a fascinating shop, whose specialities are not the sort of things we've come across all that often - which is surprising in what have been mainly rural tours. Amongst the traditional craft items on display, the corn dollies are particularly eye-catching, as are the dried flower arrangements. The emphasis seems to be on traditional skills on every hand and there are many other gifts and toys to underline the point. For anyone who missed their mid-day meal in Lavenham in their excitement, Corn Craft's also offer light lunches or cream teas (if it's that late) in their tearoom. The whole delightful experience is open daily throughout the year except on winter Bank Holidays.

On balance, I think I'd recommend some more fresh air and leg stretching at this stage, so a pause at Chelsworth would be good. We'll need clear heads and some superior map reading if we're to reach the elusive A14 in reasonable time, without too many tense silences floating around between the front and back seats.

Chelsworth it is then, for a brief stroll beside the River Brett (did you know there was one?), remembering that these are wet grasslands - which sound like another job for the wellies. If, on the other hand, you don't mind going a bit further for the sake of some drier, more conventional meadows, there's another walk along the banks of the Brett, not too far away at **BILDESTON** In a way, the need for a breather has done us a favour, as these little places can all lay claim to be minor gems.

Now for the change. We're moving towards Suffolk's central plateau, towards a terrain quite different from the land of painters and shepherds. We shan't be seeing many picturesque villages or resplendent market towns whose prosperous past has bequeathed a present of architectural perfection. In short, we're approaching an area where necessity has overridden art in the evolution of the environment, both built and otherwise.

On leaving the Valley of the Stour - and its lookalikes - we find a plateau that was once adorned with wide tracts of forests. This was never sheep country and its towns were never wool towns; this agriculture is heavily arable: its produce is cereal crops, sugar beet - and peas! Hundreds - I dare say thousands - of tons of peas. The farms are vast - we've seen their counterparts in Cambridgeshire and parts of Norfolk - but here I mean seriously vast! It is not uncommon in this area to find single operations that run to more than 3,000 acres of open fields, none of which have any real shelter from trees or hedges - the forests are long gone, I'm afraid. In fact, for those of us who think the notion of an 'agriculture industry' is a contradiction in terms, a trip to the Suffolk plateau is a real eye-opener. There it sits - with the emphasis on 'industry', it seems to me. Of course, life being what it is - and East Anglia being what *it* is - we shouldn't be surprised to find that the Soil Association, leading advocates of organic farming along traditional lines, have their major research operation here too, carrying out a programme of experiments at Haughley that have begun to turn the minds of consumers away from the produce of intensive monoculture to the tastier, more nutritious products of traditional techniques. They still grow fields of peas up the road, though, and the tonnage doesn't seem to have gone down that much.

In this productive yet somehow barren landscape, where villages huddle around greens that were created in medieval times as forest clearings, one is reminded again and again of thoughts from elsewhere, chiefly from the Fen country. This is not, in any sense, a tripper's paradise. It's an area that most of the brochures ignore as they guide their readers to the comforts of Constable Country, or to the quaint coastal communities. I'd like to think we're different, we're more discerning - we are nearly as happy being educated by a holiday as we are being cosseted in fantasy land. Not all the time - and nothing too gruelling, as we're nothing if not self-indulgent at such times - but we do like to meet reality once in a while, to discover what's actually going on.

Well, here it is - reality! There are rather a lot of us living on this small island off the coast of continental Europe - and we have to be fed. Regardless of the on-going argument between the Soil Association and ??? about how that should be done, no-one can dispute the fact that it has to be done. So, if fifty million people 'need' frozen peas or 'sugar with everything' it all has to come from somewhere. Somewhere like right here. In short, this is what our insatiable lust for frozen peas - or sugar - looks like, on the ground. Hideous it may well be, but until we change our eating habits it's a fact of life - and I make no apology for claiming that it does none of us any harm to leave our suburban, and urban, homes and gardens occasionally to wander down a country road and check it out. While we're at it we might also praise the Lord for the people who are prepared to live amongst it, to work amongst it, from one year's end to the next, to keep our stomachs full (of frozen peas)!

A word or two more on the landscape's features. Familiar church steeples - and farmhouses - are not the dominant features that they are in, say, North Norfolk. On the plateau they're overshadowed by silos and water towers - which are essential as the average annual rainfall is low, at twenty to thirty inches a year, for the demand put upon it. The farms are also moated in many cases, originally for defence or as a result of clay being taken out for building, but now to maintain the supply of stored water.

During the winter, this is not a place to be for 'softies' like us. The land is dark and bare, the huge skies are all but overbearing and there's very little comfort to be had. In summer, the endless acres of barley, wheat and oats ripple in the breeze - but even then it's not the best setting for a country walk. Finally, as all this produce has to be taken somewhere - to Ipswich, Lowestoft or Great Yarmouth, for example - the roads are something else at harvest times, with lorry loads of peas vying with trailers of sugar beet or cereals, as season succeeds season, for their slot in the road space. Not a pretty sight - a necessity it would seem, and that's all.

So, what are we doing here? Going round the edge of it, actually, while we take the point and move on to somewhere more appealing, as is our way at such times.

'Somewhere else' is Mid Suffolk, in general, and at this moment, **STOWMARKET** (Enquiries - 01449 676800) in particular. Local people speak of this town as being the focus for a 'working rural community' - and we know what that means. We've enthused more than once about the way Suffolk, as a whole, is peppered with communities and individual buildings that come close to visual perfection - because that's the icing on the cake of an approach that is, essentially, very practical. They look like this - because 'this' is what works best.

Stowmarket is a pretty little market town whose prosperity was based on its maltings that were set up there to take advantage of its position at the head of the navigable section of the River Gipping. Grain from the surrounding farms would have been brought in by wagon and than shipped down river to Ipswich and the sea. Along with this business, the town's other source of importance was its ease of access. Roads radiate from its hub to all parts of Mid Suffolk, via Ipswich and Colchester to London and northwards and eastwards into all the main areas of Norfolk and Cambridgeshire. On market days this focal function is very obvious.

Given this function, where better than Stowmarket to set up a MUSEUM OF EAST ANGLIAN LIFE (Information - 01449 612229)? We have seen plenty of museums over the days (weeks, even) but few would be able to equal, never mind surpass the presentation on this delightful, seventy acre riverside site. Many fine collections of evocative elements from the region's past are on display ranging from gypsy caravans to domestic and farming memorabilia. There's a working watermill and wind pump, craft workshops, a smithy and a tithe barn. With all the carts, wagons, steam engines and farm implements on every hand, a visit to the Museum is another one of those time warp experiences that are a speciality of many of the places we've visited.

MUSEUM OF EAST ANGLIAN LIFE

There are regular craft demonstrations at the Museum and displays of working practises, which often include the sight of Suffolk Punch horses harnessed up to drays, rollers, harrows and the like. In fact, as I see it, almost everything on show at this site is to do with work in one form or another - but what else should we expect? As the good people in the town themselves told me: "This is a 'working rural community'. To complete the picture - and to encourage recovery after the exhaustion of watching other people work - there's an opportunity for refreshments, followed by a leisurely dawdle round the gift shop. The whole package will cost us £3.85 a head and we will be welcome between April and October, from Monday to Saturday, after 10.00am and before 5.00pm. Sundays start a little later at 11.00am.

There are outdoor opportunities a'plenty around the edge of the town, but before we take a stroll, or even settle down to a relaxing picnic, it could be time to work up an appetite and take off a few millimetres around the waistline. If that's the case we need look no further than the MID SUFFOLK LEISURE CENTRE (Enquiries - 01449 674980). The Centre has just about everything for the masochist from fitness studios to indoor climbing and from squash courts to swimming pools. An hour or so of that and you're either much better - or in hospital, I suppose. Let's assume you're better, eager for the 'off', or whatever you do at such a time, and ready to picnic your way back to where you were before: it's time for COMBS FORD. Once we've fed ourselves in this sylvan setting, we can have a stroll through nearby COOMBS WOOD, an ancient woodland, all hornbeam and damp flowery woodland rides, before bounding back on the A14 to continue our journey southwards, to **NEEDHAM MARKET.**

This little town marks the most easterly extremity of our present tour. Soon we'll be turning due north along the edge of East Suffolk - our next focus for exploration - until we curve away west to absorb another bevy of small treasures on our way back to BURY. Again, we're in the midst of a pleasant market centre for the surrounding farmland, with the full range of facilities for the needs of each of its satellite communities. It's a little further down the Gipping from Stowmarket - and a little nearer the point where the river isn't called the Gipping any more but becomes the more famous Orwell instead, as it enters the eastern outskirts of Ipswich. I think all of East Anglia is odd, if you dig deep enough!

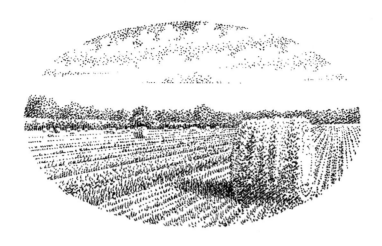

FIELDS NEAR NEEDHAM MARKET

In national terms, Needham Market is on the humble side, for no good reason that I can see, beyond the existence of its lofty neighbours with their prosperous, well endowed historics. Its own history stretches back as far as any of them and it has put its location on the, by now, well and truly navigable Gipping (what's left of it) to serious purpose as another outlet for local produce. To prove the point, it's worth taking a brief stroll along the NEEDHAM MARKET TOWN AND COUNTRYSIDE TRAIL, which takes in the best features of the town's architecture, and the points of local interest, before moving out along the river. If time and energy permitted, this stroll could turn into a full blown hike as it merges, in a sense, with the GIPPING VALLEY PATH that leads back to Stowmarket - or down to Ipswich, if we were going in that direction. In addition, if we hadn't had one picnic already today, we might have chosen to stop off at the pleasant NEEDHAM LAKE PICNIC, but we have, so we won't. We'll just have to put it on that ever growing list of 'things to do' on a later visit. Along with the farm walk at RAVENS FARM MEADOW, I suspect.

As we've plotted our general direction we might as well bring it down to daffodils. If we cross the Gipping there's a minor road to the left, before the A14, that looks interesting as it leads us via **CREETING ST MARY** to the A1120. I've noticed, by the way, that you've stopped grunting "so what?" on these occasions. All this exploration must be growing on you - and not before time! The A1120 would take us back to Stowmarket, if we let it - but we have other plans, as usual. Having turned left onto it, in next to no time we turn right off it again, and follow the lanes to MIDDLEWOOD GREEN, MENDLESHAM GREEN and COTTON where we have a date with another museum that revives memories of one of our early tours in Norfolk.

Comparisons are nearly always odious - and usually futile - so we won't get into that. Let's just say that finding the MECHANICAL MUSIC MUSEUM (Enquiries -

01449 613867) at Cotton is as much of a culture shock (no comparisons) as it was when something similar happened to the north of the county line a while ago. Here the extensive collection extends from a mighty Wurlitzer theatre pipe organ in a specially re-constructed cinema (!) to fairground organs, street pianos and polyphons. On a smaller scale there are also displays of gramophones and music boxes. All the exhibits are playable - and played - as are the many other even more unusual pieces of equipment housed in the Museum. After nature walks, Constable and medieval guildhalls this typically East Anglian contrast sparks up the sensibilities and is well worth the £3.00 admission fee. The Museum is only open on Sunday though, between June and September, from 2.30pm to 5.30pm - although groups may visit on weekdays by arrangement.

With our ears ringing - much as they were on the other occasion - and with our eyes dewy with nostalgia we must pull ourselves together for the next - rather more conventional - leg of the homeward run. We use a trace of the B1113 out of Cotton, through FINNINGHAM, before taking a left turn away from it that leads us to **WALSHAM LE WILLOWS**.

From the first glance one sees that the name is well chosen, but there are magnificent limes and beeches, as well. The village lies in the midst of parkland and is a meeting point for roads and lanes leading to other smaller villages and hamlets in the surrounding countryside. The buildings, which are weather boarded and timber framed, are arranged in a deliciously romantic, ad hoc fashion with eaves and roof levels taking every imaginable line and angle. I'll skip the church itself this time, because one of the local traditions carried on there borders on the maudlin, to my mind, and pop across to the VILLAGE MUSEUM, housed on the same site.

Here, between the end of May and August, it's possible to catch up with all the local variations on the theme of village life and to ponder on the fact that villages do vary enormously from area to area in terms of local occupations, trades, climate, geography and so on. There may be many hopeful candidates for the label 'perfect English village' but the idea of a typical village seems to be pretty meaningless. In any case, the exhibition here changes regularly so the picture is probably even more complex - and way beyond the understanding of we townees.

On from Walsham our road lies north, to WATTISFIELD, which is barely a step away. Here, it's HENRY WATSON'S POTTERIES (Enquiries - 01359 251239) that we're seeking. More than 180 years ago the pottery was established to specialise in terracotta domestic kitchen ware. Clearly the idea was a good one - and caught on - so that today we are still able to appreciate the range of products. The Factory Shop is open all year from Monday to Saturday between 9.30am and 4.30pm and on Easter Sunday. It is closed on Good Friday, from the 25th to the 27th December and on New Year's Day.

Once we've loaded our few more purchases into the groaning boot, it's time to be off again, down the A143 for another change of context, with another touch of the familiar thrown in for reassurance - in fact, it's actually two examples of a similar change, but don't worry, they're both familiar, as it happens. In between there's a 'special', to 'prime' us for our evening meal - yes, it is about time, too.

First familiar - STANTON WINDMILL (Enquiries - 01359 250622) which is actually only familiar up to a point. Most of the dozens of mills we've seen up north in Fenland, for example, were built to pump water. The post mill at Stanton fits our mental image more closely, however, as it was built in 1751 to produce stoneground flour. It can still do it, nearly 250 years later, which is a testimony to something or other quite remarkable. It is remarkably complete and, as well as being in working order, is home to a series of post mill and local interest displays. For £1.50 you can tour the building, maybe buy some flour and pick up some more tit bits of local culture. Sounds like a bargain! The mill is open at the Easter and May Bank Holidays and between July and September on Sundays and Bank Holidays from 10.00am to 7.00pm.

Now for the special: not far from the mill we'll find WYKEN HALL GARDENS AND VINEYARD (Enquiries - 01359 250240). The four acre gardens are a composite of herb, knot, rose, kitchen and woodland areas with other features, including a woodland walk to add to the attraction - not to mention the rare breed sheep! What we're after, though, is what comes out of the seven acre vineyard, as much as the produce that can be bought in the Country Store and Cafe, which are housed in a splendid 16th century barn. Dinner could be on offer, were we in that frame of mind, although it's strongly recommended that bookings be made in advance. Times of opening are 10.00am to 6.00pm on Thursdays, Fridays, Sundays and Bank Holidays between 1st February and 24th December. Dinners are served from 7.00pm on Thursdays, Fridays and Saturdays. Admission to the gardens is £2.00 a head while entry to the vineyard, store and cafe is free.

Which brings us to the last call before Bury, it's another one of Suffolk's landmarks by a fluke of fate, and a very pleasant epilogue to a colourful day's touring, I trust. PAKENHAM WATER MILL (Enquiries - 01359 270570 or 01787 247179) is situated near **IXWORTH** on the A143, which is about to lead us home. **PAKENHAM** itself is a British village with a working watermill and windmill, and has retained much of the charm of its heritage. For £1.35 one has access to a host of attractive features and points of interest arising from the milling practises - and as all proceeds are in aid of the Suffolk Building Preservation Trust, there's a double reason for pausing in our headlong flight back to the hotel.

We can expect to find the Mill's own flour in the souvenir shop, along with the inevitable ice creams and drinks, while only a step away is a picnic area (for a later visit) and the opportunity for pleasant walks out along the river bank. By the way, have you noticed that the three 'neighbourhood' rivers around lovely Bury St Edmunds are named Dove, Lark and Linnet? I love that, don't you? Meanwhile, back at Pakenham, there are excellent views for sketching and painting or - more realistically, in our case - a quick last-minute photograph. Don't worry, John Constable, you're not under threat!

And that's it! A swift dash south west down the A143 completes our circle, mentally I am still on the banks of the Stour, how I wish I could have been part of that era, had even a grain of Constables talent, perhaps God will be kind and arrange for me to meet this great artist.

THE CEDARS HOTEL
Needham Road,
Stowmarket,
Suffolk IP14 2AJ

AA ** Tourist Board 3 Crowns

Tel: 01449 612668
Fax: 01449 674704

Well served by major roads, this is an ideal hotel in which to stay for a touring holiday of Suffolk and beyond. Originally it was a 16th century farmhouse and in recent years it has been extensively and thoughtfully modernised, to offer a high standard of accommodation, dining and conference facilities, whilst retaining many original features. It stands in its own grounds on the main A1308 just one mile outside Stowmarket.

Regular visitors to The Cedars will tell you about the pleasant atmosphere that prevails throughout the hotel and the cheerful, friendly manner in which Clive Barley, Tony and Jill Carter and their well trained staff look after guests. It is interesting to see the contrasting styles of the old and modern parts of the hotel. Rooms in the old part feature genuine beams and low ceilings whilst the more recent additions reflect the more practical 'Motel' style. Every room is beautifully furnished and all the bedrooms are en-suite with direct dial telephones, television and a generously supplied hostess tray.

The hotel serves a delicious selection of English and Continental dishes (many of which are home-made) which can be enjoyed in the attractive, more formal surroundings of the restaurant or in the relaxed comfort of the bar, perhaps in front of the open fire. The Cedars is a popular meeting place for locals enjoying a meal or a drink as well as the businessmen who come to make use of the excellent conference facilities. There is a large Banqueting Suite which is suitable for every occasion and you can be sure the Proprietors will be pleased to assist with every aspect of your booking.

USEFUL INFORMATION

OPEN: All year except Dec25-31
CHILDREN: Welcome
CREDIT CARDS: Master/Visa
LICENSED: Yes
ACCOMMODATION: en-suite rooms
RATES: Sgl £42 Dbl. £47

RESTAURANT: Good choice
Range of steaks and grills
BAR FOOD: Traditional fare
VEGETARIAN: Yes
WHEELCHAIR ACCESS: Yes
GARDEN: Yes

COLLEGE FARM
Hintlesham,
Ipswich,
Suffolk
IP8 3NT

ETB 2 Crown Highly Commended.
Farm Holiday Bureau Member

Tel/Fax: 01473 652253

College Farm is a 15th century, Grade II Listed building with Tudor Chimney Stack. It oozes history and is full of character and atmosphere. Exploring its history which has connections with Cardinal Wolsey, Eton College and much more, will give you a fascinating pastime aided and abetted by your hosts Ian and Rosemary Bryce. It is to be found six miles west of Ipswich amidst arable fields in a peaceful setting conducive to relaxing and throwing off the cares of the modern day world. It has a delightful, well kept garden where one may play at Croquet or simply sit doing nothing in the Summer House. There are way-marked walks around the six hundred acre family run farm, which is mainly arable with some beef cattle.

Within this fascinating house where a warm atmosphere prevails at any time of the year, there are three guest bedrooms, a double which is en-suite, a family room and a single room with a shared private bathroom. The three rooms are charmingly equipped with antiques, pretty drapes and bed covers. Each room has a clock radio, electric blanket and a hostess tray. Downstairs the Guest sitting room with antique furniture and an inglenook fireplace, has television, books, board games and log fires in winter. There is a separate Dining Room where breakfast is served. Breakfast is a delicious meal of generous proportions, freshly cooked on the Aga and more than enough to set one up for a day's exploration or business.

From College Farm one can set out to see Lavenham and other medieval 'Wool Towns' as well as Constable Country. The Heritage coastline is nearby. For the energetic, apart from the farm walks, there is golf within half a mile, riding, swimming and fishing in three miles. It is a good area for bird-watching and sightseeing. Rosemary loves meeting people and is very happy to pass on her personal knowledge of the area helped by an abundance of local literature and maps. Both she and Ian have many interests and are very active in village life.

USEFUL INFORMATION

OPEN: Mid-Jan to Mid Dec.
CHILDREN: Over 10 years
CREDIT CARDS: None taken
LICENSED: No
ACCOMMODATION: 1dl en-suite
1fa 1sgl sharing bathroom
RATES: From £18pp pn (£2 extra for 1 night stay)
Children sharing with adults £11

DINING ROOM: Excellent breakfast
VEGETARIAN: Catered for
WHEELCHAIR ACCESS: No
GARDEN: Yes + Farm walks
PETS: No
NON-SMOKING HOUSE

GARDENERS ARMS
Moats Tee,
Combs,
Stowmarket.
Suffolk
IP13 2EY

Tel:01449 673963

In the heart of the Suffolk countryside overlooking acres of farmland and just two miles from Stowmarket at Combs, is the Gardeners Arms, a two hundred year old pub which has been tastefully and attractively modernised. It has become a very popular hostelry for those who like to escape from Stowmarket at lunch-time or in the evenings. Regulars have discovered that the Gardeners Arms is a cheerful, welcoming pub where they can be assured of a warm welcome from the landlords Julia and David Stephens-Row.

They know the Greene King quality beers are well kept and the standard of food served at very sensible prices makes eating a pleasure. You can eat either in the bar or the lounge. There is an a la carte menu which is backed by traditional and sometimes exotic Daily Specials. Home-made Lasagne is one of the most popular of dishes. Vegetarians are also catered for. A whole range of Bar snacks are also available with everything from freshly cut, well-filled sandwiches to Ploughman's and salads. The comprehensive wine list adds to the enjoyment and many wines are available by the glass. People over fifty five are offered a reduced price menu from Monday-Friday at lunch-time.

For those who enjoy a game of darts or the chance to play pool, there is a board and a table. Smoking is permitted in the bar only. In the warmer weather the enclosed Garden Patio is just the place to enjoy a drink with a meal. The newly built Children's Play Area backs on to the local cricket ground. This is a thoroughly nice pub and well worth taking time to drive out to it from Stowmarket.

USEFUL INFORMATION

OPEN: 11.30-3.30pm & 6.30-11.30pm
CHILDREN: Welcome
CREDIT CARDS: None taken
LICENSED: Full On
GARDEN: Patio & Children's Play area

RESTAURANT: Not applicable
BAR FOOD: Wide choice in Lounge & Bar
VEGETARIAN: Always a choice
WHEELCHAIR ACCESS: Yes
PETS: Bar only

THE GRANGE HOTEL
Barton Road,
Thurston,
Bury St Edmunds,
Suffolk
IP31 3PQ

3 Crown Commended

Tel/Fax: 01359 231260

The Grange Hotel has one of the most idyllic countryside settings in Suffolk, in the village of Thurston just four miles from historic Bury St Edmunds. It is a Tudor style country house hotel with a terrace overlooking the lawn gardens. The Hotel has been family run by the Wagstaff family for three generations. The proprietor today is also the inspired chef who was trained at Westminster College and some of London's finest hotels including The Connaught and Claridges. With such a pedigree, it is not surprising that its reputation reaches out far and wide.

It achieved Royal approval when Prince Edward stayed here whilst he was making his 'Crown and Country' series. What appeals to guests most is the relaxed, almost informal, atmosphere together with a friendly well-trained staff who enjoy ensuring that one has a memorable stay. There is so much to do and see in this area of Suffolk. One can play golf, shoot, ride or perhaps go further afield to take a look at Cambridge, Norwich or Ipswich, all within one hour's drive and the port of Felixstowe is just thirty minutes. For race-goers, Newmarket with its two courses and Museum is within easy reach but closer at home Bury St Edmunds is superb with its Abbey Gardens and Ruins.

Within the Hotel you will find restrained comfort, beautiful furniture and gracious rooms. The two lounge bars open onto the terrace and garden and offer a diverse menu of excellent food. They also serve a range of fine local and guest beers. The Adam room offers a more formal restaurant atmosphere where superb A la Carte lunches and dinners are served, as well as a traditional roast lunch on Sundays. The Banquet Room which seats one hundred is a popular venue for wedding receptions, dinner dances and Christmas parties. It is also used as a conference room seating up to eighty people theatre style or thirty boardroom style. The attractive Coffee Room overlooks the garden and is ideal for private dinner parties or small conferences up to twenty people.

USEFUL INFORMATION

OPEN: All year 11am-11pm
CHILDREN: Welcome
CREDIT CARDS: Visa/Master/Switch/Delta
LICENSED: Full On
ACCOMMODATION: 13 en-suite
RATES: Bargain Breaks 2 nights DB&B £80pp
Low season £34 pp.pn High Season £35pp.pn

RESTAURANT: Home-cooked fare
with Continental influence
BAR FOOD: Yes
VEGETARIAN: Catered for
WHEELCHAIR ACCESS: Yes
PETS: By arrangement

GARDEN: Terrace and lawn

RED HOUSE FARM,
Station Road,
Haughley,
Stowmarket,
Suffolk
IP14 3QP

2 Crowns Commended

Tel/Fax: 01449 673323

Beautiful Mid-Suffolk is always a good base for a holiday or a break and in the village of Haughley is Red House Farm owned by Mary and Eric Noy whose family have been Suffolk farmers and wind millers in East Suffolk for generations. The house is fascinating. It is a typical timber framed Suffolk farmhouse in which the oldest part with a low roof was built centuries ago as a barn type structure with a fire in the middle of the floor and a hole in the roof to let the smoke out. The first chimney stack with a bread oven was built on the side of the house at a later date and in due course the house was enlarged by adding the front wing of larger and higher rooms and two attic rooms. It all makes for a splendid interior full of nooks and crannies and unexpected corners. Everywhere there is evidence of the family life of the Noys with photographs and a collection of horse brasses they have acquired over the years. Some of the furniture has been in the family for generations and it all provides a wonderful, homely atmosphere in which it is a pleasure to stay.

There are four en-suite rooms, comfortably furnished and complete with a hospitality tray. Both the Lounge with television and the Dining Room have some nice antique furniture and both rooms invite one to relax. Breakfast is a typical farmhouse meal which makes a great start to a day's exploring. In addition Red House Farm has a well equipped self-catering cottage attached to the house and an established Caravan Site with Electric Hook-ups.

There are many activities within easy reach including some great walks, horse riding, bird watching, cycling and golf. It is within easy reach of the Coast and the County Town of Ipswich. Norwich and Cambridge are forty minutes away and historic Bury St Edmunds just thirteen miles.

USEFUL INFORMATION

OPEN: January-November
CHILDREN: Welcome over 8 years
CREDIT CARDS: None taken
LICENSED: No
ACCOMMODATION: 4 en-suite rooms
RATES: From £20 pp B&B
CARAVAN SITE -Electric Hook-up

DINING ROOM: Great farmhouse breakfast
VEGETARIAN: Upon request
WHEELCHAIR ACCESS: No
GARDEN: Yes + Garden games
PETS: No
SELF-CATERING COTTAGE
STRICTLY NON-SMOKING

THE RED LION
The Street,
East Bergholt,
NR Colchester,
Essex

Tel: 01206 298332

East Bergholt is a particularly interesting village set just off the A12 between Colchester and Ipswich. Not only is it attractive, it also contains a historic church unique for its bell tower which is sited at ground level. Right next to the Post Office Stores is the 15th century Red Lion Inn, steeped in history, full of character and so welcoming. The proprietor, a delightful lady, Susan Lewsey, has the ability to make everyone feel at home as soon as they walk through the bar door and that is the key to the success of the inn.

Many people like to come to the Red Lion to stay for a night or two as well as to enjoy the superb and inspired traditional pub food. There are four pretty guest rooms, comfortably furnished and each with television and a well supplied hostess tray. The Red Lion is well known for the quality and variations of its food. In the pleasant dining room one can choose from Chicken, Cheese and Mustard Pie, Pigeon in Elderberry Wine Pie, Exotic Fruit and Vegetable Curry or Leek, Mushroom and Sesame Bake. Fresh Fish is a regular feature and there are many other tasty dishes from which to choose. The lounge and public bar are comfortable welcoming places in which to enjoy a drink and perhaps join in with the cheerful local conversation.

From East Bergholt one can so easily explore John Constable country and discover why he loved it so much. Flatford Mill one of his favourite subjects is just a short walk away. There are many picturesque walks alongside the River Stour, with boating facilities, good fishing and many historic buildings. It is a paradise for camera enthusiasts and artists.

USEFUL INFORMATION

OPEN: 11-3pm & 7-11pm
CHILDREN: In dining room & garden
CREDIT CARDS: None taken
LICENSED: Full Licence
GARDEN: Yes, picnic benches
RATES: £18.50 pppn B&B

RESTAURANT: Traditional Pub Fare
BAR FOODL Wide range
VEGETARIAN: 3-4 dishes
WHEELCHAIR ACCESS: Yes
PETS: By arrangement

RYEGATE HOUSE
Stoke-by-Nayland
Suffolk
CO6 4RA

ETB 2 Crown Highly Commended

Tel: 01206 263679

Margaret and Albert Geater have created a superb atmosphere in their attractive modern house built in the style of a Suffolk farmhouse. It is situated in the pretty village of Stoke-by-Nayland within the Dedham Vale and only a short walk from the local shops, the post office, and a number of excellent pubs and restaurants. The magnificent Wool Church with a 120ft tower, dominates the landscape from the highest point in the area. The village has a long history, documented back to the mid 9th century. There are many old timber-framed houses some dating from the 13th century. From Ryegate House you can set out to explore Constable Country; the local countryside with fishing, golf courses, the historic town of Colchester, the attractive wool town of Lavenham and many other picturesque Suffolk villages, towns and coastal resorts. The ports of Felixstowe and Harwich are both within easy reach.

Ryegate House is a comfortable, well furnished home, into which you are welcomed. It has its own slogan - 'Warm Welcome - Fine Food - Restful Rooms' and that describes it perfectly. It is a totally non-smoking establishment with two double and one twin-bedded room, all have en-suite bathrooms. Each room is delightful, with colour co-ordinated soft furnishings, and they all have colour television, radio alarms, shaver points and that boon to travellers - a well supplied hostess tray. After a quiet, restful night you come down to the bright dining room, ready to enjoy an excellent breakfast, designed to suit everyone. It can be full English, continental or vegetarian - the choice is yours. There are no evening meals but with the number of excellent local eateries this presents no problem and Margaret and Albert will be happy to point you in the right direction.

The house is centrally heated throughout and is open all the year with the exception of Christmas. Children over twelve years are very welcome, there is ample off street parking and you may bring your pet providing you have made arrangement in advance. No one could fail to enjoy the genuine hospitality offered by Ryegate House.

USEFUL INFORMATION

OPEN: All year except Christmas
CHILDREN: Over 12 years
CREDIT CARDS: None taken
LICENSED: No
ACCOMMODATION: 2dbl 1 tw all en-suite B&B
NON SMOKING HOUSE

DINING ROOM: Excellent breakfast. No evening meals
VEGETARIAN: Yes
WHEELCHAIR ACCESS: No
RATES: Dbl £22 pp.pn B&B Sgl £30 pp.pn
GARDEN: Yes
PETS: By prior arrangement

THE SWAN INN
Woolpit,
Bury St Edmunds,
Suffolk
IP30 9QN

Tel:01359 240482

Woolpit is a village with over one thousand years of history. You will find it equidistant between the market towns of Bury St Edmunds and Stowmarket. Visitors are always enchanted by all Woolpit has to offer from the steeple of St Mary Church seen from the A14 and resplendent at night when it is illuminated to the magnificent double hammer beam roof of the church, thought to be one of the finest in East Anglia. It has a noble medieval porch and the brass eagle lectern is said to have been donated by Elizabeth I. The Museum, said to be the smallest in Suffolk, was started in 1985 and is run by volunteers and here you will find much of the history of the village.

In the heart of the village is the Swan Inn, a focal point of village life, serving an excellent pint of ale in pleasant and comfortable surroundings. A good selection of Scottish Malt Whiskys and Irish Whiskeys is always available from the well-stocked bar. It is an imposing red brick building believed to date back to the 14th century with extensive alterations and additions in 1759 and again in 1820-1830. All of this has merely served to make it even more attractive today. Modern times have brought modern requirements but the old log fire burns throughout the winter throwing out a delicious heat but judiciously backed up by central heating! One would not call The Swan a catering house because of the limited kitchen space, but what it does provide is some superb home-made soup with crusty bread - just the thing to warm the cockles of the heart on a winter's day. Occasionally there are very good curries. However, people mainly come to the Swan to enjoy the camaraderie and a village pub in the traditional sense.

Accommodation is available here. Four ground floor rooms are situated in the annexe, the family room having en-suite facilities. All rooms overlook the large walled garden. The four-poster room is situated in the oldest part of the pub with modern, newly decorated bathroom, and overlooks the village centre with splendid view of the church steeple. All the rooms are comfortable, centrally heated and attractively decorated. All have colour telvisions, hostess trays and alarm clock radios. For television addicts there is Sky available in the Bar.

USEFUL INFORMATION

OPEN: Noon-2pm 5-11pm Mon-Fri	RESTAURANT: Not applicable
Sat & Sun. All day	BAR FOOD: Limited
CHILDREN: Welcome	VEGETARIAN: No
CREDIT CARDS: None taken	WHEELCHAIR ACCESS: Yes
LICENSED: Full On	GARDEN: Walled Beer Garden
ACCOMMODATION: 5rooms.1 en-suite	with Boulles Pitch
RATES: From £20pp B&B Four-poster £30	PETS: Yes, if well trained

THE WHITE HORSE
Hopton Road,
Thelnetbarn
Nr Diss,
Norfolk
IP22 1JN

Tel: 01379 898298

People come from far and wide to enjoy the hospitality of The White Horse. Built over two hundred years ago it has great character, is full of nooks and crannies and we would not be surprised if it had a ghost, although one is not recorded. The atmosphere is warm and friendly and in the capable hands of Mike, Rob and Barbara Bentley, it has never been better run. The ale is well kept, there are always guest beers, every kind of spirit is available including Malt Whisky. A comprehensive wine list is made up of wines from around the world sold either by the bottle or the glass - even the house red and white are more than palatable. You will find The White Horse on the B1111 just off the main A1066 between Thetford and Diss.

This is a pub that does not pretend to be a restaurant with a bar but is a true country inn where the art of conversation is very much alive. People come to enjoy this sort of atmosphere and also to know that the food, served in the attractive, old restaurant, will be delicious, perfectly cooked and beautifully presented. The menu is all encompassing and includes English traditional fare as well as dishes with an eastern and continental flavour. Emphasis is placed on fresh and local produce wherever possible. To accompany the main course there are a selection of starters and some tempting desserts. Food is also served in the bar where you can get anything from a sandwich to a Ploughman's, a Daily Special to a steak. The White Horse understands the well-being of the inner man and also cares for his pocket.

In the summer people enjoy sitting out on the patio or the lawn enjoying the sun and a drink or two. From The White Horse you can set out to walk in delightful countryside or perhaps drive twelve miles into Bury St Edmunds, one of the oldest and most historic towns in Suffolk with a superb abbey and magnificent gardens.

USEFUL INFORMATION

OPEN: 11-3pm & 5-11pm   RESTAURANT: Excellent menu
Sat: All day Sun: 12-3pm & 7-10.30pm   BAR FOOD: Good choice
CHILDREN: Welcome   VEGETARIAN: Yes
CREDIT CARDS: All major cards   WHEELCHAIR ACCESS: No
LICENSED: Full On   GARDEN: Lawn & Patio
PETS: Well behaved

50 TEMPLE ROAD
Stowmarket,
Suffolk
IP14 1AT

ETB Listed

Tel: 01449 674673

Situated in a quiet residential area within the town centre of Stowmarket, 50 Temple Road provides a home-from home for people either on holiday or on business. It is an Edwardian House, gracious and spacious and very much a family home which is something that comes over to visitors the moment they arrive. Owned by Constance Ruegg who has a keen eye for colour, decor and furnishing, you will find the rooms attractive and comfortable. There are three guest rooms all sharing a bathroom. One is a large family room, another a double and the third a single. Each has a television and a hostess tray. Breakfast is served every morning in the pleasant dining room. The meal is delicious, freshly cooked and with a choice of either a traditional full English breakfast or the Continental variety. There are no evening meals but Stowmarket has a variety of eateries at varying prices.

USEFUL INFORMATION

OPEN: All year
CHILDREN: Welcome
CREDIT CARDS: None taken
LICENSED: No
ACCOMMODATION: 1fam.1dbl.
1sgl. Not en-suite
RATES: £16pp B&B

DINING ROOM: Excellent breakfast
No evening meal
VEGETARIAN: Yes
WHEELCHAIR ACCESS: Not suitable
GARDEN: No
PETS: Yes

THE ANGEL HOTEL
Market Place,
Lavenham, Suffolk CO10 9QZ
Tel: 01787 247388 Fax: 01787 248344

Lavenham claims to be the finest medieval town in England and has three hundred listed buildings. Everyone who goes there falls in love with it. At its heart, on the attractive Market Place, stands the 15th century Angel Hotel. The exterior had a little remodelling in Georgian times but inside many of the earlier nooks and crannies remain, and the space around the bar is divided up by half-timbered walls and partitions. It creates a wonderfully intimate atmosphere. Everywhere there are water-colours, old photos of the inn, prints of birds and animals and a carved wooden angel adorns the fireplace. If you are a resident you can escape the bars and retire to a first floor lounge, whose fine plaster ceiling dates from the 16th century. The food is of a high standard and certainly a cut above the average pub fare. You might choose to have a pork casserole with walnuts and apricots or a delicious hot Suffolk cheese and ham pie. You eat at one of the assorted scrubbed pine tables inside or in the warmer weather in the pretty garden tucked away at the rear. There are eight comfortably furnished bedrooms en-suite either with shower or bath. Each room has television, direct-dial telephone, hair dryer and room service. Children are welcome and baby-listening is offered. Wheelchair access is possible in the restaurant and to the one ground floor room.

USEFUL INFORMATION

OPEN: All year. Closed 25th & 26th Dec
CHILDREN: Welcome. Early suppers
CREDIT CARDS: All major cards
LICENSED: Full On
ACCOMMODATION: 8 en-suite rooms
RATES: Mon-Thurs B&B £65 Dbl. £39.50sgl
Weekend D B&B £105

RESTAURANT: High standard
BAR FOOD: Wide choice
VEGETARIAN: Yes
WHEELCHAIR ACCESS: Yes
GARDEN: Yes
PETS: By arrangement only

THE BLACK LION & COUNTRYMAN RESTAURANT
The Green, Long Melford,
Suffolk CO10 9DN

Tel: 01787 312356 Fax: 01787 374557

Janet and Stephen Errington are the proud, and very successful owners of The Black Lion Hotel and Countrymen Restaurant. Well they might be, for from its inception which started with the Countrymen Restaurant and then had a 17th century coaching inn added to it, they have dedicated thought, time and money into creating one of the nicest venues in Suffolk. Charmingly decorated with ragging and colour washing throughout, they show off their splendid collection of plates in the restaurant and Toby jugs in the bar. Everything about this exemplary run restaurant and hotel pleases its clientele. People come here to eat, to enjoy Stephen's exciting and varied menus in the main restaurant where you can choose from four set-price menus, or pick and mix from the a la carte. Informal options are available in the bistro/wine bar, a pleasant room overlooking the green where you can order a plate of pasta or lamb's liver and mashed potato. The nine bedrooms are charming and furnished with antiques. There are four posters and antique beds, pine furniture and stencilling in the bathrooms. Every room has television, direct-dial telephone, mini bar and hair dryer. Everything is done for the comfort and enjoyment of guests.

USEFUL INFORMATION

OPEN: All year. Restaurant closed Sun.
CHILDREN: Welcome. Early suppers
CREDIT CARDS: All major cards
LICENSED: Full On
ACCOMMODATION: 9 en-suite rooms
RATES: Sgl £50-60 B&B Dbl. £70-80
Special breaks

RESTAURANT: Varied, delicious
                menu.
BISTRO: Daily menu.
VEGETARIAN: Yes
WHEELCHAIR ACCESS: No
GARDEN: Yes
PETS: Not in public rooms

CHIMNEYS RESTAURANT
Hall Street,
Long Melford, Suffolk CO10 9JR
Three Star

Tel: 01787 379806 Fax: 01787 312294

Long Melford is full of beautiful buildings, has two historic houses, an old church and a National Trust Property. It is also the longest village in England and in its midst is the charming 16th century Chimneys Restaurant which has been meticulously and lovingly restored retaining its many original features including a wealth of exposed timbers and large inglenook fireplaces, it also boasts a beautiful walled garden. Owned by Sam Chalmers, Chimneys opens seven days a week for luncheon and dinner except Sunday dinner. It has an enviable reputation for many miles around and entices people back to enjoy its food time and time again. The menu, which changes regularly, is perfectly balanced with a choice of eight starters and eight main courses and a dessert menu which tempts the strongest willed person. Start perhaps with Baked Filo Parcels with Feta Cheese and Shrimps followed by Pot Roast Guinea Fowl with Lime and Marsala or Pan Fried Fillet of Scottish Beef with a Madeira Jus. Vegetarians always have a choice at all courses. The wine list is well chosen and offers wine and champagne by the glass. The surroundings are delightful, the friendly service quietly efficient. It would be very difficult not to enjoy Chimneys.

USEFUL INFORMATION

OPEN: 12-2pm & 7-11pm (Not Sunday dinner)
CHILDREN: Welcome
CREDIT CARDS: Visa/Master
LICENSED: Full On
GARDEN: walled & beautiful

RESTAURANT: Delicious
food, wonderful atmosphere
VEGETARIAN: Yes
WHEELCHAIR ACCESS: Yes
PETS: No

THE GREYHOUND INN
97 High Street,
Lavenham, Suffolk CO10 9PZ

Tel: 01787 247475

George and Marion Grey are the landlords at The Greyhound Inn in the High Street, Lavenham, one of the most unspoilt and beautiful villages in England. It is full of beautiful buildings and the half-timbered inn with its pink washed walls and black paint, fits into the scene beautifully. Built in the 14th century, the inn is full of nooks and crannies, low ceilings and beams. It is friendly and welcoming, a pleasant place just to have a drink if you wish but the food is also good. There is no specific restaurant but one can eat in the bars from a blackboard menu which changes regularly and offers traditional pub fare with the addition of dishes from around the world. Everything is home-cooked and served by friendly, smiling staff who are the two sons of the owners, Mike and Ben. The garden with its patio is a popular place in the warmer weather. You can sit out here and enjoy the weather whilst you have a drink or you can take your food outside as well, if you wish. Lavenham will offer any visitor great pleasure in exploration. There are many walks around the village and golf courses within easy distance.

USEFUL INFORMATION

OPEN: 9am-11pm
CHILDREN: Welcome
CREDIT CARDS: ll major cards
LICENSED: Full On
GARDEN: Yes + Patio
PETS: Public bar only

RESTAURANT: Not applicable
BAR FOOD: Blackboard menu. Traditional pub fare + world dishes
VEGETARIAN: Always a choice
WHEELCHAIR ACCESS: No

THE HARE INN,
High Street,
Long Melford,
Suffolk CO10 9DF

Tel: 01787 310379
Fax: 01787 313948

The 15th century Hare Inn stands in the High Street of Long Melford, somewhere that is world renowned for its antique shops. This brings a lot of visitors but the focal point is The Hare Inn which is a traditional inn and caters not only for the influx of visitors but for its very contented regulars who are always to be found in the bar enjoying a pint and discussing the topics of the day in a good humoured fashion. The landlords, Paul Kemp and Cathy O'Neill have been here just over a year and have made their mark. They have improved what was already a good local. The well-stocked bar seats fifty in comfort and it is here you can enjoy the home-cooked food which is mainly traditional with the emphasis on fish, chicken and steak dishes. Every day there are Daily Specials and on Sundays the Roast Lunch is very popular. If you do not want a meal you will find a good range of sandwiches, Ploughmans and other bar fare. Food is available all day from noon until ten p.m.

USEFUL INFORMATION

OPEN: 11am-11pm Sun: 12-10.30pm
CHILDREN: Welcome
CREDIT CARDS: All major cards
LICENSED: Full On
GARDEN: Yes

RESTAURANT: Not applicable
BAR FOOD: Good pub fare
VEGETARIAN: Always a choice
WHEELCHAIR ACCESS: Yes
PETS: In restricted areas

HOLIDAY FARM HOUSE
Fen Road, Hinderclay,
Diss, Norfolk IP22 1HS
ETB 2 Crown Highly Commended

Tel: 01379 898302
Fax: 01379 890107

This beautifully restored farmhouse which still retains exposed beams, has been lived in by the Aves family for over sixty years. It is very much a family home and today Dulcie Aves takes great pleasure in welcoming her guests. The house stands in one acre of delightful gardens and within fifteen acres of pastureland. It is just one hundred yards from the famous Angles Way - a popular footpath which extends along South Norfolk from the coast to Breckland. It is also within easy reach of many fascinating places to explore including National Trust Properties, Bury St Edmunds with is magnificent Abbey and both Norwich and Ipswich are three quarters of an hour away. There are two twin rooms and one double room all en-suite with baths and showers. Each room, attractively and comfortably furnished, have television, and iron, hairdryer and a hostess tray. A washing machine is also available. Breakfast is a delicious meal and as well as the traditional English fare there is fish, cheese, fresh fruit and yoghurt. No evening meals but there are many eateries close by offering all sorts of fare.

USEFUL IN FORMATION

OPEN: All year
CHILDREN: Over 10 years
CREDIT CARDS: None taken
LICENSED: No
ACCOMMODATION: 2tw 1dbl en-suite
RATES: £20pp dbl. £25 sgl

DINING ROOM: Excellent breakfast
VEGETARIAN: On request
WHEELCHAIR ACCESS: No
GARDEN: Yes
PETS: No
STRICTLY NON-SMOKING

LAVENHAM PRIORY
Water Street,
Lavenham, Sudbury,
Suffolk CO10 9RW

Tel: 01787 247404
Fax: 01787 248472

Benedictine monks originally owned this Grade I Listed house, outstandingly beautiful even amongst the wonderful buildings that constitute the beautiful village of Lavenham. Bed chambers feature crown posts, wall paintings and oak floors, with four-poster, lit bateau and polonaise beds. Visitors can relax by inglenook fires in the 13th century hall or sitting room. Breakfast and pre-dinner drinks can be enjoyed in the sheltered courtyard herb garden. Tim and Gill Pit, your hosts are charming, welcoming people and they thoroughly enjoy ensuring the welfare of their guests. It is a very definite family atmosphere and people leave here feeling they have become one of this warm-hearted family. An excellent breakfast is served every morning and dinner is by arrangement. Gilli loves cooking and this is evident in the delicious meals she prepares. Lavenham is often described as one of the finest medieval villages in England with its historic buildings and streets. Within easy walking distance of The Priory are the Guildhall, Wool Church, antique and gift shops, tea rooms, restaurants and country strolls. You can walk everywhere and simply enjoy the beauty of Lavenham.

USEFUL INFORMATION

OPEN: All year except Christmas & New Year
CHILDREN: Over 10 years breakfast.
CREDIT CARDS: Yes
LICENSED: No
ACCOMMODATION: 2dbl 1tw all en-suite
RATES: £30-45 pp.pn B&B

DINING ROOM: Delicious
Dinner by arrangement
VEGETARIAN: Upon request
WHEELCHAIR ACCESS: No
GARDEN: Yes
PETS: No

LE TALBOOTH RESTAURANT.
Gun Hill. Dedham.
Colchester, Essex CO7 6HP

Tel :- 01206 323150 Fax:- 01206 322309.

What has become known as Constable country, inspired the artist John Constable to paint pictures of such area as Falfoot Mill and in instance included this restaurant in his now famous painting of Dedham Vale, (currently housed in the National Gallery of Scotland). This charming 16th. Century timber framed house, once a Weavers cottage, was discovered by Gerald Milsom, the owner, in 1952 when it was a simple tea-room. So enchanted was he and being the entrepreneurial type saw the potential of converting it to what it is today, one of the most famous restaurants in England. Sitting on the tiered terrace one can conjure up imagination of when this was a toll booth for horse drawn traffic and river craft. In reality you are in the garden of this fine restaurant by the river, with its International reputation for excellence. Whatever the season and wherever you dine in this building or outside on the terrace or lawns, the food will be sublime, the staff unobtrusively efficient, and the ambience something you will find hard to forget. Eating in a restaurant will never be the same again after you have been here. The award winning kitchens are the heart of the coveted reputation of this fine restaurant, complemented by an extensive wine cellar. The hotel in the same ownership, just a short distance away is equally renowned, both are popular meeting places for intimate parties, wedding receptions, or more elaborate grand receptions in the restaurant or garden marquee. Please write to me if my description does not live up to your expectations, I expect no letters.

USEFUL INFORMAION

OPEN: All year.
CHILDREN: Welcome
CREDIT CARTDS: All major
LINCENCED: Yes
PETS: Not in restaurant.

RESTAURANT: Award winning fare.
VEGETARIAN: Imaginative choices.
WHEEL CHAIR ACCESS: Yes
GARDEN: Yes

MAISON TALBOOTH
Stratford Road,
Dedham, Essex CO7 6HN
3 Red AA Star. 3 RAC Stars, Blue Ribbon

Tel: 01206 322367   Fax: 01206 322752

Maison Talbooth is the essence of a Victorian country house enjoying a superb position overlooking the river valley, with water meadows stretching away to the medieval church at Stratford St Mary. A short walk along the lane is the picturesque village of Dedham with its celebrated main street and magnificent church. There are ten beautifully appointed suites, the epitome of quiet luxury. The menu in the restaurant is superb with dishes prepared and cooked in the English manner by a talented chef. Maison Talbooth can claim the rare achievement of having retained and enhanced its reputation for superb cuisine for over thirty years, complemented by an extensive and interesting wine list. Everything about Maison Talbooth points to gracious living. The beautiful garden entices people to sit and enjoy a drink, stroll a while or even eat outside in warm weather. You can play chess or croquet on the well manicured grass. The Vale of Dedham is where the river Stour forms the boundary with Suffolk. It is an area of outstanding scenic beauty. The most celebrated English painters have responded to these gentle pastoral scenes and dramatic skies.

USEFUL INFORMATION

OPEN: All year
CHILDREN: Welcome
CREDIT CARDS: All major cards
LICENSED: Full On licence
ACCOMMODATION: 10 suites
RATES: From £90-£175

RESTAURANT: Superb cuisine
BAR FOOD: Not applicable
VEGETARIAN: Always a choice
WHEELCHAIR ACCESS: Yes
GARDEN: Yes. Croquet. Chess
PETS: No

MILL HOUSE
Newton Green,
Sudbury, Suffolk CO10 0QY

Tel: 01787 372427

Sudbury is where the artist Thomas Gainsborough was born and somewhere from which he took much inspiration and it is also in what has become 'Constable Country' because of the great artist John Constable who, with his paintings, made the countryside famous and today, long after his death, still attracts many visitors to the area. At Newton Green, a quiet village, Mill House stands at the corner of an 18 hole golf course, surrounded by beautiful countryside and with a wealth of interesting places, 14th century churches, fascinating villages with their antique shops and much more for the visitor to see and do. The sporting visitor can play golf, swim in the indoor swimming pool at Mill House, enjoy country walks or go horse riding. Brenda White owns Mill House and she enjoys having guests in her comfortable relaxed home. There are four guest rooms, two doubles, one twin and one single all with wash basins and television. Brenda is renowned for the excellence of her breakfasts and whilst she does not provide an evening meal, she is happy to direct you to one of the many good eateries in the neighbourhood.

USEFUL INFORMATION

OPEN: All year
CHILDREN: Welcome
CREDIT CARDS: None taken
LICENSED: No
ACCOMMODATION: 4 rooms not en-suite
RATES: £25pp.pn

DINING ROOM: Excellent breakfast
VEGETARIAN: Upon request
WHEELCHAIR ACCESS: Yes
GARDEN: Yes. Very pretty
PETS: Yes

PIPPS FORD
Needham Market,
north of Ipswich,
Suffolk IP6 8LJ

Tel: 01449 760208 Fax: 01449 760561

Pipps Ford is a large Tudor farmhouse with inglenook fireplaces, sloping floors, low beams and historic associations. It stands on a stretch of the River Gipping in a designated area of 'outstanding beauty' in a delightful garden beyond which there is coarse river fishing in the river, where the cricket-bat willows grow, and a Roman site. From here you can easily get to such interesting places as Sandringham, Constable country, Lavenham, Aldeburgh, Southwold, Norwich, Ipswich and Bury St Edmunds as well as some very pretty villages and ancient churches. Raewyn Hackett-Jones, a charming New Zealander is your hostess. Her home-making touch is evident everywhere with her own patchwork quilts or cushion-covers for every room. There are flowers in every bedroom and many of the beds are collectors' pieces. Every room has an attractive bathroom, one is spectacular with a huge oval bath. Breakfasts are exceptional and dinner a feast. It is a delightful, relaxed, comfortable and friendly house to stay in.

USEFUL INFORMATION

OPEN: Mid-Jan-Mid Dec.
CHILDREN: Over 5 years
CREDIT CARDS: None taken
LICENSED: Residential
ACCOMMODATION: 7 en-suite rooms
RATES: From £22.50-£32.50sgl £45-£65 dbl.
PETS: Only if they sleep in the car

DINING ROOM: Exceptional breakfast
and delicious dinner
VEGETARIAN: & Vegan by arrangement
WHEELCHAIR ACCESS: Yes, 4
                              ground floor rooms
GARDEN: Yes. Tennis,

THE PYKKERELL INN
38 High Street,
Ixworth, Suffolk IP31 2HH
Good Food Guide

Tel/Fax: 01359 230398

Built in 1510 this is one of the oldest inns in Suffolk. Well before the days of coaching it was welcoming travellers but it became well known as a Coaching Inn in the 18th and early 19th century. It is complete with a Tudor Barn and still has an old stable block. One of the pleasures in coming here is its situation one hundred yards from the river, but most of all people come from miles around to enjoy the happy feeling generated by Ron and Annie Goulding, the owners, and their friendly staff. It goes without saying that the ale is well kept but until you come here you will not realise that Ron is a Wine Master and his extensive wine list provides well chosen bottles at sensible prices, as well as wine by the glass. The food here is also renowned. Home-made it features fresh fish every day, a host of Daily Specials and an a la carte menu which is tempting. In the Bar there are snacks and sandwiches served at lunch-time. Sunday evening is the only time when food is not available. If you wonder where the inn got its name, it derives from Pike caught in the river - which came first no one can relate.

USEFUL INFORMATION

OPEN: 12-3pm & 6-11pm
CHILDREN: Welcome
CREDIT CARDS: All major cards
LICENSED: Full On
GARDEN: Courtyard. Tudor Barn
PETS: Yes

RESTAURANT: Home-cooked fare
with emphasis on fresh fish
BAR FOOD: At lunch-time
VEGETARIAN: Yes
WHEELCHAIR ACCESS: Yes

THE ROYAL GEORGE
Church Street,
Barningham,
Suffolk IP31 1DD

Tel: 01359 221246

The Royal George is a 17th century thatched pub in Barningham, a rural area of Suffolk. You may wonder how a pub in a rural village acquired its name which comes from the Navy's Flagship, The Royal George, built over ten years in the early 1700s. The story is too long to retell here but Jacqui and Neil, the cheerful landlords of the inn will be happy to tell you all about it. Much of the inn retains its ancient features with old beams and huge inglenook fireplaces. It is essentially a village hostelry in which pub games, pool, darts, dominoes, cards and quizzes are encouraged and provide a lot of fun for visitors as well as the locals. The bar is well-stocked, the beer well kept and for diners there is a quiet area seating 20 in part of the front bar. It also acts as a small function room. The food is high quality, home-cooked fare. One of the specialities of The Royal George is the Steak and Ale pies; mouth-watering pastry and totally delicious. The menu covers a whole range of dishes and the bar snacks provide everything from a sandwich to a salad.

USEFUL INFORMATION

OPEN: Mon-Thurs 11-3pm &6-11pm
Fri-Sun: All day
CHILDREN: Welcome
CREDIT CARDS: None taken
LICENSED: Full On

RESTAURANT: Good food
BAR FOOD: Wide range. Home-cooked
VEGETARIAN: At least 4-5 choices
WHEELCHAIR ACCESS: Yes
GARDEN: Yes PETS: Yes

SCUTCHER'S BISTRO
Westgate Street,
Long Melford, Suffolk CO10 9DP

Tel: 01787 310200

Visitors are always enchanted with Long Melford because of its Aladdin's cave of antique shops which allows them to browse for hours. Having done that, Scutcher's Bistro is the place to make for. Owned by Nicholas Barrett who is also the chef, it offers an oak-beamed retreat after the excitement of the antiques. The menu is honest. What you see is what you get. For example Smoked Salmon with lemon is just that and the portions are more than generous. You can choose duck confit served on leek and potato mash with a balsamic just as a starter. Pork Loin Chop comes on buttered spinach with a green peppercorn sauce, pheasant is cooked in cider and served with glazed apples. The choice is vast across the board. Puddings are delectable and can be anything from a simple fruit salad to a sticky sponge pudding. There is a delicious lemon and thyme sorbet. Everything offered to you is value for money and the service is faultless. 109 wines are grouped by grape variety. Brief tasting notes are helpful. There are eight good house wines at £1.80 a glass. Bottles start from £10.50. You are expected to dress smartly albeit casually. There are forty seats in the garden. Children are welcome and have special helpings. Several choices are suitable for Vegetarians. Private parties are catered for beautifully.

USEFUL INFORMATION

OPEN: Tue-Sat 12-2pm & 7-9.30pm
Closed Bank Hols. Dec 25 &26
CHILDREN: Yes, Children's helpings
CREDIT CARDS: All major cards
LICENSED: Yes   PETS: Guide dogs only

BISTRO: Excellent menu
VEGETARIAN: Catered for
WHEELCHAIR ACCESS: Yes
GARDEN: Yes & for eating

SIX BELLS AT BARDWELL
The Green, Bardwell,
Bury St Edmunds, Suffolk IP31 1AW
ETB***Commended AAQQQQSelected.
Les Routiers 'Pub of the Year' 1993
Tel/Fax 01359 250820

If you are a fan of the television series 'Dad's Army' you may well recognise this delightful inn. It was used in the filming of the series, a photograph of the cast is displayed in the bar, and 'The Dad's Army Appreciation Society' visit once or twice a year. Easily accessible from the Bury St Edmunds to Diss road, although a little off the beaten track. The Six Bells in the pretty village of Bardwell, dates from the 16th century and is Grade II Listed. It retains many of its original festures with an inglnook fireplace in the bar and an old Suffolk range in the restaurant, which is heavily beamed. The atmosphere is terrific and the hospitality second to none. Richard and Carol Salmon are the proprietors and together with their staff they work hard to ensure everyone enjoys a visit here. The food in the restaurant and the bar, cooked by Richard and his team is traditional and imaginative. The result is superb and it is little wonder they are famed in this part of East Anglia. The nine en-suite bedrooms, all at ground level, are in a converted barn and stables adjacent to the main building with views over the field. One room has a four poster and they all have direct dial telephones, television and hostess trays. There is a small room available for private parties and conferences.

USEFUL INFORMATION

OPEN:12-2pm & 6.45-11pm Not Dec25/26th
CHILDREN: Welcome
CREDIT CARDS: Mastercard/Visa
LICENSED: Full On
ACCOMMODATION: 9 en-suite ground floor rooms
RATES: From £35pp.pn sgl £40dbl
Short Breaks from £75 pp d.B&B

RESTAURANT: Superb
imaginative, traditional cuisine
BAR FOOD: Good choice
VEGETARIAN: Always a choice
GARDEN: Yes
WHEELCHAIR ACCESS: Yes
PETS: Yes £5 per stay

THE GREAT HOUSE HOTEL & RESTAURANT
Market Place,
Lavenham, Suffolk CO10 9QZ
4 Crowns Highly Commended AAQQQQ
@Best Family Restaurant of the Year' Egon Ronay 1997
Tel: 01787 247431 Fax: 01787 248007
greathouse@surflink.co.uk

This delightful 16th century house with Georgian facade overlooks the magnificent Market Square of Lavenham, one of England's finest medieval towns. Yet with owners Regis and Martin Crepy, and their team, it is like walking into a little pocket of France. The warm 'Gaelic' welcome is the perfect start for a relaxing stay either 'en famille' or with your best friends. The beautifully decorated rooms, each with its own individual style, retain much of their original character with beams and sloping ceilings. Most are spacious with separated sitting rooms or sitting area. There are five bedrooms, each with direct dial telephone, television and a hostess tray. You can stretch in the six foot wide Jacobean Four Poster bed or if you prefer a cosy cottage look, choose the top floor bedrooms. The superb en-suite bathrooms give the last touch of luxury! French croissant and petits au chocolat are part of the English breakfast. The reputation of the restaurant in the area speaks for itself. Service is professional and friendly. The menus combine the best of French and Continental cuisine. The daily changing Set Menus offer excellent value and the extensive wine list is something to look forward to. In the summer meals can be taken 'alfresco' in the attractive colourful courtyard from breakfast in the sunshine to late dinners in the moonlight.

USEFUL INFORMATION

OPEN: Feb-Dec 12-2.30pm & 7-10.30pm
CHILDREN: Welcome
CREDIT CARDS: Visa/Master/AMEX/Switch
LICENSED: Hotel Licence
ACCOMMODATION: 5 en-suite rooms
RATES: From £35 pp Children £15

RESTAURANT: Delicious Set Menu
changing daily. Non-smoking
VEGETARIAN: Always a choice
WHEELCHAIR ACCESS: Yes
GARDEN: Walled garden & courtyard
PETS: Yes if well behaved

THE OLD RECTORY
Mickfield, NR Stowmarket
Suffolk IP14 5LR

Tel: 01449 711283

The Old Rectory has 'grown' from medieval origins. It is a delightful timber framed house quiet and peaceful, surrounded by its own lovely garden, orchard and meadow. The sort of place from which to escape from the world. It is situated right in the middle of Suffolk, secluded yet within easy reach of main roads and would make a good base for exploring the whole of East Anglia. The house is superbly furnished and at the same time essentially comfortable. Guests will appreciate the beamed Tudor dining room, gracious Georgian drawing room and the most stylish and comfortable bedrooms. Patricia Currie owns the Old Rectory and she has the instinctive ability to know how to ensure her guests comfort. Breakfast every morning is a sumptuous feast and dinner at night is optional. Now her daughters have left home, Patricia enjoys her passion for gardening and working and training her two flat coated retrievers who, along with a Labrador welcome you with waving tails.

USEFUL INFORMATION

OPEN: All year
Closed Christmas, New Year & Easter
CHILDREN: Over 8 years
CREDIT CARDS: Yes
LICENSED: No
ACCOMMODATION: 1dbl 1 tw or sgl
RATES: £29pp.pn B&B

DINING ROOM: Excellent breakfast
        Dinner optional
VEGETARIAN: Upon request
WHEELCHAIR ACCESS: No
GARDEN: Lovely. Orchard & Meadow
PETS: No

THEOBALD'S RESTAURANT
68 High Street,
Ixworth, Suffolk IP31 2HJ
AA 2 cooking Rosettes.
Good Food Guide Cooking 4.Michelin. Egon Ronay

Tel/Fax: 01359 231707

It would be so easy to miss Ixworth and that would be an enormous shame because in the High Street is Theobald's one of the nicest small restaurants in Suffolk. They say you should never judge a book by its cover and you might be excused if you thought the frontage of Theobald's so subtle and in keeping with the style of buildings around it, that it made it all but invisible! Inside it is totally charming, with good taste in both the decor and the delicious food. There is a wealth of exposed beams, a cosy little lounge with comfortable armchairs in front of an open fire providing a great welcome. The elegant dining room is separated into sections by standing timbers creating an intimate atmosphere. The menu is a tempting mixture of English and Continental dishes cooked by the owner, Simon Theobald who runs the restaurant with his friend has an instinctive flair for combining ingredients with a light touch. The service is excellent with stylishly dressed waitresses who unobtrusively care for their tables. Particularly impressive is the selection of many-flavoured bread rolls offered as soon as one is seated at table. They are so tempting that one has to be disciplined enough not to ruin the meal by an over indulgence of bread.

USEFUL INFORMATION

OPEN: All year except 2 weeks in August
Tues-Fri Lunch & Sun Lunch 12-15-1.30pm
Tues-Sat Dinner 7.15-9pm
CHILDREN: Over 8 at dinner
CREDIT CARDS: Visa/Master
LICENSED: Yes

RESTAURANT: Imaginative and
inspired menu
VEGETARIAN: Always a choice
WHEELCHAIR ACCESS: No
GARDEN: Yes
PETS: No

THE ANGEL INN,
Stoke-By-Nayland
Suffolk
Tel: 01206 263245   Fax: 01206 263373

The Angel Inn is at the cross-roads in the centre of Stoke-by-Nayland, one of Constable's favourite villages. The village stands on the bluff of land that rises above the water meadows and fields of Dedham Vale, now a conservation area. The surrounding countryside with its many footpaths and country lanes, is ideal for exploring on foot or cycling. The Angel has stood since 1536 and although much restoration work has been done over the centuries, much of the original building survives from this time. Today, The Angel continues its long tradition of hospitality to travellers. Comfortably furnished rooms, beamed bars with log fires in winter, good food, wine and local ales. There are six guest bedrooms, all with bathrooms en-suite. A full English Breakfast is included in the tariff. The restaurant offers a wonderful a la carte menu for lunch and dinner every day and on Sunday, a traditional roast lunch. Due to its popularity it is advisable to reserve a table. Lunch and supper are also served in the bar every day from an extensive chalkboard menu. The head chef, Mark Johnson's style strikes a balance between the adventurous and the traditional with the emphasis on flavour. The Angel is one of Suffolk's treasures. Miss this Inn and you will have forgone a memorable meal.

USEFUL INFORMATION

OPEN: Weekdays 11-2.30pm & 6-11pm
Sundays 12-3pm & 7-10.30pm
CHILDREN: No
CREDIT CARDS: All major cards
LICENSED: Full On Licence
ACCOMMODATION: 6 en-suite rooms
RATES: £46 sgl £59.50 dbl B&B

RESTAURANT: All fresh,
International
BAR FOOD: Wide selection.
VEGETARIAN: Two dishes per day
WHEELCHAIR ACCESS: Yes
GARDEN: Patio
PETS: No

FLATFORD MILL

IAN PETHERS

Selected venues in this chapter

' The Lord be praised if my belly's raised an inch above the table,
but we'll be damned if we are not crammed as full as we are able'
Queen Victoria

Chapter 11: East Suffolk:
Contrasts, Concerts and the Cornelian Coast
Lowestoft to Southwold, Aldeburgh & Ipswich

Let's reminisce: you remember those breakfasts in Ely? How good it was to sit over the coffee and watch the mist curtains part to reveal the huge sky over the Fens? Two, in fact, were very good - the third? Well, it was dark, we had half Lincolnshire ahead of us and every time we looked at the clock the moving minute hand made us feel guilty for not rushing through the toast. Still, we survived and the golfers, at least, got value for money during the day.

Why *are* we reminiscing? Mainly to soften the *next* blow, I have to confess. Something along the lines of: if you think *this* seems bad, remember Ely and how two out of three *weren't* bad and even the third, very tough one, had its good points. That sort of thing. In other words, if two out of three at Bury have been pretty fair and the third looks like being an absolute *monster*, we've been there before. We've survived - and some of us have done even better than that.

This does *look* bad for the moment, I must admit. We have *miles* to go before we sup, thousands of years of history to experience and several hundred tons of antiques, collectibles, curios and the other thing to collect (*between* us, not *each*). We've had a bit of a lie in too: it's gone eight and we're still sitting here.. Of course, if anyone says we're *still* wasting time, hanging around listening to my PR - and my excuses - they're quite right. We should be on our way out of Bury, towards the north east. It *will* be a long day, but it's full of contrasts - and a renewed acquaintance with the sea - so let's sit back, think of England and enjoy it.

I think we'd be sensible to take the A143 - traffic and all - to start with, to give ourselves a psychological boost by the feeling that we're actually getting somewhere. It shouldn't be as busy as the A14 - 'container way' - which, these days, takes a tremendous number of heavy goods vehicles from the Midlands through to the docks at Ipswich and Felixstowe. We've already used this road on our last trip - but as we're heading in the opposite direction this time, let's hope it *looks* different if nothing else. Another advantage of this route is that, by and large, we'll skirt round most of Suffolk's central plateau with its endless fields of sugar beet, cereals and peas, which we've touched on to help our understanding of the region, but which we wouldn't actually choose for a long term - or even a second - discerning visit. We can't miss it entirely - our first call is very much a part of 'High Suffolk' but fortunately there's plenty to restore the balance coming later.

So, it's a familiar road as far as Wattisfield and then we begin to break new ground as we ease towards the Norfolk border. Just south of Diss - and hopefully still inside Suffolk (just testing) we turn sharp right and cross the A140, after less than a mile, to take the B1077 into **EYE.** This is a gem of a small country town, which grew up around its castle. Its name means 'island', which looks unlikely nowadays but made a lot of sense in times past. It used to be virtually isolated by the little River Dove, on one side, and by impenetrable marshes on most of the rest.

We could start our visit by inspecting the CASTLE'S Norman and Medieval ruins, whilst pondering on its more prosperous past. It is open from the week before Easter to 30th September, daily between 9.00am and 7.30pm, or dusk, if earlier. Admission is free. We might then come to the 15th century CHURCH OF ST PETER AND ST PAUL, which is hugely impressive, even at first glance. The tower, described in Pevsner's 'The Buildings of England' as *"one of the wonders of Suffolk"*, is decorated in 'flushwork' to a standard barely equalled anywhere else in the county. At a height of 101 ft, it also dominates the local landscape quite effectively. The Church has a mixture of Early English, Decorated and Perpendicular styles, showing clearly that it was built in several stages as were so many structures of this type and size. The earliest visible work - in the aisle's south doorway - dates from the 13th century, while most of the rest came a hundred years later. Building didn't stop there, as the Church was heightened and given clerestory roofing and new windows when the tower was completed in the 1470s. In 1480 the superb Rood Screen, painted with figures of saints, was added. An ART EXHIBITION is held in the Church each September and there is also a gift shop in the South Porch which will be opened on request if it is closed. Opening times are 8.30am to 6.00pm daily in summer and 8.30am to 4.30pm in winter.

Although the town today appeals to visitors as much for its sleepy charm as anything, there are quite enough points of interest and relics from its historic past to justify a stroll around its streets. With this in mind, it's worth picking up a leaflet from the Mid-Suffolk Tourist Information Centre which will guide us along the EYE TOWN TRAIL. In the course of its circuit the Trail takes in no less than seventeen individual items whose attraction is either their history, their architecture - or both. At the outset, it's obvious that Eye was a centre of great importance from the time when a BENEDICTINE PRIORY was founded in 1087 by Roger Mallet, to the east of the town, until well into the 19th century. It's population peaked at 2,587 in 1851, after which it declined gradually despite later efforts to encourage trade. Nowadays, I suspect its somewhat revived state has more to do with *where* it is - and the way it looks - than with what it does, as it lies in the middle of a rectangle formed by Ipswich, Bury St Edmunds, Norwich and Lowestoft, all of which can be reached pretty easily by road.

If we tried to cover every feature thoroughly, we'd need a chapter just for Eye - *and* one each for Bungay, Beccles, Lowestoft and the rest, to the point where the book would have become an encyclopedia, an *expensive* encyclopedia! As that's not an option, I'll focus on two or three items that really held my attention, apologise for the omissions - all of which you *must* see for yourselves - and introduce you to the very personal tip of an extremely intriguing iceberg.

Just a step from the Church, along CHURCH STREET, is the late 15th century GULDHALL, a two storey building with exposed timber frames. It was carefully restored in 1875 by Lady Kerrison with the original appearance very much in mind, although there's not a lot of the truly old work to be seen apart from the carving of the Archangel Gabriel on the corner post. The Guildhall was used as a school from 1495 and in 1875, became the residence of the master and between fifteen and twenty boarders until 1909. hen it became a County Secondary School for girls as well as boys. Today we see the results of yet another change, as the old building currently houses the St Peter and St Paul Church of England Aided Primary School - with a collection of offices and a bookshop on its ground floor.

We may well have exhausted guildhalls, but both of the next two places where we'll be pausing are unique - and their associations are interesting, too. LINDEN HOUSE, which is way up LAMBETH STREET, on the right, is a late 17th century house which was given an external coat of classical red brick early in the next century. It's the early part of *this* century that holds my interest, though. Right up to the late 1950s this house was the home of the *six* Thompson sisters! Can you imagine? All of them were professional women and two were involved with the suffragette movement. Margaret Thompson had three spells of imprisonment with Mrs Pankhurst and Mrs Pethwick-Lawrence between 1909 and 1912.

Further up Lambeth Street there's something really extraordinary: a fairly lengthy stretch of 'crinkle crankle' walling. There are other examples elsewhere in the county - so it isn't *literally* unique - but it *is* a style of brickwork that many of us will not have seen before today. As well as giving a pleasing appearance, the design - which uses a serpentine plan and presents an elevation of fairly massive vertical corrugations - gives great strength from a wall that's only one brick thick. Behind the wall is a house which dates from 1811. It was occupied from 1963 to 1970 by Sir Frederick Ashton, the famous dancer, choreographer and Director of the Royal Ballet.

There's so much more to see in the course of the Trail, as one follows the circle of the streets around the focal point of CASTLE HILL, with the ruins at its summit. We may well be side-tracked, I must admit. As it happens, there are four shops that are very much what we usually have in mind. Then there's the EYE THEATRE (Information - 01379 870519), which is located in the converted 18th century Assembly Room of the former White Lion Hotel. The Theatre was re-opened by the present director in 1991 to offer comedy and drama at a reasonable price in the intimate and elegant setting of one of the smallest professional theatres in the country. Meanwhile, there are those shops.

CORNER ANTIQUES (Enquiries - 01379 871439) in Castle Street mainly specialise in porcelain, jewellery, brass, silver, clocks and furniture. Along the way, we'll come to THE TARTAN BOW COUNTRY CURIOS (Enquiries - 01379 783057), a tiny shop which is crammed with kitchen, domestic and rural bygones, in the main. Also in Castle Street we'll find TALENTS (Enquiries - 01379 870888), where two shops in one sell pine furniture, antiques and bric-a-brac together with traditional toys, local craft products and unusual gifts. The final call may well be at GIPPESWICH BOOKS (Enquiries - 01379 871439) - you'll discover the origin of the name a little later in this chapter. It lies next to the Church, has excellent parking facilities, and has good quality second hand and out of print books for sale. Opening hours are 10.30am to 5.00pm, Thursday to Saturday, with 4.30pm closing in winter.

I think this visit to Eye has been an object lesson in not knowing what you're looking for, after miles of driving around, and then finding it in a small town with everything to offer - apart from a famous name. That is what these tours are all about. By the time we switch off the engine at the end of the last tour, we'll have forgotten where we bought half the pictures that stunned us at first glance. We won't have a clue where we found the pots, the ear-rings, the mountains of collectables - but we'll remember the six sisters, the crinkle crankle wall and the ancient Guildhall that spent most of its life as a school. Which is the best kind of memory to take away from anywhere, I would have thought. Cue for departure? Absolutely - but with one local tale to ease us on our way. It's a yarn that's worth the telling, as it sounds so very familiar, even now, one hundred and fifty years after the events took place.

It seems that the railway between Stowmarket and Norwich was meant to go through Eye when it was opened in 1849. Unfortunately, and *typically* one suspects, the local squires refused to have anything to do with this new fangled nonsense on *their* land. The railway company just shrugged its shoulders - and took the trains to Diss, instead. One could say that the squires won, but the *town* lost, judging by the relative levels of prosperity in the two localities today. Don't we *all* know people like them?

While we're in Eye, if we don't feel *too* pushed for time, it sounds a good idea to wander up the odd lane to the neighbouring village of **HOXNE** (pronounced 'Hoxen', if you have to ask the way). From as far back as we go this has been a religious centre, if for no other reason than that the smart money is on the notion that St Edmund was martyred here in 870 AD. Of course, East Anglia being what it is - there also seems to be plenty of marginally *less* smart money on the view that it's all a total nonsense. Whatever - there's a nice little local story that's been built up around the idea that adds a touch of something or other. The King, it is said, tried to shelter under GOLDBROOK BRIDGE from the avenging Danes who meant to do him no good - terminally! As usual, his luck ran out and he was betrayed to his pursuers by a *bridal* party, of all things. While still in possession of his regal head, he laid a heavy curse on the bridge, and to this day it would take a very brave - or very liberated - local girl to cross it on her wedding day. After that kind of malice, no wonder the Danes finished the job!

At this point, if we fancy elevenses al fresco before pressing on along the B1117, there's a very pleasant picnic site close at hand, beside the River Dove, which *has* to be an idyllic note for the next postcard home: "this morning we had coffee and biscuits in the sunshine beside the Dove". If that *is* the mood of the moment, we should head for PENNINGS PICNIC SITE at LUDGATE CAUSEWAY.

The next stretch is a rural ride eastwards through a succession of villages that typify this area. There *are* points of interest to either side of our route, such as WINGFIELD OLD COTTAGE AND GARDENS (Information - 01379 384888) a delightful medieval timber framed great hall, now concealed behind an 18th century facade where there are garden walks, art exhibitions and home-made teas to ensnare us and CHURCH COTTAGE POTTERY (Enquiries - 01379 384523), a small pottery in a thatched cottage setting that produces domestic, garden and decorative pots in terra-cotta and stone ware. Complete with a teashop, it is open between February and December on weekdays - apart from Wednesdays - from 10.00am to 6.00pm and on Sundays from 2.00pm to 6.00pm. Admission is free.

As long as we keep going and don't get distracted by thoughts of pots and pictures, we'll come eventually, by way of the B1117, to **HEVENINGHAM** - pronounced 'Henningham', to sort out the sheep and goats - where the 18th century HALL provides us with a second chance to marvel at crinkle crankle walls. At which point we discover that, elsewhere in the county, there are *43 more* examples of this way of doing things - which is so peculiar to Suffolk - if we really want to get obsessive! Some of the finest work by James Wyatt that's still surviving is the main cause for joy inside the building. In particular, the ENTRANCE HALL, with its semi-circular vaulted ceiling, and the DINING ROOM, restored to the original plan after a fire in 1949, are truly stunning examples of his style.

The Hall overlooks a fine area of parkland laid out by Capability Brown. The gardens have an orangery as well as 'that wall' - which is even more massive in appearance than the one at Eye. I wonder how many gardens in Horsham, Newark, Aberdovey and Kilmarnock - not to mention Amiens, Little Rock, Kyoto and Kuala Lumpur, if the book goes global - will have a touch of crinkle crankle within a twelvemonth of the end of this tour?

Eased along by such schemes and dreams, we'll find the journey to **HALESWORTH**, still along the B1117, passes in no time. The next thing we know, we're parking ourselves near the town centre. Another market town blessed with bustle and business, Halesworth lies in an area of genuine - as opposed to synthesised - rural charm; complete, I'm glad to say, with the odd rough edge to give it authenticity. Clearly, the MARKET itself is worth inspecting, but there are also plenty of buildings of architectural interest, dating from the Middle Ages as well as from the Tudor, Stuart, Georgian and Victorian periods. The impressive Tudor RECTORY and the GOTHIC HOUSE, with its splendid carvings, can be found just off the ancient, winding THOROUGHFARE. At STEEPLE END, a row of Elizabethan ALMSHOUSES are to be found and these are now home to the town's ART GALLERY, where exhibits include sculpture, paintings, ceramics and textiles. The HALESWORTH AND DISTRICT

MUSEUM occupies another part of the same building and amongst its displays are items that suggest that parts of the town were actually settled at least 10,000 years ago.

Halesworth nestles in a hollow, a feature which, with its traffic free centre, makes for a pleasant and cosy environment for shopping. There's an excellent cross-section of retail outlets within the compass of a few attractive old streets - and the antique dealers, in particular, will repay some close attention. To complete the many attractions of this delightful area, I must mention the golf. There's a fine course to the south of the town and one could certainly recommend a round to soothe the withdrawals which have had next to no treatment for what seems like an age.

Heading almost due north out of Halesworth, touching the A144 to add impetus, we come to **BUNGAY**. It could be that the rather strange name comes from a French source: 'bonque' means 'good ford' while 'le bon eye' means a spit of land that juts out into a river. In this case, either would fit.

There's been quite a bit of recycling of the castle ruins over the years, with lumps of its masonry cropping up in alley walls and wherever else it could be put to use. These days there's little more to be seen, apart from some fragments. A fire in 1688 burnt down most of the original houses and even melted the bells of ST MARY'S CHURCH. To find the most pleasing streets, from our point of view, one needs to go beyond the churchyard to the land above the River Waveney. As we do so, it's worth noting that there are claims that the BUNGAY STONE, to the west of the north porch, is a Druid relic. Another connection with the stranger and more mystical aspects of East Anglia's past is found in the town sign: the castle, forked lightening and a black dog. Remember 'Black Shuck'? We first heard that tale up on the North Norfolk coast but it's said by some in *these* parts that the dog on the sign is the very same creature - who's not to be taken lightly, even this far South.

The town has a MUSEUM (Enquiries - 01986 892176) in BROAD STREET, where aspects of local history are displayed including coins, pictures and photographs. The Museum is open throughout the year from Monday to Friday between 9.00am and 1.00pm and 2.00pm to 4.00pm. The admission charge is 50p. To put some flesh of reality on the bones of the Museum's information, there's a TOWN TRAIL that reveals much of the history of this attractive old market town, with a special place reserved for the 13th century BIGOD'S CASTLE, which in its heyday dominated the area from its elevated position overlooking the river near the town centre. Admission to the castle is free, but keys need to be collected from local key holders whose names are on a notice at the site. It's open daily between 9.00am and 6.00pm. If you plan to look over the ruins as part of your walk, there's an informative leaflet available from local shops. Two obvious bonuses come out of our walk: we get the measure of the shops themselves and we learn something about Bungay's other PARISH CHURCH - HOLY TRINITY. Dating back to about 1000AD, it features a Saxon round tower which was added some forty years later.

Shopping on Market Day (Thursday) is all we've come to expect, as enthusiastic crowds gather around the town's 17th century BUTTER CROSS, which is surmounted by a figure of 'Justice', made from lead. There are many specialist shops to be discovered too, including a jewellery workshop, and NURSEY'S, a large leatherwork shop. Founded in 1790, today it produces a wide range of hand stitched sheepskin coats, mittens and hats. To round off the visit, a tour of Bungay's wealth of antique shops has to be seen as a necessity.

Before leaving the town altogether, it might be wise to offer a trace more lip service to the zeal of the golfers and even go so far as to tune up their anticipation with a foretaste of what the next town has to offer, as well. At Bungay, it's the BUNGAY AND WAVENEY VALLEY GOLF CLUB (Enquiries - 01986 892337) that seems very likely to offer a satisfying round or two. Somewhat further along our way we'll come to BECCLES GOLF CLUB (Enquiries - 01502 712244), for those who can wait that long. Those who can't will probably try for rounds at *both* venues - and never be seen again, on this tour, at least! Meanwhile, I feel redeemed: having spent days, or so it seemed, somewhere near Cambridge, without an iron or a putter so much as seeing the light of day, we have to some extent made up the lost ground. Figuratively speaking, my handicap, in guidebook terms, should be back to nought; while our corporate optimism should know no bounds (credibility is everything in this business, I always find).

As always around these parts, the last visit never really *is* the last. There's always just one more thing - and one more and one more - I wonder if we can make this the very last for the area around Bungay. 'This' is the NORFOLK AND SUFFOLK AVIATION MUSEUM (Enquiries - 01986 896644) at **FLIXTON**. Open between April and September (at times that vary with the month, so phone before your visit), this attraction features an excellent selection of World War I and II memorabilia, while the aircraft displayed include a DH Vampire TII, a Gloster Meteor F8 and a replica Supermarine Spitfire. The Museum is a member of the British Aircraft Preservation Council.

Now we turn almost due east, for a short run along more of the B1062. This takes us through two or three pleasant little villages, and brings us swiftly enough to BECCLES (Information - 01502 713196), a mellow old town best seen from the River Waveney and its tow paths. The river is still tidal at this point and part of the Broadland network. Gardens run down to the water, whose course is marked with a succession of boat-houses and landing-stages. The water side meadows are dominated by the 14th century detached bell tower of ST MICHAEL'S CHURCH which stands 97ft high and houses a peal of ten bells.

It was at St Michael's, in 1749, that Catherine Suckling married the Reverend Edward Nelson, little realising, one must suppose, that she would give birth to a son Horatio, destined to be one of her country's greatest naval heroes. For our part it's interesting to find the famous name cropping up for at least the fourth time in our travels. Another of Beccles' truly notable buildings is ROOS HALL, a distinguished, red-brick manor, typical of many similar structures that we've seen - in every respect bar one. It is said to be one of the most haunted houses in England! On Christmas Eve, so one story goes, a coach drawn by phantom horses and driven by a headless coachman pulls up at the front door.

Beccles has two museums. The WILLIAM CLOWES PRINT MUSEUM (Information - 01502 712884) in NEWGATE, tells the story of the development of printing from 1800, with displays of machinery, woodcuts, books and so forth. Entry is free and the Museum is open between June and August, from Monday to Friday, between 2.00pm and 4.00pm, with guided tours available by arrangement. At LEMAN HOUSE, in BALLYGATE, the BECCLES AND DISTRICT MUSEUM houses many local history exhibits, including a printing press that dates from the 19th century, farm implements, wherrying material, 19th century costume and the original Beccles town sign. This Museum is open from April to October, on Tuesday, Sundays and Bank Holidays, between 2.30pm and 5.00pm and admission is free. The town has many fine shops. These include BRADLEY'S workshop, where hand blown crystal is produced, an antiquarian bookshop, antique dealers and several craft shops.

After Beccles, it's main road motoring up the A143, all the way to **LOWESTOFT** (Information - 01502 523000), the most easterly town in Britain, with LOWESTOFT NESS as the most easterly point. The town is justifiably famed for the quality of its beaches, and will be a kind of symbolic gateway to the next phase of this tour, which will focus on the Suffolk coastline, in the main, all the way down to Felixstowe and Ipswich. We'll make the odd sortie inland, from time to time, but most of the way our gaze will be set firmly on the sea. Unless we're actually *driving*, of course!

It's a well nigh irresistible temptation to draw parallels between Yarmouth and Lowestoft, the Norfolk and Suffolk variations on a similar theme: holidays, herrings and the harbour. In practice the two mixes have turned out to be very different.

Fishing has been the major industry in the town since the middle of the last century, with local fortunes rising and falling with the herring catches. As we found in Yarmouth, the herring boom peaked just before the First World War, when over seven hundred drifters were based at Lowestoft. In recent years, overfishing has led to a decline in the herring catch and now fishermen struggle to make a living based on other species. One consequence of this shift has been the decimation of the fishing fleet to fewer than fifty motor trawlers.

Wide sandy beaches are another feature that Lowestoft has in common with its neighbour to the north, as is the Broadland element that lies behind it to the west. The treatment of both, I suspect, has been somewhat different - possibly because of the impact of oil and gas finds on Yarmouth, as much as anything else. In 1997, all three 'Sunrise Coast resorts' - Lowestoft, Kessinglan and Southwold - won the Tidy Britain

Group Seaside Awards, which are granted to beaches with the highest levels of cleanliness and safety. For a 'resort' beach such as Lowestoft South Beach to gain the award, bathing water must achieve a mandatory quality, while 29 other land based criteria, including management, cleansing, safety information and education must be met. In the case of 'rural' beaches, such as Lowestoft North Beach and Kessingland, eight land based criteria must be met. To complete the quality of the amenities at one end of the spectrum is the provision of a full lifeguard service between May and September; at the other is the rule banning dogs from the beach during the same period.

With a mixture of interests, Lowestoft seems to be pretty successful. Incomes from shipping, holiday making and fishing have made the town into a thriving centre whose atmosphere and character have an exhilarating quality. Somehow the local people have found a way of blending the possibilities in their location in a way that always has a positive air about it. For example, whereas the post war herring decline virtually finished Yarmouth's fishing industry, in Lowestoft the tapered down fleet, having turned its attention to white fish, went on to become the country's leading source of plaice. The fleet is reduced in numbers, but what is left has a strong base; the fish dock has been modernised and is also one of the best in the country.

SOUTH TOWN is where most of the holiday trade is located, with hotels and boarding houses along the South front. The sandy SOUTH BEACH, which is patrolled by lifeguards in summer, lies to the south of the harbour's SOUTH PIER. Swimming is generally safe as long as one keeps clear of the harbour itself. Still with more conventional holidaying in mind, we might take note of the amusement arcades on both the South Pier and CLAREMONT PIER, along with the summer theatre - but no 'pleasure beach', no 'golden mile'! Disappointed?

This 'resort' part of Lowestoft was largely set out by Sir Samuel Martin Peto in the 19th century. Even then, the town seems to have gone for 'quality', as it was Sir Samuel's firm who built Nelson's Column and the Houses of Parliament. His links with the town were forged in the 1840s when he built a railway to allow fish fresh from the market to be delivered to Manchester.

The trawler harbour and commercial docks are north of the bascule bridge that spans the narrow strip of water - LAKE LOTHING - which, otherwise, divides the town. The two halves of the bridge are raised to admit large merchant ships into the very heart of the area which includes the old town that was so badly damaged by bombs in the Second World War. Also nearby are the lighthouse and the very fine little MARITIME MUSEUM, which is packed with momentos of the herring fishing industry. This part of Lowestoft has a remarkable set of parallel lanes which run down steeply from the HIGH STREET to the level of the foreshore and which are known as 'SCORES'. The name was probably coined as a comment on the way they seem to have been 'scoured' or cut away from between the other buildings.

Whereas the main part of the port, including its dry dock and shipyard, lies upstream and is mainly involved in the grain and timber trades, the outer harbour is the location for the YACHT CLUB and the LIFEBOAT STATION, the latter being something of a monument to Lowestoft's tradition for dour courage; the *actual* monument - to the men of the Royal Naval Patrol Service who "have no graves but the sea", stands in gardens near the lighthouse. The Lifeboat Station itself was founded in 1801, 23 years *before* the Royal National Lifeboat Institution was established! A further reminder of this tradition is found nowadays in the SPARROW'S NEST (Enquiries - 01502 514402), a park which has become a local centre for entertainment, and is named after one of the Station's founders. The Maritime Museum is located here, as are a cafe, bar and other facilities.

At **CARLTON COLVILLE**, two miles to the west of Lowestoft, we'll find the EAST ANGLIA TRANSPORT MUSEUM (Enquires - 01502 518459) in CHAPEL ROAD. This is one of the country's most amazing attractions as far as its variety goes - but, more to the point, in terms of the way in which all the exhibits have been presented. Working trams and trolley buses are seen in the setting of a reconstructed 1930s street; the narrow gauge railway, battery powered vehicles, buses, lorries and cars are displayed in ways that convey the context in which they would have operated. Admission, which includes *all* the rides is a mere three quid! Which must rate as the bargain of the Millenium - eat your heart out Alton Towers! Opening times vary enormously throughout the year - or so it seems to me - so a prior phone call is advisable to ease the pain.

The other Lowestoft Museums are all within the town boundary. We've mentioned the Maritime Museum already and, while we're there, we could do a lot worse than call in at the ROYAL NAVAL PATROL SERVICE MUSEUM (Information - 01502 586250) also in Sparrow's Nest, where ship models, naval documents, uniforms, photographs and certificates add a further commemoration to those of the Service who lost their lives. The museum is open between 16th May and 17th October and between 2.00pm and 4.30pm. Sunday opening is between 2.00pm and 4.30pm and admission is free.

Again out of town, the LOWESTOFT MUSEUM (Information - 01502 511457) is located at OULTON BROAD. This inland stretch of water, fed by the River Waveney, is very popular with both the sailing and angling fraternities - occasionally to the mutual discomfort of both at peak times, when their interests aren't exactly identical. It is reached from Lowestoft via Lake Lothing and a lock. There's a certain amount of parking at THE BOULEVARD, just to the south of the Broad, which gives access to NICHOLAS EVERITT PARK, a good place for boat watching or just for enjoying a stroll. For those who fancy a trip on the River Waveney, or who'd enjoy hiring a boat, there are facilities for both at this point on the river bank.

The Museum is in BROAD HOUSE, which is also in the Park. It's displays embrace local and domestic history, Lowestoft porcelain, archaeology and geology, and extends to include fossils, flints and medieval artefacts from field searches. It is generally open between April and November, but a prior phone call would be helpful to be sure of the exact days and times. Admission is free, although donations are always appreciated.

Another pleasant trip from Lowestoft could be out to SOMERLEYTON HALL (Enquiries - 01502 730224), which was rebuilt in the 1840s in the Anglo Italian style. The Hall has fine state rooms, period furnishings and some splendid paintings. The gardens are renowned in their own right, particularly for the famous maze. To complete the visit there's a tea room and a picnic area. Guided tours are available by prior arrangement but the general opening hours, between Easter and September are on Thursdays, Sundays and Bank Holidays between 1.30pm and 5.00pm with the addition of Tuesdays and Wednesdays in July and August, although the tea rooms and gardens open from 12.30pm.

Back in the town again - and I'm sorry if we seem to be boomeranging around this neck of North Suffolk, but it does seem to trigger off an awful lot of impulses - let's turn to some of Lowestoft's festive occasions. There are several local fetes and fairs culminating in June with the LOWESTOFT FISH FAYRE AND CLASSIC CAR RALLY, which incorporates a huge range of outdoor events. At this time, too, are the MARITIME WEEK and the LOWESTOFT SMACK RACE. Then there's a SEAFRONT FESTIVAL in July, the CARNIVAL, during the first week in August, and a little way out of the town, the HENHAM STEAM RALLY and the SOMERLEYTON HORSE TRIALS, during September. Couple all these with the local events in the neighbouring towns and villages, from the BUNGAY BEER FESTIVAL in October to the BECCLES CARNIVAL at the end of July, and quite clearly there never *is* a dull moment!

As we'd expect, out and out physical activities get quite an airing, too. Because of the ever present demand, let's start with golf. Lowestoft has its own nine hole pitch and putt at DIP FARM (Enquiries - 01502 513322). Over at Carlton Colville, the ROOKERY PARK GOLF CLUB (Enquiries - 01502 560380) has a full eighteen hole course. Further afield, don't forget the clubs at Beccles and Bungay that we've visited already, should you choose to take a break based on Lowestoft and wish to vary the settings for your games. Other facilities include swimming - and all the usual range of more punishing forms of exercise - at the WAVENEY SPORTS AND LEISURE CENTRE (Information - 01502 569116 in WATER LANE, and tennis at NORMANSTON PARK (Information - 01502 565340) and at KENSINGTON GARDENS (Information - 01502 573731). This is good cycling country and, if you forgot the mountain bikes, the SUFFOLK CYCLE CENTRE (Information - 01502 585968) offer bike hire as one of their many features. Of course, if you want a more leisurely and traditional taste of Suffolk leisure pursuits, then there is archery, from BEAR BOW ARCHERY (Information - 01502 589469) and horse riding from PARKFIELD RIDING SCHOOL (Information - 01502 572257).

After our tour of the Broad we ease back into the town to pick up the A12 for the journey south, parallel to the coast. As we leave it's worth casting an eye up to the weather vane of ST MARGARET'S CHURCH, the first object in Britain to be touched by the rays of the morning sun! Amazing! Our route takes us first through **PAKEFIELD**, a southern extension, in a sense, of Lowestoft proper, with a sand and shingle beach below grassy banks. ST MARGARET AND ALL SAINTS CHURCH originates from the 14th century and was two churches in one until 1748, when the two parishes, with their two rectors, were combined. The church was badly bomb damaged in the War, but has been rebuilt since.

This is caravan and bungalow country, not to mention the holiday camps, so we shan't be tempted to dally as we move down the coast towards **KESSINGLAND**, home of the SUFFOLK WILDLIFE PARK (Information - 01502 740291). Advertised as 'a walk on the wild side', the park is set in a hundred acres of coastal parkland and has a wide range of species in residence, from lions and cheetahs to lemurs, giraffes, otters and aardvarks. There are even snake handling sessions to help visitors become better acquainted with Burmese pythons. The Park is open daily from 10.00am, except on Christmas and Boxing Days. A phone call is suggested for further details and prices of admission.

SUFFOLK WILDLIFE PARK

South of Kessingland the coast adopts a more tranquil quality, mainly because the road sweeps inland making access to the water more difficult. At BENACRE NESS, for example, it takes a one and a half mile walk down a road that is closed to cars to reach the shingle headland. This is the second most easterly point in England after Lowestoft Ness, and is not a place for swimming as the currents sweeping past the point are at least as dangerous as one might imagine.

We can loop back towards the sea from the village of **WRENTHAM** to call in at **COVEHITHE**, which is remarkable for the ruined ST ANDREWS CHURCH. Within the roofless and windowless nave of the original 15th century building is a much smaller, thatched church, built in 1672 when the parishioners decided that the original was too large for their needs. It's a lonely, dramatic spot between heath land and the beach but there is no access to the sand and shingle for some distance, because of the dangerous state of the cliffs. There *is* a footpath just across from the church, however, which crosses the heath to a point where one can see across to the distant roofs of Southwold, which will be our next goal.

The whole coastline from Kessingland to Felixstowe has been invaded by Romans, Angles and Danes - almost as a way of life until the Normans arrived and put an end to that sort of nonsense. The nearest anyone else came to more bother was in 1672, when the Dutch fleet confronted a combined French and English fleet off Covehithe at the Battle of Sole Bay. The Dutch were eventually beaten off after a bitter struggle. There have been no more human incursions since then - but the sea itself has more than made up for that. The shelly sand is no match for the combination of tides and vicious storms whose assaults have removed whole towns over the years. On the plus side, beach-combing is often rewarding in such circumstances: occasional pieces of amber have been found along with many samples of cornelian. Meanwhile, because of the relentless erosion, it's never made any sense to run a continuous road along the shore, so separate roads feed out to the coastal towns and villages from the main A122, until one reaches the southern end where it's possible to ease out of Woodbridge and take a series of lesser 'A' and 'B' roads as far as Blythburgh.

SOUTHWOLD (Information - 01502 724729) is one of England's favourite seaside resorts and one of the jewels of the SUFFOLK HERITAGE COAST, the largely unspoilt and often lonely area of shingle, sand, marsh, heath and crumbling cliffs that has been left almost untouched by the modern world because of the siting of the main roads inland, away from erosion. Another factor affecting the siting of these roads has been the presence of estuaries which wind in leisurely loops and also force lines of communication away from the sea. In short, Nature has provided Suffolk with a wonderful chance to take a breather from the pressures of 20th century life and this coast is tailor made for lovers of peace, quiet and wide open spaces - not to mention walking, sailing, bird watching, sea food and real ale.

The special character of Southwold stems from the informal groupings of houses around a series of pleasant greens; a planning decision that was taken after a devastating fire in 1659 destroyed much of the original, congested little town. Today's elegance is founded on 17th century rebuilding and Victorian extension and embellishment. GUN HILL and NORTH PARADE overlook rows of perky beach huts from striking Victorian terraces and the whole is reminiscent of the traditional English seaside as it was before the First World War.

Southwold is built on what amounts to an island as it is cut off to the north by Buss Creek and to the south by the last mile or so of the River Blyth, which is lined by boatyards and huts selling fresh fish. The sandy beach is, as one might expect, safe for swimming as long as one keeps away from the mouth of the harbour.

SOUTHWOLD

The PARISH CHURCH OF ST EDMUND is one of the finest in Suffolk, with a superb painted screen that dates from around 1500 - and managed to escape both Henry VIII's and Cromwell's bouts of vandalism. The Church is also home to 'Southwold Jack', the 15th century figure of a man at arms, carved from oak, and carrying a sword and battle-axe, which strikes a bell at the pull of a cord to signal the start of services and the entry of the bride at a wedding.

The other features of Southwold relate to its streetscape and to a traditional occupation that *doesn't*, for once, relate to the sea - the former connects strongly with the latter, as we'll see. In the introduction to this chapter, I mentioned the horse drawn drays that deliver beer from ADNAMS BREWERY. While they might look a little odd in some contemporary settings we've seen, they look absolutely right in this town with their magnificent pairs of percheron horses taking the brewery's products in such a sedate and dignified manner along streets lined with red brick and flint cottages and colour washed houses.

Southwold has three museums amongst its range of attractions. The TOWN MUSEUM (Information - 01502 722437) in VICTORIA STREET houses an impressive range of items relating to the history, natural history, geology, and archaeology of the area along with exhibits of domestic bygones, memorabilia, photographs and posters. It is open daily from Easter to September between 2.30pm and 4.30pm and also between 11.00am. and 12.30pm in August. Admission is free.

There is a small LIFEBOAT MUSEUM (Information - 01502 723600) on Gun Hill, with a collection of items relating to the Lifeboat Service in general and to Southwold in particular. Opening hours are from 2.30pm to 4.30 pm between the Spring Bank Holiday and September, although a phone call is recommended to confirm the details. Admission is free. Down on EAST STREET, the town's third museum is located in the SOUTHWOLD SAILORS' READING ROOM, a charitable institution founded and built in 1864. On display are maritime exhibits including pictures, models of ships and figureheads. The Reading Room is open throughout the year between 9.00am and 5.00pm and admission is free, although donations are always much appreciated.

It wouldn't be right to leave Southwold without some kind of nautical interlude and, with this in mind, OSPREY BOAT TRIPS (Information - 01502 722287) deserve a recommendation. Between May and September, for a modest fee, a range of pre-booked voyages are available on the River Blyth, from 11.00am to 5.00pm. As a guide-line, a fiver will buy you a two hour trip, which could include bird watching and time for a picnic.

Across the estuary of the Blyth, as we'll see from the boat, lies the village of **WALBERSWICK -** and that's as close as we'll get without making the eight mile journey inland to Blythburgh and out again. I leave the choice to you as regards this detour: the place certainly merits a visit, but your time may be too pressing for all the extra driving involved.

This village was once a busy port but is now popular with small boat sailors. It's river shore is muddy and subject to strong currents but the actual beach which lies at the end of an unmade road is sandy and offers safe swimming. Inland there is a pleasant residential community with large houses and well kept gardens.

On, then, to **BLYTHBURGH,** where the scale and magnificence of the CHURCH OF THE HOLY TRINITY - 'The Cathedral of the Marshes' - is sure to stop us dead in our tracks. When it was built, in the 15th century, the town was an important place with a busy quay beside the River Blyth where merchants, who had grown rich through the Suffolk wool trade, went about their business. Unfortunately, as we have seen elsewhere, the ships grew bigger while the Blyth silted up - and the rest is history. Today's village is all that is left of the once thriving urban community, where the church is the overwhelming point of interest.

Cromwell's men did their worst to the interior - but they passed and were all but forgotten. Although some of the marks of their passing remain the true glories of the place are undiminished by the senseless time of desecration. Meanwhile, the building still gives passers by food for thought as it towers above the common and the mud flats beloved of so many water birds and wild fowl.

A detour from the B1125 would take us into **DUNWICH** which was also a large port in medieval times - and a bishopric, with many monasteries and abbeys. King John gave the borough its charter - but the sea had little respect for any of it. Today, the many religious buildings are fathoms deep, as they say, with the last - All Saints Church - going over the eroding cliffs during the course of this century. All that is left - unless that's gone since I last saw the place - is a solitary gravestone near the edge of the cliff.

Erosion of the cliffs was not the only reason for the demise of Dunwich. Although the Norman inhabitants had generally managed to keep the waters at bay with fairly simple defence measures, the storm in January 1326 made a total mockery of their efforts. During just one night, a million tons of sand and shingle were dumped across the mouth of the harbour, diverting the River Blyth, cutting the port off from the sea and, to all intents and purposes, killing off trade. People moved away, Dunwich was left to the elements, which made the most of it, and by 1677 the sea was lapping across the market place. The MUSEUM (Information - 01728 648796) tells the history of the town and pays particular attention to its disappearance beneath the waves. It is open daily between March and October although opening times are best checked by a phone call. Admission is free.

On a more positive note, south of Dunwich lies one of Britain's best known RSPB reserves, at MINSMERE. This 1500 acre expanse at the mouth of the Minsmere River is home to more than a hundred species of birds within its mixed habitat of reed beds, artificial lagoons and islands as well as heath and woodland - in fact, it shelters the widest range of breeding birds of any reserve in the country. Shore-birds can be observed from a big public hide that lies along the coast from the National Trust car park, on DUNWICH HEATH. To visit the main reserve, we need permits from the Reception Centre and information regarding times and dates from the RSPB.

At this point we could take a look at SIZEWELL, not being too interested in Nuclear power we decided to turn inland, and a look at LEISTON ABBEY (Information - 10728 830764) a magnificent ruin to the right of the B1122 which dates from the 14th century. The brick and flint remains are quite extensive and extend to the transepts, presbytery and lady chapel. Inside the ruins stands a Georgian House which is used as a religious retreat. Much of the village of **LEISTON** itself was built in the 19th century by Richard Garrett, whose company designed and built the Garrett railway engine.

From Leiston, we stay on the B1122 and head south east, noting as we do that the eccentricities of **THORPENESS**, a holiday village laid out before the First World

War by dramatist and author Glencairn Stuart Ogilvie around a specially dug 65 acre lake, will be worth a visit at a later date, when we have more time. For now we need all the time we can spare for **ALDEBURGH** (Information - 01728 453537).

This flourishing town, with its fine hotels and a pleasant mixture of street scapes, managed to survive the destruction of its medieval ship building and fishing industries by the sea to become one of Suffolk's - and England's - cultural centres. The poet George Crabbe was born in Aldeburgh in 1754 and his best known poem, 'The Borough', which describes the harshness of the daily round for the local people, was the source of inspiration for Benjamin Britten's opera 'Peter Grimes', which is set in the town. By way of another one of those total contrasts, Elizabeth Garrett Anderson, Britain's first woman doctor, has Aldeburgh connections beyond those of her professional and private life. She became the country's first woman mayor, too - here, in this very town.

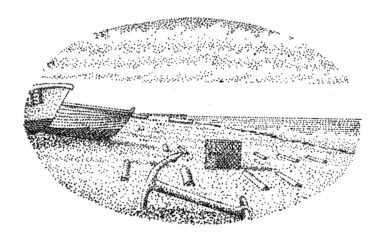

THE BEACH, ALDEBURGH

Crabbe and Britten weren't the only creative spirits to forge strong links with this locality. M.R.James and Wilkie Collins both had a love for its nature and atmosphere as did Kathleen Hale, the author of the series of children's books that focussed on the doings of Orlando, the Marmalade Cat. In fact, her story, 'A Seaside Holiday', is set in 'Owlbarrow on Sea' which, by its easily recognisable features and characters, is to be identified with Aldeburgh. E.M.Forster regularly visited his friends Benjamin Britten and the singer, Peter Pears here, while Sir Laurens van der Post wrote regularly in the southern lookout tower, which was close to his home in the town. Ruth Rendell is associated with the area too, as are many famous painters, including Turner and John Piper.

Aldeburgh became a seaside town in the early 19th century but it was the creation, in 1848, of its annual MUSIC FESTIVAL, held in June, which brought it into the limelight. By the time he died, Britten had been directing the Festival for thirty years - he is commemorated in the CHURCH OF ST PETER AND ST PAUL by a memorial window designed by John Piper, while a memorial to Crabbe is on a nearby wall.

Out of the Festival grew the SNAPE MALTINGS (Information - 01728 688303/ 5), a magnificent red brick Victorian complex originally built for the barley industry on the bank of the River Alde but largely converted since 1967. The first development was a CONCERT HALL for the Festival, but following a devastating fire in 1969 (and restoration in 1970), the Maltings Complex now extends to the inclusion of a tea shop, art gallery, craft centre - and the BRITTEN-PEARS SCHOOL FOR ADVANCED MUSICAL STUDIES, named after the composer and his fellow supporter in the cause of the Festival. The Maltings are open all year, daily from 10.00am to 5.00pm in summer and to 5.00pm in winter. Naturally there are other concerts throughout the year in addition to the June Festival.

Aldeburgh has at least as many other attractions as one could possibly predict for a community of its size. For example, there's the MOOT HALL MUSEUM, that we mentioned a couple of chapters ago, situated in a Tudor building and still used as the TOWN HALL. The COUNCIL CHAMBER, featured in the opening scene of 'Peter Grimes', contains maps and paintings of the neighbourhood. Other rooms house further paintings and photographs; displays of local birds, butterflies and moths; exhibits of fishing techniques and coastal erosion and objects from the SNAPE SHIP BURIAL, which are even older than those from the more famous Sutton Hoo. The Museum is open from Easter to October, at weekends, between 2.30pm and 5.00pm. From June to the end of September this is extended to daily opening between 2.30pm and 5.30pm, with morning opening, as well, from 10.30am to 12.30pm in July and August. Admission is 45p. Aldeburgh has two sailing clubs, an eighteen hole and a nine hole heathland golf course, tennis and bowls facilities and a small independent cinema. It also has an interest in model yachts! The BOATING LAKE is situated on MOOT GREEN, while model yachts can be bought in the newsagents and gift shops. Which brings us, naturally enough, to the town's considerable potential for shopping in general.

There's everything you might expect amongst a wide range of local businesses, so I'll just pick out the odd one or two of special interest - with my customary apologies to all the rest. First off, there's THOMPSON'S GALLERY (Enquiries - 01728 453743), in the HIGH STREET, which offers a fine selection of Victorian oils, water colours, modern British and contemporary paintings, sculpture and furniture. Then there are the ALDEBURGH GALLERIES (Enquiries - 01728 453963), also in the High Street, home to an antiques and collectables centre. Further along the street is the AMBER SHOP (Enquiries - 01728 4524310), which reflects the finds that I mentioned earlier and is Britain's oldest and largest specialist amber shop. Finally and somewhat inevitably, also in the High Street is the ALDEBURGH BOOKSHOP (Enquiries - 01728 452389), which has a large range and is able to obtain special orders often within twenty four hours.

The River Alde, its banks bedecked with small boats, cuts in tight behind the yacht club and divides the mainland from ORFORD NESS, an incredibly long marshy spit, before joining the Rive Ore. On its way to HAVERGATE ISLAND, a nesting place for avocets, it passes **ORFORD** on its west bank.

The winding road to this attractive little village passes through the ancient STAVERTON FOREST and the 14th century gate-house of BUTLEY PRIORY before bringing us to a small square amidst mellow houses with a road leading down to its quay. The near perfect and quite stunning keep of ORFORD CASTLE (Information - 01394 450472) is a tribute to the days when the village enjoyed rather more importance than it does today. Henry II built the Castle in 1165 to keep the wealthy, free spirited East Anglians in order - and also with a view to the defence of this stretch of coast. The Castle is open daily from 10.00am to 6.00pm between 1st. April and 30th September and from 10.00am to 6.00pm between 1st. October and 31st March. It is closed on Christmas, Boxing and New Year's Days and admission costs £2.60.

The National Trust now owns a large part of Orford Ness, which is the largest feature of its kind in Europe. This spit of land saw use as a top secret military testing area during both World Wars but is now a haven for bird lovers along with the nearby RSPB sanctuary at Havergate Island. The existence of the Ness and the Island have led to the setting up of a very pleasant river cruise attraction on board the 'Lady Florence' (Enquiries - 0831 698298 Mobile) Sailings are available throughout the year, with brunch, lunch or dinner - and a bar and open fire in winter to add to the delights. To reach the Ness from Orford means taking "PUFFIN" FERRY from Orford Quay (Enquiries - 01364 45007). The ferry runs other trips on the River Ore, while the "Regardless" (Enquiries - 01364 450884) offers trips around the RSPB sanctuary at Havergate.

These are the 'special' attractions of time spent in Orford, attractions which relate to its unique situation and geography. There is more, though! Wouldn't you just *know* it? Above ORFORD CRAFTS (Enquiries - 01364 450678) on FRONT STREET, is the SUFFOLK UNDERWATER STUDIES CENTRE (Same phone number). Covering the Suffolk coastline, displays show the underwater exploration of a number of major marine sites, especially medieval Dunwich.

That's more or less it, apart from GALLERY GIFTS (Enquiries - 01364 450420) and CASTLE ANTIQUES (Enquiries - 01364 450100) and several rather special places to eat - with seafood, particularly Orford Fish and Chips, seeming to be a local 'must try'. All in all, another bit of Suffolk's best balanced approach, is Orford.

ORFORD CASTLE

From Orford we turn north west and head via the B1078 to the A12 for the last leg of this stage which takes us in a big pear shaped loop through three more classic Suffolk towns, before we return to the coast at Felixstowe. Unfairly, perhaps, we'll only have time for a cursory glance at **SAXMUNDHAM**, before we turn inland and arrive, by way of the B1119, at **FRAMLINGHAM.**

This market town is dominated by another CASTLE (Information - 01728 724189), which is also classed as an ancient monument. Built in the 12th century, it is one of the finest examples of a curtain walled castle in the country, and much of it has been preserved and partly restored, including a walk linking nine of the towers and an outer bailey. Opening times are the same as at Orford. The helmet of Thomas Howard, made Duke of Norfolk after defeating the Scots at Flodden, is in the CHURCH, as are the tombs of the Howard family. The building itself has several notable features which include an unusual wall painting dating from 1400, a splendid hammer beam roof and the Tamar Organ, which was built in 1674. More details of its history are given on information boards, although the point is well made that it is primarily a place of worship, and not another museum.

The street scene is ideal for our interests, consisting as it does of a rich selection of shops selling art and craft work and antiques in a variety of settings amidst pleasant side streets. All in all one would have to say that Framlingham is almost ideal for 'trail type' exploration. With this very much in mind, the Town Council has produced a remarkable leaflet on the subject, copies of which are available from the Tourist Information Centres at Southwold and Lowestoft. There are no less than 28 points of interest listed, including the Castle and ranging from the Parish Church to FRAMLINGHAM COLLEGE MERE, owned by the College and managed by the Suffolk Wildlife Trust as a delightful nature reserve. Then there are the ALMSHOUSES, the GUILDHALL, the LANMAN MUSEUM, the late 17th century timber framed ANCIENT HOUSE, QUEEN'S HEAD ALLEY and THE COURT HOUSE. This is, in short, one Trail that shouldn't be overlooked.

Framlingham's history has centred on the Castle since 1100 AD. It was the seat of the Earls and Dukes of Norfolk, one of the most powerful families in the country - just how powerful can be seen at a glance by visitors, even today. The Town also benefited from the prosperity that accumulated at the Castle, as can be seen in the splendour of its Church and the quality of the architecture on every hand throughout its streets. Around the town there are also several pleasant villages, such as **DENNINGTON** and **PARNHAM**, well worthy of our interest in a return visit.

From Framlingham the B1116 takes us south again, and back to the A12 by means of which, with just a touch of pressure on the loud pedal, we should arrive at **WOODBRIDGE** (Information - 01394 382240) in next to no time. This bustling town is set on sloping ground overlooking the River Deben at one of its prettiest points. It gained its prosperity from the manufacture of sail cloth, rope making and boat building but now it's better known for the construction of yachts, motor cruisers and sailing dinghies. SHIREHALL on MARKET HILL was built by Thomas Seckford in the 16th century, like so many of the local delights. WOODBRIDGE MUSEUM (Enquiries - 01394 380502) has an exhibition reflecting the town's history, including details of the lives of Seckford and Edward Fitzgerald. Also on display is an exhibition that focuses on the Anglo Saxon sites at BURROW HILL and more famously at SUTTON HOO, which is a mile away on the opposite side of the Deben, and was excavated in 1939 to reveal the remains of a Saxon ship and a vast hoard of treasure.

While we're in the Hall, we must just nip upstairs to the SUFFOLK HORSE MUSEUM (Information - 01394 380643), which is dedicated to the story of the oldest breed of heavy working horse in the world - the Suffolk Punch (which, to our great delight, we've seen more than once during the course of these tours). On display are many items relating to the history of the breed and its Society, to the horse's place in Suffolk life, its work and the way it was kept - backed up with examples of harness and of the work of the blacksmith. Finally, there is an account of the steps that have been taken to rescue the breed from near extinction.

WOODBRIDGE

Other points of interest in the town are the attractive shopping environment that's been created amidst a network of narrow streets; WOODBRIDGE TIDE MILL (Enquiries - 01473 626618), a rare example of its type that has been restored to full working order; and BUTTRUM'S MILL (Enquiries - 01473 583352) a 19th century tower mill with particularly fine machinery. Woodbridge is very much a floral Town, too. It has been in the Finals of the 'Britain in Bloom' Competition (small towns category) for the last ten years, consistently winning the 'Anglia in Bloom' title while it was at it - not to mention the 'England in Bloom' award in 1988. With this in mind, a visit to NOTCUTTS GARDEN CENTRE (Enquiries - 01394 445400) on the IPSWICH ROAD should be worth our while, as should the CROWN NURSERY (Enquiries - 01394 460755).

Other opportunities for topping up our various collections seem to relate mainly to the world of fine art. A wide choice is offered by two galleries and a saleroom: the DENNIS TAPLIN GALLERY (Enquiries - 01394 386603), the FRASER GALLERY (Enquiries - 01394 387535) and NEAL SONS AND FLETCHER'S FINE ART SALEROOM (Enquiries - 01394 382263). While we're in Woodbridge, no doubt some of us will want to take even more advantage of the golfing opportunities in this part of the world by trying rounds at either - or both - of the nearby courses. SECKFORD HALL GOLF CLUB (Enquiries - 01394 388000) is at **GT BEALINGS**, while the UFFORD PARK HOTEL (Enquiries - 01394 383555) has a challenging eighteen hole play and pay course that sounds rather beguiling.

From Woodbridge we follow another curve, by way of the A12 and the A14, to return briefly to the sea, as promised, at**FELIXSTOWE** (Information - 01394 276770), another bustling seaside resort, but one that's been transformed, in conjunction with Harwich, by the boom in container traffic to become one of the busiest and largest operations of its kind in Europe. The town became fashionable as a resort after a visit by the German Empress Augusta and her children in 1891 - but there is no legacy of historic mansions, no pretensions, just a large measure of brash good cheer. There *are* sedate Victorian hotels and other architectural features that range from houses of a similar age to modern seafront pavilions and amusement centres.

Felixstowe is located in a gently curved bay between the estuaries of the Deben and the Orwell which has created a two mile long beach of shingle, pebbles and sand. This is backed by a wide promenade with lawns and flower gardens. The MARTELLO TOWER, built as a defensive measure against the French in 1810, is one of the town's oldest buildings; the fort on LANDGUARD POINT was another defence measure, only this time the date is early 16th century. FELIXSTOWE MUSEUM (Information - 01394 277985) is open from Easter to September on Wednesdays, Sundays and Bank Holidays, between 2.00pm and 5.00pm. It contains a wide range of exhibits of local and national historical interest and charges a £1.00 entry fee.

All of which brings us to the run into Ipswich, Suffolk's largest town, and a place that I seem to have found almost worth a chapter in itself. We approach it in a north westerly direction back up the A14, parallel with the Orwell Estuary. We leave the main road before the ORWELL BRIDGE and take the A1156 into FORE STREET, which leads to an encounter that hasn't been - and won't be - repeated anywhere else in this entire book. We're talking about a combination of elements here, each *one* of which we *have* seen but which are not found together anywhere else in the region.

IPSWICH (Information - 01473 258070) is bigger than Norwich - but it has no cathedral and isn't a city. It's even bigger than Cambridge - but was over five hundred years behind in opening a university. If those two snippets sound odd, there are footnotes to both which border on the weird: no Cathedral - but there *are* twelve medieval churches, which is the third greatest number in any one place in the whole of England, after Norwich and York (*both* of which *are* cities). Meanwhile, the brand new UNIVERSITY COLLEGE OF SUFFOLK, which opened for the Autumn Term in 1997, is the first - and only - University in the *whole* of Suffolk. Before it admitted its initial intake, university education was totally unavailable in a county that was the birthplace of Gainsborough, Constable and Thomas Wolsey and beloved of Dickens, Defoe, Munnings and Benjamin Britten. But *not* of counterparts to Isaac Newton, Samuel Pepys, Francis Bacon or Macaulay, one notices. Sounds like a "Catch 22" thing here: the presence of a university seems to be both a magnet *and* a stimulus - but you don't *get* the university without a particular kind of local talent in the first place. Curious.

So we have a great deal of history in Ipswich as in most of East Anglia; a great many churches, as in Norwich; a university - at last - as, again, in Norwich - but we also have a major port, a river estuary and the inescapable influence of the sea, in all its guises. This, as I have suggested, must be unique in our experience. So is it's size - which may mean we need even more good luck than usual to come to grips with it.

Over the first couple of thousand years of the town's history, following that day when an early group of nomads saw the River Orwell's possibilities and set up home, it grew from a Stone Age settlement, via some Iron Age and Roman Action, to an Anglo Saxon town by the name of Gippeswick. Undeterred by that disadvantage (and there's *plenty* in a name: imagine Arsenal v 'Gippeswick' in the Cup Final) the town went downhill even further between 884 and 1069, as waves of Vikings behaved very badly all over it. The last wave - the Danes - stayed put and tried to make it their own. They might have succeeded if King Harold hadn't lost the plot at Hastings after one away fixture too many - also against the Danes - at Stamford Bridge (Lincs not London). The new chap, William the Conqueror, seems to have been rather efficient, for a Frenchman, especially at dealing with objections - from Saxons, Celts, Danes or whoever - so we shouldn't be too surprised to find Ipswich settling down under Norman rule, with precious few tantrums.

The upshot of 'settling' was rather a lot of prosperity. Ipswich had been a port almost forever - certainly since the days of the Romans - and by the time William arrived it was the largest in England. Unless you come from Lincolnshire, of course, in which case you'll claim the title for Boston! In 1200, King John took the point and granted the town a charter, largely because its trading graph looked set to go off the top of the chart. It was the wool trade that created the boom during the Middle Ages and by 1404 Ipswich gained the status of 'Staple port', that is one from which wool could be exported legally. This pleased everyone, as the export of the highly prized Suffolk cloth - and wool - was really a very nice little earner to add to the long term dealings in skins, leather and fish. The graph went even higher, while the rich got richer and built big houses, as they do at such times. This process attracted the attention of Geoffrey Chaucer, who satired the merchants of Ipswich in his 'Canterbury Tales'. As his family had owned a pub in the town it's just possible his words were more about settling scores than objective social comment.

At this point I'm strongly tempted to act on impulse and take time out from peering at the pages of history. D'you fancy a bus ride? It's not that I've taken leave of my senses - far from it. What's suddenly occurred to me is that we'll never get under the skin of this town by trying to do the traditional tourist thing as soon as we park the car. There *is* plenty of scope for sight-seeing but in Ipswich, as I see it, that comes later, as does all the biographical stuff to get us ready for it. It's the port, the Orwell and the way to the open sea that keeps the town's heart beating, as it has done for more than ten centuries. That's where we need to be - now! Before we do anything else. Don't you agree? We had a taste of the kind of thing I have in mind a couple of chapters ago at Boston, when we took a boat trip down the Haven to the Wash. Being a coward from the cradle, I don't fancy another boat on this occasion; there's a lot of water out there and the opposition tend to be very big - kind of inexorable - very busy and very impatient with self drive motor-boats that get in their way. We *could* find a cruise boat - but there's a chance of the 'been there, done that' syndrome in the idea that could start a row. So, why *not* bus? Let's try IPSWICH BUSES (Information - Freephone 0800

819390). *'Freephone'*? I'm impressed already: that's the first one of *those* we've had! Ipswich Buses do a CIRCULAR TOUR of the PARKS, DOCK and BREWERY. Now there's a thing: *and* the Brewery, note! Sounds like a wonderful way to wind up a touch of exploring, wouldn't you say? I gather we take in CHRISTCHURCH PARK, CHANTRY PARK, HOLYWELLS PARK, THE DOCKS and the ORWELL BRIDGE (en route to the Brewery) so we'll be well on the way to getting the clear idea we need before we come back to the history, the galleries, the shops and the theatres. I'm definitely up for it, so let's leave the car in one of the car parks off CHARLES STREET - or at TOWER RAMPARTS - and hop on a bus!

The maritime heritage of Ipswich is crystal clear the moment we ease down towards NEPTUNE QUAY. Here, to the north east of the river, stands the OLD CUSTOM HOUSE built in 1845; still with a job to do as the headquarters of the Ipswich Port Authority. It's the work of the same architect who designed St John's Church, Woodbridge, J. M. Clark. You'd have to say the style fits the function: it look serious, the kind of place that wouldn't take any old buck from tetchy seafarers. On the other hand, it's also a bit over the top, in the Victorian way of things, with the balconies, balustrades and neo-classical columns. As a temple to trade what else would you expect?

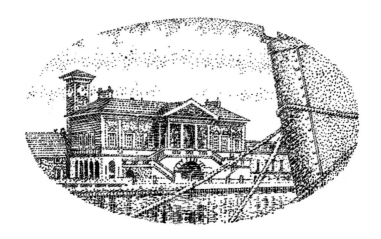

WEST DOCK & CUSTOM HOUSE

In fact, it's not the river that faces us as we look out past the quay from the bus. What we're looking at is known as the WET DOCK and, when it was opened in January 1842, it was the largest enclosed dock in the country.

The dock was built to solve a problem that had dogged Ipswich increasingly for more than two hundred years since trade had peaked in the 15th century. Not only did it have to contend with French pirates and with the Dutch wars, it's prosperity was disastrously under threat from the silting up of the river. A canal was dug, but that didn't help: the port fell into decline that began to look terminal as the silt choked up the quays. The crisis was averted when a group of merchants got together in 1805 and lobbied for the setting up of river commissioners to widen, deepen, clean and generally improve the state of the waterway.

The commissioners sorted things out in time, dredged everything in sight, and trade began to pick up again - as did the revenue from harbour dues and the like. Spurred on by their success, the commissioners suggested that an enclosed dock should be built on the north bank of the river, to turn success into a major triumph. The idea caught on - and the rest is even more spectacular. Today the Wet Dock combines the roles of commercial port and marina, of business and pleasure - a double pleasure as it's become a very pleasant place for a stroll, between the bars and restaurants. Admit it: suddenly you're *very* glad you came. I suppose we could even get off the bus now and leave the parks for later. Get thee behind me!

If the early Middle Ages saw a boom in Ipswich, thanks to its port, the recent years are more like a nuclear explosion, with the fastest growth in its entire history. It's still expanding, trading globally by means of bulk carriers, container ships and roll on - roll off ferries. We can't see much of *that* from the bus, as the developments needed to handle this traffic have all taken place down river of the Wet Dock so that the complex, as a whole, now extends for more than a mile. I don't know about you, but I could be getting a taste for this and a definite yearning to wander down past the Orwell Bridge to see more of it. We're committed to the bus, though - *can't* waste the tickets - so let's take in the parks and then come back for a second round.

CHRISTCHURCH PARK, just north of the town centre and near to where we parked the car, is a pleasant 65 acre stretch of tranquil parkland in the heart of which we'll find CHRISTCHURCH MANSION (Enquiries - 01473 253246). This beautiful Tudor mansion, built in 1548, is furnished as an English country house, with splendid collections of furniture and ceramics. What people *really* come to see though, is the most important assemblage of works by the local boys - Gainsborough and Constable - outside London. There is also an extensive collection of paintings, drawings, prints and sculpture by other Suffolk artists from the 17th century to the present day.

Nevertheless, everyone *does* come for the star attractions and remembering what we said on the banks of the Stour a while ago, we'd better join the crowd. At a time like this I find the best approach is to whizz round until something holds my attention and then give it my all, in a manner of speaking. I wonder why I'm surprised that it's the most famous Constables that stop me in my tracks. Perhaps I was too sure of my independence, too convinced that I knew better than to follow the herd. Not so! This time the herd seem to be on the ball: the Willy Lott's cottage views are masterpieces and definitely where I want to spend most of my visit to the Mansion.

There's a question that's still floating from the last chapter - something like: do we get so much out of Constable country because the paintings have showed us how to do it? Or is there something in the places, that we recognise in an instant and that speaks clearly to each of us? The more I look at the pictures, the more I think it's Constable. Once anyone has picked up his perspectives, one tends to see what he saw and fill out most of the rest almost without realising. Obviously, we *all* try to filter out the cafes and the car parks, if modern day living hasn't smashed up *all* our sensibilities, but I'm sure it goes further than that, to the point where it's almost the case that if it isn't in the picture it isn't there. Or, if it is and it doesn't seem to look quite as Constable painted it, then it's nature that's wrong - and *not* the artist. It gets worse - or better, perhaps, if you're a painter yourself - as soon after this, when one is back in Milton Keynes or Horley, it's the painting of Flatford Mill that floats in the eye of the mind, that is so easy to recall - and *not* the original, whatever one's aversion to one way lanes. I wonder if you'll agree, after you've spent half an hour or so looking at the Stour on canvas.

Once we've settled this issue - and I'm sure there'll be many different responses - it could be worthwhile popping through to the purpose built WOLSEY ART GALLERY, which is entered via Christchurch Mansion, to observe yet another perspective on the painter's art. This new facility specialises in a changing programme of temporary exhibitions, which includes national and touring presentations. From our stand-point it serves as a pointer to Constable's (and Gainsborough's) true stature and as a further comment on the issued I raised a moment ago.

While we're up for galleries, so to speak, it's worth noting that Ipswich is up with the best of them in this respect. It's nine galleries compare very favourably with those of Plymouth - another port town - which has double the population, but only three more. Apart from Christchurch and Wolsey, most of the others offer mainly temporary exhibitions of works that are for sale.

Time to move on, noting as we do so that the Mansion is open from Tuesday to Saturday, plus Bank Holidays, from 10.00am to 5.00pm. It is open on Sundays from 2.30pm to 4.30pm but closed on Good Friday, from 24th to 26th December and on 1st January. The house closes at dusk in winter and admission is free at all times. Finally, if you'd prefer a guided tour, these are available every Wednesday from June to September and at other times by arrangement.

The other parks on the circuit are more 'parkish', if you understand, though none the worse for that, but Christchurch is definitely a one off. So CHANTRY PARK and HOLYWELLS PARK are not to be dismissed, if one's hoping for the usual park facilities or even a bit of a stroll in the fresh air. On that subject, I must say that there is something about a park, even if one has just spent hours, days or even weeks in the open countryside, au naturel. It's not just that it's a welcome break from the sea of concrete and tarmac, no it's more that. Maybe 'The Park' is actually one of those legacies of Victorian municipal opulence that actually still work. In a well conceived and maintained park, with its artistically laid out flower beds, shrubs, summer houses and ornamental lakes or ponds; trees, paths and railings we all feel enriched, more elegant and even a bit sophisticated. Sadly there's been a tendency to turn 'parks' into 'recreation grounds' which makes them very useful - but much less to do with anything *remotely* resembling elegance.

Which just leaves the Brewery. Just? Who *am* I trying to kid? The splendid TOLLY COBBOLD BREWERY (Enquires - 01474 231723) has been a major feature in Ipswich for over a century. On a tour of the two brewhouses one can see the country's largest collection of commemorative bottled beers before tasting the malt and smelling the hops. The magnificent Victorian brewery was featured in the BBC's 'Trouble-shooter' with Sir John Harvey-Jones and is open all year daily from 12 noon between May and September and at varied times between October and April - a phone call for details is advisable.

That's the 'academic' bit - the BREWERY SHOP is where the interest level really perks up, as there are cases of beer on offer at 'brewery prices'. If you draw the line at cracking a case open in public, there's always THE BREWERY TAP, a traditional pub for real ale lovers and anyone else who fancies a taste of old fashioned pub atmosphere - which is one atmosphere you really *can* 'taste'! Late in the evening you can probably cut it as well - but that's another story altogether As a gesture to magnanimity 'The Tap' can provide other drinks too, including tea and coffee. To top off the occasion, we might even go as far as one of the pub's freshly prepared snacks or meals.

By any reckoning we should be well primed for a return to the Orwell, but not just to the Wet Dock this time. We'll start off at WHERRY QUAY, right enough, a watersport centre where yachts and sailing dinghies are moored or dragged out of the water in place of the barges and 'tall ships' that made the place's name a century ago, but then we'll move along down stream, as promised. The Quay has the same strolling crowd of bar and restaurant character that have adopted the area as a whole, but this is not to say the changes jar with the old port's essence - quite the reverse. Even the old maltings, where the tidal stream is taken under Stoke Bridge by the New Cut, have been converted into stylish apartments without spoiling their traditional appearance. Once the whole programme is finished the residential and recreational developments could become an asset to the location as a whole, with all the qualities of a port village as it used to be, brought up to date in a quite gratifying way.

However, it's time to leave the crowded streets for a while, to put off the shopping and the bargain hunting and take to the by-ways. The Felixstowe road is the one I have in mind, which takes us down to Nacton and Levington. Our way out of Ipswich takes us along a curving route through the south west of the town. From time to time there are glimpses of the port extension, which is part of what we've come for, and then one is skirting round the north of the airport and approaching a junction with the A14. Once past that, and back on our minor road, we're soon running parallel with the estuary and passing a golf course. For once, in the light of our current 'intrepid explorer' routine, that temptation has to be resisted, so that in the rosy glow of self denial we soon find ourselves arriving at **NACTON**.

There's a track to the east of ORWELL PARK SCHOOL that takes us down to the water's edge, which along this stretch is basically an expanse of tidal flats with panoramic views to be enjoyed to the accompaniment of the cries of curlews bubbling over the top of the lapping wavelets. During the 18th century Admiral Sir Edward Vernon (1684-1757) lived at ORWELL PARK. He had the nickname 'Old Grog' because he was rarely seen wearing anything more stylish than a suit of coarse cloth made of mohair and wool known as grogram. He it was who introduced the navy to the idea of a daily ration of rum mixed with water - known ever afterwards as 'grog'!

Beside the house is a domed, 19th century observatory while across the lane we'll find a medieval church, but it *is* the House that's the main point of interest so let's stroll back to look at it in more detail. It's another of the magnificent mansions that have become such a feature of our travels, with grounds sweeping down to the river. Along with those of the adjacent BROKE HALL these parklands have been designated an Area of Outstanding Natural Beauty, so they should stay unspoiled whatever the developments up and downstream.

Towards the end of the Victorian period, Before Orwell Park became a school, it was the home of Colonel George Tamline, who was well heeled, but something of a recluse, by all accounts. Nevertheless, he did have vision, in that he it was who laid the plans for the first dock at Felixstowe from which the great - and incredibly busy - modern port has developed. What, one wonders, would 'Old Grog' have made of this idea, coming from the occupant of his own home more than a century later? Another century later, had he seen the container handling facilities that currently dominate the port, he might have needed more than the traditional grog ration to recover from the shock!

Broke Hall, the Park's neighbour, also has a tale or two to tell. This splendid Gothic Mansion with its fine views of the estuary had another famous admiral among its occupants over the years. Sir Philip Bowes-Vere Broke won honour in one of the British Navy's legendary encounters when his ship, the 'Shannon', captured the American frigate 'Chesapeake' in a short, sharp struggle off Boston in 1813.

The lane between the two estates, which we've noticed already, is worth following a little further as it leads to a path that runs along the side of the river, to **LEVINGTON CREEK**, from whose wooded, cliff edge point of vantage extends a view over the entire estuary to the skyline of Harwich. We could follow these lanes and paths all the way to Felixstowe if we chose, but the nearer we came to the port the more the peace of the river bank would begin to evaporate and, in any case, we haven't finished with Ipswich itself yet, so it's a bit early to start dabbling in somewhere else. Of course, we *haven't* finished with Ipswich and this little outing was only a diversion, a means to the end of locating the town in its historical, geographical and economic settings. Since we've followed the line of the port's expansion and influence from the original 'Wet Dock' to a point halfway down the estuary, we could be said to have 'done' it. So let's go back to the town centre, park the car and think about life in some of its other forms and fantasies - over *lunch*!

On our way back from Nacton we might like to reflect on one local tale that links the village with a bout of 18th century romance and which, in its own way, has brought a certain amount of fame to the area. Most of that fame has its origins in a book, written in 1846, by the Rev. Richard Cobbold, which made the name of its heroine known a long way beyond the boundaries of the parish. That the said heroine had once been in service with the Cobbold family claimed to add to the authenticity of the tale; that *the author* seems to have been a archetypal Victorian to my mind points more to the likelihood of its having been seriously distorted, in keeping with the taste of the times for a particular variety of morbid sentimentality. However, to 'enliven' our journey back to urban reality, I'll pass on the details, for what they're worth. Margaret Catchpole was a wilful, passionate young woman who lost her heart to one Will Laud, smuggler of the parish. Came the day when she got a message, apparently from Laud, that he was waiting for her in London. Off she rode, on a horse stolen from her master's stable, only to find a distinct absence of her lover at the appointed meeting place. In a blast of initiative, she tried to sell the horse at Aldgate - only to be arrested for having stolen it! She might have been executed for the crime but the Cobbolds pulled rank and got her a reprieve and a reduction in the sentence - to transportation to Australia! I suspect some of us would have actually preferred the rope - but there we are.

Unfortunately, bureaucracy being what it is in *any* century, the powers that be must have got the files muddled because poor Margaret found herself in Ipswich gaol instead of on the beach at Botany Bay. Undaunted, Will Laud - and John Luff, who'd recruited him into 'the trade' - planned to spring her so she and Will could escape to the Netherlands where he planned to go straight. As usually happens in these Victorian melodramas, fate decided otherwise. All three of them managed to reach the beach at Orford Ness, where a ship had been laid on to collect them, only to find that the gaoler from Ipswich, plus a posse from the Revenue, had been hot on their trail. Naturally there was a fight and, just as naturally, Will and John were killed. Finally, to a theme from Mendelsohn - or was it Schubert - played on muted strings, our heroine was packed off to Australia, alone, after all. All of which brings us, in the nick of time, to the car park, the 20th century and a further taste of what passes for 'reality' these days.

We left the history of Ipswich at the point where Chaucer was waxing sarcastic at the prospect of the local merchants making names for themselves. Another local boy who made very good indeed was Thomas Wolsey (1475-1530), whose potential turned out to be far in excess of the wildest imaginings of his father - an Ipswich butcher - who can have had no idea, as he hacked at the sirloin, of what young Tom was going to do with *his* life. Thomas seems to have made quite an impression with the Church hierarchy as he rose through its ranks to become Cardinal and, eventually, Chancellor of England. He was an important patron of the arts and learning, which came to a climax in 1528 when he commissioned the building of a major college in Ipswich. Had he lived more than another two years who knows what might have followed? The college *could* have become a University, history *could* have followed a different course - but *he* didn't, it didn't and the University idea had to wait another 470 years or so for an education committee to get it off the ground.

Apart from the burning of the Protestant 'Ipswich Martyrs' on CORNHILL, in 1555 -as part of Mary Tudor's PR for Catholicism - not a lot happened.. Money was still being made, so life wasn't *all* bad, but in the wings trouble was learning its lines ready for a big entrance as the 'French pirate - Dutch War - river silting' syndrome we talked about during our bus ride and its aftermath. In the midst of all this, between 1611 and 1634, some smarter than average East Anglians - and others from elsewhere in England - must have read some promising stories of the possibilities in the Americas, while they sat on the banks of the Orwell watching the mud pile up.

New England (I'll bet the local red Indians had some views on that little label) seems to have caught on better than most and Ipswich became a major centre for emigration. It was organised by the Town Lecturer, Samuel Ward, whose brother Nathaniel became fist minister of Ipswich, Massachusetts and co-author of the New England law code.

Another lull, another century - with more mud and a fair bit of domestic activity, it would appear. We'll come to the ANCIENT HOUSE in more detail later, if we ever get away from the gossip and look at the Town's architectural pretensions. For now, we'll just mention its 'pargetting' - a highly decorative form of plasterwork - that was added to the exterior, along with the Royal Coat of Arms, by Robert Sparrow in 1660. In 1699 the UNITARIAN MEETING HOUSE was built as one of the first non-conformist chapels allowed by the 'Act of Tolerance'. Half a century later, Cobbolds started their brewery at Cliff Quay, using water from Holywells, while in between the 'Ipswich Journal' went to press for the first time in 1720.

My guess is that most of the mental energy of the 18th century in Ipswich was glutinously focused on the mud, with the French and Dutch seen less and less as a threat and more as a temporary irritant to the over ruling Britannia - especially when the name of almost local boy H.Nelson and his peer group started making a few broadsides, not to mention names for themselves. The trouble was that while ruling the *waves* might be second nature to traditional Brits, ruling the silt and mud that the waves tended to shift around was just a touch too technical - you couldn't shift a sandbank with a discharge of cannon balls and a boarding party.

As there was only marginal progress - and the odd bad idea, like the canal - over the next 120 years of the port's existence, attention is still best kept on the rest of the town. A famous name arrived in 1789 - at least, it's a name engraved on *my* memory from years of adolescent grass cutting - when Robert Ramsome opened his plough works, in OLD FOUNDRY ROAD. After forty years of that the company broadened its base in 1832, by putting the world's first lawnmower into production. I must say that, 120 years afterwards, I for one wished they hadn't bothered - the more the grass grows, the more I hate the green machine that I have to keep on trundling backwards and forwards across it.

Meanwhile, on the arts front, it must be recorded that Gainsborough arrived in Ipswich for a fairly brief stay, between 1755 and 1759. While he lived in the house in FOUNDATION STREET, he picked up his first commissions, to paint local worthies, on the success of which he eventually took off for London and the true 'big time'. Dickens, on the other hand, left 'the smoke' for a while to visit the town where he found inspiration in the local characters and events. These crop up most notably in 'Pickwick Papers; although the references and influences are found more than once in his other stories. At this point on the time scale the commissioners came up with the idea for the Wet Dock, the railway interests came up with the idea of a line to Ipswich - and life was suddenly *very* different. So different, in fact, that they even started a football team, albeit an amateur one. The bustle in the Orwell was renewed and increased as a seemingly endless stream of ships sailed back and forth again. Sail gave way to steam, new designs of ferries, bulk carriers and container ships rolled off the stocks in yards all over the world and Ipswich settled into another prosperous phase in its long, long history.

Talk of yards, stocks and shipbuilding reminds one of another aspect of the town's industrial strength. For centuries it was known for its shipyards which, over the years, spread downstream from the present dock area as far as Nacton, would you believe. As long ago as 1292, Ipswich was building war galleys for Edward I and, when the various problems arose during the 17th century to limit its trading activities, the emphasis shifted further to the point where the flourishing ship-building operation was largely responsible for keeping the place alive, one can imagine. It was certainly one of the main forces behind the drive towards a lasting solution to the problems with the river which the merchants eventually caused to be overcome, as we have seen. Of course, once the crisis was finally past, a new balance between the yards and the docks had to be struck - a balance which must have come down finally - and terminally, for the shipyards - in favour of the port. During this century, as the quantities of cargo going through the port increased astronomically, the point was reached where, in the 80s for example, it was already well in excess of two and a half million tons a year! You don't waste time building ships when there's that kind of traffic in the estuary.

All this talk of industry, effort and endeavour has quite worn me out. Did we ever get round to lunch, I wonder? It was certainly high on the list just now, somewhere between the mud and the mowers, as I recall. Whether we did or not, I feel hungry again, so let's look at Ipswich as a place to eat in, by means of a quick run through the possibilities in general terms. The town has 53 places where we could get a meal - that's four restaurants (or cafes etc.) for every one church! Or six for every art gallery! Does this form a picture in our minds? Something to do with the laws of supply and demand? Of course, that comparison could be utterly unfair to the local population. I mean, if it were a valid yardstick, what on earth would we make of 18th and 19th century Crowland which, as you'll remember, had 34 pubs to its one church and a chapel? On the other hand, there is *something* underlying it all - if only one could analyse it.

TOWN CENTRE CAFE, IPSWICH

Whatever one's conclusion, it's obvious that with a choice like that Ipswich has to have somewhere to suit our immediate need. Within the 'grand total', there are some utterly fascinating sub-divisions: the familiar Chinese, Indian Greek and Italian restaurants are joined by Thai and Mexican establishments, along with others whose brand of 'International Cuisine' is somewhat less specific. At the opposite end of the spectrum we find ten cafes, some with a French influence and others very definitely English, alongside eleven pubs, four wine bars - and two 'themed restaurants', whose specialities I suspect I'm too old to understand. To complete the list, there's a vegetarian restaurant and a trio of establishments often referred to in 'Tourist Guides' as 'High Street Favourites' - although I have to say I've never looked twice at any of them whenever I've been in a High Street as, for years, I honestly thought 'fast food' was a label for the kind of cooking that drove one to fasting (I lie - but only just).

If we can assume that the list came up trumps, that we found 'the very thing' - and felt the better for it, I suggest a return to the more traditional aspects of the urban tour by congregating around the statue of 'Grandma' in PRINCES STREET. This unique (and for once I mean it) statue immortalises the famous character created by Giles, the much loved cartoonist because I'm convinced that just as Constable played a major part in shaping our perceptions of the rural idyll, so Giles played a part of his own in the way we see 'us', and the way we live; the things we do right down to our attitudes, our fears and all the things we fuss about. Giles worked in the town, and lived nearby, so it seems reasonable to assume that much of what he drew he saw in these streets; in other words he recorded 'us' in Ipswich. Let's follow 'us' around for a while and see what we get up to.

What we get up to is shopping. It has to be. There must have been hundreds of cartoons of the English in shops, going to shops, coming back from shops - we will shop, I suggest, and observe the thousands of others like ourselves who are traipsing around with their cartons and carrier bags in pursuit of bargains, treasures, necessities - or something to keep the kids quiet for a couple of hours.

Ipswich continues to develop as a regional shopping centre and has two large malls to complement the traditional shopping area in the town's historic streets. To me - and I'm sure this is absolutely the wrong idea - that means that a gratifying number of the items I wouldn't dream of buying and an even more gratifying number of the places that sell them are conveniently tucked away under identifiable roofs - easily identifiable and hence, praise the Lord, just as easily avoidable. Which leaves those historic streets to local businesses, specialist shops and outlets where the staff know rather more about the goods they sell than the bar codes. In these streets we'll find enough of the things we really like for us to build up another bootful of pictures, pots, plants and positively the last unusual glass ornament we'll ever buy for the people across the road who always go to Majorca and always bring us leather bags.

To be fair, the BUTTERMARKET and TOWER RAMPARTS MALLS do what they do with plenty of style and panache, so that if you're a local resident and you want a new electric kettle, a set of sheets, a video or a packet of drawing pins they're ideal - and if you want all four you wouldn't dream of going anywhere else, what with the parking and so forth. How often do tourists want kettles, sheets or videos, though? Next to never, I imagine, so, regrettably, the Malls get a 'not today thank you' as we head off to the MARKET, which is held on Tuesdays, Fridays and Saturdays beside the CIVIC CENTRE. After that, we'll be away to the side streets, the lanes and anywhere else we can fine that looks promising. Most of the area that we'll be exploring is pedestrianised, with easy access from half a dozen car parks, so we may not emerge for hours - otherwise known as 'tea time'!

If our shopping has taken us towards the top end of WESTGATE, we're well poised to bring another touch of variety into the day. Just up the HIGH STREET from the intersection, we'll find the IPSWICH MUSEUM (Information - 01473 213761) where history is brought to life in vivid displays and reconstructions amidst the setting of a remarkably fine Victorian building. These include the Natural History Gallery, which reflects the Museum's 19th century origins; the Suffolk Wildlife Gallery, which has everything from a lifesize woolly mammoth downwards; the Bird Gallery; the Suffolk Geology Gallery and the Peoples of the World Gallery.

On from these we find the Roman Suffolk Gallery, which includes a reconstruction of a Roman villa and a neighbouring display which shows how the town grew from an Anglo Saxon settlement to the trade capital of East Anglia. Amongst the many items featured are a reconstructed workshop, a burial, a loom, replicas of treasures from the royal burial site at Sutton Hoo and an interactive touch screen computer installation. It is hoped to add an exhibition to these displays that focuses on the architectural decorations of Tudor and Stuart times that were such a feature of the houses of prosperous merchants in the town. The Museum is open throughout the year from Tuesday to Saturday between 10.00am and 5.00pm, except on Good Friday, 24th to 26th December and 1st January, when it is closed all day. Admission is free.

While we're back with museums, there's one collection in the town that will be irresistible to anyone like me who wonders what they did with the trolleybuses - and actually misses them! THE IPSWICH TRANSPORT MUSEUM [Information - 01473 715666] in COBHAM ROAD, used to be a trolley bus depot . So *that*'s the answer. A very 'green' form of transport I'd have imagined. Today it houses the largest collection of transport exhibits in the country to have been drawn from a single area. Everything one sees was made, or used, in Ipswich, from prams and cycles to horse-drawn carriages, fire engines and buses. The collection is also extended to include uniforms, photographs and models which are used to present railway and water-borne transport. Having aired one's enthusiasm, there's an opportunity to relax in the Museum's tea room or to visit the gift shop for a memento of one's experiences. It is recommended that a prior phone call be made to check on opening times, special events and prices of admission.

The Transport Museum is all about local transport but, as we've seen, travel round the Town on foot is just as rewarding for the visitor, in its own way. Having realised as much, the Tourist Information Centre has produced one of the most comprehensive sets of 'Town Trails' leaflets I've ever seen. Even at this stage, it's an excellent idea to pop in to ST STEPHEN'S and collect a set - if only to make sure that nothing important has been missed. Perish the thought! Almost every aspect of the Town's history, activities and traditions is given full coverage, from its maritime heritage to a circuit in pursuit of the local ghosts! Not only do these leaflets add tremendously to one's experience of the town but the whole package - leaflets, walks and all - adds up to an absorbing way of filling many hours that is absolutely free - apart from admission charges to any particularly interesting places that are met en route.

I'd like to think it's not too much of a gulf to bridge between talk of museums and of town trails and thoughts of the 'performing arts' - although I can't quite see the exact connection at the moment. I suppose it's possible that they do actually have two features in common in Ipswich, when you think about it: both aspire to the grand scale and both set a high standard of excellence in their presentations, unusual even today when the entertainment industry is very much 'big business'. The town claims to offer a "vibrant and varied entertainment scene" and surely no-one would want to disagree.

The spectrum from 'performing arts' to 'live entertainment' is offered in three main centres. The IPSWICH REGENT [Box Office - 01473 281480 and 215544] is the largest theatre in East Anglia, with 1780 seats. It seems to specialise in extravaganzas and attracts the big names in music and comedy. The CORN EXCHANGE, which is nearby and which shares the same box office phone number as the Regent, is an arts and entertainment complex whose wide variety of presentations extends from concerts and shows to exhibitions and line dancing.

A stone's throw away, off CIVIC DRIVE, we'll find a quite different approach. The WOLSEY THEATRE [Box Office - 01473 253725] is one of Britain's leading provincial repertory theatres. The productions it stages are generally considered to be of a very high standard and make a pleasing counterpart, in terms of scale and range, to those of the more intimate WOLSEY STUDIO, which is operated as a 'sister auditorium'. For those of us who prefer the 'silver screen' to the stage, there's also plenty of scope in Ipswich to enjoy a good night out. The five screen ODEON [Enquiries - 01473 287287] is the place for block-busters, while the two screen IPSWICH FILM THEATRE [Enquiries - 01473 215544]' which is another part of the Corn Exchange Complex, offers the latest releases as well as specialist, independent and foreign films.

The Tourist Information Centre offers a 'Whats On' service for the price of a phone call, covering all these venues. As a result, at any given time of the year one can find oneself faced with a selection that might range from 'Titanic' to a symphony concert, from a rock concert to a touring ballet company or from a modern comedy show to the English National Opera. 'Spoilt for Choice' sounds rather more apt than usual and suggests that we could fill every evening in Ipswich with no trouble at all - especially when one adds in the restaurants for a meal before or after the show. Suppose we had just had ourselves such an evening: a few drinks before the concert or play, a late dinner afterwards, a few more drinks after that, and so on: a picture of fin de siecle sophistication, wouldn't you say? Fine - so what more could thoroughly modern people possible want? Five seconds thought and the answer is so obvious it's barely worth stating: something to pull ourselves together the next morning to face another full day behind the wheel, that's what!

Amazing Ipswich comes up trumps again, of course. In spades! How many times have we pulled each other's legs on these tours about the price of our over indulgence and the suffering needed to repair the damage? In the midst of the banter, we've usually found a sports centre in a small town, somewhere, and heaved, jumped and pounded - or dashed off the lengths in the pool - for all of seven minutes, in the fervent hope that some of it might take off the inches, loosen the liver and [please] ease the guilt.

In Ipswich, there are no less than four centres and a pool as well as an 'entertainment centre', if you think Ten Pin Bowling or Roller skating would solve the problem - till next time. In fact, looking at the whole range, one would have to say that this is one town where they've turned physical recreation into an *industry*. All four centres have indoor and outdoor facilities - and all four sets of indoor facilities include a sports hall and squash courts. From there, each offers what appear to be specific - and different - combinations of opportunities for exercise. At WHITTON SPORTS AND COMMUNITY CENTRE [Enquiries 01473 462711] they also provide a fitness suite, a snooker room and a solarium. Not to mention the community room and bar - which would probably defeat *our* particular point in being there. Come to think of it, all four centres have bars - one could obviously grow to like keeping fit the Ipswich way! MAIDENHALL SPORTS CENTRE [Enquiries 01473 680644] adds a gymnasium to sports and squash; NORTHGATE SPORTS CENTRE [Enquiries 01473 711211] has the sports, the squash, the gym *and* a practice hall and solarium and, finally, GAINSBOROUGH SPORTS AND COMMUNITY CENTRE [Enquiries 01473 713088] parallels Whitton, with an identical range of opportunities.

A couple of phone calls, a quick booking and everyone who feels the need should be able to satisfy it - if not at a sports centre then almost certainly at CROWN POOLS [Information - 01473 219231] in CROWN STREET, which has three pools of varying degrees of earnestness - as well as a solarium, sauna, fitness studio and a rather quaintly titled facility for something called 'Adult Beach Parties', which sound the kind of experience that could lead almost anywhere other than back to the car, rejuvenated and ready for miles and miles of happy motoring! Especially at our age.

By the time you've finished your work-out you'll probably be ready for anything and anxious to tell me all about it. Excellent: you'll find me, as usual, in a little cafe, on my third black coffee [Sumatra, naturally], my second eclair and - and I promise to listen to your *every* word. Care to join me?

Which just about sums it all up: another day, another town, another cup of coffee, while we mull it all over. Ipswich might not fit everyone's image of the perfect holiday town, at a superficial level, but the fact is that you can do everything there that people *say* they've done - at a price -at locations with much more trendy auras - apart from jumping off the patio on to the beach. The more the globe shrinks, the more the package packed 747s roar out to its furthest extremes, the harder it becomes to find anywhere that *isn't* like Ipswich, give or take rather more sunshine and the odd tropical plant in a pot. Seriously, you can dine, dance, swim, shop, sunbathe, waterski, drink and play tennis virtually anywhere these days - so why *not* Ipswich?

We'll let that question float in the air, shall we, as we climb aboard the motor, fire up the horses and head off out of it. Our route is away from the town, south west along the A12 to our next - and last - base: Colchester, in Essex. It's quite a short run - and fairly quick, compared to some we've known - so we shouldn't be too tired to enjoy an evening in our new surroundings. Tomorrow, we begin our final series of encounters with East Anglia - for the moment. As I've said more than once, though [Shades of John Wayne]: we'll be back!

ABBE HOUSE HOTEL
322 London Road South,
Lowestoft,
Suffolk
NR33 OBG

AA 4Q's ETB 2 Crowns
Highly Commended

Tel/Fax:01502 581083

Abbe House Hotel is superbly positioned for a holiday. It is about two hundred yards from Lowestoft's award winning Victoria beach and is a short stroll away from the beautiful Kensington Gardens with its Bowling Greens, Boating Lake, Tennis Courts and Aviary. If you are tempted to leave all that Lowestoft has to offer then you are only two miles from the Norfolk Broads, the American Theme Park is close by and there are many National Trust properties within striking distance. If you enjoy the noisy fun of a resort then Gt. Yarmouth is just nine miles up the road. Lowestoft is the furthest point East in Britain.

The house is Victorian, approximately one hundred and thirty years old, and designed by Sir Samuel Peto who designed the Houses of Parliament. It is a gracious house with lofty rooms, tall windows and a sense of spaciousness. In the summer the front entrance is a mass of colourful hanging baskets and tubs full of flowers. Inside the house has its own charm. Every room is individually decorated and is spotlessly clean. In fact, in recognition of the very high standard of hygiene and the varied choice of healthy options which the menus offer, the hotel has been awarded both the Good Hygiene Certificate and the prestigious 'Heartbeat Award'. Diane and Nick Murphy, the owners believe that 'Small is Special'. Because the rooms are limited they are able to provide the very highest standards for their guests. All three non-smoking guest bedrooms are immaculately appointed with two of them en-suite, additionally each room has television, radio alarms, hairdryers, together with an extensive hospitality tray, as well as many other extras such as bath robes and luxury toiletries. The hotel is centrally heated throughout making it an ideal place to stay in winter as well as summer. This is not a house for children.

The menu both at breakfast and dinner offers a choice of beautifully cooked food - Abbe has been nominated for the BBC Good Food Programme's 'Best B & B Award'. At dinner you dine by candlelight on dishes that are a mixture of English and Continental. The Hotel is licensed and has an extensive wine list to complement the meal. Snacks and Sandwiches are available from the bar and a picnic basket can be provided, given notice.

USEFUL INFORMATION

OPEN: All year
CHILDREN: No
CREDIT CARDS: None taken
LICENSED: Yes
ACCOMMODATION: 3 rooms 2 ensuite
Non-smoking
RATES: £36 standard £42 ensuite

DINING ROOM: High standard both at
Breakfast and Dinner
BAR FOOD: Snacks & Sandwiches
VEGETARIAN: Upon request
GARDEN: No
PETS: No
WHEELCHAIR ACCESS: No

THE ALBANY HOTEL
400 London Road South
Lowestoft,
Suffolk
NR33 0BQ

2Crown RAC Acclaimed AA Listed

Tel: 01502 574394
Fax: 01502 581198

The Albany Hotel is situated on the A12 to the South of Lowestoft town centre just three minutes from the award winning golden beaches of the Sunrise Coast and Kensington Gardens with its Bowling Green and Tennis Courts. Lowestoft is where Broadlands meets the sea and is an important fishing port with a picturesque fishing quarter which is the site of the first recorded lighthouse in England. Lowestoft is the home of the famous Lowestoft porcelain, birthplace of Benjamin Britten as well as several museums with a maritime flavour. The town is a wonderful base for a holiday and staying in the Albany Hotel is the ideal place. The Hotel was formerly a fine turn of the century terraced town house and became a hotel about twenty five years ago. Today's owner Geoff Ward has made sympathetic alterations to the building including the addition of a Victorian style conservatory at the back to extend the elegant spacious dining area. The Albany has already been refurbished throughout internally in a style which compliments the understated elegance of the house. Here you will find a warm, friendly welcome, a relaxed informal atmosphere and an efficiently run hotel.

The well-appointed eight bedrooms, six of which are ensuite, have a strong period flavour although the comfortable beds, one of which is a four-poster, are of the 1990's rather than a century ago! Each room has television and a well supplied hostess tray. The delightful dining room is one of the nicest in the hotel. The food is delicious, freshly cooked, with a selection of breakfasts, in the evenings the table d'hôte menu is home-cooked using as much local produce as possible. The Bar is a focal point in the evenings where you will find Geoff or his General Manager Den Grosvenor dispensing the drinks and chatting about their lives in Show business, if encouraged, which are extensive and fascinating. With this entertainment world experience the street-wise owners extend a welcome to everyone without prejudice.

USEFUL INFORMATION

OPEN: All year
CHILDREN: Welcome
CREDIT CARDS:
Master/Visa/Diners/AMEX/Switch
ACCOMMODATION: 8 rms 6 ensuite
RATES: From £17.50 B&B

DINING ROOM: Excellent home-cooked
BAR FOOD: Sandwiches, Salads
VEGETARIAN: Catered for
LICENSED: Residential
PETS: Yes
GARDEN: No

THE ANGEL HOTEL
The Thoroughfare,
Halesworth,
Suffolk
LP19 8AH

Tel: 01986 873365
Fax: 01986 874891

Halesworth is an historic market town which became established centuries ago at the highest navigable point of the River Blyth which flows into the sea at Southwold. The 16th century Angel Hotel is located right in the heart of the town in the award winning pedestrianised Thoroughfare. The skilful manner in which this has been done has enhanced the centre of the town enormously even if it does mean that the Angel forfeited a large amount of its gardens.

Visitors enjoy The Angel for many reasons. Firstly it is steeped in history and has great character which has been maintained although many alterations have been carried out to make it the comfortable inn it is today. Secondly the welcoming and friendly atmosphere, which is the hallmark of The Angel, is complimented by many of the public areas being candlelit throughout the evening. The owners, Richard Rhodes and Simon and Cleone Tennant have that wonderful knack of making everyone welcome and even if you have never visited Halesworth or The Angel before you will leave feeling you have been with friends.

The downstairs layout has changed over the years but now features the original two bars one generally for local drinkers and the other larger one for bar meals and a quiet drink before dinner. Both bars are reached from the central courtyard - a light, airy room with natural stone floor and high glass roof. The conditions suit the many plants climbing and thriving in the room including bay trees and a passion flower. On the other side of the courtyard is the well established Italian Restaurant, Cleone's, with its stained wood floor, collection of old pine tables, and walls covered in paintings and pictures of Italy. Where it was once a carpeted function room, a little corner of this Mediterranean country has emerged complete with real masks from Venice, contemporary Italian music, pasta displays and more living greenery. The seven, comfortable, individually designed twin and double rooms all with private bath, shower and toilet and furnished with locally made practical pieces, reflect the rural heritage of the Hotel. The rooms can easily be adapted to accommodate families.

USEFUL INFORMATION

OPEN: 11am-11pm (10.30pm Sun)   RESTAURANT: Great food.
CHILDREN: Welcome Continental influence
CREDIT CARDS: All major cards   BAR FOOD: Wide variety
LICENSED: Full On   VEGETARIAN: Always a choice
ACCOMMODATION: 7 ensuite rooms   WHEELCHAIR ACCESS: Yes
RATES: B&B from £27.50pp double £36 single Special short break rates

THE BLINKING OWL
30 Marine Parade,
Lowestoft,
Suffolk
NR33 0QN

Tel/Fax :01502 563717

Lowestoft prides itself on being the most easterly town in Britain. It has an award winning, Blue Flag, safe bathing beach patrolled by Lifeguards, and it is facing the beach on Marine Parade that you will find the Blinking Owl Guest House. It is an enviable position and ideal for holidaymakers at anytime of the year except Christmas. It is one of the imposing Victorian houses on the sea front which has been the home of Pauline and Alan Payne for the last twenty years.

They are a friendly, hospitable couple who enjoy having guests in their house and do everything within their power to make sure the stay is a memorable one. From the Blinking Owl you can set out for many places and many activities if you do not want to spend the day lazing on the beach. The American Style Theme Park, Pleasure Hills, Kessingland Wildlife Park, Fritton Lake & Country Park, the glorious Somerleyton Hall and Lowestoft's own Marina Theatre, are all there for your enjoyment. For the sports minded there are six excellent golf courses nearby, a Yacht Marina, Sea fishing, Coarse fishing and Broads cruising. You could never be bored here.

The Blinking Owl has five attractively appointed bedrooms with very comfortable beds, three of which are ensuite and two have private bathrooms. They can be either twin or double beds. Each room has multi-channel colour television, a radio, a hostess tray and they are all centrally heated, making it a warm and cosy place to stay at any time of the year. Breakfast is a delicious, substantial meal. Children are very welcome but regrettably because of the number of stairs, there is no access for wheelchairs. Pets are welcome if they are well behaved!

USEFUL INFORMATION

OPEN: All year except Christmas
CHILDREN: Welcome
CREDIT CARDS: None taken
LICENSED: No
ACCOMMODATION: 5 ensuite rooms
RATES: From £15 pp.pn B&B Child £5

DINING ROOM: Excellent breakfast
No evening meal
VEGETARIAN: Upon request
WHEELCHAIR ACCESS: No
GARDEN: No
PETS: Yes

BROAD OAK FARM
Bramfield,
Halesworth,
Suffolk
IP19 9AB

2Crowns Commended EATB.
4 Q's Selected AA

Tel:01986 784232

Farmhouse Bed and Breakfast always has an appealing ring to it and Broad Oak Farm is a delightful find. It is a 16th century farmhouse surrounded by meadow land and attractive gardens just a third of a mile from the road and three quarters of a mile from the village of Bramfield which is on the A144. It is close to the North East Heritage Coast and Minsmere R.S.P.B reserve and only eight miles from the popular Edwardian sea-side town of Southwold. Riding, golf, cycle hire and fishing are all available as well as excellent walking on heath land and along the wild sand-dune coasts. Wonderful medieval churches and castles are in abundance and just ask to be explored.

Broad Oak farmhouse is full of character with exposed beams and large fireplaces. It was carefully modernised in 1980 but still retains its period features. It is the centre of a working farm but separated from the dairy and cattle buildings. There is an attractive paved area on the west side of the house overlooking a large lawn, herbaceous borders and water areas. A tennis court is there for the use of guests. Patricia Kemsley runs the house with her husband, Peter, giving his support in welcoming visitors, when he is not busy on the farm. The house is beautifully furnished with a nice mixture of antiques and other pieces. The Guest sitting room has a wood burning stove, television and video and a piano. The Dining Room is light and airy and it is here you will be served a delicious farmhouse breakfast and if you are dining in you will find all kinds of traditional meat dishes on the menu, using a specialist local butcher and organic grown vegetables. Fish is served frequently and is locally caught. Patricia excels herself with the wonderful home-made sweets and fruit pies.

Three double bedrooms, one double with ensuite bathroom and cot, one twin ensuite shower and the third can be either a double or twin with private bathroom and separate toilet. All the rooms are attractively furnished, warm and comfortable and each has a hostess tray as well as a radio. Staying here is relaxed, friendly and you are quietly made aware of the Kemsleys concern about environmental and green issues.

USEFUL INFORMATION

OPEN: All year
CHILDREN: Welcome
CREDIT CARDS: None taken
LICENSED: No
ACCOMMODATION: 3 rooms ensuite
RATES: From £16 low season.

DINING ROOM: Splendid farmhouse
breakfast and home-cooked evening meal
VEGETARIAN: If required
WHEELCHAIR ACCESS: Yes but no
special accommodation

BURLINGTON LODGE,
30 Burlington Road,
Ipswich,
Suffolk
IP1 2HS

Tel: 01473 251868
E Mail:
nortonburlodge@msn.com

There are some nice historical facts about Burlington Lodge which is situated in a quiet suburb on the western edge of Ipswich's medieval town centre. Built in 1870 on land that belonged to a Quaker family and was subsequently used to provide large residences for Ipswich's Victorian businessmen, the house is gracious, high ceiling and has great warmth and light. Here, the East Anglian artist Edward Smythe spent the final years of his life when the house belonged to his daughter. Several of his paintings can be seen in the Christchurch Mansion and the Ipswich Museum, two places which should be visited by everyone coming to the town, if only to enable them to absorb the depth of history. Ipswich is a delight to explore and having had your fill of history, you will find there are many good restaurants and pubs in which to find refreshment.

Staying here you are within easy walking distance of the town centre. Peter and Lesley Norton are the owners and it is Peter who is chef and Maitre de hotel at which he is talented. He retired from the Army in 1994 but Lesley is still working as a Civil Servant and one tends to see more of her at weekends. The house is efficiently run, spotlessly clean and has a warm and welcoming atmosphere which Peter and Lesley have worked hard to create.

There are five bedrooms, three twins and two doubles. They all have private showers. One double with full ensuite facilities is on the ground floor. The upper floor comprises the other four rooms and two separate toilets. All the rooms may be let as single. Every room has television, radio/alarm, hairdryers and a hostess tray. Breakfast is a feast and no one could possibly leave the table feeling hungry! Vegetarian and Special Diets are available by prior request. Smoking is permitted in the bedrooms but nowhere else. Children are not encouraged, but there are facilities for a child to share with parents.

USEFUL INFORMATION

OPEN: All year
CHILDREN: By arrangement
CREDIT CARDS: None taken
LICENSED: No
ACCOMMODATION: 5 rooms
4 with shower, 1 ensuite
RATES: From £22 sgl pp pn B&B

DINING ROOM: Delicious breakfast
No evening meals
VEGETARIAN: Upon request
WHEELCHAIR ACCESS: No.
adapted for wheelchair access
PETS: Yes

Café 152
152 High Street,
Aldeburgh,
Suffolk

Mentioned in Round Up Section
Good Food Guide 1997 & 1998

Tel/Fax: 01728 454152

Its simple name belies the gastronomic experience to be had at Café 152 and it is much more than just eating here which makes the place unforgettable. Owned by Claire Bruce-Clayton and Richard Lawson , a great bear of a man, over six feet and with a dark, thick beard; their joint personalities reach out to all their customers, many of whom are devotees and make a beeline for the Café 152 whenever they can. It did not surprise us to learn that the ebullient Richard is a voluntary tractor driver for Aldeburgh lifeboat.. There are only a dozen or so tables in the colourful restaurant with its crab coloured walls, covered in pictures and with a large overmantel taking stock of diners. There are books on the fireplace, newspapers hang alongside one wall. The whole is thoroughly pleasing and entirely the right environment to enjoy the exciting food produced by Claire who is a talented chef, and having travelled the world, she brings the culinary knowledge gained to the kitchen and the end product is truly sensational. You might start with steamed mussels with garlic, tarragon and lemon or a creamy spinach and mushroom risotto with shaved parmesan - both dishes can also be had as main courses. The main course menu is well planned, making it difficult to choose, but breast of duck on braised red cabbage, apples and thyme with roasted shallots is a firm favourite and so too is griddle fillet steak on potato and parsnip rosti, with a red wine sauce. The desserts are equally tempting and whether you come for lunch or dinner, it will be an unforgettable experience. The Adnams wine list, simply and well explained, is comprehensive and competitively priced.

Apart from having a superb position between the shingle beach and the High Street in Aldeburgh, superb food and wine, Café 152 seems to take everything in its stride. No matter how busy they are, they have time for individual customers. Children are genuinely welcome and the whole atmosphere is redolent of contentment. Maybe it has something to do with Aldeburgh which is a quiet unspoilt resort with a long fishing heritage. Fresh fish is still sold daily from the fishermen's huts on the beach. It is famous for its lifeboat and has been, and is, the home of many writers and artists. It first became famous when written about by John Betjeman and then with the advent of Benjamin Britten and Peter Pears who started the world famous Aldeburgh Festival.

USEFUL INFORMATION

OPEN: All year Lunch & Dinner
Pre & Post Concert Dinners during
the summer season
CHILDREN: Welcome but please
under 7's out by 8pm
CREDIT CARDS: Visa/Master/Delta/Switch
LICENSED: Full On.

RESTAURANT: Superb, innovative
food
VEGETARIAN: Wide variety
WHEELCHAIR ACCESS: Yes
COURTYARD: Tables outside in summer
PETS: No

THE CHEQUERS INN
Kettleburgh,
Woodbridge,
Suffolk

Tel: 01728 723760

What a delightful site The Chequers Inn stands on. It is totally rural in every direction and at the rear of the pub there is a large garden that runs down to the banks of the River Deben. The building is not very old having been built in 1912 as a replacement for an ancient inn which sadly was destroyed by fire.

At one time Kettleburgh was a place of some importance with its own Market and Fair. In those days the now small Deben would have carried barges up to the docks at Debenham. Plague ravaged the village in the Dark Ages and the then Lord of the Manor took flight and removed his residence to an adjacent hill where he thought he would be safe from the infected village. You can still see the original site of his moated home next to the old church. Nearby is Brandston village where in the 17th century, they hung their octogenarian vicar for witchcraft. Also in Brandeston is the cottage of one Margaret Catchpole whose misdeeds caused her to be transported to Australia.

The infamous lady is supposedly related to the present landlord of The Chequers through his Great-grandmother. Keith Wilson and his wife Judith have been here for ten years and there is no likelihood of them being transported! It is far more likely that the customers will be transported with delight at the excellence of the Real Ale and the large selection of Malt Whiskeys. The Restaurant menu offers a super choice of dishes all at realistic prices. Children can choose from their own list and in the bar snacks and light meals are served. Try the Kettleburgh Ploughman's with various accompaniments - absolutely delicious and very filling.

USEFUL INFORMATION

OPEN: Mon-Sat 11-2.30pm & 6-11pm
Sun: 12-3pm & 7-10.30pm
BAR FOOD: Fresh home-cooked fare
CREDIT CARDS: All major cards
except AMEX/Diners
GARDEN: Large with Children's play area
PETS: Well behaved

RESTAURANT: Wide range
traditional home-cooked food
CHILDREN: Welcome. Play area
VEGETARIAN: 3 home-made dishes
LICENSED: Full On
WHEELCHAIR ACCESS: At
front door

CHUFFERS
14-16 Great Eastern Square,
Felixstowe,
Suffolk
IP11 7DY

Tel:01394 270132
Fax: 01394 270890 (Bureau)

Everything about Chuffers is charming and different. For starters it is situated in the centre of the renovated Victorian Railway Station, a unique building comprising other small businesses. It overlooks the old platform and small, traditional market with a free parking area. Chuffers retains much of the past including the original station 'steel' or cast iron metal work and canopies, all superbly restored. There are many reasons to come here that are totally independent of the excellent food served all day. Firstly it is owned and run by Mick and Roger, an unlikely pair who have become a perfect team for running a restaurant. Mick is an ex long distance lorry driver, a keen gardener, super cellarman and a great wit and story-teller. Roger is an ex-Harwich deep sea tug mate, he is a brilliant chef and one of life's special characters. The combination is irresistible! Together with their friendly, caring and efficient staff, they achieve the perfect atmosphere for this Continental Restaurant with Bar and Patio.

Open all the year, the Cafe starts at 8.30am for breakfast and shuts at 11pm. The Bar is open from 11am-11pm. It is an ideal place to go to at anytime of the day for a quiet drink and a meal, a cup of coffee or a delicious afternoon tea. One of the great things about Chuffers is that the prices will suit every pocket. To start dishes can be had from as little as £1.50, a whole range of pasta and rice dishes offering ample portions at £4.50. There are fish dishes, Vegetarian dishes, meat dishes - the dish of the day includes a sweet and all for less than £5. Fry and grills are always popular. Jacket potatoes with varied fillings, salads, Ploughman's, French bread fillings and burgers complete the main dishes but desserts will no doubt tempt you with anything from home-made apple pie and custard to chocolate pudding with chocolate sauce. Teas and coffees of all kinds are served either in a cup or a mug. Fresh home-grown, organic vegetables are served every day. The place buzzes with laughter and it is a pleasure to eat here. Do take note of the vast amount of railway memorabilia decorating the interior. In the summer the patio on the platform with its tables and benches is very popular. Quiz nights are held regularly. There is full disabled access and facilities both within the bar and the complex.

USEFUL INFORMATION

OPEN: All year 8.30-11pm Bar 11-11pm   RESTAURANT: Good value fare
CHILDREN: Welcome   VEGETARIAN: Catered for
CREDIT CARDS: None taken   WHEELCHAIR ACCESS: Yes
LICENSED: Full On   GARDEN: Patio with tables
PETS: No   Designated smoking & non-smoking areas

COVENTRY HOUSE
8 Kirkley Cliff,
Lowestoft,
Suffolk
NR33 0BY

Tel: 01502 573865

Built in the middle of the 19th century,, Coventry House is typical of the period. The rooms are spacious, the ceilings high and the whole light and airy. This Guest House has the advantage of calling the sea front its garden, so it has a perfect position for holiday makers at anytime of the year. Indeed many people come here out of season to enjoy the warmth and hospitality offered by the owners Chris and Jill Alden and to watch the ever changing seas, from the shore on good days or from the comfort of the lounge on a stormy winter's day when the waves pound the shore. From Lowestoft you are only one mile from the Norfolk Broads and just a half a mile from the centre of this nice old town, which itself deserves exploration. For those who enjoy the razzmatazz of a seaside resort for a short space of time, Great Yarmouth is only nine miles away.

With Coventry House you will find charming decor, and furnishings in keeping with the age of the house but in the case of the beds especially, the emphasis is on the 1990's! There are seven guest rooms, with four doubles, twins or family, ensuite. Each bedroom is well-appointed and has television, alarm clock radio and a beverage tray - what a boon the latter is to the traveller; nothing like being able to make a drink whenever you wish. Breakfast is a super, freshly cooked meal with several choices, cereals, fruit juices, toast and preserves, freshly made coffee and piping hot tea. Every evening, except Friday, an evening meal is available at the very reasonable price of £7. It is a set menu of four courses, home-cooked and excellent value for money. Coventry House is not licensed but you are welcome to bring your own wine. Vegetarians are catered for with advance notice please.

USEFUL INFORMATION

OPEN: All year
CHILDREN: Welcome
CREDIT CARDS: None taken
LICENSED: No. BYO
ACCOMMODATION: 7 rooms 4 ensuite
RATES: From £16pp pn £18 sgl £24 ensuite sgl £38dbl

DINING ROOM: Good home-cooking
VEGETARIAN: With advance warning
WHEELCHAIR ACCESS: No
GARDEN: Sea front
PETS: Well behaved dogs

EDINGWORTH GUEST HOUSE
395/7 London Road South,
Lowestoft,
Suffolk
NR33 0BJ

ETB 'Listed Commended'

Tel/Fax: 01502 572051

Edingworth Guest House in Lowestoft with its award winning south beach, makes an excellent base for people wanting to explore the Norfolk Broads, Oulton Broad and Waveney Valley, to take in historic Norwich with its magnificent cathedral. Constable Country is approximately one hour's drive south. It is an area with numerous golf and pitch and putt courses within an hour's reach. If you like the razzmatazz of a 'mini-Blackpool' for just a few hours, then Gt. Yarmouth is just a half an hour away.

Edingworth, built in Victorian times still retains many of the original features which give it graciousness and a certain elegance which is highlighted by the excellent manner in which Gwen and Keith Wicks, the owners, run the house. It sparkles with cleanliness and the welcome is warm and genuine. People comment on the home-from-home atmosphere as well as the delicious food - you can read many flattering comments in the well-filled visitors book. There are nineteen guest bedrooms, fourteen in the main house and five in the annexe a few yards away. Six ensuite rooms contain a double bed and a single.

They are all very spacious and furnished to a high standard. One ensuite room is on the ground floor. An enormous family room is available with a double bed and two singles and there is a good size single room. In addition there are ten standard rooms either twin or double. Every room has television and a hostess tray. Cots are available but not cot linen without a surcharge. The comfortable residents lounge has multi-channel television by request. In the dining room you will enjoy a great breakfast frequently featuring kippers or smoked haddock if you give advance notice of your preference.. In the evenings the meal is home-cooked using as much local produce and fresh vegetables as possible.

USEFUL INFORMATION

OPEN: All year except Dec25th & 26
CHILDREN: Welcome
CREDIT CARDS: None taken
LICENSED: No
ACCOMMODATION: 19 rooms
7 ensuite
RATES: Standard £20 single pppn, Standard £15.50 dlb pppn
              Ensuite £20 single pppn, Ensuite £18 dbl pppn

DINING ROOM: Super home-
                              cooked food
VEGETARIAN: On request
WHEELCHAIR ACCESS: No
GARDEN: No
PETS: Small dogs by arrangement

FRANKLINS BRASSERIE
14 Sea Road,
Felixstowe,
Suffolk
IP11 8BB

Tel: 01394 270462

Down in the basement of 14 Sea Road, Felixstowe there is the most unexpected and delightful find, Franklins. There is nothing usual about this place from the owner Tim Franklin to the food he produces. He will tell you that there is sausage and mash and then there is his version of sausage and mash - a world apart! Is he Felixstowe's answer to Cornwall's Rick Stein - a man he admires enormously - well maybe, but we would prefer to say he is an original who has absorbed all that is good in the world of cuisine and continues to do so. On Mondays, his day off, he takes off for London to seek out what is new in the restaurant world and then returns to translate his finds into new and exciting dishes, always with the Tim Franklin finish. In a short space of time Franklins has become the 'In Place' to be in Felixstowe. He can count, among his clients, Delia Smith, Jimmy White, Barbara Cartland, Griff Rhys Jones and Robert Dougal. He can lay claim to having pureed fillet steak for the baby Prince William when he worked for the late Earl Spencer. A man of many parts, his enthusiasm, his innate charm and the self-mockery make him an ideal restaurateur.

There is nothing formal about the forty cover restaurant but it none the less has a great deal of charm. The napery is crisp and fresh, the glasses sparkle and the silver gleams. The menu, in addition to the A la Carte, is displayed on blackboards, highlighting the Special of the Day. Light lunches are available in the Spring and Summer. The mouth-watering starters can be anything from thinly sliced marinated salmon served with a dill and mustard sauce to Vine tomato 'tarte tatin' with parmesan flakes and basil. Breast of Suffolk chicken sliced on to a sweetcorn and potato chowder, Open 'Toad-in-the-Hole' with roasted kidneys, crispy bacon and onion gravy or the finest Scotch sirloin sliced on to a cracked peppercorn and ale mustard sauce, are just three of the delicious main courses. The sweets are equally delectable and the cheese selection varied. From time to time there are Gourmet Evenings with Wine Tasting, very popular occasions. With a friendly, efficient, fun loving staff, Tim Franklin has success at his finger tips. Franklin's Brasserie is a must for anyone living in East Anglia, and certainly for those visiting the port.

USEFUL INFORMATION

OPEN: All year except 1st 2 weeks Jan.
12-2.30pm & 7-10pm
CHILDREN: Welcome
CREDIT CARDS: Visa/AMEX
LICENSED: Full On
GARDEN: No

RESTAURANT: Innovative food
VEGETARIAN: Pasta dishes
WHEELCHAIR ACCESS: No
PETS: No

THE GRIFFIN
The High Street,
Yoxford,
Suffolk
IP17 3EP

Listed

Tel/Fax: 01728 668229
ygriffin@netcomuk.co.uk

This fine old village inn, in the heart of Yoxford has served travellers since approximately the early 1500's. Before that date it was used as a Manorial Court. Today, although it has seen alterations, it is still full of old world charm, nooks and crannies, low beams and oak frames have been exposed in the Restaurant and other rooms. You will find The Griffin and Yoxford just off the A12 in what is known as the Garden of Suffolk. Unusually it has a railway station one mile away and it is near to Framlingham and Orford Castle, Minsmere Nature Reserve and the seaside towns and villages of Southwold, Walberswick, Dunwich and Aldeburgh. Snape Maltings and the Aldeburgh Festival are close by.

You will find the bar used by locals who have helped create, together with the landlords Ian Terry and Sara Paton, a wonderful, warm and cheery welcome. The beer is well kept and apart from Benskins Bitter there is always a Guest Ale and two in summer. The small restaurant seating thirty six, is charming and intimate, furnished with old wooden tables, tapestry, weapons, gargoyles and Boars head on the walls. It serves delicious and frequently innovative food such as chicken pasty lombard, a medieval dish of chicken breast, bacon, leek and verjuice in a pastry case or pumpes - a medieval dish of balls of pork with apple, herbs and spices coated with an almond milk batter, served with a light mustard sauce. There are traditional favourites as well, displayed on the blackboard as well as delectable desserts and a good range of Bar snacks. A Children's menu is available. Vegetarians have their own dishes. Wine by the glass as well as the bottle is available and there are always seven house wines to choose from.

For those wanting to stay in this pretty village, The Griffin has three guest bedrooms, one double ensuite, one double and one twin with private bathrooms. The rooms are all attractively furnished, warm and comfortable and have television and hostess trays. Breakfast like the rest of the food at The Griffin, is of a very high standard and a substantial meal. Our researcher ranked this one of the best pubs he had stayed at in East Anglia.

USEFUL INFORMATION

OPEN: All year
Food served 12-2.30 & 7-9.30pm
CHILDREN: Welcome
CREDIT CARDS: None taken
LICENSED: Full On
ACCOMMODATION: 1dbl ensuite
1dbl & 1 tw with private bathrooms
RATES: From £22.50pp pn 10% discount after day one

RESTAURANT: Excellent and sometimes
innovative menu
BAR FOOD: Wide range available
VEGETARIAN: Catered for
WHEELCHAIR ACCESS: Yes
GARDEN: Yes
PETS: Yes

HEDGEHOGS
Main A12, Kelsale,
Nr Saxmundham,
Suffolk
IP17 2RF

3 rating in
Good Food Guide

Tel: 01728 604444
Fax: 01728 604499

There is nothing prickly about Hedgehogs! This delightful 16th century thatched restaurant is set in its own landscaped gardens, a place of tranquillity and good food. You will find it on the edge of the A12 main London- Gt. Yarmouth Coast road and within easy reach of sandy beaches and picturesque thatched Suffolk villages. The name Hedgehogs was decided on following the discovery of a family of hedgehogs whilst renovation work was being undertaken many years ago - needless to say they were safely rehoused and spotted from time to time in the undergrowth of the landscaped tea gardens.

Stephen Yare is the owner and the chef. He is talented, imaginative and innovative as one would expect having being trained by such super chefs as Raymond Blanc, Albert Roux, Pierre Koffman, and the late Francis Coulson. He creates a very special ambience and runs the restaurant with professional expertise with the emphasis on the enjoyment of the delicious food in an atmosphere of style and elegance. The menu which is revised seasonally, is complemented by a selection of 'Specials' from the blackboards, might start with smoked sprats with spicy tomato and coriander salsa or crispy courgettes with hot bacon salad and garlic dip. Grilled sea bass with saffron & olive risotto, roast shank of lamb with chunky onion sauce or confit of duck served crisp with pea and lovage puree.

The own-baked desserts and puddings are irresistible. There are theme nights, such as Tapas, Italian, Starters and Pudding Club (a regular happening), plus cookery demonstrations. There is also an outside catering and bar service. Conference facilities for up to twenty people to lighten the tedium of the most taxing business meetings. What more romantic setting could there be for a wedding reception than the old world sophisticated elegance of Hedgehogs.

USEFUL INFORMATION

OPEN: 12-1.30pm 7-9.00pm Tues-Sat
Sun: 12-2pm Mondays by prior arrangement only
CHILDREN: Yes
CREDIT CARDS: All major cards
LICENSED: Restaurant Licence
VEGETARIAN: Selection

RESTAURANT: Innovative
delicious food
WHEELCHAIR ACCESS: Yes
GARDEN: Landscaped
PETS: Yes

HINTLESHAM HALL
Hintlesham,
NR Ipswich
Suffolk
IP8 3NS

Tel: Hotel 01473 652268/652334
Golf Club 01473 652761
Fax: 01473 652463

Set in over one hundred and seventy five acres of rolling Suffolk countryside, Hintlesham Hall is a haven of gracious living, with supremely comfortable accommodation, excellent food and wine, and attentive service - ensuring a level of hospitality difficult to surpass. It is privately owned and since 1984 when Robert Carrier sold what was his restaurant and cookery school, Hintlesham Hall has been sensitively transformed into the prestigious hotel and restaurant it is today.

Since 1990 when the Hotel reached its present size, David Allan, the proprietor and managing director, has undertaken many other developments ranging from replanting areas of garden and reviving elderly trees to the construction of a national award winning Clubhouse. This fine building provides attractive alternative bar and dining services and spa facilities as well as serving the Hall's own excellent eighteen hole golf course.

Everything about Hintlesham Hall is gracious from the grandeur and elegance in the Salon, the largest of the three dining rooms to the supremely comfortable and perfectly appointed bedrooms, all with modern bathrooms, direct dial telephones, television and teletext, radio, mini bars, hair-dryers, towelling robes, mineral water and a profusion of toiletries. It is an outstanding venue for dinner parties, wedding receptions, special celebrations and corporate entertainment. The conference facilities are very efficient and discreet. As well as golf, many other leisure pursuits are available including trout fishing, tennis, snooker, croquet and The Orangery Pool. Clay pigeon shooting, horse riding and days at the races are also features of Hintlesham life. Guests may explore picturesque and historic Suffolk, perhaps using the Hintlesham Hall Antiques Guide.

USEFUL INFORMATION

OPEN: All year
CHILDREN: Not under 10 years
CREDIT CARDS: All major cards
LICENSED: Yes. 500 bin wine list
ACCOMMODATION: 33 ensuite rooms
RATES: Sgl from £89 Dbl. from £115 room only
Short Breaks from £160 small dbl. inc. D.B&B

PETS: Yes

RESTAURANT: 3 elegant dining rooms
Superb cuisine. English & Continental
VEGETARIAN: Separate menu
WHEELCHAIR ACCESS: Yes. 8 ground
floor rooms
GARDEN:175 acres
18 hole golf course
Croquet, Snooker, Gym

HOPE HOUSE
High Street,
Yoxford,
Suffolk
IP17 3HP

Tel/Fax: 01728 668281
HopeHouseYoxford@compuserve.com

This delightful 17th century house with recorded 15th century origins, was re-styled in the early eighteenth century. It is situated in Yoxford, a village described as 'The Garden of Suffolk', because of the way it nestles in between four stretches of parkland. The owners, Michael Block and Roger Mildren, clearly love the house, and ensured that none of the wealth of period detail was lost, when they renovated the property. All work was carried out with loving care and an eye for detail. Throughout the house antique and modern furniture form a happy marriage. The graceful panelled drawing room is decorated in warm yellows, and furnished with handmade blue and yellow carpets and matching upholstery. Whether it be the roaring log fires in the winter or the cool tranquillity in summer, this is always a most restful and refreshing room. Throughout the house the paintings, decorative objets d'art, furniture and flowers add to the feeling of well being. All of the bedrooms are equally well appointed. Comfortable armchairs, writing tables and every creature comfort in well proportioned rooms, with well equipped facilities, make this the most perfect place to relax. Whatever the length of your stay, you will leave feeling pampered and revived. The gardens to the rear of the house are walled and in a formal style with exuberant plantings. There is no nicer place to take tea than on the south facing terrace, amidst the scent of roses and lavender. For Bed and Breakfast there is no better. For House Parties, exclusive use is given to the party. It is then that Michael will display his excellence as a chef, and delicious dinners will be served in the stunning candlelit dining room. Both Michael and Roger genuinely enjoy having people to stay in their beautiful home and have made many friends with their guests. Hope House is certainly a rarity and one is privileged to be able to enjoy the atmosphere and the beauty. There are two double bedrooms and one twin-bedded room, and single accommodation can be arranged. One of the double rooms has a Hepplewhite four-poster bed refurbished in fabulous red and gold silk brocade. The ingenious en-suite facilities ensure that the proportions and historic styles of the bedrooms have not been diminished. From Yoxford many places of interest are accessible including the Suffolk coastal towns of Southwold and Aldeburgh, Minsmere Bird Sanctuary, Framlingham Castle, Helmingham Hall and Orford Castle You will find Yoxford on the A1120 at its junction with the A12 between Woodbridge and Lowestoft. Hope House is at the west end of the village set well back from the road

USEFUL INFORMATION

OPEN: All year
CHILDREN: No
VEGETARIAN: Upon request
WHEELCHAIR ACCESS: Not suitable
LICENSED: No
ACCOMMODATION: 3 ensuite rooms
RATES: High Season £50. Low Season £35.
Pppn. B/B. Dinner available.

DINING ROOM: Best breakfast in
                              Suffolk
CREDIT CARDS: None taken
GARDEN: Beautiful walled garden
PETS: Well behaved dogs

KINGS HEAD
Gorams Mill Lane,
Laxfield,
Suffolk
IP13 8DW

Egon Ronay recommended

Tel: 01986 798395

This charming, old world pub stands on a quiet country lane, with no passing traffic and opposite the upper reaches of the River Blyth. It is unusual not to see at least one horse tethered in front of the pub, as the locals still arrive by horse and cart and there is a steady flow of horse and carriages hired from nearby Tannington Hall. The Kings Head has remained unchanged for centuries. It is a maze of small, quaint rooms with traditional settles and open fires. There is no bar andll drinks are served from the taproom with its row of barrels on the ancient stillages. No fruit machines, pool tables, piped music or other modern distractions disturb the animated conversation. In the immaculate garden unusual cross legged tables and seats stand under creeper clad oak arches, surrounded by flowers and shrubs. The pub overlooks the old village bowling green, which now forms the lawn and here stands the original pavilion with its unusual curved windows. To one side of the lawn is the recently built Millenium Arbor. Made of local oak salvaged from the 1987 hurricane, it is cloaked by vines whose cuttings were taken from England's oldest vines that were given to Henry VIII. Visitors to the pub love sitting here, relaxing, enjoying a drink or eating, sheltered from the sun by the leafy canopy.

You may well hear locals calling the Kings Head, the Low House, because it is situated in the Blythe valley and was the lowest of the four pubs that once served the village. Whatever it is called it is a welcoming hostelry where Adrian and Sylvia Read are mine hosts. Their friendly welcome stretches out to everyone. You could be excused for thinking that you were back in Dickensian times when you step through the door. It has a warm, cosy atmosphere with high-backed settles and open fires. Because there is no bar, drinks are served at table and you summon service by banging your glass on the table or ringing the bell. In a slightly more modern vein, the chef at the Kings Head is gaining a great reputation for the quality of his cuisine. He makes a delicious vegetable broth for example and some tempting, time honoured favourites like beef stew and dumplings, liver and bacon or steak kidney pie and some delectable old-fashioned puddings.. It is all excellent value for money.

USEFUL INFORMATION

OPEN:11am-11pm at landlord's discretion
CHILDREN: Welcome
CREDIT CARDS: None taken
LICENSED: Full On
GARDEN: Yes
PETS: Yes

RESTAURANT: Great
traditional English country cooking
BAR FOOD: Home-cooked
VEGETARIAN: Yes
WHEELCHAIR ACCESS: Yes

'THE KNOLL'
182 Church Road,
Kessingland,
Suffolk
NR33 7SG

Tel: 01502 740354

Jill Thurston has lived in this comfortable house for over eighteen years and it was not until nine years ago that she made the decision to share it with guests. The decision has been a good one for those lucky enough to stay at The Knoll. Built just before the turn of this century, the house has great character and is surrounded by mature gardens, beautifully maintained and full of colour in the summer months. Inside it is warm, friendly and welcoming with lots of pictures everywhere, a happy mixture of furniture and pleasant decor. There are four guest bedrooms, all of which are ensuite and have pretty drapes, bed covers etc. as well as television and tea and coffee making facilities. The beds are comfortable and the peaceful situation of the house makes for a quiet, restful night's sleep.

Every morning Jill provides an excellent breakfast in the attractive dining room. Everything is freshly cooked to your order and as well as the traditional full breakfast with cereals, fruit juices, toast, preserves, freshly made coffee and piping hot tea, there is a Continental breakfast for those whose preference it is. Jill is also able to provide vegetarian and special diets given due notice. Evening meals are not available but Jill knows all the best places to eat in the area from pubs to restaurants. In addition Jill opens her home for functions from private parties to wedding receptions. The Knoll is licensed.

Kessingland is a splendid place for a holiday. The beach is two minutes walk from The Knoll, you can go sea fishing, take part in water sports, play golf on one of two courses within two miles, and there are horses for hire at the local riding school. Kessingland is only three miles from Lowestoft and the Norfolk Broads. There are National Trust properties to visit as well as Minsmere Bird Sanctuary. It is a great area for those who enjoy walking but if you prefer exploring towns, you will find that historic Norwich is only forty five minutes by car.

USEFUL INFORMATION

OPEN: All year
CHILDREN: Welcome
CREDIT CARDS: None taken
LICENSED: Yes
ACCOMMODATION: 4 ensuite
RATES: £18pp pn B&B

DINING ROOM: Excellent breakfast
No evening meals. Private functions
VEGETARIAN: Yes + special diets
WHEELCHAIR ACCESS: Not to
bedrooms. Function rooms only
GARDEN: Yes
PETS: No

MAGPIE INN
Norwich Road,
Stonham Parva,
Stowmarket,
Suffolk IP14 5JY

Tel: 01449 711287

Parts of the Magpie Inn date back to 1390 and it has had a miscellany of uses. It was a coaching inn, has been a post office and housed the RAF who stayed in attic rooms upstairs during World War II. Needless to say it has a ghost, if not more than one, who have been haunting the Magpie, in a friendly way, ever since the days of Dick Turpin and also probably because convicts used to be hung from the gibbet just across the road from the inn - it is still there today, as is the pub's sign which is listed and stretches right across the road - one of only three to do this in the country.

Inside this friendly, welcoming inn, Colin and Linda Buttle are mine hosts. Two cheery people who enjoy meeting people and have a knack of making everyone feel at home. Used by locals regularly, there is always something going on here. They are a mine of information about the area, something they are happy to share with visitors. Take a look around and you will still see all the trappings of bygone centuries including exposed beams, an original fireplace in the restaurant and witches markings! Colin is very proud of his cellar; the beer is excellent. Colin is also in charge of the food which is renowned in the area for its quality and for good value. The steaks and mixed grills are always popular and the home-made steak and kidney and game pies are delicious. There is also a range of traditional bar fare and Daily Specials usually consisting of time-honoured favourites. The freshly cut and filled sandwiches are huge and make a meal in themselves. Linda takes care of the front of the house.

The Magpie has three guest rooms, not ensuite but with very comfortable beds, one room has a king size bed. All three rooms have television and a hostess tray. Breakfast is a substantial and delicious meal which will set you up for the day. Stonham Parva is a friendly village and close to many visitor attractions including Helmingham Hall and Framlingham Castle. Stonham Barns Countryside Leisure Centre is two miles away and so is the Birds of Prey Centre at Stonham Aspel and Mickfield Fish Centre. Colchester is twenty three miles, Norwich thirty five miles and Great Yarmouth forty five miles. There is a Caravan Site attached to the inn.

USEFUL INFORMATION

OPEN: 11-11pm Mon-Sat 12 noon-10.30pm Sun
CHILDREN: Yes up to 8pm
CREDIT CARDS: Visa/Delta/Master
LICENSED: Full On
ACCOMMODATION: 3 rooms not ensuite
RATES: £45 per room B&B
GARDEN: Yes. Patio. Pond. Landscaped

RESTAURANT: Good
traditional fare
BAR FOOD: Wide range
Huge sandwiches
VEGETARIAN: Catered for
WHEELCHAIR ACCESS: No
PETS: Guide dogs only

THE MARLBOROUGH HOTEL
Henley Road,
Ipswich
Suffolk
IP1 3SP

AA 2 Rosettes
RAC Merit Award

Tel:01473 257677
Fax: 01226927

Just a stone's throw away from the beautiful Christchurch Park in Ipswich is the elegant family owned and run Marlborough Hotel. It is in a quiet residential area of Ipswich and provides an ideal centre for business clients and the weekend guest looking for a little luxury. The twenty two bedrooms are perfectly appointed, all ensuite and with direct-dial telephone, television and hostess trays. The inviting comfort of the public rooms reflects the relaxed yet sophisticated atmosphere of the hotel. This together with the award winning Two Rosette Victorian restaurant which overlooks the secluded floodlit garden means that the Marlborough appeals to both the business client travelling away from home and to weekend guests keen to explore Suffolk.

The Marlborough has facilities for wedding receptions, parties, conferences and meetings. Ample car parking means that they regularly cater for very large parties. The Tapestry Room provides the perfect atmosphere for small meetings. Whilst the Henley Room is ideal for private dinner parties and functions. Snape Maltings, home of Benjamin Britten's Aldeburgh Festival is just a few miles away. Nearby rise the glorious castles of Orford and Framlingham. At Pin Mill, on the River Orwell is one of the best British pubs, The Butt & Oyster, be careful with the tides. And Constable's Dedham Vale is just fifteen minutes away.

USEFUL INFORMATION

OPEN: All year
CHILDREN: Welcome
CREDIT CARDS: All major cards
LICENSED: Full On
ACCOMMODATION: 22 ensuite rooms

RESTAURANT: Award winning food
VEGETARIAN: Always a choice
WHEELCHAIR ACCESS: Yes
GARDEN: Beautiful grounds
PETS: By arrangement

RATES: Room only Sgl from £68, Dbl. £72 Suite £90
Special weekend rates & Getaway Breaks. Friday night Jazz Dinners

MOCKBEGGARS HALL
Claydon,
Ipswich,
Suffolk
IP6 0AH

ETB Listed Highly Commended

Tel: 01473 830239
Fax: 01473 833001

The name Mockbeggars Hall would attract attention in its own right but this charming house set in its own grounds of thirteen acres surrounded by farm land, stands on the side of a hill looking across at Claydon church and village, providing the visitor with a supremely relaxed and restful place in which to stay. The house is a Jacobean Manor first owned by the Bishop of London, John Aylmer, in 1621 but possibly built before that time. It still has the original turret staircase and many other features even though it was adapted for modern living by Victorians. The Dutch style gables are mentioned in a book 'Suffolk Houses' by Eric Sandon F.R.I.B.A. The present owners, Nick and Priscilla Gibson have a keen and knowledgeable interest in Holistic work with animals and their owners, for which they run courses in Animal Reiki and Mahayani Chi. and others. Holiday activities are also planned to include riding - you can bring your own horse for which there is stabling - gardening, cycle routes, walking and possibly tapestry, painting, machine knitting, painting and drawing weekends and flower arranging, if the interest is shown. In such a great setting it would be a super place in which to stay and learn at the same time. From Mockbeggars Hall there is easy access to and from the A14 and A12. It is just five miles from Ipswich town centre, a fifteen minute drive to Constable Country, and Bury St Edmunds, Colchester and Felixstowe beach are within thirty minutes drive.

Within this comfortable and welcoming house, the rooms are all stylishly furnished with a happy marriage of antique and other pieces. There are three guest bedrooms. one double ensuite with a half tester bed, one double with a king size bed and one family room sharing a bathroom - if the family room is not let, the double becomes ensuite. Each room has television, in house video, hairdryer and a hot drinks tray. The sitting room is charming with antique furniture and lots of pictures and ornaments. A log fire burns in the grate in cooler weather and on warm days the French windows open onto the garden where one can play croquet and table tennis in summer. The warmer evenings also lend themselves to Barbecues which are good fun. Priscilla enjoys cooking and provides a delicious breakfast and dinner if ordered in advance. She always discusses menus with her guests so that a meal is designed to their wishes. Horse livery rates are available on application.

USEFUL INFORMATION

OPEN: All year	DINING ROOM: Excellent breakfast
CHILDREN: Welcome	Dinner by arrangement
CREDIT CARDS: None taken	VEGETARIAN: Any diet catered for
LICENSED: No	WHEELCHAIR ACCESS: No
ACCOMMODATION: 3 rooms	GARDEN: Yes. Croquet. Table tennis
RATES: From £20 pp B&B	Barbecues
Discount for more than 4 nights stay	PETS: Outside. Stables

THE OLD RECTORY
Campsea Ash,
Nr Woodbridge,
Suffolk
IP13 0PU

Good Food Guide; Good Hotel Guide;
Which Hotel; Egon Ronay

Tel/Fax: 01728 746524

Winner of many accolades, The Old Rectory is a delightful Georgian house furnished quite beautifully but always with the comfort and ease of the guests in mind. It could not be a better location for those who enjoy walking. The coast is nearby at Orford, Aldeburgh and Southwold. At Aldeburgh you can watch the fishermen land their catch and buy fish straight from the sea. There is a Riding Stable close by and for those who love music, Snape Maltings has superb concerts all year round. Historic Castles at Framlingham and Orford provide pleasure for the explorer and also at Orford one can embark on river trips. The world famous Minsmere Bird Reserve is another 'must' on a visitor's itinerary.

Stewart Bassett is the owner and the chef. His love of food and wines produces a perfect combination for meals. You dine in the elegant Dining Room on produce that is always fresh. The set menu has three courses with daily changes and always an emphasis on seasonal dishes. It is a great way to end a day, sitting at table, enjoying good wine and afterwards taking coffee in the well furnished Drawing Room where smoking is permitted - the only room in the house. Here there is an Honesty Bar, television, and hidden away in a cupboard, board games. Tina Morford is Stewart's 'Right-Hand Person'. Her friendly smiling face greets every guests and she constantly works to ensure that everyone is content and enjoying their stay. The house is well-maintained with a regular programme of re-decoration and improvement to sustain the high standards. The pretty, well laid out garden entices guests on warm evenings.

Eleven guest bedrooms, all ensuite, are attractively and comfortably furnished with beds that are guaranteed to ensure a good night's sleep. Each room is centrally heated and has a plentifully supplied hostess tray. You come down in the morning to a delicious, freshly cooked breakfast or perhaps a Continental one if you prefer something lighter. The Old Rectory is a retreat from the busy outside world and it is not surprising that so many people come back time after time.

USEFUL INFORMATION

OPEN: All year. Closed 1 week at Christmas
CHILDREN: Welcome
CREDIT CARDS: Visa/Master/AMEX
LICENSED: Fully licensed
ACCOMMODATION: 11 ensuite rooms
RATES: From: £29 pp inc. breakfast
Children £6 per child sharing

DINING ROOM: Home-cooked, seasonal fare. Set menu
VEGETARIAN: If pre-booked
WHEELCHAIR ACCESS: No
GARDEN: Yes
PETS: Yes

PARK FARM
Sibton,
Saxmundham,
Suffolk
IP17 2LZ

ETB 2 Crowns Commended.
Member FTB

Tel: 01728 668324
Fax: 01728 668564

Park Farm is a working farm seven miles from the sea, and in the midst of a world of music with the Aldeburgh Festival and Snape Maltings providing music all the year round. The village itself is heavily involved in trying to save its beautiful church and some super concerts and flower festivals are planned to raise money. It is also ideally situated for many places including Wingfield, Eye and Framlingham, centres for artists who are drawn by the beauty of the East Anglian skies. There are many pretty villages within easy reach and for bird-watchers it is a paradise. Cycling and walking enthusiasts all delight in the countryside around Sibton.

David and Margaret Gray own Park Farm and whilst David farms Margaret cares for her guests in a delightful, relaxed, friendly manner which ensures their comfort and makes for a memorable stay. The rooms are spacious and relaxing. The Sitting Room has a log fire to cheer one on gloomy days and the Dining Room is a very pretty room with beautiful furniture. Here you breakfast in style and dine at night by candlelight.
The restful bedrooms, two twins with ensuite facilities and one double with a private bathroom, are individually 'dressed' and provided with several thoughtful touches including good books and a hostess tray, although Margaret will happily bring Morning Tea to the bedrooms. Margaret is an excellent cook and produces super meals using as much farm and local produce as possible. The results are mouth-watering.

Both David and Margaret have many interests and are heavily involved in the life of the village. Margaret is a Quilter and her quilts adorn the house, as well as many fine paintings by local artists and two by long standing guests. People will tell you that they arrive here as strangers and leave as friends.

USEFUL INFORMATION

OPEN: All year except Christmas
CHILDREN: Welcome
CREDIT CARDS: None taken
LICENSED: No
ACCOMMODATION: 3 ensuite rooms
RATES: From £17pp pn B&B
Children 1/3 reduction

DINING ROOM: Delicious home-cooked fare
VEGETARIAN: Welcome
WHEELCHAIR ACCESS: No
GARDEN: Yes. Farm walks
PETS: Dogs, well behaved by arrangement

THE QUEENS HEAD INN,
Brandeston,
Woodbridge,
Suffolk
IP13 6 AD

Tel: 01728 685307

The four hundred years old Queens Head Inn in the centre of the quiet village of Brandeston, just three miles from Framlingham, takes one back into a more restful era. It is a charming hostelry with the added touch of two ponds, home to ducks! It hasn't always been so serene however, In 1645 John Rowes, the vicar of Brandeston was tried by Matthew Hopkins, the witch-finder, in a room in the Inn, accused of being a witch. He was found guilty and was subsequently hanged in Bury St Edmunds. The village itself has quite a lot of history; tales which are happily told to visitors frequenting the Inn.

Today the Queens Head is family run with Tony and Doreen Smith at the helm, ably assisted by their daughter Louise. It is Tony who welcomes customers whilst Doreen and Louise produce the excellent fare for which the Inn is well known. Some of the dishes are outstandingly popular including very good home-made soups , a delicious lamb hot pot and that essentially English dish, Toad in the Hole. It is essentially a village Inn rather than anything else and you will always find locals at the bar, happily chewing the cud whilst they enjoy a pint or two of the very well kept ale, on which Tony prides himself. For visitors with young children, there is a Family Room. The Inn always has a friendly, happy air about it, whatever the time of the day or year, built up no doubt over the centuries but certainly enhanced by the Smith family.

You can stay here in one of the two guest rooms. They are comfortably furnished and have hand basins but share a bathroom. One is a double and the other a family room. There is extensive parking and a function room which caters for private parties.

USEFUL INFORMATION

OPEN: 11.30-2.30pm & 6-11pm
Sun: 12-3pm & 7-10.30pm
CHILDREN: Welcome. Family room
CREDIT CARDS: None taken
LICENSED: Full Licence
ACCOMMODATION: 1dbl 1fam not ensuite
RATES: £17pp pn B&B

BAR FOOD: Extensive, home-cooked
fare 7 days a week
VEGETARIAN: Good selection
WHEELCHAIR ACCESS: Yes
GARDEN: Yes
PETS: Well behaved, yes.

RANDALLS
18 Ballygate
Beccles,
Suffolk
NR54 9NA

Tel: 01502 716100

From the terraced gardens of Randalls, one of the nicest restaurants in Suffolk, one can sit and watch the activity on the River Waveney; a restful, pleasant occupation whilst studying the comprehensive and enticing menu. Ballygate is full of character buildings and not the least enchanting is Randalls, a 16th century town house which Alan Randall and his partner Gail Goldspink have lovingly restored and decorated. They have created a peaceful atmosphere with a gentle yellow decor, soft lighting, rich gold, green and terracotta checked curtains, interesting hot air balloons hanging from the beams and a splendid inglenook fireplace. The immaculately laid tables with gold linen napery, have sparkling glass and shining silver. A local artist displays her work on the walls; delightful, soft water colours, totally in keeping with the restaurant. There are thirty covers, small enough to be intimate and to appreciate the personal service offered by Gail and her staff. Alan is the chef; he has a wealth of experience gained from working for many high class establishments and this experience he has brought to Randalls, adding his own inspired touches to an exciting menu.

You may lunch or dine at Randalls. The menus change regularly and Alan uses fresh local produce and vegetables. The starters at dinner might include an unusual soup, cream of spinach and nutmeg for example or smoked haddock baked with Welsh rarebit. The main course is equally well chosen. Breast of duck with a plum chutney and rosemary jus, loin of lamb wrapped in a Tarragon mousse, carved around ratatouille with sautéed sweetbreads or baked halibut surrounded by a pear and chervil sauce. The desserts are irresistible and the cheese board tempting with Chef's selection of cheeses from Bailey's Delicatessen with home-made grape chutney. There is a set price which at the moment is, Two course dinner £15.50 and Three course dinner £19.95. Great value for money as is the carefully selected wine list. Vegetarians are catered for. Children are welcome at lunch-time and in the afternoon. This is a non-smoking restaurant.

USEFUL INFORMATION

OPEN: 11.30-2pm 3-5pm & 7-9pm
CHILDREN: Daytime only
CREDIT CARDS: All major cards
LICENSED: Yes
GARDN: Yes. Terraced

RESTAURANT: Intimate, charming
innovative menu.
VEGETARIAN: Always a choice
WHEELCHAIR ACCESS: Yes
PETS: No

ROMA RISTORANTE ITALIANO
6 Church Street,
Framlingham,
Suffolk
IP13 9BH

Tel: 01728 724283

Roma Ristorante Italiano could not be situated in a better place. Across the road is the old parish church of St Michaels dating from fourteen hundred, and nearby is the famous 12th century castle. Church Street was thought to be the inner moat at the time when the mote and bailey castle was built and was once known as Bow Street, the main shopping area. Ciro and Vanessa Cappiello's restaurant is a Grade II Listed building and has what is accepted as a rarity in Framlingham; the upper floor incorporates ceilings with formalised Tudor roses and decorative plaster work.

There is a wonderful Latin atmosphere in this delightful restaurant, largely created by Ciro and Vanessa, who are two very friendly, outgoing people, who firmly believe that the customer is all important. The decor is fresh and clean, with Continental elegance, soft music plays in the background,

Ciro is a talented and inspired chef with a wealth of experience gained both in Rome and in Europe. His food is renowned far beyond Framlingham. Every dish is produced using the freshest of ingredients and vegetables, the best olive oils and a sense of seasoning that only the Italians know how to use. There is a wide choice on the menu and everything is cooked freshly to order which means that at busy times you must have a little patience. The result is worth every minute of waiting time. The choice of wines is comprehensive but naturally with an emphasis on those from Italy. Add the superb food to the delicious wine, the friendly, efficient service and you have all the ingredients for a meal that is memorable. A restaurant not to be missed. Please book in advance.

USEFUL INFORMATION

OPEN: Evenings from 6.30pm	RESTAURANT: Delightful atmosphere
CHILDREN: Welcome	Wonderful food
CREDIT CARDS: All major cards	VEGETARIAN: Always a choice
LICENSED: Yes	WHEELCHAIR ACCESS: Yes
GARDEN: No	PETS: No

BOOKING IS ESSENTIAL

THE ROUND HOUSE RESTAURANT
Thorington,
Saxmundham,
Suffolk
IP17 3RE

Tel: 01502 478220
round@dial.pipex.com

This has to be one of the most interesting buildings in which a restaurant is housed, in the whole of Suffolk. Built in 1890, it was originally a gamekeepers cottage. Standing in a sylvan setting, it is constructed of brick and pebblestone with a thatched roof and it is literally almost round. Thorington is near an area of the Suffolk coast which is renowned for its natural beauty, very close to Southwold, Minsmere, Aldeburgh and Snape Maltings. The Round House is easily found located on the main A12 at the Thorington turn off approximately two miles south of Blythburgh.

Glen and Alison Allenby are the owners of this delightful restaurant. They are very experienced in their craft and have the knack of making it all appear so simple - the sign of a true professional. The Round House has three rooms in use for the restaurant, each attractively decorated and charmingly furnished with table linen, matching glasses and oil lamps. Before dinner on a summer's evening it is blissful to sit out on the terraced area, enjoying an aperitif and studying the very good menu which can be either a la carte or an excellent value three course dinner with coffee and half a bottle of wine, currently at the very reasonable price of £25 per head. Lunch-time menus of two and three courses with coffee at £12.50 and £14.50 are very popular. At dinner time hot canapés are always offered with complimentary mineral water. All of the menus include some interesting starters and irresistible puddings.

From the main courses on offer, one can choose anything from seared Escalopes of salmon and tuna with creamy tagliatelle or roast monkfish with lobster sauce to crispy roast duck with a sauce of peaches, redcurrants and Cointreau or rack of lamb with garlic and rosemary sauce. The menu changes regularly and takes account of the seasons. Dining here is a true gourmet experience and this is especially highlighted on the monthly Gourmet evenings and the unusual and popular 'starters and puddings' evenings which are regular events. The Round House has a mailing list which keeps its very contented clientele up to date with forthcoming evenings. The varied wine list with a wide choice of European and New World wines completes the picture. Last orders are at the closing times listed below.

USEFUL INFORMATION

OPEN: Tues-Sun: Lunch 12-2pm
Tues-Sat: Dinner 7-9.30pm
CREDIT CARDS: Visa/Master/Switch
LICENSED: Yes. Restaurant
GARDEN: Yes & Terrace

RESTAURANT: Superb
CHILDREN: Welcome
VEGETARIAN: Small menu
WHEELCHAIR ACCESS: Yes
PETS: No

THE SANDCASTLE
35 Marine Parade,
Lowestoft,
Suffolk
NR33 OQN

Tel: 01502 511799

The Sandcastle enjoys a great sea front position overlooking Lowestoft's Award Winning Beach. It is a gracious Victorian house, built in 1847 by Sir Morton Peto, who brought the railway to the town. The Guest House opened in 1997 and has a happy feel about it and bright, light and airy rooms with each room individually decorated and furnished. Tony and Susie Gittins are the owners and they have brought to the business a wealth of experience in the hospitality industry including several winners running ski chalets in the French Alps. The easy going, informal atmosphere of the ski slopes has almost been recreated here replacing snow and ice with sea and sand. Their aim is to ensure the comfort and well being of their guests and making sure they will wish to return to The Sandcastle next time they come to Suffolk.

The guest bedrooms have been furnished in an attractive but practical manner which makes it a very comfortable place for families especially. Every bedroom has television and a hostess tray, quality soft furnishings and bed linen. The rooms are not ensuite but there is a lovely Victorian style bathroom and very powerful shower in the separate shower room.

Food is always important on holiday and here you will be fed on a delicious mix of French and English cuisine professionally cooked and always using the best quality ingredients. All the meat comes from local farms, the bacon is dry cured locally from free range pigs, eggs from local farmers and kippers from the local smokehouse. Everything is cooked on an Aga and you will certainly not find supermarket meats at The Sandcastle. Children are very welcome but sadly it is entirely unsuitable for anyone needing to use a wheelchair - there are too many stairs. Pets are not allowed and there is a strict No-Smoking rule throughout the house.

USEFUL INFORMATION

OPEN: All year
CHILDREN: Welcome
CREDIT CARDS: Yes
LICENSED: No
ACCOMMODATION: Well furnished rooms
RATES: £18pppn sgl £35 dbl.
Children under 10 £7.50 10-15 £10.
Babies in cots free.

DINING ROOM: French/English cuisine
VEGETARIAN: Upon request
WHEELCHAIR ACCESS: No
GARDEN: No
PETS: No
NON-SMOKING HOUSE

STERNFIELD HOUSE
Church Hill,
Sternfield,
Saxmundham,
Suffolk
IP17 1RS

Tel: 01728 602252
Fax: 01728 604082

Sternfield House is a fine example of Double-Bow Queen Anne architecture and retains inside much of its original features despite of being used as the Divisional Headquarters for the 3rd Armoured Division in the Second World War. It has its claim to fame in a quieter manner because it was owned by a Comptroller of the Royal Household and he and his family were quite used to receiving Royal guests on private visits. They found it a retreat from the busy world in just the same manner that guests do today. You approach the house, which nestles in a dell amid 25 acres, through a parkland drive and in the background there is the old historic. church which looks as though it was part of the property. It is idyllic and the friendly welcome you get from the owner, Jenny Thornton emphasises what a welcoming home this has been through the centuries.

Sternfield is only a small village but it is within easy reach of Saxmundham, Framlingham Castle is no distance nor is Snape Maltings, where there are concerts throughout the year or Minsmere Bird Sanctuary with its profusion of rare birds and wildlife in general. There are only two guest rooms in this non-smoking house , and every guest feels privileged, relaxed and pampered after a night spent either in a luxurious king-size bed in a very large ensuite room overlooking the gardens and parkland or in the smaller double which has a Queen size bed, is also ensuite and has the same view. The rooms are beautifully furnished with a happy mixture of antiques and other pieces. Both rooms have television and a hostess tray. The Garden entices many guests with its beauty, its tennis court, its swimming pool and the opportunity of playing Croquet. Breakfast is a delicious meal, freshly cooked to your order and always includes free range eggs and as much local produce as possible. An evening meal is available upon request.

USEFUL INFORMATION

OPEN: All year except Christmas
CHILDREN: Over 12 years
CREDIT CARDS: None taken
LICENSED: No
ACCOMMODATION: 2 dbl. ensuite
RATES: Sgl from £30 Dbl. from £50
Short breaks: 3 nights for the price of two

DINING ROOM: Delicious
freshly cooked breakfast
VEGETARIAN: Upon request
WHEELCHAIR ACCESS: Yes
GARDEN: 25 acres. Tennis
Swimming pool. Croquet
PETS: No

STRICTLY NON-SMOKING HOUSE

TANNINGTON HALL
Tannington,
Woodbridge,
Suffolk
IP13 7NH

Tel: 01728 628226
Fax: 01728 628646

Tannington Hall is situated in deepest rural Suffolk surrounded by rolling farmland. The setting is perfect with beautifully kept grounds and fishing for carp in the moat. Here you may have a clay shoot nearby or play golf on a course close to hand. There are many places locally to visit including the working windmill at Saxtead, Framlingham Castle, Minsmere Bird Sanctuary and Snape Maltings but more importantly Tannington Hall itself has 12 carriage horses in regular work taking guests and the public for pleasure drives in traditional vehicles and gypsy caravans. There are a range of Carriage Drive options. You may relax in your private carriage and let your coachman drive you through peaceful country lanes, and maybe stop off at the King's Head at Laxfield for a snack, a meal or just a drink. On evening trips you can enjoy the romantic experience of the drive back to the Hall with lamps shining on your carriage. Once back at the Hall enjoy a lunch or candlelit dinner chosen by you in advance from the extensive menu and cooked especially for your party. After lunch, spend a pleasant hour or so walking round the gardens, stables and the collection of horse-drawn vehicles. Tannington Hall caters for parties of between two and sixty, you must remember to bring your own wine because the Hall is not licensed. Gypsy Picnics are a firm favourite with children and the young at heart. You arrive at the Hall with your picnic and are driven off in a genuine gypsy caravan to a quiet spot in a woodland clearing. While the horse grazes nearby, collect sticks for the fire and when all is ready the kettle and frying pan are hung over the fire on a special hook. Children and adults, sitting on rugs or logs, watch with eager eyes as the sausages sizzle in the pan and kettle boils for tea. A wonderful outing.

Tannington Hall was a monastery before the Dissolution and the house contains many unusual features, a moulded Jacobean ceiling in the drawing room, a solid oak staircase - a horse was once ridden up these stairs - and listed fireplaces. In the grounds, black swans roam and there is a unique round half-timbered building with eleven different styles of brickwork. Horse drawn carriages enter and leave the courtyard, as in the old coaching days. Guests are invited to enjoy a carriage drive down local lanes and view the collection of fifty traditional vehicles. You may stay in the Hall if you wish. There are four guest rooms, two ensuite double and one with a private bath and one ensuite twin bedded room. It is a very happy, informal and relaxed place to stay and you will certainly be well fed. Judith Vaudrey who owns Tannington Hall with her father, Tony Harvey, is Cordon Bleu trained.

USEFUL INFORMATION

OPEN: All year
CHILDREN: Welcome
CREDIT CARDS: None taken
LICENSED: No BYO
ACCOMMODATION: 4 ensuite rooms
RATES: £25pp pn B&B Children 1/2 price

RESTAURANT: Cordon bleu
                                       cooking
VEGETARIAN: Upon request
WHEELCHAIR ACCESS: No
GARDEN: Beautiful grounds
PETS: Yes

WOODLANDS FARM
Brundish,
Framlingham,
Suffolk
IP13 8BP

Tourist Board 2 Crown
Highly Commended.
AA 4Q Selected

Tel:01379 384444

You will not find a more welcoming or happier place to stay in the county than the non-smoking Woodlands Farm, the home of John and Jill Graham who have lived and loved the county of Suffolk for the majority of their lives and are always ready to help guests in any way they can. It is a traditional Suffolk Longhouse style built about two hundred years ago and still retaining the atmosphere of the past enhanced by lots of beams, inglenook fireplaces in the Sitting and Dining Rooms. Every room has been furnished with loving care and the whole creates a warm, friendly atmosphere. You are invited to enjoy the beautiful garden and relax sitting under the huge Weeping Willow overlooking the water lilies on the pond in summer evenings and listen to birds singing and the occasional horse trotting along the lanes. On cooler evenings after a brisk walk you come back to a welcome cup of tea in front of a roaring log fire.

Woodlands Farm has three guest rooms, two ensuite and the other one with private bathrooms. The beds are strictly of the 1990s but the rooms are delightful. Antique furniture and beams give them an olde world feeling. Each room has a generously supplied hostess tray. Jill is renowned for her delicious food which is quite apparent every day when you are served breakfast and if you dine in, the excellence of the meal cooked from locally produced meat and most vegetables, and soft fruit, grown in their own garden. It is good farmhouse fare and Vegetarians are catered for imaginatively.

Set close to orchards in peaceful countryside in the Heart of Suffolk, six miles north of Framlingham, Woodlands Farm is ideally situated for exploring the half-timbered market towns, medieval churches and castles, the Heritage Coast, Minsmere Bird Reserve, Snape Maltings and Constable Country. It is great countryside for both walkers and cyclists.

USEFUL INFORMATION

OPEN: All year excluding Christmas
CHILDREN: Over 10 years
CREDIT CARDS; None taken
LICENSED: No
ACCOMMODATION: Ensuite rooms
RATES: From £18pp B&B

DINING ROOM: Delicious home-cooked farmhouse fare
VEGETARIAN: Catered for
WHEELCHAIR ACCESS: No
GARDEN: Yes, beautiful
PETS: No

STRICTLY NON-SMOKING

THE CAPTAIN'S TABLE
3 Quay Street,
Woodbridge,
Suffolk
IP12 1BX

Tel: 01394 383145

For those who have enjoyed the delicious food and impeccable service at The Captain's Table in the past, you will be delighted to know that the tradition is now to be carried on by Joanna Moussa and Pascal Pommier who are accomplishing their dream of opening their own restaurant in an area they call home. They are a talented pair whose enjoyment of good food and wine has been an integral part of their lives for many years and now they hope to have the opportunity of sharing that with you. They want The Captain's Table to continue its long established tradition of providing memorable meals in a comfortable environment and to this end you can be sure of the freshest ingredients being used with flair, service being friendly and a bill that reflects value for money. The wide selection of dishes will include local fish and seafood as it has always done. The wine list is a good selection of carefully chosen wines from all over the world. It is quite apparent that Jo and Pascal, who have high standards, will bring a new and exciting ambience to this well tried and well loved 16th century, yellow washed restaurant.

USEFUL INFORMATION

OPEN: Tues-Sat: 12-2 & 6.30-9.30pm
(Fri & Sat 10pm) Sun 12-3pm
CHILDREN: Welcome
CREDIT CARDS: Visa/Master/Switch
LICENSED: Yes
GARDEN: Walled with patio
PETS: No

RESTAURANT: Superb cooking
with flair and imagination
BAR FOOD: Wide range
VEGETARIAN: Yes. Vegan &
others by arrangement
WHEELCHAIR ACCESS: Yes with ramp

CATHERINE HOUSE
2 Ringsfield Road,
Beccles, Suffolk NR34 9PQ
2 Crowns commended

Tel/Fax: 01502 716428

Beccles is on the Norfolk Broads and part of the National Park with Bird Watching Reserves. Close by are the seaside town of Gt. Yarmouth and the historic city of Norwich. Situated in a quiet road just five minutes from the picturesque town is Catherine House at No.2 Ringsfield Road. This beautifully maintained home looks out over the Waveney Valley . The owners Karen and William Renilson are naturally friendly people and they clearly enjoy welcoming guests to their attractive house. All the rooms are decorated and furnished to a very high standard and the three bedrooms are well appointed with antique pine furniture, television and video, a hostess tray, wash hand basins, hairdryers and shaving points. One room has a four-poster bed, one family room is ensuite and there is also a single room. A cot and high chair are available. A full English Breakfast is served every morning with a choice and using fresh local produce. No evening meals but there is an extensive choice of restaurants, pubs and wine bars in the town centre. Guests are welcome to use the garden and can play croquet upon request.

USEFUL INFORMATION

OPEN: All year
CHILDREN: Welcome
CREDIT CARDS: None taken
LICENSED: No
ACCOMMODATION: 3 rooms 1 ensuite
RATES: From £20.00pp B&B

DINING ROOM: Great breakfast
VEGETARIAN: Upon request
WHEELCHAIR ACCESS: No
GARDEN: Croquet. Sun Lounges
PETS: No

FIDDLERS HALL
Cransford, Framlingham,
Woodbridge, Suffolk IP13 9PQ

Tel: 01728 663729

Fiddlers Hall is a 15th century moated farmhouse and a working farm in a secluded peaceful setting. It has lost nothing of its old world charm with heavily beamed inglenook fireplaces, wattle and daub walls . To stay here is to feel removed from the stress of the 1990s and with the opportunity to recharge your batteries before you face the world again. This feeling is enhanced by having the opportunity to feed the animals, milk a goat, search for the free range eggs and perhaps scratch the backs of the very rare pigs from New Zealand. There is a Shetland Pony and a Suffolk horse to ride. Jennie Mann is your hostess and it is immediately apparent that she loves having, and caring, for her guests. There is a Guest Lounge with a roaring log fire in winter, television and roomy, comfortable armchairs and sofas. The large dining room is where you will be served a true Suffolk farmhouse breakfast with everything home produced. Add this to grapefruit, cereals and fruit juices as well as plenty of toast, home-made marmalades and jams, and you will have enjoyed a sample of Suffolk produce. There is a charmingly furnished double bedroom with ensuite shower, toilet and hand basin plus a family room with large private bathroom. Fiddlers Hall is near the coast and two miles from Framlingham Castle.

USEFUL INFORMATION

OPEN: All year
CHILDREN: Welcome
CREDIT CARDS: None taken
LICENSED: No
ACCOMMODATION: 1dbl ensuite
Family room with large private bathroom
RATES: From £20pp pn B&B

DINING ROOM: Excellent breakfast
VEGETARIAN: Upon request
WHEELCHAIR ACCESS: No
GARDEN: Yes + Farm
PETS: No

NO 3 CAUTLEY ROAD,
Southwold,
Suffolk IP18 6DD

Tourist Board 2 Crowns Commended

Tel: 01502 723611

Southwold remains today much as it was many years ago. A great place in which to take a break or a holiday. Where better to stay than the elegant Edwardian Number 3 Cautley Road where Barry and Helen Collis personally look after the welfare of their guests. It is only four minutes walk to the beach and shops. Inside this beautifully appointed house, the rooms are spacious with high ceilings. In the very comfortable lounge you will find a chesterfield suite, exposed floor boards and, in winter, a roaring fire. It all resembles the style and atmosphere of an old Gentleman's Club. The Breakfast Room where you will be served one of the best breakfasts in Suffolk, is charming and just the place to start your day. At night you will sleep peacefully in one of the three ensuite guest rooms, each with large beds. Each room has a hostess tray, television, a radio alarm and a hairdryer. Open all the year, it is ideal for those on business or pleasure.

USEFUL INFORMATION

OPEN: All year
CHILDREN: Welcome
CREDIT CARDS: None taken
LICENSED: No
ACCOMMODATION: 3 ensuite rooms
RATES: From £25 pp B&B

BREAKFAST ROOM: Great breakfast
VEGETARIAN: Upon request
WHEELCHAIR ACCESS: Not really
GARDEN: Yes. Bicycle storage if needed
PETS: Yes

THE OLD BOOT HOUSE
Main Road,
Shotley, Ipswich,
Suffolk IP9 1EY

2 AA Rosettes
Good Food Guide recommended
Tel: 01473 787755

Nestled on the peninsular between the rivers Stour & Orwell in Shotley, just Southeast of Ipswich, The Old Boot House in the Main Street, is a charming restaurant offering the essence of country cooking. It is a delightfully informal place surrounded on all sides by wheat, barley, beet and free range pigs. The menus are inspired by the location and incorporate as much seasonal local goodies as possible, with a hint of the exotic. John Downie crab apple trees provide the restaurant with plenty of scented amber crab apple jelly to serve with the slow roasted pork shanks with caraway flavoured cracking for Sunday lunch. Ian and Pamela Chamberlain, the welcoming owners, use their own Hidcot lavender jelly to accompany the potted goose at Christmas. The menu is delicious and includes Starters like fresh east coast crab sausage with pickled samphire, followed perhaps by baked hare fillets wrapped in butter puff with Suffolk black bacon and elderberry sauce. If, after this you have room for one of the tempting desserts, try the rose petal and raspberry tart - the roses are grown on the front of the restaurant.

USEFUL INFORMATION

OPEN: All year
CHILDREN: Welcome menu.
VEGETARIAN: By arrangement
CREDIT CARDS: Barclaycard/Access/Visa
GARDEN: No

RESTAURANT: Non-smoking. Inspired
Booking advised
WHEELCHAIR ACCESS: Yes
LICENSED: Restaurant Licence
PETS: No

ROSE CORNER GUEST HOUSE
5 Glenavon Road,
Ipswich, Suffolk IP4 5PJ
Tourist Board Listed &Approved
Tel: 01473 728041

Once having stayed in Rose Corner Guest House you will understand why so many people from all over the world have stayed here as often as they are in this part of East Anglia. Marlene and Brian Snell are the owners and their constant endeavours to ensure their guests comfort has produced this result. They are both friendly, outgoing people who genuinely enjoy visitors. Within this homely atmosphere there are four guest bedrooms. Two of the rooms are ensuite and the others have showers and basins. They are all attractively decorated and both television and hostess trays are there for the benefit of guests. There is a comfortable Guest Lounge with television and a pleasant Dining Room where Breakfast in the true English fashion, is served every day. Rose Corner, within easy access to the A14, is on the east side of Ipswich and backs onto the Rushmere Golf Course. There are no less than four other courses within three miles and four Bowls Clubs within two miles who welcome the touring visitor. Ten Pin Bowling, Squash Court and Health Club are half a mile along the road. Local bus services to the town centre run every fifteen minutes from the end of Glenavon Road. Ipswich is an historic Anglo-Saxon town with much to interest the visitor including Christchurch Mansion with a wealth of paintings on display including Constable and Gainsborough. Thomas Wolsey's Gate, Ipswich Museum and a tour of a local brewery. There are guided tours around the town which are well worth joining.

USEFUL INFORMATION

OPEN: All year
CHILDREN: Welcome
CREDIT CARDS: None taken
LICENSED: No
ACCOMMODATION:2 ensuite
2 with showers
RATES: £18pppn Children under 5 FOC 5-16 £9

DINING ROOM: Excellent home-cooked
VEGETARIAN: Catered for
WHEELCHAIR ACCESS: Yes
GARDEN: Yes
PETS: Yes

THE SOLE BAY INN
7 East Green,
Southwold,
Suffolk IP18 6JN

Tel: 01502 723736
Fax: 01502 72456

Southwold lies in the centre of an area of great natural beauty - a paradise for the walker, the naturalist, the bird-watcher. The ancient borough was granted a Charter by Henry VII in 1489 and somehow not much has changed through the centuries. It is still away from 'the madding crowd' a peaceful existence for its residents and a place of sheer delight for visitors. To many, the distinctive charm of Southwold stems from the haphazard grouping of houses of differing architectural designs, resulting in an unique blend. In amongst all this is The Sole Bay Inn, a welcoming hostelry which is all one could wish for. Built in the 19th century, it is a comfortable, friendly hostelry much used by local people but equally welcoming to strangers. Tony and Rose Fisher are the cheerful landlords. Tony is a Fellow of the British Institute of Innkeepers. The running of the Inn leaves no one in any doubt that the accolade is well earned. The food is simple, traditional, pub fare and the ale well kept. The bedrooms are comfortable and well furnished and each has both television and a hospitality tray. A happy place to stay and ideal for exploring this glorious part of Suffolk.

USEFUL INFORMATION

OPEN: 11am-11pm
CHILDREN: Yes, if well behaved
CREDIT CARDS: None taken
LICENSED: Yes
ACCOMMODATION: Comfortable rooms
RATES: £35 per room B&B

BAR FOOD: Traditional fare
VEGETARIAN: Upon request
WHEELCHAIR ACCESS: No
GARDEN: Small patio
PETS: No

THE WEAVERS TEA ROOMS
The Knoll, Peasenhall,
Saxmundham, Suffolk IP17 2JE

Tel: 01728 660548

Situated in a quiet part of Peasenhall and within an atmospheric listed building, The Weavers Tea Rooms is a regular haunt for locals and a place to be sought out by visitors. The quality of everything served here and the pleasing ambience ensures a contented clientele. Everything is home-made - the cakes, scones and cream teas are irresistible. On the menu you will find traditional English fare with the additions of Daily Specials which more often than not are time honoured favourites. You are as welcome to pop in for a coffee as you are for a full blown meal. Trudy Hollands is the owner and both she and her staff set great store in welcoming customers. In the evenings after 6.30pm it is necessary to book a table. Children are welcome and their tastes catered for as well as vegetarians. Weavers is not licensed but you are very welcome to bring your own wine.

USEFUL INFORMATION

OPEN: 9-6.30pm
CHILDREN: Welcome
CREDIT CARDS: All major cards
LICENSED: No BYO
PETS: Well behaved dogs

RESTAURANT: Home-cooked fare
Evening bookings only
VEGETARIAN: Yes
WHEELCHAIR ACCESS: By request

Selected venues in this chapter

' Never eat anything at one sitting that you can't lift.
Always use one of the new - and far more reliable - elastic measuring tape,
to check your waistline'...
Miss Piggy.

Chapter Twelve: N. ESSEX:
Oysters, Charm and Ancient Towns
Colchester to Maldon, Halstead & Saffron Waldon

We're at our last base: **COLCHESTER** (Information - 01206 282920). Last night I found myself wondering why. How many people do *you* know who'd be getting excited about a holiday in *Essex*? I don't necessarily mean Clacton or Frinton, either. I mean *inland* Essex, somewhere between where we're sitting over one more breakfast and Stanstead, where you can't hear yourself think above the racket of jet loads of holiday packages coming and going. It all sounds *really* attractive, wouldn't you say?.

Actually it hides many treasures for the tourist, coupled with some typically English oddities. For example, Suffolk has grabbed *all* of Constable for itself - but the village of Dedham is actually in Essex. Then talk of castles may draw the mind to the Welsh Borders, while Norwich has plenty to say about its own castle (now a museum, as we've seen). Yet the largest surviving Norman keep ever built in Europe is right here, in Colchester. Town walls? We've seen plenty of stretches of those in our tours, but nothing to touch remotely the one and a half *miles* of wall, complete with the country's largest remaining Roman gateway - again in Colchester. By contrast, over to the west of the area, one finds a host of unspoilt villages where comments like 'enchanting' and 'lovely' are almost understatements for places whose streets and squares are some of the most photographed in England.

Meanwhile, fame and anonymity walk unpredictably over rolling, wooded hills. Thaxted and Dumow are familiar names - but who remembers the equally attractive Finchingfield or Wendens Ambo? Again, how many of the people who *do* know that Colchester Castle is huge have even heard of Castle Hedingham which, in reality, runs it pretty close? Finally, while the Civil War battles of Edgehill, Naseby and Marston Moor are familiar enough for folklore, how many details do any of us know of the Parliamentarians' eleven week siege of Colchester in 1648? And so it goes on. And on, apparently - with the country's tallest Tudor gate-house down the road, the home of connoisseur's jam a little further still and a bevy of vineyards all over the place. Not to mention the oysters, the cream teas, the fish, the French cuisine and much else.

So, abandon prejudice all ye who are dawdling over coffee; turn procrastination to positive action - and let's get stuck into this place.

COLCHESTER CASTLE

Before our wanderings take up a particular direction we need to fix one fact firmly in our minds: we are about to take on the oldest recorded town in England. By the time the Romans arrived in 43AD, the settlement was already seven hundred years old and had been the capital of Cunobelin - Shakespeare's Cymbeline, the King of south east England - since the early days of the 1st Century. Despite being protected to the west by ramparts, parts of which can still be seen, Camulodunum, as it was called, was overrun by the Roman invaders who established their own first colony in Britain nearby. Not for long though: in AD60 nemesis arrived in the form of Boadicea and an army of Britons who had a marked lack of enthusiasm for the new regime. To make their point, they sacked the city and wrecked the temple, leaving a mass of wreckage that somehow lacked the status of the original - for years. The Romans didn't get where they got by giving in though, and they rebuilt the place as a major town during the 2nd Century. In other words, the Romans laid down the streets that have since become those of modern Colchester something like 1800 years ago and the 'old quarter' is still surrounded by their original walls, pierced by the monumental West, or BALKERNE GATE.

When the Romans finally ran out of steam early in the 5th Century, under pressure from various bunches of 'barbarians' (i.e. people who *weren't* Romans and hence had rather different, horrid habits), Britain was, to all intents and purposes, up for grabs. The Saxons duly grabbed and immediately took over Camelodunum and renamed it Colchester - "the Roman fortress on the River Colne." Either they weren't as barbaric as the Roman propaganda made out, or the atmosphere of the town had a soothing effect, because the community prospered under their control throughout the next six hundred years, until the Norman Conquest. By the time this latest bunch of invaders crossed the Thames and headed north, they would have found Colchester well established as a large, vigorous borough - just the kind of place, in other words, that would need a *very* large castle and some *extremely* vigorous men at arms to keep it under control. These were duly provided - the Castle being even bigger in those days, with two more storeys than we see today and a ground plan fifty percent larger than that of the White Tower at the Tower of London! The men at arms must have been well up to scratch too, as there's not much sign of later interruptions in the general scheme of getting seriously richer.

Along with most of East Anglia the town built up its share of the riches during the Middle Ages on the back of the wool and cloth trades, to which, in this case, were added profits from its fishery and market. The cloth trade dropped away in the 1550s but was revived some twenty years later by a contingent of five hundred Flemish protestant refugees who arrived to settle in the town. The half-timbered and plastered houses (some of which were built long before the 16th Century) around STOCKWELL STREET are even today known as the DUTCH QUARTER, which appears to make up nearly a third of the town.

The town was also an important port at the time, and THE HYTHE is still in use, although it's been somewhat out gunned by developments further round the coast at Harwich, Felixstowe and Ipswich. Meanwhile, seventy years passed with little more turmoil than anywhere else - until the Civil War. Colchester backed the eventual losers, unfortunately, and suffered severe damage as a result of the eleven week siege by the Roundheads that duly followed in 1648. The town was taken, the two Royalist leaders were executed as rebels and an uneasy settlement ensued until the Restoration - whereupon life returned, more or less, to what passed for normality in those days and remained that way until the Napoleonic Wars, around a hundred years later, when Colchester found itself formed into a garrison town.

Around this time the cloth trade finally reached the end of its terminal decline and disappeared. The gap it left was soon filled by an engineering industry that restored the town's income and nowadays clothes manufacture and agriculture play their part as well. In the meantime, the Hythe also seems to have recovered from the reduction in trade caused by the coming of the railway in the 19th Century, even in the shadows of its neighbours, with more than 2,000 ships involved in coastal trading here every year.

We've looked at Colchester's strategic and economic ups and downs - what of its relations with the Church? ST JOHNS ABBEY was founded by the Benedictine Order in 1096, but all that is left of it since the efforts of Henry VIII is the splendid 15th Century GATEHOUSE. Two storeys high, it has battlements and octagonal turrets. Another monastic building, also dating from the 11th Century is ST BOTOLPH'S PRIORY which remains as the ruin created by the Roundhead battering in 1648 with only the west front, its splendid doorway and part of the nave still recognisable.

Suppose we leave the historical sites for a moment and take a break in a Museum or two - or four! There are a couple quite close to the Priory, while the visit to the fourth will take us right into the centre of the main shopping area. Need I say more? If we continue up ST BOTOLPH'S STREET into QUEEN STREET and cross over, a step or two will bring us to Colchester's NATURAL HISTORY MUSEUM for a start. The idea here is a 'hands on' approach to matters concerning the local environment, from the Ice Age right up to the present day. Admission is free and opening times are from Tuesday to Saturday between 10.00am and 5.00pm, with a break for lunch from 1.00pm to 2.00pm.

Crossing the road again, half right into UPPER CASTLE PARK, we come to HOLLYTREES MUSEUM in the HIGH STREET. In this elegant Georgian townhouse, dating from 1718 we find interiors set out as they would have been over two hundred years ago, complete with many items and fittings that would have been the height of fashion in those days. Admission is again free with opening times as for the Natural History Museum, except that lunch is taken earlier, between noon and 1.00pm.

If we head roughly west at this stage, across the Park to the Castle, we can call in next at the CASTLE MUSEUM, which is not free but is open longer - from Monday to Saturday, throughout the year, between 10.00am to 5.00pm with Sunday opening as well, between 2.00pm and 5.00pm from March to November. Last admissions are at 4.30pm. The charge is £3.50 a head for adults and it is suggested that a phone call is made to 01206 282931/2 before a visit, to check on group discounts, guided tours and special events.

Having got all that out of the way, what do we find? We find an Aladdin's cave of a place, but on the grand scale, with many different collections whose importance - nationally and internationally - could only be surpassed rarely. As you'd expect there's a fairly strong emphasis on the town's past, with exhibits ranging from the mysterious four thousand year old Dagenham Idol to a tour round the dungeon - with the splendid Roman Middleborough Mosaic as a bonus. Again there are various hands on displays, which seem to be growing in popularity. Whatever your particular interests, it's a place that's not to be rushed and two to three hours is recommended for the average visit.

When we come out of the Museum, all the pointers will tend to dictate a spell of fresh air - coffee al fresco, even. With a shade more of the Aladdin touch, it's all available on site, so to speak, as the CASTLE PARK AND GARDENS are right in front of us: an "oasis of horticultural splendour" in a town that must have more square feet of public parks and gardens per head of the population that anywhere we've seen in East Anglia. Whatever street you're in it seems there's always a view of green spaces, flowers and trees within a pace or two. Of the 180 acre total, 33 acres are laid out around the Castle so, as that's where we happen to be at this very moment, let's see what all the excitement's about.

Colchester is rightly proud of its Victorian Castle Park and Gardens. A town guide said it's *"one of the prettiest jewels in Colchester's crown"* and many visitors spend more time there than at any other one feature in the locality. With justification, I have to say. It's no distance at all to the shops and yet here we are amongst delightfully landscaped gardens with terraces, riverside walks and a boating lake and pond. This award winning concept re-creates the classic Victorian park atmosphere and, as we head up the hill for coffee at the cafe by the bandstand we can re-capture the charm and the quiet elegance of such places at their best, just as though we had stepped back in time.

The other side of park life is also taken into account. There's Pitch and Putt in the summer, plenty of scope for children - especially where the boating lake is concerned - and festivals, fairs, displays and open air concerts throughout the year, whose organisers see Castle Park as the perfect venue. For us it's a refreshing pause in a busy day, a place for people watching and a chance to air our reactions to the museums and the history among our companions. Another coffee? Mine's black, if you remember - Sumatra if possible. Looking out over the flower beds I'm reminded by the display of exquisite pink roses that Colchester is home to one of the best respected specialist rose growers in the country: CANT'S OF COLCHESTER (Information - 01206 844008). Their colourful nurseries at NAYLAND ROAD, MILE END, just up the A134 Bury St Edmunds road, are an obvious source of delight to gardeners, especially as amongst all the many varieties there's one called 'Colchester Beauty' which would make a marvellous perennial souvenir of one's visit.

With the promise of a tour of the shops very much in mind, let's leave the Park for a while and wander across the High Street and down TRINITY STREET to the last Museum on our current short list. TYMPERLEYS CLOCK MUSEUM feels like a first for us, even after all the visits we've made since we arrived in the region. However many clock collections we've seen, there can't have been more than one or two that could come anywhere near the quality and variety of the collection in this 15th Century timber framed house, especially when one realises that all of the 18th and 19th Century pieces on display were actually made in the town. Indeed, so impressive is the collection that it caught the eye of the BBC who featured it on the 'Antiques Roadshow' programme. Yet again admission is free and the Museum is open from April to October, Tuesday to Saturdays, between 10.00am and 5.00pm with what seems to be the obligatory lunch break around here between 1.00pm and 2.00pm. Time having ticked away dramatically at Tymperleys we find ourselves as close to the centre of the shopping area as we have any right to expect - so, let's get stuck in. Even on the brief look that we had on our way to the Museum, it's obvious that Colchester is another one of East Anglia's real treats when it comes to *our* kind of shopping. Of course there are the modern facilities: ST JOHN'S, CULVER and LION WALK shopping centres are big, bright and bursting with familiar outlets for everything from toothpaste to toys to television. Mercifully the town has recognised that tourism requires a different, more local approach and has met that requirement handsomely.

As one would imagine in a town of this antiquity, the older areas are mazes of narrow alleyways and lanes and these are packed with small specialist shops that are likely to keep us occupied for hours at a time. It's all a very special experience across the spectrum from galleries and antique shops to street traders - as well as the MARKET, on Fridays and Saturdays. Let's start with Colchester's own exclusive, independent department store, shall we? WILLIAMS & GRIFFIN (Enquiries - 01206 571212) is on the High Street and operates on six levels, each with its own distinctive character. The store has all the character and quality that one would expect from such a place and no more so than at Christmas, when Santa Claus is in residence amidst all the glitter of magical, seasonal displays.

Talk of Christmas, Santa Claus and toys must lead us straight away back down to SIR ISAAC'S WALK and THE BEAR SHOP (Enquiries - 01206 577345). We've seen teddy bears before - and we've decided that comparisons are a waste of energy on tours like these - but have we *ever* seen anything quite like *this* place? Everybody seems to have had at least one in the course of their lives - but the Bear Shop gives an idea of the possibilities in the furry beasties that borders on the stunning. They've got literally hundreds of them from tiddlers about an inch high to monsters that are several feet from top to toe. There's a price range to match, where a little one will set you back a modest few quid while a limited edition collector's item has the sort of appealing expression that would make parting with fifty or sixty pounds an act of kindness! Not to be missed - and we don't hand out *that* accolade too often.

On the other hand, we *might* be about to hand out one more! Just south of all the bears, on ST JOHN'S STREET, is the PAM SCHOMBERG GALLERY (Enquiries - 01206 769458), which is open between 10.30am and 5.00pm, Monday to Saturday. These things come down to a matter of taste as much as anything - provided the technical skills are there in the first place. As far as my own feelings are concerned, if someone gave me a blank cheque and a supermarket trolley, I'd next be seen emerging from Schomberg's fully laden - and that would include my jacket pockets. To me, the exhibits, whether they're in ceramics, glass, textiles, wood or metal, are as exciting as anything you'll find in any other town in Britain. The jewellery is probably of the same order, but I'm not a jewellery person, particularly, so I won't offer more than an approving grin, on this occasion. We've seen many excellent galleries and craft centres on our earlier tours - and this is *definitely* one time I'll avoid all idea of comparisons or pecking orders - so, if you enjoyed them and found the odd item or two to delight you, go to Schomberg's.

After you've gone there you might just be tempted to push your acquaintance with contemporary art a shade closer to the cutting edge. Put more simply, that would add up to another stroll across town to the east end of the High Street where we'll find THE MINORIES (Enquiries - 01206 577067), headquarters of FIRSTSITE, Colchester's premier contemporary visual arts organisation, and the location for one of East Anglia's foremost contemporary art exhibition programmes. Housed in a converted town house that is predominantly Georgian, the changing displays are presented throughout the year. They include sculpture, painting and photography which are exhibited within the Minories' many galleries.

There's more - again! As we must have realised by now, a place of this kind in Colchester is bound to have a garden - and it has. Quite a garden. Enough of a garden, in fact, to have attracted the attention of Lucien Pisarro, who once worked here and who, one can imagine, must have been very taken with the tranquillity of it all, particularly in the walled area. Or was it the Gothic folly that inspired him?

Given the sylvan setting, there's one more essential feature - and that hasn't been overlooked either. Colchester is a town where eating out is treated as a pastime of ritualistic - even mystic - significance for the visitor. At the Minories there's a GARDEN CAFE so, however avant garde one's artistic tastes, however many of the exhibits one has coveted, one can, in the end, retreat to the reassurance of home-made cakes and speciality coffees, or even a light lunch if the time is right. These people think of everything! Actually they do: the cafe even has a licence, bless it. Opening hours are from 10.00am to 5.00pm, Monday to Saturday throughout the year. Between Easter and October, however, closing time is an hour earlier at 4.00pm.

I don't know about you, but after such a spectacular stream of visual delights, topped off with a cup or two of Sumatra (black, two sugars) I'm just about ready for something completely different. Now what on earth might *that* be? No, the shopping trip hasn't been abandoned all together - or even for the rest of the day - I just have an irresistible desire to rush off somewhere out of the ordinary. Is Colchester up to it? Well, there's ROLLERWORLD and QUASAR, all roller skates and laser guns with lights, smoke and pounding music to take us out of ourselves - permanently. No, I think not. Not this time. How about the ESSEX SECRET BUNKER, then? What *is* it? It's the former Essex County Nuclear War HQ, preserved just as it was when it was released from the official secrets list. Not the thing for a holiday, perhaps, even if they do have a cafe. Ah! I have it. The very thing - and I'm absolutely positive we haven't done one of these, yet. You're going to love the idea - if not, *you* go roller-skate or walk round the bunker and *I'll* see you later at AQUA SPRINGS (Information - 01206 282010) in COWDRAY AVENUE.

They call it "the ultimate relaxation for adults" and I'm not about to argue. The prices match the experience, I've no doubt, but every once in a while there has to be a time when you *need* to say: "Honey, I don't give a damn! Hang the expense!" This is one of those times. I won't quibble about the phrase "Mediterranean sauna" being a bit of a geographical contradiction, as the essence of the place is so luxurious I wouldn't care whether the Swedish population of Monte Carlo do it every day or not. Whoever thought of the combination, it works, and that's what we're paying for. Of course, with four separate saunas, massage, aromatherapy, steam room and hot spa bath - complete with fountain and waterfall - it *ought* to work. Some don't, though, while others try to mix these ultimate delights of self indulgence and cosseting with the brutalities of diets, fitness suites and weight training - as if you ought to torture yourself afterwards, like good northern puritans, to exorcise your guilt. Forget it. Let's have the works - and then get ready for dinner.

Some of the more eager souls may be away from Aqua Springs in time for tea in one of Colchester's delightful - and typically English - tea rooms. The rest of us may well have to be dragged out kicking and screaming to cram in a couple of cocktails before adjourning for something more substantial. After all it's the kind of place where time stays firmly on the back burner for the duration.

We know already that there's ample variety in the menus of the town's restaurants and hotels to make the start of the evening a source of joy, so what might come next? That, of course, depends on how high a 'high brow' you are: let's not forget that Colchester is the home town of 'Blur' - and you can't get much higher than that! Or do I mean 'cooler'? More cool? Please *don't* show your age by asking who or what is, or are Blur? That would be 'un-cool', I gather. Anyway, there's plenty more where they came from and we'd have to be unbearably fussy or stuffy (or both) not to find a host of ways of enjoying the final phase of the day.

Four main venues suggest themselves at once, but there are many other pubs, clubs and the like where entertainment is all part of the service. I'm told that there's live music, for example, going on somewhere in Colchester every night of the week and that ranges from symphony concerts to pub rock. If you had a concert in mind then you'd need to look no further than CHARTER HALL (Information - 01206 577301), the town's largest venue. In fact the Hall plays host to an enormous spectrum of entertainment and artists: the symphony concert is very much a possibility - but so are show bands, rock groups, comedy stars, exhibitions and fairs. Charter Hall is just north of the River Colne; if you'd prefer music on a slightly smaller, more intimate scale - with rather more of an up beat, perhaps - then COLCHESTER ARTS CENTRE (Infoline - 01206 282020) might suit. This is yet another contrast. Because of the smaller scale economics, experimental work can be presented as can acts who don't expect lottery scale cheques every time they step on to a stage. The result is the liveliest imaginable mix of music styles - from jazz to rock to folk - with comedy shows, drama and workshops to complete the bill of fare. An added enticement, as I've said, is that the Centre is on the fringe of the day time shopping area where there are plenty of opportunities for a touch of refreshment after the show and before turning in.

We're still only halfway down the list, as there are still two more fascinating possibilities yet to be explored. The first, because it's still within the boundaries of the town - and only a matter of yards from the Arts Centre along BALKERNE HILL - is the MERCURY THEATRE (Information - 01206 573948), the town's own top class repertory theatre which sets very high standards in presenting the best in today's British talent.

Two miles to the east of Colchester at Wivenhoe Park, stands the UNIVERSITY OF ESSEX, which was founded in 1961. The LAKESIDE THEATRE (Information - 01206 873261) is based on the campus and presents a varied programme of touring theatre, student drama, music and exhibitions. Its near neighbour is the UNIVERSITY GALLERY, making a further contribution to the town's spectrum of opportunities to encounter the very best in contemporary art.

As so often, when we're looking at live entertainment in a town, we feel the need to turn aside to see what's on offer for 'silver-screen' enthusiasts. Colchester has an ODEON CINEMA (Enquiries - 01206 544869), once again not far from the Arts Centre, but this time in CROUCH STREET. This complex has six screens showing a wide selection of the latest films, although the word is that it's advisable to book in advance. Yet again, because of its location, it's well suited to making a night of it with a drink or a late supper after the block-buster. After the supper, and after the block-buster, it's probably time to pass out back at the hotel, so let's take a natural break before looking a little further afield at the attractions on offer in Colchester's suburbs and beyond. After *that* - we'll see, but there could be some more history and the odd glance at one or two of the town's impressive civic buildings.

On the morning after, once we've recovered our composure, the way lies south along the B1025 to BOURNE MILL (Enquiries - 01206 572422). The National Trust property was built originally as a fishing lodge, in 1591. Converted later to a mill, it features stepped 'Dutch' gables. Much of the machinery is still intact, including the water-wheel ,and the picturesque mill pond is worth inspecting. Admission costs £1.50 and opening times during July and August are between 2.00pm and 5.30pm on Tuesdays and Sundays. Otherwise it is open on all Bank Holiday Sundays and Mondays at the same times.

For our next call we need to cut across country, westwards to **LAYER DE LA HAYE**, where we'll find the 1200 acre ABBERTON RESERVOIR. This is a site of Special Scientific Interest, in general terms, but is also a particular attraction for bird-watchers as it is a major nesting area for migrating species and an important site for wintering ducks. It's also claimed to be home to more wildfowl than any other reservoir in Britain. The well stocked shop at CHURCH ROAD offers telescopes, binoculars and bird books as well as other gift ideas. The Reservoir is open to visitors six days a week (not Mondays) apart from Christmas Day and Boxing Day, although it *is* also open on Bank Holiday Mondays throughout the year. Times of opening are between 9.00am and 5.00pm, although another exception here is that 'late night' opening is available during the summer months until dusk on Thursdays and Sundays. Admission is free, but donations are always welcome. As there are various events and open days organised during the year, a phone call to 01206 738172 would be well advised.

Another short cross-country stretch of minor roads brings us to the B1022 and to what is frequently voted the "Best Visitor Attraction in East Anglia". I think I'll stay neutral on this one, although I can see why COLCHESTER ZOO (Enquiries - 01206 330253) is so highly regarded by conservationists: it actively *supports* its resident species rather than just containing them for display. It's also good to know that the zoo is doing such excellent pioneering work with endangered species such as orang-utangs, snow leopards and Siberian tigers. All in all, some 175 different kinds of animal are to be found within its forty acres of beautiful gardens, with other attractions including breeding chimpanzees, penguins and elephants. The Zoo is open daily from 9.30am, except on Christmas Day. Last admissions are at 5.30pm in summer, and one hour before dusk at other times of the year. Admission will cost us £7.50 a head.

There's no doubt in my mind that Colchester Zoo is a great asset to the area, nor that its contribution to the future welfare of wild animals is of a very high order. The admission cost is money well spent on an absorbing experience that is likely to take up most of the day. Full marks for all of it - but 'Best' tourist attraction? I really wouldn't want to make a subjective claim like that, myself. After all, how many *other* attractions have we seen so far? Five hundred? A thousand? And is the Zoo really better than any of them? Put it another way: how on earth would you begin to compare, say, Fakenham Gas Museum, The Thursford Collection, Norwich Cathedral and the Spalding Flower Festival in terms of 'Best'? Common sense suggests it's better not to try. Some you like; some you don't. Which is exactly as it should be, variety being the spice of life's rich pageant. Comparisons and 'league tables' are for the odd balls who compile nonsenses like the 'Classical Music Charts': "The 'best' symphony in the world this week, folks, is Beethoven's Ninth; next week we'll see if it's knocked off its perch by Elgar's Second!" Come *on*! It's a wonderful Zoo - I wouldn't recommend it if it wasn't - so let's chat up a chimp, have a peek at the penguins and leave the rest to the spin doctors.

Since we're on the B1022, we might as well profit from the fact and take in two other attractions, even though that might be pushing the boundaries of our area just a bit too far south. Having come this far though, it would be a shame to miss them for the sake of an extra hour or two and a few miles added to the journey back to Colchester.

LAYER MARNEY TOWER (Information - -01206 330784) is the tallest Tudor gate-house in Britain and is exquisitely decorated in the early 16th century Italianate style. There are magnificent, sweeping views to reward those intrepid - and fit - travellers who climb to the top, while at ground level there are a host of less energetic diversions for the rest of us, including delightful gardens, deer park, farm walk, tea room and a gift shop. It is open from 1st April to 4th October (except Saturdays) between noon and 5.00pm plus Bank Holiday Sundays and Mondays between 11.00am and 6.00pm. Admission will set us back £3.25.

The next call before our return to Colchester for another brief encounter with its ancient urbanity pays further homage to our penchant for gluttony. Remember childhood? Remember those daydreams of sitting down with a whole pot of jam and a spoon and stuffing yourself witless? You never had dreams like that? Get on! Everybody had dreams like that back in the fifties, especially if they'd lived through even part of a wartime childhood when jam, chocolate and sweets only *existed* in dreams. What has any of that got to do with the Essex of the 1990s? Everything, as I'm about to reveal at **TIPTREE**.

The management at WILKIN'S OF TIPTREE (Information - 01621 815407) might not have day dream bouts of gluttony in mind, exactly (although *anything's* possible these days, at a price) but the world famous Tiptree jams still have a large touch of magic about them, even if health conscious discerning travellers of our age are more likely to spread the wondrous stuff thinly on Ryvita than stuff it down with a dessert spoon. I don't know though. Of course it *could* be one of those 'big moments', a bit like Easter Sunday? You know the kind of thing: 364 days a year people in our stage of imminent senility count the calories, watch the waistline and, at worst, toy with an After Eight - once in three weeks! We are perpetually caught up in a major effort to stay healthy and live forever. Until 'That Day', in late March or early April, when we rip the wrapping off the eggs from hell - or, more accurately, from the kids, the wife, the husband, the lover, the milkman and somebody from the golf club who didn't know what got into him. Tear off the plastic, the cardboard, and the aluminium foil, then get stuck in to milk chocolate, plain chocolate, white chocolate, bitter chocolate. Chocolate with caramel, mint, coffee cream, fudge, truffles, nuts, liqueurs, green cream, pink cream, orange cream - oh my good lord! You've never done anything like that? Well, you'll probably hate Tiptree, too - but you won't spoil the fun for the rest of us.

Seriously - or rather, *more* seriously, as Easter chocolate *is* serious in its own way - this is really a place for connoisseurs rather than gluttons, I suppose - although, even for gourmets, a dollop of Wilkin's strawberry on a dollop of clotted cream on a fresh baked scone has more style than the 'spread thinly on crispbread' syndrome. And if this place elevates the business into some kind of a religion, with its jam shop (for delicious gifts for the family), its Museum and its tea room, so what? Indulgence, to be gratifying, needs to have a touch of naughtiness built in, I always find, so let's get stuck in.

After that we need air - fresh air - lungfuls of it, with a touch of muscular activity thrown in - all of which sounds like a good reason for visiting FINGRINGHOE WICK NATURE RESERVE (Information - 01206 729678) as part of a roundabout way of getting back to the hub of things. As a bonus we might even find out how anywhere on earth - let alone in Essex - ever got a name like *that*? Something the Vikings left behind, I imagine. We'll need a trace of the B1022 northwards, and a fair bit of map reading through the lanes, but it'll be worth it if only to damp down our consciences and revive our appetites.

The Headquarters of the Essex Wildlife Trust, Fing. etc. (I can't get my tongue round that at all, not after three jam scones, I can't) is a wonderful venue for bird watchers and nature lovers in general, as it's situated on the edge of the Colne Estuary, where a much-needed breath of sea breeze wafts over the tidal banks. It's open all through the year from 9.00am to 5.00pm and until 6.00pm in summer. Admission is free, although all donations are gratefully received.

Revived, refreshed and with our guilt exorcised, we should be ready to drive back into the townscape -so, what's on offer this time? The High Street, I would have said, for a look at the TOWN HALL. Completed in 1902, this monument to well justified civic pride dominates its surroundings in an elegant, Italianate way. The splendid, tall clock tower is topped with the figure of St Helena, mother of Constantine, according to one story. According to another, she was the daughter of Cunobelin, the British chieftain mentioned earlier, who is said to be the reality behind the 'Old King Cole' figure of children's nursery rhymes. Of course, she could have been *both*, I suppose, but it's hard to be sure as that period of British history is all rather vague.

Seeing the Roman influence is another reminder of connections and origins, of all the aspects of provincial life that must have been so vital in Colchester during the first couple of centuries AD. We saw some of the finds in the Castle Museum including, let's not forget, the bronze boar and the bronze Mercury, one of the finest Roman figures ever discovered in Britain. So, looking up at the tower of the Town Hall, seeing the almost geometric regularity of the town plan and remembering these archaeological finds one must be aware of a sense of continuity that borders on the comforting. There is another side, of course.

The main room of the Town Hall, known as the MOOT HALL, is where the COLCHESTER OYSTER FEAST is held in October each year, commemorating the fame of the local oysters that have been cultivated in the lower stretches of the River Colne since the days of the Romans - who weren't slouches when it came to delighting the inner man. The oyster season is declared open in September by the mayor, who dredges up the first oysters on a ceremonial cruise downstream and then drinks the Queen's health in gin, accompanied by gingerbread. The actual Oyster Feast itself goes back to the time of Charles II, as far as official records can be traced, but the word is that it was celebrated for centuries before then on the first day of the FAIR OF ST DENYS, a major annual event locally. The oddity here ought to prove something: oysters weren't eaten as a delicacy or an aphrodisiac or whatever. No, their main claim to fame was that they were almost the only edible items that could be taken out of the river without having to *pay* someone!

Talk of oysters, gastronomy and archaeological finds tends to focus one's mind for a moment on the relationship between the Romans and the British tribes in this area. The bronze boar we've spoken about recently was a Celtic symbol for fearlessness in battle, whereas a silver medallion found in the same grave has the head of Augustus cast on it. In other words, during the lifetime of the king buried there the two cultures must have been fairly thoroughly mixed, as the top dogs in Rome didn't give medals to people they didn't trust. The date of the boar is AD10, that of the medallion AD16 - yet some 45 years later *another* bunch of Brits led by Boadicea, as we've seen, ripped into the place and tore it to bits. Interesting. For example, is one to conclude that the one time owner of the boar and medal was to be seen as a rather unpleasant form of collaborator, a quisling, while the avenging Queen was the patriot, the Champion of freedom? Or were the bulk of the burghers of Colchester perfectly happy with *any* form of government - Roman or otherwise - just as long as they were left in peace to get on with the sensible business of making money? In that context, Boadicea looks a bit different, I'd suggest. Less the freedom fighter and more the egocentric protector of her own interests, perhaps. Certainly, a little over 250 years later, the Roman Emperor Constantine came to power largely on the strength of his support from the legions stationed in Britain - and presumably with a fair bit of acceptance from the local population. Maybe it was mainly a question of alternatives by then: if there weren't any Romans there were going to be Vikings who did unpleasant things with battle-axes, wrecked churches - and never even took a bath afterwards. I'm sure we'd have voted for Constantine too - in the circumstances. Back to the present.

Another piece of all but overpowering architecture in the town is to be found at the west end of the High Street, opposite the Mercury Theatre. It's a gigantic water tower, as it happens, which for some reason has been named JUMBO, after the huge African elephant resident in the London Zoo at the time when the tower was built, in 1882. Having been drawn by a whim to this side of the town, it seems logical to start our first major tour in this direction and head out on the A120. This route also takes us in the vicinity of the remaining dykes and ramparts, such as GRIME'S DYKE and TRIPLE DYKE built nearly two thousand years ago to protect the original Camulodunum.

Our goal is **COGGESHALL**, a small town with a tradition of wool and lace making that goes back to the Middle Ages, which is on the route of the old Roman STANE STREET. The ruins of a 12th century ABBEY are to be found on the banks of a fast-flowing mill stream, but the chief place of interest is PAYCOCKE'S (Information - 01376 561305), a National Trust property that was built around 1500.

Located on WEST STREET, Paycocke's started life as a merchant's house and stands today as a fine example of the half-timbered style of architecture. The interior is of great interest too, as it contains unusually rich panelling and wood carvings. In keeping with Coggeshall's fame for its lace there are examples of particularly high quality work of this kind on display and, to complete the pleasure of the visit, the house is set in a delightful garden. Paycocke's is open from 3rd May to 4th October on Sundays, Wednesdays and Bank Holiday Mondays between 2.00pm and 5.00pm, with additional opening in August on Thursdays and Saturdays, between the same hours.

Not far from Paycocke's is another National Trust property which, although not as well known, perhaps has an even stronger claim on our attention. COGGLESHALL GRANGE BARN (Information - 01376 562226) on GRANGE HILL, is the oldest surviving timber framed barn in Europe. Dating from the 12th century, it was originally part of a Cistercian Monastery. It was restored in the 1980s by the Coggeshall Barn Trust, Braintree District Council and Essex County Council and contains a small collection of farm carts and wagons. The Barn is open between 29th March and 11th October on Tuesdays, Thursdays, Sundays and Bank Holiday Mondays between 1.00pm and 5.00pm. Admission to the Barn costs £1.50 and to Paycocke's £2.00. A joint ticket is available at a price of £3.00. It's also worth noting that parking at the Barn is definitely the best bet of the two.

From COGGLESHALL the A120 remains our road, as it takes us further west to **BRAINTREE** (Information - 01376 550066), where textiles have been the key to prosperity for over four centuries. In common with most of East Anglia, the wool trade set the scene for expansion, but whereas many towns we have seen virtually died when that trade went downhill in the 19th century, Braintree attracted the attention of the Courtauld family, who introduced silk weaving, an industry that still contributes significantly to the town's economy - although a lot of other people seem to spend their time making steel windows.

Braintree is also on Stane Street, which was the Roman's link between their major cities of St Albans and Colchester. The town's PARISH CHURCH OF ST MICHAEL actually has some Roman bricks incorporated in its structure. Further evidence of the antiquity of the town is found in its MARKET, held on Wednesdays and Saturdays, which was first granted a charter in 1199.

Onward ever onward along the A120 brings us to the District of Uttlesford, in general, and to **GREAT DUNMOW** in particular, which is an intriguing place in its own right as well as being, in a sense, the gateway to an area of great beauty and tranquillity to the north of the main road, in the direction of Thaxted and Saffron Walden, both of which we shall be visiting shortly. We shall also be dropping in on several of the little villages that are a characteristic of the area and are held to be so attractive that more than one writer has observed that no-one can talk accurately about the beauty of a classic English village unless he knows these places well. Sounds appealing? Of course, so let's have a look at Great Dunmow as an introduction.

GREAT DUNMOW

Stane Street crossed another Roman road near the River Chelmer (from which Chelmsford takes its name) and the town of Great Dumow grew up around the intersection. Although it has an attractive timbered GUILDHALL, an old inn and a pond where the first lifeboat experiments were carried out, today its fame rests almost totally on the business of the 'Dumow Flitch'.

The Flitch - a large chunk of bacon - is awarded every two years to any married couple *"who have not had a brawl in their home nor wished to be unmarried for the last twelve months and a day."* A 'trial' takes place before the award is made, complete with bewigged judge and counsel - all amateurs, of course! It is conducted with due solemnity, even though that is actually assumed. The uniquely English tradition dates from 1104, when the Lord of the Manor of Little Dunmow, Robert Fitzwalter, brought in the Breton idea of a flitch award for marital harmony. The tradition lapsed with the Dissolution of the Monasteries in the 16th century, but was revived in 1885 by the historical novelist Harrison Ainsworth. The successful couple are chaired through the streets before being presented with the flitch and the 'bacon chair' itself can be seen in the PARISH CHURCH in **LITTLE DUNMOW**.

Rather than drive into the countryside north of Dunmow for a tour of the villages, we must delay that pleasure for a while as there are still a couple of things to be seen further east. We will come to them though, and might enjoy the experience even more for having put it off somewhat. So, staying with the A120/Stane Street route let's move along now to **STANSTED MOUNTFICHET**, which is about as far as we go in this direction, if we're to avoid wandering into Hertfordshire. True, as we've noticed, there are some people who think we should; who see Herts as being part of the East. Now, as then, one would have to retort by asking where they proposed drawing the line - or would it come down to everywhere being east of somewhere?

Nowadays, Stansted is less of a name to conjure with than it was a few decades ago, when this part of England seems to have come nearer to civil war than at any time since the days of O.Cromwell. As I'm sure you'll remember, it was all about the so-called 'Third London Airport' and local tempers reached incandescence at the thought of a great tract of countryside, not to mention some 540 buildings of architectural interest, vanishing under acres of runways, hangars and jumbo jets. Many years on, the airport is there, the jets make the skies hideous with their racket - but, somehow or another, life goes on, while battalions of eager packagees whiz off to the Costa Gorblimey without a thought for lost cornfields, Tudor houses or anything else, I suppose. Does *any* of it make sense, I ask myself. Ever?

Back to reality: the town suffers from traffic noise as well as from the rumblings up above, but as we're not here for any of that, we can do a Nelson and look elsewhere, as we've grown used to doing. 'Elsewhere', as so often, should turn out to be worth the journey. In passing, (with our fingers in our ears) we should note the medieval CHURCH, the site of the Norman motte and bailey CASTLE and finally STANSTED WINDMILL, considered to be one of the best preserved tower mills in the country. Built in 1787, it was used continuously until 1910 and most of the original machinery has survived intact. It is open for inspection between 2.00pm and 6.00pm on the first Sunday of each month from April to October, every Saturday in August as well and also on Bank Holiday Sundays and Mondays. Fine though the Mill undoubtedly is, even the most dedicated lover of such things would have to admit that the Castle tends to steal a trace of its thunder these days.

MOUNTFICHET CASTLE has been reconstructed on a scale that would do credit to Stephen Spielberg and is the only reconstructed Norman wooden structure of its kind in the world. The work has been done on the original site of the Castle of the Duke of Boulogne, cousin of William the Conqueror, where before had stood first an Iron Age fort and then a Saxon and Viking settlement. All in all, this is an inspiring site and an inspiring example of what can be done to bring history 'to life' - the more so as much of the village that once surrounded the castle has also been reconstructed so that visitors can wander amongst the cottages and animals and all but experience some of the realities of everyday Norman life. That experience, I have to say, leaves the 'virtual reality' of what are fondly known as 'hands on' computerised simulations trailing way behind. In short, Mountfichet is a smashing effort that easily earns its place in our short list of 'must sees'. It's open from 8th March to 15th November, daily between 10.00am and 5.00pm and admission costs £4.00. With an idea of village origins in our minds, this would be a good time to move off the main road for a while to look at some of their current counterparts, with a couple of towns thrown in for good measure. So let's leave the Stansted area by the B1051 and direct ourselves first to **BROXTED**. This pleasant village is particularly noteworthy for its CHURCH OF ST MARY THE VIRGIN. It has two quite remarkable stained glass windows, dedicated in 1993, which commemorate the captivity and release of the Beirut hostages.

From Broxted, a few miles more of the B1051 brings us to our next town, **THAXTED**, a small country town of unique character and with a recorded history that goes back to before the Domesday Book. As it freely admits, it is not a place that sees itself as a backdrop to a set of tourist attractions; it is today what it has always been: a thriving community that keeps abreast of 'progress' but never at the expense of its heritage. Its past is as much a part of daily life as anything that happened last week - or last year - which creates a truly delightful situation for residents and visitors alike.

THAXTED GUILDHALL

As with so many pleasant towns we've seen, Thaxted grew up around a Saxon settlement which, in this case, had been built beside a Roman road. There have been a number of Roman 'finds' over the years and Roman tiles have actually been built into the tower of the great PARISH CHURCH OF ST JOHN THE BAPTIST, whose cathedral-like structure dates from the 14th century. The Manor of Thaxted was granted to Gilbert, Earl of Clare, in Suffolk, in 1066. The pattern of the main streets - with the grand width of TOWN STREET, scene of the early medieval and Tudor markets - survives to this day.

By the mid 14th century Thaxted had become renowned for its cutlery and for its place in the general East Anglian boom in the wool trade. This period also saw the start of a 150 year rebuilding programme for the Church whose spire dominates the townscape and has been described as one of the finest of its kind in the country. It also makes a remarkably fine background for the 15th century GUILDHALL, which is an excellent example of a building type and style that has become increasingly rare. As far as the records go, it seems to have been built between 1393 and 1420, possibly by the Cutlers Guild. It actually occupies what must be seen as a strategic position between the bustle of the Market Place and the magnificence of the Church. Sadly it is only open on Sundays and Bank Holiday Mondays from April to September between 2.00pm and 6.00pm.

Thaxted is the setting for a MUSIC FESTIVAL, held over four summer weekends: the last two in June and the first two in July. It attracts internationally respected performers and is renowned for its ambitious repertoire which includes orchestral and choral works. Talk of the Festival leads on to another of the town's 'musical connections', in this case with the composer Gustav Holst, who established the tradition when he was organist at the Church. The house in Town Street where he lived in the early part of this century and drafted part of the 'Planet Suite', had been 'modernised' during the 18th century vogue for altering old properties to the popular 'Georgian style' to reflect an upturn in the Town's fortunes.

The WINDMILL (Information - 01799 613799) at Thaxted was built in 1804 by John Webb, a local farmer, at a time when there was an increase in the demand for milled wheat and malt. It stands on the site of the earlier Church Mill and was constructed of local bricks. Having been used to grind corn into flour until some time between 1900 and 1907 it fell gradually into disrepair until the Thaxted Society began work to restore it, in 1973. It is open on Saturdays, Sundays and Bank Holiday Mondays between May and September from 2.00pm to 6.00pm.

The MILL, which also houses a rural museum, nestles behind the Church along with a picturesque row of ALMSHOUSES, at the top of one of the most photographed streets in the county: STONEY LANE. The attraction is the delightful array of timber framed, overhanging houses whose equals are unlikely to be met anywhere else. Across from the Church CLARANCE HOUSE, a jewel of an example of Queen Anne architecture, creates the perfect balance with the character of these older properties. It is now a Community Education Centre, where services are available for County employees, and a venue for Adult Education classes.

One final Thaxted event worth noting before we move on is the FAYRE AND GARDENER'S WEEKEND, held in September each year. A procession of floats winds its way through the main streets and a fair and stalls are set up on the RECREATION GROUND. The other side of the business takes the form of a display and competition open to the Town's gardeners which is held at the Guildhall.

Our route now lies roughly north west along the B184 through **HOWLETT END** to **SAFFRON WALDEN** (Information - 01799 510444), whose 'den' ending signifies that it lies in a valley. The river responsible for the feature, by the way, is the Cam (or Granta) that we met further north a few chapters ago. The whole name - 'Walden' - means 'valley of Britons' and the early settlement that first bore the name would have been closer to the river, to the south and west of the present town. The 'saffron' reference shows the importance of the valuable *crocus sativus* crop between the 15th and 18th centuries which was grown for use as a medicine, a dye and a flavouring. The town was the major English centre for the production of the Saffron Crocus until cheaper saffron was imported from Spain and the Middle East and more artificial dyes were developed.

Following the Norman Conquest the manor was allocated to the De Mandervilles, who most probably built the CASTLE some time in the 11th or 12th centuries, the remains of which are seen today as massive flint rubble walling. At the time, and for some centuries afterwards, the castle dominated the whole area while its enclosure dictated the present day street pattern. With the castle's impact more than somewhat diminished these days, the town is crowned by the largest and one of the most beautiful parish churches in Essex, especially since the spire was added in 1832. The CHURCH OF ST MARY THE VIRGIN is nearly 200ft in length and was largely rebuilt between 1450 and 1525 as an outcome of the years of prosperity enjoyed by the saffron industry.

Around the corner from the Church is the OLD SUN INN, at the junction of MARKET HILL and CHURCH STREET, which is part of a magnificent group of buildings dating from the 14th century. The gateway displays outstanding pargetting from the 17th century which shows Tom Hickathrift fighting the Wisbech Giant armed with an axle and a wheel for a shield. According to local legends, this was the Inn where O.Cromwell and General Fairfax lodged on their way through the area during the Civil War.

OLD SUN INN, SAFFRON WALDEN

Notable residents of the Town have included Gabriel Harvey, an Elizabethan poet and astrologer; Henry Winstanley, a man of many parts but best known for designing the first Eddystone lighthouse in 1699 and, last but far from least, the Gibson family. Well known Quakers, the Gibsons began in Saffron Walden as brewers but eventually formed the Gibson Bank. This became the founding company of the present Barclays Bank, the local branch of which was originally built in 1874 for Gibson's. The Bank building has splendid long transomed windows, with four lights and a parapet decorated with rosettes. The family presented the DRINKING FOUNTAIN, which faces the Bank, to the town to celebrate the wedding of the Prince of Wales to Princess Alexandra in 1863. Prior to that it had been shown at the Great Exhibition.

On the opposite side of the square to the Bank, and beyond the Fountain, stands the CORN EXCHANGE. This elaborate Italianate building was erected in 1847-48 to the design of Robert Tress and now houses the town's library. If we stroll a few yards south from the Bank we'll come to THE ROWS, medieval traders' streets divided into simple stalls which later evolved into shops. Each 'row' was dedicated to a specific trade: butchers, tanners, mercers and drapers.

We need to backtrack in a northerly direction now, towards MUSEUM STREET and the Castle, in general terms. We've seen many museums in our travels but the SAFFRON WALDEN MUSEUM (Information - 01799 510333) is definitely up with the best. Standing between the Church and the Castle its displays cover the range of human activities that lie between these two symbols of differing ideals and aspirations. That, however, is only the starting point, in case one thought its field of interest might be largely parochial.

Certainly there are exhibits of local geology and wildlife and a 'Town and Country' section which tells the tale of later growth and change in the area and follows on from the 'Ages of Man' gallery which deals with archaeology and very early history. In addition there are fine Ancient Egyptian and Greek displays and the 'Worlds of Man' gallery which exhibits objects of international interest from the peoples of Africa, the Americas, Australia and the Pacific which were mainly collected during the 19th century.

All in all the Museum represents a wonderful quids worth. It's open all year, Mondays to Saturdays, from 10.00am to 5.00pm (4.0 pm between November and February) with Sunday and Bank Holiday opening from 2.30pm to 5.00pm (4.30pm between November and February). It is closed on Christmas Eve and Christmas Day. One final thought: isn't it a nice touch for the Museum to sell saffron crocus each August, for autumn flowering?

The Mandeville family, who built Walden Castle, also founded a priory at **AUDLEY END**, about a mile to the west of the Town on the B1383. It was dissolved during Henry VIII's anti-monastic rampage and the land passed to Thomas Howard, Earl of Suffolk, eventually. He had AUDLEY END HOUSE (Information - 01719 733434) built in 1603, but the building as seen today shows the substantial work of Robert Adam, in the 18th century, as much as anything. The grounds and lake designs are attributed to Capability Brown. There is a further royal connection with Audley House, which was at one time one of the largest houses in the country. Charles II bought it in 1669 for actual use as a Royal Palace which was visited in 1677 by Samuel Pepys as he made a point of recording in his diary.

AUDLEY END HOUSE

The House, which is an English Heritage property, is presented very much as it was in the 18th and 19th centuries, with its magnificent Jacobean style Great Hall and many fine 17th century plaster ceilings. Apart from the Adam interiors, other points of great interest include the Braybrooke silver collection in the Butler's Pantry and a quite splendid Dolls House. Audley House is open to the public from April to September, daily (apart from Mondays and Tuesdays) between noon and 5.30pm and also on Bank Holiday Mondays. Admission is £5.75.

Back in Saffron Walden, briefly, as our further journeyings lie in that direction from Audley End, there's a trace of true tourism to be done before we move on. Undoubtedly the finest medieval building in the Town is the late 15th century house on the corner of MYDDYLTON PLACE. Now a youth hostel, it has a fine carved dragon post, while along its south side are two fine oriel windows. To the east of the Town, the COMMON, defined by COMMON HILL and EAST STREET, was formerly the CASTLE GREEN where a Royal Tournament was held in 1252. The MAZE, located at the far end of the Common was almost certainly constructed during the Middle Ages and is said to be the largest Turf Maze in England.

At another extremity of Saffron Walden, we'll find BRIDGE END GARDENS AND HEDGE MAZE, near the ANGLO-AMERICAN WAR MEMORIAL. This is another creation of the ubiquitous Gibsons, as Atkinson Francis Gibson was responsible for the start of the gardens, around 1790. They are of a superb quality and are a remarkably intact reminder of early Victorian elegance. The Maze, constructed initially in 1838-39, has been replanted recently to the original design. A key to the Maze is available by appointment, through the Tourist Information Centre.

Our course on leaving the town takes us almost due east initially, and then with a trace of north in it, along the B1053 to **HEMPSTEAD** and then the B1054 close to the Suffolk border, beyond **STEEPLE BUMPSTEAD**. From there, we turn right, down the A604 from **BAYTHORN END** to our next call, at **CASTLE HEDINGHAM**. This little medieval town is dominated by yet another huge Norman keep, all that remains of the castle built in 1140 by the powerful de Veres, Earls of Oxford. There is also a Norman church and a Georgian squire's house, snuggled below the great castle mound. And there is *also*, on a more nostalgic note, access to the COLNE VALLEY RAILWAY (Information - 01787 461174). This steam railway runs through one of the prettiest parts of the Colne Valley and there's the added attraction of a large woodland riverside area for a touch of refreshment after the trip. Opening times are 10.00am to 5.00pm from 1st March to 23rd December. Admission costs £2.00 generally and £5.00 for 'Steam Days'.

Were we enjoying a picnic at this stage, it would be a good moment for a pause while we reflect on some general aspects of Essex north of the A12. We've seen some of its towns and a few of its villages, but the accent is on 'few'. This area is literally peppered with picturesque little places to make your heart leap and your eyes pop. For example, amongst the many we've had to by-pass for lack of time are the **RODINGS**, eight farming villages with names like ABBESS RODING and BERNERS RODING which lie along the valley of the River Roding. In a sense, they're just a bit remote from our area of interest at the moment, which tends to be focused on Stane Street, but a visit would involve such a short detour that they really ought to be taken into account, with their old churches, moated manors, clap-board or half-timbered cottages, all set in great swathes of rolling ploughland, grassland and woods. This is an individual and enchanting world which was a favourite with Anthony Trollope and is a peculiarly English facet of rural life.

Above the A120 there are also the **BARDFIELDS**, which lie along the little River Pant. **GREAT BARDFIELD**, once a market town, has many houses dating from the Middle Ages and from the Georgian period, a windmill that has been restored and the mainly 14th century ST MARY'S CHURCH, which is worth visiting for its fine stone screen. There's quite a large contingent of artists living in the village nowadays, attracted, no doubt, by its picturesque qualities seen to great advantage in its HIGH STREET. **LITTLE BARDFIELD** and BARDFIELD SALING are smaller but just as attractive, with the HALL at Little Bardfield dating from around 1580 being of special merit, as is ST KATHERINE'S CHURCH, especially for its Saxon tower and its organ which was constructed in 1700 or thereabouts.

And so it goes on. To **ASHDON**, near the Bartlow Hills to the north of Saffron Walden, and the location of the finest examples or Romano-British burial grounds in England. Or to **FINCHINGFIELD**, a chance grouping of houses of many different types and periods that has grown up around a church on a hill, a stream, a duck-pond and a green that combines in a scene that is utterly delightful. To the clap-board

WATERMILL at **STEBBING**, on the Stebbing Brook, which is one of the prettiest in the country. And so it definitely goes on!

It's also 'Lovejoy Country', where the antiques business seems to be the second major religion after orthodox Christianity, with shops, stalls, dealers and auction rooms queuing up in droves to be marvelled at, browsed through or lost in for the rest of one's natural life. In fact, if you put the Lovejoy factor in with the countryside and the cottages, I'd be pretty surprised if more than three of you ever leave the area once you've seen it. There aren't that many golf courses, though!

Let's take to the rural rides out of Castle Hedingham, while we have the image of idyllic Essex villages in mind. We can take a quick look at **GREAT MAPLESTEAD** and **LITTLE MAPLESTEAD** before crossing the A131 and moving out in the direction of Bures which we visited as part of our Mid-Suffolk tour a couple of chapters ago. From there, a meander or two through the lanes southwards will bring us to **CHAPPEL**, home of the EAST ANGLIAN RAILWAY MUSEUM (Enquiries - 01206 242524).

EAST ANGLIAN RAILWAY MUSEUM, CHAPPEL

We have here a collection that spans a century of railway history, while spanning the river valley is a massive railway viaduct that is a splendid feat of Victorian engineering. As well as the full size exhibits, there's a MODEL RAILWAY EXHIBITION on 6th and 7th June together with a shop selling transport books and gifts, a buffet and a picnic area. The Museum is open daily through the year between 10.00am and 5.00pm (or dusk, if earlier) with the exception of Christmas Day. Admission is £2.50, or £4.50 on 'steam days'.

From Chappel our direction is north east again, crossing the B1508 above **WEST BERGHOLT** and the A134 north of **GREAT HORKESLEY**. Our goal is **BOXTED** where we'll find the home of CARTERS VINEYARDS (Enquiries - 01206 271136). "Sunshine into wine," they say, is the theme for this five acre vineyard set in forty acres of conservation landscape on the borders of Constable country. A vineyard trail through the New Zealand style trellising leads on to a nature ramble around lakes, wildflower meadows and new stretches of woodland. Day fishing licences are available for the lakes.

ESSEX COUNTRY SCENE

There are several different styles of wine available for tasting, all produced using organic techniques, while the electricity for the winery is produced by solar cells and a wind driven generator. The Vineyards are open from Easter to the end of September, between 11.00am and 5.00pm. Admission is £2.50, which includes the tasting and the tour.

Having returned to the fringe of the Stour Valley, our next call will take us to within hailing distance of the area around Constable's birthplace that we explored when visiting East Bergholt. This time we're on the Essex side of the county line which permits us to look, in this chapter, at **DEDHAM** itself. The attractions here - apart from the associations with the artist - lie, once again, in the architecture. The HIGH STREET has some excellent upper storeys over its shop fronts while the ELIZABETHAN FREE GRAMMAR SCHOOL features excellent brickwork. The 16th century CHURCH is worth visiting for its own sake as well as for a close up view of the famous spire which is so familiar from 'the paintings'! The insignia of the Weavers Guild and the Millers Guild are combined in an heraldic shield in the roof to mark the rich endowments from which the building benefited. As a total contrast, there are medallions on one of the pews to commemorate the first moon landing, in 1969.

Sir Alfred Munnings KCVO, lived and painted in and around Dedham for forty years. His house, set in delightful gardens, is now an ART MUSEUM (Information - 01206 322127) and, with its studios and galleries, contains a large collection of paintings, drawings, sketches and other items that represent his life's work. The house and garden are open from 3rd May to 4th October, on Sundays, Wednesdays and Bank Holiday Mondays between 2.00pm and 5.00pm and also on Thursdays and Saturdays, at the same times, during August. Admission is £3.00.

There's one more call to make at Dedham before we swing away to follow the edge of the Stour Estuary for a survey of this part of the Essex coastline. The DEDHAM VALE FAMILY FARM (Enquiries - 01206 323111) has a large selection of farm animals for us to encounter - although it *also* has a playground and 'Pets Paddocks' to cater for children and *might* be a little on the boisterous side. How young at heart do we *really* feel? Nonetheless, it's a pleasant attraction with the additional features of a picnic area and gift shop, so it has to be well worth a thought as we prepare to brace ourselves for the creeks, beaches and islands that make up the final stage of our final tour - along the Essex coast.

Regardless of the terrain, the built environment goes so far from one extreme to another - almost to the point of caricature - as to leave one all but speechless. Just think of Clacton, Southend - and Frinton! You take the point? You don't? Put it like this, then: at the height of the season one could expect Southend on Sea to make the total amount of *all* the bustle we've encountered *everywhere* else - with the possible exception of Great Yarmouth - seem rather quieter than that cliché of a vicarage tea party. Frinton? Frinton is *genteel*. Frinton is self consciously above all that kind of thing. The last time I was there (briefly) in the late 80s it was still the only holiday resort in the country, on that scale, without a single *pub*! *Now* you take the point. A few miles further down the coast, Clacton on Sea is second only to Southend when it comes to glitz.

I don't believe there's a stretch of coastline in the country of similar length that manages to cram as much *variety* into a more or less uniform natural environment as this bit does. It's not just the range, from the unbelievably brash to the all but impenetrably exclusive, either. Some towns have retained most of their historical character, regardless of events on their outskirts, while others have dived head first into 20th century 'improvement' vandalism and come up dripping with neon, burger bars, UPVC windows and 'theme parks' in every other back yard. Of course, if you stand on the water's edge, with your back to most of it, the sea is still the sea, wherever you are - in between the water skis, windsurfers, jet skis, paragliders, marinas and other things.

One could write an entire 'Four Seasons Guide' just about the Essex coast - and maybe that'll happen, one day. For now, there just isn't the space or the time, so we'll do a brief circuit, to pick up the essence of the area, and pick out one or two pleasant spots to link the impressions with the geography.

If we start with **MANNINGTREE**, we'll find ourselves in a pleasant town, once an active port, and now better known for its swans and as the home of a number of the old sailing barges that are kept sea-worthy by enthusiasts for this almost vanished form of transport. There are numerous Victorian and Georgian houses to commemorate the town's former prosperity and a punt regatta every July.

ESSEX SEAFRONT

In the 17th century Manningtree was used as a base by Matthew Hopkins for his tours of East Anglia as 'Witch Finder General', a role in which he seems to have revelled as he spread fervour wherever he went. In 1647 life's familiar irony caught up with him: he was accused of witchcraft himself and put to 'the test'. He was bound and thrown into the water, where he floated, thereby proving his guilt. There was only one possible penalty and, shortly afterwards, he was hanged.

We can't come this far without calling in briefly at **HARWICH** (Information - 01749 677633) which has seen so many of England's famous mariners sail from its quays and whose waters today offer the spectacle of an A to Z of vessel types, from fishing boats to cargo boats to ferries linking East Anglia with a range of ports on Europe's western seaboard. Even the 'Mayflower' in which the Pilgrim Fathers sailed from Plymouth in 1620 had come from Harwich at one stage. The town also has connections with Samuel Pepys who has popped up repeatedly during our tours. Not only was he Charles II's Secretary of State for the Admiralty at one time but he was also MP for Harwich.

Along with all the other east coast ports we've visited, Harwich has had a prosperity peak in recent years. This is most apparent on the quayside, which is so busy with lorries that the authorities have had to take positive steps to discourage sight-seers. At the HALFPENNY PIER - so called because the toll for the ferry trip over to Felixstowe was a halfpenny at the time it was first opened - the tempo is a little slower and, in summer, one can linger there while waiting for an evening cruise on the Stour or the Orwell.

Just past HARWICH GREEN is the resort of **DOVERCOURT**, where holiday-makers can enjoy a sandy beach backed up by a sea wall. Low wooden groynes have been set up to reduce erosion and one of the landmarks is a couple of abandoned lighthouses on stilts that were replaced by buoys in 1917.

Following the line of the coast a little way inland on the B1414 and the B1033-1034 we arrive next at **WALTON ON THE NAZE**. The word 'naze' has the same origin as 'ness' (which we saw at Orford) and refers to a wide neck of sandstone, gorse and grass that runs north from the town. Here we have another family resort that blossomed from the 1830s onwards and which is characterised by its safe, sandy beach - that all but vanishes at high tide. Its enormous pier is only exceeded in length by the one at Southend. The pier is the second to be built at Walton: the first was built in 1875 to cater for paddle steamers from London but, unfortunately, low tides left it stranded. Another stroke of fate saw it destroyed in a violent storm, to be replaced in the 1880s by the present structure, which is currently privately owned. A wide variety of holiday attractions is on offer along its half mile length during the summer, from the giant wheel to sideshows, as well as fishing for cod, dab, haddock, hake, whiting, brill and sole.

The Naze itself provides several sources of interest. Its 40ft sandstone cliffs, which drop straight to the beach, yield rich fossil finds that date from the Ice Age. On the other hand, its one and a quarter mile NATURE TRAIL would give us the chance to see butterflies such as the Painted Lady and Essex Skipper in summer and many species of migrating birds in autumn and winter.

The next town would be Frinton which is so lovely and peaceful, to visit it would take up the rest of our day, therefore I propose by-passing it and going for the quickest of quick looks at **CLACTON ON SEA** (Information - 01255 423400), which is another of those places that will take you back to your youth. These days, it seems like a huge fairground, not just *by* the sea but mainly *on* the sea, as its name suggests. For this conclusion we have to thank its greatly widened pier, from which the 'young at heart' retreat to hotels and boarding houses in the small hours, totally exhausted, to sleep up enough energy to rush back the next day and do it all again. Fine - if you've got the stamina - but 'know your limitations' is one adage I accept without reservation.

If any of the local residents have managed to wade this far through the 'Guide', I'm sure their faces will be reddening as they mutter "Unfair," into their cups of tea or gin and tonics. I'm just as sure that they're probably right, bearing in mind the Town's THEATRES, its ZOO, MARINE PARADE, SCENIC RAILWAY, CINEMAS, NORMAN CHURCH and its PUBLIC GARDENS. As we can't get round the seaward side of COLNE POINT, we need to turn inland along the B1027 to reach our next destination, **BRIGHTLINGSEA**, an old port on the Colne Estuary known for its fishing and yachting. There's a fine house, JACOBES HALL, dating from the Middle Ages, which is now a hotel, and a CHURCH whose magnificent 94ft tower is one of the finest to be found anywhere in East Anglia. Built in the Perpendicular style, the church contains more than two hundred wall plaques which commemorate seamen who were killed in battles or who drowned whilst out fishing.

The key to the town's current fame is probably its ramp for launching boats, which is undoubtedly the best for miles around and helps make the place a centre for vessels of every kind. This asset continues its history extremely well as boat building and fishing have been its main occupations for hundreds of years. When the church was built it was an important port too, and was the only associate member of the Cinq Ports outside Kent and Sussex. To underline the point, the officials of the town still take an oath of allegiance to the Mayor of Sandwich as part of a ceremony held on the first Monday after the 30th November (St Andrew's Day).

The Town, which is surrounded by water on three sides and only accessible by the road we used to reach it, is also the Headquarters of the Smack Preservation Society, an organisation committed to the preservation of these fine, traditional Essex fishing boats, most of which were among those built at the turn of the century. There is a race for these smacks - and large sailing barges - every September from Brightlingsea to Clacton and back. The 'beach', for want of a better word, is muddy sand with sprinklings of shingle while strong, erratic currents make for dangerous bathing. But who cares? It's not that kind of a place. At Brightlingsea you hire, buy, beg, borrow or steal a boat - any boat - and stretch out on that to pick up your suntan!

Our next leg of the journey lies north west, inland from the course of the River Colne, but parallel with it almost as far as Colchester as we can't cross the river until we reach **WIVENHOE**. Before we get as far as the University, however, we turn left and then head south west on the B1025 for a glance or two over **MERSEA ISLAND**. As we cross THE STROOD, a narrow causeway that may be under water at high tide, we find ourselves very quickly in an area that really can be described as "a world of its own". Lanes wind across countryside that rises and falls with no particular sense of urgency.

WEST MERSEA is the crowded main resort and boating area with pleasant old fishing cottages still managing to survive in the older areas. There is a CHURCH which displays a mixture of Norman and 14th century styles and a small MUSEUM but, apart from the boats, the main attraction is probably the 'West Mersea Natives', local oysters that can be bought and eaten at stalls on the foreshore near the old oyster storage pools.

EAST MERSEA is altogether quieter and is set amidst reasonably unspoilt farmland and grazing marshes. Saltings lead on to mud flats backed by sand and shingle and there are walks in both directions along the sea wall. However, as there's a firing range nearby - which has led to the public being warned of the danger of unexploded shells - it might be better to take the air, if you've a mind to, at CUDMORE GROVE COUNTRY PARK whose thirty five acres offer walks, a picnic area and access to the beach. Yet again, potential bathers should beware the dangerous currents off the end of the island.

At this stage, wisdom would direct that we call it a day and give the loud pedal some welly in the general direction of Colchester, for a drink or two, a meal and a good night's sleep, as is our wont. However, we are on holiday, just, and holidays are more about impulse than wisdom, so let's finish the tour with a couple of contrasts.

Beyond Mersea, overlooking the estuary of the River Blackwater, we'll find the big village of **TOLLESBURY**. In a sense, particularly in its remoteness off the beaten track, it represents much of what has been our stock in trade throughout all the miles we've travelled. It has a fine Medieval CHURCH - and a MARINA for the modern counterpart of its fishing fleet which numbered more than a hundred sailing smacks around the beginning of this century. The sails and rigging from these vessels were usually kept in wooden boat houses, a row of which, some carefully restored, lie behind the Marina.

Now for the contrast - although I'm not putting forward a case for making another detour at this stage. The contrast - with Tollesbury, Orford, Brightlingsea and nearly anywhere else we've been - *has* to be Southend-on-Sea. The existence of this amazing phenomenon on the Thames estuary, several worlds away from Thaxted or Saffron Walden but still very much in Essex, will make an excellent footnote to this chapter - and, in a sense, to the whole book. As a concept, to be held in the mind. We won't go there - at least, not yet we won't - we'll think about it while we go somewhere else instead.

We're midway between where we've been and the mental image of where we may go some other time. In short, we're in **MALDON** (Information - 01621 856503). Shortly after the First World War, my father had his first summer holidays in the town. He has spoken ever afterwards, with the mists of nostalgia clouding his old eyes, of the idyll he enjoyed. It isn't *quite* the same these days (and he's changed too, come to that) but more than seventy years on, I can still see what he means. There's not a lot in this direction - and this close to London - that has a prayer of staying 'unspoilt', but Maldon has done its best and its success is much appreciated.

The essence is the same old Essex coastal thing: the miles of creeks, the myriad boats and the cries of birds make a marvellous mixture. Given that the boats on the Blackwater tend to belong to fishermen or to people whose lives are driven by the urge to preserve old Thames barges, the visual delights are beyond debate. Maldon is on a hill above the water, where Anglo-Danish troops led by one Brynoth were fought to a standstill, in 991 AD by some untypically stubborn Vikings who seem to have put their more normal 'fast in, fast out' tactic on the back burner, for once. The battle, which ran for an unbelievable three days, is commemorated in an epic poem of the 10th century known as 'The Battle of Maeldune'.

Three centuries later some ecclesiastical eccentrics decided to build ALL SAINTS' CHURCH in the town - with a *triangular* tower. They were true eccentrics, as things turned out, for the structure remains the only one of its kind in the country. The surrounding countryside has its moments, too. Among the places worth a visit is BEELEIGH ABBEY, a mile upstream, with its fine CHAPTER HOUSE and its splendid carp ponds set in charming gardens. For those in need of refreshment, it's also worth noting that BEELEIGH FALLS, which are not far from the Abbey, make a wonderful spot for a picnic.

Just as you can't claim to *know* English villages until you've seen them in East Anglia, I suspect you can't claim to know England at all - and certainly not the *English* - until you've visited **SOUTHEND ON SEA** (Information - 01702 - 215120). One of the largest seaside towns in Britain, it is famed for having the longest pier in the country, which stretches for more than a mile into the estuary of the River Thames.

It all began as little more than a modest hamlet, known as the South End of Prittlewell. Today it has a population of around 200,000 and has spread to swallow up neighbouring **LEIGH ON SEA, WESTCLIFF, PRITTLEWELL** and **THORPE BAY**. There are fun fairs, winkle stalls, jellied eels, pubs - and acres and acres of mud. Out of season, Southend presents shadowy reminders of its past as a 'select watering place' to which the Prince Regent sent his Princess Caroline to spend some time in what is, today, ROYAL TERRACE. *In* season, however, you can forget all that and join the crowds in the midst of what's been *the* day-trippers' delight for the past hundred years, since paddle-steamers first splashed their way down stream to put crowds of Londoners ashore at the pier for their day out of the smoke.

As you would expect, there are droves of attractions in and around the town from the HISTORIC AIRCRAFT MUSEUM to the SOUTH-EAST ESSEX MUSEUM, set in acres of parkland at PRITTLEWELL PRIORY which, almost unbelievably, is less than two miles inland from the Pier. Then there is shopping to die for, with multi-storey complexes of such proportions that continental visitors arrive by the ferry load with no other object in mind. An amazing phenomenon, as I say; perhaps not really a part of a truly discerning guidebook but it's very much there, in a county that I hope we've really come to appreciate. So it has to be seen - perhaps as part of a cruise down the Thames from London?

Heaven knows how many miles we've covered together during these chapters. Having started out on the North Norfolk coast, from King's Lynn to Cromer, having spent our first nights in Dersingham and, possibly most of all, having come to accept 'contrast' almost as a way of life in East Anglia, I find the thought of ending the book contemplating a day trip on a boat to Southend about as perfect an idea as I've ever stumbled across. After the boat trip we will drive back up the B1022 from Maldon to our Colchester hotel.

Now it is time to conclude this story of our trips throughout East Anglia. I sincerely hope that you will enjoy your travelling and the places that have given us so much pleasure, should you visit places that you feel should be included in the next edition, please do write to me.

Finally all the venues included in this guide have been especially selected for their comfort, quality, and value for money. We have tried to include places across the price spectrum, so whatever your budget there will be a venue for you to suit your needs.

When using any of the prestigious venues in this guide, please mention that you found them in the Discerning Visitor Guide.

Bon voyage.

THE BENBRIDGE HOTEL
The Square,
Heybridge,
Maldon,
Essex
CM9 4LT

Tel: 01621 857666
Fax: 01621 841966

This comfortable hotel, currently being refurbished, has a welcoming atmosphere and many regular guests. It is situated on the River Chelmer, near a small industrial area and during World War II became a hostel for local apprentices. One cannot imagine it being used for this purpose today! It is attractively decorated throughout and each room has new furniture, new beds, desks in reclaimed wood. The rooms are all ensuite and some have baths, some showers. Every room has television, direct dial telephone, trouser presses, hairdryers and a generously supplied hostess tray. The hotel is warm and comfortable and ideal for anyone at anytime of the year. Amanda and Rob Loman run the hotel with a degree of professionalism and efficiency that ensures every guest is well cared for. For this reason many business people choose to stay here because they feel at home.

The restaurant serves excellent food with a menu that tends to be traditional but also provides a number of interesting dishes from around the world. In the bar, snacks and light meals are available. The hotel has a large conference room which is used regularly for business, is in demand for weddings and functions. Every occasion is given attention to detail ensuring that whatever the function, it is a memorable one for all the right reasons.

If you like to take a stroll you can meander along the canal all the way to Goldhanger. Close by is Maldon town which houses the Moot Hall and All Saints Church dating back to the 13th century. Maldon Promenande once a year hosts the Maldon Spectacular, a weekend of Modern and Classical Music.

USEFUL INFORMATION

OPEN: All year. Normal pub hours for non-residents
CHILDREN: Welcome
CREDIT CARDS: All major cards
LICENSED: Yes
ACCOMMODATION:14 ensuite rooms
RATES: Sgl from £30 Dbl from £40 Children £5

RESTAURANT: Traditional fare
BAR FOOD: Wide choice
VEGETARIAN: Always a choice
WHEELCHAIR ACCESS: Yes
GARDEN: Local canal behind hotel
PETS: Yes

BROMANS FARM
East Mersea (Mersea Island)
Colchester,
Essex
CO5 8UE

E.A.T.B classification Listed:
Highly commended

Tel: 01206 383235

Within walking distance of the sea, Bromans Farm is a much sought after place in which to stay. Those who come here and sample the hospitality offered by Ruth and Martin Dence will all tell you it is second to none for several reasons. The first has to be the very warm welcome afforded to everyone, the second the comfort throughout the house, the third the excellent food and finally the sheer beauty of this 14th century house. It is blissfully quiet and just the place in which to relax and recharge your batteries before facing the rigours of the 20th century world again. The atmosphere built over the centuries is added to by the oak beams and the open log fires in winter. Central heating and double glazing, features of this century, have been carefully installed to increase your comfort. From Bromans Farm there are all sorts of places you can explore. There are fine walks along the estuary, a vast country park and nature reserve, excellent bird watching from the Country Park. It is Twenty minutes from historic Colchester while West Mersea's shopping, sailing, yachting and surfing plus other sporting facilities are only minutes away. The house is very convenient for London which is one hour by train and for the ports of Harwich and Felixstowe. If you just feel like doing nothing then Bromans secluded garden offers a retreat from the world.

Guests arriving at Bromans are greeted with refreshments and offered a choice of single, double or family rooms with use of bathroom. Guests are encouraged to unwind in the delightfully furnished sitting and dining rooms. In the latter you will be served a delicious and traditionally substantial Breakfast. There are three bedrooms in all, each beautifully furnished and decorated, warm and comfortable, and one has a private bathroom. Each room has a hostess tray.

USEFUL INFORMATION

OPEN: All year
CHILDREN: Welcome
CREDIT CARDS: None taken
LICENSED: No
ACCOMMODATION: 3 rooms.
1 with private facilities
RATES: From £19 pp pn B&B

DINING ROOM: Substantial breakfast
GARDEN: Yes. Secluded
VEGETARIAN: Upon request
WHEELCHAIR ACCESS: Not suitable
PETS: Yes, but not in the house

EMSWORTH HOUSE
Ship Hill,
Bradfield,
Near Manningtree,
Essex CO11 2UP
ETB Commended

Tel: 01255 870 860
Fax: 01255 870869
Mobile 04674 77771

Emsworth House, previously the Vicarage is owned by Penny Linton, a practising artist and teacher.

Bradfield is on the Essex/Suffolk border and on the 'Essex Way'. Emsworth House is set in a much loved large mature garden and has spacious rooms, with pretty drapes and decor and stunning views of the countryside and River Stour. It is restful and relaxing in an informal atmosphere - perfect for a holiday or a break from the hurl burly of life! The area is very unspoilt and history is around every corner. For exploring, sailing, swimming, fishing, bird watching or walking, it is ideal.

It is very convenient for visiting 'Constable Country' - Dedham, Flatford and East Bergholt as well as the old Roman town of Colchester with it's castle and equally historic Ipswich, both with excellent shops, theatres, restaurants, pubs etch are twenty five minutes drive. Harwich is also very near and convenient for travel to or from the Continent. London, Liverpool Street is fifty five minutes on the train. For your evening meal there are many local restaurants and pubs serving delicious home-cooked food.

All the bedrooms have television, radio, tea/coffee making facilities and use of direct dial telephone. All tastes are catered for and breakfast is served in a sunny, large Dining Room overlooking the river. Emsworth House is a perfect place to stay! For more information write or ring for a brochure.

USEFUL INFORMATION

OPEN: All year
CHILDREN: Welcome breakfast
VEGETARIAN: Choice of menu
WHEELCHAIR ACCESS: Not practical
LICENSED: No
ACCOMMODATION: ensuite rooms
RATES: £27sgl £38sgl ensuite
£38dbl £48dbl ensuite Camp Bed £12 Cot £6

DINING ROOM: English or Continental

CREDIT CARDS: No
GARDEN: Lovely. Croquet. Badminton
PETS: Yes £5 charge

THE HENNY SWAN
Henney Street,
Great Henny,
Sudbury,
Suffolk CO10 7LS

Tel: 01878 269238

Great Henny is a picturesque village in the Stour valley, just over the Essex border but it is more readily approached via Sudbury from which you take the minor B road to Lamarsh. Great Henny is just before Lamarsh and you cannot miss the 17th century Henny Swan, once an old barge house which is on the left of the riverside, where the willows bend to caress the water as it rushes along to drop spectacularly over a weir. Majestic swans glide along ignoring the presence of visitors who can do nothing but stand back and enjoy the scene.

From the outside you will see there is a large barbecues area which is very popular in summer. There is also plenty of parking space. Inside the lounge bar is open plan and spacious making it ideal for meals. Mark Smith is the cheerful and congenial landlord who runs his domain smoothly and efficiently and at the same time creating a delightfully relaxed atmosphere. The restaurant offers an a la carte range of English and foreign dishes, all of which are well cooked and attractively presented. In the Bar the menu has daily specials including an excellent steak pie as well as Ploughman's and succulent steaks. Everything is home-cooked.

There are all sorts of things you can do if you visit The Henny Swan. One can fish on a stretch of the river, take one of the thirty local walks or perhaps take to the water with a River Trip on the Stour. The trips start either from Henny or Sudbury and run from Easter to early October. The Henny Swan itself boasts a Hobby Farm on site.

USEFUL INFORMATION

OPEN: All year 11-3pm &6-11pm
CHILDREN: Welcome
CREDIT CARDS: All major cards
LICENSED: Full On
GARDEN: Yes & River Bank Garden

RESTAURANT: A la Carte English
and Foreign Dishes
BAR FOOD: Wide choice
VEGETARIAN: Yes
PETS: Yes

THE OLD POST OFFICE
Church End,
Broxted,
Dunmow,
Essex
CM6 2BU

ETB 2 Crowns

Tel/Fax: 01279 850050
TOPO@CLARA.NET

One finds it quite hard to believe that the noise and activity of Stansted International Airport is only three miles away from the peaceful village of Broxted. It is a delightful rural area with easy access to London by either road or rail taking approximately forty five minutes. In the centre of the village is The Old Post Office part of which was built in 1821 and was used as a working Post Office until the mid-1950's. It was then that two cottages were joined on to enlarge the existing house with a further extension in the 1980's making it the attractive place it is today.

Peter and Sandy Russell are the owners and they share their home with visitors from all over the world who have come to love the informal, friendly and welcoming atmosphere that pervades the house. It is seldom that the house does not have one guest who has not been many times before. Peter and Sandy both used to work in aviation but they have taken to their change of life style with an ease that would be envied by many who have been in the hospitality business all their lives. They both believe that guests should be cared for in the same manner that they would wish to find if they were staying away from home. There are six guest rooms, three of which are ensuite including a Family Room which has a double bed, a single bed and a cot, if required. All the rooms are charmingly decorated and furnished with a happy mixture of modern and antique pieces with original pine beds and wardrobes.. Pretty drapes and bedcovers, colour television and videos, hairdryers and tea and coffee making facilities complete the picture. The house is pleasantly warm in winter making it ideal for winter breaks. Breakfast is a delicious, substantial meal, freshly cooked and offering a choice. Vegetarians are catered for upon request and a Continental breakfast is always available. The Old Post Office is not licensed at present but a license has been applied for. In the meantime you are very welcome to bring your own.

USEFUL INFORMATION

OPEN: All year
CHILDREN: Welcome
CREDIT CARDS: Visa/Switch/Master/Charge
LICENSED: Applied for
ACCOMMODATION: 1fam. 2dbl ensue
1dbl.2sgl standard rooms
RATES: £25pp.pn Children £12.50

DINING ROOM: Excellent breakfast
VEGETARIAN: Upon request
PETS: No
WHEELCHAIR ACCESS: Not suitable
GARDEN: Yes

THE PRINCE OF WALES.
The Street.
Inworth.
Essex. CO5 9SP.

Tel: 01376 570813.

Inworth is a small village on the B 1023 between Kelvedon and Tiptree. It is a friendly place with a close community which focuses on the only pub, The Prince of Wales, The Grange and Church. Paul & Sharon Allen are the landlords, who after may years working as Golf stewards all over Britain, have returned to their native East Anglia, an area they both love. They are keen golfers and animal lovers, something that becomes apparent when you see the many pictures on the walls. Canine visitors are greeted with fresh water and biscuits, making their owners feel immediately welcome and relaxed. There is lot to see and do locally with picturesque villages, many of which are featured in the Lovejoy television series. There are historic towns, seaside resorts, interesting country-side offering invigorating walks along the river, in woodland or on the many beaches. Animal and bird enthusiasts will enjoy Layer Marney Tower Deer Park and the Rare Breeds Farm, Abberton Reservoir and Finringhoe Nature Reserve. For the golfer there is the Five Lakes Golf & Country Club at Tolleshunt Knights, which is not far away.

The Prince of Wales is a Firehouse. The original part of the pub is a farm house dating back to 1850, this is connected to a 17th.Century barn by a modern annexe. Part of the bar area is where bodies were laid out prior to burial at the Church, no such morbid happenings today. You now enter a happy pub, offering well kept ales and sumptuous food. Paul & Sharon have decided ideas of their own when to comes to furnishing, hence the bars are good to look at, comfortable to relax in, with a slightly different decor to the norm, there is a feel good ambience in this pub. The music is unobtrusive with no juke box, there are a variety of pub games available on request.

You will not find factory prepared food, chips or fry ups in the establishment. Dishes range from Eastern, Mediterranean, Oriental, traditional English, fish and Vegetarian and much more. One could say that the emphasis is on healthy eating, only fresh vegetables are used. You will be extremely pleased with the meal, whatever you choose. The well chosen wine list reflects the enthusiasism of the Landlords to please their clients, with old favourites, New World wines, and a vast choice to suit every pocket An outstandingly good pub, where you will get value for money.

USEFUL INFORMATION

OPEN: Winter 12-2.30 & 6 - 11pm.
Summer: Normal licensing hours..
CHILDREN: Welcome if supervised
CREDIT CARDS: No.
GARDEN: Yes

RESTAURANT: Wholesome healthy food
BAR FOOD: Wide choice.
VEGETARIAN:5 Dishes
WHEEL CHAIR ACCESS: Yes.
PETS: Very welcome.

REDGATES BED AND BREAKFAST
Redgates Farmhouse,
Redgate Lane,
Sewards End,
Saffron Walden,
Essex
CB10 2LP

2 Crowns Highly Commended

Tel: 01799 516166

There are some stunning views of the countryside from Redgates Farm House at Sewards End just outside Saffron Walden. Alison Colbert is the owner of this delightful 15th century farmhouse which she has lovingly and carefully renovated retaining much of the original features including inglenook fireplaces in which log fires blaze in colder weather.. It is a warm and welcoming house and Alison believes that the welfare and comfort of her guests is paramount. There are only two guest bedrooms, each with private bathroom, colour television and hostess tray.

This allows her to provide a very personal service for those who choose to stay here. Her guests come from all over the place, some on holiday and some who have business in Saffron Walden and who find the peaceful, relaxed house a great place to unwind at the end of a day's work. There is a charming sitting room, furnished with some nice antique pieces and deep chairs. The dining room where Alison serves breakfast is an equally delightful room. Her breakfasts are memorable and plentiful. You start with fruit juice and cereal and follow it with a traditional full English breakfast of bacon, sausage, mushrooms, tomato and egg and finish the meal with as much toast and preserves as you wish for. Piping hot tea and freshly brewed coffee complete breakfast. There are evening meals but Alison will happily direct you in the right direction to find a suitable eatery if you would rather eat out.

There are times when Alison uses the house for business meetings and then she provides lunch for the delegates. She is also happy to arrange and cook for dinner parties. She is an accomplished cook and revels in the task of showing what she can do. When we spoke to her she was planning to provide accommodation for horses as well as their owners. There is no doubt the animals would be equally well cared for.

There are many places in and around Saffron Walden to interest the visitor. The town itself is old and has a fascinating one hundred and fifty year old museum of local history and much else. Chilford Hall Vineyard is to be found in an interesting old building. Linton Zoo is a privately owned Zoo with fine Zoological Gardens and then there is Duxford Imperial War Museum, Europe's top Aviation Museum, which will provide hours of entertainment.

USEFUL INFORMATION

OPEN: All year
CHILDREN: Welcome
CREDIT CARDS: None taken
LICENSED: No
ACCOMMODATION: 2 rooms private bathrooms
RATES: £25sgl £40double Child £15

DINING ROOM: Excellent breakfast
VEGETARIAN: Upon request
WHEELCHAIR ACCESS: Not suitable
GARDEN: Yes
PETS: No

THE ROSE HOUSE HOTEL
21-23 Manor Road,
Westcliff-on-Sea,
Essex
SSO7SR

RAC Recommended

Tel:01702 341959
Fax: 01702 390918

In recent years The Rose House Hotel has been restored to it's former glory as a Victorian Hotel. The bedrooms boast such splendid names as the Edwardian Suite, the Queen Victoria Room, the Princess Alexandria Room, the Rose Room and the Halftester Room, capturing the flavour and style of the Victorian era. Many of the rooms have ensuite facilities and all have colour multi-channel television, tea and coffee hospitality trays, radio intercom and baby listening service.

Situated opposite Westcliff station and just one hundred and twenty yards from the Sea Front promenade, it is a very popular hotel and has many visitors who come year after year. It is also a home-from-home for many stars appearing at the Cliffs Pavilion. It is a relaxed, comfortable establishment in which one can feel at ease. Furnished throughout with some nice antiques mixing happily with other pieces, every room is stylish. The Dining Hall which can seat up to fifty guests has the distinction of a number of Wall Mirrors and a large collection of Wall Plates. It has magnificent chandeliers, a clock collection, an Electric Organ and Pianola. Definitely out of the ordinary. The food is well-cooked and beautifully presented with the emphasis on good, traditional English fare. The cosy bar is a popular meeting place and here you can enjoy a snack. Thoughtfully a non-smoking television lounge has been provided for guests, who are offended by the smells of the weed.

Westcliff-on-Sea has much to offer the visitor, with glorious sea views, a fine beach, two theatres and glorious gardens. A thirty minute walk will take you to nearby Leigh-on-Sea. People come here for a restful holiday, away from the razzmatazz of more garish resorts. At Rose House Hotel you will be well-cared for with standards of service and hospitality which might well have come directly from Victorian times - times when guests were of prime importance - here they still are.

USEFUL INFORMATION

OPEN: All year
CHILDREN: Welcome
CREDIT CARDS: All major cards
LICENSED: Full On
ACCOMMODATION: 12sgl 8dbl 3fam 1tw
RATES: £25sgl £40dbl
Fam of 4 £55 Fam of 3 £45

DINING HALL: Good, traditional fare
BAR FOOD: Snacks available
VEGETARIAN: Yes
WHEELCHAIR ACCESS: Yes
GARDEN: Yes
PETS: Yes

THE THATCHERS ARMS
1 North Street,
Tolleshant D'Arcy,
Essex CM9 8TF

Parliamentary Beer Club
Good Food Guide

Tel/Fax: 01621 860655

In the heart of a traditional English village is The Thatchers Arms, an old hostelry with a great atmosphere and surrounded by fields en-capturing some very beautiful and very English landscapes. The pub is not thatched, as one might expect, but gets its name from being a meeting place for Thatchers and Gleaners; a craft not having a Union or a Guild. It is a lively, friendly place where the landlord is a devout Arsenal fan and lets everyone know how thrilled he is at them achieving the double in the 1997/8 season. The Thatchers is just one and a half miles from Five Lanes Country Club with its PGA rated Golf Course. Mersea, East and West is near enough to enjoy yachting and fishing and The Thatchers is just five minutes from Abberton Reservoir and Bird Sanctuary.

Everyone who comes here enjoys the friendly, relaxed atmosphere. One bar has multi-channel television with a big screen for special events. The beer is renowned for being well kept and you will always see locals at the bar enjoying their favourite beverage and chewing over the topic of the day - frequently football! To add to the fun, the Bar Manager, Tommy, who is a Greek hailing from Sunderland, has earned himself the nickname of 'The Singing Barman'! There are two roaring log fires in winter, a gleaming brass collection. Darts and pool have their own areas and most weekends there is live entertainment especially at Bank Holidays.

You will be well fed on a range of dishes from freshly caught sea bass, lamb kleftico, succulent steaks to simple well filled sandwiches. The menu changes regularly and every day mine host, who is an inventive chef, produces something extra special.

USEFUL INFORMATION

OPEN: 11.30-3pm & 6.30-11pm
All day Sundays
CHILDREN: Welcome to eat
CREDIT CARDS: None taken
LICENSED: Full On
GARDEN: Yes. Swings and slides

RESTAURANT: Imaginative
 menu. Good value
BAR FOOD: Baguettes, Sandwiches etch
VEGETARIAN: 6-10 dishes daily
WHEELCHAIR ACCESS: Yes
PETS: Only in garden

THE BELL INN & HILL HOUSE
High Road,
Horndon on the Hill,
Essex SS17 8LD
Tel: 01375 673154
Fax: 01375 361611

This historic inn bears a blue plaque on the outside recording that Thomas Higbed was burned at the stake for his Protestant faith in 1555 in the courtyard. Everyone who comes to the Bell Inn today has total faith in its welcome and its high standards, and none need fear such an untimely end as Thomas Higbed. Christine and John Vereker accord guests of any faith a similarly warm welcome and at the same time the warmth of centuries spreads a comforting air over the whole inn. The bar has wooden settles on stone flags, old photos on the walls remind us of days gone by and a ninety year old tradition of nailing hot-cross buns to the beams is still evident. Reminders of the past crop up in the choice of the suites. Anne Boleyn has a half-tester and large Chinese rug, while Lady Hamilton's bathroom is a splendid affair, containing a huge claw-foot bath. Hill House, a couple of doors away is under the same ownership but is two hundred years younger than The Bell. Food for both comes from the kitchen of The Bell and in the case of Hill House is served in an elegant dining room. The rooms at Hill House are less expensive than The Bell and less imaginative except for the amazing Captain's Cabin in the converted stable block where the bed is perched aloft in a gallery reached by a wooden ladder. Good wine, good food , total comfort and a warm welcome is what you will get from both The Bell and Hill House.

USEFUL INFORMATION

OPEN: All year	RESTAURANT: Delicious fare
CHILDREN: Yes	BAR FOOD: Wide range
CREDIT CARDS: All major cards	VEGETARIAN: Yes
LICENSED: Yes	WHEELCHAIR ACCESS: No
ACCOMMODATION: 14 ensuite rooms	GARDEN: No
RATES: Tw £50pn room only dbl. £55	PETS: Bedrooms only

Suite weekdays £65 Weekends £75   Children sharing with parents free

CAFFE BROWNS
30 Rosemary Road,
Clacton-on-Sea,
Essex
CO15 1NA

Tel: 01255 475972
http://www.caffe.demon.co.uk

This restaurant is charming and unusual. It is a Victorian building which has many of its original features with wooden floors, window fronts and painted woodwork and recently it has been totally refurbished combining traditional Victorian features with a fresh Mediterranean feel providing diners with a delightful, warm, relaxed and friendly atmosphere. The Patio is terrific with a spectacular mural, romantic lighting and heating. Kay and Ian Jackson are the proprietors and their outgoing personalities combined with the excellence of their well trained staff ensures every diner enjoys a meal here. The menu is varied and extensive catering for all tastes. You are as welcome for a coffee as you are for a traditional English breakfast or a succulent steak. Children have their own menu and every day there are delicious Daily Specials. Smoking and non-smoking areas are available. Cafe Browns also caters for functions, small or large.

USEFUL INFORMATION

OPEN: Winter 9-3pm weekdays	RESTAURANT: Wide range
Sat: 9-4pm Summer: 9am-10pm	VEGETARIAN: Always a choice
CHILDREN: Yes. Own menu	WHEELCHAIR ACCESS: Yes + toilets
CREDIT CARDS: None taken	GARDEN: Patio seats 26
LICENSED: Full On	PETS: Guide dogs only

THE BULL
2 Maldon Road,
Great Totham.
Essex CM9 8NH

Tel : 01621 893385
Fax: 01621 893367

If you enjoy village pubs you will certainly enjoy The Bull. It overlooks the village cricket field with the River Blackwater in the near distance. Carole and Ray Ibbotson are the cheerful landlords and together with their well-trained friendly staff, everyone is welcomed. You will always find regulars at the bars enjoying the well kept ale. The Saloon bar is a traditional beamed area with a brick built fireplace and the Public Bar has a pool table, darts, juke box and Sky TV with a big screen. The pub is known for the high standard and quality of its food including the chef's speciality Kleftico. The menu is wide ranging with something for everyone including fish, curries, succulent steaks, pies and pasta dishes. The pretty restaurant decorated in a dusky pink with draped curtains, is restful and just the place to enjoy a good meal complemented with wine from the well chosen list. Bar food is available and provides anything from a freshly cut, garnished sandwich to Ploughman's and salads. Several country walks start from the Bull ,there are four golf clubs within a few miles and the old town of Maldon with a strong sailing fraternity, is a pleasant place in which to wander.

USEFUL INFORMATION

OPEN: 11am-11pm Mon-Sat.
Sun: 12noon-10.30pm
CREDIT CARDS: All major cards
CHILDREN: Welcome
LICENSED: Full On+Supper licence
GARDEN: YEs. Beer Garden & Car Park

RESTAURANT: Good choice. High quality

BAR FOOD: Very wide selection
VEGETARIAN: Always a good choice
WHEELCHAIR ACCESS: Yes+ ramp
PETS: Yes, on leads

THE CROWN
51 High Street,
Manningtree Essex
CO11 1AH

Tel: 01206 396333

This 16th century inn is full of atmosphere and character although it has been sympathetically modernised over the year. It stands in the busy High Street of Manningtree with pleasant views over the river from the restaurant and the bar. It is a friendly, welcoming hostelry, much enjoyed by local people and by the stream of visitors who call in during the season. The busy restaurant with seventy covers has an all encompassing menu with something for everyone's taste and pocket. Bar snacks and light meals are served every day from an equally extensive menu. From The Crown one can set out for a good walk in attractive countryside, go fishing or play a round of golf as well as explore this part of Essex and nearby Suffolk with Constable Country. The Crown has four ensuite guest rooms, simply and comfortably furnished with the addition of television and a hostess tray. There is a pleasant terrace to sit out on in the warmer weather and whatever the weather you can be assured of a friendly and warm welcome from Julie and Joe Bain, the landlords and their able staff.

USEFUL INFORMATION

OPEN: All day every day
CHILDREN: Welcome
CREDIT CARDS: All major cards
LICENSED: Full On
ACCOMMODATION: 4 ensuite rooms.
RATES: From £15pp B&B

RESTAURANT: Extensive menu
BAR FOOD: Wide choice. Great value
VEGETARIAN: Always a choice
WHEELCHAIR ACCESS: Yes
GARDEN: Terrace overlooking river
PETS: By arrangement

FOUNTAINS HOUSE & DEDHAM HALL
Brook Street,
Dedham, Essex CO7 6AD
Good Food Guide,
Good Hotel Guide, Michelin Guide

Tel:01206 323027 Fax: 01206 323293

The Vale of Dedham lies about 70 miles from London between the towns of Colchester and Ipswich. It is a wide valley through which runs the River Stour, the boundary between Essex and Suffolk. The Vale is most generally known by John Constable's famous landscapes and fortunately Dedham Vale has been declared an area of outstanding beauty and National importance, making sure that it still appears much as Constable painted it. Dedham Hall is situated in 6 acres of grounds set back from the village. From the lawns one can see the well known tower of Dedham Church rising above the trees. Part of it dates back to 1400 and the building is listed as an Historic House of special interest. It offers you a peaceful holiday in tranquil surroundings. All the bedrooms have en-suite bath or shower rooms and early morning tea making facilities. The residents lounge, dining room and bar are in the 15th century cottage and overlook a scheduled walled garden. The Fountain House Restaurant is well known for careful and imaginative cooking at very reasonable prices. It is complemented by a modern and adventurous wine list, which over the years has received high praise. The restaurant, open to non-residents, overlooks the pond and gardens of The Hall. Booking a table in advance is advisable.

USEFUL INFORMATION

OPEN: All year
CHILDREN: Welcome at reasonable prices
CREDIT CARDS: All except AMEX/Diners
LICENSED: Yes
ACCOMMODATION: En suite rooms
RATES: Sgl £45 B&B £60 D.B&B   Dbl. £65 B&B £95 D.B&B

RESTAURANT: Acclaimed food

VEGETARIAN: Yes
WHEELCHAIR ACCESS: Yes
GARDEN: Yes

ELM HOUSE
14 Upper Holt Street,
Earls Colne, Essex CO6 2PG
Tel: 01787 222197

Elm House is a charming Queen Anne house and the home of Lady Larcom, who thoroughly enjoys her guests and is delighted to share all that the house has to offer. It is warm and welcoming and well-appointed with beamed ceilings and open fires. The walled garden is beautiful and here on a summer's morning you may breakfast on the terrace. A perfect start to the day. Every room is furnished with style and elegance. The Drawing Room is the only room in the house where smoking is permitted. The large library has an open fire and deep chairs - great for reading in quiet contentment. Lady Larcom is a gifted cook and dinner served in the dining room with its Georgian furniture, is one of the highlights of staying here. Her dishes are always prepared using as much of local and her own produce as possible. There are three guest rooms. All the rooms are spacious, with an ensuite double that has a brass Victorian framed bed and a garden view, a twin bedroom adjacent to the bathroom furnished in the William Morris style and another double sharing a bathroom with wrought iron Victorian beds. The countryside around Earls Colne is stunning, there is a wealth of history, architectural interest and antique shops in the area. In the drawing room there are two box files full of leaflets on places to visit within easy reach of Elm House.

USEFUL INFORMATION

OPEN: All year except Christmas
and New Year
CHILDREN: Welcome
CREDIT CARDS: None taken
LICENSED: No
ACCOMMODATION: 3 rooms .1dbl ensuite
RATES: £19 or £25pp.pn B&B PETS: By arrangement
Long stay discounts. Children under 10 half price, up to 2 years free

DINING ROOM; Delicious home-
cooked fare
VEGETARIAN: If requested in advance
WHEELCHAIR ACCESS: Possible
but no special facilities. Ground floor only
GARDEN: Delightful walled garden

THE ESPLANADE HOTEL
Marine Parade East,
Clacton-on-Sea,
Essex CO15 1UU
ETB 3 Crown Approved

Tel: 01255 220450 Fax: 01255 221800

The sea front location of the Esplanade Hotel makes it a sought after establishment and add to that its style and friendliness and you have found somewhere very good to stay for either a break or a longer holiday. It is close to the Pier and Clacton's many attractions and only 5 minutes from the town centre taking a gentle stroll along the front. Clacton is renowned for its beautiful gardens and there is much that would make one reluctant to explore elsewhere but it would be a pity not to take advantage of Clacton's close proximity to 'Constable Country' and to Colchester, half an hour away, the oldest recorded town in England. The Esplanade Hotel is a relaxing place to stay. Its resident proprietors and 8 well trained staff bend over backwards so that everyone can feel at ease and ready to appreciate all that is on offer. Good food is available at every meal. Sunday Lunch is a traditional affair , and there are bar snacks. Live entertainment is provided during the season and there are also games and quizzes frequently organised by the staff. There are twenty nine comfortable bedrooms of which twenty seven are ensuite and two have private facilities. All the rooms have direct dial telephones, television and a hostess tray. A great place to stay at sensible prices.

USEFUL INFORMATION

OPEN: All year
CHILDREN: Welcome
CREDIT CARDS: Visa/Master/Switch/Delta
LICENSED: Full On
ACCOMMODATION: 29 ensuite rooms
RATES: From £25pppn B&B £20 room only

RESTAURANT: Excellent food
BAR FOOD: Wide range
VEGETARIAN: Yes
WHEELCHAIR ACCESS: Yes + toilets
GARDEN: Yes

Single £5 surcharge - 2,3 & 4 night Breaks from £59 pp Half Board - Children £5 + meals

---

THE FLEECE
27 West Street,
Coggeshall, Essex
CO6 1NS

Tel: 01376 561412

Built in 1505, The Fleece has been a popular hostelry for centuries, offering its customers excellent ale and a friendly welcome. Alan and Maureen Potter, the licensees today carry on the tradition of centuries and both he and his staff ensure that everyone entering the doors of The Fleece feels relaxed and in good company. There are many walks one can take from the pub and it is on the Essex Way from Epping to Harwich. There are many Tudor buildings in Coggleshall which make it an attractive village to visit. The pub is known too for its involvement in charities and there is almost always something going on or being planned. Next door to The Fleece is Paycock House belonging to the National Trust. Traditional pub fare best describes what is on the menu. Home-cooked it is plentiful in portion and sensible in price. On Sundays there is a traditional roast lunch which is very popular and for which it is advisable to book a table. Simple snacks are available like jacket potatoes with fillings, Sandwiches with crusty fresh brown or white bread, toasted sandwiches and filled baguettes.

USEFUL INFORMATION

OPEN: 10am-11pm
CHILDREN: In the garden & to eat
CREDIT CARDS: None taken
LICENSED: Full On
GARDEN: Yes
PETS: Yes

RESTAURANT: Traditional pub fare
BAR FOOD: Sandwiches, Jacket
potatoes etch
VEGETARIAN: Yes
WHEELCHAIR ACCESS: Yes

THE GREEN DRAGON
Upper London Road,
Young's End, Great Notley,
Braintree, Essex CM7 8QN

Tel: 01245 361030 Fax: 01245 362575
green dragon@virgin.net.

Situated on the A131 Braintree-Chelmsford Road (Braintree two miles-Chelmsford eight miles) and near the new Great Notley Village. The Essex County Show ground is also close by. The Green Dragon is only eighteen miles from Stansted Airport and within easy reach of Colchester and Constable Country. The inn is approximately two hundred and fifty years old and is a traditional country inn which at one time had a farm attached. The Barn area now houses a good A La Carte restaurant on the ground floor with a newly converted, non-smoking hayloft gives additional restaurant space and is also available for parties and meetings. The inn has a great deal of atmosphere and charm enhanced by excellent landlords, Bob and Mandy Greybrook and their well-trained staff. The food is of a very high standard. The Blackboard Menu features seasonal fare and there is also an extensive fish menu, mostly supplied from nearby Mersea Island, famed for its Colchester oysters. The Bar Menu is innovative and is changed on a regular basis. The A La Carte menu features mainly British dishes but there is a first class curry. There is an extensive wine list together with Greene King Real Ales and Seasonal and Guest Draught Beers.

USEFUL INFORMATION

OPEN:11.30-3.30 & 6pm-11pm daily
CHILDREN: Well behaved welcome
CREDIT CARDS: Master/Visa/Switch
LICENSED: Full On
GARDEN: Yes
PETS: Garden area only

RESTAURANT: High standard
               with wide choice
BAR FOOD: Innovative
VEGETARIAN: Always a choice
WHEELCHAIR ACCESS: Yes
               limited access

THE GREEN MAN
The Street,
Gosfield, Nr Halstead
Essex CO9 1TP

Tel: 01787 472746

This is a real, old fashioned pub, run by a jovial landlord who believes in upholding all that is good in traditional inn-keeping. You will not find keg beer here. The Green Man is really in keeping with Gosfield, which in spite of its fair share of development over the years has managed to hide it away, and so the character has not been destroyed. Without doubt the place to go for good food and a cheery welcome and a thoroughly enjoyable outing, is The Green Man. From a food point of view you should be warned that the dishes are upmarket, and if you are concerned about cholesterol levels or diets, John Arnold, mine host, will tell you that health and fitness are no part of the menu! Actually he is joking, the cooking is of a very high standard and anyone needing to watch what they eat will find that these dishes are available. You will relish the Pheasant Casserole, drool over the asparagus and probably decide that you have not seen a better cold table for miles around. The interior decor is most attractive and well lived in, which makes it hospitable. Tables are laid with pretty cloths in colours that blend with the furniture. the walls have their fair share of interesting pictures, and the low beams help to create the intimate, warm and friendly atmosphere. The amount of 'Pub Tatt' is kept to a minimum. Another favourite place of mine, miss this one and you will have forgone a meal to remember.

USEFUL INFORMATION

OPEN:11-3pm & 6.30-11pm
CHILDREN: Tolerated
CREDIT CARDS: AMEX/Visa/Master/Switch
LICENSED: Full On
PETS: Please ask first WHEELCHAIR ACCESS: Yes

RESTAURANT: Excellent, honest English
BAR FOOD: Traditional
VEGETARIAN: 2 dishes
GARDEN: Large and well kept

THE HORSE AND GROOM
20 Rayne Road,
Braintree,
Essex
CM7 2Q11

Tel:01376 343513

This nice pub is good for all ages and is one of those rare places where a woman on her own can feel at ease. Built in the 17th century The Horse and Groom is essentially a locals pub where conversation is far more important than juke boxes and fruit machines which are banned. Furnished throughout in a comfortable fashion, it is relaxing. The ale is well kept and both Richard and Lorraine Martin know how to run a hostelry efficiently and yet with a degree of informality. The food is good value and of a high standard. Best described as traditional pub fare, the chef is renowned for his pies which can be anything from steak and kidney to game. There are lots of other dishes including daily specials and simple things like sandwiches as well. You order from the bar and then it is brought to table for you. In fine weather you can wander out into the garden with a drink and have your food there as well. There are some interesting places around the Braintree area including Heddlingham Castle and Silk Mill.

USEFUL INFORMATION

OPEN: 11am-11pm
CHILDREN: Yes
CREDIT CARDS: Visa/Master/AMEX
LICENSED: Full On
GARDEN: Yes

RESTAURANT: Not applicable
BAR FOOD: Good pub fare. Pies
a speciality
VEGETARIAN: Yes
PETS: Public Bar only

THE KINGS ARMS
Broad Green,
Coggeshall, Essex CO6 1RU

Tel: 01376 561581

Mick and Miriam Overy are the welcoming landlords at The Kings Arms in Coggleshall. This 18th century inn is full of character and in summer the whitewashed and green painted exterior is ablaze with colourful hanging baskets and tubs. You can sit outside as well at rustic tables with benches - very popular in the warm weather. Regulars come to the pub because of the well kept beer and knowing that the bar will invariably have a familiar face to talk to. Visitors come here as strangers and leave as friends. Food is served every day and is an eclectic mixture of traditional fare, home-cooked and full of taste and interest. There are always daily specials and at the bar one can order a simple snack, just a sandwich if that is all you require. The sandwich will be freshly cut, well filled and garnished. Equally the daily specials are invariably time-honoured favourites and very tasty. Everything is sensibly priced and great value for money. Food is served every day at lunch and in the evenings. Coggleshall with its fine Tudor buildings and other places of interest is a great place to explore before or after visiting The Kings Arms.

USEFUL INFORMATION

OPEN:11.30-11pm Sun:12-3pm & 7-10.30pm
CHILDREN: Yes with adults
CREDIT CARDS: None taken
LICENSED: Full On
GARDEN: Yes

RESTAURANT: Good pub fare
BAR FOOD: Wide range
VEGETARIAN: Yes
WHEELCHAIR ACCESS: Yes
PETS: On Leads

THE KINGS HEAD
1 High Street,
Tollesbury,
Essex
CM9 7PB

Tel: 01621 869203

Located in the peaceful village square adjacent to the old church, The Kings Head built about 1650 is the oldest surviving inn left. The church is famous for its full set of bells which ring out every Thursday and The Kings Head has been a welcoming hostelry over the centuries and still opens its friendly doors both to locals and visitors today. The locals have many lurid tales to tell and visitors enjoy hearing the stories as they enjoy a drink. Paul Yull is the cheerful landlord whose outgoing personality and good humour are two of the reasons why people come to The Kings Head. His ale is well kept and his good home-made traditional fare is sensibly priced and always tasty. You can play pool, throw a dart or watch the big screen Sky television. A thoroughly nice, unpretentious village inn with a great ambience. It is hoped to have Bed and Breakfast accommodation soon and it would certainly be a happy place to stay.

USEFUL INFORMATION

OPEN: 11am-11pm
CHILDREN: Welcome
CREDIT CARDS: None taken
LICENSED: Full On
ACCOMMODATION: B&B coming soon
PETS: Yes

RESTAURANT: Not applicable
BAR FOOD: Traditional home-cooked
VEGETARIAN: Upon request
WHEELCHAIR ACCESS: Yes. Ramp
GARDEN: Yes

PAXTON DENE
Church Road,
Brightlingsea, Essex CO7 0QT
Tourist Board Commended

Tel: 01206 304560
Fax: 01206 302877

Nora Reynolds is the owner of Paxton Dene, a cottage built some sixty years ago and which spells out a warm welcome from the moment you walk through the front door. Spotlessly clean and furnished throughout with good furniture and pretty decor, it is comfortable and one feels immediately relaxed and at home. Fresh flowers everywhere add to the sense of well-being. There are three ensuite bedrooms, individually decorated and furnished, each with television, hairdryer, radio alarm and a very welcome hostess tray. Breakfast is a freshly cooked, substantial meal which will set you up for the day and if you require an evening meal that is available upon request. Brightlingsea is a sailing town and if this is not your sport or your pleasure you will find many places of interest within easy reach including Dedham in Constable Country and Colchester, the oldest recorded town in England. It is excellent walking country. Guests are welcome to stroll or sit within the half an acre of gardens.

USEFUL INFORMATION

OPEN: All year
CHILDREN: No
CREDIT CARDS: None taken
LICENSED: No
ACCOMMODATION: 3 ensuite rooms
RATES: Sgl £25 Dbl. £38

DINING ROOM; Excellent breakfast
Evening meal by arrangement
VEGETARIAN: By arrangement
WHEELCHAIR ACCESS: Yes
GARDEN: 1/2 acre
PETS: By arrangement

Guests are requested not to smoke in the house

THE QUEENS HEAD HOTEL
The Hythe,
Maldon,
Essex
CM9 5HN

Tel: 01621 854112

The Queens Head Hotel has been a hostelry since the 15th century and it has a wonderful atmosphere that has grown steadily over the centuries and today, in the capable, friendly hands of Neil and Jean Yardley, the owners, it has never been better. It is a much loved pub frequented by many local people, especially local fishermen. Comfortably and attractively furnished, the walls are covered with old riverside photographs. The position of the Queens Head is great for anyone who enjoys a walk before a pint. The sea wall from Bradwell ends at the inn. On a nice day there is nothing pleasanter than to take a drink out to the garden where, at the bottom, the river flows gently along. It is peaceful and therapeutic. Neil Yardley is a dedicated chef who enjoys creating dishes and at the same time excels in the traditional pub fare, giving customers time-honoured favourites such as home-made steak and kidney pie. This is a genuine inn and one to be enjoyed for its unpretentious hospitality.

USEFUL INFORMATION

OPEN: Normal pub hours
CHILDREN: No
CREDIT CARDS: None taken
LICENSED: Full On
GARDEN: Yes to river bank

RESTAURANT: Traditional fare
BAR FOOD: Wide range. Daily specials
VEGETARIAN: Yes
WHEELCHAIR ACCESS: Yes
PETS: Yes

THE WHITE HART
Great Yeldham,
Essex CO9 4HJ

Tel: 01787 237250
Fax: 01787 238044

Great Yeldham stands on the borders of Essex, Suffolk and Cambridgeshire surrounded by delightful places to visit like Lavenham, Long Melford, Sudbury, Clare and numerous other picturesque villages. On the edge of the village is The White Hart built in 1505. A charming place, it became part of the Huntsbridge Group in 1995 when it was restored carefully to its former beauty whilst ensuring its capacity to trade successfully into the Millennium. It is now one of England's finest inns. Chef Patron Roger Jones has moved from another Huntsbridge Inn, The Pheasant at Keyston. His style shows the influence of Britain's greatest Italian Chef, Franco Taruschio of the Walnut Tree in Abergavenny, with whom he trained for six years. Robust flavours are combined with a lightness of touch that has won Roger accolades in all the good food guides. The White Hart is neither pub nor restaurant. Guests can eat whatever they wish from the long menu, wherever they wish. Real ales and the wine list are to Huntsbridge's usual standards. Wedding parties particularly benefit from the huge gardens, running down to a river. The 'Brewhouse' is an excellent private room for meals or meetings.

USEFUL INFORMATION

OPEN: 12-2pm 7-10pm
CHILDREN: Yes
CREDIT CARDS: All major cards
LICENSED: Yes
GARDEN: Yes, huge
PETS: No

RESTAURANT: Eat wherever and
whatever you wish from a superb menu
BAR FOOD: Yes. Special price lunch
during week
VEGETARIAN: Always a choice
WHEELCHAIR ACCESS: Yes

THE STARR RESTAURANT WITH ROOMS
Market Place,
Gt. Dunmow,
Essex CM61AX

AA Level 4 2 Rosette AA RAC ETB
Tel:01371 874321 Fax: 01371 876337
www.zynet.co.uk\menu\starr

Gt. Dunmow is a small bustling market town mid way between London and Cambridge, just off the M11 Motorway very close to London Stansted Airport. Probably best known for its famous Dunmow Flitch Trials dating back to medieval times which seeks out the married couple who have not quarrelled for a year! In the Market Place is The Starr Restaurant which also has excellent guest bedrooms. This award winning restaurant is a favourite with local people and for others from many miles around. The owners, Brian and Vanessa Jones, will tell you that they do like things done properly but in a very friendly way. Although they have a very good reputation for food and service it is not in the least a snooty or stuffy place. It is attractively furnished in a comfortable manner and with sufficient space between the tables to make the diner feel able to converse without his conversation being overheard. Recently a lovely and elegant conservatory overlooking the courtyard has been added to the building making another delightful place in which to eat. Everyone is made to feel very welcome. It is remarkable in this day and age to have a staff who have been at The Starr for many years. It makes for a very special atmosphere. The Starr opens for lunch seven days a week and for dinner six nights, closing on Sunday after lunch. There is a two course lunch for £10 Monday to Saturday and on Sunday two courses for £17.50 or three courses £22.50. Dinner on Monday to Friday is £22.80 or £32.50 Saturday Dinner is £35. The menus are full of delicious dishes with starters that might include watercress and Parmesan soufflé with a wild mushroom ragout or a fresh crab custard tart on a salad with pink grapefruit and fresh coconut followed by fillet of sea bass in crispy filo pastry, new seasons rack of English lamb with Spring vegetables and pink rosemary butter sauce or steamed turbot with saffron moules mariniere and fresh herbs. If, after these gourmet delights you can find room for a dessert, they are equally mouth-watering. The Starr has two private rooms on the first floor; ideal for a special party or for meeting. Eight delightful bedrooms have been built in the converted stable block in the courtyard. They are charmingly furnished, ensuite and each is different. The Oak Room, for example, boasts a cast iron bath and a fine oak four poster. The Pine Room has male and female hand basins set in marble with gold taps and a corner bath. All the rooms have direct dial telephones, television and a hostess tray as well as many other nice touches for the comfort of guests. Gt. Dunmow is surrounded by many interesting places to visit including Thaxted the ancient capital of the steel trade and the ancient town of Saffron Walden where Oliver Cromwell resided during the Civil War.

USEFUL INFORMATION

OPEN: All year except 1st week Jan.
CHILDREN: Welcome
CREDIT CARDS: All major cards
LICENSED: Restaurant Licence
ACCOMMODATION: 8 ensuite rooms
RATES: £60sgl £90 dbl. Child: £15

RESTAURANT: Imaginative
dishes beautifully presented
VEGETARIAN: Wide choice
WHEELCHAIR ACCESS: Yes
GARDEN: No
PETS: Yes

THE WALTON TAVERN
30-32 The Parade,
Walton-on-the-Naze,
Essex

Tel: 01255 676000

The Walton Tavern has an enviable position on the seafront at Walton-on-the-Naze overlooking the bay. Once it was three buildings but in 1971 it was skilfully converted into the friendly, welcoming hostelry that it is today. Attractively and comfortably furnished throughout in a modern, fresh style it is a very pleasant place in which to enjoy a drink and have a snack or have a first class meal in the restaurant which has a full A la Carte and Table d'hote menu. If your appetitie is particularly good you will probably relish the Tavern Special, a mixed grill of gargantuan size. Everything is reasonably priced, for example Rack of Lamb with vegetables will only cost you £6.50. Fresh fish is always a popular item on the menu. English home-made fare is on offer at the bar. The Walton Tavern has nine guest rooms which have recently been refurbished. Four of the rooms are ensuite and the others share bathrooms. Every room has television and a generously supplied hostess tray. Wheelchair access is restricted to the ground floor and not to the bedrooms.

USEFUL INFORMATION

OPEN: 10am-11pm
CHILDREN: Welcome
CREDIT CARDS: Applied for
LICENSED: Yes
ACCOMMODATION:9 rooms 4 ensuite
RATES: £22.50 ensuite pp.pn B&B
£17.50 not ensuite Children under 12 free

RESTAURANT: A la Carte & Table d'hote
BAR FOOD: Wide range, home-cooked
VEGETARIAN: Yes to order
WHEELCHAIR ACCESS: Ground floor only
GARDEN: No. Sea front
PETS: No

THE WHITE HORSE
39 Church Street,
Sible Hedingham,
Essex CO9 3NT

Tel: 01787 460742

The White Horse stands at the cross roads of this large, prosperous village, close to pleasant walks, Hedingham Castle, the Steam Railway and many interesting churches. It is also close to many pretty villages including Finchingfield and the old town of Sudbury with its busy market on Thursday and Saturday. The inn, built in the 14th and 15th centuries is full of atmosphere. It has a plethora of original beams, a priest hole, a bible in the inglenook fireplace to be used for exorcising the building every seven years! What was the Malt House still stands outside and there is a delightful garden with a stream and a pond. Everything about The White Horse is warm, welcoming and comfortable. You eat in the Lounge in a small eating area. The food is good home-made pub fare. In summer there are Barbecues which are well attended. For anyone wanting to enjoy the hospitality of the pub and stay a night or two, there are three guest rooms, not en-suite but each has television and a well-stocked hospitality tray.

USEFUL INFORMATION

OPEN: 12-3pm & 7-11pm (Not Xmas night)
CHILDREN: Welcome
CREDIT CARDS: Visa/Master/Switch/Delta
LICENSED: Full On
ACCOMMODATION: 3 rooms not ensuite
RATES: £15pp.pn
PETS: No

RESTAURANT: No
BAR FOOD: Good pub fare
VEGETARIAN: Yes
WHEELCHAIR ACCESS: No
GARDEN: Yes. Stream &
                    Pond. BBQ

THE WHITEHALL HOTEL.
Church End.,
Broxted.. Essex CM6 2BZ
ETB **** Highly commended. AA***RAC 78%. AA Two Rosettes.

Tel:- 01279 850603. Fax:- 01279 850385.

This classic Elizabethan Manor House is set in its own grounds, overlooking the rolling country side of North Essex. It is conveniently situated close to Stansted Airport, Cambridge, Audley End and the Imperial War Museum at Duxford. The hotel has an interesting history, the original house on this site dates back to 1150AD, being then the founding house of the Knights of St.John. Later it became the home of a Lord Chancellor of England, namely the Duchess of Warwick and Lord |Butler. The atmosphere today is friendly, professional without being over bearing,. The service is superb and the quality simply prestigious. There are twenty five rooms, ranging from doubles, twins, suits and singles, all en-suite and furnished in pleasingly bright colours. The Public rooms are charming, the forty seat restaurant is a spectacular vaulted timbered room over-looking the Tudor garden.. With the accolades you would expect the food to be sumptuous, you will not be disappointed. There are conference facilities for up to one hundred delegates, with all the equipment required.

USEFUL INFORMATION

OPEN; All year, except Christmas day.
CHILDREN: Welcome
CREDIT CARDS: All major.
LINCENSED: Restaurant
ACCOMMODATION:- 25 ensue rooms.
Six ground floor rooms.
RATES:- Dbl.£110 to £140. Sgl. £80.
Breakfast is available as an extra charge.

RESTAURANT: Award winning fare.
VEGETARASIN: Imaginative choices.
WHEELCHAIR ACCESS: Yes
GARDEN: Yes

Cities, Towns, Villages and Hamlets in this Guide

Cities, Towns, Villages and Hamlets in this Guide

Cities, Towns, Villages and Hamlets in this Guide

Cities, Towns, Villages and Hamlets in this Guide

Cities, Towns, Villages and Hamlets in this Guide

THE FOUR SEASONS
DISCERNING VISITOR GUIDE Series.

Titles currently available in this series are:-

DEVON & CORNWALL	**£6.95**
WESSEX & EXMOOR	**£7.95**
EAST ANGLIA	**£7.95**

AVAILABLE FROM LEADING BOOK SHOPS.

Titles in the series for the Millennium..

COTSWOLDS & THAMES & CHILTERNS.
THE HEART OF ENGLAND.
THE MIDSHIRES.
SOUTH & SOUTH EAST ENGLAND.

Also available from Kingsley Media Ltd.

HEALTHY OPTIONS   **£9.95**
A book that no health conscious person should be without.

To order any of the above titles direct from the publisher, please add £3.77. post
and packing, and send you order to:-

ABA BOOKS, 138 ALEXANDRA ROAD, FORD, PLYMOUTH PL2. 1JY.

You may use postal order, cheque, or Visa.(Please do not send cash via the post)

Your can also order via the Internet, please **e-mail: kingsley@hotels.u-net.com**
When ordering on the Internet please remember your Visa number, it is fully
protected.

READERS COMMENTS

Please use this page to tell us about venues and places of interest that have appealed to you especially and to suggest suitable establishments to include in future publications.

We will pass on your recommendations and approval, and equally report back any complaints. We hope the latter will be few and far between.

Please post to:
Kingsley Media Ltd
Freepost PY2100
The Hoe
Plymouth
PL1 3BR

Name of Establishment:

Address:

Comments:

Your Name: (Block Caps Please)

Address:

Your name and details will not be used for any other commercial purpose

Glossary of Places To Visit

FEB: Market, **King's Lynn**.

MAR: Races, **Fakenham**.

MAY: Races, **Fakenham**.
            Festival, **Downham Market**.

JUN: Music Week, **Wymondham**.
            Royal Norfolk Show, **Costissey, Nr. Norwich**.
            Carnival, **Caister**.
            Festival, **Fakenham**.
            Festival of Arts, **Hunstanton**.
            Carnival, **Hunstanton**.

JUL: Lord Mayor's Weekend, **Norwich**.
            Inter-County Grass Courts Championships, **Cromer**.
            Carnival, **North Walsham**.
            Festival, **Worstead**.
            East International Exhibition, **Norwich**.
            Arts Festival, **King's Lynn**.
            Lavender Harvest Time, **Heacham**.
            Flower Show, **Sandringham**.
            Sheepdog Demonstrations, **Castle Acre**.
            World Snail Racing Championships, **Congham**.
            Firework Concert, **Sandringham**.

AUG: Carnival, **Great Yarmouth and Gorleston**.
            Carnival, **Cromer**.
            Junior Tennis, **Cromer**.
            Senior Tennis, **Cromer**.
            Festival, **Mundesley**.
            Carnival, **Wells-next-the-Sea**.
            Carnival, **Sheringham**.
            Miracle Dinghy National Championships, **Hunstanton**.

SEPT: Royal Norfolk Showground Spectacular, **Norwich**.
            Herring Festival, **Great Yarmouth**.

OCT: Norfolk and Norwich Festival, **Norwich**.
            CAMRA Beer Festival, **Norwich**.
            Races, **Fakenham**.
            Norfolk Conker Championships, **Downham Market**.

DEC: Races, **Fakenham**.

Glossary of Places To Visit

JAN: Straw Bear Festival, **Whittlesey**.

MAR: Shire Horse Show, **Peterborough**.

APR: Daffodil Weekend, **Thriplow**.

MAY: Cheese Rolling, **Stilton**.
May Fayre, **Boston**.
Spring Festival and Flower Parade, **Spalding and South Holland**.
Beer Festival, **Cambridge**.
South Holland Arts Festival, **Spalding**.
British Motorcycle Rally, **Peterborough**.
Folk Festival, **St Neots**.
Beer Festival, **Wisbech**.

JUN: Air Show, **Duxford,**
Carnival, **Huntingdon**.
May Week, **Cambridge**.
Festival, **Chatteris**.
Strawberry Fair, **Cambridge**.
Show, **Crowland**.
'Jazz Plus' Music Festival, **Wisbech**.
Carnival, **Boston**.
Shakespeare at the George, **Huntingdon**.
Cathedral Festival, **Peterborough**.

JUL: Air Show, **Duxford**.
World Pea-Shooting Championships, **Witchan, Nr. Ely**.
Rose Fair, **Wisbech**.
East of England Show, **Peterborough**.
Folk Festival, **Cambridge**.
Folk Festival, **Ely**.

AUG: CAMRA Beer Festival, **Peterborough**.
Rowing Regatta, **Peterborough**.
Horticultural Show, **Ely**.
Fenland Country Fair, **Stow-Cum-Quy**.
Flower Festival, **Crowland**.

SEP: Pumpkin Fayre, **Soham**.
Steam Engine Rally, **Haddenham**.
Show, **Boston**.
Burghley Horse Trials, **Stamford**.
Flying Display, **Duxford**.

OCT: Flying Display, **Duxford**.

NOV: Fireworks Fiesta, **Peterborough**.
Fireworks Display, **Midsummer Common, Cambridge**.

DEC: Festival of Nine Lessons and Carols, **Cambridge**.

Glossary of Places To Visit

FEB: St Valentine's Fair, **Ipswich.**

MAR: Schools Music Celebration, **Aldeburgh.**

APR: Easter Festival, **Aldeburgh.**
        Spring Fair, **Lowestoft.**

MAY: Horse Show, **Woodbridge.**
        World OSY 400 Championship, Motor Boat Club, **Oulton Broad.**
        Historic Vehicle Run, **Ipswich,**
        Championship Fete, **Lowestoft.**
        Air Show, **Mildenhall.**
        Lions Club Fete, **Southwold.**
        Suffolk Show, **Ipswich.**
        Springtime Garden Show, **Bungay.**
        RAC Classic Car Rally, **Ipswich.**

JUN: Festival, **Aldeburgh.**
        Trinity Fair, **Southwold.**
        Maritime Fair, **Ipswich.**
        Maritime Week, **Lowestoft.**
        Charter Day, **Ipswich.**
        Fish Fayre, **Lowestoft.**
        Flower Show, **Ipswich.**
        Smack Race, **Lowestoft.**
        Classic Boat Festival, **Ipswich.**
        Classic Vehicle Run, **Ipswich.**

JUL: Barge Match, **Pinmill.**
        Festival, **Bungay.**
        National Gallery Week, **Ipswich.**
        Summer Antiques Market, **Bungay.**
        Seafront Festival, **Lowestoft.**
        Carnival, **Beccles.**

AUG: Snape Proms, **Aldeburgh.**
        Carnival, **Ipswich.**
        Carnival, **Lowestoft.**
        Horticultural and Flower Show, **Oulton Broad and Lowestoft.**
        Regatta Week, **Oulton Broad.**

SEP: Beer Festival, **Ipswich.**
        Horse Trials, **Somerleyton.**
        Steam Rally, **Henham.**

OCT: Beer Festival, **Bungay.**
        Firework Display, **Ipswich.**
        Christmas Lights Switched On, **Ipswich.**

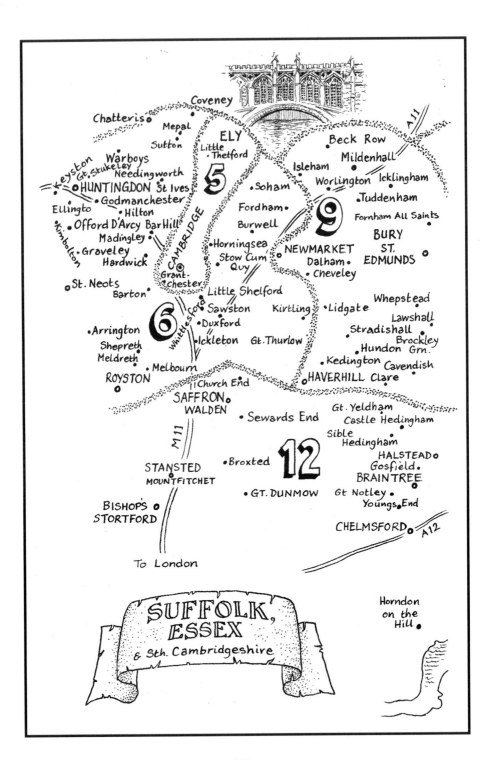

Chatteris

Coveney

Mepal

Sutton

ELY

Beck Row

Mildenhall

Keyston
Gt.Stukeley
Warboys
Needingworth

Little
Thetford

Isleham

Worlington
Icklingham

HUNTINGDON St Ives

5

Soham

Tuddenham

Godmanchester

Ellingto
Hilton

Fordham

9

Fornham All Saints

Offord D'Arcy Bar Hill

Burwell

Kimbolton
Madingley

CAMBRIDGE

Horningsea

BURY
ST.
EDMUNDS

Graveley

Hardwick

Stow Cum
Quy

NEWMARKET

Dalham

St. Neots

Grant-
chester

Cheveley

Barton

Little Shelford

Whepstead

Sawston

Kirtling

Lidgate

Lawshall

Arrington

6

Duxford

Stradishall

Whittlesford

Ickleton

Gt.Thurlow

Brockley

Shepreth

Hundon Grn.

Meldreth

Kedington

Cavendish

Melbourn

HAVERHILL Clare

ROYSTON

Church End

SAFFRON
WALDEN

Gt.Yeldham

Castle Hedingham

Sewards End

Sible
Hedingham

M 11

12

HALSTEAD

STANSTED
MOUNTFITCHET

Broxted

Gosfield

BRAINTREE

GT. DUNMOW

Gt Notley
Youngs End

BISHOP'S
STORTFORD

CHELMSFORD A12

To London

SUFFOLK,
ESSEX
& Sth. Cambridgeshire

Horndon
on the
Hill

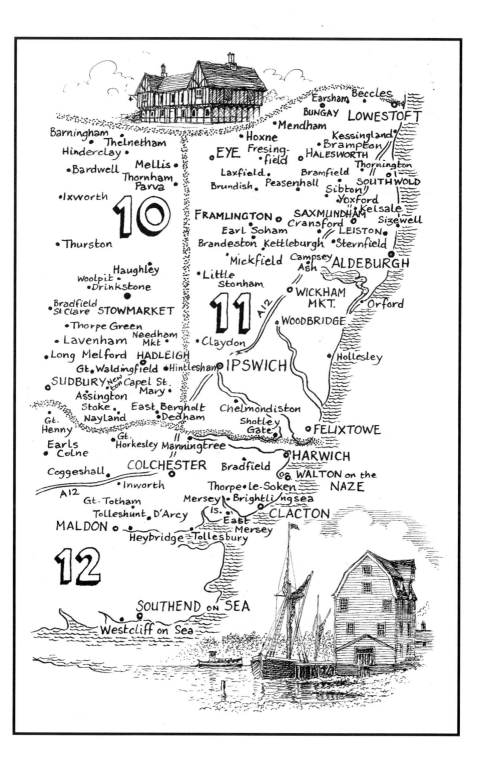

Earsham • Beccles
BUNGAY • LOWESTOFT
• Mendham
• Hoxne Kessingland •
EYE Fresing- • Brampton
• field HALESWORTH
Laxfield • Bramfield • Thornington
Brundish • Peasenhall SOUTHWOLD
Sibton •
Yoxford •
FRAMLINGTON • SAXMUNDHAM Kelsale
Cransford • Sizewell
Earl Soham • LEISTON •
Brandeston • Kettleburgh • Sternfield
Mickfield Campsey ALDEBURGH
• Little Ash
Stonham WICKHAM
MKT. • Orford
WOODBRIDGE

Barningham
• Thelnetham
Hinderclay •
• Bardwell Mellis •
Thornham
Parva •
• Ixworth

10

• Thurston

Haughley
Woolpit • Drinkstone
Bradfield •
St Clare STOWMARKET
• Thorpe Green
• Lavenham Needham
Mkt •
• Long Melford HADLEIGH
Gt • Waldingfield • Hintlesham
SUDBURY New Capel St.
ton Mary •
Assington
Stoke • East Bergholt Chelmondiston
Gt • Nayland • Dedham Shotley
Henny Gate
Earls Gt • Manningtree
• Colne Horkesley

COLCHESTER Bradfield •
• Inworth HARWICH
A12 WALTON on the
Gt • Totham Thorpe • le-Soken NAZE
Tolleshunt • D'Arcy Mersey • Brightlingsea
Is. East CLACTON
MALDON • Mersey
Heybridge • Tollesbury

12

SOUTHEND on SEA
Westcliff on Sea

11

A12

• Claydon

IPSWICH

• Hollesley

• FELIXTOWE

599

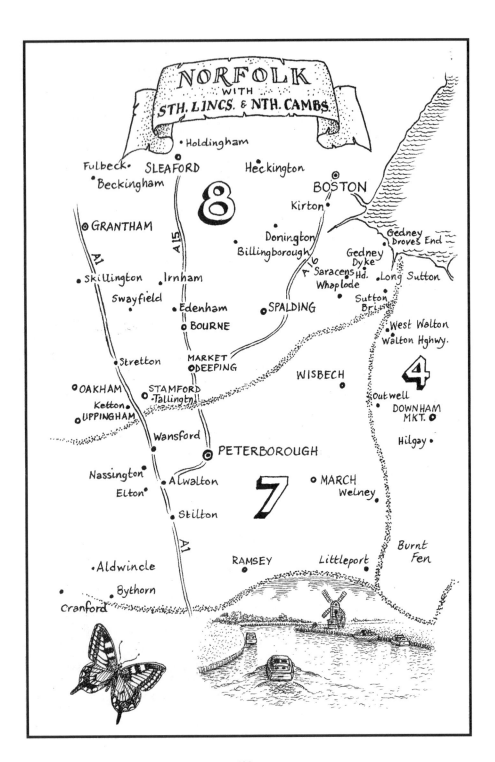

NORFOLK
WITH
STH. LINCS. & NTH. CAMBS.

• Holdingham

Fulbeck • SLEAFORD   Heckington
• Beckingham   BOSTON

                              Kirton •

⊙ GRANTHAM

                    Donington   Gedney
              Billingborough   Droves End
• Skillington   Irnham   Gedney
      Swayfield   Saracens Dyke
                              Hd.
                      Whaplode • Long Sutton
        • Edenham   SPALDING   Sutton
        ⊙ BOURNE   Bri...

                                   • West Walton
                                   • Walton Hghwy.
        • Stretton   MARKET
                    ⊙ DEEPING   WISBECH   4
⊙ OAKHAM   STAMFORD
  Ketton • ⊙ Tallington   Outwell
⊙ UPPINGHAM   DOWNHAM
        Wansford   MKT. ⊙
                                   Hilgay •
              ⊙ PETERBOROUGH
Nassington   7
        • Alwalton   ⊙ MARCH
  Elton •   Welney

        • Stilton

                              Burnt
                              Fen
• Aldwincle   RAMSEY   Littleport
    • Bythorn
Cranford

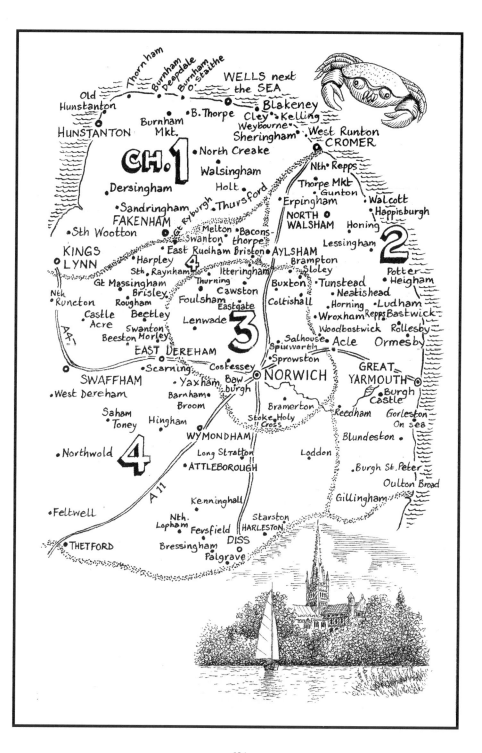

Thorn ham
Burnham Deepdale
Burnham O' Staithe
WELLS next the SEA
Old Hunstanton
B. Thorpe
Blakeney
Cley Kelling
Weybourne
Sheringham
West Runton
CROMER
HUNSTANTON
Burnham Mkt.
North Creake
CH.1
Nth Repps
Walsingham
Thorpe Mkt.
Gunton
Holt
Erpingham
Walcott
Happisburgh
Dersingham
Tatterburgh
Thursford
Sandringham
FAKENHAM
NORTH WALSHAM
Honing
Sth Wootton
Melton
Bacons thorpe
Swanton
Lessingham
East Rudham
Briston
AYLSHAM
KINGS LYNN
Harpley
4
Brampton
Sloley
Potter Heigham
Sth. Raynham
Itteringham
Gt Massingham
Thurning
Buxton
Tunstead
Neatishead
2
Nth Runcton
Brisley
Cawston
Coltishall
Horning
Ludham
Rougham
Foulsham
Eastgate
Wroxham
Repps Bastwick
Castle Acre
Beetley
Lenwade
Woodbastwick
Rollesby
Swanton Morley
3
Salhouse
Acle
Ormesby
Beeston
Spixworth
EAST DEREHAM
Costessey
Sprowston
GREAT YARMOUTH
Scarning
NORWICH
SWAFFHAM
Yaxham
Bow burgh
Burgh Castle
West Dereham
Barnham Broom
Bramerton
Reedham
Gorleston On sea
Saham Toney
Hingham
Stoke Holy Cross
Blundeston
WYMONDHAM
Loddon
Northwold
4
Long Stratton
ATTLEBOROUGH
Burgh St. Peter
Oulton Broad
Kenninghall
Starston
Gillingham
A11
HARLESTON
Feltwell
Nth. Lopham
Fersfield
Bressingham
DISS
THETFORD
Palgrave

601

Notes

Notes

Notes

Notes

Notes

Notes

Notes